The I-Series

Microsoft® Office
Access 2003

Complete

D0139111

Stephen Haag

University of Denver

James Perry

University of San Diego

Merrill Wells

University of Denver

McGraw Hill **Technology Education**

Boston   Burr Ridge, IL   Dubuque, IA   Madison, WI   New York   San Francisco   St. Louis
Bangkok   Bogotá   Caracas   Kuala Lumpur   Lisbon   London   Madrid   Mexico City
Milan   Montreal   New Delhi   Santiago   Seoul   Singapore   Sydney   Taipei   Toronto

THE I-SERIES: MICROSOFT® OFFICE ACCESS 2003, COMPLETE

Published by McGraw-Hill/Technology Education, a business unit of The McGraw-Hill Companies, Inc., 1221 Avenue of the Americas, New York, NY, 10020. Copyright © 2004 by The McGraw-Hill Companies, Inc. All rights reserved. No part of this publication may be reproduced or distributed in any form or by any means, or stored in a database or retrieval system, without the prior written consent of The McGraw-Hill Companies, Inc., including, but not limited to, in any network or other electronic storage or transmission, or broadcast for distance learning.
Some ancillaries, including electronic and print components, may not be available to customers outside the United States.

This book is printed on acid-free paper.

1 2 3 4 5 6 7 8 9 0 WEB/WEB 0 9 8 7 6 5 4

ISBN 0-07-283076-X

Editor-in-chief: *Bob Woodbury*
Publisher: *Brandon Nordin*
Senior sponsoring editor: *Donald J. Hull*
Development editor: *Jennie Yates*
Editorial assistant: *Veronica Vergoth*
Marketing manager: *Andy Bernier*
Executive producer, Media technology: *Mark Christianson*
Lead project manager: *Mary Conzachi*
Senior production supervisor: *Rose Hepburn*
Lead designer: *Pam Verros*
Senior supplement producer: *Rose M. Range*
Senior digital content specialist: *Brian Nacik*
Cover design: *Asylum Studios*
Interior design: *Mary Christianson*
Typeface: *10.5/12 Minion*
Compositor: *GAC Indianapolis*
Printer: *Webcrafters, Inc.*

Library of Congress Cataloging-in-Publication Data
Haag, Stephen.
    Microsoft Office Access 2003 : complete / Stephen Haag, James Perry, Merrill Wells.
       p. cm.—(I-series)
    Includes index.
    ISBN 0-07-283076-X (alk. paper)
    1. Microsoft Access. 2. Database management. I. Perry, James T. II. Wells, Merrill. III.
    Title. IV. Series.
QA76.9.D3H237 2004
005.75'65—dc22   2004043923

www.mhhe.com

MCGRAW-HILL TECHNOLOGY EDUCATION

At McGraw-Hill Technology Education, we publish instructional materials for the technology education market, in particular computer instruction in post-secondary education—from introductory courses in traditional 4-year universities to continuing education and proprietary schools. McGraw-Hill Technology Education presents a broad range of innovative products—texts, lab manuals, study guides, testing materials, and technology-based training and assessment tools.

We realize that technology has created and will continue to create new mediums for professors and students to use in managing resources and communicating information to one another. McGraw-Hill Technology Education provides the most flexible and complete teaching and learning tools available, and offers solutions to the changing world of teaching and learning. McGraw-Hill Technology Education is dedicated to providing the tools for today's instructors and students that will enable them to successfully navigate the world of Information Technology.

- McGraw-Hill/Osborne—This division of The McGraw-Hill Companies is known for its best-selling Internet titles, Harley Hahn's *Internet & Web Yellow Pages*, and the *Internet Complete Reference*. For more information, visit Osborne at www.osborne.com.

- Digital Solutions—Whether you want to teach a class online or just post your "bricks-n-mortar" class syllabus, McGraw-Hill Technology Education is committed to publishing digital solutions. Taking your course online doesn't have to be a solitary adventure, nor does it have to be a difficult one. We offer several solutions that will allow you to enjoy all the benefits of having your course material online.

- Packaging Options—For more information about our discount options, contact your McGraw-Hill sales representative at 1-800-338-3987 or visit our Web site at www.mhhe.com/it.

McGraw-Hill Technology Education is dedicated to providing the tools for today's instructors and students

THE I-SERIES PAGE

By using the I-Series, students will be able to learn and master applications skills by being actively engaged— by *doing*. The "I" in I-Series demonstrates Insightful tasks that will not only Inform students, but also Involve them while learning the applications.

How Will the I-Series Accomplish This for You?

Through relevant, real-world chapter opening cases.

Tasks throughout each chapter incorporating steps and tips for easy reference.

Alternative methods and styles of learning to keep the student involved.

Rich, end-of-chapter materials that support what the student has learned.

I-Series Titles Include:

Computer Concepts

Computing Concepts, 2e, Introductory

Computing Concepts, 2e, Complete

Microsoft Office Applications

Microsoft Office 2003, Volume I

Microsoft Office 2003, Volume II

Microsoft Office Word 2003 (Brief, Introductory, Complete Versions) 11 Total Chapters

Microsoft Office Excel 2003 (Brief, Introductory, Complete Versions) 12 Total Chapters

Microsoft Office Access 2003 (Brief, Introductory, Complete Versions) 12 Total Chapters

Microsoft Office PowerPoint 2003 (Brief, Introductory Versions) 8 Total Chapters

Microsoft Office Outlook 2003 (Brief, Introductory Versions) 8 Total Chapters

Microsoft Office FrontPage 2003 (Brief Version) 4 Total Chapters

Microsoft Office XP, Volume I

Microsoft Office XP, Volume I Expanded (with Internet Essentials bonus chapters)

Microsoft Office XP, Volume II

Microsoft Word 2002 (Brief, Introductory, Complete Versions) 12 Total Chapters

Microsoft Excel 2002 (Brief, Introductory, Complete Versions) 12 Total Chapters

Microsoft Access 2002 (Brief, Introductory, Complete Versions) 12 Total Chapters

Microsoft PowerPoint 2002 (Brief, Introductory Versions) 8 Total Chapters

Microsoft Internet Explorer 6.0 (Brief Version) 5 Total Chapters

Microsoft Windows

Microsoft Windows 2000 (Brief, Introductory, Complete Versions) 12 Total Chapters

Microsoft Windows XP (Brief, Introductory, Complete Versions) 12 Total Chapters

For additional resources, visit The I-Series Online Learning Center at www.mhhe.com/i-series

GOALS/PHILOSOPHY

The I-Series applications textbooks strongly emphasize that students learn and master applications skills by being actively engaged—by *doing*. We made the decision that teaching how to accomplish tasks is not enough for complete understanding and mastery. Students must understand the importance of each of the tasks that lead to a finished product at the end of each chapter.

Approach

The I-Series chapters are subdivided into sessions that contain related groups of tasks with active, hands-on components. The session tasks containing numbered steps collectively result in a completed project at the end of each session. Prior to introducing numbered steps that show how to accomplish a particular task, we discuss why the steps are important. We discuss the role that the collective steps play in the overall plan for creating or modifying a document or object, answering students' often-heard questions, "Why are we doing these steps? Why are these steps important?" Without an explanation of why an activity is important and what it accomplishes, students can easily find themselves following the steps but not registering the big picture of what the steps accomplish and why they are executing them.

I-Series Applications for 2003

The I-Series offers three levels of instruction. Each level builds upon knowledge from the previous level. With the exception of the running project that is the last exercise of every chapter, chapter cases and end-of-chapter exercises are independent from one chapter to the next, with the exception of Access. The three levels available are

Brief   Covers the basics of the Microsoft application and contains Chapters 1 through 4. The Brief textbooks are typically 200 pages long.

Introductory   Includes chapters in the Brief textbook plus Chapters 5 through 8. Introductory textbooks typically are 400 pages long and prepare students for the Microsoft Office Specialist (MOS) Core Exam.

Complete   Includes the Introductory textbook plus Chapters 9 through 12. The four additional chapters cover advanced-level content and the textbooks are typically 600 pages long. Complete textbooks prepare students for the Microsoft Office Specialist (MOS) Expert Exam. The Microsoft Office User Specialist program is recognized around the world as the standard for demonstrating proficiency using Microsoft Office applications.

In addition, there are two compilation volumes available.

Office I   Includes introductory chapters on Windows and Computing Concepts followed by Chapters 1 through 4 (Brief textbook) of Word, Excel, Access, and PowerPoint. In addition, material from the companion Computing Concepts book is integrated into the first few chapters to provide students with an understanding of the relationship between Microsoft Office applications and computer information systems.

Office II   Includes introductory chapters on Windows and Computing Concepts followed by Chapters 5 through 8 from each of the Introductory-level textbooks including Word, Excel, Access, and PowerPoint. In addition, material from the companion Computing Concepts book is integrated into the introductory chapters to provide students with a deeper understanding of the relationship between Microsoft Office applications and computer information systems. An introduction to Visual Basic for Applications (VBA) completes the Office II textbook.

STEPHEN HAAG

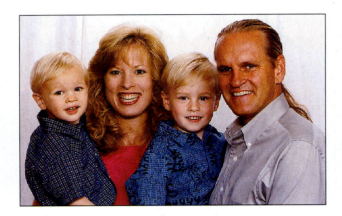

Stephen Haag is a professor and Chair of Information Technology and Electronic Commerce and the Director of Technology in the University of Denver's Daniels College of Business. Stephen holds a B.B.A. and M.B.A. from West Texas State University and a Ph.D. from the University of Texas at Arlington. He has published numerous articles appearing in such journals as *Communications of the ACM, The International Journal of Systems Science, Applied Economics, Managerial and Decision Economics, Socio-Economic Planning Sciences,* and the *Australian Journal of Management.*

Stephen is also the author of 20 other books including *Interactions: Teaching English as a Second Language* (with his mother and father), *Case Studies in Information Technology, Information Technology: Tomorrow's Advantage Today* (with Peter Keen), and *Excelling in Finance.* He is also the lead author of the accompanying I-Series *Computing Concepts* text, released in both an Introductory and a Complete version. Stephen lives with his wife, Pam, and their four sons—Indiana, Darian, Trevor, and Elvis—in Highlands Ranch, Colorado.

JAMES PERRY

James Perry is a professor of Management Information Systems in the University of San Diego's School of Business. He holds a B.S. in mathematics from Purdue University and a Ph.D. in computer science from The Pennsylvania State University. Jim has published several journal and conference papers. He is the co-author of 60 other textbooks and trade books including *Using Access with Accounting Systems, Building Accounting Systems, Understanding Oracle, The Internet,* and *Electronic Commerce.* His books have been translated into Chinese, Dutch, French, and Korean. Jim teaches both undergraduate and graduate courses at the University of San Diego and has worked as a computer security consultant to various private and governmental organizations including the Jet Propulsion Laboratory. He was a consultant on the Strategic Defense Initiative ("Star Wars") project and served as a member of the computer security oversight committee. Jim lives with his wife, Nancy, in San Diego, California. He has three grown children: Jessica, Stirling, and Kelly.

PAIGE BALTZAN

Paige Baltzan is a professor of Information Technology and Electronic Commerce in the University of Denver's Daniels College of Business. Paige holds a B.S.B.A. from Bowling Green State University and an M.B.A. from the University of Denver. Paige's primary concentration focuses on object-oriented technologies and systems development methodologies. She has been teaching Systems Analysis and Design, Telecommunications and Networking, Software Engineering, and The Global Information Economy at the University of Denver for the past three years. Paige has contributed materials for several McGraw-Hill publications including *Using Information Technology* and *Management Information Systems for the Information Age.*

Prior to joining the University of Denver Paige spent three years working at Level(3) Communications as a Technical Architect and four years working at Andersen Consulting as a Technology Consultant in the telecommunications industry. Paige lives in Lakewood, Colorado, with her husband, Tony, and her daughter, Hannah.

AMY PHILLIPS

Amy Phillips is a professor of Information Technology and Electronic Commerce in the University of Denver's Daniels College of Business. She holds a B.S. degree in environmental biology and an M.S. degree in education from Plymouth State College. Amy has been teaching for more than 18 years: 5 years in public secondary education and 13 years in higher education. She has also been an integral part of both the academic and administrative functions within the higher educational system.

Amy's main concentration revolves around database driven Web sites focusing on dynamic Web content, specifically ASP and XML technologies. Some of the main core course selections that Amy teaches at the University of Denver include Analysis and Design, Database Management Systems, Using Technology to Communicate, and Using Technology to Manage Information. Her first book, *Internet Explorer 6.0,* written with Stephen Haag and James Perry, was published in September 2002.

MERRILL WELLS

Merrill Wells is a professor of Information Technology and Electronic Commerce in the University of Denver's Daniels College of Business. Merrill holds a B.A. and M.B.A. from Indiana University. Although her goal was to teach and write, she followed the advice of her professors and set out to gain business experience before becoming a professor herself.

Merrill began her nonacademic career as a business systems programmer developing manufacturing, accounting, and payroll software using relational databases. Throughout her first career Merrill worked in the aerospace, manufacturing, construction, and oil and gas industries. After years of writing technical manuals and training end users, Merrill honored her original goal and returned to academia to become an active instructor of both graduate and undergraduate technology courses.

Merrill is the author of several online books including *An Introduction to Computers, Introduction to Visual Basic,* and *Programming Logic and Design.* Merrill lives with her husband, Rick, in Denver, Colorado. They have four children—Daniel, Dusty, Victoria (Tori), and Evan—and foster twins Connor and Gage.

Each textbook features the following:

Did You Know Each chapter has six or seven interesting facts—about both high-tech and other topics.

Sessions Each chapter is divided into two or three sessions.

Chapter Outline Provides students with a quick map of the major headings in the chapter.

Chapter and Microsoft Office Specialist Objectives At the beginning of each chapter is a list of 5 to 10 action-oriented objectives. Any chapter objectives that are also Microsoft Office Specialist objectives indicate the Microsoft Office Specialist objective number.

Chapter Opening Case Each chapter begins with a case. Cases describe a mixture of fictitious and real people and companies and the needs of the people and companies. Throughout the chapter, the student gains the skills and knowledge to solve the problem stated in the case.

Introduction The chapter introduction establishes the overview of the chapter's activities in the context of the case problem.

Another Way and Another Word Another Way is a highlighted feature providing a bulleted list of steps to accomplish a task, or best practices—that is, a better or faster way to accomplish a task such as pasting a format into an Excel cell. Another Word, another highlighted box, briefly explains more about a topic or highlights a potential pitfall.

Step-by-Step Instructions Numbered step-by-step instructions for all hands-on activities appear in a distinctive color. Keyboard characters and menu selections appear in a **special format** to emphasize what the user should press or type. Steps make clear to the student the exact sequence of keystrokes and mouse clicks needed to complete a task such as formatting a Word paragraph.

Tips Tips appear within a numbered sequence of steps and warn the student of possible missteps or provide alternatives to the step that precedes the tip.

Task Reference and Task Reference Summary Task References appear throughout the textbook. Set in a distinctive design, each Task Reference contains a bulleted list of steps showing a generic way to accomplish activities that are especially important or significant. A Task Reference Summary at the end of each chapter summarizes a chapter's Task References.

Microsoft Office Specialist Objectives Summary A list of Microsoft Office Specialist objectives covered in a chapter appears in the chapter objectives and the chapter summary.

Making the Grade Short answer questions appear at the end of each chapter's sessions. They test a student's grasp of each session's contents, and Making the Grade answers appear at the end of each chapter so students can check their answers.

Rich End-of-Chapter Materials End-of-chapter materials incorporating a three-level approach reinforce learning and help students take ownership of the chapter. Level One, Review of Terminology, contains fill in the blank, true/false, and multiple choice questions that enforce review of a chapter's key terms. Level Two, Review of Concepts, contains review questions and a Jeopardy-style create-a-question exercise. Level Three contains Hands-On Projects (see the paragraph following this one). Level Four, Analysis, contains short questions that require students to step back from the details of what they learned and think about higher level concepts covered in the chapter.

Hands-On Projects Extensive hands-on projects engage the student in a problem-solving exercise from start to finish. There are seven clearly labeled categories that each contain one or two questions. Categories are Practice, Challenge!, E-Business, On the Web, Around the World, Analysis, and a Running Project that carries throughout all the chapters.

We understand that, in today's teaching environment, offering a textbook alone is not sufficient to meet the needs of the many instructors who use our books. To teach effectively, instructors must have a full complement of supplemental resources to assist them in every facet of teaching, from preparing for class to conducting a lecture to assessing students' comprehension. The **I-Series** offers a complete supplements package and Web site that is briefly described below.

INSTRUCTOR'S RESOURCE KIT

The Instructor's Resource Kit is a CD-ROM containing the Instructor's Manual in both MS Word and .pdf formats, PowerPoint Slides with Presentation Software, Brownstone test-generating software, and accompanying test item files in both MS Word and .pdf formats for each chapter. The CD also contains figure files from the text, student data files, and solutions files. The features of each of the three main components of the Instructor's Resource Kit are highlighted below.

Instructor's Manual Featuring:

- Chapter learning objectives
- Chapter key terms
- Chapter outline and lecture notes
  - Teaching suggestions
  - Classroom tips, tricks, and traps
  - Page number references
- Additional end-of-chapter practice projects
- Answers to all Making the Grade and end-of-chapter questions
- Text figures

PowerPoint Presentation

The PowerPoint presentation is designed to provide instructors with comprehensive lecture and teaching resources that will include

- Chapter learning objectives followed by source content that illustrates key terms and key facts per chapter
- FAQ (frequently asked questions) to show key concepts throughout the chapter; also lecture notes, to illustrate these key concepts and ideas

- End-of-chapter exercises and activities per chapter, as taken from the end-of-chapter materials in the text
- Speaker's Notes, to be incorporated throughout the slides per chapter
- Figures/screen shots, to be incorporated throughout the slides per chapter

Test Bank

The I-Series Test Bank, using Diploma Network Testing Software by Brownstone, contains over 3,000 questions (both objective and interactive) categorized by topic, page reference to the text, and difficulty level of learning. Each question is assigned a learning category:

- Level 1: Key Terms and Facts
- Level 2: Key Concepts
- Level 3: Application and Problem-Solving

The types of questions consist of 20 percent Multiple Choice, 50 percent True/False, and 30 percent Fill-in-the-Blank Questions.

ONLINE LEARNING CENTER/ WEB SITE

To locate the I-Series OLC/Web site directly, go to www.mhhe.com/i-series. The site is divided into three key areas:

- **Information Center** Contains core information about the text, the authors, and a guide to our additional features and benefits of the series, including the supplements.

- **Instructor Center** Offers instructional materials, downloads, additional activities and answers to additional projects, answers to chapter troubleshooting exercises, answers to chapter preparation/post exercises posed to students, relevant links for professors, and more.

- **Student Center** Contains chapter objectives and outlines, self-quizzes, chapter troubleshooting exercises, chapter preparation/post exercises, additional projects, simulations, student data files and solutions files, Web links, and more.

RESOURCES FOR STUDENTS

SimNet

SimNet is a simulated assessment and learning tool for either Microsoft® Office XP or Microsoft® Office 2003. SimNet allows students to study MS Office skills and computer concepts, and professors to test and evaluate students' proficiency, within MS Office applications and concepts. Students can practice and study their skills at home or in the school lab using SimNet, which does not require the purchase or installation of Office software. SimNet includes:

Structured Computer-Based Learning SimNet offers a complete computer-based learning side that presents each skill or topic in several different modes. *Teach Me* presents the skill or topic using text, graphics, and interactivity. *Show Me* presents the skill using an animation with audio narration to show how the skill is used or implemented. *Let Me Try* allows you to practice the skill in SimNet's robust simulated interface.

Computer Concepts Coverage! SimNet includes coverage of 60 computer concepts in both the Learning and the Assessment side.

The Basics and More! SimNet includes modules of content on:

Word	Windows 2000
Excel	Computer Concepts
Access	Windows XP Professional
PowerPoint	Internet Explorer 6
Office XP Integration	FrontPage
Outlook	

More Assessment Questions! SimNet includes over *1,400* assessment questions.

Practice or Pre-Tests Questions! SimNet has a separate pool of over *600* questions for Practice Tests or Pre-Tests.

Comprehensive Exercises! SimNet offers comprehensive exercises for each application. These exercises require the student to use multiple skills to solve one exercise in the simulated environment.

Simulated Interface! The simulated environment in SimNet has been substantially deepened to more realistically simulate the real applications. Now students are not graded incorrect just because they chose the wrong submenu or dialog box. The student is not graded until he or she does something that immediately invokes an action—just like the real applications!

DIGITAL SOLUTIONS FOR INSTRUCTORS AND STUDENTS

PageOut PageOut is our Course Web Site Development Center that offers a syllabus page, URL, McGraw-Hill Online Learning Center content, online exercises and quizzes, gradebook, discussion board, and an area for student Web pages. For more information, visit the PageOut Web site at www.pageout.net.

Online Courses Available OLCs are your perfect solutions for Internet-based content. Simply put, these Centers are "digital cartridges" that contain a book's pedagogy and supplements. As students read the book, they can go online and take self-grading quizzes or work through interactive exercises.

Online Learning Centers can be delivered through any of these platforms:

McGraw-Hill Learning Architecture (TopClass)

Blackboard.com

College.com (formerly Real Education)

WebCT (a product of Universal Learning Technology)

Did You Know?

A unique presentation of text and graphics introduce interesting and little-known facts.

CHAPTER one

1

Creating Worksheets for Decision Makers

did you
know?

one-third *of online shoppers abandon their electronic shopping carts before completing the checkout process.*

goldfish *lose their color if they are kept in a dim light or if they are placed in a body of running water such as a stream.*

electric *eels are not really eels but a type of fish.*

in *1963, baseball pitcher Gaylord Perry said, "They'll put a man on the moon before I hit a home run." Only a few hours after Neil Armstrong set foot on the moon on July 20, 1969, Perry hit the first and only home run of his career.*

Chapter Objectives

- Start Excel and open a workbook
- Move around a worksheet using the mouse and arrow keys
- Locate supporting information (help)—MOS XL03S-1-3
- Select a block of cells
- Type into worksheet cells text, values, formulas, and functions—MOS XL03S-2-3
- Edit and clear cell entries—MOS XL03S-1-1
- Save a workbook
- Add a header and a footer—MOS XL03S-5-7
- Preview output—MOS XL03S-5-5
- Print a worksheet and print a worksheet's formulas—MOS XL03S-5-8
- Exit Excel

Chapter Objectives

Each chapter begins with a list of competencies covered in the chapter.

Task Reference

Provides steps to accomplish an especially important task.

task *reference*   Opening an Excel Workbook

- Click **File** and then click **Open**
- Ensure that the Look in list box displays the name of the folder containing your workbook
- Click the workbook's name
- Click the **Open** button

SESSION 1.1

Making the Grade

Short-answer questions appear at the end of each session, and answers appear at the end of each chapter.

making the grade

1. A popular program used to analyze numeric information and help make meaningful business decisions is called a _____ program.

2. _____ analysis is observing changes to spreadsheets and reviewing their effect on other values in the spreadsheet.

3. An Excel spreadsheet is called a(n) _____ and consists of individual pages called _____.

4. Beneath Excel's menu bar is the _____ toolbar, which contains button shortcuts for commands such as Print, and the _____ toolbar containing button shortcuts to alter the appearance of worksheets and their cells.

5. The _____ cell is the cell in which you are currently entering data.

Modifying the left and right margins:

1. With the Print Preview window still open, click the **Setup** button. The Page Setup dialog box opens

2. Click the **Margins** tab and double-click the **Left spin control box** to highlight the current left margin number

3. Type **0.5** to set the left margin to one-half inch

4. Double-click the **Right spin control box** to highlight the current right margin number

5. Type **0.5** to set the right margin to one-half inch

6. Click **OK** to close the Page Setup dialog box

tip: If you still cannot see the entire worksheet on one page, you can force the worksheet to fit by clicking the **Page** tab in the Page Setup dialog box and then click the **Fit to** option button in the Scaling section of t...
it fits on a single page

7. Click the **Close** butto... and return to the wo...

Step-by-Step Instruction

Numbered steps guide you through the exact sequence of keystrokes to accomplish the task.

Tips

Tips appear within steps and either indicate possible missteps or provide alternatives to a step.

Screen Shots

Screen shots show you what to expect at critical points.

---

hands-on projects

practice

LEVEL THREE · CHAPTER ONE

1. Creating an Income Statement

Carroll's Fabricating, a machine shop providing custom metal fabricating, is preparing an income statement for its shareholders. Betty Carroll, the company's president, wants to know exactly how much net income the company has earned this year. Although Betty has prepared a preliminary worksheet with labels in place, she wants you to enter the values and a few formulas to compute cost of goods sold, gross profit, selling and advertising expenses, and net income. Figure 1.26 shows an example of a completed worksheet.

1. Open the workbook **ex01Income.xls** in your student disk in the folder Ch01

2. Click **File** and then click **Save As** to save the workbook as **Income2.xls** in the folder Ch01

3. Scan the Income Statement worksheet and type the following values in the listed cells: Cell C5, **987453**; cell B8, **64677**; cell B9, **564778**; cell B10, **-43500**; cell B15, **53223**; cell B16, **23500**; cell B17, **12560**; cell B18, **123466**; cell B19, **87672**

4. In cell C10, write the formula =SUM(B8:B10) to sum cost of goods sold

5. In cell C12, type the formula for Gross Profit: =C5-C10

6. In cell C19, type the formula to sum selling and advertising expenses: =SUM(B15:B19)

7. In cell C21, type the formula =C12-C19 to compute net income (gross profit minus total selling and advertising expenses)

8. In cell A4, type **Prepared by** <your name>

9. Click the Save button on the Standard toolbar to save your modified worksheet

10. Print the worksheet and print the worksheet formulas

FIGURE 1.26
Income statement

EX 1.41
EXCEL

www.mhhe.com/i-series

End-of-Chapter Hands-On Projects

A rich variety of projects introduced by a case lets you put into practice what you have learned. Categories include Practice, Challenge, On the Web, E-Business, Around the World, and a running case project.

---

another word   . . . on Cell Ranges

A SUM function can contain more than one cell range. For example, the function =SUM(A1:A5,B42:B51) totals two cell ranges. Place commas between distinct cell ranges within the SUM function. The collection of cells, cell ranges, and values in the comma-separated list between a function's parentheses is its *argument list*

Another Way/ Another Word

Another Way highlights an alternative way to accomplish a task; Another Word explains more about a topic.

---

task reference summary

Task	Location	Preferred Method
Opening an Excel workbook	EX 1.00	• Click **File**, click **Open**, click workbook's name, click the **Open** button
Entering a formula	EX 1.00	• Select cell, type =, type formula, press **Enter**
Entering the SUM function	EX 1.00	• Select cell, type **=SUM(**, type cell range, type), and press **Enter**
Editing a cell	EX 1.00	• Select cell, click formula bar, make changes, press **Enter**
Saving a workbook with a new name	EX 1.00	• Click **File**, click **Save As**, type filename, click **Save** button
Obtaining help	EX 1.00	Obtaining help

Task Reference Summary

Provides a quick reference and summary of a chapter's task references.

What does this logo mean?

It means this courseware has been approved by the Microsoft® Office Specialist Program to be among the finest available for learning *Microsoft Word 2003, Microsoft Excel 2003, Microsoft PowerPoint® 2003, Microsoft Access 2003, Microsoft Outlook® 2003*. It also means that upon completion of this courseware, you may be prepared to take an exam for Microsoft Office Specialist qualification. The I-Series Microsoft Office 2003 books are available in three levels of coverage: Brief, Introductory, and Complete. The I-Series Introductory books are approved courseware to prepare you for the Microsoft Office specialist exam. The I-Series Complete books will prepare you for the expert exam.

What is a Microsoft Office Specialist?

A Microsoft Office Specialist is an individual who has passed exams for certifying his or her skills in one or more of the Microsoft Office desktop applications such as Microsoft Word, Microsoft Excel, Microsoft PowerPoint, Microsoft Outlook, Microsoft Access, or Microsoft Project. The Microsoft Office Specialist Program typically offers certification exams at the "Core" and "Expert" skill levels.* The Microsoft Office Specialist Program is the only program in the world approved by Microsoft for testing proficiency in Microsoft Office desktop applications and Microsoft Project. This testing program can be a valuable asset in any job search or career advancement.

More Information:

To learn more about becoming a Microsoft Office Specialist, visit www.microsoft.com/officespecialist.

To learn about other Microsoft Office Specialist approved courseware from McGraw-Hill Technology Education, visit www.mhhe.com/i-series/mos.

*The availability of Microsoft Office Specialist certification exams varies by application, application version, and language. Visit www.microsoft.com/officespecialist for exam availability.

Microsoft, the Microsoft Office Logo, PowerPoint, and Outlook are trademarks or registered trademarks of Microsoft Corporation in the United States and/or other countries, and the Microsoft Office Specialist Logo is used under license from owner.

acknowledgments

The authors want to acknowledge the work and support of the seasoned professionals at McGraw-Hill. Thank you to Bob Woodbury, Editor in Chief, for his leadership and a management style that fosters creativity and innovation. Thank you to Craig Leonard, Associate Sponsoring Editor. Craig took on the very difficult task of both developmental editor and then sponsoring editor with eagerness and did a splendid job of bringing all the pieces together.

Thank you to Victoria Hampton, a Rose-Hulman Institute of Technology engineering student, who assisted in editing, created some of the data files, and captured many screen shots. We also wish to thank our schools, the University of Denver and the University of San Diego, for providing support including time off to dedicate to writing.

If you would like to contact us about any of the books in the I-Series, we would enjoy hearing from you. We welcome comments and suggestions. You can e-mail book-related messages to us at i-series@McGraw-Hill.com. For the latest information about the I-Series textbooks and related resources, please visit our Web site at www.mhhe.com/i-series.

dedication

To my wonderful family:

Rick, Daniel, Dusty, Tori, Evan, Connor, and Gage

For all that they do to support me when writing isn't easy and to celebrate the times when it goes well.

M.W.

brief *brief* contents

table of contents

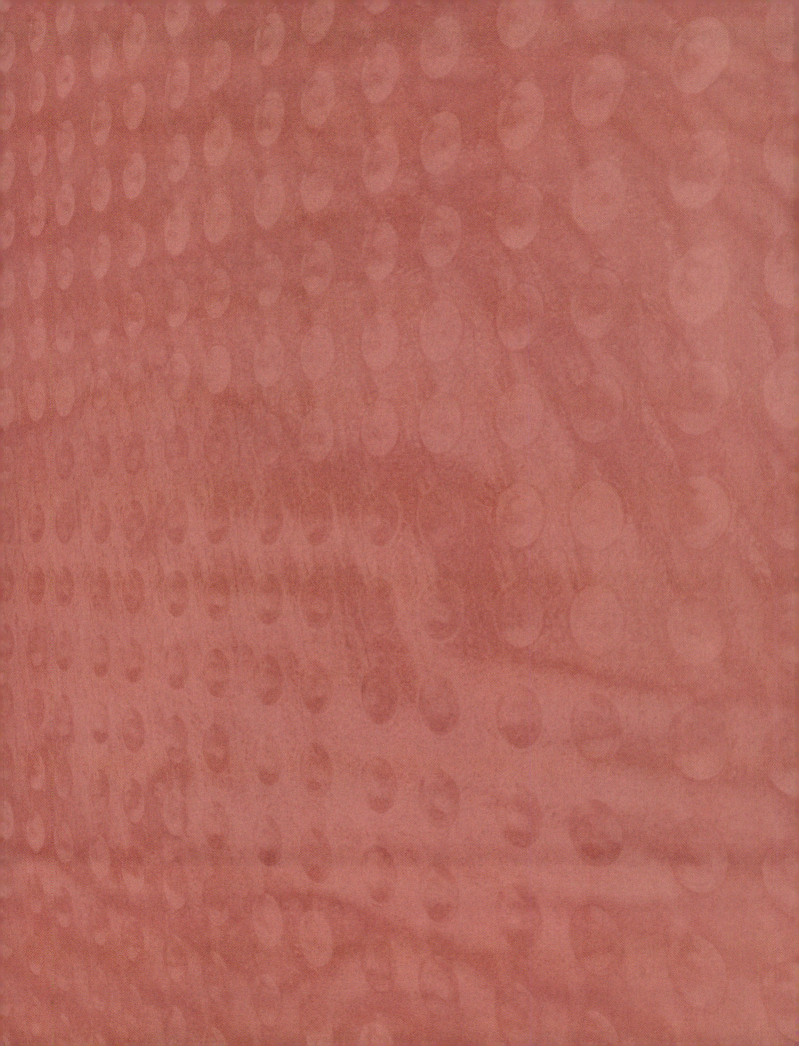

Understanding Relational Databases

did you know?

a *NUKE InterNETWORK poll found that 52 percent of Internet users have cut back on watching TV in order to spend more time online; 12 percent have cut back on seeing friends.*

Time *magazine named the computer its "Man of the Year" in 1982.*

dating *back to the 1600s, thermometers were filled with brandy instead of mercury.*

Bill Gates *formed a company to sell a computerized traffic counting system to cities, which made $20,000 its first year. Business dropped sharply when customers learned Gates was only 14 years old.*

a *1999 survey of 25,500 standard English-language dictionary words found that _____ percent of them have been registered as .coms.*

to *find out how many English-language words had been registered as .coms by the middle of 1999, visit* www.mhhe.com/i-series.

Chapter Objectives

- **Learn what relational databases are and how they function**
- **Define the terms *field, record, table,* and *database***
- **Understand the use of primary keys, aggregate keys, and foreign keys**
- **Navigate Access records—MOS AC03S-2-2**
- **Create an Access database using a Wizard—MOS AC03S-1-1**
- **Create a query with the Simple Query Wizard—MOS AC03S-1-7**
- **Build a table with the Table Wizard—MOS AC03S-1-2**
- **Create an AutoForm—MOS AC03S-1-8**
- **Print table design—MOS AC03S-4-3**
- **Print data in a form and datasheet—MOS AC03S-4-3**

KoryoKicks: Starting a Personal Business

Missy and Micah Hampton are twins who have been practicing martial arts for as long as they can remember. Their parents are both master instructors who participated in international competitions representing the United States when they were in college and now coach international competitors. Missy and Micah have been leading youth classes at their parents' martial arts studio and entering competitions since they were eight years old. Both are second-degree black belts.

The twins are away from home in college and are members of their college's martial arts team. Both have also made the national team. Although their course and workout schedules are very full, they need more spending money and want to go into business for themselves. Since they can no longer work for their parents but are familiar with martial arts, they have decided to offer self-defense classes to their fellow college students.

To begin, they contacted each fraternity and sorority on campus and secured permission to offer self-defense classes in the house. They then conducted demonstrations at each house willing to participate. The exhibitions consisted of forms, sparring, and board breaking emphasizing that these skills are designed to help individuals defend themselves. Students were recruited and payment accepted at the demonstrations. Classes were scheduled for two nights a week in any house with 10 or more committed students.

FIGURE 1.1
Martial arts supplies

For the first classes, Micah accepted payments and handwrote the receipts while Missy collected contact information such as name, phone number, and previous self-defense experience. Unfortunately, over time this methodology proved inadequate. They were unable to keep track of when a student started, when they could test for a belt, or when they needed to pay for additional sessions.

To project a more professional image and aid in student tracking, they decided to automate by using Word for receipts and invoices and Excel to track profits and expenses. After six months the partially automated business was a success, but data were still inadequate to meet business reporting and scheduling requirements.

What had started out as a way to earn a little extra cash had grown into a complex organization with a need to collect and track multifaceted data.

They had stacks of paper relating to students, classes attended, payments, invoices, locations, customers, demonstration schedules, house contacts, and supplies (see Figure 4.1). The problem was that finding information needed to make a business decision was onerous. Something as simple as determining how many people owed money or who to contact to extend classes required a frustrating manual search.

It is obvious that the data organization and reporting capabilities of a database could help, but the twins have no experience in this area. They ask you to help them determine how best to automate data gathering and evaluation. KoryoKicks will be used throughout this book to demonstrate the data needs of an entrepreneurial business and the use of Access to develop effective data applications.

SESSION 1.1 INTRODUCING RELATIONAL DATABASES

Before evaluating the specific needs of KoryoKicks, you decide to review your knowledge of databases. Because relational databases are the most efficient way to store and manipulate data, you will focus your research on those concepts.

Uses and Benefits of Relational Databases

All organizations maintain and use data for day-to-day business operations, history, and performance analysis. Data are stored about members of the organization (employees, customers), products of the organization (services, goods), suppliers (vendors, consultants), and transactions (sales, purchases). The data maintained are determined by the needs of the organization. Schools keep data on employees, students, and business operations such as ordering products and paying for products and services.

Data are a valuable organizational resource. Good data and information retrieval technology can improve the organization's ability to compete in an industry, deliver products to consumers, and evaluate opportunities. The loss or contamination of an organization's data can contribute to failure.

A *database management system (DBMS)* is the software that is used to store data, maintain those data, and provide easy access to stored data. Good DBMSs provide users with

- Common interfaces to share data
- Software tools needed to design the storage area for data
- Facilities to maintain stored data
- Tools to create screens (forms) used to view and update data
- Query services to obtain fast answers to questions about the data
- Report generation capabilities
- Utilities to secure, back up, and restore data

Relational database management systems (RDBMSs) are a type of DBMS that store data in interrelated tables. Tables are related by sharing a common field as shown in Figure 1.2. The tblVendor and tblSoftware tables share the common field VendorCode. If you select a product like Math Tester from tblSoftware, the VendorCode from that table can be matched to the VendorCode in tblVendor to retrieve data about Academic Software, the Math Tester vendor.

RDBMSs are flexible, reliable, and efficient because they use data storage and retrieval methodology based on mathematics. *Data integrity* is the term used to describe

F I G U R E 1.2

Using related tables

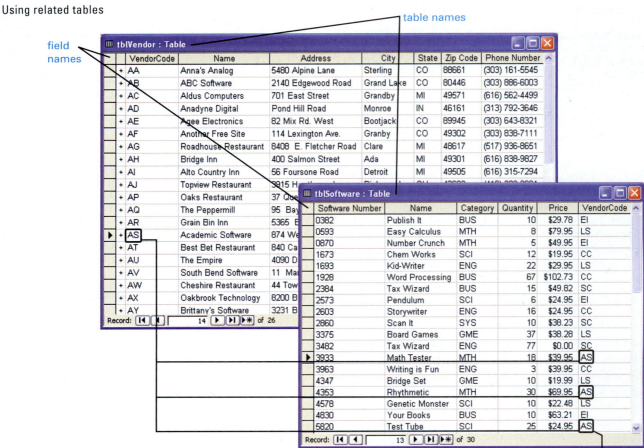

the VendorCode for Math Tester is used to look up the vendor in tblVendor

the reliability of data. Data stored in a relational database are more likely to be correct because

- They are validated as they are entered using **data validation rules** to ensure that entries are within appropriate bounds
- A specific piece of data such as customer name is stored only once—thereby avoiding the errors that could be introduced by making the same update to several files. Having one update point is said to reduce **data redundancy**
- Database security ensures that only authorized people can access and update data

Relational Database Concepts

In the computing world where software becomes obsolete almost before it can be implemented, relational database technology is relatively old and stable. Relational database theory was developed by E. F. Codd, a researcher at IBM in the 1960s. The first RDBMS was released in the mid-1970s for IBM mainframes. Since then RDBMS software has been developed for every size computer and operating system. Better implementations and graphical user interfaces (GUIs) have been produced, but the basic technology remains the same.

RDBMSs provide a **data definition language (DDL)** for structuring the data tables and their relationships and a **data access language (DAL)** for rapidly retrieving and organizing stored data. Questions or queries are posed to a relational database using **Structured Query Language (SQL)**. Most database management software, including Access, provide graphical interfaces that allow users to create tables, queries, forms, and reports without knowing the underlying language.

Relations

As previously demonstrated, relational databases store data in tables. The formal name for a table is a relation. A relation (table) consists of rows and columns of related data. Each row represents the unique data for one **entity** (person, place, object, idea, or event) and also can be referred to as a **record** or tuple. Each column represents a unique property of an entity such as LastName, BirthDate, or Quantity and also can be referred to as a **field** or attribute. The intersection of a row and column contains data pertaining to one attribute of one entity and is called a **data value**. For example, $39.95 is the Price (attribute) associated with SoftwareNum 3963 (entity identifier) in Figure 1.3. A **relational database** is a collection of such relations.

All entries in the table for one attribute belong to the same **domain**. The domain is the list of all possible values of an attribute. For example, the list of all Software Names is the domain for the Name attribute in tblSoftware.

Since each cell in a table represents the value for one entity and one attribute, the order in which the columns and rows are stored is irrelevant. You can view columns and rows in any order without impacting the validity of the data. The only restriction is that a column contains data values for only one attribute and a row represents the data for one entity.

Keys

Keys are table attributes that perform a special function in the relation. The **primary key** uniquely and minimally identifies an entity with one and only one row of data. In tblSoftware above, the field Software Number holds a unique value for each software company, identifying each as a distinct entity in the table. A primary key can identify one and only one row in the table. An error message will be generated and the update aborted by the RDBMS if a duplicate primary key is entered. To meet the minimal requirement of the primary key definition, the key must contain no unnecessary data. For example, the Software Number and Name fields could be used in combination to

F I G U R E   1.3
Example of a relation (table)

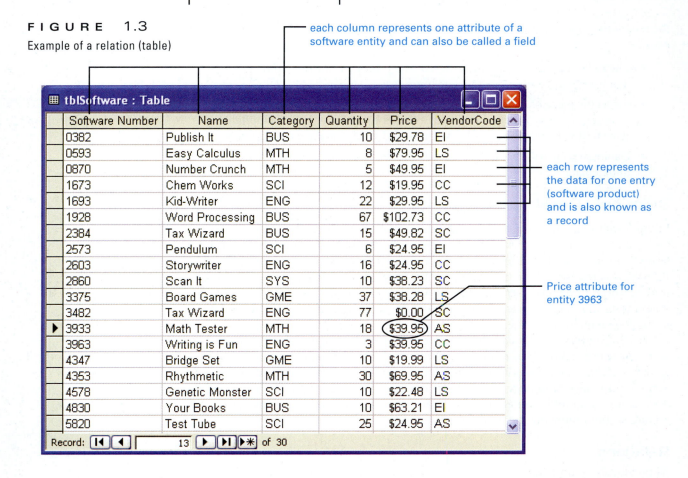

each column represents one attribute of a software entity and can also be called a field

each row represents the data for one entry (software product) and is also known as a record

Price attribute for entity 3963

uniquely identify each row of data in tblSoftware; however, the combination does not meet the minimal test because Software Number alone is a unique identifier.

Sometimes there is no one attribute (column) in a table with values that can uniquely identify each row of data. In such cases the designer looks for a combination of attributes that can act as the table primary key. When multiple columns of data are used for the primary key, the result is a **composite key**. As an example, a composite key is advisable when storing data about U.S. cities. The city name alone is not sufficient since multiple U.S. cities carry the same name (for example, Bloomington, IN, and Bloomington, IL). In this case, both the city and state columns would be required for a unique key.

In many instances, there are multiple attributes in the table that each could serve as the primary key of that table. Each attribute that could be defined as the primary key is called a **candidate key**. One of the candidate keys is assigned as the primary key and the others are called **alternate keys**. In tblSoftware Software Number and Name each uniquely and minimally identifies one row in the table and is therefore a candidate key. Software Number was named the primary key, so Name remains an alternate key.

A **foreign key** (see Figure 1.4) is used to match the values from one table to those in another table. VendorCode in tblSoftware is a foreign key that matches values in the tblVendor VendorCode attribute. In tblVendor VendorCode is the primary key. Most designers will give the same name to attributes stored in multiple tables so it is obvious that they are really the same attribute.

F I G U R E   1.4

Software database demonstrating one-to-many relationship

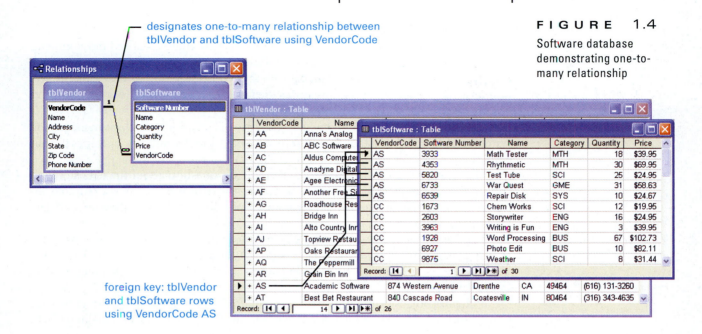

designates one-to-many relationship between tblVendor and tblSoftware using VendorCode

foreign key: tblVendor and tblSoftware rows using VendorCode AS

Because there are so many types of keys, the word *key* used alone can seem ambiguous, but it is not. When the word *key* is used without identifying the type of key (i.e., foreign key), it always means the primary key.

Relationships

When a foreign key from a table is used to link to the data in another table, it is called *joining*. Join relationships take one of the three forms discussed in the following paragraphs.

One-to-one (abbreviated 1:1) relationships exist when one row of the first table matches to one and only one row of the second table and both tables have the same primary key. One-to-one relationships are unusual because such closely related data would normally be stored in a single table. When table requirements exceed Access's limit of 255 columns per table, two tables with a one-to-one relationship are created to hold all of the data. Security and privacy issues also can cause closely related data to be stored in multiple tables. For example, in the medical community some patient data must be reported and some must be held private. Even though all of the data are for patients, it makes sense to store the private data in a separate table and use a one-to-one relationship to join it with the more public data.

One-to-many (abbreviated 1:M or 1:∞) relationships exist when one row of the first table matches to multiple rows in the second table. One-to-many relationships are the most common. Figure 1.4 shows the tables needed to keep inventory information for a small business like KoryoKicks. The tblSoftware table is used to store inventory information while tblVendor stores data about vendors who provide the software.

Many-to-many (abbreviated M:N or ∞:∞) relationships exist when one row in the first table matches with multiple rows in the second table and one row in the second table matches with multiple rows in the first table. Many-to-many relationships can't be directly modeled in relational databases but are broken into multiple one-to-many relationships.

Relational Database Objects

In general an object is a reusable template or structure that will speed development. Relational database objects assist in developing the components for the database. All RDBMSs support table, query, report, form, index, and stored procedure objects. The *database* file is a container that organizes the tables, queries, forms, reports, and other objects.

The *Table* object is the fundamental structure of a relational database management system. The function of a table object is to store data about a category of things such as employees in records (rows) and fields (columns).

The *Query* object will allow you to formulate a question about the data stored in your tables, or a request to perform an action on the data and store it as a reusable object. A query can bring together data from multiple tables to serve as the source of data for a form, report, or data access page.

The *Form* object allows you to create a custom interface for taking actions or for entering, displaying, and editing data in fields. A typical form, like the one in Figure 1.5, displays one row of data from a table in contrast to the default table grid that displays several rows of data.

A *Report* object prints information formatted and organized according to your specifications. Examples of reports are sales summaries, phone lists, and mailing labels.

Indexing

When storing more than a few records in a table, it is important to optimize the table so that data can be efficiently retrieved. Conceptually, storing and accessing data in tables are straightforward, but scanning tables for values or sorting the rows for output can be very inefficient. Consider looking for a specific topic in this book like *Saving Access as HTML*. One approach would be to scan the pages of this book until you found the topic. A second approach would be to find the topic in the index and then proceed to the correct page(s). In the vast majority of searches, the index approach would provide the fastest and most complete results.

F I G U R E   1.5

Tabbed form from the Northwind sample database

company data fields for one employee

tab to access second page of form

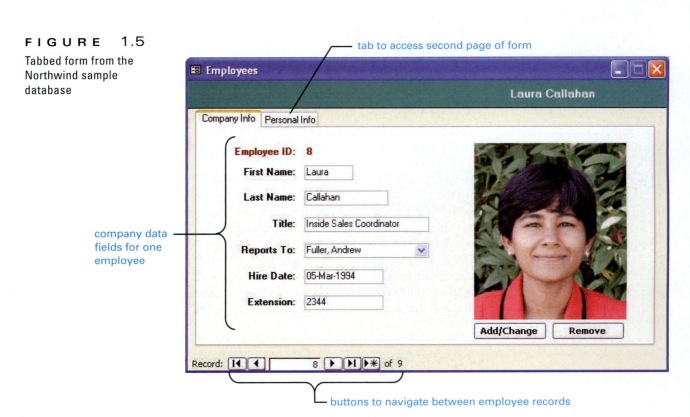

buttons to navigate between employee records

FIGURE 1.6

Indexes for the Customers table

Customers table design

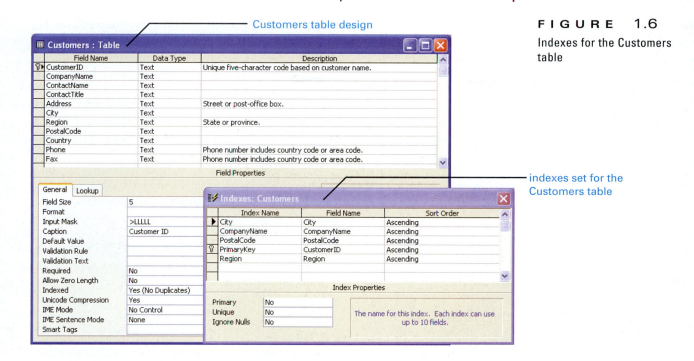

indexes set for the Customers table

Table *indexes* can be applied to improve table search performance and are similar in function to the index of a book. A table index tracks where the rows for a particular value are stored in the table so that the values can be accessed without scanning through the entire table. When you have a primary key, a unique index is automatically defined for the key values. Any other fields that are frequently used to search for values or sort data are also candidates for indexing. Figure 1.6 shows the fields and indexes for a Customer table. Notice that indexes have been set for the PrimaryKey (CustomerID) and PostalCode because both fields are frequently used to sort and retrieve data.

Indexes are automatically updated as table data are added or changed. There are no restrictions on the number of indexes applied to a table. Indexes can be added and deleted as they are needed using table Design View.

Database Management Systems

Database management systems are the various software products that allow organizations to store data in a central location using a standard format. While we are concentrating on the relational database model that stores data in tables, it is important to understand where the relational model fits in the overall data storage scheme. There are also hierarchical, network, and object-oriented models for database management systems.

DBMS Models

Hierarchical and network database management system models are older and more restricted than the relational model. Both the hierarchical and network models depend on predefined data relationships, while the relational database model allows new relationships to be defined at any time. There are, however, situations where users have fixed storage and reporting requirements where the older models will outperform relational databases.

Evolving user needs and emerging technologies have given rise to object-oriented DBMS models. In addition to handling conventional rows and columns of data, an object-oriented database will store documents, diagrams, graphics, multimedia, and more. In an object-oriented database, each item stored is an *object*. An object is virtually anything—traditional data, a moving image, people talking, a photograph, narrative, text, music, or any combination. Objects can be accessed individually or in combination. For example a graphic and a voice recording each could be a stored object in a database. These objects could be accessed individually or combined into a new object comprised of both the graphic and sound. Regardless of what is stored and how it will be used, the idea is to have a natural-looking way to interact with all types of data.

No leader has emerged in object-oriented database technology, and most current implementations are actually object-relational databases. An object-relational DBMS is a relational database that can store other objects such as graphics, video, audio, methods, and procedures describing how the objects will behave.

There are a wide variety of products that can be used to manage object-relational data access. Each product has strengths and weaknesses that should be understood before using the product. A few RDBMSs that, to one extent or another, can store objects are

- Microsoft Access—widely used on personal computers
- Microsoft SQL Server—used to share data on Microsoft NT networks
- Oracle—popular Web-commerce database
- DB2—IBM mini and mainframe data storage software

Client/Server DBMS

Besides looking at the model used to store the data, DBMSs can be divided into two basic categories: *personal databases* and *client/server databases*. Many of the same concepts apply to both DBMS categories. The differences lie largely in the amount of data that can be stored, the number of concurrent users supported, networking capabilities, and the level of data security provided.

Personal database management systems like Microsoft Office Access 2003 work best in single-user environments. The ideal environment is one user updating and reporting on the data from one PC. Although personal database management systems can be networked and shared, the general rule-of-thumb is that there should be no more than 10 concurrent users. If security, network traffic, or the ability to recover from system failures is important, a client/server DBMS would be a better choice.

Client/server DBMSs are designed to support multiple users in a networked environment. Powerful servers store and process large quantities of organizational data, while client PCs can request data from the server and then query, update, and report on it locally. A typical client/server application has a front end like Microsoft Office Access 2003 that runs on the local client workstation and a back end like Microsoft SQL Server that runs on the server. In these implementations, the front end provides the local user interface on a PC, while the back end has the power to store and process data from multiple users on a network server.

For example, the client (you at your PC) could request a listing of August computer sales. The server database holds the information for all organizational sales and must run a query to retrieve August computer sales, which it then passes to the requesting client (your computer). You now have a local copy of August computer sales that you can use your local client software to manipulate. Depending on the application, you might make changes to the local data and then the client could send updates to the server that are then applied to the organizational database.

Client/server applications are cost effective and scalable. They also can take advantage of common PC software like Microsoft Office Access 2003 on the client, making them easy for users to learn and use. On the down side, shared data are never as secure as centralized data stored on a mainframe.

Opening an Access Database

Access 2003 software can be opened from the Start menu or by opening an Access document directly. When an Access database file is double-clicked, Access is launched and then the database is loaded in one step.

Starting Access and opening a blank database:

1. Verify that Windows has loaded and is ready to launch programs

2. Click the **Start** button on the Windows Taskbar and then pause over **All Programs** to list the programs available on your computer

3. Pause over **Microsoft Office 2003** and then select **Microsoft Office Access 2003** to launch Access

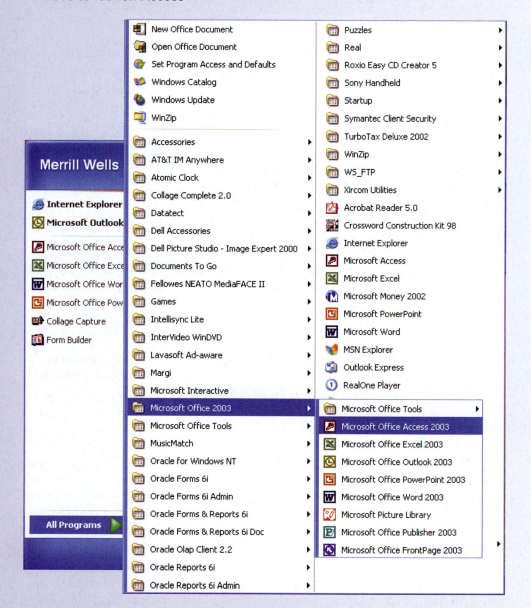

F I G U R E   1.7

Launching Access from the Start menu

tip: *Your screen may differ from what is depicted due to the settings on your computer, the operating system parameters, and what software has been installed*

If Microsoft Access is not listed in your Programs menu, you will need to either install Access or seek technical assistance

4. After a short pause, the Microsoft Access 2003 copyright information is displayed on the screen and then the Microsoft Access 2003 window displays

FIGURE 1.8

The Microsoft Access window

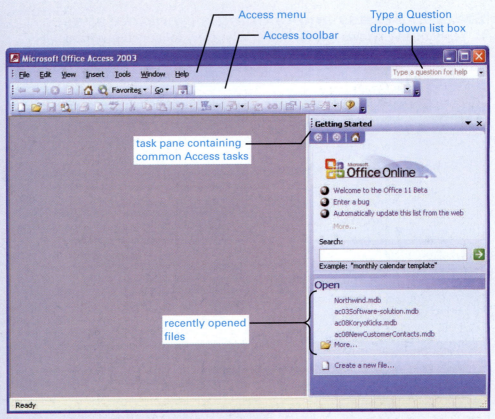

tip: *The specific files listed in the Open a file list will reflect database files loaded on your system. If the task pane is not displayed, use the Toolbars option of the view menu to display it*

5. In the task pane, click **Create a new file** and then click **Blank Database**
   a. Use the Save in drop-down list to select a location for your database
   b. Change the default filename to **ac01Blank.mdb**
   c. Click **Create**

The Access database, ac01Blank.mdb, created in the previous steps is an empty container ready to store objects. The only object that can be built in an empty database is a table. After at least one table is added, query, form, and report objects to manipulate table data can be created and stored.

Database Window

Like all Microsoft Office System applications, the Access 2003 opening page contains a menu, a toolbar, an edit pane, and a task pane. Once the Access program has been initiated, the task pane displays on the right-hand side of the screen. The initial file options in the task pane are to open an existing file, create a new database file, use an existing database file to create a new database, or use one of Microsoft's templates to create a new database. The last option in the task pane is a check box that will turn off the task pane so that it does not show each time Access loads. If you don't need the task pane, it can be closed using the Close button in its Title bar.

Remember that a database file is used to organize related tables, queries, forms, and reports. A prototype of the Customer database for KoryoKicks has been created using the customer information Missy and Micah provided.

Opening the Customers database:

1. Verify that Access is running and make sure that the data files for this course are in the proper drive

2. If the task pane is not displayed, click **View**, pause over **Toolbars**, and click **Task Pane**

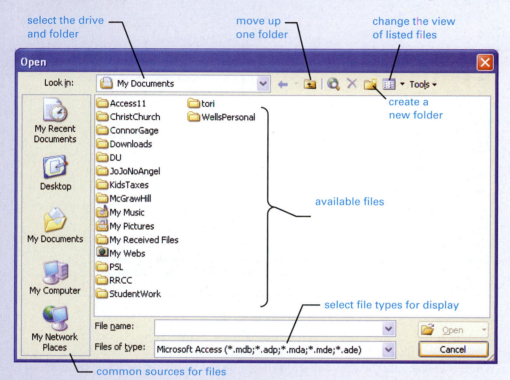

select the drive and folder

move up one folder

change the view of listed files

create a new folder

available files

select file types for display

common sources for files

FIGURE 1.9

Microsoft Access Open dialog box

3. If the **ac01Customers.mdb** database displays in the task pane, select it and *skip to step 5*

4. If the ac01Customers.mdb database does not display, click the **More files** option in the task pane to display a standard Open file dialog box

tip: *The Open dialog box will display the files from My Documents on your computer, so the files and folders displayed will be different on each computer*

5. Click the **Look in** drop-down arrow and select the drive and folder containing your data. Open the folder for Chapter 1 and select the **ac01Customers.mdb** file

6. Once the file is selected, click **Open** to load the database into Access

Windows and Toolbars

The Access 2003 user interface consists of a series of windows that display inside the main *Access Window*. As you can see in Figure 1.10, when a database is open, it displays in its own window called the *Database Window*. Tasks that are common to all Access operations reside on the Access Window, while those specific to a database are accomplished from the Database Window. Other windows will be discussed as we explore more features of Access.

Each open window has a toolbar with operations that are relevant to the functions of that window. For example, the toolbar in the Database Window contains options for

FIGURE 1.10
The Customers database

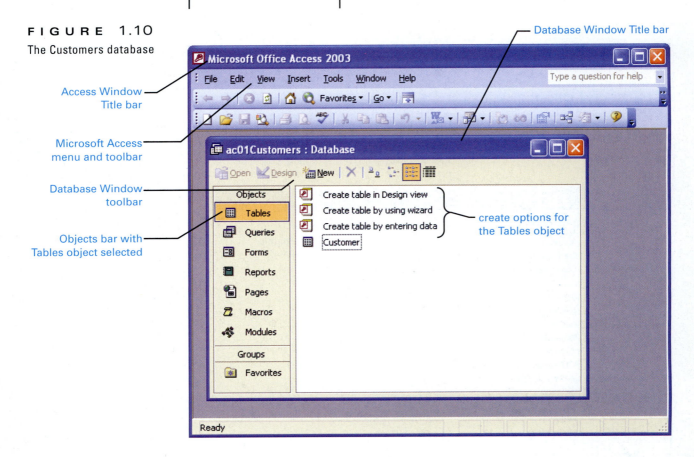

Access Window Title bar

Microsoft Access menu and toolbar

Database Window toolbar

Objects bar with Tables object selected

Database Window Title bar

create options for the Tables object

opening and creating database tables while the Access Window has common features used to open files, save files, and use the Office Clipboard. The toolbar in the Access Window enables and disables selections based on the needs of the active window.

Identifying Access Database Objects

The Database Window is made up of panes. The left pane holds the Objects bar and the Groups bar. The right pane displays the selections made from the left pane. The **Objects bar** displays icons for each of the objects that can be created for the open database. Clicking one of the Objects bar selections displays options for that object in the main pane of the Database Window. The **Groups bar** allows the user to group database objects for easier manipulation.

Tables

Clicking Tables in the Objects bar will display a list of tables for the open database. The Tables object is the backbone of a database, meaning that if there are no tables in the database, none of the other database objects can function. It should make sense that to query (ask questions of) a table, the table and its data must already exist.

For relational databases, tables are designed using a process called normalization, their structures are defined during the table creation process, and then data are entered. Notice in Figure 1.10 that the first three options presented when the Tables object is selected are tools used to create new tables in the database. Each table that has already been built is listed below the Create table tools.

Queries

Selecting Queries from the Objects bar will display valid query options for the open database. Queries are used to view, change, and analyze data in different ways. They also

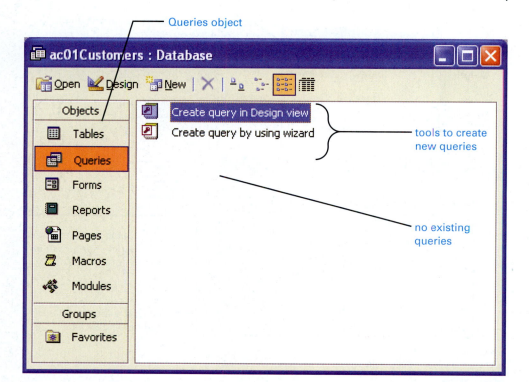

can be used to select and sort data for forms, reports, and data access pages. Access 2003 provides both QBE (Query by Example) and SQL (Structured Query Language) interfaces. Several types of queries are available in Microsoft Access 2003.

Select queries are the most common and are used to retrieve data from one or more tables. Select queries also can perform simple calculations and organize the data. Selected data can be updated or used for other processes like reporting.

Parameter queries are select queries that prompt the user for criteria that will be used in selecting data from the database. For example, the user might be prompted for two dates and then the query would display sales that occurred between the dates entered.

Crosstab queries are used to analyze data. They group data and calculate values for each group. If you have worked with Excel, it is very similar to crosstab reporting in that application.

Action queries update the data in a database in some fashion. Action queries can be used to delete a group of records that meet a criterion, to update a group of records, to add records to an existing table, or to add records to a new table. Action queries are very powerful and are most effective when used to update or move large quantities of data. For example, suppose that your database was very large. To improve performance, you decide to move data for customers who have not purchased anything in the last year to an inactive table. You could review and move records manually or use an action query with criteria for inactive accounts to select the records and move them to the inactive table in a single operation.

Forms

A form is a database object used primarily to enter and display database data. Forms also can be used to create a user interface for a database. Forms that create a user interface are called switchboards. A switchboard would contain options to open the tables, queries, forms, reports, and other objects of the database (see Figure 1.12). A dialog box is also a form that accepts user input and carries out an action based on the input. All forms are used to make it easier for a user to interact with the database.

F I G U R E   1.12

Examples of forms—
switchboard, input, and
dialog box

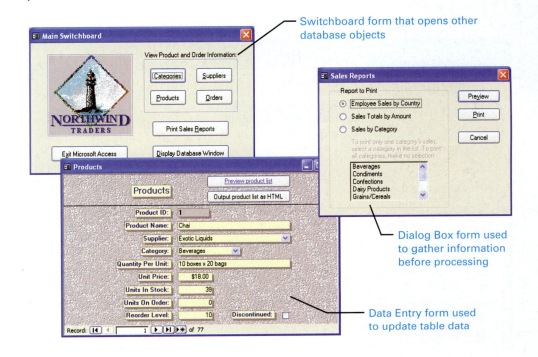

Switchboard form that opens other
database objects

Dialog Box form used
to gather information
before processing

Data Entry form used
to update table data

Reports

The Reports object is used to display database data in print. Reports can be as simple as mailing labels or contain complex formatting and graphics. Normally a report is based on the result of a query. Using a query to select the data ensures that the report contains only the desired rows and columns.

Once the data are selected, the report design specifies how those data will be displayed. The design includes specifications for the report title, sort order, and grouping and summarizing of data. Expressions can be used to create calculations based on data values. For example, if you were creating a sales report, you might want subtotals for the sales by month or by department.

Locating database objects:

1. From the Objects bar of the Database Window select **Tables**

tip: *It may already be selected. The Customer table object should display*

2. Click **Queries** in the Objects bar. No queries have been created so there are no objects to view

3. Explore the remaining database objects (which are all empty) and then return to **Tables**

help yourself *Use the Type a Question combo box to view the Help topics by typing **tables**. Review the contents of About Tables. Close the Help window when you are finished*

Pages

The Access 2003 Pages object supports the creation and deployment of Web pages. There are three types of Web pages that are related to data in a database. How the data will be used determines which type of page should be created.

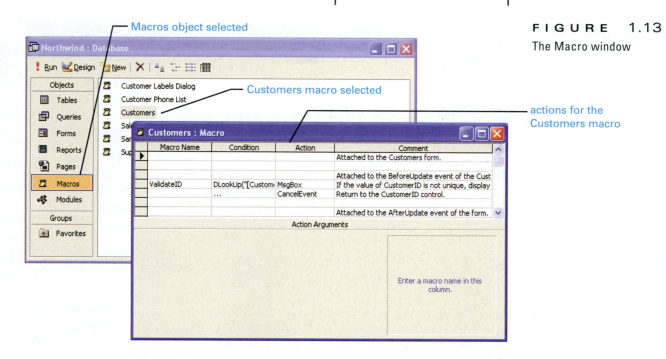

Data Access Pages allow a Web browser to be used to view and update table data. A Data Access Page has a live connection to the data in your database. It can be used on an intranet or published to the Internet using DHTML (Dynamic HTML) technology.

An **Active Server Page (ASP)** is designed to display up-to-date read-only data. The data are selected by the server and displayed in a table format. Opening or refreshing an ASP file from a Web browser causes the page to be dynamically created from current values and sent to the browser.

Finally, **static HTML** pages can be used to publish a snapshot of the data. Static pages can be based on tables, queries, forms, or reports. Each object will display in a format consistent with its on-screen appearance. No user action can cause a static page to update. If the data change, you must update the HTML pages and post them to the Web again. HTML template files can be used to create a consistent publishing format for static pages.

Macros

Macros are used to automate repetitive database tasks. The basic building block of a macro is an action: a self-contained instruction or command like Open Table. Actions are selected from a drop-down list box (see Figure 1.13) and include options for manipulating tables, queries, reports, and forms.

Modules

Modules are used to customize the way tables, forms, reports, and queries in your database look and function. Modules are written in Visual Basic (VB), a programming language used to develop Windows applications. A **module** is a collection of Visual Basic statements and procedures that are organized and stored together to be accessed as a unit. You can create simple event procedures that are initiated by a user action such as clicking or double-clicking. Complex custom functionality also can be added with a solid understanding of programming concepts.

ACCESS

making *the grade*

1. RDBMS is an acronym for _____.

2. SQL (Structured Query Language) is _____.

3. Tables are joined using shared _____.

4. A table attribute that uniquely and minimally identifies each row in the table is called a(n) _____.

5. Go back and review the KoryoKicks case at the beginning of this chapter. Considering the twins' business needs, create a list of data attributes (fields) the KoryoKicks database would need to store about its customers.

SESSION 1.2 INTRODUCING MICROSOFT ACCESS

Now that you have reviewed your understanding of database management systems and opened Access, it is time to introduce Missy and Micah to Access and begin to formulate a plan for KoryoKicks. Since KoryoKicks has some standard business needs like storing customer data, it makes sense to look at customer tables first.

Opening an Existing Table

Tables are the central objects of a database. They store the data on which all other Access objects operate. To view or update table data, the table must be opened.

Viewing Table Data

Since relational databases store data in tables, the default layout used to display Access data is a table or *Datasheet View*. In the datasheet, you can move to a new row by clicking the *record selector* button to the left of a record. An entire column of data can be selected using the *field selector* button above the column. The record selector is also called a row selector and the field selector can be called the column selector.

TRADITIONAL NAVIGATION.   The Tab key can be used to advance from cell to cell in the datasheet. Arrow keys also will move from cell to cell and have the added advantage of moving up and down between rows. When using keyboard navigation, the default is for the entire contents of a cell to be selected. This can be effective if you want to type and replace existing contents. If, however, you want to move character by character in a cell, you will need to choose Options from the Tools menu and change the Keyboard options to either Go to start of field or Go to end of field. You also can click in any cell using a pointing device or use the navigation buttons below the datasheet. Navigation buttons are outlined in Figure 1.14.

VOICE NAVIGATION.   Access 2003 is enabled to use speech for both dictation and command control. This feature is only effective if speech recognition training has been completed (covered in general Office Topics) and you own a good microphone headset. Activate speech recognition by selecting Speech from the Tools menu. The Language Bar—shown in Figure 1.15—will float over the Access Title bar, allowing you to control language options.

F I G U R E   1.14

Datasheet navigation buttons

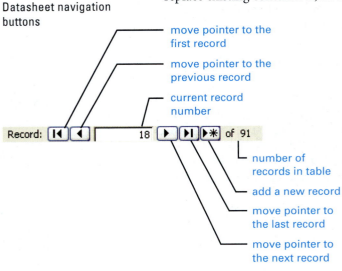

move pointer to the first record

move pointer to the previous record

current record number

number of records in table

add a new record

move pointer to the last record

move pointer to the next record

FIGURE   1.15
Language Bar

Voice commands can be issued by choosing Voice Command from the Language Bar and speaking menu options such as File Print. Because of the complexity of the Access interface, dictation is time consuming to learn and of limited functionality. Speaking keywords such as Tab moves from cell to cell in a datasheet, but dictating data values is challenging. For example, speaking "CustmrNmbr 048" (zero four eight) results in "zer" being stored in the field because speech recognition tried to write out zero but the field only allows 3 characters. Speaking "forty-eight" places 48 in the cell when 048 is the correct value. Similar problems arise when speaking dates and phone numbers.

---

task reference   Opening an Access Object

- Click the type of object that you would like to open in the Database Window's Objects bar

- Select the object that you would like to open

- Click the **Open** button

Opening the Customer table:

1. If you are not continuing from the previous session, start Access and open the ac01Customers.mdb database. Verify that the **Tables** object is selected in the Database Window

    tip: *Refer to Figure 1.10 to find the Tables object*

2. Double-click the **Customer** table. The contents of the table will display in Datasheet view

3. Navigate the table data by clicking in several cells

4. Select the record for Ben Katz by clicking the record selector (the gray button before the record)

5. Select the State column by clicking the column selector (the gray button above the data labeled State)

6. Click in any cell and use the Tab and Shift+Tab keys to navigate forward and backward through the cells

anotherway
. . . to Open Database Objects

Select the object and use the **Open** button of the Database Window toolbar.

OR

Right-click an object and select the **Open** option from the shortcut menu

---

Adjusting Column Widths and Row Heights

Besides navigating table data, you can adjust the appearance of datasheet contents. When the datasheet loads, default sizes for rows and columns are used. Often the column is larger or smaller than the data it contains. Resizing the columns and rows will make the data more readable.

ACCESS

FIGURE 1.16

The Customer table

current record
indicator

navigation bar

Customer : Table

CstmrNmbr	LastName	FirstName	Street	City	State	ZipCode	Phone	FirstContact
01	Wagoner	Sam	5480 Alpine Lane	Sterling	CO	88661	(303)161-5545	05/25/1999
02	Calahan	Eliza	2140 Edgewood Road	Grand Lake	CO	80446	(303)886-6003	05/25/2001
03	Lake	James	701 East Street	Grandby	MI	49571	(616)562-4499	08/25/1999
04	Meadows	Sara	Pond Hill Road	Monroe	IN	46161	(313)792-3646	02/28/1999
07	Calahan	Casey	82 Mix Rd. West	Bootjack	CO	89945	(303)643-8321	04/03/1999
21	Smith	Alto	114 Lexington Ave.	Granby	CO	49302	(303)838-7111	06/02/1996
22	Lewis	Ronnie	8408 E. Fletcher Road	Clare	MI	48617	(517)936-8651	04/12/1999
23	Chinn	Bridgett	400 Salmon Street	Ada	MI	49301	(616)838-9827	04/17/2001
25	Katz	Ben	56 Foursone Road	Detroit	MI	49505	(616)315-7294	06/12/2001
27	Gray	Monica	3915 Hawthorne Lane	Richmond	OH	43603	(419)332-3681	07/29/2001
28	Rivers	Ramona	37 Queue Highway	Lacota	MI	49063	(313)329-5364	04/20/2002
29	Amstont	Sandy	95 Bay Boulevard	Jenison	CO	80428	(616)131-9148	04/27/2000
31	Hill	James	5365 Bedford Trail	Eagle Point	CO	80031	(906)395-2041	05/01/2000
33	Florentine	Haven	874 Western Avenue	Drenthe	CA	49464	(616)131-3260	05/03/2001
35	Calahan	Thomas	840 Cascade Road	Coatesville	IN	80464	(316)343-4635	05/11/2001
36	Benton	Cleo	4090 Division St.	Borculo	OH	49464	(616)838-2046	05/11/2002
43	Pointe	Bryson	11 Marsh Rd	Shelbyville	IN	46344	(616)379-5681	10/24/1999
47	Krizner	Jean	44 Tower Lane	Mattawan	MI	49071	(517)630-4431	09/18/2000

Record: 1 of 26

Changing Customer table column widths and row heights:

1. Verify that the Customer table is open in Datasheet View

2. Place the pointer on the right edge of the State field selector until the pointer has left- and right-pointing arrows, as demonstrated in Figure 1.17

FIGURE 1.17

Adjusting column widths
and row heights

adjust State column width

adjusting the
height of one
row changes
all rows

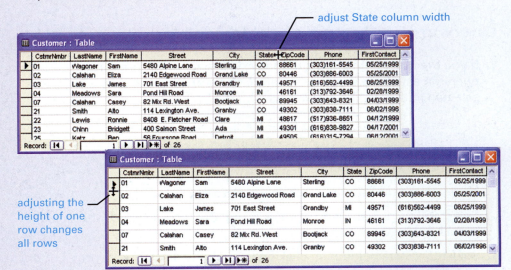

3. Click and drag the State column until it is just wide enough to display the data

4. To allow Access to automatically size a column based on the data it contains, double-click the right edge of the field selector. Use this method to adjust the width of the Street column

5. Place the pointer between any two record selectors and drag the rows to the desired height. Notice that all rows are adjusted to the same height

Changes to the column and row dimensions cannot be reversed with the Undo command from the toolbar or the Edit menu. When you close the datasheet, you will be prompted to save the changes to the layout of the table. Select Yes to retain the size adjustments, No to discard them, and Cancel to return to the datasheet.

Printing Table Data

Access print features are very similar to those of other Office products. There are two common methods for printing Access objects:

- Click the Print 🖨 button on the toolbar to print an open datasheet or other open object. If there is no datasheet open, the Print button will cause the selected object to print

- Alternatively, you can use the Print option of the File menu, which will open the Print dialog box. The Print dialog box provides options for setting up your output page, changing the printer, controlling printer properties, and printing multiple copies

The toolbar's Print Preview button is an excellent way to verify the content and format of output before printing. The Print Preview toolbar contains options to control the zoom (magnification) of the output and the number of pages that display for review and to change the printer setup. If you have made and saved formatting changes such as column widths or fonts to the datasheet, they will be reflected in the printed output.

Viewing Table Design

The *Design View* for a table displays the attributes of each field in the table called the table structure. Design View can be used to build tables from scratch or make changes to the design of existing tables. You and the twins will take a look at the design of the KoryoKicks Customer table prototype.

Displaying the Customer table's design:

1. If the Customer table is open, close it. From the Database Window, select **Table** from the Object bar and **Customer** from the main pane

2. Click the **Design View** 🗹 button from the Database Window toolbar

3. Review the attributes of the CstmrNmbr field

4. Close the Customer table Design View

In table Design View, the key icon in the CstmrNmbr selector (see Figure 1.18) indicates that it is the primary key. The Text data type means that it will accept any text entered (letters, numbers, or punctuation), a Field Size of 3 denotes that a maximum of three characters can be stored, and an Indexed value of Yes indicates that the field has been indexed.

F I G U R E   1.18
Customer table Design
View

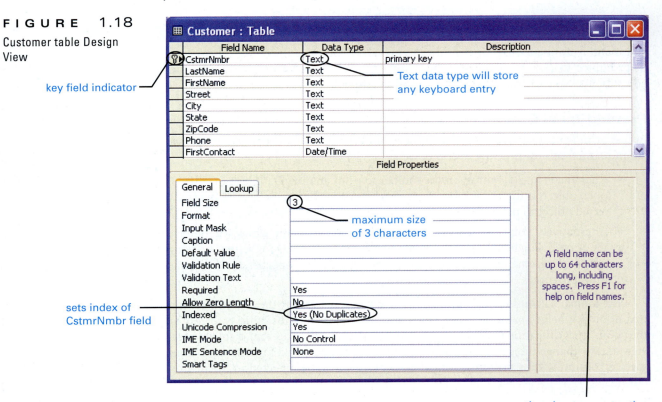

F I G U R E   1.18
Customer table Design
View

key field indicator

Text data type will store
any keyboard entry

maximum size
of 3 characters

sets index of
CstmrNmbr field

A field name can be
up to 64 characters
long, including
spaces. Press F1 for
help on field names.

tips about current action

---

anotherword . . . on Changing Views

Many Access objects support multiple views like the table object. The Design View allows you to see and update the table design while the Datasheet View allows you to see and update the stored data. You can move easily from one object view to another using the View button on the toolbar. The View button is a drop-down button that will display the valid views for the open or selected object. The two most common views are Datasheet and Design.

Printing Table Design

It is a good idea to keep paper documentation outlining the design of your tables. Printing table design *cannot* be accomplished using the Print option of the File menu, as you would expect. Special tools are used to analyze and document the design of Access objects. The documentation feature of the Database Analyzer includes the ability to print table designs.

Printing the Customer table's design:

1. From the **Tools** menu, select **Analyze** and then **Documenter**

   tip: *No particular object or view is necessary for this operation*

2. The Documenter dialog box will display to allow you to select the object to be documented and the options for the documentation

3. Verify that the **Tables** tab is selected and **check** the Customer table check box

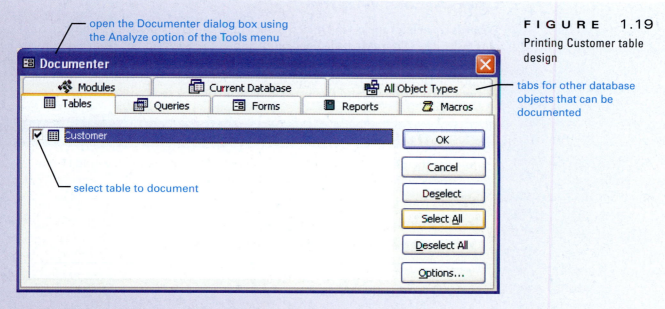

open the Documenter dialog box using the Analyze option of the Tools menu

tabs for other database objects that can be documented

select table to document

FIGURE 1.19
Printing Customer table design

tip: *The table to be documented must be checked; highlighting is not sufficient*

4. Click the **Options** button to display the Print Table Definition dialog box. The options selected here determine what documentation will print for the Customer table. The default values are shown in Figure 1.20

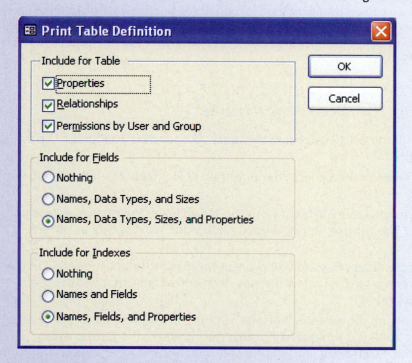

FIGURE 1.20
Print Table Definition dialog box settings

5. Click **OK** to exit the Print Table Definition dialog box

6. Click **OK** in the Documenter dialog box to generate a preview copy of the documentation

7. Select the **Printer** button from the toolbar to complete the Table Design. Print as you would print any other document

Using Access Wizards

Wizards are helpful applets in Office System Applications that walk users through complex tasks. The Wizards installed on your computer are determined by the options selected when Access was installed. To work along with the instructions in the section, you will need the Wizards for creating tables, forms, queries, and reports. If these Wizards are not present, run the installation again or seek technical assistance.

---

task reference   Activating Access Wizards

- Click the object (Queries, Forms, Reports) whose Wizard you would like to access in the Database Window's Objects bar
- Click **New** in the Database Window's toolbar
- The available Wizards will be listed
- Select the Wizard and respond to its questions

The Simple Query Wizard

The Simple Query Wizard allows columns (fields) to be specified for retrieval from one or more tables in a database. Simple calculations such as COUNT, SUM, or AVERAGE can be added to the results. This Wizard does not allow criteria for selecting specific rows of data, so all rows of the table(s) are included in the return set.

The Simple Query Wizard displays a series of dialog boxes requesting the information needed to complete the query. Each Wizard dialog box contains navigation buttons that will allow you to move to the previous dialog box (Previous), move to the next dialog box (Next), cancel the operation (Cancel), or complete the task with the data entered so far (Finish).

anotherway

. . . to Initiate the Simple Query Wizard

Once the Queries object is selected, double-click on Create query by using Wizard. The Simple Query Wizard dialog box will open in one step

Querying the Customer table:

1. Verify that the ac01Customers database is open and contains a Customer table with data

2. Click **Queries** in the Objects bar and then select **New** from the Database Window toolbar

3. Select **Simple Query Wizard** from the New Query dialog box, and then click **OK**. The Simple Query Wizard dialog box will display as shown in Figure 1.21

4. The Simple Query Wizard will prompt for the information needed to create a query. Use the Tables/Queries drop-down list box to select the **Customer** table

5. Practice using the selector buttons outlined in Figure 1.22 to select and unselect fields for the query. For this query, select the **CstmrNmbr**, **LastName**, **FirstName**, and **Phone** columns and then click **Next**

6. The Next dialog box allows the creation of a custom title for your query output. The default of Customer Query does not need to be changed. Click **Finish**

7. The query results are displayed in Datasheet View and can be manipulated, formatted, updated, or printed using the same techniques as when reviewing an entire table in Datasheet View

8. Close the datasheet and notice that Customer Query has been added to the list of Queries as shown in Figure 1.23

Simple Query Wizard

select the Queries object

click New

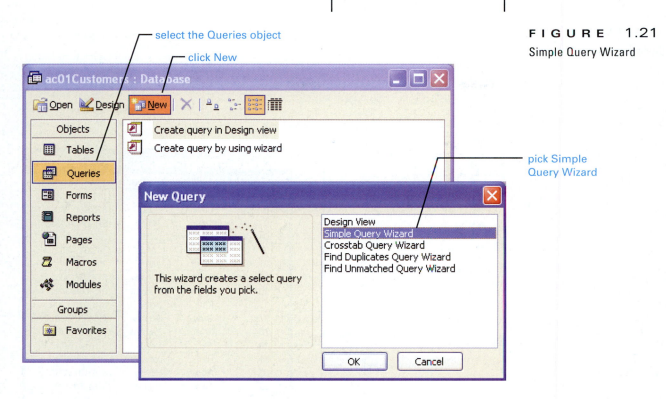

pick Simple
Query Wizard

Select table and fields for
query

select table to be queried

move all Available Fields to
Selected Fields

move highlighted Available
Fields to Selected Fields

remove highlighted
Selected Fields

remove all Selected Fields

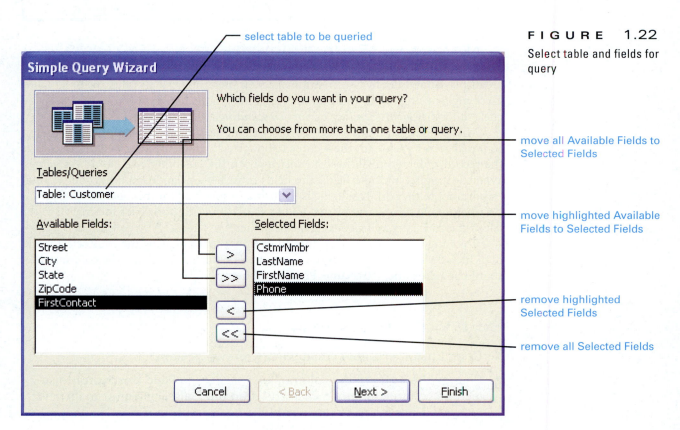

FIGURE   1.23

Customer query results

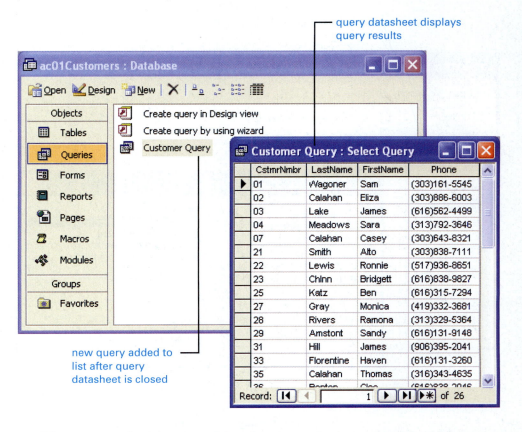

The query results are not saved, but the query criteria are stored for future use. A saved query can be reopened by double-clicking the title. By default, the query results are displayed in order by CstmrNmbr since it is the primary key of the Customer table. To change the order of the output, click anywhere in the field that you want to sort and click either the *Sort Ascending* or *Sort Descending* toolbar button.

Missy and Micah want to use the query results as a phone book of their customers, so it makes more sense for the records to be sorted by the customer's name. To change the record order, you will need to sort by both the customer's last and first names. When sorting by multiple fields, the fields must be contiguous and in order of their importance to the sort. LastName is the primary sort field for this query and must appear before the secondary sort field, FirstName. Typically sort fields are moved to the left of the datasheet to make using the list easier.

To change the order of the columns, select the column using the Field selector and drag the selected column to its new location. For this phone book, the column order should be LastName, FirstName, Phone, and CstmrNmbr.

Sorting the query results:

1. **Open** Customer Query created in the previous steps

2. Change the order of the columns by clicking the **Field Descriptor** to select the column, and then click and drag the Field Descriptor to its new location. Repeat this process until the column order is LastName, FirstName, Phone, and CstmrNmbr

tip: *The Field Descriptor is the box with the field name above each column of data*

3. Place the cursor in the LastName field and click the **Sort Descending** button on the toolbar

FIGURE 1.24

Reordering Customer
Query results

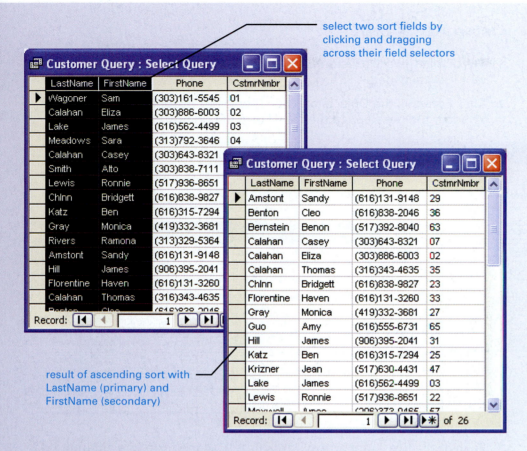

select two sort fields by
clicking and dragging
across their field selectors

result of ascending sort with
LastName (primary) and
FirstName (secondary)

4. Notice that while the data are sorted correctly by last name, the first names are not correctly ordered. The Calahans are not sorted by their first names. If you click in FirstName and sort, the data are no longer sorted by LastName

5. To sort both fields simultaneously, use the Field Selectors to select both the FirstName and LastName columns by clicking and dragging across both Field Selectors

6. When both the FirstName and LastName columns are selected, click the **Sort Ascending** button on the toolbar (see Figure 1.24)

7. Now that the data are arranged, the datasheet can be printed using the **Print** button of the Access toolbar

8. When you close the sorted query results, you will be prompted to save the layout changes that you have made. Choose **Yes** so that the next run of the Customer Query will be sorted by customer name

The Form Wizard

Forms are primarily used to display or update database data on a computer screen. There are two ways to create simple forms. AutoForm is the fastest and most efficient when you want a form displaying all fields from a single table. The Form Wizard will create more complex forms involving multiple tables and formatting.

Using AutoForm:

1. Verify that the ac01Customers database is open and that the Customer table contains data

2. Click **Forms** in the Objects bar, and then select **New** from the Database Window toolbar to open the New Form dialog box

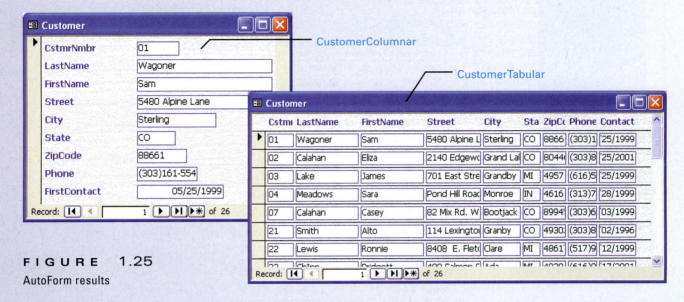

FIGURE   1.25

AutoForm results

3. Each of the five AutoForm Wizards produces the form in a different layout. Datasheet is the default form with which you have already worked. Select **AutoForm: Columnar** to produce a single-column form

4. Select the **Customer** table from the drop-down list and click **OK**

5. Close the Form saving it as **CustomerColumnar**

6. Repeat the process for **AutoForm: Tabular**. Compare the results of the two types of AutoForms

7. Use the Close button in the Form toolbar to close the tabular AutoForm, naming it **CustomerTabular**

Save any form specifications that will be used in the future. Forms also can be printed. Clicking the Printer button on the toolbar will print out all records in the table. Choosing Print from the File menu provides options to print all or a subset of the records.

Printing forms with data:

1. Open the **CustomerColumnar** form created in the previous steps

2. Use the navigation bar to move to the fourth record

3. From the Access menu select **File** and then **Print** to open the Print dialog box

4. The Print Range options determine what records print. All will print all table records. Pages From will print the specified range and Selected Record(s) will print the current selection. Choose **Selected Record(s)** to print the fourth record

FIGURE 1.26

Printing forms with data

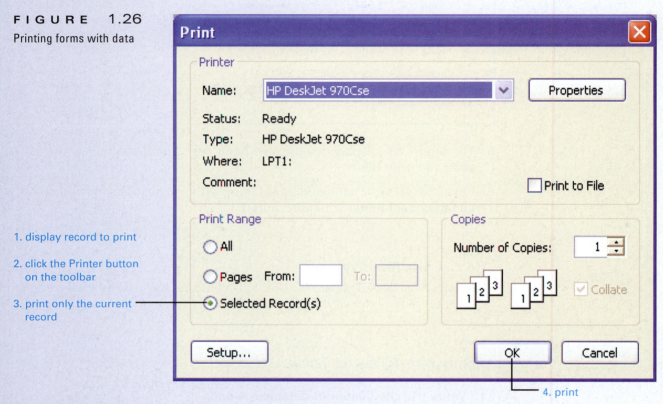

1. display record to print

2. click the Printer button on the toolbar

3. print only the current record

4. print

5. Click **OK** to print the record

6. Close the form

The Report Wizard

Reports are primarily used to consolidate and format data for printing. There are two types of report Wizards available. The AutoReport Wizard creates default reports from one table or query. The Report Wizard will create multitable reports with calculations and custom formatting.

Using the Report Wizard:

1. Verify that the Customer database is open and that the Customer table contains data

2. Click **Reports** in the Objects bar and then select **New** from the Database Window toolbar. The New Report dialog box will open

3. Click **AutoReport: Tabular** to create a report in rows and columns

4. Select the **Customer** table from the drop-down list and click **OK**

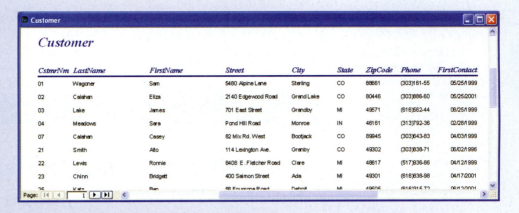

5. The report will display in a preview pane, where you can review the results and print them

6. Close the preview pane and save the report specifications for future use as **CustomerTabular** when prompted

The Create Table Wizard

The Create Table Wizard provides a collection of business and personal database tables to be used as the basis for creating your table.

Using the Create Table Wizard:

1. Verify that the Customer database is open

2. Click **Tables** in the Objects bar, double-click **Create table by using Wizard** to open it without viewing the intermediate dialog boxes (see Figure 1.28)

3. Review the Business table samples provided by the Wizard

4. Click the **Personal** table category

5. Select the **Household Inventory** from the list of Sample Tables. Move **HouseholdInvID**, **RoomID**, **ItemName**, **Description**, **Manufacturer**, **PurchasePrice**, and **AppraisedValue** from the Sample Fields list to the Fields in my new table list. Click **Next**

6. Name the table **Household Inventory**, choose to set a primary key, and click **Next** (see Figure 1.29)

7. Ensure that your new table is not related to other tables in the database

8. Click **Finish**

9. Enter at least five of your possessions into the Household Inventory table

10. Print table data using the Standard toolbar's Print button

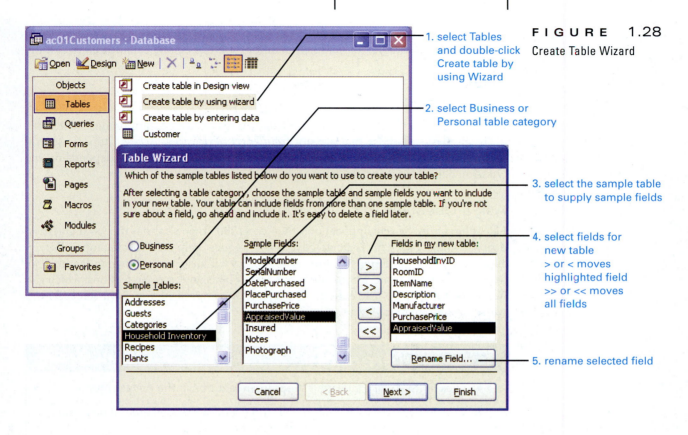

Create Table Wizard

1. select Tables and double-click Create table by using Wizard

2. select Business or Personal table category

3. select the sample table to supply sample fields

4. select fields for new table
   > or < moves highlighted field
   >> or << moves all fields

5. rename selected field

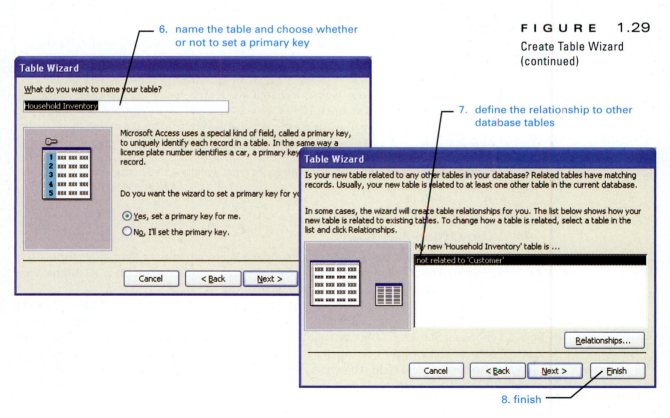

Create Table Wizard (continued)

6. name the table and choose whether or not to set a primary key

7. define the relationship to other database tables

8. finish

ACCESS

It is important to remember that the Create Table Wizard uses templates to build the fields of a new table. All field names and properties can be customized to suit the current use.

Getting Help

Even people who work with Access on a daily basis need direction on how to accomplish new tasks or those that are not frequently performed. Access supports several methods of obtaining help. The technique selected for getting help depends on the question being posed and the work style.

Ask a Question

Like other Office System applications, the Access 2003 menu bar has the Ask a Question drop-down list box. This is an effective way to request help on a specific topic. Type in a question and press Enter. A list of related topics will display, as shown in Figure 1.30. When you select a topic, Microsoft Access Help opens with more selections, which can be clicked to bring up instructions. The instructions can display on your screen as you work through them in Access.

---

task reference   Getting Help

- Click in the Type a Question drop-down text box in the Access menu

- Type in keywords relevant to your topic. Full sentences are not necessary and do not improve the performance of the search

- Press **Enter**

- Select from the topics provided or adjust the keywords and search again

---

Once Microsoft Access Help is initiated, the search results are displayed in the task pane. Click a result link to open Help topic. As you can see in Figure 1.30, Help topics contain additional links allowing you to select and view information directly related to your question.

help yourself *To learn more about creating new Access tables, type **new table** in the Type a Question box and review the topics presented. Close the Help window when you are finished*

The Office Assistant

Dropping down the Help menu in the Access Window displays a complete list of Help options. The available options are to start Help, initiate the Office Assistant, view Sample Databases, access help on the Web, or use the What's This tool.

The Office Assistant is the animated interface to Microsoft Office Help and can be initiated by pressing F1, choosing Microsoft Access Help from the Help menu, or choosing Show the Office Assistant from the Help menu (see Figure 1.31). Regardless of how the assistant is initiated, typing a question and clicking Search will open Microsoft Access Help (shown in Figure 1.30) with topics related to your search.

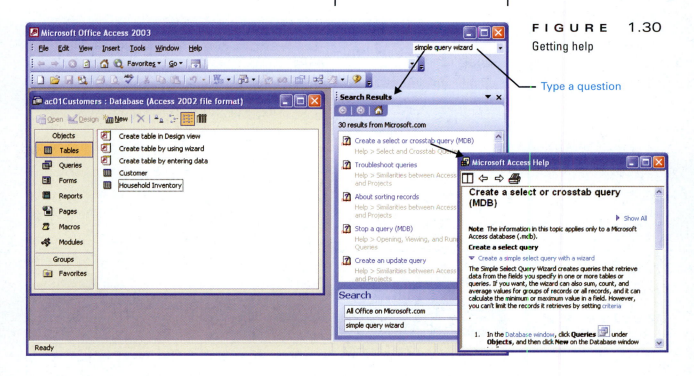

FIGURE 1.30

Getting help

Type a question

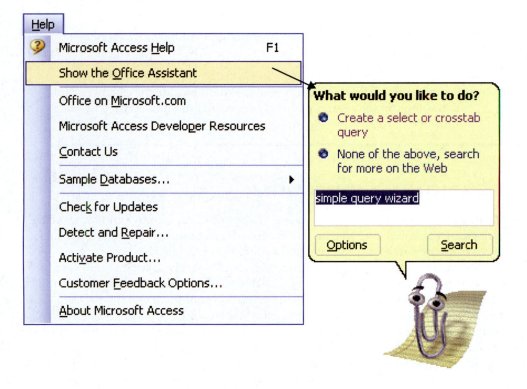

FIGURE 1.31

Help menu and Office
Assistant

Right-clicking the Office Assistant displays options that control how the assistant works. The visual presentation gallery includes Merlin the magician, a robot, a cat, and a dog. If he is left active and set to do so, the assistant will provide tips as you work. He can also be hidden or disabled.

Exiting Access

Exiting Access is accomplished by choosing the Close button of the main Access Window. The Exit option of the File menu also will close Access. Regardless of the exit method employed, all open objects will be closed before Access is closed. If you have made unsaved changes to open objects such as a table or datasheet, you will be prompted to save or abandon changes. When all open objects have been successfully closed, Access will close.

Exiting Access:

1. Select **File** and then **Exit** from the menu
2. If prompted to save changes, do so

SESSION 1.2

making the grade

1. Access database objects include _____, _____, and _____.

2. T F   Changes made in the Datasheet View such as widening columns are automatically saved when the view is closed.

3. Describe the purpose of the Documenter (Tools|Analyze|Documenter) menu option.

4. Create a query from the KoryoKicks Customer table that will be used to create mailing labels. The query results should include the customer's full name and complete street address. The records should be sorted by ZipCode.

SESSION 1.3 SUMMARY

Relational database management systems are powerful data storage and retrieval technologies. Data stored in RDBMSs have reduced data redundancy and increased data integrity and use data validation rules to improve data reliability.

Raw data are stored in tables where they can be accessed and manipulated using Queries, Forms, and Reports objects. Each table column represents an attribute or field of an entity. For example, Gender is a common column in a table storing data about employees. All of the attributes for one entity are stored in a row or record, so all data stored for one employee are in the same row. All of the possible values of an attribute are called its domain. Indexes are used to speed data retrieval and output sorting.

Ideally each table should have a primary key that uniquely and minimally identifies each row of data. Social Security Number is one likely primary key when storing data about people. Tables are joined to each other using shared fields. A field that can be used to join to another table is called a foreign key. When tables are joined, they have definable relationships such as one-to-one or one-to-many.

Wizards are an easy way to create simple queries, forms, and reports. Queries are a way to ask questions of the database data by specifying what data to retrieve and how to organize them. Queries also can be used to update multiple rows of data in one step. Forms are a user-friendly way to view and update data on a computer screen. Reports allow you to format data for printing.

Database objects support multiple views. Personal preference and the operation to be performed determine the view to be used. For example, a table's Datasheet View is used to view, navigate, and maintain data while the Design View is used to change the structure of the table.

Visit www.mhhe.com/i-series/ to explore related topics.

MICROSOFT OFFICE SPECIALIST OBJECTIVES SUMMARY

- Create Access databases using the Wizard—MOS AC03S-1-1
- Find and move among records—MOS AC03S-2-2
- Create tables using Table Wizard—MOS AC03S-1-2
- Create Select Queries using the Simple Query Wizard—MOS AC03S-1-7
- Create forms using the Form Wizard—MOS AC03S-1-8
- Print database objects and data—MOS AC03S-4-3

making the grade *answers*

SESSION 1.1

1. relational database management system.

2. the standardized language used to ask questions of data stored in relational databases.

3. columns, attributes, fields, or foreign keys. Each is an acceptable answer.

4. primary key.

5. A wide range of answers can be considered appropriate for this. There are some key components that all acceptable answers should contain. At a minimum, the answer should contain fields for FirstName, LastName, StreetAddress, City, State, and ZipCode. Better answers would also contain fields for OrderDate, Product, and OrderQuantity and address the need to find a unique key to identify each customer.

SESSION 1.2

1. Any answers from the following list are correct: Tables, Queries, Forms, Reports, Pages, Macros, or Modules.

2. False. The user is prompted to save them when they close the view.

3. One of the features of the Documenter is the ability to create printed documentation about an Access object such as a table. The chapter example used the Documenter to print the Customer table design.

4. The query results should include the customer's full name and complete street address. The records should be sorted by ZipCode.

task reference *summary*

Task	Page #	Preferred Method
Opening an Access object	AC 1.19	• Click the type of object that you would like to open in the Database Window's Objects bar • Select the object that you would like to open • Click the **Open** button
Activating Access Wizards	AC 1.24	• Click the object (Queries, Forms, Reports) whose Wizard you would like to access in the Database Window's Objects bar • Click **New** in the Database Window's toolbar • The available Wizards will be listed • Select the Wizard and respond to its questions
Getting help	AC 1.32	• Click in the Type a Question drop-down text box in the Access menu • Type in keywords relevant to your topic. Full sentences are not necessary and do not improve the performance of the search • Press **Enter** • Select from the topics provided or adjust the keywords and search again

TRUE/FALSE

1. Reports are designed to be viewed on a computer screen.

2. Wizards are helpful applets that walk you through complex operations like creating a table.

3. A table must be open in Design View to print the design of the table.

4. Tables, forms, reports, and queries are examples of Access database objects.

5. Access database indexes are similar to an index of a book and are used to speed looking up data values.

6. Relationships allow data from multiple tables to be used together in queries, forms, and reports.

7. The data in one cell of a table are called a data value.

FILL-IN

1. The Access object used to create printed output is the _____ object.

2. Database _____ ensures that only authorized people can access and update database data.

3. _____ is the language used to define the structure of a database table.

4. When using the Simple Query Wizard, the _____ button will add the current field to those that will appear in the query results.

5. The _____ is one way to obtain help in Access.

6. A(n) _____ key is a field that could have been defined as the primary key but was not.

MULTIPLE CHOICE

1. A database management system (DBMS) provides
   a. facilities to maintain data.
   b. the ability to store data.
   c. tools to build reports and forms.
   d. all of the above.

2. A relational database
   a. stores data in tables.
   b. stores data in a hierarchical structure.
   c. stores data in a dominion.
   d. stores data in a networked structure.

3. The primary key is important to data stored in a database because it
   a. is used to define many-to-many relationships.
   b. allows data from other tables to be retrieved.
   c. uniquely identifies each row of data stored.
   d. is a required database object.

4. In the relational database environment an object is
   a. the foreign key.
   b. an item that can be stored like a table or form.
   c. a client/server database.
   d. an Access Window.

5. A query
   a. creates a formatted printout of data.
   b. can select and calculate based on criteria.
   c. is a member of the Groups bar.
   d. is initiated using the field selector.

review of concepts

REVIEW QUESTIONS

Each of the following topics should be addressed in one to three paragraphs.

1. Discuss at least two ways to open an Access database.

2. Discuss the benefits and difficulties of using database management systems.

3. How does reduced data redundancy decrease errors in database data?

4. Outline at least two Customer data queries that might benefit KoryoKicks.

5. Discuss the various types of keys introduced in the chapter and how they are used in relational databases.

6. What are the benefits of storing data in a relational database? Are there any negative issues that must be dealt with?

7. Describe the various ways that data in relational database tables can be joined.

CREATE THE QUESTION

For each of the following answers, create the question.

ANSWER	QUESTION
1. They are specific to each Access object and appear at the top of a window	_____
2. Setting a primary key automatically creates the first one for a table	_____
3. The object that allows you to create a custom user interface to display and manipulate data	_____
4. A reusable template that will speed the development of Access database components such as tables and queries	_____
5. The Table view used to change the Table structure	_____

FACT OR FICTION

For each of the following, determine whether the statement is fact, fiction, or both and present your arguments for that conclusion.

1. Relational databases are the only databases in use by today's businesses.

2. The Office Assistant is the only way to obtain Access help.

3. The Query Datasheet toolbar can be displayed while viewing a form.

4. A query is another way to store data.

5. The Print button can be used to print the design of a table.

6. The Simple Query Wizard allows you to select columns that will be returned by a query, but not the rows.

1. Working with a Database for Curbside Recycling

Curbside Recycling is a Muncie, Indiana, recycling organization that picks up recyclables from homeowners. Neighborhoods subscribe to the service so that pickup is cost effective. Curbside provides special containers to subscribers for sorting recyclables: a blue container for paper products and a purple container for aluminum, plastic, and glass products.

Subscribers place their recycling containers on the curb for biweekly pickup. Each recycling container is weighed before being emptied. Curbside drivers carry handheld recording devices used to track each pickup. Subscribers receive quarterly profit-sharing checks based on their contributions. If Curbside does not make a profit, subscribers don't get paid for their recyclables. If Curbside makes a profit, subscribers share in that profit. Curbside has asked you to help develop a database that will effectively track subscribers using the data downloaded from the drivers' devices. Eventually, there will be multiple tables in the database. The Customers table will hold static customer information such as name, address, and phone. The CustomerRecords table holds data about each recyclable pickup. It currently contains test data and is the one with which you will be working.

1. Make sure that you have access to the data from your data disk

2. Start Access and open the **ac01CurbsideRecycling.mdb** database from your Chapter 1 files

FIGURE 1.32

Customer table update form

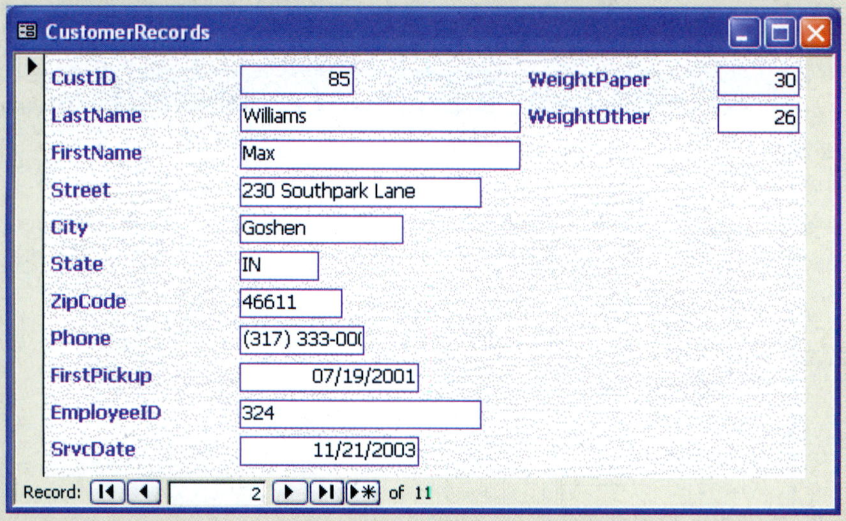

3. Open the **CustomerRecords** table, add records for yourself and a friend with CustID 30 and 31, today's date as both the SrvcDate and FirstPickup, and EmployeeID 902

4. Sort the datasheet rows by EmployeeID, SrvcDate, and CustID. Print the result

5. Make the following updates to existing data:

   CustId 2, SvcDate 11/22/2003 WeightOther should be updated to **17**

   CustID 20, SvcDate 11/22/2003 WeightOther should be updated to **26**

6. Sort the CustomerRecords datasheet. Use EmployeeId as the primary sort and WeightOther as the secondary sort. Print the results and save the format changes to the table. Make the sort fields the leftmost columns

7. Use the Simple Query Wizard to create a query containing EmployeeID, WeightPaper, and WeightOther. When prompted, choose Summary and set the Summary Options to Sum WeightPaper and WeightOther. The query should be named **EmployeeTotals** and display one row of totals for each employee

8. Use AutoForm: Columnar to create a data entry form with all fields from the Customer table. Display the Max Williams record for Svc Date 11/21/2003 and print it. Close the form saving it as **CustomerUpdate**

9. Use the Report Wizard to create a tabular report. Print the result. Close the report saving it as **CustomerReport**

10. If your work is complete, exit Access; otherwise, continue to the next assignment

2. Working with a Database for Lalier Construction

Lalier Construction Inc. (LCI) is a Colorado company started by Mike and Niki Lalier. LCI's primary business is commercial roofing, but also includes residential roofing and small remodeling jobs. During the off-season LCI provides work for only eight full-time employees, while at the height of a construction season it can employ over 300 people on 25 or more projects. Mike manages initial client contact, project bids, and the various construction crews. Niki recruits and hires crew employees, handles customer follow-up, and keeps all of the company books.

LCI uses bookkeeping software for billing, receivables, and financial statements but has been tracking employee contact and effectiveness data on 3 × 5 cards. Because the business is seasonal and the workforce is temporary, a better way to recruit and manage employees is needed. Niki has started creating a Microsoft Access database to track employees who have already worked for LCI and any potential employees that come to her attention. The goal is to have a ready resource for rapidly staffing any project that Mike contracts.

1. Make sure that you have access to the data from your data disk

2. Start Access and open the **ac01LalierConstruction.mdb** database from your Chapter 1 files

3. Open the **Employees** table and add records for yourself and at least three of your friends. Each new record should be for a JobSkill of **Roofing**, BillingRate of **$70**, and an HourlyRate of **$40**

4. Sort the datasheet rows by City. Make City the leftmost field and print the result

5. Sort the datasheet rows by FirstName within LastName (first sort field). Make the following updates to existing data and then print the result

   • Justin Modahl's *Home Phone* should be updated to **3039285729**

   • Evan Navaro's *Billing Rate* should be updated to **$75**

   • Garrett Stiefler's JobSkills should be updated to **Texture**

6. Use the Simple Query Wizard to create a query containing EmployeeID, LastName, FirstName, and HomePhone. Save the query as **PhoneList** and print the resulting datasheet

7. Use AutoForm: Columnar to create a data entry form. Display the Adam Kiernes record and print it. Save the form as **EmployeeUpdate**

8. Use the Report Wizard to create the default tabular report. Print the result. Close the report saving it as **EmployeeReport**

9. If your work is complete, exit Access; otherwise, continue to the next assignment

FIGURE 1.33

EmployeeUpdate and EmployeeReport

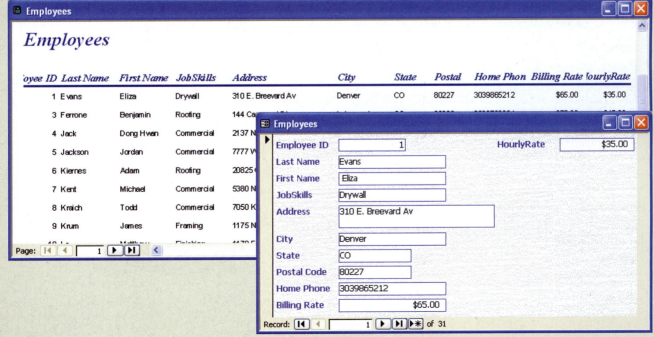

challenge!

1. Tracking Employees at Little White School House

Samuel Mink is the director of the Little White School House, a small private mountain community school. There are 142 students from preschool through grade 6. The staff consists of eight teachers, the director, a secretary, and community volunteers. Current records for the school are kept manually or in an Excel spreadsheet. Samuel would like more automation, consistency in record keeping, and reporting capabilities. You have met with Samuel and he has provided you with sample forms and a copy of the current data.

Your plan is to begin by putting employee tracking into an Access database according to the criteria listed below.

1. Use Microsoft Word to create a list of employee attributes that should be contained in the Little White School House Employee table

2. Open Access, create a new database (select Blank Database from the New category of the task pane), and name it **ac01LittleWhiteSchoolHouse**

3. Use the Table Wizard to create an Employee table with a primary key. Remember that while you need to store personal data, payroll data, and contact information, this is a small organization, so all of the suggested fields are not needed

4. Enter the following data:

<your name>	Secretary	22,400
Samuel Mink	Director	58,929
Margaret Frost	Preschool teacher	31,211
Rachael Dawson	1st grade teacher	28,452
Robert Gibbs	2nd grade teacher	36,283
Randi Evans	3rd grade teacher	45,879
Asayah Muhammad	4th grade teacher	44,962
David Mackall	5th grade teacher	30,980
Kasey Johnson	Music teacher	30,281
Ennis Johnson	Art teacher	30,486

5. Add two of your friends as volunteers (0 salary) and make up the remaining data so there are no blank cells in the table

6. Update Margaret Frost's salary to **31,311**

7. Sort the table by employee first and last name. Make the name fields leftmost fields and print

8. Sort the table by decreasing salary. Make Salary the leftmost field and print

9. Print the table design

10. Use the AutoForm: Columnar Wizard to create a form for this table. Print the form with the data for Asayah Muhammad showing (Figure 1.34). Name the form **Employees**

11. Use AutoReport: Tabular to create the default report from this data. Name the report **Employees**

12. Close the database and exit Access if your work is complete

F I G U R E   1.34

Employee table form

2. Tracking Your Recordings

Personal databases can be used to track and report on your personal assets, possessions, and plans. Sometimes this tracking can simply catalog a collection or collections. Other times, a database is an effective way to produce reports needed for taxes, other government reporting, banking, or personal business uses. To experience the simplicity of building and populating a database of a personal collection, you will create a database and table to hold information about your personal recording collection.

1. Open Access, create a new database (select Blank Database from the New category of the task pane), and name it **ac01<yourname>Recordings.mdb**

2. Use the Table Wizard to create a new table. Use the **Recordings** sample table in the **Personal** Table Category to add the following fields to your table

   - RecordingId
   - RecordingTitle
   - RecordingArtistID renamed to **RecordingArtist**
   - MusicCategoryID renamed to **MusicCategory**
   - RecordingLabel
   - YearReleased

3. Name the table **MyMusic**

4. Open the table in Design View. Modify the table design by setting the Data Type of both RecordingArtist and MusicCategory to **Text**

5. Switch to Datasheet View saving the table when prompted. Remember that RecordingID is automatically generated as you enter the data shown in Figure 1.35

6. Enter the data for at least 15 of your own recordings (use your friends' if you do not have 15 of your own). Be sure to add music in at least two different MusicCategory values

7. Use the Simple Query Wizard to produce a list containing MusicCategory, RecordingArtist, and RecordingTitle. Save the query as **MusicCategory**

8. Use AutoForm: Columnar to create a data entry form from the **MyMusic** table. Display the John Coltrane record and print it. Save the form as **MyMusicUpdate**

9. Use the Report Wizard to create the default tabular report for the MyMusic table. Print the result. Close the report saving it as **MyMusicReport**

10. If your work is complete, exit Access; otherwise, continue to the next assignment

FIGURE 1.35

MyMusic data and MyMusicUpdate form

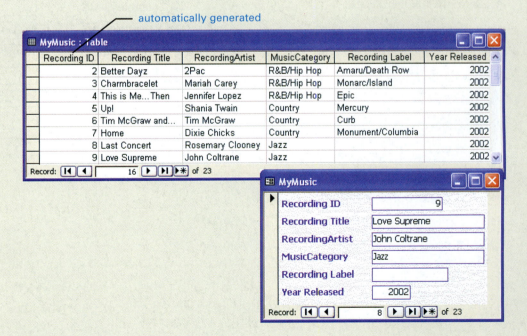

automatically generated

Recording ID	Recording Title	RecordingArtist	MusicCategory	Recording Label	Year Released
2	Better Dayz	2Pac	R&B/Hip Hop	Amaru/Death Row	2002
3	Charmbracelet	Mariah Carey	R&B/Hip Hop	Monarc/Island	2002
4	This is Me...Then	Jennifer Lopez	R&B/Hip Hop	Epic	2002
5	Up!	Shania Twain	Country	Mercury	2002
6	Tim McGraw and...	Tim McGraw	Country	Curb	2002
7	Home	Dixie Chicks	Country	Monument/Columbia	2002
8	Last Concert	Rosemary Clooney	Jazz		2002
9	Love Supreme	John Coltrane	Jazz		2002

Record: 16 of 23

MyMusic

Recording ID: 9
Recording Title: Love Supreme
RecordingArtist: John Coltrane
MusicCategory: Jazz
Recording Label:
Year Released: 2002

Record: 8 of 23

1. Exotic Flora Price List

Exotic Flora is a worldwide consortium of small florists who provide unique fresh flower arrangements for every occasion. Each florist pays a membership fee and agrees to deliver ordered arrangements within 24 hours of payment verification. All arrangements are guaranteed to match the order and to last for at least 10 days.

The bulk of flower orders is generated through an e-storefront that accepts orders, verifies payment, and forwards the order to the appropriate florist. Forty-two percent of the profit for each order goes to the e-storefront management organization, 10 percent goes to the Exotic Flora association, and the florist who delivers the flowers keeps the remainder.

For the e-storefront to work effectively, the member florists must provide product data to the storefront managers in a convenient format. After some trial and error, the florists have settled on Access as the tool that best suits their needs. Each member florist provides a weekly table of available arrangements with the arrangement name, price, picture, availability dates, and maximum quantity that can be delivered. The e-storefront manager consolidates the Access tables provided by the various florists into a large Oracle database that is used to generate the e-storefront site.

Gabriella Juarez is a small florist in Pahoa, Hawaii, who has decided to join Exotic Flora to increase her business. She has no experience with computers and has asked you to build the database that she needs.

1. Open Access, create a new database (select Blank Database from the New category of the task pane), and name it **ac01ExoticFlora**

2. Use the Table Wizard to create a Products table:
   a. From the Products sample table select ProductID, ProductName, ProductDescription, and UnitPrice
   b. From the Employees sample table select Photograph
   c. Set ProductId as the primary key that is automatically generated

3. Enter the data from Figure 1.36 into the table. Instructions for adding the jpg image are in the Tip

tip: *Click the Photograph cell, choose Object from the Insert menu, click Create from File, and browse to find this chapter's pictures. The actual photograph is not visible in this view. You can change the photograph by deleting the current cell contents and inserting a new photo*

4. Sort the data by product name and print

5. Print the table design

6. Use the AutoForm: Columnar Wizard to create a form for this table

tip: *Later chapters will teach you to customize forms to fully display labels and pictures*

Print the form with the data for Kea Mix showing

7. Close the ExoticFlora database and exit Access if your work is complete

FIGURE 1.36

ExoticFlora data and form

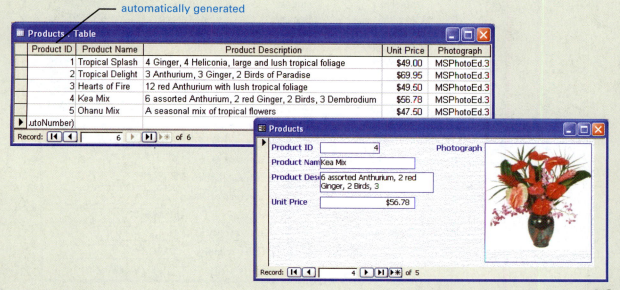

AC 1.43

ACCESS

2. Tracking Customers at Delroy Ocean Travel

Rolfe Delroy is the owner of Delroy Ocean Travel (DOT), a small private travel agency specializing in ocean-related adventures. The DOT staff consists of eight agents, a promotions manager, a secretary, and Rolfe. Current customer and cruise records are kept manually or in an Excel spreadsheet. Rolfe would like more automation, consistency in record keeping, the ability to use customer lists from other businesses, and the enhanced reporting capabilities available from a database. You have met with Rolfe and he has provided you with sample forms and examples of how the current data are stored. Your plan is to begin by putting customer tracking into an Access database.

1. Open Access, create a new database (select Blank Database from the New category of the task pane), and name it **ac01DelroyTravel.mdb**

2. Use the Table Wizard to create a new table. Use the **Customers** sample table in the **Business** Table Category to add the following fields to your table design

   - CustomerID
   - ContactLastName renamed to **CustomerLastName** using the Wizard's Rename Field button
   - ContactFirstName renamed to **CustomerFirstName** using the Wizard's Rename Field button
   - City

   - StateorProvince renamed to **State** using the Wizard's Rename Field button
   - PhoneNumber

3. Set CustomerID as the automatically generated primary key and save the table naming it **DOTCustomer**

4. Remember that CustomerID is automatically generated as you enter the data shown in Figure 1.37

5. Add two of your friends with their correct data. There should be no blank cells in the table

6. Sort the table by CustomerFirstName within CustomerLastName (first sort field) and print

7. Sort the table by descending state and print

8. Print the table design

9. Use the Simple Query Wizard to produce a list containing CustomerLastName, CustomerFirstName, and PhoneNumber. Save the query as **CustomerList**

10. Use the AutoForm: Columnar Wizard to create a form for this table. Print the form with the data for yourself showing. Save the form as **CustomerUpdate**

11. Use the Report Wizard to create the default tabular report. Print the result. Close the report saving it as **CustomerReport**

12. Close the database and exit Access if your work is complete

FIGURE 1.37

CustomerUpdate data and form

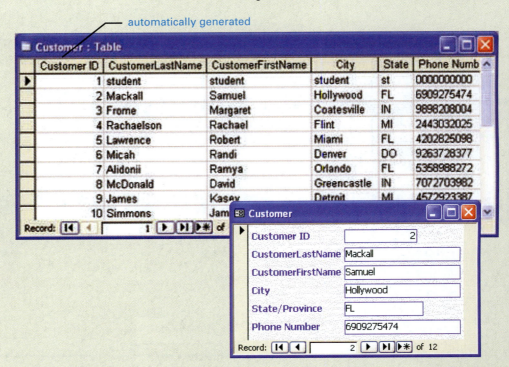

automatically generated

Customer ID	CustomerLastName	CustomerFirstName	City	State	Phone Numb
1	student	student	student	st	0000000000
2	Mackall	Samuel	Hollywood	FL	6909275474
3	Frome	Margaret	Coatesville	IN	9898208004
4	Rachaelson	Rachael	Flint	MI	2443032025
5	Lawrence	Robert	Miami	FL	4202825098
6	Micah	Randi	Denver	DO	9263728377
7	Alidonii	Ramya	Orlando	FL	5358988272
8	McDonald	David	Greencastle	IN	7072703982
9	James	Kasey	Detroit	MI	4572923387
10	Simmons	Jam			

Record: 1 of

Customer

Customer ID	2
CustomerLastName	Mackall
CustomerFirstName	Samuel
City	Hollywood
State/Province	FL
Phone Number	6909275474

Record: 2 of 12

1. Searching for Service Organizations

The Wheeler Helping Hand Association (WHHA) is an alliance of missions, food banks, and service organizations supporting central Indiana. The goal of the group is to provide assistance to people who need food, shelter, clothing, job training, and counseling. The organization has two full-time staff to organize and coordinate hundreds of volunteers. Volunteers are the backbone of the organization, doing everything from cooking to counseling.

All supplies are donated through charitable contributions. Most of the contributions are received through churches, but there is also an annual Thanksgiving phone drive and a new Internet contributions site. The Internet contributions site has two purposes. The first is to let people know what the current needs of the organization are by posting a list of the most needed food, clothing, and services. The second is to promote the Wheeler Helping Hand vision and accept monetary contributions.

You have volunteered and have been asked to use your computer expertise to support the services being provided. You know that the Internet is a great resource and have decided to look for better ways to promote the association and support the volunteers. One of your ideas is to provide a database of Web sites that have useful services for WHHA clients. Although the clients are unlikely to have computer access, volunteers who need to be able to provide support without much training would find the information useful.

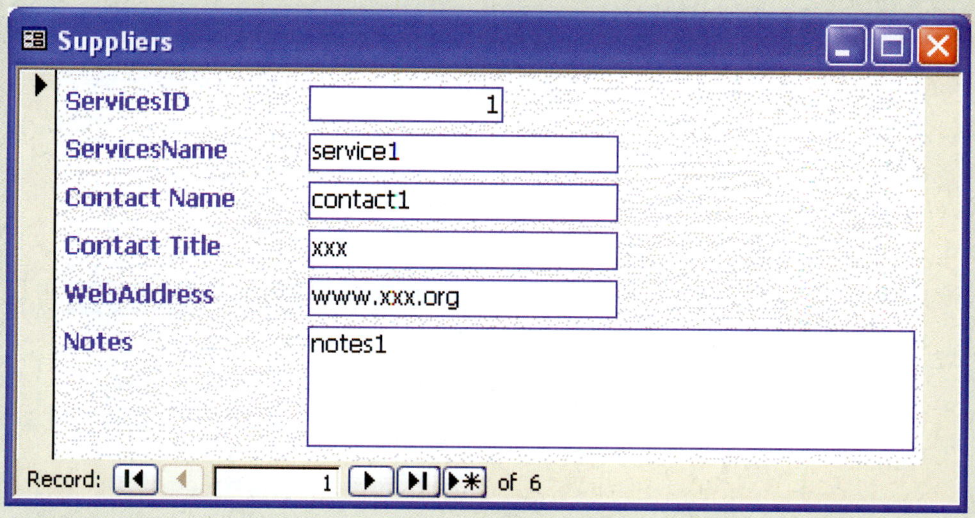

1. Use your favorite search engine to find organizations and services that could benefit the WHHA clientele

2. Record the information from at least six sites to be entered into the volunteer database

3. Open Access, create a new database (select Blank Database from the New category of the task pane), and name it **ac01WHHA.mdb**

4. Use the Table Wizard to create a **Services** table
   a. From the Suppliers Sample Table select SupplierID, SupplierName, ContactName, ContactTitle, PhoneNumber, EmailAddress, and Notes
   b. Rename (click the Rename Field button with the field selected) SupplierID to **ServicesID**, SupplierName to **ServicesName**, and EmailAddress to **WebAddress**
   c. Set ServicesId as the automatically generated primary key

5. Enter the data from your Web search in the Services table. Make up the contact data if needed and include your comments about the services and the Web site in notes. Do not leave any blank cells

6. Print the table design

7. Use the AutoForm: Columnar Wizard to create a form for the Services table named **WHHA**. Print the form with the data for your third record showing (see Figure 1.38)

8. Close the WHHA database and exit Access if your work is complete

FIGURE 1.38

WHHA form

around the world

1. Tracking International Trade Consultants

The Alliance for Global Commerce (AGC) is an organization that tracks and rates businesses participating in international trade. The three businessmen who founded AGC were able to navigate the various cultures and rituals participating in trades, but had a persistent problem with knowing which other traders were reliable. Since trial and error had proved costly, they started AGC.

The AGC vision was to create something like the Better Business Bureau on an international scale. Initially the three men gathered data on trade incidents necessary to support their own trade activities and then published the data in a newsletter distributed to trade, retail, and wholesale organizations. After that, the newsletter recipients reported trade incidents that were tracked and published in the newsletter. Incidents are any behavior of a trade organization that negatively impacts the viability of the trade pact. The most common incidents are failure to pay and shipments over one week late. Initially there was a concern that false incident reports would be a problem, but they proved not to be.

The founders now believe that as international commerce increases, the problems with unreliable and unscrupulous traders will become more prevalent, increasing the need for tracking and analysis. They have hired you to spearhead the data gathering and analysis. You have begun by building a table of traders and searching for new trade organizations.

1. Start Access and open the **ac01AGC.mdb** database

2. Open the Traders table and become familiar with its contents

3. Add the following data for TraderNmbrs 80, 81, and 82

   South Side Imports, 3850 S. Emerson Ave., Indianapolis, IN, 46121, (317)786-8188, Automobiles, 0

   Titan International, 4515 W 16th St., Dayton, OH, 48378, (383)484-9195, Automobiles, 2

   Auto Network, 8441 Castleton Corner Dr., Atlanta, GA, 30301, (290)748-2070, Clothing, 0

   tip: *Commas are used to separate the fields and should not be entered*

4. Look in your local phone book and find four international trade businesses. Enter the data into the Traders table. Use TraderNmbrs 83 through 86

5. Sort by TraderNmbr and print

6. Make TradeArea the first column, sort by it, and then print

7. Make BusinessName the first column, sort by it, and then print

8. Make Incidents and Business Name the first columns. Sort the table by descending Incidents and Business Name and print

9. Print the table design

10. Use the AutoForm: Columnar Wizard to create a form for this table. Print the form with the data for AutoNetwork showing

11. Use the AutoReport: Tabular Wizard to create and print a report

12. Close the AGC database and exit Access if your work is complete

FIGURE 1.39

AGC form and report

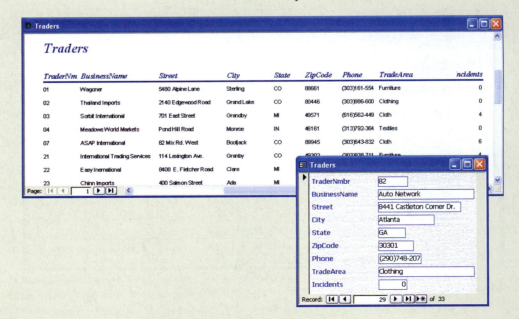

running project: tnt web page design

Beginning the TnT Database

TnT is a custom Web page development company founded by Victoria (Tori) Salazar and her college roommate Tonya O'Dowd. Tonya was an art major learning graphic design and Tori was a computer science major studying programming languages. The company was born when both had final projects due at the end of their second semester. Tonya was creating custom graphics and Tori was using Java to automate a Web site when they decided that they could create a killer site if they combined their talents.

Their first project was to put the college newspaper online. As a result of this project, both were hired as interns at the local newspaper.

After college, Tonya was hired as a graphic artist at a Web design company and Tori was hired as a Web software developer by a Fortune 500 company. They lived in different parts of the country but maintained contact via e-mail. After a few years Tori began picking up some extra work doing e-commerce development for fun and contracted with Tonya to create the graphics. The women liked working together and having control of what they worked on and decided to pick up more contracts. As business grew, both women quit their other jobs to concentrate on Web development.

They are frequently asked for customer references and samples of their work, and it has become tedious to maintain the Web site that provides this information. Tori and Tanya ask you to develop a database that will support their business. At some point they would like to store links to their customers and the sites that they have developed and update their Web site automatically. The first step is to create the Customer table.

1. Make sure that you have access to the data disk
2. Start Access and open the **ac01TnT.mdb** database
3. Open the **tblCustomers** table in Datasheet View
4. Sort the table by CusCountry and CusName. Make the sort field the leftmost column. Print the results
5. Print the table design
6. Use the Simple Query Wizard to create a query displaying the customer name, city, state, country, and phone. Sort by customer name. Print and save
7. Add yourself and two of your friends as customers
8. Create a columnar form and print your record
9. Create a tabular report. Save and print
10. Close the database and exit Access if your work is complete

FIGURE 1.40
TnT form

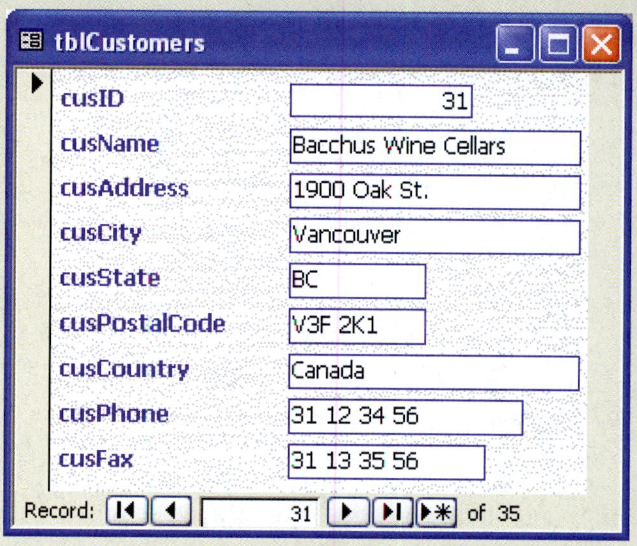

1. Create a Personal Database

Evaluate your personal needs and select an area such as classes, grades, or belongings that could benefit from a database. Describe how the database will be used, being sure to document your database needs and the benefits that you expect to gain by creating the database.

Create a new blank database named **ac01<your-name>.mdb**. Use the Wizards introduced in this chapter to create table(s) in the database. Populate at least one table with 10 or more records. Use the Wizards to create an update form, simple query, and simple report for the populated table. Print the design of each table. Print each object created.

2. Start a Personal Business

Assume that you are starting a personal services business such as mowing lawns or tutoring. Document the type of data that you would need to track in order to effectively run your business. Describe how a database could be used to improve storage and access to the data needed for your business. Are there valid reasons to create a database? Not to create a database?

Create a new blank database named **ac01<your-name>Business.mdb**. Use the Wizards introduced in this chapter to create table(s) in the database. Populate at least one table with 10 or more records. Use the Wizards to create an update form, simple query, and simple report for the populated table. Print the design of each table. Print each object created.

Maintaining Your Database

did you know?

according *to Dennis Changon, spokesman for the International Civil Aviation Organization in Montreal, Canada, if all of the commercial planes in the world were grounded at the same time, there wouldn't be space to park them all at the gates.*

Colonel *Waring, New York City Street Cleaning Commissioner, was responsible for organizing the first rubbish-sorting plant for recycling in the United States in 1898.*

early *models of vacuum cleaners were powered by gasoline.*

honey *is used as a center for golf balls and in antifreeze mixtures.*

the *first commercial passenger airplane began flying in 1914.*

focus *group information compiled by CalComp revealed that _____ percent of computer users do not like using a mouse.*

to *find out how many computer users don't like using a mouse, visit* www.mhhe.com/i-series.

Chapter Objectives

- **Maintain table data using various methods to add records, delete records, and update field data—MOS AC03S-2-1**

- **Learn to organize and find table data using Datasheet View**

- **Understand how to design relational database tables**

- **Create and save Access table definitions using table Design View**

- **Use the Clipboard to copy records between tables**

- **Format datasheets—MOS AC03S-3-4**

- **Sort records in Datasheet View—MOS AC03S-3-5**

KoryoKicks: Starting a Personal Business

Missy and Micah are pleased with the progress that has been made in evaluating the database needs of KoryoKicks. The twins have significantly improved their understanding of databases and are happy with what they have learned by manipulating the Customer table prototype. Now they understand enough to help you design and develop a database to support the full data requirements of their business.

You know that education for database users is critical to the success of any database development project. If you build a wonderful database but the customer doesn't know how to use it, the result is an ineffective product. To avoid this situation, the process of familiarizing Missy and Micah with Access needs to continue. You want to ensure that they are comfortable organizing, maintaining, and using the stored data. Additionally, both are interested in learning how to design and develop databases so that they have a better understanding of potential applications for their data. They understand that Access can help them to market their martial arts classes and supplies using e-commerce.

Missy and Micah have provided you with paper copies of the Excel spreadsheets and manual reports that are currently being used. You have evaluated these documents to understand their business and get a better idea of how to design a database to support it. The preliminary assessment of the organization's database requirements indicates that tables are needed for customers (both students and people who purchase products are customers), orders, products, and suppliers. The Customer table prototype was built in Chapter 1 and is already in use. The Orders table would hold data about each order including order number, product ordered, and quantity ordered. The Products table would list products with their availability such as supplier, quantity on hand, and lead time needed to order. The Suppliers table would contain contact information and performance history for vendors who supply products to KoryoKicks.

Although you have a good idea of the tables Missy and Micah need, it is always a good idea to spend some time using a formal design process before developing tables. You will proceed with a more detailed analysis of data requirements and then develop a prototype for each table specified in the design process. You have decided to begin by looking at the data necessary to bill customers using the sample invoice from Figure 2.1. Missy and Micah will be involved throughout the analysis, design, development, and implementation steps of this process.

FIGURE 2.1

KoryoKicks customer
invoice form

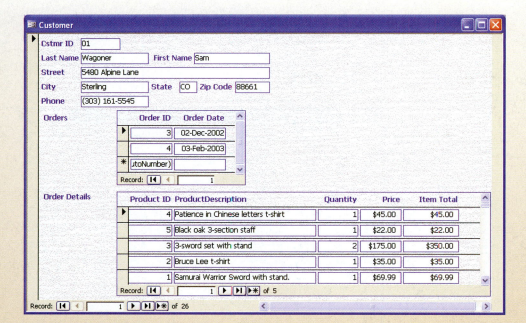

SESSION 2.1 MAINTAINING ACCESS DATA

To be effective, data stored in a database must be kept current. The process of keeping data current is called maintenance. Maintenance tasks include adding new records, removing old records, and changing values in existing records. Missy and Micah will both use KoryoKicks data, but there will be only one copy of the database and one user at a time. It is critical that they each understand how to sort, find, and update table data. They also need to develop a methodology for sharing maintenance tasks.

Ordering, Finding, and Entering Data

Access table data can be maintained many ways. The best way to maintain data will depend on the size of the tables, the frequency of updates, the design features that have been applied, and personal preferences. Because all Access objects support updates from the Datasheet View, you will review that method with Missy and Micah first.

Recall from the previous chapter that the Datasheet View displays stored values in a tabular format. Each row of data is a record and each column is a field. You can use the record selector to select an entire record, the field selector to select a column, and the Tab key to move from cell to cell. While this might be all the navigation that you need in a small database, the deficiencies of these methods should be obvious when contemplating the maintenance of tables containing hundreds or thousands of records.

Sorting Records

Database data are physically stored in what is called natural order, or the sequence the records were added to the table. By default the datasheet shows data in order by the primary key if there is one. Many times the primary key is wonderful for uniquely identifying records, but not an effective tool for humans to use in finding records. For example when you are looking for data on a specific person, you would have a hard time finding him or her by Social Security Number, the most likely primary key. However, it would be relatively easy to find him or her using the last and first names.

FIGURE 2.2

Various sorts of the
Customer table

sorted by LastName
and FirstName

sorted by State

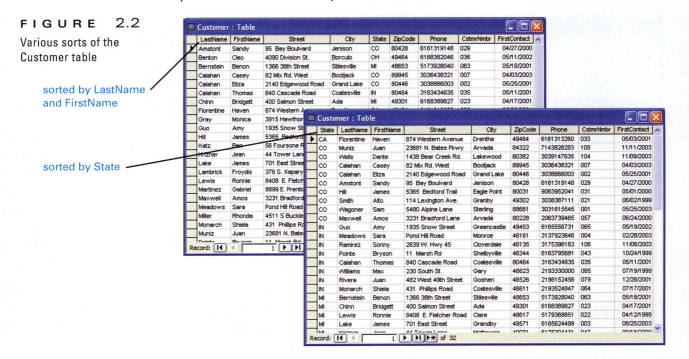

Finding and updating the correct row and column of data are critical to the integrity of database data. A simple way to improve your ability to find specific records in a large table of data is to sort the records in a manner related to the way they are being used. The same table data can be displayed in various sort orders that match the assorted ways that the data are used (see Figure 2.2). Normally the sort fields are placed to the left of the data to simplify visual searches of the list.

Moving Table Columns

Sorting table data in Datasheet View works in much the same way as sorting query output, which was introduced in the previous chapter. The first step in changing the order of the records is typically to move the sort column(s) to the left of the datasheet to visually indicate which field has been used to order. Most users expect data to be sorted by the first column(s) displayed for a table.

Changing the column order significantly improves the usability of a datasheet and has no impact on how the data are actually stored. When the column order reflects how the data are sorted (leftmost fields) and matches the way it is used (source documents like drivers licenses), updates are much more likely to be valid.

Micah lets you know that when he takes orders for martial arts supplies or signs up a student, he asks for the customers' name, address, city, state, zip, and then phone number. He would like the Customer table data to display in that order.

Reorganizing datasheet columns:

1. Open the Customer table of the **ac02Customers.mdb** database in Datasheet View

2. Use the field selector to select the CstmrNmbr column

3. Click and drag the column until it is between Phone and FirstContact

help yourself *Use the Type a Question combo box to improve your understanding of reorganizing table columns in the datasheet by typing **move table column**. Review the contents of* Move a column. *The contents of* Tutorial: Formatting and Printing a Table *are also helpful. Close the Help window when you are finished*

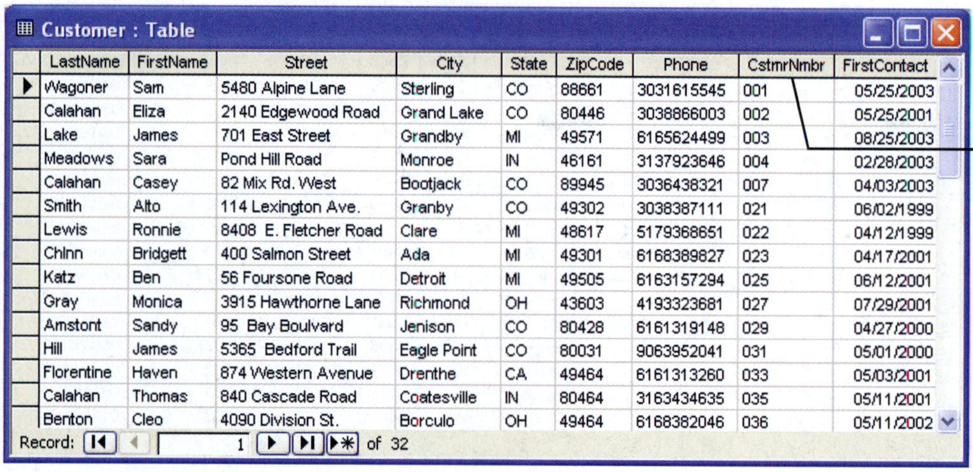

FIGURE 2.3

Customer table with new column order

repositioned CustmrNmber column

Organizing Records

Sorting by one field is as simple as clicking anywhere in the column and selecting the Sort Ascending or Sort Descending key from the toolbar. Unless a sort field contains unique values for each row in the table, multiple sort fields are needed to completely organize the data. For example, LastName is a nonunique field that can contain multiple rows with the value, Hampton for instance. When a sort field has multiple rows with the same value in the *primary sort* field, a *secondary sort* field like FirstName is needed to organize records. Access will allow you to select two or more adjacent columns for a sort. The order of the columns determines the importance of the field to the sort. Access will sort by the leftmost column first and then continue sorting with each of the other selected columns moving from left to right.

To achieve the desired order for the Customer table, you will show Missy and Micah how to sort by both the customer's last and first names. LastName is the primary sort field and must appear in the table before the secondary sort field, FirstName. To sort the data, select both the LastName and FirstName columns and then select the appropriate sort key button from the Access toolbar.

Sorting the Customer table:

1. Verify that ac02Customers.mdb is open

2. Open the Datasheet View of the Customer table

3. Verify that the column order is set so that LastName is the primary sort field and FirstName is the secondary sort field

4. Select both the LastName and FirstName columns and click the **Sort Ascending** button on the toolbar (see Figure 2.4)

5. When you close the datasheet, you will be prompted to save the layout changes that you have made. Choose **Yes** so that the next time you open the Customer table it will still be sorted

The impact of ascending and descending sorts on various types of data is represented in Figure 2.5. If you need to sort nonadjacent columns or use an ascending sort on some fields and descending sort on others, this can be accomplished in a query.

sorted by FirstName
within LastName

	LastName	FirstName	Street	City	State	ZipCode	Phone	CstmrNmbr	FirstContact
▶	Amstont	Sandy	95 Bay Boulvard	Jenison	CO	80428	6161319148	029	04/27/2000
	Benton	Cleo	4090 Division St.	Borculo	OH	49464	6168382046	036	05/11/2002
	Bernstein	Benon	1366 36th Street	Stilesville	MI	48653	5173928040	063	05/18/2001
	Calahan	Casey	82 Mix Rd. West	Bootjack	CO	89945	3036438321	007	04/03/2003
	Calahan	Eliza	2140 Edgewood Road	Grand Lake	CO	80446	3038866003	002	05/25/2001
	Calahan	Thomas	840 Cascade Road	Coatesville	IN	80464	3163434635	035	05/11/2001
	Chinn	Bridgett	400 Salmon Street	Ada	MI	49301	6168389827	023	04/17/2001
	Florentine	Haven	874 Western Avenue	Drenthe	CA	49464	6161313260	033	05/03/2001
	Gray	Monica	3915 Hawthorne Lane	Richmond	OH	43603	4193323681	027	07/29/2001
	Guo	Amy	1935 Snow Street	Greencastle	IN	49453	6165556731	065	05/19/2002
	Hill	James	5365 Bedford Trail	Eagle Point	CO	80031	9063952041	031	05/01/2000
	Katz	Ben	56 Foursone Road	Detroit	MI	49505	6163157294	025	06/12/2001
	Krizner	Jean	44 Tower Lane	Mattawan	MI	49071	5176304431	047	09/18/2000
	Lake	James	701 East Street	Grandby	MI	49571	6165624499	003	08/25/2003
	Lambrick	Froydis	376 S. Xapary Dr	Minneapolis	MN	55102	5522873587	292	01/04/2003

Record: ◀ ◀ | 1 | ▶ ▶ ▶* of 32

Type of Data	Ascending Sort Behavior	Descending Sort Behavior
Number	Sorts from lowest to highest value	Sorts from highest to lowest value
Text	Sorts from A to Z	Sorts from Z to A
Date	Sorts from oldest to newest date	Sorts from newest to oldest date
Time	Sorts from oldest to newest time	Sorts from newest to oldest time
Yes/No	Sorts Yes or checked first	Sorts No or unchecked first

Finding Records

Access provides a Find tool for locating specific records. It can be used in many of the views of a database including the Datasheet View. Click in the column whose values will be searched and then click the Find button on the toolbar or select the Find option of the Edit menu.

The Find and Replace dialog box is used to set the criteria for a search. Valid criteria are outlined in Figure 2.6.

The Find and Replace dialog box can be used to find and replace values. It is best to test the Find criteria and then add the Replace value so that data are not accidentally destroyed. In the next exercise you will replace the word "Road" with the abbreviation "Rd." in the Customer table's Street addresses column.

anotherway

. . . to Initiate
**Access Operations
for the Current
Column**

Pressing **Ctrl+F** will
initiate the Find and
Replace dialog box
for the active column

task reference   Finding Specific Data Values

- Click in the column to search
- Click the **Find** 🔍 button
- Enter the Find What criteria using data values and wildcards to create a search pattern. Remember that a question mark (?) can be used as a wildcard for one character and an asterisk (*) is a wildcard for multiple characters
- Click the **Find Next** button. If multiple rows match the Find What criteria, repeat this step until the desired row is found

Find and Replace Dialog Box		
Criteria	**Action**	
Find What	Sets the value that will be matched in the search	
Look In	Determines what will be searched. The default is the active column, but you also can choose to search the entire table.	
Match	Any Part of Field	Matches if the *Find What* value is anywhere in the field
	Whole Field	Matches if the *Find What* value is all that is in the field
	Start of Field	Matches if the *Find What* value is at the start of the field
Search	All	Searches for a match in the entire *Look In* area
	Up	Searches for a match above the cursor in the *Look In* area
	Down	Searches for a match below the cursor in the *Look In* area
Match Case	Matches the case of *Find What* when clicked on	

FIGURE 2.6
Find and Replace dialog box components

Finding and replacing values in the Customer table:

1. Verify that the Customer table of ac02Customers.mdb database is open in Datasheet View

2. Click in the **LastName** column and activate the Find and Replace dialog box using the **Find** 🔍 button on the toolbar

3. Enter **Calahan** in the Find What text box and click **Find Next**. The first Calahan occurrence should highlight. Click **Find Next** again to display the second occurrence and again to find the third occurrence

tip: *When Find Next is clicked after all occurrences of a value have been found, a dialog box displays stating "Microsoft Access finished searching the records. The search item was not found"*

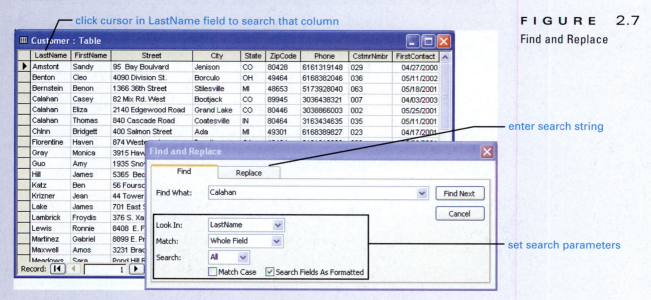

click cursor in LastName field to search that column

enter search string

set search parameters

FIGURE 2.7
Find and Replace

4. Click in the Street column and enter a Find What value of **Road** and set Match to **Any Part of Field**. Click **Find Next** repeatedly to step through all of the values

tip: *Be sure that only the word "Road" is being selected from the street address. When the replace is applied in the next step, it will replace everything selected—not just the Find What value. If the entire contents of the Street are being selected, double-check the Match setting*

5. Now that the Find works, lets replace "Road" with the abbreviation "Rd." in all of the addresses. Click the **Replace** tab of the Find and Replace dialog box. Enter **Rd.** in the Replace With text box

6. Click **Replace All** to update all of the records at once

7. Verify that the replace worked correctly

Wildcards

When entering the Find What criteria, wildcards are used to create a pattern match (see Figure 2.8). A question mark (?) can be used to represent any single character in a pattern. Let's say, for example, that you were looking for a female Tony, but are not sure of the spelling. A search for Ton? would return both Toni and Tony. It would also return Tone, Tong, and Tons if they were stored in the field. The asterisk (*) wildcard will replace any number of characters so that searching for Ton* would return Tonaba, Toni, Tony, Tons, Tonka, Tonanbaum, and so on.

It is important to note that wildcards are not meant to be used with date, time, and numeric data types. Using wildcards with these data types can cause incomplete or erroneous data retrieval. Confusion arises because wildcards on numeric fields often appear to work and sometimes produce the correct results. Ideally wildcards are used on text data when you only know part of the value or want to find data that match a pattern.

FIGURE 2.8

Access wildcards

Character	Description	Example
*	Matches any number of characters; it can be used as the first or last character of a search value	wh* Finds what, who, whale, and wham
?	Matches any single alphabetic character	b?ll Finds bill, bell, ball, and bull
#	Matches any single numeric character	b#98 Finds b098, b98, and b998
[]	Matches any one of the characters contained in the brackets	b[ae]ll Finds ball and bell
	! Negates a condition	b[!ae]ll Finds bill, and bull because they do not contain a or e
	- Specifies a range of conditions	B[a-g]ll Finds ball, bbll, bcll, bdll, bell, bfll, and bgll

Access Wildcards

Using wildcards to find Customer table data:

1. Verify that the Customer table of ac02Customers.mdb database is open in Datasheet View

2. Click in the **Street** column and activate the Find and Replace dialog box using the **Find** 🔍 button on the toolbar

3. Enter ***hill*** in the Find What area

tip: *This Find What criterion will find any street addresses containing the characters "hill"*

4. Repeatedly click **Find Next**, evaluating each found address until there are no more matches

5. Click in the **FirstName** column and activate the Find and Replace dialog box by clicking it

6. For this exercise we would like to retrieve first names with three letters. Type **???** in the Find What text box. Set the Match to **Whole Field**

7. Repeatedly click **Find Next**, evaluating each name found until there are no more matches

8. Click in the **State** column and activate the Find and Replace dialog box by clicking it

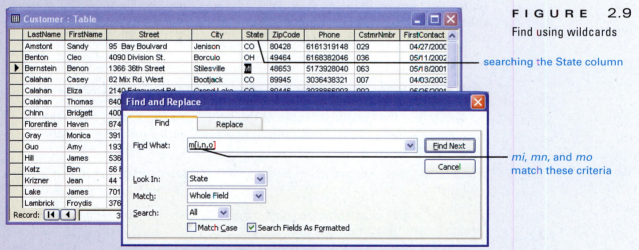

F I G U R E   2.9

Find using wildcards

← searching the State column

mi, mn, and *mo* match these criteria

9. For this exercise we would like to retrieve data for the states of Michigan (MI), Missouri (MO), and Minnesota (MN), so you will need to enter **m[i,n,o]** in the Find What text box and click **Find Next**. The first matching occurrence should highlight. Click **Find Next** until you have reviewed all selected records (see Figure 2.9)

Adding Table Records

The order of table data display has nothing to do with the order in which it is stored. It is therefore *not* important to view table columns in a consistent order to insert new records in any particular order. The primary key or a user-defined sort criterion will determine the order of records displayed for a user.

Whether a table simply needs some new records added or is empty because it has just been built, the datasheet is a simple place to create new records. When you open a table, the default is to display the data in Datasheet View. Unless the field order has been changed, the columns display in the order they were defined when the table was built.

FIGURE 2.10

Customer table in
Datasheet View

current record indicator

new record indicator

FIGURE 2.10

Customer table in
Datasheet View

current record indicator ──

new record indicator ──

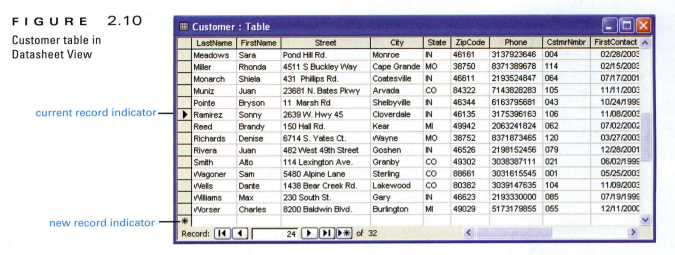

The last row displayed in the datasheet is blank with an asterisk in the record indicator, as shown in Figure 2.10.

Clicking in the new record row will change the record indicator to an arrow, meaning that it is the current record. As you begin to enter data in the row, the record indicator changes to a pencil to point out that the record is being edited. Once the record is in edit mode, you can key in field data using the Tab key to advance to the next field and Shift+Tab to move to the previous field. Moving to the next empty record or to any other row of the datasheet will automatically save newly entered data. If a required field such as the primary key has been left blank, an error message will display.

Adding new records to the Customer table:

1. Verify that the Customer table of the ac02Customers.mdb database is open in Datasheet View. Find the current record indicator, a right-pointing arrow in the record selector

2. Click the **New Record** ▶* indicator, an * in the record selector, or toolbar button

tip: *The record indicator should convert to a pencil as you begin making modifications to indicate that the record is in edit mode*

3. Verify that the empty record is the current record and then enter the data in Figure 2.11 using the Tab key to move from cell to cell

FIGURE 2.11

New data for the
Customer table

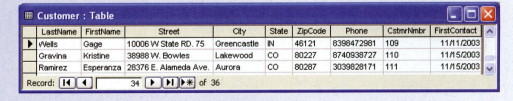

tip: *Correct typing errors by using the Backspace key to delete characters to the left of the insertion point or the Delete key to remove characters to the right of the insertion point, or by double-clicking a data value to select the entire value and overtype it*

4. Add yourself as customer 108

5. Re-sort the table contents by LastName and FirstName and then print the table using the Print button from the toolbar

Updating Data

Besides adding new records to database tables, existing data must be updated to keep them current. Customers move, changing their address information; get married or divorced, changing their name; or sometimes the original data were entered erroneously and must be corrected. Whatever the cause, deleting old data and updating existing data are critical to the integrity of a database.

Deleting Data

Database data need to be removed from tables when they are no longer useful. Unnecessary rows of data slow processing and confuse users. Most businesses do not simply delete old data because they could be useful as history or may need to be retained for legal reasons (tax and personnel data must be retained for periods specified by laws). In such cases, the data are backed up or stored to an alternate location before they are deleted from the active table.

   Actually deleting a single record is a simple process. Use the record selector to highlight the record to be deleted and then press the Del key on the keyboard. There is also a Delete button on the toolbar, a Delete Record option in the Edit menu, and a Delete Record option in the pop-up menu. Once completed, the delete process *cannot* be reversed, so be careful to verify that you are deleting the correct record.

Deleting a record from the Customer table:

1. Verify that the Customer table of the ac02Customers.mdb database is open in Datasheet View

2. Use the record selector to choose the record for Monica Gray

3. Press the **delete** ✗ button on the toolbar or the **Del** key on your keyboard

4. Answer **Yes** to the warning that the delete can't be undone

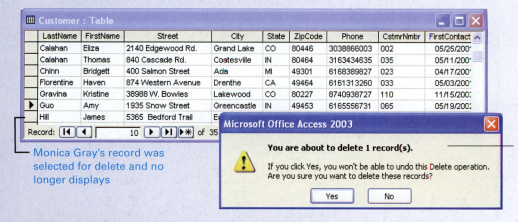

Monica Gray's record was selected for delete and no longer displays

dialog box warning that the delete cannot be recovered

FIGURE 2.12
Deleting a Customer table record

5. Make CstmrNmbr the first column and sort the data by it

6. Close the Customer table saving your changes

   Using Find to locate records for deletion is an effective way to ensure that the correct record is selected. It is also possible to delete a group of records. Use click and drag across multiple record selectors to highlight several contiguous records. Any of the previously mentioned delete methods will remove all selected records. The warning dialog box will list the number of records selected for deletion.

Modifying Data

Modifying data is the process of changing specific values in a record or records. Access navigation can be customized to simplify the editing process. When using *keyboard navigation* (Tab and arrow keys), Access's default navigation settings cause the entire contents of a cell to be selected when the cell is entered. Typing while all contents of a cell are selected will replace the entire data value. If, however, the goal is to move character by character in a cell, choose Options from the Tools menu and change the Keyboard options to either Go to start of field or Go to end of field.

In *navigation mode* (Tab selects the entire cell contents), using the Home and End keys will move the cursor to the first and last cell in a record, respectively. The arrow keys move the cursor from cell to cell. In edit mode (Go to start or end of field), the Home and End keys move the cursor to the beginning and end of a field. The left and right arrow keys move the cursor character by character within the cell.

The mouse also can be used to navigate during editing operations. Clicking an insertion point in the text of a field will allow new characters to be added to the existing data. Click and drag to select multiple characters of a data value for typeover. When editing with the mouse, each table cell is edited like a word-processing document.

Using Undo

When editing records in Datasheet View, the Undo feature of Access 2003 will allow changes to be reversed. Undo can be accessed from the Edit menu or via the toolbar button. As edits are completed, Undo stores each action. Before they are saved, actions on a single record can be undone one at a time or from a point backward using the Undo button.

Once the cursor moves to another record or the view is exited, any changes made to a record are saved to the database and Undo is cleared. At that point selecting Undo Saved Record from the Edit menu will restore the original record (see Figure 2.13).

Updating with the Microsoft Office Clipboard

The Windows Clipboard is a temporary storage area that will hold cut or copied information from any Windows program. Stored information can be pasted into any open

FIGURE   2.13

Undo saved record

text changes to match the action that can be undone

Can't Undo indicates that nothing can be undone

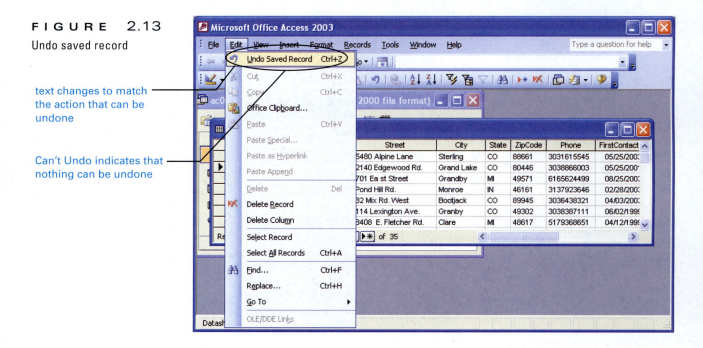

Windows program. The Windows Clipboard holds only one item. By contrast, the Microsoft Office Clipboard allows multiple text and graphic items from any number of *Office* programs to be collected and then pasted into any open *Office* document. For example, some text from a Microsoft Word document, some data from a Microsoft Excel spreadsheet, a bulleted list from Microsoft PowerPoint, and some text from Microsoft FrontPage or Microsoft Internet Explorer could all be copied to the MS Office Clipboard and then pasted into a Microsoft Access datasheet.

Like the Windows Clipboard, the Office Clipboard works with the Cut and Copy buttons on the toolbar. The Office Clipboard, however, will hold up to 24 items. Items remain on the Office Clipboard until all Office applications are closed or the Clipboard is cleared. The Paste button on the toolbar pastes the contents of the *Windows* Clipboard, which is also the last entry from the Office Clipboard. The Office Clipboard opens as soon as two items are cut or copied from the same application. The contents of the Office Clipboard are viewed in the task pane by selecting Office Clipboard from the Edit menu or pressing Ctrl+C twice.

The Office Clipboard can be used to copy values from one row of a database table to another row or rows to speed repetitive data entry and reduce errors. The Clipboard can also be used to copy entire records and move data from other Office System applications. Each Clipboard item carries the icon of the originating Office System product (see Figure 2.14). Items can be selected and pasted individually or the Paste All button can be used to paste the entire Clipboard contents at once.

Notice in Figure 2.14 that when multiple fields are copied, Access data are placed on the Clipboard with the field name as well as the copied contents. The field name is informational and will not be pasted. The selection can be any part of a field, an entire column, multiple fields of a record, an entire record, or multiple rows of a table to be placed on the Clipboard. When pasting data from multiple fields to a datasheet, make sure the columns match the order of the data you want to copy or move.

In the next series of steps, the Office Clipboard will be used to copy the records of customers with billing problems to a new table.

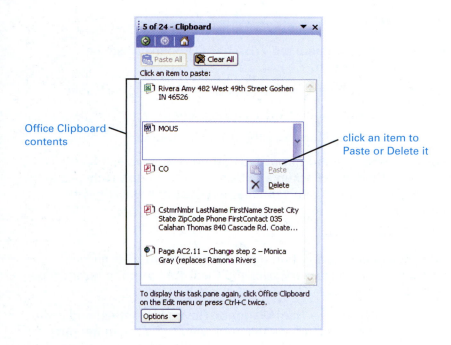

FIGURE 2.14

The Office Clipboard

---

task *reference*   Using the Office Clipboard

- Collect items to paste
  - Display the Office Clipboard by selecting **Office Clipboard** from the **Edit** menu
  - Select the item to be copied
  - Click the **Copy** or **Cut** button in the Standard toolbar
  - Continue placing items on the clipboard (up to 24) until you have collected everything that you need

- Paste collected items
  - Display the Office Clipboard if it is not already present. If the Office Clipboard option of the Edit menu is not available, you are in an application or view that does not support the Office Clipboard
  - Click or select the area where you want to place items
  - Do one of the following:
    - Select the **Paste All** button to paste the entire contents of the Office Clipboard
    - Select a Clipboard item and choose **Paste** from its drop-down menu

- Remove Office Clipboard items when it is open
  - To clear one item, click the arrow next to the item you want to delete and then click **Delete**
  - To clear all Clipboard contents, click the **Clear All** button
  - Placing more than 24 items on the Clipboard will replace existing items beginning with the oldest item

---

Using the Office Clipboard with the Customer table:

1. Verify that the ac02Customers.mdb database is open. Close the Customer table if it is open

2. Use the Windows Clipboard to make a copy of the Customer table

   a. Select the **Customer** table in the Database Window

   b. Select the **Copy** button from the Standard toolbar

   c. Select the **Paste** button from the Standard toolbar. Name the copied table **CustomerBackup** and select the **Structure Only** paste options. This will create a new table named CustomerBackup with no data

3. Open the **Customer** table

4. Select the **Office Clipboard** option of the **Edit** menu to view current Clipboard contents. If necessary, click the **Clear All** button to remove existing Clipboard contents

5. There are three customers—Sam Wagoner, Haven Florentine, and Jean Krizner—with billing problems whose data need to be put in the new table. Select each record and copy it to the Clipboard using the Copy button

6. Close the Customer table

7. Open the **CustomerBackup** table, which should contain no records

row selected for paste

FIGURE 2.15
Pasting records from the
Office Clipboard

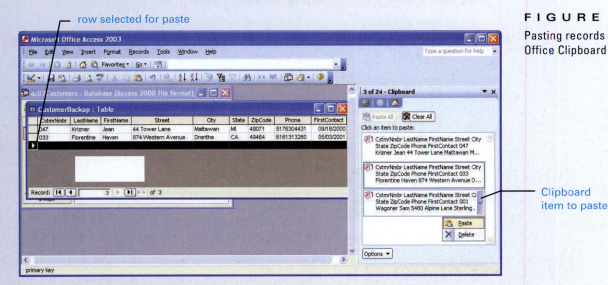

Clipboard
item to paste

8. Select the new record row of CustomerBackup and select the **Paste** option for the first item on the Office Clipboard. Repeat this process for the other two items on the Office Clipboard

tip: *If you get a paste error, verify that the entire row of CustomerBackup is selected before trying to paste a record from the Office Clipboard*

9. Close CustomerBackup

When pasting multiple fields, it is important for the paste area to match the size and shape of the copy area (same number of cells). When pasting multiple cells or entire rows of data, it is important for the field names of the paste area to match the field names of the copy area.

In Access only one database can be open at a time. Using the Office Clipboard it is possible to move or copy data between databases by opening the first database, placing data on the Clipboard, opening another database, and then pasting the Office Clipboard contents.

Organizing a Datasheet

Datasheets are often bigger than your computer screen, making data updates difficult. Hiding and freezing columns can improve your ability to enter data in the correct rows and columns.

Hiding and Unhiding Columns

When there are columns in a datasheet that are not relevant to the task at hand, they can be hidden. Hiding removes columns from display but does not remove the stored data. When only the needed columns are displayed, more of the table will fit on the screen, you do not have to tab through unwanted data, and only the displayed columns will print.

task *reference*   Hiding and Unhiding
                                             Datasheet Columns

- Open a table, query, or form in Datasheet View
- To Hide a column
  - Click the field selector of the column to be hidden
  - Click **Hide Columns** on the **Format** menu
- To Unhide a column
  - On the **Format** menu, click **Unhide Columns**
  - Select the names of the columns to show from the Unhide Columns dialog box

---

*another***word**   . . . on Hiding and Unhiding Columns

The Unhide Columns dialog box can be activated when no columns are hidden. It is a convenient way to hide multiple columns by unchecking them. The shortcut menu containing the Unhide Columns option can be activated by right-clicking the datasheet window outside the data area (for example, in the Title bar)

Hiding and unhiding columns of the Customer table:

1. Open the Customer table of the ac02Customers.mdb database in Datasheet View
2. Click the column selector for State
3. Select the **Format** menu and then select **Hide Columns**. The column will remain hidden until it is unhidden or until you close the datasheet without saving the formatting changes
4. To unhide columns, select **Unhide Columns** from the **Format** menu
5. Check the **State** checkbox in the Unhide Columns dialog box and click **Close**

Freezing and Unfreezing Columns

Freezing columns is useful when the datasheet is wider than the viewing area of your screen. As you move to the far-right columns, the leftmost columns scroll off the screen, making it difficult to determine what entity's record is being edited. Freezing the column containing entity identification information causes that column or columns to stay on the screen while scrolling through the remaining columns.

task reference — Freezing and Unfreezing Datasheet Columns

- Open a table, query, or form in Datasheet View
- Select the column(s) to freeze or unfreeze
- To Freeze column(s), select **Freeze Columns** on the **Format** menu
- To Unfreeze column(s), select **Unfreeze All Columns** on the **Format** menu

Freezing and unfreezing columns of the Customer table:

1. Verify that the Customer table of ac02Customers.mdb database is open in Datasheet View

2. Narrow the datasheet window to display only five columns of data by dragging its right corner to the left. Use the Tab key to navigate through a record to demonstrate that the identifying values (CstmrNmbr, LastName, FirstName) scroll out of the viewing area

3. Select both the **LastName** and **FirstName** columns by clicking and dragging across their field selectors

4. Select the **Format** menu and then select **Freeze Columns**. The LastName and FirstName columns will be moved to the first columns of the datasheet

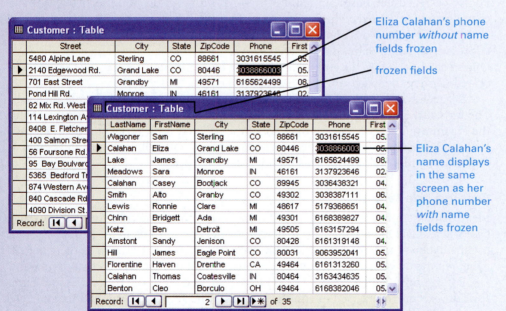

Eliza Calahan's phone number *without* name fields frozen

frozen fields

Eliza Calahan's name displays in the same screen as her phone number *with* name fields frozen

FIGURE 2.16

Unfrozen and frozen Customer table columns

5. Tab through the columns of a record. Notice that the frozen fields stay visible while the remaining fields scroll

6. To unfreeze columns, select **Unfreeze All Columns** from the **Format** menu

7. Close ac02Customers.mdb

making *the grade*

1. What is the significance of an asterisk in the row selector of a table?

2. Discuss the use of wildcards when finding data in a table.

3. When/how are changes made to a record stored in the table?

4. Discuss the importance of column order when sorting by multiple fields.

5. T F   Rows deleted from a table can be restored.

6. T F   The Windows Clipboard and the Office Clipboard are the same thing.

SESSION 2.2 DESIGNING AND BUILDING A DATABASE

Now that Missy and Micah are comfortable with the Customer table, it is time to assess the remaining data requirements for KoryoKicks. The twins are interested in learning how to design and develop databases and have asked to work through this process with you. Involving users in the design process helps to ensure that their needs will be met by the completed database.

Assessing Information Needs

The longevity and effectiveness of a database are rooted in the quality of its design. Poorly designed databases are tedious to work with and do not effectively adapt to changing business needs. The 90/10 rule is often cited. It states that 90 percent of your effort should go into designing the database structure so that only 10 percent of your effort is required to maintain the structure after it is implemented and contains data. Once a database is live, the emphasis should be on maintaining and using the data, not on redesigning the structure.

Regardless of the size of the project, the first step is to assess the information needs. The formality and duration of this process are governed by the size of the project and the organization responsible for the development. There are a variety of tools and procedures that can be used to define information needs. You will use paper and pencil to walk Missy and Micah through a simplified design process.

Outline the Mission

Identifying the mission of a database involves determining specifically what the database will and will not accomplish. To determine the mission, talk to the people who will use the database and document the tasks that they want it to perform. If there are existing reports or forms, collect them; otherwise, sketch out the reports that users want.

For example, with KoryoKicks, you have reviewed all of the paper files and Excel spreadsheets currently used to run the business. The review determined that current tracking fits generally into one of the following areas:

- Tracking customer orders
- Determining product availability
- Tracking suppliers
- Tracking payments
- Tracking class schedules

The next step is to find out what the current system won't do that the new system needs to do. A simple way of determining requirements is to write down the business questions the database should be able to answer. Missy and Micah tell you they are generally happy with the data they have, but it is taking too much time to find and consolidate.

The business questions they consider most important are

- What are the total sales for each month?
- What do my customers owe me?
- How many multiple-order customers do I have?
- Which suppliers provide the best service?
- What do I owe suppliers?
- How much of each product do I have available?

These questions define the outputs that are required of the KoryoKicks database and are used to determine what fields (inputs) need to be stored in database tables. The questions are also a very good start at outlining the forms, queries, and reports needed to provide answers.

Establish Table Subjects

Each table in a database contains data about only one subject (one type of entity). Determining table subjects is not always as easy as it sounds. The business questions that establish the results needed from the database correspond nicely to queries, reports, and forms but *do not* dictate table structure. Categorizing the information into tables is done by evaluating the impacts of various table configurations on the effectiveness of the database. A formal set of steps called normalization often is used to help ensure effective table design. This session will demonstrate an informal application of normalization rules. Common sense and good judgment help in this process.

Let's consider an invoice for a KoryoKicks customer (see Figure 2.17). The invoice would contain information such as the invoice number, invoice date, customer's name and address, product identification, product description, product price, quantity ordered, item total, tax, shipping, and invoice total. While all of these appear on one invoice, it would be problematic to store everything in one table. A customer can order multiple products at a time, which would mean that there would be a row of data for each product ordered. If a customer ordered three products, everything would be entered in the table three times. That is great for the data that change each time, but static data such as the customer's name and address would also be entered three times, significantly multiplying the chance of data entry errors. Duplication also increases maintenance by requiring multiple records to be updated if the customer moves.

To reduce the storage of duplicate data, put the data that do not change often in one table and the changing data in another. The data that do not change often are referred to as *static data* while frequently changing data are called *transaction data*. The Customer table will hold the static data about the customer. It is also apparent that a table holding data about products would be beneficial. Common shorthand used to describe tables is to list the table name with its attributes (fields) in parentheses after it. In this notation, the primary key is underlined. Using this notation with the invoice data, we can demonstrate the tables currently being evaluated as shown in Figure 2.18.

The next step is to review the unassigned attributes to be certain that they do not belong in either the Customer or Product table. The question to ask to determine whether the field belongs in the Customer table is "Does this attribute belong to the customer?" Similarly, ask if the attribute belongs to the Product table. For all of the unassigned values shown in Figure 2.18, the answer to both questions is no, meaning that at least one more table is needed.

FIGURE 2.17

Customer invoice form

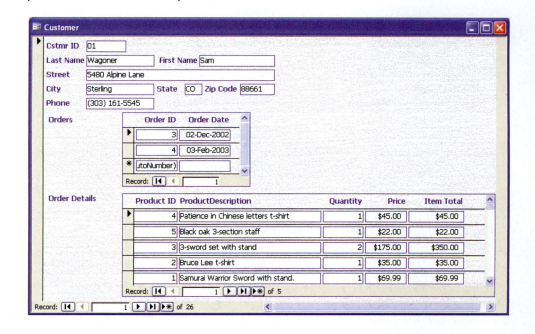

While the formal rules of normalization have not been presented, this informal process is achieving the same result. One further rule holds that derived or calculated data should not be stored in tables. Following that axiom, tax, shipping, and invoice total should be calculated when the invoice is created, not stored in a table, so they can be removed from consideration. The remaining unassigned attributes of invoice number, invoice date, and quantity ordered could all be considered to be order data. Each of these fields is frequently updated with information generated by customer orders. This design stage is shown in Figure 2.19.

help yourself *Use the Type a Question combo box to solidify your understanding of database design by typing* **database design***. Review the contents of* About designing a database. *Be sure to click to expand all topics. Close the Help window when you are finished*

This evaluation process needs to be completed for each output defined in the mission statement. The result will be a list of tables and possible attributes covering most of the user's requirements.

FIGURE 2.18

First table design break out

Customer (name, address)

Product (product identification, product description, product price)

Unassigned (invoice number, invoice date, quantity ordered, item total, tax, shipping, and invoice total)

FIGURE 2.19

Table design after removing calculated values

Customer (name, address)

Product (product identification, product description, product price)

Order (invoice number, invoice date, quantity ordered)

Establish Table Fields

Now that the table entities (subjects) and what they should store are established, it is time to determine exactly what attributes need to be stored in each table and how they will be named. In general, field names should be descriptive and not contain spaces or special characters. Here are some tips for defining fields:

- Each field must directly describe the subject of the table. A field that does not describe the subject belongs in another table

- Store data in their smallest logical part. It is easy to merge attributes in queries, forms, and reports, but very difficult to access part of a data value. Combined data values also make it difficult to retrieve and analyze the data. Create separate fields for each part of a person's name and address. Consider breaking up any field that you might want to access part of, such as a part number with embedded information. For easy reporting, such a part number could be broken into PartCategory and PartID, which combine to make a unique part number

- Assign a primary key field to each table. The primary key field(s) should uniquely and minimally identify a specific entity or row of data in the table. If there is no naturally occurring primary key, one should be generated. For example, because names can be duplicated in the data, use either Social Security Number or a sequential number to uniquely identify each person

Applying these tips to the previous design results in creating multiple fields for the customer's name and address and adding CstmrID as the key to the customer table (see Figure 2.20). ProductID is added as the key for the Product table and OrderID is made the key of the Orders table.

At this point it is wise to return to the information gathered while creating the mission statement. Be sure that all of the data to create the defined outputs are assigned to a table. Further ensure that all of the questions documented for the design can be answered from the data assigned to tables.

Defining Relationships

The power of relational databases is their ability to rapidly locate and organize data stored in multiple tables. For example, the current design stores the data to create a customer invoice in three tables. Data from multiple tables are joined by matching values in a shared field. Those relationships have to be identified and foreign key fields added to the tables so this joining can take place.

Decide what tables are related and then how they are related. Remember that table relationships are classified by how many records in the first table are related to how many records in the second table. One-to-many relationships are the most common and occur when one record in Table A relates to many records in Table B. For example, one customer can have many orders. In a one-to-one relationship, one record from the first table can be related to one record of the second table. One-to-one relationships are created when there are too many fields for one Access table, or there are fields that are blank for most of the rows.

Customer (*CstmrID*, LastName, FirstName, Street, City, State, Zip)

Product (*ProductID*, ProductDescription, ProductPrice)

Order (*OrderID*, OrderDate, QuantityOrdered)

FIGURE 2.20

Table design with field names and primary keys assigned

ACCESS

Many-to-many relationships are the most complex because many records from one table are related to many rows in another table. For example, one customer can buy many products and one product can be purchased by many customers. Since relational databases can't directly model many-to-many relationships, a new table is added that has a one-to-many relationship with each table in the many-to-many relationship.

One way to determine relationships is to diagram them. There are usually multiple ways to set the relations in a database; choosing the best fit takes practice. Begin by drawing a rounded box for each table and placing the table name in it. Connect tables that are related with a line and label the line with a brief description of the relationship.

Figure 2.21 presents one possible model of the Customer, Product, and Order relationships. These diagrams are read from entity to entity as shown in the relationships figure notes.

Notice that the relationship between products and orders is many-to-many. To model this relationship, an intermediate table having a one-to-many relationship with each table in the many-to-many relationship must be added to the design. In this case, OrderDetail has been added as the intermediate table (see Figure 2.22). It has one-to-many relationships to both the Order and Product tables. Each row in OrderDetail represents one invoice line item (the order for one product). To complete the design, the primary key from the table on the one side of the relationship is added to the table on the many side as a foreign key, enabling the tables to be joined. The final design is described in Figure 2.22.

F I G U R E   2.21

Preliminary entity diagrams for invoicing design

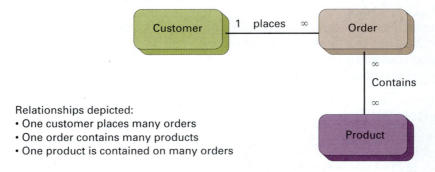

Relationships depicted:
• One customer places many orders
• One order contains many products
• One product is contained on many orders

F I G U R E   2.22

Invoicing design with two one-to-many relationships replacing a many-to-many relationship

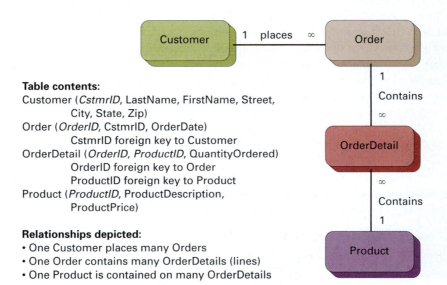

Table contents:
Customer (*CstmrID*, LastName, FirstName, Street,
     City, State, Zip)
Order (*OrderID*, CstmrID, OrderDate)
     CstmrID foreign key to Customer
OrderDetail (*OrderID*, *ProductID*, QuantityOrdered)
     OrderID foreign key to Order
     ProductID foreign key to Product
Product (*ProductID*, ProductDescription,
     ProductPrice)

Relationships depicted:
• One Customer places many Orders
• One Order contains many OrderDetails (lines)
• One Product is contained on many OrderDetails

Designing a Prototype

Once the tables, fields, and relationships are designed, it is time to build a prototype for testing. Create the tables, specify the relationships, and enter some test data. The test data should be representative of the data the table will actually hold in order to successfully evaluate the design. Create rough drafts of the queries, forms, and reports to see if they contain the data needed to answer the questions outlined in the mission statement.

As you work with the prototype, note where the design can be improved. Are any data missing? Are data repeated? Are the primary keys working correctly? Can tables be joined effectively? Update the prototype and continue testing until it is ready for production.

Building Access Tables Using Design View

In Session 1.2 a table was built using the Table Wizard. Now it's time to take a look at what is going on behind the Wizard. There are many table attributes automatically set by the Table Wizard. The attributes of a table determine how data will be stored, displayed, and processed. Field attributes include a field's name, data type, size, and key. Building tables in Design View allows control over all table attributes.

Field Names

The *Field Name* property is used to retrieve data from a column in queries, forms, and reports. Although the design already specifies field names, it is important to understand the rules that govern name selection. In Microsoft Access field names must be unique within a table and can

- Be up to 64 characters long
- Include any combination of letters, numbers, spaces, and special characters except a period (.), an exclamation point (!), an accent grave (`), and brackets ([ ])
- *Not* start with a space
- *Not* contain control characters

Although Access allows spaces within field names, it is best to capitalize the first letter of each word and not use spaces. So while both Customer number and CustomerNumber are valid field names, CustomerNumber is the better choice. Finally, short but descriptive names are best since the assigned names will be used frequently.

Data Types

The *Data Type* property of a field establishes what data values it can store and what other properties can be set for the field. For example, setting the OrderDate field to a Date data type ensures that only valid dates and/or times can be stored. Figure 2.23 outlines Access data types. Notice that numbers not used in calculations are best stored in Text fields.

In addition to determining what data can be stored in a field, the Number, Date/Time, Currency, and Yes/No data types have display formats. Display formats define what the user sees as output from these fields.

You, Missy, and Micah add data types to the table design as outlined in Figure 2.24. CstmrID is a field that contains numbers that won't be used in calculations and will not be automatically generated. Such numbers are faster to search, sort, and process when they are stored in a Text field.

F I G U R E   2.23
Microsoft Access data type overview

Data Type	Use for	Size
Text	Text or combinations of text and numbers, such as addresses. Also numbers that do not require calculations, such as phone numbers, part numbers, or postal codes	Up to 255 characters
Memo	Lengthy text and numbers, such as notes or descriptions	Up to 64,000 characters
Number	Numeric data to be used for mathematical calculations, except calculations involving money. Set the FieldSize property to define the specific Number type	Dependent on the field size chosen
Date/Time	Dates and times	8 bytes
Currency	Currency or other values with 4 or fewer decimals. Accurate to 15 digits to the left of the decimal point and 4 digits to the right. Calculations do not round	8 bytes
AutoNumber	Unique sequential (incrementing by 1) or random numbers automatically inserted when a record is added	4 bytes
Yes/No	Fields that will contain only one of two values, such as Yes/No, True/False, On/Off	1 bit
OLE Object	Objects (such as Microsoft Word documents, Microsoft Excel spreadsheets, pictures, sounds, or other binary data), created in other programs using the OLE protocol, that can be linked to or embedded	Up to 1 gigabyte (limited by disk space)
Hyperlink	Field that will store hyperlinks. A hyperlink can be a UNC path or a URL	Up to 64,000 characters
Lookup Wizard	A field that allows you to choose a list of values from another table using a combo box. Choosing this option initiates a Wizard to define this for you	The same size as the primary key field that is also the Lookup field; typically 4 bytes

Field Sizes

The *Field Size* property is available for Text, Number, and AutoNumber data types. The other data types either have a fixed field size or adjust to fit the data entered. Field size determines the maximum value a field can store, how much storage space it requires, and how fast it processes. In general, use the smallest field size that will meet your needs.

For fields with a Text data type, the field size can be set from 0 to 255 characters. The default text field size is 50 characters. Text fields only store the data entered without any trailing spaces, so setting a smaller field size does not reduce storage requirements. Smaller text field sizes do improve the validity of stored data. For example, if a company has 15-character part numbers, setting the field size to 15 stops the user from entering more than 15 characters. The valid field sizes for Number data types are outlined in Figure 2.25.

If the DataType property is set to AutoNumber, the FieldSize property can be set to Long Integer or Replication ID, as outlined in Figure 2.25. AutoNumber fields are frequently used to generate unique primary keys for records without a natural primary key. It is important to note that the currency field size is not just for tracking dollars and cents. The currency field size will provide faster fixed-point calculations than either Single or Double and should be used for all noncurrency data of one to four decimal places.

FIGURE 2.24
Table design with data types

Table	Field Name	Data Type
Customer	CstmrID	Text
	LastName	Text
	FirstName	Text
	Street	Text
	City	Text
	State	Text
	Zip	Text
Order	OrderID	AutoNumber
	CstmrID	Text
	OrderDate	Date/Time
OrderDetail	OrderID	Number
	ProductID	Number
	QuantityOrdered	Number
Product	ProductID	AutoNumber
	ProductDescription	Text
	ProductPrice	Currency

FIGURE 2.25
Microsoft Access field sizes for number data type

Field Size	Description	Decimal Precision	Storage Size
Byte	Stores numbers from 0 to 255 (no fractions)	None	1 byte
Decimal	Stores numbers from $-10^{28}-1$ through $10^{28}-1$	28	12 bytes
Integer	Stores numbers from $-32,768$ to $32,767$ (no fractions)	None	2 bytes
Long Integer	(Access Default) Stores numbers from $-2,147,483,648$ to $2,147,483,647$ (no fractions)	None	4 bytes
Single	Stores numbers from 3.402823E38 to 1.401298E$-$45 for negative values and from 1.401298E$-$45 to 3.402823E38 for positive values	7	4 bytes
Double	Stores numbers from -1.79769313486231E308 to -4.94065645841247E$-$324 for negative values and from 1.79769313486231E308 to 4.94065645841247E$-$324 for positive values	15	8 bytes
Replication ID	Globally unique identifier	N/A	16 bytes

FIGURE 2.26

Database design with field sizes

Table	Field Name	Data Type	Field Size
Customer	CstmrID	Text	5
	LastName	Text	30
	FirstName	Text	30
	Street	Text	30
	City	Text	30
	State	Text	2
	Zip	Text	5
Order	OrderID	AutoNumber	LongInteger
	CstmrID	Text	5
	OrderDate	Date/Time	N/A
OrderDetail	OrderID	Number	LongInteger
	ProductID	Number	LongInteger
	QuantityOrdered	Number	Integer
Product	ProductID	AutoNumber	LongInteger
	ProductDescription	Text	30
	ProductPrice	Currency	N/A

The database design with field sizes added is shown in Figure 2.26.

Building a Table Definition

It's finally time to build the KoryoKicks table definitions in Access using Design View and set all of the attributes that have been outlined. Before you begin, review the Order table design in Figure 2.27.

FIGURE 2.27

Order table design

	Order Table Design		
Table	Field Name	Data Type	Field Size
Order	OrderID	AutoNumber	LongInteger
	CstmrID	Text	5
	OrderDate	Date/Time	N/A

---

task reference   Defining a Table Field

- Click **Tables** in the Options bar
- Click the **Design View** button on the toolbar
- Enter a field name
- Select a data type
- Define other field attributes as needed

Building the Order table:

1. Open the ac02KoryoKicks.mdb file. The Customer and Products tables have already been built. Use both Design and Datasheet Views to review the existing tables

2. Click the **Tables** object in the Database Window and select the **New** button on the toolbar

3. Select **Design View** from the New Table dialog box and click **OK**

4. Review the Design View grid. Note the default table name, Table1. Find the columns for Field Name, Data Type, and Description. As you create fields, the General tab at the bottom of the page will display other attributes such as Field Size

5. The first field of the Order table is OrderID. To create that field, type **OrderID** in the Field Name column of the first row. Tab to or click in Data Type to activate the drop-down list. Select **AutoNumber** as the Data Type and leave the Field Size as **LongInteger**

tip: *The Description attribute is for the developer's notes about the design and contents of a field. The value can be up to 255 characters and will display in the Access status bar when the field is active in Datasheet View*

6. Repeat step 5 for the CstmrID field using Figure 2.27. Be sure to set the Field Size for CstmrID on the General tab

7. Repeat step 5 for the OrderDate field using Figure 2.27

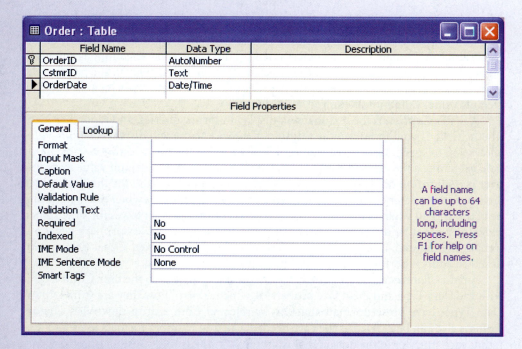

FIGURE 2.28

Field definitions for the Order table

8. Set the table primary key by clicking the record indicator for the OrderID field and then selecting the **Key** button from the Access toolbar

9. Close the Design View window and answer **Yes** to Do you want to save changes to the design of table 'Table1'?

10. Enter **Order** in the Save As dialog box and click **OK**

FIGURE 2.29

Order table listed in the
Database Window

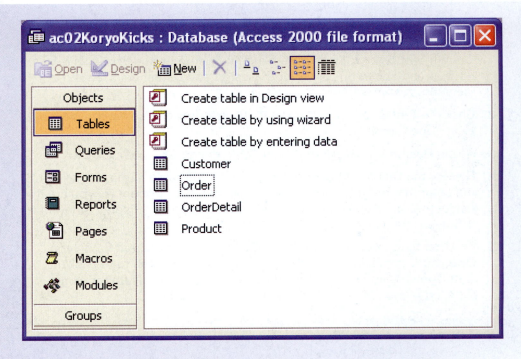

11. Verify that your new Order table is listed in the Database Window
(see Figure 2.29)

General Tab Attributes

Let's take a look at some of the other table attributes. The attributes that display on the General tab in Design View are determined by the Data Type selection, as shown in Figure 2.30. A brief description of the selected attribute will display in the panel to the right of the General tab. Attributes that are common to all data types include Caption, Default Value, Validation, Required, and Indexed.

A field's *Caption* is the text that will display in forms, queries, and reports to identify the field. If you do not set the Caption, the Field Name will display. *Default Value* allows you to speed data entry by automatically placing the most common value in the field each time a new record is added. The user can override the default value by typing over it. *Validation* holds the rules that govern what data are valid for the field, which are covered in a later chapter. The *Required* attribute is set to yes when the field cannot be blank and no when blank entries are acceptable. *Indexed* is set to yes for a field when indexing by that field will improve database performance. A table's primary key is automatically indexed. In general, foreign keys also should be indexed. Other fields are indexed to address performance issues when the database is in use.

A field's *Format* attribute controls how data are displayed to the user. Contrast this with the Data Type and Field Size properties, which control how they are stored. Many Data Types have preset formats that can be selected from a drop-down list. Custom formats also can be created as they are needed. Custom Number formats use a # to represent each number in the output. For example, ###.### would cause all number values to display with three decimal places.

Custom date formats are more complex, using the symbols outlined in Figure 2.31. A Date/Time field is capable of storing both the date and time in the same field. If both are stored, the format can be set to display either one or both. Custom time formats are not covered here.

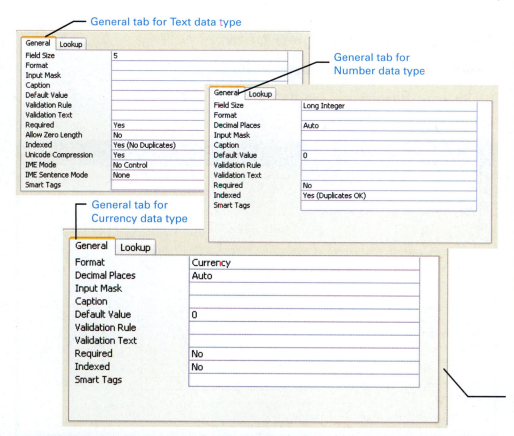

General tab for Text data type

General tab for Number data type

General tab for Currency data type

description of selected General tab attributes

FIGURE   2.30

General tab attributes for Text, Number, and Currency

FIGURE   2.31

Custom date format symbols

Symbol	Uses
/	Date separator
d	Formats the day of the month
	d—day of the month without leading zeroes (1–31)
	dd—day of the month in two digits (01–31)
	ddd—weekday abbreviations (Sun–Sat)
	ddddd—full weekday (Sunday–Saturday)
w	Sets week formats
	w—day of the week (1–7)
	ww—week of the year (1–53)
m	Formats the month
	m—month without leading zeroes (1–12)
	mm—two-digit month (01–12)
	mmm—month abbreviations (Jan–Dec)
	mmmm—full month name (January–December)
y	Formats the year
	yy—two-digit year (01–99)
	yyyy—full year (0100–9999)

Setting General tab attributes:

1. Verify that the ac02KoryoKicks.mdb file is open

2. Open the **Order** table in Design View

3. Select the **OrderDate** field

FIGURE 2.32

OrderDate format

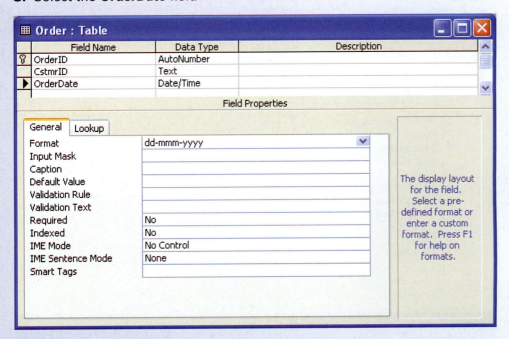

4. Enter the custom format **dd-mmm-yyyy**. Dates entered in this field will display with a two-digit day, a three-character month abbreviation, and a four-digit year (15-Jul-2002)

5. Verify your custom format and close the Design window

6. Answer **Yes** to save the design changes that you have made

If a Number field is set to Currency format (not the same as Currency field size), it will display values based on the regional settings in the Windows Control Panel. Changes made to the regional settings in the Windows Control Panel will be automatically reflected in table fields set to currency format.

To complete the database prototype, the OrderDetail table must be built and table relationships defined. You will build OrderDetail in the next series of steps. Setting relationships is covered later.

Building the OrderDetail table:

1. Verify that the ac02KoryoKicks.mdb file is open

2. Open a new table by selecting **Tables** from the Object bar and clicking **New** on the toolbar

3. Use what you have learned to build the table fields outlined in Figure 2.33

Table	Field Name	Data Type	Field Size	Other Attributes
OrderDetail	OrderID	Number	LongInteger	
	ProductID	Number	LongInteger	
	QuantityOrdered	Number	Integer	Required, Default value 1

FIGURE 2.33
OrderDetail fields and attributes

4. Click and drag over the record indicators for OrderID and ProductID to select them both. Use the key icon in the Access toolbar to set them as the composite primary key

tip: *If you are successful, both fields should have a key icon in their record selector*

5. Verify your fields and field attributes

6. Close the Design window and save the table as **OrderDetail**

7. Open the **OrderDetail** table in Datasheet View. The table is now ready to hold data

8. Close OrderDetail

9. Close the ac02KoryoKicks.mdb database

Using Undo and Redo when Defining Tables

The Microsoft Access Undo feature has more options in Design View than it does in Datasheet View. The difference stems from the way the two views save data. Design View saves data on exit. The Datasheet View updates the database as soon as the cursor moves to a new record.

In Design View Access keeps a list of the 20 most recent actions that can be undone. The Undo button on the Access toolbar has a drop-down list that displays those actions. Clicking an action to undo will also undo all actions above the selection on the list. One action at a time can be undone by repeatedly typing Ctrl+Z.

The Redo button stores the 20 most recent undone actions. Like the Undo button, when redoing an action, the Redo button reinstates all actions above it on the list. Both the Undo and Redo lists are cleared when the view is changed.

*another***word** ... on Saving Table Designs
You will be prompted to save your changes when you access another view, but you can save them at any point by clicking the Save button on the Access toolbar

Working with New Tables

New tables have now been created using both the New Table Wizard and Table Design View. Table Design View provides the developer with much more control than using a Wizard. Many developers use the Wizard to create the first draft of a table and then use Design View to customize the table generated by the Wizard. Regardless of how you choose to build tables, the ability to move comfortably between table views and add data are critical.

Navigate between Views

When working with Access objects, it is tedious to close an object to use a different view. Fortunately Access provides an easy way to move between views using the View

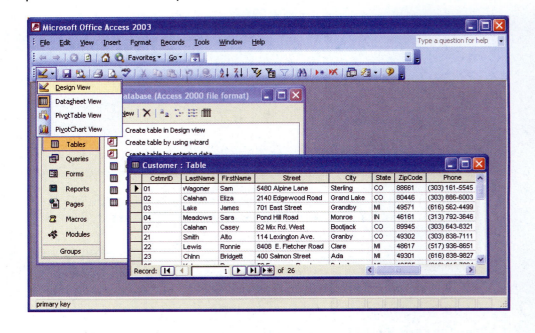

button on the Access toolbar. The View button is a drop-down list box that displays valid options for the current or open object (see Figure 2.34).

Remember that the undo and redo buffers are cleared when you change views, but the Clipboard is not cleared. Changes made in one view can impact data in another view. Be especially careful when changing the design of an object. The impacts of table design changes are discussed in a later chapter.

Populate New Tables

Session 2.1 covered adding, deleting, and updating records in a table. As has been noted, table Datasheet View is a simple way to enter and maintain data. Forms and queries also can be used to add and maintain table data. The Clipboard can copy data that exist elsewhere and paste them into the table. Finally, data can be imported from existing documents maintained by other Office products like Excel.

Regardless of how tables are being populated, there are dangers in entering data before the entire database has been built and table relationships set. The defined relationships between tables enforce integrity of the data that are entered. With the independent tables that are in the KoryoKicks database now, an order could be entered for a customer who is not in the Customer table. Similarly an order could be entered for a product that is not in the Product table. Because building table relationships is outside the scope of this presentation, a copy of KoryoKicks.mdb has been created with the table relationships set. The relationships will keep you from entering orders for nonexistent customers and products.

The ac02KoryoKicks2.mdb prototype will be used in the remaining steps. Table relationships have been set and the Customer and Product tables have already been populated. You will be entering orders.

Populating the Order table:

1. Open the **ac02KoryoKicks2.mdb** database

2. Explore the table designs using Design View—they are the same as what you built earlier in this session

3. Explore the data in the Customer and Product tables

4. Select **Relationships** from the **Tools** menu to view the table relationships that have been set up (see Figure 2.35)

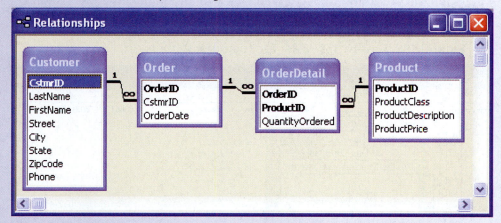

F I G U R E   2.35
KoryoKicks table relationships

5. Open the **Order** table in Datasheet View and add a record for customer **5** on **12/15/03**. You will receive the error shown in Figure 2.36 because customer 5 is not in the Customer table

F I G U R E   2.36
Table relationships being enforced

tip: *The ESC key is used to abandon the update*

6. Enter the records shown in Figure 2.37 for customers 01 and 02 who have already been added to the Customer table

7. Close the Order table

8. Open the **OrderDetail** table. The one-to-many relationship between Order and OrderDetail means that Order must be entered before OrderDetail (line items) can be added for that order. If you try to add a nonexistent OrderDetail, you will receive the error shown in Figure 2.36

9. Enter the records shown in Figure 2.38. These data represent the product and quantity (invoice detail lines) for orders 03 and 05

F I G U R E   2.38
Records for the OrderDetail table

F I G U R E   2.37
Records for the Order table

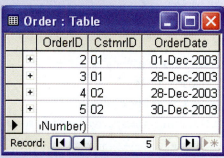

	OrderID	CstmrID	OrderDate
+	2	01	01-Dec-2003
+	3	01	28-Dec-2003
+	4	02	28-Dec-2003
+	5	02	30-Dec-2003
▶	(Number)		

Record: 5

	OrderID	ProductID	QuantityOrdered
▶	2	4	1
	2	8	1
	2	38	4
	3	1	1
	3	10	1
	4	11	10
	4	29	2
	4	37	3
	5	15	8
	5	19	2
	5	20	35
	5	21	4
*	0	0	1

Record: 1   of

10. Close the OrderDetail table

11. Open the **Customer** table. You can view all of the linked table data in a subdatasheet by clicking the plus sign in front of the customer record. The Order and OrderDetail records for Customer 01 are shown in Figure 2.39. Review the order for customer 2

FIGURE 2.39

Order and OrderDetail rows for Customer 01 shown in subdatsheets

12. Close the ac02KoryoKicks2.mdb file

These steps demonstrated how properly designed relational databases force data to be entered in an order that is consistent with the defined relationships. The data on the one side of the relationship must always be present before data on the many side of the relationship can be added. Conversely a parent record (one side of the relationship) cannot be deleted when there are child records. You entered two orders for customer 01. The Customer record for customer 01 could not be deleted unless the Order and associated OrderDetail were deleted first.

When relationships are built between tables, Access uses **subdatasheets** to display data from related tables. When viewing data from the parent or primary table in Datasheet View, a plus sign indicates that a subdatasheet can be displayed. To view the related data, click the plus sign. To remove the subdatasheet, click the minus sign.

Access Limitations

The general specifications for Microsoft Access are very broad and reflect optimal implementations. The model of computer, available memory, and use of the database can reduce the maximums significantly. An Access database can

- Be up to 2 gigabytes
- Store up to 32,7678 objects such as tables, queries, forms, and reports
- Have 64 characters in an object name
- Have 14-character passwords
- Support up to 255 concurrent users

Microsoft Access tables can

- Have up to 64 characters in each field name
- Have up to 255 fields
- Be one of 2048 concurrent open tables
- Be up to 2 gigabytes minus the space needed to store system objects
- Have 32 indexes

making *the grade*

1. When fields are listed in parentheses after the table name, how is the primary key identified?

2. T F   The Format attribute controls how data values are stored in the table.

3. What is the maximum number of characters a text field can store?

4. To enter the most common value of a field automatically you would set the _____ attribute.

5. T F   The Undo button on the Access toolbar can be used to undo 20 items when entering data in Datasheet View.

6. T F   Currency format is dependent on the regional settings of the computer.

SESSION 2.3 SUMMARY

To keep data accurate, it must be maintained. In Datasheet View the rows and columns of a table can be reorganized to make maintenance easier without impacting the underlying table structure or data. When sorting by multiple columns, the sort columns must be adjacent and in order of their importance (primary sort field first). Columns such as the primary key can be frozen so that they remain on the screen to identify records when scrolling to the right in a datasheet to ensure updates are being made to the correct record. Columns can be hidden when they are not relevant to the current operation.

Adding, deleting, and editing existing records can easily be accomplished in Datasheet View. A NewRecord indicator (*) displays in an empty row at the bottom of a table's datasheet. Click in the NewRecord row to enter new data using the Tab key to move between table columns. Updates made to table data are saved automatically when the cursor is moved to another record—the Save File button is not needed. The Microsoft Office Clipboard operates between Office products with storage for 24 items.

Find and Replace allows both a search criterion and a replace value to be specified. By clicking the Find Next button, each occurrence of the search value can be found and replaced with the new value. Wildcards such as * and ? can be used to search for specific patterns of data such as Ton? or Ton*.

The Undo feature operates differently in the various Access views. In the Design View where the table file is not updated until you leave the view, both Undo and Redo are available for 20 actions. In table Datasheet View, Undo is available for the last action and the last record update can be reversed from the Edit menu.

Database design is critical to the development of a stable database with valid data. The 90/10 rule states that 90 percent of the time should be spent designing the database structure so that only 10 percent of the time is spent maintaining it. The design process includes outlining the mission, determining the outputs, listing fields, assigning fields to tables, defining table relationships, and building a prototype. Once the database design is complete, the tables are built by defining their fields, field attributes, and relationships.

Visit www.mhhe.com/i-series/ to explore related topics.

MICROSOFT OFFICE SPECIALIST OBJECTIVES SUMMARY

- Enter, edit, and delete records—MOS AC03S-2-1
- Format datasheets—MOS AC03S-3-4
- Sort table data—MOS AC03S-3-5

making the grade answers

SESSION 2.1

1. Indicates the new record row.

2. Wildcards are used to set match values for searching text. * replaces any number of characters. ? replaces a single character. [] can be used to include alternative values such as [jf].

3. The Access table file is updated with changes made in a record when the pointer is moved to a new record.

4. The column order is important when sorting because the first field is primary and the second field is secondary—only used to break ties in the first value.

5. False.

6. False.

SESSION 2.2

1. Underline the primary key.

2. False.

3. 255.

4. default.

5. False.

6. True.

task reference summary

Task	Page #	Preferred Method
Finding specific data values	AC 2.6	• Click in the column that you would like to search • Click the **Find** button • Enter the Find What criteria using the data value that you would like to find. Remember that a question mark (?) can be used as a wildcard for one character and an asterisk (*) is a wildcard for multiple characters • Click the **Find Next** button. If multiple rows match the Find What criteria, you may need to repeat this step until the row you are searching for is found
Office Clipboard: collect items to paste	AC 2.14	• Display the Office Clipboard by selecting **Office Clipboard** from the **Edit** menu • Select the item to be copied • Click the **Copy** or **Cut** button in the Standard toolbar • Continue placing items on the Clipboard (up to 24) until you have collected everything that you need

Office Clipboard: paste collected items	AC 2.14	• Display the Office Clipboard if it is not already present. If the Office Clipboard option of the Edit menu is not available, you are in an application or view that does not support the Office Clipboard
		• Click or select the area where you want to place items
		• Do one of the following:
		  • Select the **Paste All** button to paste the entire contents of the Office Clipboard
		  or
		  • Select a Clipboard item and choose **Paste** from its drop-down menu

task reference *summary*

Task	Page #	Preferred Method
Office Clipboard: remove items	AC 2.14	When the Clipboard is open • To clear one item, click the arrow next to the item you want to delete and then click **Delete** • To clear all Clipboard contents, click the **Clear All** button • Placing more than 24 items on the Clipboard will replace existing items beginning with the oldest item
Hiding datasheet columns	AC 2.16	• Open a table, query, or form in Datasheet View • Click the field selector of the column to be hidden • Click **Hide Columns** on the **Format** menu
To unhide a column	AC 2.16	• On the **Format** menu, click **Unhide Columns** • Select the names of the columns that you want to show from the Unhide Columns dialog box
Freezing and unfreezing datasheet columns	AC 2.17	• Open a table, query, or form in Datasheet View • Select the column(s) that you want to freeze or unfreeze • To freeze column(s), select **Freeze Columns** on the **Format** menu • To unfreeze column(s) select **Unfreeze All Columns** on the **Format** menu
Defining a Table field	AC 2.26	• Click **Tables** in the Options bar • Click the **Design View** button on the toolbar • Enter a field name • Select a data type • Define other field attributes as needed

TRUE/FALSE

1. A subtable displaying related data can be accessed by clicking the plus sign (+) in front of a record displayed in Datasheet View.

2. The format property of a field controls how values stored in the field will display to the user.

3. The table on the many side of a relationship is referred to as the parent or primary table.

4. Hiding a table field causes it to stay on the screen while the remaining columns scroll.

5. The Default Value property of a field causes a value to be automatically displayed for that field.

6. The mission of a database defines exactly what it will and will not accomplish.

7. Undo buffer is cleared by deleting the contents of the Clipboard.

FILL-IN

1. The _____ View of a table has more levels of undo than the _____ View.

2. Access has a maximum capacity of _____ open tables.

3. The _____ dialog box is used to enter criteria for searching a table.

4. The first sort field is the _____ sort.

5. A table column that does not scroll off the screen is said to be _____.

6. A _____ is a rapidly developed test copy of the database used to test design.

7. The _____ holds up to 24 Office items that can be pasted into any Office document.

MULTIPLE CHOICE

1. The maximum size for an Access database is
   a. 1 user.
   b. 2 gigabytes.
   c. 2,000,000 fields.
   d. all of the above.

2. A subdatasheet
   a. opens on top of a datasheet.
   b. displays data from another table.
   c. is activated by clicking a plus sign (+).
   d. does all of the above.

3. The _____ attribute of a field should be set to yes when the field cannot be left blank.
   a. Required
   b. No Blank
   c. Compulsory
   d. Mandatory

4. The data type of a field controls
   a. appropriate field names.
   b. the table a field belongs to.
   c. what type of data it can store.
   d. how the field's data values display.

5. In table design the underlined field of a table is the
   a. primary key.
   b. index.
   c. foreign key.
   d. table name.

review of concepts

REVIEW QUESTIONS

Each of the following topics should be addressed in one to three paragraphs.

1. Explain the meaning of the following:
   Product (*ProductID*, ProductDescription, ProductPrice).

2. Explain how at least two of the rules used to assign fields to tables are used.

3. What is the process of modeling tables with a many-to-many relationship?

4. Assume that you are designing a Products table for a candy manufacturer. The fields that you are considering are CandyType, CandyFilling, CandyCost, CandyPicture, QuantityOrdered, TotalYTDProduction. How would you determine what fields to include in the table? Is there a natural primary key for this table?

5. If you were to build a database to store information on your CD collection, what fields would you consider? How many tables? What would be the key field(s)? Why?

6. Explain how Undo works in Datasheet View while maintaining data.

7. Describe how to use wildcards in a Find and Replace operation.

CREATE THE QUESTION

For each of the following answers, create the question.

ANSWER	QUESTION
1. Things that you can do to improve the order of columns in Datasheet View	_____
2. Secondary sort field	_____
3. The entry in the Find What text box	_____
4. ?	_____
5. When the cursor is placed in another record	_____

FACT OR FICTION

For each of the following determine whether the statement is fact, fiction, or both and present your arguments for that conclusion.

1. An edit on a record can be undone after moving to another record and storing the edit from the second record.

2. Setting the Caption property of a field changes the label that displays with the field data without any further impact.

3. There are no problems with entering data into tables before all of the table relationships have been defined.

4. Records entered into a table are physically stored in the order that they were entered so there is no "insert" operation that places a record in a specific table location.

5. When building new tables with the New Table Wizard, you have complete control over all of the field properties.

1. Creating BBs Shoes Database

BBs Shoes is a family-owned shoe store specializing in athletic shoes. Roberto and Benita Lopez started the store to provide name-brand shoes at a discount price. They are dedicated to being a neighborhood resource, by providing needed shoes and jobs to the neighborhood. Benita has decided that a database would help track inventory. She has asked you to build it for them.

1. Start Access and open a new blank database. If a database is already open, use the **Toolbars** option of the **View** menu to open the **Task Pane**

2. Name the database **ac02BBsShoes.mdb**

3. Create the table shown in Figure 2.40 using Design View

4. Save the table as **Shoes**

5. Add the data in Figure 2.41

6. Although there are not enough data to make a Find truly operational, practice using Find with wildcards. Use Find to locate all inventory stored in aisle A. What Find What value did you use? How many did you find?

7. Enter three more records with data about your favorite shoes. Give each a unique stock number and a storage location of B1

8. Update the data as follows:
   - Change *Nike Tiemp 2000 D* to **Nike Tiempo 2000 D**
   - Change *Rio Zoom* to **Rio Zoom Hrdgrnd**
   - Use **Undo** to reverse the previous change. If you have already saved the update by moving to another record, use **Undo Saved Record** from the **Edit** menu

9. Delete the record for AR17208

10. Hide the StockNbr column, sort by descending price, and print the result. Close the table and save your changes

11. What forms and reports using these data can you think of to help Benita?

12. Are there other tables that could benefit this business? What would they track?

FIGURE 2.40

Shoes table design

Field Name	Data Type	Field Size	Notes
StockNbr	Text	7	Primary key
ShoeDescription	Text	30	
ShoePrice	Currency		
QtyOnHand	Number	Integer	
Location	Text	3	Aisle and shelf location

FIGURE 2.41

Shoes table data

StockNbr	ShoeDescription	ShoePrice	QtyOnHand	Location
AG87473	Adidas Gazelle	$59.95	78	B3
AR17208	Air Roma II	$69.95	15	B1
NT17165	Nike Tiemp 2000 D	$89.95	28	A2
NT17166	Nike Tiempo 2000 M	$84.95	45	C3
PC19435	Puma Cellerator	$149.95	20	A1
PS19439	Puma Sting	$74.95	36	C1
RK19387	Rio Zoom	$119.00	22	C2
*		$0.00	0	

Record: 1 of 7

2. Creating the Snow Rentals Database

Jagitt Jain is the proprietor of Snow Rentals, an Alberta, Canada, company that rents recreational equipment. As the name implies, Snow Rentals specializes in snow-related equipment with the bulk of its rentals involving downhill snow skis, cross-country snow skis, and snowboards. Jagitt has several store locations located near resort areas. Each location has a local supply of rental equipment and the ability to "borrow" from a central warehouse when demand for an item exceeds the local supply.

Jagitt is still using a paper-based checkout system to keep track of which store has "borrowed" from the central warehouse. Each warehouse item has a card (similar to an old library card) kept with the item when it is in the warehouse. To check an item out, the card is removed and the name of the borrower, date checked out, and return date are written on the card before it is filed with other checkout cards.

As the organization grows, this system is proving cumbersome and inadequate. Jagitt has to thumb through thousands of cards to determine what items have not been returned on time or to find out where to look for a lost item.

1. Start Access and open a new blank database. Name the database **ac02SnowRentals.mdb**

2. Create the **Store** and **Inventory** tables shown in Figure 2.42 using Design View

3. Enter the table data shown in Figure 2.43. Remember that StoreID and InventoryID are automatically generated

FIGURE 2.42

Store and Inventory table designs

Store Table

Field Name	Data Type	Field Size	Notes
StoreID	AutoNumber		Key
StoreName	Text	25	
StoreManager	Text	25	
Phone	Text	13	

Inventory Table

Field Name	Data Type	Field Size	Notes
InventoryID	AutoNumber		Key
InventoryClass	Text	25	
InventoryDescription	Text	25	
QtyInStock	Number	Integer	

4. Verify your data entry and make any needed changes

5. If your work is complete, exit Access; otherwise, continue to the next assignment

FIGURE 2.43

Store and Inventory table data

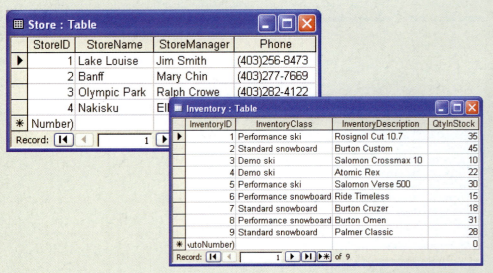

challenge!

1. HealthCare2Go Employee Tracking

HealthCare2Go is a temporary services agency providing short-term employees to the medical community. Temporary employees are scattered across the United States and travel to their temporary positions. Riki Lee is charged with tracking the availability of employees and needs help building an effective database.

1. Start Access and open a new blank database. If a database is already open, use the **Toolbars** option of the **View** menu to open the **Task Pane**

2. Name the database **ac02MedTemps.mdb**

3. Create the table shown in Figure 2.44 using Design View

4. Print the table design

5. Use the Office Clipboard to copy records from the **ac02TempEmployees.mdb** table into your Employee table

6. Use Find with wildcards to locate all RNs and LPNs. What Find What value did you use? How many did you find?

7. The JobClass field was too small and has truncated data. MedTe should be **MedTech**. Use Find and Replace to change the field values. Document how you accomplished this

8. Test field size by trying to change the JobClass for Cecilia Wong to **Operations Manager**. Document the result

9. Add the data in Figure 2.45. Make up the addresses and phone numbers using your city, state, zip code, and area code. Remember that EmployeeID is generated for you

10. Sort the table data by last and first names. Order and resize the columns appropriately. Print the result

FIGURE 2.44

Employee table design

Field Name	Data Type	Field Size	Notes
EmployeeID	AutoNumber		Key
LastName	Text	25	
FirstName	Text	25	
Address	Text	30	
City	Text	30	
State	Text	2	
Zip	Text	5	
Phone	Text	10	
JobClass	Text	10	

FIGURE 2.45

Employee table data

LastName	FirstName	Phone	JobClass
Andersen	Tom	314-404-0000	RN
Andersen	Sam	874-588-5234	LPN
Bartlen	Connie	874-588-5234	LPN
Anderson	Nancy	887-582-5835	MedTech
Callaway	Lois	879-502-3303	LPN
Carter	Mary Jane	306-588-9302	RN
Decett	Lana	113-563-8751	MedTech
Drennen	Leo	932-587-2193	RN
French	Jennifer	773-500-8370	MedTech
Hampton	Dan	425-557-5368	RN
Harris	Jerry	291-546-8297	LPN
Ricker	Ricky	128-532-7321	RN
Werner	Paul	761-598-9891	LPN
Waxman	Sue	412-593-3232	LPN

Record: 1 of 14 (Filtered)

2. Tracking Video Rentals

Video Extravaganza is a rural Ohio video store run by Vaughn and Linda Aimes. Inventory, customer lists, and checkouts are currently being maintained on Excel spreadsheets. Vaughn and Linda believe that an Access database will simplify their record keeping and reduce expenses caused by lost and misplaced inventory items. They have asked you to begin developing their database.

1. How would you go about designing a database for this organization?

2. Open Access, create a new blank database, and name it **ac02VideoExtravaganza.mdb**

3. Create the Movie table outlined in Figure 2.46

4. Print the design of the table

5. Open **ac02NewVideoReleases.mdb.** Use Copy and Paste to place all 94 records from the NewReleases table in the Movie table

6. Enter the data shown in Figure 2.47

7. Use Find with wildcards to locate Dramas in the Movie table. What Find value did you use? How many did you find?

8. Use Find and Replace to change Action Category values to **Action/Adventure** in the Movie table

9. Make Category the leftmost column and then sort the Movie table by Category. Save this layout update

10. Hide the ID field in the Movie table. Save this layout update

FIGURE 2.46

Video Extravaganza Movie table design

Field Name	Data Type	Field Size	Notes
ID	AutoNumber	Long Integer	Key
StreetDate	Date/TIme		
Title	Text	40	
YearReleased	Text	4	
Rating	Text	5	
Actor	Text	30	
RentalAvailability	Text	25	
Category	Text	25	

FIGURE 2.47

Video Extravaganza data

Title	YearReleased	Rating	Actor	RentalAvailability	Category
Basic Instinct	1992	R	Sharon Stone	VHS/DVD	Suspense
X2: X-Men United	2003	PG-13	Hugh Jackman (more)	VHS/DVD	Action/Fantasy
Bad Boys II	2003	R	Will Smith (more)	VHS/DVD	Action/Comedy
Chasing Papi	2003	PG	Roselyn Sanchez (more)	VHS/DVD	Comedy

1. SportBabies.com Product List

SportBabies.com is an online storefront selling replica sports uniforms for babies and toddlers. It carries products for all NFL, NHL, NBA, Major League Baseball, National League Baseball, and college teams. The uniforms are exact replicas of those currently worn on the field and come in standard baby and toddler sizes. Product manufacturers include Champion, Nike, Russell, and Wilson. Classic player gear is also available.

The current Web site is based on static HTML, which means that it must be manually maintained each time products and prices change. To automate this heavy maintenance project, a database is being created. The database will be maintained and generate updates to the Web site. You have been asked to build the ProductList database. You will be using NFL products for testing.

1. Start Access and open a new blank database. If a database is already open, use the **Toolbars** option of the **View** menu to open the **Task Pane**

2. Name the database **ac02SportBabies.mdb**

3. Create the table shown in Figure 2.48 in Design View

4. Add the data in Figure 2.49

5. Add records for three non-NFL players with a price of $30

6. Add yourself and a friend as NBA players with a price of $48

7. Make League, Team, and Player the first columns of the datasheet by hiding the ProductID column. Sort by League, Team, and Player and print the result

8. Print the table design

9. Use Find with wildcards to locate records for NFL and NBA players. Document the Find criteria

10. Sort the data by descending price. Make Price the first column and print

11. Document at least three business questions that could be answered using these data

FIGURE 2.48
ProductList table design

Field Name	Data Type	Field Size	Notes
ProductID	AutoNumber		Key
League	Text	3	
Team	Text	30	
Player	Text	25	
Price	Currency		

FIGURE 2.49
ProductList data

ProductList : Table

ProductID	League	Team	Player	Price
1	NFL	49ers	Rice	$29.99
2	NFL	Bears	Enis	$31.48
3	NFL	Bengals	Dillon	$24.52
4	NFL	Bengals	Warric	$28.92
5	NFL	Broncos	Davis	$32.45
6	NFL	Broncos	Greese	$35.32
7	NFL	Broncos	Price	$25.68
8	NFL	Cowboys	Sanders	$21.15
9	NFL	Cowboys	Galloway	$21.15
10	NFL	Cowboys	Smith	$20.44
11	NFL	Jets	Martin	$20.44
12	NFL	Jets	Johnson	$23.83
13	NHL	Avalanche	Foresburg	$34.88
14	NHL	Oilers	Gretzky	$185.99
15	NHL	Avalanche	Roy	$42.38
16	NBA	Bulls	Pfeifer	$25.00
17	NBA	Jazz	Audette	$25.00

Record: |◀ ◀ 20 ▶ ▶| ▶* of 22

2. Tracking Services for xXtreMeSportz

Casey Lewis, Evan Roach, and Wei Wong are extreme sports enthusiasts. They play hockey, skateboard, and snowboard. After talking to many of their friends the three decided to create a cooperative organization for extreme sports aficionados. The main goal of the co-op would be to act as a clearinghouse for equipment and events so that members would be able to purchase supplies, clothing, and event tickets at a bulk reduced rate.

After enlisting over 300 local members, the partners launched the www.xXtreMeSportz.com Web site to communicate their services and recruit additional members. Keeping the Web site updated has become too time-consuming so the partners have agreed to use an Access database to store their services. The Web site will be automatically updated from the database.

1. Open Access and create a new blank database named **ac02xXtreMeSportz.mdb**

2. Use Design View to create the Event table outlined in Figure 2.50

3. Print the table design

4. Add the data shown in Figure 2.51

5. Open **ac02Calendar.mdb**. Use Copy and Paste to place all 109 records from the Calendar table into the Event table of ac02xXtreMESportz.mdb

6. Verify your data entry and then use Find and Replace to change all occurrences of ASP WQS 6 in the Sponsor field to **ASP WQS 8**

7. Use Find and Replace with a **null** Find What value to set empty sponsor fields to **ASP WQS 8**

8. Make Sponsor the first column and add a descending sort by that field. Close and save

9. Close the database and exit Access if your work is complete

F I G U R E   2.50

Event table design

Field Name	Data Type	Field Size	Notes
EventID	AutoNumber		Key
Category	Text	30	
StartDate	Text	15	
EndDate	Text	15	
EventTitle	Text	50	
Venue	Text	50	
Sponsor	Text	20	
Contact	Hyperlink		

F I G U R E   2.51

Event table data

EventID	Category	StartDate	EndDate	Event Title	Venue	Sponsor	Contact
1	SURF	May-24	May-27	Local Motion Surf Into Summer	Honolulu,Oahu-Hawaii	ASP WQS 1	http://www.aspworldtour.com/
2	SURF	May-26	Jun-7	Quiksilver Pro	Tavarua/Namotu-Fiji	ASP WCT	http://www.aspworldtour.com/
3	SKATE	May-30	Jun-2	Mountain Dew National Championships	Cleveland, Ohio	Vans TC	http://www.vans.com/
4	BMX	May-31	Jun-3	CBF II Bikes, Boards and Blades	Wheatfield, NY		http://www.hsacentral.com/
5	IN-LINE	Jun-1	Jun-6	ASA Pro Tour	Cincinnati, OH	ASA	http://www.asaskate.com/
6	SURF	Jun-5	Jun-9	SMAS	Newport Beach,California-USA	SMAS	http://www.vanssmas.com/
7	BMX	Jun-6	Jun-9	Mervyn's Beach Bash	Hermosa Beach, CA		http://www.hsacentral.com/

on the web

1. Toy Purchase Statistics by Internet Research Inc.

Internet Research Inc. (IRI) is a statistical evaluation organization specializing in Internet commerce. The evaluations are based on many facets of commerce including product price, shipping costs, timely delivery, ease of Web site navigation, product quality, and return policies. The statistics generated by IRI are published on a Web site for consumers and used by Shopping Bots to rank and evaluate shopping requests entered by users.

You have been hired by IRI to maintain the statistical evaluations of toy sales sites. As a training exercise, you will gather data manually and use Access to evaluate the results. You will begin by researching toy prices and building an Access table to hold your findings. The goal is to familiarize you with the sites and tools you will be evaluating and provide an understanding of the underlying research methodologies.

1. Use a Shopping Bot such as www.mysimon.com or a search engine to find at least two sites that sell toys

   a. At your first site, determine the lowest priced Barbie (you can choose another popular toy with multiple models)

   b. Find the price for the same toy at the second site

   c. At the second site determine the highest priced Barbie

   d. Find the price for the same toy at the first site

   e. Perform the previous steps for a third toy of your choice

2. Start Access and open a new blank database. If a database is already open, use the **Toolbars** option of the **View** menu to open the **Task Pane**

3. Name the database **ac02IRI.mdb**

4. Create the table shown in Figure 2.52 in Design View

5. Print the table design

6. Input the data from your search, use a unique key value for each record, verify your data entry, and make any necessary edits

7. Further testing of the table uncovers a need for a ReviewDate field. Switch to table Design View and add it as the last table field with an appropriate data type and format

8. Test your update by adding review dates to all of the records

9. Sort the table data by ascending ToyName. Order the columns so that the sort field is first and adjust the column width to fit the data. Print the results

10. Sort the table data by ascending Web site. Order the columns appropriately. Print the results

FIGURE 2.52

Toys table design

Field Name	Data Type	Field Size	Notes
ToyID	Text	3	Key
WebSite	Hyperlink		
ToyName	Text	25	
ToyDescription	Text	50	
Price	Currency		

LEVEL **THREE**

CHAPTER TWO

around the world

1. Getz International Travel Corporate Customers Database

Getz International Travel is the largest travel agency in the world. The organization consists of over 5,000 full-time employees working in offices in San Francisco, Los Angeles, Phoenix, Chicago, Detroit, Indianapolis, Orlando, London, Budapest, Warsaw, Taiwan, and Paris. Getz arranges every facet of travel for both domestic and international treks.

Schedules are happily arranged for individuals, small groups, and large groups of up to 300. Arrangements include airfare, tours, hotels, car rentals, and more.

The over 5,000 corporate customers are the backbone of the organization. Currently, all customers are kept in the same table. You have been assigned the task of creating a separate table for corporate customers because they are being assigned to a new division of the organization.

1. Start Access and open a new blank database. If a database is already open, use the **Toolbars** option of the **View** menu to open the **Task Pane**

2. Name the database **ac02Getz.mdb**

3. Create tblCustomers shown in Figure 2.53 in Design View. Make the lengths of text fields fit the data

4. Print the table design

5. Add the data in Figure 2.54.

6. Create a format for the CustomerID field that will cause the five digits to display with a dash after the first two digits (03-129)

7. Due to a data entry error, you need to use Find and Replace to change all of the area codes from 303 to 313

8. Add five local businesses to the table. Use your friends' names for primary and secondary contacts

9. Sort the table data by CompanyName. Order and resize the columns appropriately. Print the results

10. Sort the table by City within State. Order the columns appropriately. Print the results

11. Create a Find that will locate Colorado records. Document the Find What criteria

FIGURE 2.53

Corporate customers table design

	Field Name	Data Type	Description
🔑▶	CustomerID	Number	Customer identification number
	CompanyName	Text	Company Name
	Contact	Text	Contact person within company
	2ndContact	Text	Secondary Contact person
	Address	Text	Street address or Post Office Box
	City	Text	City
	State	Text	State (two character abbreviation)
	ZipCode	Text	Five-digit ZIP code
	PhoneNumber	Text	Telephone number
	FaxNumber	Text	Facsimile phone number
	CreditLimit	Number	Credit Limit

FIGURE 2.54

Corporate customers table data

	CustomerID	Company	Contact	2ndContact	Address	City	State	ZipCode	PhoneNumber	Fax
▶	1768	Alpine Construction Group	James Darling		805 W. 44th Ave.	Wheat Ridge	WI	20321	(103) 674-1753	
	1873	Eye Wear Inc.	Kathleen Paduano		60605 US Hwy 285	Pine	CO	80637	(303) 674-2114	
	2048	1st Bank	Marie Baal		3560 Evergreen Pkwy.	Evergreen	CO	80453	(303) 674-7809	
	2718	Vision Land Consultants	Ramona Hyde		30960 Stagecoach Blv	Arvada	FL	30932	(803) 674-3025	
	2892	Arvada Villa	Jim Rogers	Betty Truett	5453 West 57th Avenu	Arvada	CO	80004	(303) 422-3123	
	3312	Block's Plumbing & Heating	Elliott Waterman	Sam Patterson	3121 West 80th Avenu	Thornton	CO	80131	(303) 428-5300	
	4312	Integrative Physical Therapy	Sandra Dawson	Lynn Bryant	2200 South Federal	Denver	CO	80231	(303) 441-9882	
	5132	Quest Academy	Jennifer Botts	Nancy Kind	3005 30th Street	Boulder	CO	80321	(303) 441-7887	
	7312	Sportline	George Jenson	Angela Alston	6510 Wadsworth Blvd.	Arvada	OH	50004	(503) 422-1312	
	20931	Sutton Attorneys	Bill Skewes		30752 Southview Dr.	Evergreen	CO	80439	(303) 674-7041	
*	0									

Record: ◀◀ ◀ 1 ▶ ▶▶ ▶* of 10

running project: tnt web page design

Create a New TnT Table

TnT is a custom Web page development company founded by Victoria (Tori) Salazar and Tonya O'Dowd. The background for this case was presented in Chapter 1. Go back and review it if necessary.

1. Use Windows to create a copy of ac01TnT.mdb and rename the copy **<yourname>TnT.mdb**. Replace ac02<yourname> with your last name and first name (e.g., WellsJim)

2. Start Access and open the <yourname>TnT.mdb database

3. Open **tblCustomers** in Datasheet View

4. Use Find and Replace to remove the parentheses () and the dash (-) from the cusPhone and cusFax fields

5. In Design View, add a format to each field that will display the deleted characters even though they are not stored in the field

6. Create a new table in Design View

   a. The first table field is custID with a Number data type and LongInteger field size because it will join to the custID field of tblCustomers carrying an AutoNumber data type

   b. The second table field is SiteNumber with a Number data type and Integer field size

   c. The third field is URL with a Hyperlink data type

   d. Set the combination of custID and SiteNumber as the primary key

   e. Close the Design View and save the table as **tblCustomerSites**

7. You will need to build a one-to-many relationship between these two tables, since each customer can have more than one site built by TnT

   a. Open the Relationships window by right-clicking in the database window and choosing **Relationships**

   b. Right-click in the Relationships window and choose **Show Table…**

   c. In the Show Table window click **Add** to add the tblCustomerSites (it is selected by default) table to the Relationships window

   d. In the Show Table window select **tblCustomer** and click **Add** to add it to the Relationships window

   e. Close the Show Table window

   f. In the Relationships window click the custID field in CustomerSites and drag to the cusID field in tblCustomers. The Edit Relationships window should open

   g. Click the check boxes as shown in Figure 2.55 and choose **Create**

   h. A one-to-many relationship should now display in the Relationships window

   i. Close the Relationships window, saving the relationship

8. Close CustomerSites

9. Open tblCustomers and review the data you entered in the subdatasheets

10. Print both tables and exit Access

FIGURE 2.55
Edit Relationships window settings

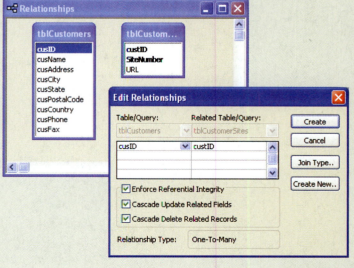

analysis

1. Evaluate Database Requirements

Yoko Yim is a small-business owner who would like to track personal data about her customers. Yoko provides various types of massage and personal training in clients' homes. The primary goal for the database is to be able to send follow-up thank-you messages to new customers and appropriate holiday greetings. Her customers are from many cultural and religious backgrounds. She would also like to know the last date a service was provided and what that service was. The business is run on a cash basis, so there is no need to create invoices.

Document your evaluation of Yoko's database needs. Describe how Yoko will be able to use the database to support her stated business needs. Create a new blank database named **ac02YimCustomers.mdb**. Use Design View to build the tables you designed.

2. Start a Database for Your Hobby

Assume that you are starting a database to store data about your hobby or pastime. Document the type of data that you would need to track. Use the design techniques outlined in the chapter to design tables for your database. Describe how you could use this database. Are there valid reasons to create a database? Not to create a database?

Create a new blank database named **ac02<your name>Hobby.mdb**. Use Design View to build the tables for your database. Populate at least one table with 10 or more records.

3

Introducing Queries, Filters, Forms, and Reports

did you know?

the *scientist Anders Celsius developed a measuring scale with freezing at 100 degrees and boiling at 0 degrees. Fellow scientists waited until Celsius died to reverse the scale.*

cooking *and salad oils with an additive developed by Penn State chemical engineers performed as well as commercial oils when used to lubricate machinery, such as cars and boats.*

the *first video game was Pong, introduced in 1972 by Noel Bushnell, who then created Atari.*

in *Rome, the world's first paved streets were laid out in 170 B.C. The new streets were popular as they were functional in all types of weather and were easier to keep clean, but they amplified the city's noise level.*

to *make a daguerreotype, an early photograph, required a 15-minute average exposure time.*

to *find out what percentage of computer data loss cases are due to human error, visit www.mhhe.com/i-series.*

Chapter Objectives

- **Filter data in Datasheet View—MOS AC03S-3-6**

- **Create and run Select Queries—MOS AC03S-1-7**

- **Create and modify calculated fields and aggregate functions in Query Design View—MOS AC03S-3-1**

- **Construct and customize simple forms—MOS AC03S-1-9**

- **Create, customize, and print simple reports—MOS AC03S-1-10**

- **Modify form layout—MOS AC03S-3-2**

KoryoKicks: Using Access to Evaluate Products and Markets

Missy and Micah need to make some tough business decisions. Their martial arts classes and products are selling very well. KoryoKicks is successful and, as is often the case with personal businesses that take off, the twins are unable to keep up with demand. They are considering:

- Limiting the number of classes offered to what they can personally teach
- Reducing the number of martial arts products they provide

- Moving the business into a storefront so they can hire additional help
- Finding a partner or partners to share the workload
- Selling the business

To evaluate the viability of these options, the twins need information about their business (see Figure 3.1). The only thing that they are sure of at this point is that current profits are not sufficient to support even a part-time employee. To decide how to proceed, they need to evaluate the additional

FIGURE 3.1

Potential KoryoKicks queries and reports

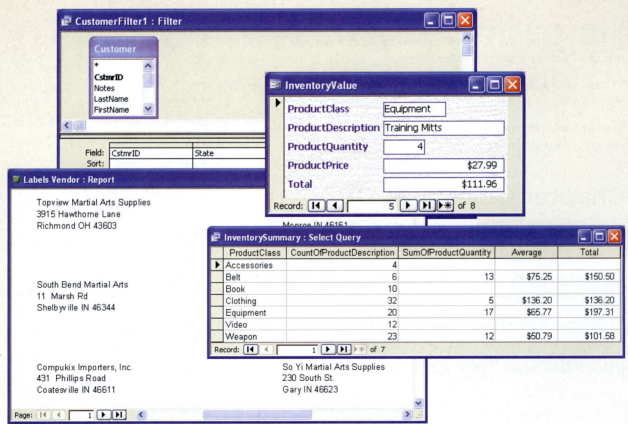

potential of their products and markets. Is the market sufficient to allow increased product and class sales? Can the existing suppliers support an increase in product sales? Have all customers paid their bills? Invoices are being sent out, but there is currently no way to track payments. It is possible that adding tracking and follow-up to the current system could significantly increase profits. Another way to increase profits is to cut costs. The twins would like to know if there are products that can be discontinued because they are unprofitable.

Although existing data are limited, the twins can see the potential of Access query and report fa-

cilities to answer their business questions. Queries and reports can be used to organize and analyze their business data to help make decisions. While no amount of information can guarantee the result of a business decision, timely and effective information can significantly improve the likelihood of a positive outcome. Missy and Micah have asked you to guide them through the process of creating effective queries and reports for their business. They plan to use this information to help determine how to best proceed.

SESSION 3.1 SELECTING AND ORGANIZING DATA

Access provides an array of options for selecting and organizing data into useful information. This session evaluates the effectiveness of various filters and introduces select queries.

Selecting Data with Filters

Filters are used to restrict (limit) the rows of data displayed in the current datasheet so that a subset of the data can be manipulated. An ideal time to use filters is to maintain or print only some of the rows in a table. Missy and Micah are curious about how filters can be used with KoryoKicks data. They do not understand the functionality of the various types of filters and have asked you to show them.

Introducing Filters

There are four ways to apply filters to the datasheet. The first, *Filter By Selection*, returns records matching the datasheet selection. The second, *Filter By Form*, presents an empty version of the current datasheet where match values can be typed. *Filter For Input* accepts a value or expression to restrict the records. The *Advanced Filter/Sort* window presents a design grid used to build filter criteria. Regardless of the type of filter being applied, the goal is to display only records that meet specific criteria. Creating the criteria is slightly different for each type of filter. You will experience each type of filter using the KoryoKicks prototype database to gain an understanding of their utility.

Creating Filter by Selection Criteria

Filter By Selection is not only the most intuitive filtering tool, but also the most limited. All or part of a data value in any field can be selected to control which records will display. The selection is evaluated as described in Figure 3.2.

FIGURE 3.2
Filter By Selection criteria

Selection	Action	City Field Example
Click in a field	The whole field value will be used to search that field for matches	Click in the value Berlin and only records for Berlin will be selected
Select an entire field	The whole field value will be used to search that field for matches	Select the value Berlin and only records for Berlin will be returned
Select the first character(s) of a field value	Records starting with the selected characters will be returned	Select the characters "Ber" and all records starting with Ber will be retrieved (i.e., Berlin, Berlington, Berton, etc.)
Select character(s) after the first character	Records that contain the selection anywhere will be returned	Select "er" from Berlin and all records containing er will be retrieved (i.e., Anderson, Berlin, Merlin, Waterberry, etc.)

---

task reference   **Filter By Selection**

- Open the table in Datasheet View
- Select the field and character(s) of the search criteria (see Figure 3.2)
- Click the **Filter By Selection** toolbar button to return values matching the selection

  or

- Right-click and choose **Filter Excluding Selection** to filter the selection out of the data
- Evaluate the results of the filter
- Click **Remove Filter** on the Access toolbar

Filtering the Customer table:

1. Open the **Customer** table of the **ac03KoryoKicks.mdb** database in Datasheet View
2. Click in the City cell containing the value **Coatesville**
3. Click the **Filter By Selection** toolbar button (see Figure 3.3)
4. Click the **Remove Filter** toolbar button
5. Select **on** in any City value
6. Click the **Filter By Selection** toolbar button
7. Click the **Remove Filter** toolbar button
8. Select **G** in any City value where it is the first character
9. Click the **Filter By Selection** toolbar button

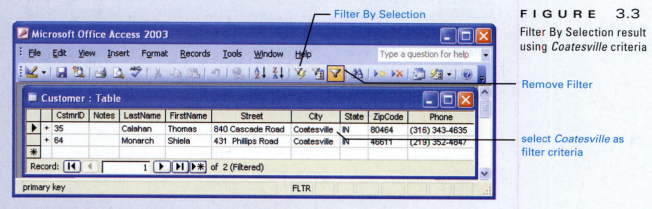

FIGURE 3.3

Filter By Selection result using *Coatesville* criteria

10. To demonstrate that filters are cumulative, select **IN** as the State value and click **Filter By Selection** again

    By combining two filters, you were able to retrieve Indiana cities that begin with the letter G

11. Click the **Remove Filter** toolbar button to remove all active filters

Filters also can be used to exclude the selection. Select a value and then right-click to bring up the pop-up menu. Select *Filter Excluding Selection* from the pop-up menu and all records containing that value will be excluded from the datasheet.

Excluding records from the Customer table:

1. Verify that the Customer table of the ac03KoryoKicks.mdb database is open in Datasheet View

2. Click in any **CO** State value

3. Right-click on the selection to bring up the pop-up menu

4. Select **Filter Excluding Selection**. The datasheet should not display Colorado records

5. Click the **Remove Filter** toolbar button to remove all active filters

Filters are cumulative, so a second filter can be applied to the result of the first filter. The results of a filter stay in effect until *Remove Filter* is selected or the datasheet is closed.

Creating Filter By Form Criteria

Clicking Filter By Form presents a blank datasheet containing two tabs where filter values can be selected from a drop-down list box or typed manually. Unlike Filter By Selection, Filter by Form accepts multiple criteria. Conditions entered in the Look for tab must all be true to retrieve a record. The Or tab allows alternate values to be entered for the same field.

Like many Access operations, Filter by Form has its own unique toolbar that is visible only in this view. Besides the Standard toolbar options such as Print, Cut, Copy, and Paste, there are also some unique toolbar options such as Open Filter and Save Filter. To leave the view, use the Close button on the Filter by Form toolbar.

ACCESS

task reference   **Filter By Form**

- Open a table in Datasheet View
- Click the **Filter By Form** toolbar button
- Build the filter criteria by selecting from the drop-down list for a field or typing your own value
- Click the **Apply Filter** toolbar button
- Review the filtered data to be sure they are what you expected
- Work with the filtered data
- Click **Remove Filter** on the Access toolbar when you are done

Filtering the Customer table with Filter by Form:

1. Verify that the Customer table of the ac03KoryoKicks.mdb database is open in Datasheet View

2. Click the **Filter By Form** button on the Access toolbar

3. Remove any existing criteria by selecting them and pressing **Delete**

4. You want to retrieve records for customer numbers greater than five from Indiana. To accomplish this, enter the criteria shown in Figure 3.4 and click **Apply Filter**

5. Review the records to be sure that the results are what you expected

FIGURE 3.4

Filter By Form using compound criteria

Filter By Form toolbar ──

CstmrNmbr criteria ──

use this tab to enter multiple criteria for one field ──

filter results ──

tip: *When sorting or filtering numbers stored in text fields, 0s are important. Leading 0s (005) are entered so that the numbers sort correctly. They also must be entered when filtering or the records returned will be inappropriate (5, 05, and 005 each returns a different result). You must match what is stored in the table*

6. Click the **Remove Filter** toolbar button to remove all active filters

When filtering, double quotes ("") are required around match values for fields containing text data. Access adds the double quotes for you if you forget. As you have just seen, Filter by Form uses relational operators (=, >, <, >=, <=, and <>). The equal condition is the default and does not need to be stated, as was demonstrated with the "IN" criterion for State. All other operators must precede the value in the criteria, as was demonstrated with the > "05" criterion for CstmrID. Criteria also can be entered using keywords including In, Like, and Between. More detail on building criteria will be presented in the next session.

Filtering the Customer table with an Or condition:

1. Verify that the Customer table of the ac03KoryoKicks.mdb database is open in Datasheet View

2. Click the **Filter By Form** button on the Access toolbar

3. Remove any existing criteria by selecting them and pressing **Delete**

4. You want to retrieve records for customers in Colorado, Indiana, or California. The Or tab will be used to enter each of the alternate state abbreviations. Enter **CO** in the State field of the Look for tab

5. Click the **Or** tab at the bottom of the window. Enter **IN** in the State field of the Or tab

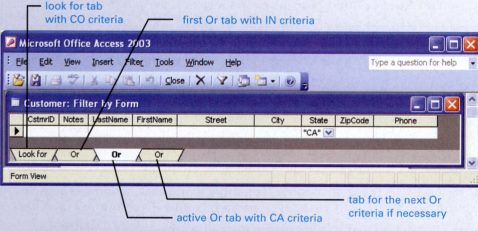

FIGURE 3.5
Filter By Form using *Or* criteria

6. Click the second **Or** tab and enter **CA** in its State field

7. Click the **Apply Filter** toolbar button

8. Review the records to be sure that they match the filter criteria (see Figure 3.5)

9. Click the **Remove Filter** toolbar button to remove all active filters

Filter by Form also can be used to see the filter criteria created by other types of filters. Did you notice that when you first opened the Filter by Form grid, it contained the criteria from the last Filter by Selection filter that you applied?

Creating Filter for Input Criteria

Filter for Input allows filter criteria to be entered from the pop-up menu. Simply right-click in the field to be filtered and type your criteria in the Filter For text box. Filter for criteria can include combinations of identifiers, operators, wildcards, and values.

---

task reference   **Filter for Input**

- Open a table in Datasheet View
- Right-click the field to be filtered
- Type the filter criteria in the Filter For text box using wildcards, operators, and values
- Press **Enter** to activate the filter
- Review the filtered data to be sure they are what you expected
- Work with the filtered data
- Click **Remove Filter** on the Access toolbar when you are done

---

Filtering the Customer table with Filter For:

1. Verify that the Customer table of the ac03KoryoKicks.mdb database is open in Datasheet View

2. Right-click in any data value of the FirstName field

3. You want to select all records for people with "am" anywhere in their first name. To accomplish this type ***am*** in the Filter For text box

4. Press **Enter** to activate the filter (see Figure 3.6)

5. Evaluate the filter results

6. Click **Remove Filter** on the Access toolbar

After a criterion is typed in the pop-up menu, the Tab key can be clicked instead of pressing Enter to keep the pop-up menu open and add criteria for the current field. Because filters are cumulative, opening the pop-up window for another field will accept criteria to further filter data.

Creating Advanced Filter/Sort Criteria

The Advanced Filter/Sort grid allows criteria to be entered on multiple fields and sorted in one step. The grid is very similar to the Query by Example grid that will be covered in the next topic.

FIGURE 3.6

Filter For criteria and results

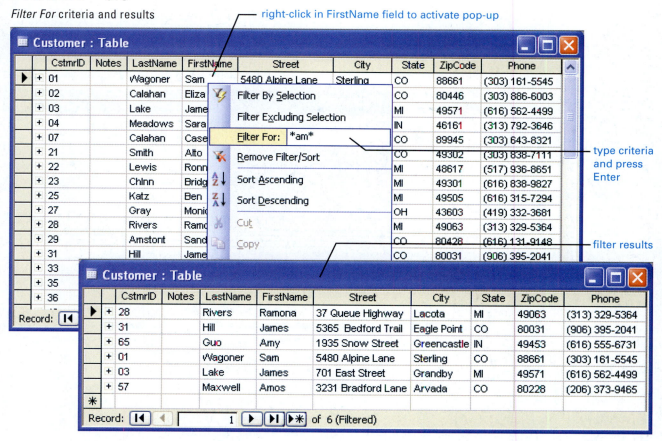

task reference · Advanced Filter/Sort

- Open a table in Datasheet View
- On the **Records** menu, point to **Filter**, and then click **Advanced Filter/Sort**
- Add criteria fields to the design grid
- Enter the filter and sort criteria
- Click the **Apply Filter** ![filter icon] button on the toolbar
- Review the filtered data to be sure they are what you expected
- Work with the filtered data
- Click **Remove Filter** ![filter icon] on the Access toolbar when you are done

Filtering the Customer table with Advanced Filter/Sort:

1. Verify that the Customer table of the ac03KoryoKicks.mdb database is open in Datasheet View

2. Click **Remove Filter** ![filter icon] to remove any active filters

3. On the **Records** menu, point to **Filter**, and then click **Advanced Filter/Sort**

4. To select records for CstmrID over 5 and from both Colorado and Indiana, enter the criteria shown in Figure 3.7

FIGURE 3.7

Advanced Filter/Sort grid with criteria

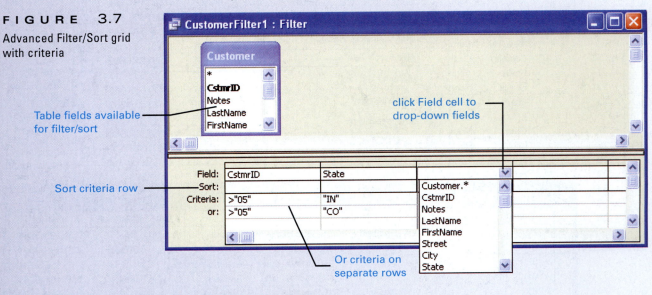

5. Click **Apply Filter**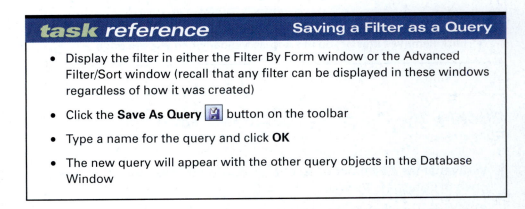

6. Evaluate the filter results

7. Click **Remove Filter** on the Access toolbar

As you can easily see, the Advanced Filter/Sort is the most powerful and the most complex filtering tool. The type of filter used depends on the complexity of the filter criteria and the user's comfort with the filtering options.

Saving a Filter as a Query

Filters are not one of the Access database objects and so they cannot be stored. To remedy this situation, a filter can be saved with a table, form, or query object. In each case, a query, which is more powerful than a filter, is saved. A saved filter can be reapplied without reentering the criteria.

---

task reference   Saving a Filter as a Query

*   Display the filter in either the Filter By Form window or the Advanced Filter/Sort window (recall that any filter can be displayed in these windows regardless of how it was created)

*   Click the **Save As Query** button on the toolbar

*   Type a name for the query and click **OK**

*   The new query will appear with the other query objects in the Database Window

Limitations of Filters

While filters are valuable tools when selecting and organizing data, there are some significant limitations in what they can accomplish. The most obvious limitation of filtering data is that all table fields must display in the filtered result. There is no way to select specific fields or even change the order in which fields are displayed. It is true that you can manually hide fields and change column order, but that becomes tedious.

> **another word**   . . . on Filters
>
> Besides filtering data in Datasheet View, filters can be used to restrict data displayed in a form or a sub-datasheet. One filter can be associated with each form so that it activates when the form is opened. This is useful when multiple users share a database and each only wants access to his or her specific data

Finally, only one table can be filtered at a time—there is no join capability. Only one filter can be associated with a table or form; however, any number of filters can be saved as queries. The functions that are missing in filters are the strength of queries.

Selecting Data with Queries

Queries are used to view and analyze data in different ways. They are much more powerful than filters because they can retrieve data from multiple tables and perform calculations on the results. Stored queries also can be used to select records that will be displayed in a form or report.

Introducing Queries

Queries are commonly used to support the business decision-making process. For example, Missy and Micah could use a query to profile their customers so they can understand how to better market their products. They also could find out if there are any products that have never been purchased so they can discontinue them. In addition, a query could list customers who have not been billed so that invoices can be sent to them.

To answer such questions, the necessary data must be stored in one or more tables in the database. For example, the current KoryoKicks database could not provide much demographic information on who customers are because no data are stored about the customer's gender, age group, income, or other factors that are generally used to set advertising strategy.

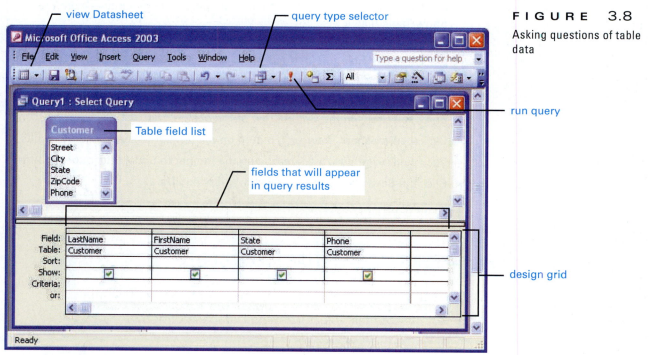

FIGURE 3.8

Asking questions of table data

The most common type of query is a Select Query. Select Queries retrieve data from one or more tables and display the results in Datasheet View. Once displayed, the records can be updated. Select Queries can

- Display selected rows of data
- Display selected columns of data
- Sort query results
- Calculate within records (e.g., calculate gross pay for each employee record)
- Group records and create subtotals (e.g., subtotal expenses for each department)
- Calculate totals such as sums, counts, and averages

You have already created a query using a Wizard. As with other Wizards, the Simple Query Wizard asks questions and produces a query based on your answers but does not provide a way to use the full scope of query capabilities. Informational queries are better developed in query Design View.

Specifying Simple Query Criteria

In query Design View a Query by Example (QBE) grid is used to enter question criteria. The *design grid* is used to provide examples of the information to be retrieved and Access will select all data matching the criteria. Since the most popular type of query is a Select Query, that is the QBE default.

One of the queries that the twins are interested in building is a phone list for customers. On the phone list, they want the customer's full name, state, and phone number. This is a select query that you will create in query Design View.

---

task reference   **Create a Select Query**

- Select the **Queries** object from the Database Window
- Click **New** from the toolbar
- Select the **Design View** [icon] button from the New Query dialog box and click **OK**
- Double-click the name of each table that contains relevant data from the Show Table dialog box
- Double-click each table field that is to be contained in the query result to place it in the Field row of the design grid. The order of the columns is the order of the output
- Enter sort criteria in the Sort row of the design grid
- Enter selections in the Criteria row of the design grid
- Click the **Datasheet View** [icon] button on the toolbar to see the query results
- Click the **Design View** [icon] button on the toolbar to update the query criteria
- Click the **Save** [icon] button to save the query criteria

---

Creating a Customer table query:

1. Close the Customer table of the ac03KoryoKicks.mdb database
2. Select the **Queries** object from the Database Window
3. Click **New** on the toolbar

4. Select **Design View** from the New Query dialog box and click **OK**

5. Double-click on the **Customer** table in the Show Table dialog box to add it to the design grid (see Figure 3.9)

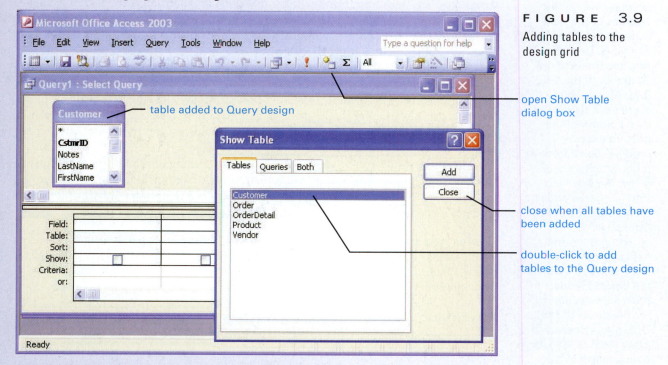

FIGURE 3.9

Adding tables to the design grid

open Show Table dialog box

close when all tables have been added

double-click to add tables to the Query design

6. Click **Close** in the Show Table dialog box

7. Double-click the **LastName, FirstName, State**, and **Phone** fields from the Customer table field list, adding each to the Field row of the design grid

tip: *If you place an undesired field in the design grid by mistake, delete it by clicking the cursor on the bar above the field to select the column. When the column is selected, press the **Delete** key to remove the column from the grid*

If fields are selected in the wrong order, move a column by clicking the cursor on the bar above the field to select the column. When the column is selected, click and drag it to the desired location

8. Click the **Datasheet View** button to see the query results (see Figure 3.10)

9. Click the **Design View** button to return to the query Design View

10. Click the **Save File** button

11. Name the query **PhoneList**

FIGURE 3.10

PhoneList query results

LastName	FirstName	State	Phone
Wagoner	Sam	CO	(303) 161-5545
Calahan	Eliza	CO	(303) 886-6003
Lake	James	MI	(616) 562-4499
Meadows	Sara	IN	(313) 792-3646
Calahan	Casey	CO	(303) 643-8321
Smith	Alto	CO	(303) 838-7111
Lewis	Ronnie	MI	(517) 936-8651
Chinn	Bridgett	MI	(616) 838-9827
Katz	Ben	MI	(616) 315-7294
Gray	Monica	OH	(419) 332-3681
Rivers	Ramona	MI	(313) 329-5364
Amstont	Sandy	CO	(616) 131-9148
Hill	James	CO	(906) 395-2041
Florentine	Haven	CA	(616) 131-3260
Calahan	Thomas	IN	(316) 343-4635

Record: 1 of 2

The query Design Window contains the tables that will be queried and the design grid that is used to enter query criteria. The Title bar of the Design Window contains the query name and the type of query, or *Query1: Select Query* by default. The Query Type button on the toolbar also reflects the query type as well as allowing the selection of a different query type.

Each table in the Design Window displays the field list for that table. The first option of each table field list is the asterisk (*) wildcard (see Figure 3.11). To be included in the query results, the fields must be moved from the field list to the design grid. Clicking and dragging a field, double-clicking a field, or clicking in the Field row of the design grid and selecting from the drop-down list are alternative ways to move fields into the design grid. Placing the wildcard (*) in the design grid causes all fields from that table to be included in the output. The order of field columns in the design grid determines their order in the query results.

Each column in the design grid contains a field and the selection criteria for that field. Query criteria include *Sort, Show, Criteria,* and *Or. Sort* allows ascending or descending sorts on each field. If sorts are set on multiple fields, the leftmost is primary. *Show* determines whether the field is visible in the query results. *Criteria* is a selection value similar to that entered in a filter. The *Or* row allows the entry of alternative criteria for a field.

The query results can be viewed at any time by clicking the Datasheet View button. Clicking the Design View button will return to the design grid. It is important to remember that the datasheet displayed from a query is a temporary subset of the data. Updates made to data in the query datasheet are applied to the table data.

help yourself *Use the Type a Question combo box to improve your understanding of queries by typing* **select query***. Review the contents of* About queries *including* About types of queries, About select and crosstab queries, *and* Create a select or crosstab query. *Close the Help window when you are finished*

Modifying Datasheet Appearance

As with the table datasheet, query results displayed in query Datasheet View can be formatted for better viewing. Columns can be hidden or reordered or have their width adjusted. Formats can be saved with the query or abandoned on exit.

The appearance of a datasheet can be modified for readability, or to visually distinguish it from other datasheets, using the Datasheet Formatting toolbar (see Figure 3.12). Turn on the toolbar by selecting *Formatting (Datasheet)* from the Toolbars option of the View menu. Formatting toolbar options apply to the entire datasheet—not just the selection.

F I G U R E   3.11

Designing a query

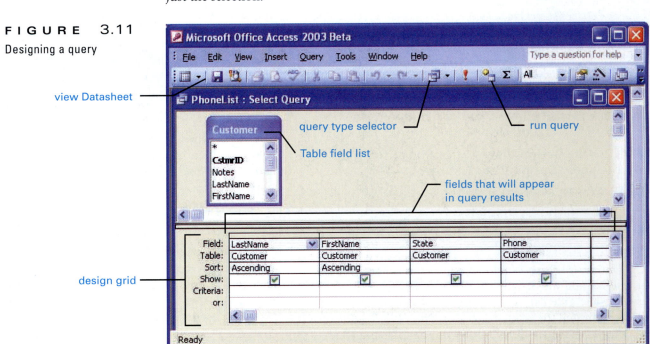

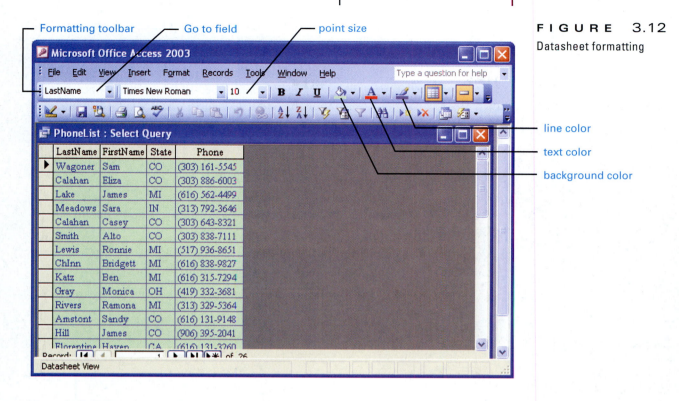

FIGURE 3.12
Datasheet formatting

Figure 3.12 demonstrates Access's datasheet formatting capabilities. The point size (8 is the default), background color, text color, and line color have all been modified. The options were not selected for visual appeal but for ease of identification.

Formatting the Customer table query:

1. Verify that the PhoneList query of the ac03KoryoKicks.mdb database is open in Datasheet View

2. Activate the Formatting toolbar by selecting **Formatting (Datasheet)** from the **Toolbars** option of the **View** menu

3. Select **Phone** from the Go to Field box to place the cursor in the Phone field (see Figure 3.12)

4. Change the font to **Times New Roman** and the point size to **10**

5. Choose background, text, and line colors that you think look appealing

6. Click the **Print** button to print the results

7. Close the Datasheet Window without saving the formatting

Sorting Query Data

Sorting data is critical to making it simple to use. The current PhoneList query is in order by CstmrID, because it is the primary key of the source table. Most users would expect a phone list to be in order by LastName and FirstName so a phone number could be easily retrieved.

There are two ways to sort query results. The first is to use the Sort Ascending and Sort Descending buttons on the toolbar. This technique works exactly as presented in the discussion about sorting table datasheets. It is simple but has the drawback of not being stored as part of the query criteria. Each time the query is opened, the sort process must be applied.

Fortunately, the QBE grid has a sort row that allows the sort order for the query results to be part of the query. This sort will be stored as part of the query and therefore automatically will be applied each time the query is opened. The PhoneList should open sorted by LastName and FirstName, so you will add those criteria to the QBE grid.

Sorting the Customer table query:

1. Open the PhoneList query of the ac03KoryoKicks.mdb database in Design View

2. Verify that the field order is LastName and then FirstName so that LastName is the primary sort and FirstName is the secondary sort

3. Add Ascending to the Sort criteria of each field as shown in Figure 3.13

FIGURE 3.13

The PhoneList query with sort criteria

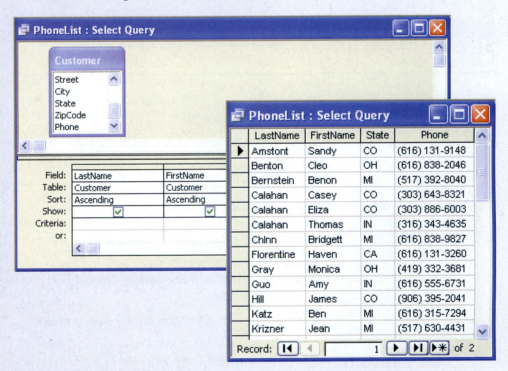

4. Click the **Datasheet View** 📊 button to see the query result

5. Click the **Design View** ✎ button to return to the query Design View

6. Click the **Save File** 💾 button to save the sort criteria with the query

7. Close the Query window

---

*another***way**

. . . to Run a Query

The instructions for viewing query results have used the Design View button, which automatically runs the query. The Run query button on the toolbar will accomplish the same task

SESSION 3.1

making **the grade**

1. What happens when part of a field is selected and then Filter By Selection is applied?

2. T F   Filters restrict the columns that display for the filtered table.

3. How can you exclude a value from the results of a filter?

4. T F   Filters remain in effect until another filter is executed.

5. What is the purpose of Or in filters?

6. What is the benefit of saving a filter as a query?

SESSION 3.2 SELECTING AND CALCULATING WITH QUERIES

Queries are a powerful analytical tool that will allow complete control over which fields and records from a table or tables display. In this session power will be added to select queries by entering record selection criteria and performing simple calculations.

Selecting Records in Queries

Query record selection criteria are entered in the Criteria rows of the QBE grid using conditions. Conditions define how records will be selected and are placed in the field to which they will be applied. A typical condition uses a relational operator and a value, such as > 30000 in the Salary field, to tell Access which records to include in the query result. All records for which the condition is true will be incorporated into the query result.

Relational operators were briefly presented in the discussion on filters. Figure 3.14 gives a more complete presentation on the meaning of the various comparison operators.

FIGURE 3.14

Relational operators

Operator	Function	Example
=	Returns records that match the value exactly. It is optional because it is the Access default	"CA" #11/23/02#
>	Returns records with values greater than the condition value	> 30000 > "Collins"
>=	Returns records with values greater than or equal to the condition value	>= 30000 >= "Collins"
<	Returns records with values less than the condition value	< 45 < "Simes"
<=	Returns records with values less than or equal to the condition value	<= 89 <= "Sam"
<>	Returns records that are not equal to the condition value	<> 4 <> "Smith"
Between	Returns records with values between the two stated values. Both values are included in the result	Between 12 And 28 Between "e" And "k"
In	Returns records with values that match those in the condition list	In ("Jan", "Mar", "Sep") In (1998, 2001)
Like	Returns records with values that match the pattern stated with wildcards	Like "Pren*"

The KoryoKicks database for this chapter contains a Product table that holds data about the various martial arts products that Micah and Missy sell. Additional data are stored about the vendors that supply these products. These data are ideal for practicing selection queries and implementing calculations. Such queries can be used to evaluate the effectiveness of current offerings.

Selecting Product table records:

1. Open the ac03KoryoKicks.mdb database
2. Open the **Product** table and familiarize yourself with the data
3. Select the **Queries** object from the Database Window
4. Click **New** on the toolbar
5. Select **Design View** on the New Query dialog box and click **OK**
6. Double-click on the Product table in the Show Table dialog box to add it to the design grid
7. Click **Close** in the Show Table dialog box
8. You'll start by creating a current inventory list. Place ProductClass, ProductDescription, ProductPrice, and ProductQuantity in the Field row of the QBE grid
9. Click the **Datasheet View** button to see the query results
10. Return to **Design View**
11. This list is to display products currently in inventory. To accomplish this enter the criterion **>0** in the ProductQuantity column Criteria row
12. Click the **Datasheet View** button to see the query results (see Figure 3.15)

FIGURE 3.15

CurrentInventory query

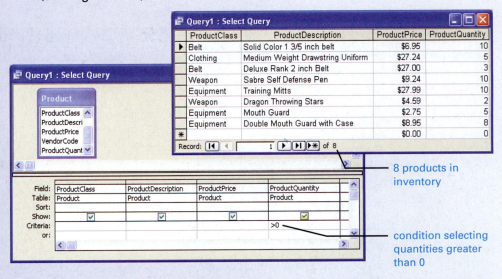

8 products in inventory

condition selecting quantities greater than 0

13. Save the query as **CurrentInventory**. The criteria will be saved and run weekly to generate a current list of products to order

The greater than (>) relational operator was used to state the condition in the previous example, but any of the other operators could have been applied. The operator is determined by the question that is being posed. There are currently several products

FIGURE 3.16
Data type delimiters

Data Type	Delimiter	Example
Number, Currency, AutoNumber	None	>5302.28
Text	Double quotes ("") delimit text match values	"Miller"
Date/Time	Pound signs (##) delimit date and time values	<#3/30/02#
Yes/No	Keywords True/False or Yes/No are used to select data in Yes/No fields	Yes

FIGURE 3.16
Data type delimiters

not carried in inventory but available for order. To retrieve items that could be ordered the criteria <=0 would be used. Although there should not be any negative quantity values in the table, it is a good idea to use <= rather than = to verify the lack of negative values. If you want to know what products are purchased from So Yi Martial Arts Supplies (SC), a criterion of SC in the VendorCode of the Product table would return that list. Remember that the equals (=) sign is optional when stating equality conditions.

When stating queries, delimiters are required for each match value. The data type of the field being matched determines the appropriate delimiter, as shown in Figure 3.16. Access QBE adds these delimiters to conditions entered without them.

Adding Calculations to Queries

When the KoryoKicks database was designed, the calculated fields were purposely not stored. One of the rules of normalization precludes storing calculated values because they can be re-created with current data each time a report or query is run.

Calculated Fields

To calculate a value for each row of data in a table, you must add a ***calculated field*** to the QBE grid. A calculated field holds a mathematical expression whose results will be displayed in the field. A typical expression contains database fields, constants, and mathematical operators. The database fields in an expression must be Number, Currency, or Date/Time data type. Access does not support mathematical operations on other data types. Constants must be numeric values such as 8238 or 0.36.

The mathematical operators are +, −, *, /, and ^. When several operators are used in a single formula, the algebraic order of precedence outlined in Figure 3.17 applies. If a formula contains operators with the same precedence— for example, if a formula contains both a multiplication and division operator—the operators are evaluated from left to right. To change the order of evaluation, enclose the part of the formula to be calculated first in parentheses.

FIGURE 3.17
Mathematical order of precedence

Order	Operation	
1	−	Negation (as in −1)
2	^	Exponentiation
3	*, /	Multiplication and division
4	+, −	Addition and subtraction

A calculated field can be entered directly into the Field row of a QBE grid, or the ***Expression Builder*** can be used to select the components of the calculation. Because the space in the QBE grid is fairly small, a large text box called a ***Zoom box*** can be opened to provide greater visibility for complicated expressions. Click in a Field cell of the QBE grid and then press Shift+F2 to open a Zoom box.

> ### task reference — Create an Expression Using Expression Builder
>
> - Click in the Field row of the QBE grid column that will display the calculation
> - Click the **Build** button in the query Design toolbar
> - Select expression elements and operators to create the desired calculation
> - Click **OK** to place the calculation in the QBE grid

The Product table contains data about the price and quantity on hand for each KoryoKicks product. The inventory value of each product was not stored but can be calculated when needed for queries and reports. Inventory value provides information needed to answer questions about the value of a company or where costs could be cut in the current system.

Creating an expression field with the Expression Builder:

1. Verify that the ac03KoryoKicks.mdb database is open

2. Select the **Queries** object from the Database Window

3. Double-click **Create query in Design View** to open the QBE grid and Show Table dialog box

4. Double-click on the **Product** table in the Show Table dialog box to add it to the design grid

5. Click **Close** in the Show Table dialog box

6. Place **ProductClass**, **ProductDescription**, **ProductQuantity**, and **ProductPrice** in the Field row of the QBE grid

7. Click in the empty Field row to the right of ProductPrice and activate the **Expression Builder**

FIGURE 3.18

Expression Builder

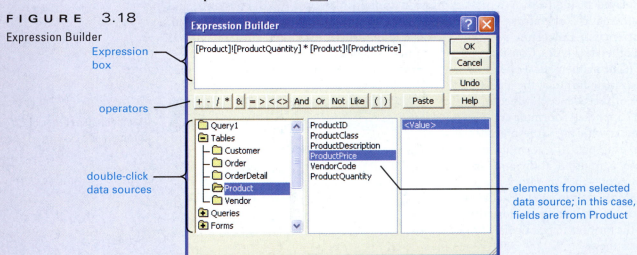

Expression box — [Product]![ProductQuantity] * [Product]![ProductPrice]

operators

double-click data sources

elements from selected data source; in this case, fields are from Product

8. Double-click **Tables**, then **Product** to list the fields that will be used in the calculation

9. Build the expression by double-clicking **ProductQuantity**, clicking the **multiplication** button, and then double-clicking **ProductPrice** (see Figure 3.18)

tip: *If you make a mistake, you can make edits directly in the Expression box. Notice that Access includes the table name with each field so that you can perform calculations involving multiple tables. Square brackets [] enclose table and field names*

10. Click **OK** to close the Expression Builder and place the expression in the QBE grid

11. Place **>0** in the Criteria row of ProductQuantity to select only in-stock items

FIGURE 3.19
Expression in the QBE grid

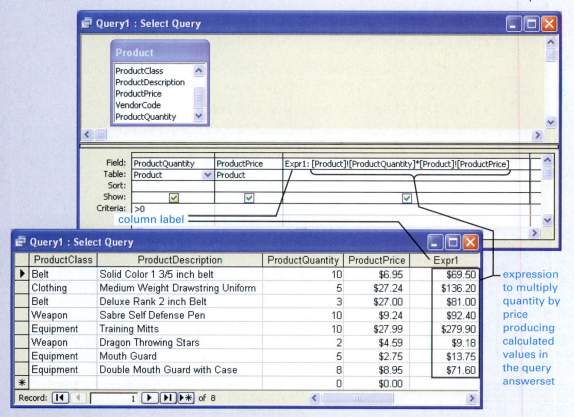

12. Click the **Datasheet View** [icon] button to see the query results (see Figure 3.19)

13. Return to **Design** [icon] View

Notice that the Expression Builder has a folder of functions. Functions are predefined calculations for common operations. Available functions include calculating the difference between two dates (DateDiff), determining a loan payment (Pmt), and averaging values (Avg). When using a predefined function, the appropriate calculation values must be provided in the correct order, a task that Expression Builder supports.

Notice also that the Expression Builder always places extra punctuation ([]!) in the expression. Access requires a field name that is used as the column heading for every column and provides one if you do not. Consider the following expression.

```
Expr1: [Product]![ProductQuantity]*[Product]![ProductPrice]
```

The colon (:) separates the column heading from the expression. The default column heading is Expr1 for the first expression, Expr2 for the second, and so on. If you provide a value to the left of the colon, it will be used. The exclamation point (!) is the delimiter or separator that differentiates between the table name and the field name. The table name is optional unless there are fields from different tables with the same name. For example, Product!VendorCode and Vendor!VendorCode need the table name to differentiate the two fields. The square brackets [] are only required when there are spaces in a field or table name, so VendorCode does not require them, but [Vendor Code] does. You may choose to eliminate the extra punctuation or leave it since it only impacts the readability of an expression, not the performance.

Creating an expression by typing:

1. Return to the previous query design

2. Verify that **ProductClass**, **ProductDescription**, **ProductQuantity**, and **ProductPrice** from the Product table are in the design grid

3. Select and delete the expression built with Expression Builder

4. Click in the empty Field row to the right of Price and type **Total:ProductQuantity*ProductPrice**

tip: *When field names are unique, the table name does not need to be included in the expression. The value to the left of the colon (:) is the column label. Square brackets [] are only required when field or table names contain spaces, but Access will add them*

FIGURE   3.20

Typed expression in QBE grid

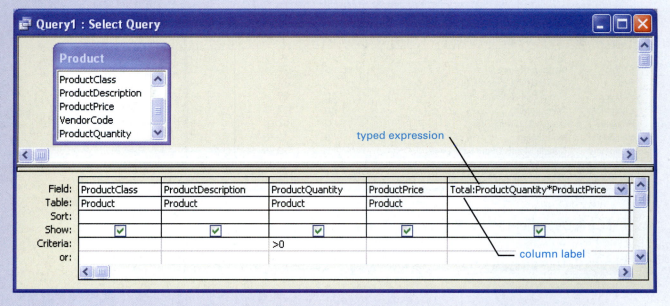

5. Click the **Datasheet View** button to see the query results

6. Close the query and save it as **InventoryValue**

For short, well-defined calculations, typing in the expression is usually faster than using the Expression Builder and results in less expression punctuation. It is important to know when the punctuation must be included. To recap the earlier discussion:

- The colon (:) separates the column heading from the expression

- The exclamation point (!) separates a table name from its field name. The table name is only required if you are using multiple tables with identical field names

- The square brackets [] are required to enclose both field names and table names that contain spaces

FIGURE 3.21
Aggregate functions

Aggregate Function	Use	Data Types
Sum	Totals the field values for selected records	AutoNumber, Currency, Date/Time, and Number
Avg	Averages the field values for selected records	AutoNumber, Currency, Date/Time, and Number
Count	Counts the number of selected records	AutoNumber, Currency, Date/Time, Memo, Number, OLE Object, Text, and Yes/No
Max	Returns the highest field value	AutoNumber, Currency, Date/Time, Number, and Text
Min	Returns the lowest field value	AutoNumber, Currency, Date/Time, Number, and Text

Aggregate Operations

Aggregate operations are used to calculate summary data such as averages and sums. These operations make use of the predefined functions mentioned in the previous topic and are outlined in Figure 3.21. *Aggregate functions* can be applied to all of the data in a table or any subset specified by the query. Because only one aggregate function can be applied to a table column, multiple copies of the same field must be placed in the design grid to achieve multiple aggregate operations on one field.

Suppose that Missy and Micah need to evaluate their product mix and want to know how many products they carry (Count ProductDescription), the average number of items on hand (Avg ProductQuantity), the total number of products on hand (Sum ProductQuantity), the average inventory cost of a product (Avg ProductQuantity* ProductPrice), and the total inventory cost (Sum ProductQuantity*ProductPrice). Such information is valuable when determining the cost of adding new products or discontinuing existing products. The following steps produce this query.

Summarizing selected data with aggregate functions:

1. Verify that the ac03KoryoKicks.mdb database is open

2. Open a new query in Design View with **Product** as the table being queried

3. Create the QBE fields outlined in Figure 3.22

4. Click the **Totals** Σ button to insert the Total row into the QBE grid

5. In the Total row, select the aggregate function for each column, as shown in Figure 3.22

6. Click the **Datasheet View** button to see the query results

7. Double-click the column borders to resize them

8. Return to **Design View**

9. Change the Field row for ProductDescription to read **Nmbr of Product: ProductDescription** to customize the field heading

FIGURE 3.22
Aggregate functions assigned to each field

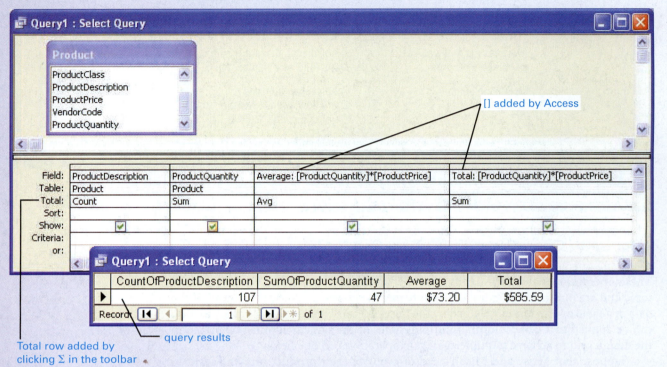

10. Click the **Datasheet View** button to see the revised query results

11. Close the query and save it as **InventorySummary**

Notice that Access created a unique field heading for each column by combining the aggregate function with the field name. The default name can be overridden by providing your own column headings before the colon in the field name, as demonstrated in the previous steps.

Record Group Calculations

Another calculation requirement is to create subtotals for specific groups of records. Returning to the Product table, we could use record group calculations to determine statistics for each ProductClass. Record group calculations are accomplished using the *Group By* operator in the Total row of a query.

Summarizing grouped data:

1. Verify that the ac03KoryoKicks.mdb database is open

2. Open the **InventorySummary** query in Design View

3. To the right of the last field, add the field **ProductClass**, select the ProductClass column, and drag it until it is the leftmost column

4. Verify that the Total row of ProductClass is set to **Group By** since we want summaries for each vendor

FIGURE 3.23

Using Group By to summarize data by ProductClass

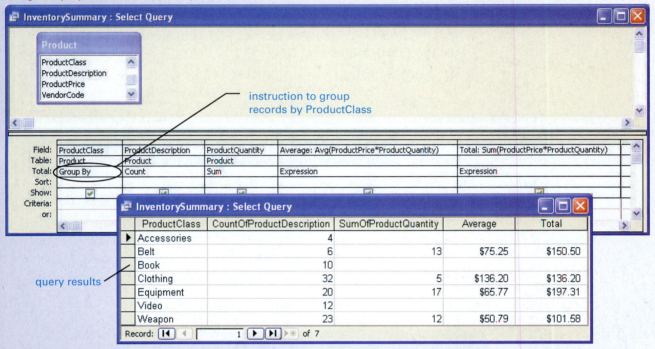

5. Click the **Datasheet View** button to see the query results
6. Double-click the column borders to resize them
7. Select **Save As** from the **File** menu and name the revised query **ProductClassSummary**

Once a query has been saved, it is listed as a Query object in the Database Window. Only the query specifications are saved, so the next time the query is run, all calculations will be computed based on the current table data. Running a saved query is as simple as double-clicking its name.

Creating and Using Forms

A form is an Access object like a query, meaning that its design is specified, saved, and then run against current data on demand. Access forms are used to organize and display data on the screen in a more effective format than Datasheet View. Typically, forms display only one record at a time.

Like queries, forms support multiple views: Design View, where the form layout and content can be altered; and *Form View,* where the data are displayed for maintenance, selection, printing, and other data update and analysis tasks.

Building a Simple Form

There are five types of AutoForm Wizards that work like the tabular and columnar forms explored in the first chapter. Each *AutoForm Wizard* will allow one table and a form layout to be specified, but nothing more. The **Form Wizard** allows fields to be selected from one or more tables and the display format to be specified, and then it creates the form based on that input. Finally a form can be created in Design View with control over fields, formats, and calculations. Let's start by creating a form based on the InventoryQuery built earlier in this session.

Using the Form Wizard:

1. Verify that the ac03KoryoKicks.mdb database is open

2. In the Database Window, select the **Forms** object and **Create form by using wizard**, then select **New**

3. Select **Form Wizard** and click **OK**

tip: *There is no need to select a table before entering the Form Wizard as you did with AutoForm*

4. Fields for this form can be selected from any existing tables and queries. Select **Query: InventoryValue** from the Tables/Queries drop-down list

5. Use the **>>** button to select all of the fields for the form and click **Next**

6. Click on each of the Layout options and preview the result. Select **Columnar** for this form and click **Next**. A sample of the layout appears on the left side of the dialog box

7. Preview all of the styles and then select **Sumi Painting** and click **Next**

8. Name your form **InventoryValue** and then click **Finish**

FIGURE 3.24

Completed form displaying the Training Mitts record

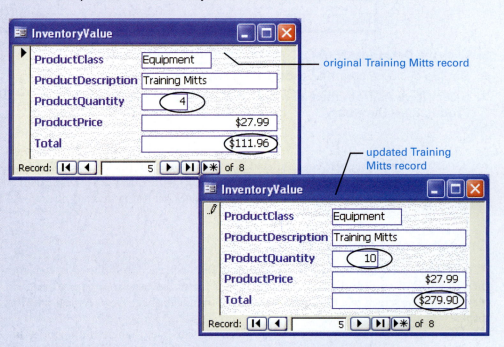

original Training Mitts record

updated Training Mitts record

9. Use the navigation bar to move through the data to the **Training Mitts** record

10. Notice that the Training Mitts Total value is $111.96. Change the Quantity to **10**, move to the next record, and then back to the Training Mitts record. Notice that the Total has also updated

11. Click the **Print Preview** 🔍 button to see how your forms would print if you clicked the **Print** 🖨 button. The Print option of the File menu contains options for printing only the current record or a range of records

As was just demonstrated, forms can be used to maintain the data in a database. Calculated fields (expressions) display in the form but cannot be updated. Calculation values are automatically updated when edits made to the expression fields are saved (when you move to another row of data).

Finding, editing, and deleting data are accomplished with the same techniques used in table Datasheet View. The same Sort, Filter, Find, New Record, and Delete buttons appear on the toolbar. Sorts can be applied to change the presentation order. Filters allow a subset of the data to be manipulated and Find will find records that meet a criterion. As when editing data in the datasheet, deletes cannot be undone.

Customizing a Form

Forms created with the Wizard can be modified in Design View. Developers frequently create the first cut of a form with the Wizard and customize to achieve the desired result.

task reference	Modify the Format of a Form

- Open the form in Design View
- Click the **AutoFormat** button in the Form Design toolbar
- Select from the same formats that were available in the Wizard

Changing the AutoFormat of the InventoryValue form:

1. Open the **InventoryValue** form in Design View
2. Select the **AutoFormat** button from the Form Design toolbar
3. Select the format that appeals to you
4. Click the **Options** button. You can choose portions of the format to apply. Click each option to see the impact
5. Click the **Form View** button to see the full impact
6. Move back and forth between Design View and Form View until you get the effect you desire
7. Close the form saving your changes

A word of caution: when using forms that do not display all of the fields of a table, users can update only the displayed fields, which can cause problems with finding and entering the data later on.

Producing Reports

Reports are used to effectively format and print data from tables and queries. All aspects of a report can be customized, including formatting and graphics.

The Report Wizards

The AutoReport Wizard was introduced in Chapter 1 to provide an overview of what the report object does. Like tables, queries, and forms, the report object stores the criteria for creating a report.

InventoryValue form in
Design View

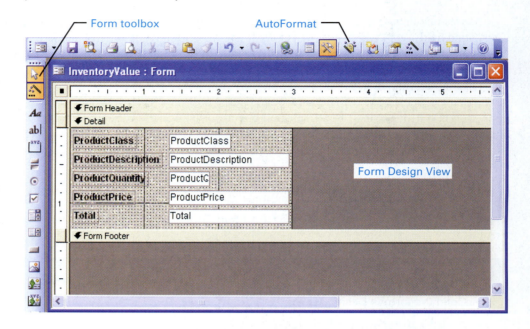

When a report opens, the saved report criteria are run against current data. Data displayed in a report can be drawn directly from a table, a group of related tables, or a query. Expressions can be used to calculate values for every record, subtotals for groups of records, or report totals. Charts and graphics also can be added.

The AutoReport Wizard presented in Chapter 1 is the most restrictive way to create a report. It allows you to select only one table or query as the data source and uses a default layout. The Report Wizard is very similar to the Form Wizard. It will allow you to choose fields from multiple tables and queries, control the order of those fields, define calculations, and select a report layout.

Using the Report Wizard:

1. Verify that the ac03KoryoKicks.mdb database is open

2. In the Database Window select the **Reports** object, then double-click **Create report by using wizard** (the fastest way to start the Report Wizard)

3. Fields for this query can be selected from any existing tables and queries. Select **Query: InventoryValue** from the Tables/Queries drop-down list

4. Use the **>>** button to select all of the fields for the form and click **Next**

5. Grouping will create subtotals. This report needs to be grouped by ProductClass. Select **ProductClass** from the list of available fields and click the **>** selection button to group by ProductClass and then click **Next** (see Figure 3.26)

6. Select **ProductDescription** from the first sort list to cause the records to be sorted by ProductDescription within ProductClass. Click on **Summary Options** to add summary calculations

7. For the ProductPrice field, click on **Avg** to calculate average price by class (the group you set). For the Total field, click on both **Sum** and **Avg** to calculate both the total inventory value by category and the average inventory value by category. Click **OK** in the Summary Options dialog box and then **Next** in the Report Wizard dialog box (see Figure 3.27)

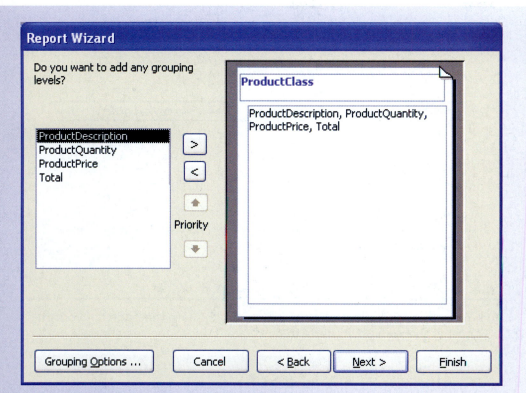

FIGURE 3.26
ProductClass added as a group to the form

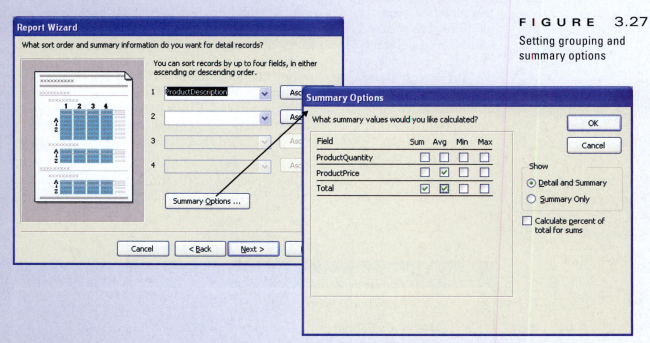

FIGURE 3.27
Setting grouping and summary options

8. Explore the various sort layouts by clicking each and reviewing the sample. Select **Stepped** and click **Next**

9. Explore the styles by clicking each and reviewing the sample. Select **Corporate** and press **Next**

10. Name the report **InventoryValueByClass**, verify that **Preview the report** is selected, and click **Finish** (see Figure 3.28)

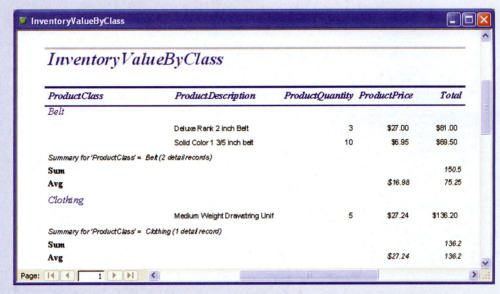

11. Your report will display in Print Preview. Explore the pages of your report and review the criteria to correlate them to the results

Grouping records is an important concept. Reports without grouping cannot contain subtotals. When records are grouped, the group value (ProductClass in our example) is used to create a header that appears above the records of that group. A group footer is also created to contain any summary statistics for the group. Up to 10 fields can be grouped with summary statistics for any or all of the 10.

The Report Wizard displays option buttons to Show Detail and Summary records or Summary Only records as the report is being built. Detail reports display each row from the selected input, like the report just created. Summary reports display only the summary statistics, for example, the ProductClass footer from the previous report.

Formatting Reports

To format reports, it is necessary to use Design View. The simplest change is to choose another AutoFormat. This process is the same as changing the AutoFormat of a form.

---

task reference   Modify the Format of a Report

- Open the report in Design View

- Click the **AutoFormat** button in the Report Design toolbar

- Select from the same formats that were available in the Wizard

Changing the AutoFormat of the InventoryValueByClass report:

1. Open the **InventoryValueByClass** report in Design View 🖊️ ▾

2. Select the **AutoFormat** 📇 button from the Form Design toolbar

3. Preview the available formats (they are the same as those presented in the Wizard) and select the format that appeals to you

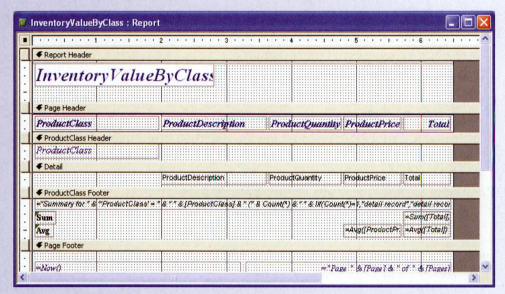

FIGURE   3.29

InventoryValueByClass report in Design View

4. Click the **Options** button. You can choose portions of the format to apply. Click each option to see the impact

5. The **Customize** button allows you to save your custom format. Click **OK**

6. Click the **Form View** 📇 ▾ button to see the full impact

7. Move back and forth between Design View and Form View until you get the effect you desire

8. Return to **Corporate** style

9. Save your changes

Access forms and reports consist of objects called controls. Each control performs a specific task. For example, a label displays text; a text box displays the value of a field and accepts input from the user. In Design View, you can see that each field is composed of two controls: a label that holds the field's caption and a text box that will display the field's value.

All of the objects displayed on a form or report can be modified. Modifications include altering the labels, moving labels and text boxes, and adding new objects. To add objects, use the toolbox containing Controls and the Control Wizards.

Adding descriptive column names is accomplished by editing the labels on the form or report. To edit a label, select it and click an insertion point. Once the text is changed, the label may need to be resized to properly display the complete content. The InventoryByClass report should be updated with labels that better describe the data.

Changing the labels of the InventoryValueByClass report:

1. Open the **InventoryValueByClass** report in Print Preview . Page through the report and notice that the report title would look better with spaces and that the complete ProductDescription does not always display (Black V-neck Elastic Waist unif)

2. Change to **Design View** 🖍 ▾

3. In the Report Header, select the title (InventoryValueByClass). Insert spaces between the words and lengthen the text box so that all of the title is displayed (see Figure 3.30)

4. Use **Print Preview** 🔍 to evaluate your changes

5. Return to **Design View**

6. Add spaces to the ProductClass, ProductDescription, ProductPrice, and ProductQuantity Page header labels. Use the Formatting Form/Report toolbar to right-align the Product Price and Total headings

FIGURE 3.30

Labels and corresponding text boxes selected

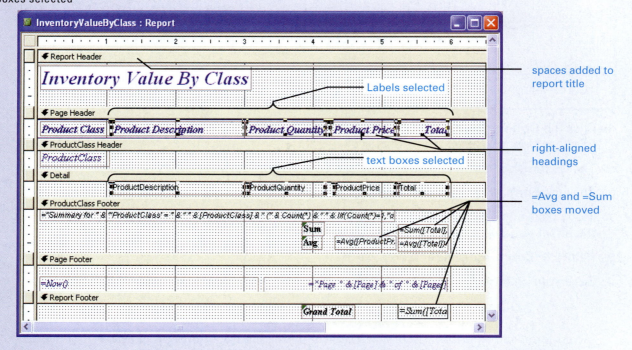

7. Click the **Product Class** text box in the Product Class Header and drag the right border to the left reducing its width by about 1/3. Adjust the ProductClass label to match

8. Move to **Print Preview** and verify that all ProductClass data display correctly. Make any necessary adjustments in **Design View**

9. Click the **Product Description** label in the Page Header and then hold down the Shift key while clicking the **ProductDescription** text box in the Detail section. With both the label and text box selected, drag the left border to the left increasing their width by about 1/3

10. With both the ProductDescription label and text box still selected, drag them to the left so that they are 2 dots away from ProductClass

11. Use the same techniques to move the remaining columns to the left and adjust their widths

12. In the Product Class Footer move the =Avg and =Sum boxes to align with the ProductPrice and Total columns. Similarly adjust the controls in the Report Footer

13. Click the Save button to save your changes and preview the report (see Figure 3.31)

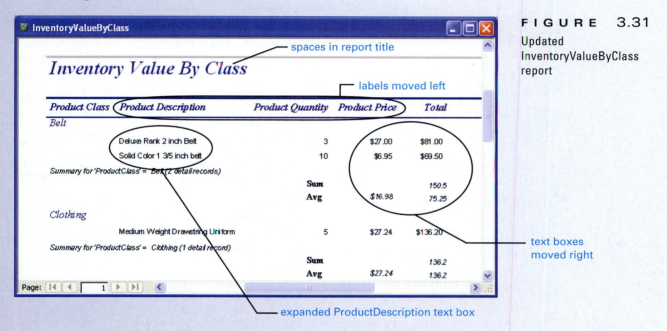

FIGURE 3.31
Updated
InventoryValueByClass
report

Notice that in Design View, the report title is placed in the Report Header section of the design, causing it to appear once at the beginning of the report. The labels for a field appear in the page header section, causing them to appear once at the top of each page of the report. The text boxes that will display the values of a field appear in the Detail section of the report, which repeats for each value.

Producing Mailing Labels

Producing mailing labels is a common business task made easy by Access. The Report Wizard has options to format labels for standard business forms (available from office supply stores).

Making mailing labels for KoryoKicks vendors:

1. Verify that the ac03KoryoKicks.mdb database is open

2. In the Database Window, click the **Reports** object and then **New**

3. Select the **Label Wizard** and **Vendor** as the data source and click **OK**

4. The next step selects the type of mailing label. We will use **Avery, J8162**, a popular label type, and click **Next** (see Figure 3.32)

5. Select Arial **10** point as the label font and click **Next**

F I G U R E   3.32

Selecting label type and font

2. select product

1. select manufacturer

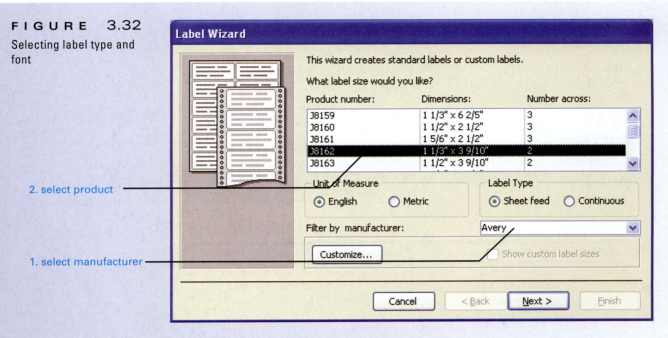

6. Build the label content as follows:
   a. Double-click **Name** and press **Enter**
   b. Double-click **Address** and press **Enter**
   c. Double-click **City** and type a comma and a space
   d. Double-click **State** and type a space
   e. Double-click **Zip Code**
   f. Click **Next**

F I G U R E   3.33

Formatting the mailing label

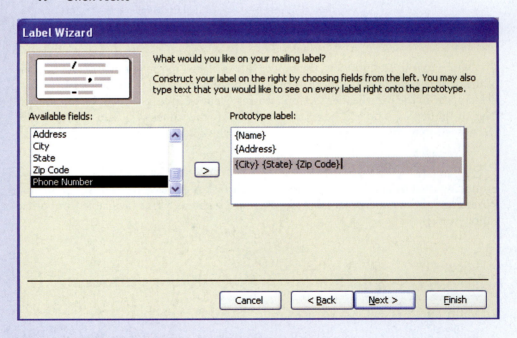

7. Sort the labels by **ZipCode** and press **Next**

8. Name the report **LabelsVendor** and click **Finish** (see Figure 3.34)

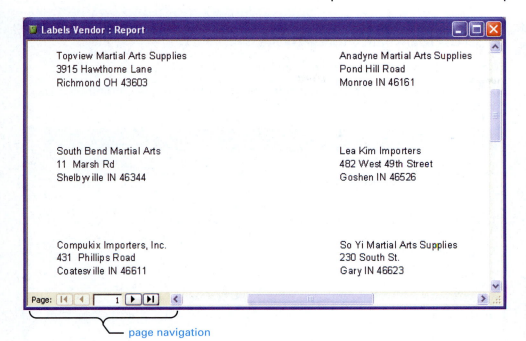

FIGURE 3.34
Mailing labels in Print
Preview

page navigation

Adding Graphics to Reports and Forms

Although graphics do not usually add to the functionality of a report or form, they do improve visual appeal. They also can promote brand identity or distinguish one type of form or report from another. Graphics are added to reports and forms with the same technique, so only a form example is provided.

help yourself *Use the Type a Question combo box to enhance your understanding of how to adjust form and report controls by typing* **move or resize controls**. *Review the contents of* About customizing a control and Resize a control, *and* Move one or more controls to a new position. *Close the Help window when you are finished*

---

task *reference* Add a Graphic to a Report or Form

- Open the report or form in Design View
- Select the section that is to display the graphic
- Select **Picture** from the **Insert** menu
- Navigate to the folder containing the image and change the file type selector to the image file type
- Select the file and click **OK**
- Move and size the image as needed

Adding a graphic to InventoryValueByClass:

1. Verify that the ac03KoryoKicks.mdb database is open

2. Open **InventoryValueByClass** in Design View

3. Click the Report Header (you must click the report or form section where you want the graphic to appear)

4. Select **Picture** from the **Insert** menu

5. Change the Files of type setting to **.gif**

6. Select the **ac03KoryoKicksLogo.gif** file from the Chapter 3 data files list and click **OK**

FIGURE 3.35
Selecting a picture

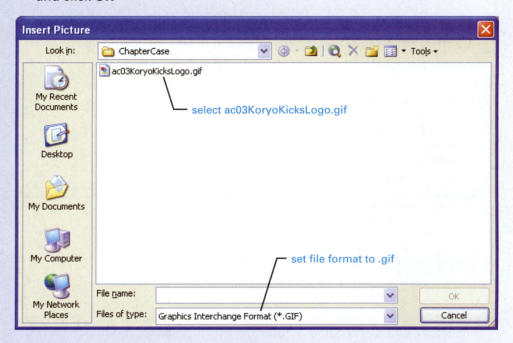

7. The image loads over the report title. Select the report title and drag it to the right of the image until all of the text displays and it is aligned with the bottom of the image

8. Use Print Preview to see the result (see Figure 3.36)

9. Save changes to the report and close Access

SESSION 3.2

making *the grade*

1. When would you use a form? A report?

2. T F   Forms cannot display data from a query.

3. What is the difference between the > and the >> buttons used to select fields in Access queries?

4. Why and how would you add an expression to a query?

5. What is the difference between a field label and a field text box in the Design View of reports and forms?

6. Describe grouping in reports.

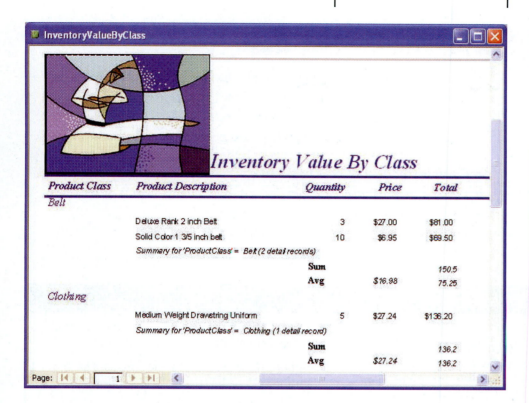

FIGURE 3.36

Form with image in the Report Header section

SESSION 3.3 SUMMARY

Access provides an array of options for selecting and organizing data into useful information. The strength of relational databases lies in the simplicity and flexibility of the analytical tools provided.

Filters are used to restrict rows of data to work with a subset of a table. The simplest filter is Filter By Selection, which allows the selection of all or part of a datasheet value and then retrieves records that match the selection. Filter By Form, Filter For Input, and Advanced Filter/Sort are other filtering tools. Each filtering tool has a different interface and provides progressively more functionality. Filter Excluding Selection allows the selected value to be excluded from the filter return set. Filters are cumulative and remain in effect until specifically removed. Filters must be saved as a query to be reusable.

Select Queries are a more powerful data analysis tool that can retrieve and organize data from multiple tables. With queries, both columns and rows can be selected and sorted. Calculated fields can compute based on data in detail records or summarize data based on defined groups. Query criteria are built in a Query By Example (QBE) grid. Relational operators are used to state the conditions to retrieve records. Query results can be formatted for better viewing by changing the column width and adjusting the font.

Forms can be used to display and maintain data from multiple tables and queries. Find, sort, edit, delete, and filter operations work in forms in exactly the same way that they do in datasheets. Deleted records cannot be retrieved.

Reports are used to format printed output based on table data. Data from multiple tables and queries can be grouped, sorted, and summarized before printing. The print can include only detail records, detail and summary records, or only the summary records.

Forms and reports are similar in Design View. Each section of a form or report has a specific function, such as to format the detail record. Graphics can be added to forms and reports from the Insert menu.

MICROSOFT OFFICE SPECIALIST OBJECTIVES SUMMARY

- Creating Select Queries using the Simple Query Wizard—MOS AC03S-1-7
- Adding a calculated field to queries in query Design View—MOS AC03S-3-1
- Creating forms using the Form Wizard—MOS AC03S-1-8
- Modifying specific form controls (e.g., text boxes, labels, bound controls)— MOS AC03S-1-9
- Creating reports—MOS AC03S-1-10
- Using aggregate functions in queries (e.g., Avg, Count)—MOS AC03S-3-1
- Aligning and spacing controls—MOS AC03S-3-2
- Filtering records by form and by selection—MOS AC03S-3-6

making the grade answers

SESSION 3.1

1. If the selection is at the beginning of a field, records that begin with the selected values will be retrieved. If the selection is in the middle of a field, records with the selected characters anywhere in their value will be selected.

2. False. Filtering restricts the rows.

3. Select the value to be excluded, right-click on it, and choose Filter Excluding Selection.

4. False. Filters are cumulative until the Remove Filter instruction is executed.

5. The Or tab in Filter By Form and the Or row in the Advanced Filter/Sort both allow you to enter multiple criteria for the same field.

6. The first benefit is that you can execute the filter again without re-creating the criteria. Secondly, the saved filter could be used as the basis for creating forms, reports, or a more complex query.

SESSION 3.2

1. A Form object is used to create a custom format for input and display of data from tables or queries. A report is used to design printed output from tables and queries.

2. False. The Form Wizard allows you to select fields from multiple tables or queries.

3. Both buttons are used to select fields. The > button selects the current field, while the >> button selects all available fields.

4. Expressions are used to calculate values that are not stored in tables such as gross pay. An expression is entered in the Field row of the QBE grid to create a calculated field.

5. Labels and text boxes are the controls that make up forms and reports. The label contains the heading or descriptive text for the field, while the text box holds the field value from each record.

6. Setting the Grouping in a report is the same as setting the Group By option in a query. Both allow you to select a field or fields that will control summary statistics. For example, to create an inventory report by department, you would want totals for each department, so department would be the group field.

task reference summary

Task	Page #	Preferred Method
Filter By Selection	AC 3.4	• Open the table in Datasheet View • Select the field and character(s) of the search criteria (see Figure 3.2) • Click the **Filter By Selection** toolbar button to return values matching the selection or • Right-click and choose **Filter Excluding Selection** to filter the selection out of the data • Evaluate the results of the filter • Click **Remove Filter** on the Access toolbar
Filter By Form	AC 3.6	• Open a table in Datasheet View • Click the **Filter By Form** toolbar button • Build the filter criteria by selecting from the drop-down list for a field or typing your own value • Click the **Apply Filter** toolbar button • Review the filtered data to be sure they are what you expected • Work with the filtered data • Click **Remove Filter** on the Access toolbar when you are done
Filter For Input	AC 3.8	• Open a table in Datasheet View • Right-click the field to be filtered • Type the filter criteria in the Filter For text box using wildcards, operators, and values • Press **Enter** to activate the filter • Review the filtered data to be sure they are what you expected • Work with the filtered data • Click **Remove Filter** on the Access toolbar when you are done
Advanced Filter/Sort	AC 3.9	• Open a table in Datasheet View • On the **Records** menu, point to **Filter** and then click **Advanced Filter/Sort** • Add criteria fields to the design grid • Enter the filter and sort criteria • Click the **Apply Filter** button on the toolbar • Review the filtered data to be sure they are what you expected • Work with the filtered data • Click **Remove Filter** on the Access toolbar when you are done
Saving a filter as a query	AC 3.10	• Display the filter in either the Filter By Form window or the Advanced Filter/Sort window (recall that any filter can be displayed in these windows regardless of how it was created) • Click the **Save As Query** button on the toolbar • Type a name for the query and click **OK** • The new query will appear with the other query objects in the Database Window
Create a Select Query	AC 3.12	• Select the **Queries** object from the Database Window • Verify that **Create query in Design View** is selected • Click **New** on the toolbar • Select the **Design View** button from the New Query dialog box and click **OK** • Double-click the name of each table that contains relevant data from the Show Table dialog box • Double-click each table field that is to be contained in the query result to place it in the Field row of the design grid. The order of the columns is the order of the output • Enter sort criteria in the Sort row of the design grid • Enter selections in the Criteria row of the design grid • Click the **Datasheet View** button on the toolbar to see the query results • Click the **Design View** button on the toolbar to update the query criteria • Click the **Save** button to save the query criteria

ACCESS

task reference *summary*

Task	Page #	Preferred Method
Create an expression using Expression Builder	AC 3.20	• Click in the Field row of the QBE grid column that will display the calculation • Click the **Build** button in the Query Design toolbar • Select expression elements and operators to create the desired calculation • Click **OK** to place the calculation in the QBE grid
Modify the format of a form	AC 3.27	• Open the form in Design View • Click the **AutoFormat** button in the Form Design toolbar • Select from the same formats that were available in the Wizard
Modify the format of a report	AC 3.30	• Open the report in Design View • Click the **AutoFormat** button in the Report Design toolbar • Select from the same formats that were available in the Wizard
Add a graphic to a report or form	AC 3.35	• Open the report or form in Design View • Select the section that is to display the graphic • Select **Picture** from the Insert menu • Navigate to the folder containing the image and change the file type selector to the image file type • Select the file and click **OK** • Move and size the image as needed

TRUE/FALSE

1. Relational operators include +, −, *, and /.

2. An aggregate function with no Group By returns a value for every detail record.

3. Only bitmaps (.bmp) format images can be displayed in Access forms and reports.

4. Each section of a form or report is used to define a different output component. For example, the header appears once at the beginning of a form or report.

5. Summary reports display only statistical or summarized data and suppress the detail line prints.

6. To add a calculation to a query, an expression containing the calculation *must* be typed directly into the query grid.

FILL-IN

1. Graphics are placed in a form or report using the _____ menu.

2. The title of a report that appears only on the first page is placed in the _____ section of the design.

3. A field from a table or query is composed of a _____ control and a _____ control when displayed on a form.

4. When using Wizards _____ determines the background and text color applied.

5. The Form Wizard allows you to select from a list of fields in a table or query. The field list displayed is determined by _____.

6. To create a query that calculates total expenses by department, you would _____ on the Department field.

7. The format for the output of each record in a report is defined in the _____ section.

MULTIPLE CHOICE

1. Which of the following relational operators could be used to retrieve a contiguous range of values defined by an upper and lower limit in a query?
   a. Between
   b. In
   c. Like
   d. all of the above

2. Which of the following presents a blank datasheet containing all the fields of a table for the entry of filter criteria?
   a. Filter by Selection
   b. Filter for Input
   c. Filter by Form
   d. all of the above

3. A filter can be saved as a
   a. filter.
   b. form.
   c. table.
   d. query.

4. What views are supported for the query object?
   a. Design and Report
   b. Datasheet and Design
   c. Datasheet and Report
   d. Form and Datasheet

5. Which of the following is not a control used to design a form?
   a. label
   b. image
   c. expression
   d. text Box

REVIEW QUESTIONS

Each of the following topics should be addressed in one to three paragraphs.

1. Discuss what you would need to do to create mailing labels for the dog owners in the Clients table of the Westside Vet Clinic database.

2. Discuss the difference between detail and summary reports and when you would use each.

3. How do you decide to what groups to apply summary statistics in a grouped report?

4. In a table containing a record for each class a student has taken this semester, how would you calculate the student's GPA? The record consists of the student ID, class ID, class credits, and a score representing the letter grade (0 = F, 1 = D, 2 = C, 3 = B, 4 = A).

5. Discuss the methods that could be used to return a contiguous range of values in a query.

6. Describe how many rows will result from using an aggregate function in a query.

CREATE THE QUESTION

For each of the following answers, create the question.

ANSWER	QUESTION
1. It doesn't have to be stated in query criteria because it is the default	_____
2. They can only operate on all fields of one table	_____
3. The only way to retrieve such a record is to restore it from a backup made prior to the update	_____
4. Double-clicking a field in the field list, clicking and dragging a field from the field list, and selecting from a drop-down list box are all ways to do this	_____
5. Doing this will cause all of the fields of a table to be displayed in the output without placing each field in the QBE grid	_____
6. Because you can select from fields in all of the tables in the database, operators, and Access functions to create an expression	_____
7. These are only required in an expression when the field name or table name contains spaces	_____

FACT OR FICTION

For each of the following, determine whether the statement is fact, fiction, or both and present your arguments for that conclusion.

1. In the expression Extended Total:Quantity*Price, the colon (:) is optional.

2. Aggregate functions can only be applied to the entire contents of a table or query.

3. The query, form, and report objects of a database store only specifications that can be used to re-create the object, not data.

4. The Form Wizard is one of the five types of AutoForms.

5. The Count aggregate function can be used on nonnumeric data.

practice

1. Creating Filters, Forms, Queries, and Reports for Curbside Recycling

Curbside Recycling was introduced as a Hands-on Project in Chapter 1; review the organization's background if needed. You have added the CustomerRecords table to Curbside's database prototype. The Customers table holds static customer information such as name, address, and phone. The CustomerRecords table holds data about each recyclable pickup. Enough test data have been added to each table to test filtering, queries, reports, and forms.

1. Make sure that you have access to the data from your data disk

2. Start Access and open the **ac03CurbsideRecycling.mdb** database from your Chapter 3 files

3. Use a filter to select records for customers who had their first pickup in October of 2002
   a. Document the filtering method you used. (*Hint:* Two Filter by Selection filters are required; only one Filter by Form filter is required.)
   b. Sort the filtered data by service date and print the result

4. Use a filter to
   a. Select all customers who live on a street that has "hill" anywhere in the street address
   b. Save the filter as a query named **HillCustomers**

5. Create a form (see Figure 3.37) to be used to enter new customers and update existing customers. The columnar form should
   a. Contain all of the Customer table data
   b. Use the SandStone AutoFormat
   c. Display the logo in ac03Curbside.tif (located with the Chapter 3 data files) in the Form Header
   d. Use spaces and complete words in the field labels (e.g., CstmrNmbr changes to Customer Number)
   e. Print the form displaying the record for Alice Arston
   f. Save the form as **Customer**

FIGURE 3.37
Curbside form and report

6. Create a report named **PhoneList** to be used as a customer phone list. The report should
   a. Contain only the fields LastName, FirstName, and Phone
   b. Be sorted by the full customer name
   c. Use the Casual AutoFormat
   d. Display the logo in **ac03Curbside.gif** (located with the Chapter 3 data files) in the Report Header. Select and delete the default title
   e. Have the column widths narrowed to better fit the data (see Figure 3.37)

7. Use a query on CustomerRecords to determine the total and average weights of Paper and other products each customer has had picked up
   a. Print the query results
   b. Save the query as **CstmrWeights**

8. Create a detailed report with summary records displaying the Average and Total of Paper and Other weights from the CustomerRecords table. Save the report as **CstmrWeights**

9. If your work is complete, exit Access; otherwise, continue to the next assignment

2. Evaluating Data in the BestBakery Database

Montgomery (Monty) Best started the Best Bakery and Catering Company 30 years ago in Orlando, Florida. The organization has been very successful with several bakeries throughout the Orlando area. Best products are marketed through grocery stores, delis, and event catering. Catering is available for any event from a small gathering of 8 to a banquet for 700.

Monty is frequently asked to share the recipes that have led to his success. While there are many specialty recipes that Monty is not willing to share, many commonly prepared dishes can easily be scaled down for home use. Monty has begun developing a database of the recipes he is willing to share. The goal is to create kiosks in grocery stores and delis where customers can browse and print their personal favorites.

1. Start Access and open **ac03BestBakery.mdb**

2. Open the **Recipes** table in Datasheet View

3. Locate the record for Italian Meatballs and notice that the Category is Mead. Use a filter to locate any other Mead records. Document the filter used and then change all Mead Categories to **Meat**. Print the filtered data. Save the filter as a query named **MeadUpdates**

4. Use a filter to select all Bread recipes. Save the filter as a query named **BreadRecipes**

5. Create a form (see Figure 3.38) to be used to enter new recipe data and update existing data. The form should

   a. Use the **Columnar** layout and **Ricepaper** style

   b. Contain all table fields

   c. Include the **ac03Food.jpg** graphic sized and placed as shown in Figure 3.38

   d. Have spaces in the field labels

   e. Print the form displaying the Irish Spaghetti record

   f. Save the form as **RecipeUpdate**

6. Create a query using the RecipeKeywords and NumberofServings fields to retrieve all chocolate recipes that will serve 24 or more people. Name the query **ChocolateLarge**

7. Create a query that counts the number of recipes in each Category. Name the query **RecipeCount**

8. Create a detailed report with all Recipes table fields and no calculations. Group the records by **Category** and sort by **RecipeName**. Include the **ac03Food.jpg** graphic. Adjust the image size and put spaces in the headings. Name the report **Recipes**

9. If your work is complete, exit Access; otherwise, continue to the next assignment

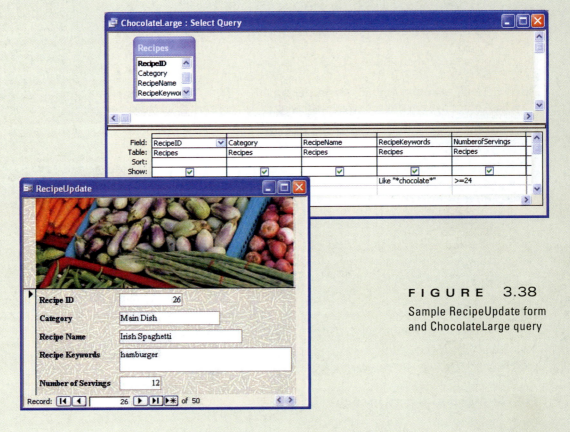

FIGURE 3.38

Sample RecipeUpdate form and ChocolateLarge query

1. Tracking Employees at Little White School House

Little White School House was introduced as a Challenge project in Chapter 1; review the organization's background if needed. You are in the process of converting the existing spreadsheets into database tables. You have cleaned up some of the data, but the transition is not going well because the spreadsheet data have not been normalized. Samuel Mink is anxious to see the reporting capabilities of Access before paying for a complete conversion. You have successfully converted a subset of the spreadsheet containing student data into a table called Students in the ac03lwsh.mdb. The StdntID is an AutoNumber field because the school has only used names in the past.

1. If you did not complete this assignment in Chapter 1, open **ac03Lwsh.mdb** and skip to step 2. If you completed this assignment in Chapter 1, retrieve your **ac01LittleWhiteSchoolHouse** database. Import the Students table from ac03Lwsh.mdb

   a. Use the **Import** option of **Get External Data** from the **File** menu

   b. Select **ac03Lwsh.mdb** and click **Import**

   c. Select the **Students** table and click **OK**

2. Review the Students table data to become familiar with them. Notice that the student's name needs to be broken up into two fields

3. Use a filter to select only students from Pine

   a. Print the result

   b. Save the filter as a query named **Pine**

4. Create a form that can be used to enter new students and update existing student records. The form should

   a. Use columnar format

   b. Use the Expedition AutoFormat

   c. Display the logo in **ac03Lwsh.gif** (located with the Chapter 3 data files) in the Form Header

   d. Print the form displaying the record for Ricky Maus

   e. Save the form as **Students**

5. Create a query that counts the number of students on each bus. The query should display one row per bus. Save the query as **BusCount**

6. Create a report that lists students grouped by their teacher. The report should

   a. Display all fields

   b. Sort by student name

   c. Use Landscape orientation

   d. Use Bold AutoFormat

   e. Display the logo in **ac03Lwsh.tif** (located with the Chapter 3 data files) in the Form Header

7. Be saved as **StudentsByTeacher**

8. Close the database and exit Access if your work is complete

FIGURE 3.39

Little White School House form and report

2. Tracking Software Inventory and Vendors

The ac03Software.mdb database contains data about the software inventory of a small retailer and the vendors that sell each software product.

1. Start Access and open **ac03Software.mdb**

2. Use Design View to create a new query based on the tblSoftware table. Include the **Name**, **Category**, **Quantity**, and **Price**. Select products that have fewer than 10 copies on hand and therefore need to be reordered. Name the query **ReorderList**

3. Create a new query in Design View based on the Products table that includes the **Name**, **Category**, **Quantity**, **Price**, and a calculated field named **Total** that multiplies Quantity by Price. Sort by Name and save the query as **InventoryValue**

4. Create a new query in Design View based on the tblSoftware table that counts the number of software products in each category, averages the quantity, averages the inventory cost of each product, and sums the inventory cost of each product (see Figure 3.40). Add custom headings to each column and name the query **InventoryValueSummary**

5. Use the InventoryValueSummary query to create a new query that returns one calculated row for all data. Delete the Category column. Name the query **InventorySummary**

6. Create a **Columnar** report based on the InventoryValue query. Include all query fields, group by Category, sort by Name, sum the Total field, use **block** layout, and use the **Corporate** style

   a. Adjust the title to include spaces

   b. Adjust column widths as needed

   c. Include the graphic ac03Software.gif in the report header and reposition the title to the bottom-right corner of the image

   d. Name the report **InventoryValue**

7. Create a columnar form for tblSoftware. Include all fields and use the **Sumi Painting** style. Use the form to update the Tax Wizard record. Change Quantity to **8** and verify that the Total also changed. Name the form **tblSoftware**. Print the form displaying this record

8. Use the Vendor table to create **Avery J8162** mailing labels. Sort by ZipCode. Name the report **LabelsVendor**

9. If your work is complete, exit Access; otherwise, continue to the next assignment

FIGURE 3.40

InventoryValueSummary query

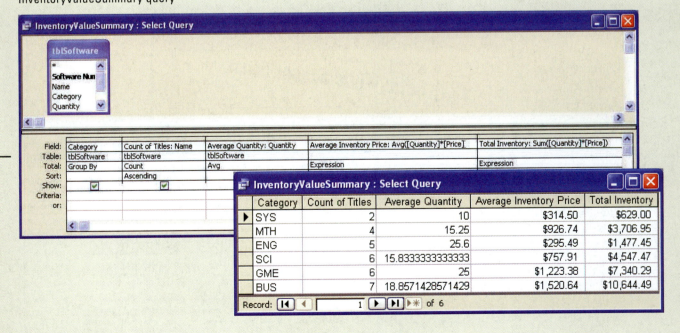

e-business

1. ScaleClassics.com Product Lists

Ricardo (Rico) Juarez runs a body shop that specializes in restoring classic cars. Rico owns three classics and began collecting scale models when his wife put her foot down and said no to building more garage space for his cars.

Although Rico frequently used the Internet and e-mail, he had never considered starting an e-business. The Scale Classics Web site began as a technology class project for Rico's son Marcel. Marcel created a basic text and graphics informational site. Rico liked the site, but wanted a complex site dedicated to the serious collector. He envisioned a storefront, auction house, and collector's forums and had been unable to find such a site in his online searches. Rico hired a local consultant to build the site, found a processing house to manage orders and payments, and began shipping scale models from the body shop.

The storefront is largely for American classic cars, which come in 1/18, 1/24, 1/43, and 1/64 scale. Popular foreign cars are also available. Rico has hired you to maintain the Product List and product analysis, which is in Access.

1. Retrieve the **ac03Cars.mdb** database

2. Review the **Catalog** table data to become familiar with them

3. Use Find and Replace to correct the spelling of Chevrolet

4. Use a filter to select any record with "coupe" in the model name

    a. Print the result

    b. Save the filter as a query named **Coupe**

5. Create a form that can be used to enter new classics and update existing records. The form should

    a. Use columnar format

    b. Use the SandStone AutoFormat

    c. Display the logo in **ac03ClassicCars.gif** (located with the Chapter 3 data files) in the Form Header

    d. Print the form displaying the record for the Dodge 1957 Pick-Up

    e. Save the form as **Cars**

6. Create a query to select the models that cost less than $35. The query should display all of the table fields and sort the result from the highest to the lowest price. Save the query as **LT35**

7. Create a report listing classic cars grouped by their make. The report should

    a. Display all fields

    b. Sort by the model

    c. Calculate the average price for each make

    d. Use Align Left 2 layout

    e. Use the Formal AutoFormat

    f. Display the logo in **ac03ClassicCars.gif** (located with the Chapter 3 data files) in the Form Header

    g. Be saved as **CarsByModel**

    h. Adjust the titles and headings to match Figure 3.41

8. Close the database and exit Access if your work is complete

FIGURE 3.41

Scale Classics form and report

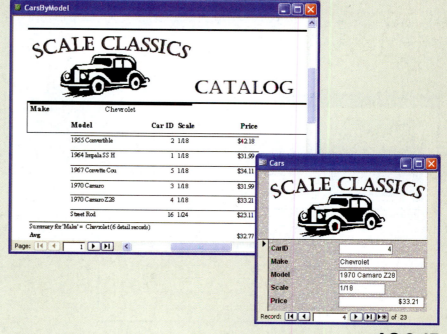

2. Tracking Enrollment at Governor's University

Governor's University is a consortium of 28 colleges and universities. The consortium was formed to allow students to take courses from any member and have them apply toward a degree. The goal is to offer the best curriculum at all 28 locations so that students have the widest possible choice and do not lose credits by moving or changing degree plans. To accomplish this, registration, enrollment, counseling, and all student services are available from the Web. A new Access database for course listings that will drive interactive Web pages is being tested. You will create queries, a form, and a report on this database to help test it.

1. Open Access and open **ac03GovernorsUniversity.mdb**

2. Open the **Courses** table and review the contents. Close the table

3. Create a query that will select all courses taught by a professor named Lewis. Include all fields in the result. Sort by Department, CourseNumber, and Section. Name the query **LewisClasses**

4. Create a query listing the Department, CourseNumber, Section, Title, Instructor, and Seats Remaining. Seats Remaining is calculated by subtracting Enr from Seat. Name the query **AvailableSeats**

5. Use a filter to find any record with the word Study in the course title. Save the filter as a query named **IndependentStudy**

6. Low enrollment courses are often canceled. Create a query listing the Department, CourseNumber, Section, Title, Instructor, and Enr of all non-Independent Study courses with eight or fewer students enrolled. Name the query **LowEnrollment**

7. Create a form that can be used to enter and update data. The form should
   a. Use columnar format
   b. Use the **SandStone** AutoFormat
   c. Display **ac03Study.gif** in the Detail section of the form
   d. Print the form displaying the record for BIOL 1021 section 1
   e. Save the form as **Classes**

8. Create a query listing with Department, CourseNumber, Section, Title, Enr, and Seats Remaining (Seats − Enr). Use this query to create a report. The report should
   a. Include all of the query fields
   b. Group by Department
   c. Sort by CourseNumber and Section
   d. Use **Align Left 2** layout and **Corporate** style
   e. Sum Enrollment and Seats Remaining
   f. Display **ac03Study.gif** in the Form Header
   g. Be saved as **DeptStats**
   h. Have titles and heading adjusted as shown in Figure 3.42

9. Close the database and exit Access if your work is complete

FIGURE 3.42

Governor's University form and report

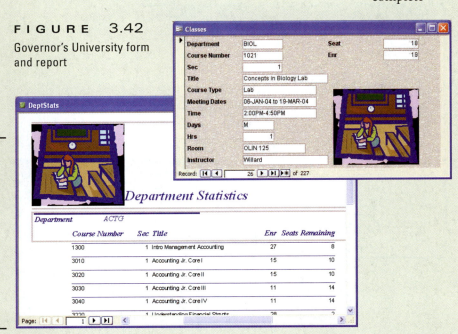

on the web

1. Toy Purchase Statistics by Internet Research Inc.

Internet Research Inc. (IRI) is a statistical evaluation organization specializing in Internet commerce that was introduced in Chapter 2. You have been asked to maintain statistical information on the various Web sites selling toys. The statistics are used to rank the sites and aid Shopping Bots in their searches for products. As a training exercise you have been manually retrieving price comparison information. You still need to retrieve a few more pieces of data and then you will be ready to create reports with groups and calculations to evaluate what you have gathered.

1. Use a Shopping Bot like www.mysimon.com or a search engine to find at least two sites that sell popular toys (www.eToys.com and www.ToysRUs.com are good sites, but there are many others). Select a video or computer game that you would like to purchase for a relative or friend
   a. Determine the price of the game at the first site
   b. Find the price for the same game at the second site
   c. Repeat this process for another game

2. Add your new research to the data that already exist in the ac03IRI.mdb database Toys table

3. Use a filter to select only Barbie items. There should be 22 rows in this answerset
   a. Print the result
   b. Save the filter as a query named **Barbie**

4. Create a form that can be used to enter new toy data and update existing Toys records. The form should
   a. Use columnar format
   b. Use the Expedition AutoFormat
   c. Display the logo in **ac03IRI.jpg** in the Form Header
   d. Include spaces in the field labels
   e. Print the form displaying one of the computer game records
   f. Save the form as **Toys**

5. Create a query that counts the number of prices for each Web site. The query should display one row per Web site. Save the query as **SiteCount**

6. Create a report that lists ToyName grouped by Web site. The report should
   a. Display all fields except ToyID (see Figure 3.43)
   b. Sum all of the prices for a Web site
   c. Sort by ToyName
   d. Use the Align Left 1 Layout
   e. Use the Corporate AutoFormat
   f. Display the logo in **ac03IRI.jpg** (located with the Chapter 3 data files) in the Form Header
   g. Be saved as **SiteTotals**

7. Close the database and exit Access if your work is complete

F I G U R E   3.43

IRI Report

around the world

1. Tracking the World's Population

Brandon Pryor is a middle school geography and civics teacher who is trying to make faraway places seem real to his students. Each of his students has an e-mail pen pal in another country and has researched his or her lineage and reported on one of the countries of his or her ancestors.

His classes participate in a Web forum by posting daily weather conditions and events. The name of each participating school has been entered on a sheet of paper and placed into a lottery box. Every day, the class draws a school from the lottery box and then spends time reviewing the information recorded by those students.

The next project is geared toward helping students understand the size of other cities in the world. Mr. Pryor has created an Access database of world populations for the students to analyze. You are assisting Mr. Pryor and his students in this process.

1. Open the **Cities** table of the **ac03Populations.mdb** database

2. Mr. Pryor's students are in Denver, Colorado, so the first task is to find out how many people live there. Use Filter by Form to determine the population of Denver and print the results. Save as a query named **Denver**

3. Now that you know how large Denver is, use separate filters to determine what cities around the world are the same size, larger, and smaller. Save each filter as a query and print each result

4. Use a query with an aggregate function to determine the smallest city in the table. Display only the population. Print the results and save the query as **SmallestPopulation**

5. Now use a query to determine the largest city. Print the results of and save the query as **LargestPopulation**

6. Create a form for entering and maintaining the population data. The form must
   a. Use Columnar layout
   b. Use the Sumi Painting style
   c. Contain **ac03Globe.gif** in the header
   d. In Design View, adjust the size and position of the text boxes as needed
   e. Save the form as **PopulationUpdate**

7. Average the city population in each country to determine which country has the largest cities. Create a report containing the city, country, and population
   a. Group the data by country
   b. Sort by city name and average the population. Display summary rows only
   c. Use **Block** layout and Corporate AutoFormat
   d. Add the Clip Art used in the form
   e. Update the title as shown in Figure 3.44
   f. Save the report as **AvgPopulation**

8. Close the database and Access if your work is complete

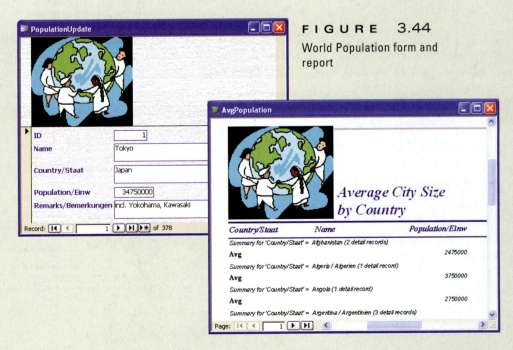

FIGURE 3.44
World Population form and report

running project: tnt web design

Querying TnT Customer Data

The TnT database now consists of two related tables. The tblCustomers table holds the static data about the organization's customers. The CustomerSites table contains the URLs for the sites TnT has built. The CustomerSites table has a Lookup field for the customer name so that you do not have to remember CustomerID values when entering data. Tori is very pleased with the progress that you are making on the TnT database. She has asked for a copy of the database so that she can begin exploring its design and content.

1. Start Access and open the **ac03TnT.mdb** database
2. Use a filter to select non-United States records from tblCustomers. Print the result and save the filter as a query named **OutsideUSA**
3. Create a columnar form that can be used to enter and update customer data. The form should
   a. Include all customer data
   b. Use a columnar format
   c. Use the Sumi Painting style
   d. Save the form as **CustomerUpdate**
   e. Display the logo from the file **ac03TnT.gif** in the Form Header

f. Change the cusID label to read **Customer ID**
g. Remove cus from the remaining labels
h. Print the form with the record for Ross & Homer

4. Create a query that lists the customer name and address (excluding other fields) by country, state, and city. Print the result. Save the query as **CityList**
5. Tori wants a phone list for U.S. customers. Create a phone list report named **PhoneListByState** that
   a. Includes the state, customer name, and phone information only
   b. Groups by state and sorts by customer name
   c. Uses the **Corporate** style
   d. Displays the logo from the file **ac03TnT.gif** in the Report Header
   e. Has spaces in the title and cus removed from the column headings
6. Create mailing labels with the following attributes:
   a. Use Avery C2163 labels
   b. Contain the customer's full name and address with each field on a new line
   c. Use 12-point Garamond font
   d. Change the text color to dark blue
   e. Sort by Postal Code
   f. Print one page of labels
   g. Save the report as **CustomerLabels**
7. Close the database and exit Access if your work is complete

FIGURE 3.45

CustomerUpdate form and CityList query

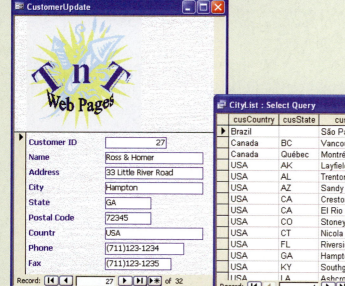

analysis

1. Evaluate Courses at Your School

Create an Access database that could be useful for your school. For example, you could track people who have been contacted as potential students, enrollment, student athletes, alumni, financial donors, student activities, or the like. The database you develop should contain data that can be grouped and used to create subtotals. Document the purpose of your database being sure to include a description of how it can be used. Include a form that can be used to maintain all fields in a table. Create at least one report with grouping, a sum, and an average. Create at least one simple Select Query and at least one query with a calculation. Call the database **ac03MySchool.mdb**.

2. Start a Database for Your Hobby

If you started a database for your hobby in Chapter 2, you can enhance it; otherwise, assume that you are starting a database to store data about your hobby or pastime. Document the type of data that you would need to track and how the database will be used. Name the database **ac03<yourname>Hobby.mdb**. Include a form that can be used to maintain all fields in a table. Create at least one report with grouping, a sum, and an average. Create at least one simple Select Query and at least one query with a calculation.

4 Compound Queries and Database Utilities

did you know?

an *ostrich's eye is bigger than its brain.*

Maine *is the only U.S. state that borders only one other state.*

in *the world of dolls, Midge Hadley was Barbie's best friend in the 1960s.*

the *U.S. Congress passed a law in 1832 requiring all American citizens to spend one day each year fasting and praying.*

Antarctica *is the only continent without any reptiles or snakes.*

to *find out the first product to have a bar code on its package, visit* www.mhhe.com/i-series.

Chapter Objectives

- **Build, run, and save compound queries using In, Like, Between, And, and Or**

- **Understand and use Crosstab Queries—MOS AC03S-1-7**

- **Modify Access table definitions by adding fields, deleting fields, and changing field properties—MOS AC03S-1-3 and MOS AC03S-1-4**

- **Add an input mask to a field—MOS AC03S-1-4**

- **Create Lookup fields—MOS AC03S-1-3**

- **Schedule and execute database backups—MOS AC03S-4-5**

- **Repair damaged databases—MOS AC03S-4-6**

KoryoKicks: Analyzing Data with Crosstab Queries

Missy and Micah have found the Select Queries you and they created very useful. They now know that sales volumes are greater than previously believed and that only a handful of customers have not paid their bills. They were able to calculate the average monthly income and expense for KoryoKicks and to project future income and expenses. KoryoKicks is continuing to grow and the twins are no closer to making a decision about how to handle the volume and money issues. Simple Select Queries are nice (see Figure 4.1), but they don't provide the analytical power needed to understand the purchasing behavior of their customers. It is important to chart the current purchasing behavior of customers to accurately project future purchases.

To understand who buys their products and in what quantities, Missy and Micah need to learn to create queries using multiple conditions. Using multiple conditions, data retrieved can be restricted using several values or a combination of values from multiple fields. For example, they would like to analyze sales from the last quarter and compare them to the previous quarter. That would require selecting records in three-month groups.

Missy and Micah would also like to cross-tabulate KoryoKicks data to see the relationship between two values simultaneously (see Figure 4.2). Crosstab Queries will allow the twins to analyze sales by month and state in one table. Sales data can also be simultaneously evaluated by both date and product.

Databases are critical to the operation of the organization using them. When data are lost, the ability to bill customers, order products, and support the business decision-making process also is lost. An important aspect of using a database is to know how to properly back up and restore tables

FIGURE 4.1

First quarter KoryoKicks sales

OrderID	CstmrID	OrderDate	QuantityOrdered	ProductDescription
41	Calahan	01-Jan-2004	2	Solid Color 1 3/5 inch belt
41	Calahan	01-Jan-2004	5	Bo Case
41	Calahan	01-Jan-2004	10	Chest Protector
41	Calahan	01-Jan-2004	8	Rank Belt 2 1/2 inches
41	Calahan	01-Jan-2004	10	Wushu Kung Fu Dragon Head Kwandao
41	Calahan	01-Jan-2004	28	Simplified Tai Chi
42	Calahan	15-Jan-2004	10	Satin Kick-boxing Shorts
37	Wagoner	15-Jan-2004	1	Knife Techniques
42	Calahan	15-Jan-2004	5	Nothern Shaolin
42	Calahan	15-Jan-2004	5	Training Mitts
42	Calahan	15-Jan-2004	35	Shaolin Long Fist Kung Fu
42	Calahan	15-Jan-2004	10	Chen Style Tai Chi Chuan
37	Wagoner	15-Jan-2004	3	Deluxe Rank 2 inch Belt
37	Wagoner	15-Jan-2004	1	Maple Bo

Record: 1 of 112

FIGURE 4.2

KoryoKicks sales by product and state

ProductByStateCrosstab : Crosstab Query

ProductDescription	Total Of QuantityOrdered	CA	CO	IN	MI	OH
1001 Street Fighting Secrets	5		3		2	
3-sword set with stand	163	15	36	69	37	6
A Woman's QiGong Guide	10					10
Ancient Chinese Weapons	14	2	10		2	
Bag Gloves	17		15		2	
Balisong Butterfly Knive	10				10	
Bamboo Dragon Fighting Fan	5			1	4	
Bamboo Short Staff	16		6		10	
Black oak 3-section staff	33		22	1		10
Black V-neck Elastic Waist Uniform	6				6	
Bo Case	5		5			
Bruce Lee t-shirt	129		35	75	14	5
Chen Style Tai Chi Chuan	11		10	1		
Chest Protector	26		21	5		
Chrome Sais	5		5			
Closed-chin Head Gear	17			15		2

Record: 1 of 74

or entire databases. Tables should be backed up before major update operations such as changing table design. Such backups protect against possible data loss. Scheduled backups should be conducted regularly to protect against data loss caused by unforeseen events such as a hardware failure. Backups reduce the likelihood of lost data and thereby protect the organization's ability to continue doing business.

SESSION 4.1 USING QUERIES TO ANALYZE DATA

Queries are the central tool in the database arsenal providing the ability to perform complex analysis on table data. Besides creating analytical information to support the decision-making process, queries allow appropriate data to be retrieved before creating formal reports. Queries also can be used to calculate totals or select data for forms when a user's view is restricted to a subset of the data. In the previous chapter, simple queries were used to retrieve rows and columns of data based on one condition. Most of the time, you will need to use multiple conditions when retrieving data.

Specifying Complex Query Criteria

Compound queries specify multiple conditions for data retrieval. The conditions can be as simple as using a list of values or as complicated as connecting a series of expressions and controlling their order of evaluation.

Selecting Records with In, Between, and Like

Using the Between, In, and Like conditional operators was briefly introduced in the previous chapter but warrants further exploration. Each of these operators allows a specific group of match values to be stated for a table field. Between provides an upper and lower selection limit. All values between those limits will be selected, including the limits. So a condition of Between 12 And 14 will retrieve records with values of 12, 13, and 14.

The twins want to retrieve sales information for the first quarter of 2004 so that they can compare it to the current quarter. You will create the first quarter query using an existing query.

Selecting Customer table records with Between:

1. Verify that the ac04KoryoKicks.mdb database is open

2. Select the **Queries** object in the Database Window

3. Double-click **Create query in Design View** (this is a faster way to initiate a Design View query)

4. Click the **Queries** tab of the Show Table dialog box

5. Add **CustomerOrdersJoin** to the query design grid and choose **Close** in the Show Table dialog box

6. Add all of the fields to the design grid

tip: *Double-click in the Title bar of CustomerOrdersJoin, click on the selected fields, and then drag them to the field row of the first query grid column*

7. Enter the condition **Between #1/1/2004# And #3/31/2004#** in the Criteria row of the OrderDate field to retrieve first quarter data

tip: *You do not have to enter the #s around the date values. Access will insert them*

8. Add an ascending sort to the OrderDate field

FIGURE 4.3

Selecting first quarter sales data

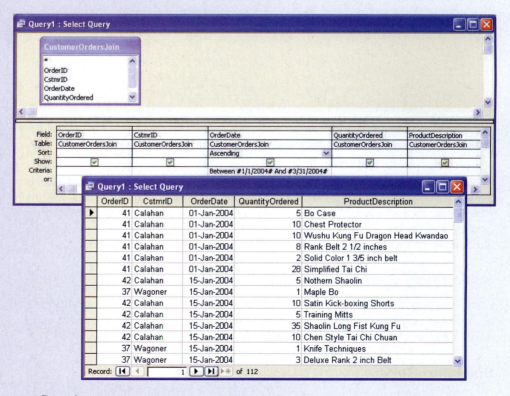

9. Run the query

10. Save the query as **FirstQuarter2004**

As was just demonstrated, an existing query can be used as the data source for other queries. In this case, the original query joined the data from three tables and then a new query was built to select first quarter data from the results of the join query.

The In operator allows a list of match values to be specified. This is effective when the match values are not logically grouped. For example In ("CA","CO","IN") would retrieve records for California, Colorado, and Indiana. The parentheses are a required part of the condition syntax for the In condition. Double quotes are a required delimiter when entering match values for Text data type fields. Suppose the twins need a list of customers that live in Coatesville, Greencastle, and Monroe, Indiana.

Selecting Customer table records with In:

1. Close any open windows except the Database Window in ac04KoryoKicks.mdb

2. Select the **Queries** object in the Database Window

3. Double-click on **Create query in Design View**

4. Add the **Customer** table to the query design and **Close** the Show Table dialog box

5. Put all of the fields except CstmrID and Notes in the design grid

6. Enter the criteria **In ("Coatesville","Greencastle","Monroe")** in the City field

7. Because all of the cities are in Indiana, it is not necessary to display the State field. Click the Show check box for State off

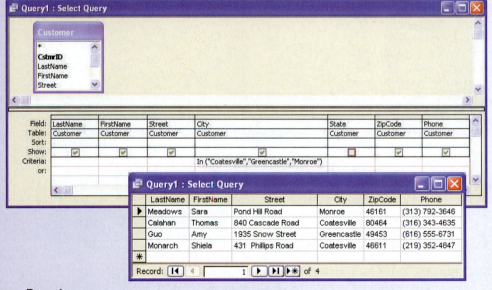

FIGURE 4.4

Customers from Coatesville, Greencastle, and Monroe

8. Run the query

9. Save the query as **INCustomers**

Each field in the QBE grid has a Show check box. When the check box is checked, values for that field will be displayed in the query results. When the check box is unchecked, the field will not display in the query results.

help yourself: *Use the Type a Question combo box to improve your understanding of Like query conditions by typing* **wildcards***. Review the contents of* Like Operator *and* About using wildcard. *Close the Help window when you are finished*

The Like operator allows a pattern to be matched using wildcards. Wildcards are designed to be used with Text fields and can provide haphazard results with other data types. Recall that the wildcards are ? to replace one character, * to replace multiple characters, and # to replace one numeral.

Let's assume that the twins need to talk to a customer, but can't remember the full name or that customer's city. They believe that the city name starts with or contains *grand*. You could use the condition *Like "*grand*"* to retrieve all records with the word "grand" anywhere in the city.

Selecting Customer table records with Like:

1. Verify that the ac04KoryoKicks.mdb database is open

2. Select the **Queries** object from the Database Window

3. Double-click **Create query in Design View** to open the QBE grid and Show Table dialog box

4. Double-click on the **Customer** table in the Show Table dialog box to add it to the design grid

5. Click **Close** in the Show Table dialog box

6. Place **LastName**, **FirstName**, and **City** in the Field row of the QBE grid

FIGURE 4.5

Customer records for cities containing *grand*

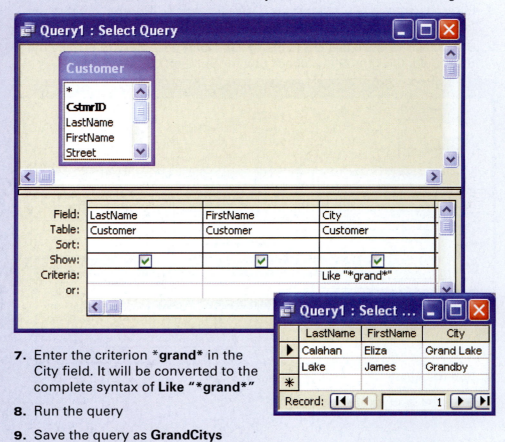

7. Enter the criterion ***grand*** in the City field. It will be converted to the complete syntax of **Like "*grand*"**

8. Run the query

9. Save the query as **GrandCitys**

In addition to selecting values that are In, Between, and Like, users often need to apply multiple selection criteria in a query. For example, to retrieve female employees who make less than $15 per hour would require a criterion for selecting records by gen-

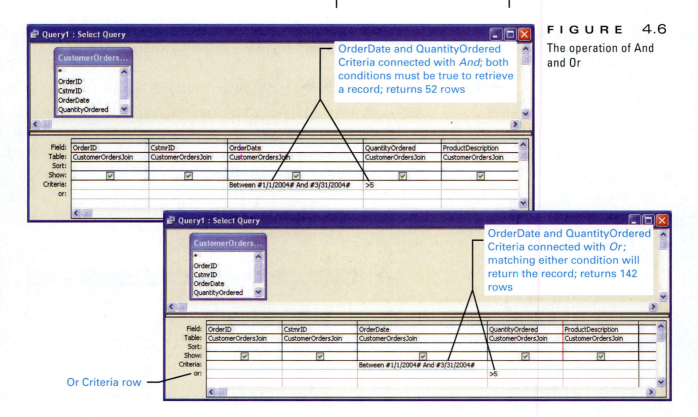

FIGURE 4.6

The operation of And and Or

der and a criterion for selecting records by hourly rate. The next section discusses how to place these conditions in the query design grid.

Using Logical Operators

Logical operators are used to join multiple criteria for selecting records. Conditions can be joined with **And** or **Or**. Use *And* to join two or more conditions when all of the conditions must be true to retrieve the record. Use *Or* to join two or more conditions when any of the conditions can be true to retrieve the record.

When using the QBE grid, conditions placed in the same row are connected with And, while those places in separate rows are connected with Or. Take a look at the conditions demonstrated in Figure 4.6.

Selecting Customer table records with compound criteria:

1. Verify that the ac04KoryoKicks.mdb database is open

2. Select the **Queries** object in the Database Window

3. Double-click **Create query in Design View**

4. Click the **Queries** tab of the Show Table dialog box

5. Add **CustomerOrdersJoin** to the query design grid and choose **Close** in the Show Table dialog box

6. Add all of the fields to the design grid

7. Enter the condition **Between #1/1/2004# And #3/31/2004#** in the OrderDate field's Criteria row to retrieve first quarter data (see Figure 4.6)

ACCESS

8. In the same Criteria row enter **>5** in the QuantityOrdered column (see Figure 4.6)

9. Run the query to view the results and then return to Design View

10. Delete the >5 condition for QuantityOrdered and enter **>5** in the Or row of QuantityOrdered (see Figure 4.6)

11. Run the query (see Figure 4.7)

F I G U R E 4.7

Results of And and Or compound queries

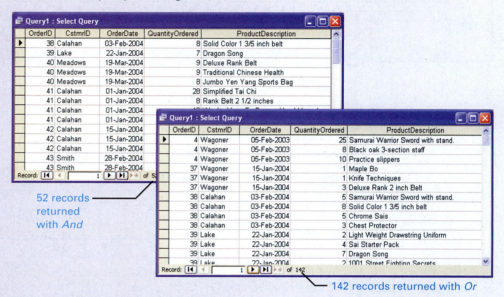

52 records returned with *And*

142 records returned with *Or*

12. Save the query as **HighVolume**

As was just demonstrated, compound conditions connected with And retrieve fewer records because both conditions must be true to return a row. Connecting conditions with Or retrieves more records because only one of the conditions has to be true to return the row. It is important to correctly use And and Or to retrieve valid query results.

Using the Not Operator

The **Not** logical operator negates a condition to select nonmatching values. Not can be placed in front of any condition created with any of the other operators ($=, >, <, >=, <=, <>$). For example, the condition *Not > 10* would retrieve records where the value of that field is less than or equal to 10.

Selecting Customer table records with Not:

1. Verify that the ac04KoryoKicks.mdb database is open

2. Select the **Queries** object from the Database Window

3. Click the **InCustomers** query and then click the **Design View** button to open the design

4. Place **Not** in front of the In condition (see Figure 4.8)

5. Run the query

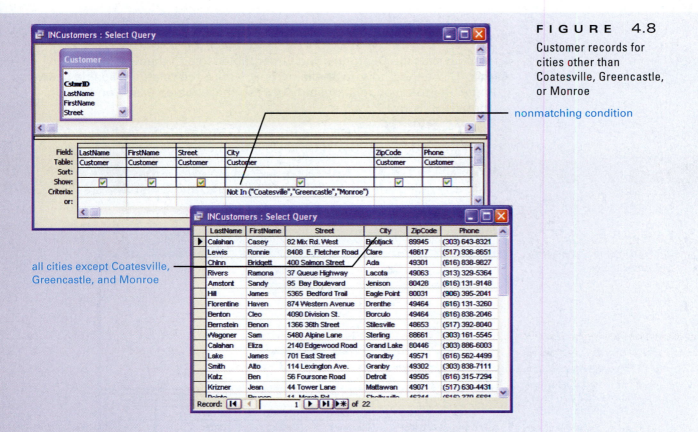

FIGURE 4.8
Customer records for cities other than Coatesville, Greencastle, or Monroe

nonmatching condition

all cities except Coatesville, Greencastle, and Monroe

6. Use the **Save As** option of the **File** menu to save the query as **NotInCustomers** and close the query window

The previous example also demonstrated how to modify an existing query and save the modification with a new name. It is often easier to use this technique than it would be to create a new query from scratch.

Joining Two Tables with a Query

Database users should be able to retrieve any data regardless of where they are stored. Multitable queries merge the data from two or more tables into one query result. The process of retrieving data from two or more tables is referred to as joining. To join tables, they must share a common column of data that can be used to match rows from one table to related rows in the second table. When the relationships between tables have been properly designed and built (covered in Chapter 6), it is just as easy to build a query to retrieve data from multiple tables as it is to build a query based on a single table.

The twins would like to review orders placed by their customers. They believe that most customers have multiple orders, but the twins have nothing to support this view. You will create a list of customers with their orders that can be reviewed to validate or disprove this belief.

Joining the Order and Customer tables in a query:

1. Verify that the **ac04KoryoKicks.mdb** database is open

2. Select the **Queries** object from the Database Window

3. Double-click the **Create Query in Design View**

4. Double-click the **Customer** and **Order** tables to add them to the design grid. Close the Show Table dialog box. Notice the relationship line showing a one-to-many relationship between these tables based on the common field CstmrID

5. Add LastName and FirstName from the Customer table to the query design grid. Add OrderID and OrderDate from the Order table to the query design grid

6. Add ascending sorts to LastName, FirstName, and OrderID

7. Run the query

FIGURE 4.9

Query using the Customer and Order tables

relationship between Customer and Order tables based on CstmrID

62 rows joined where CstmrID in the Customer table = CstmrID in the Order table

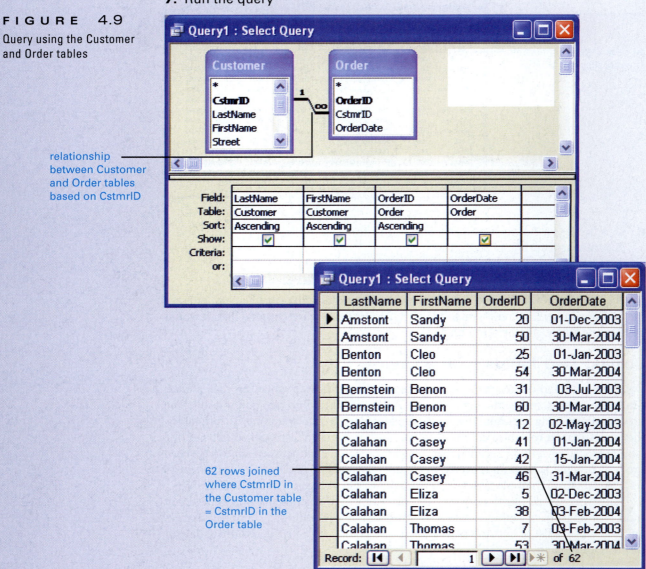

8. Close and save the query as **CustomerOrderList**

Missy and Micah would like a list of their products that are in inventory and the customers who have purchased those products. These data are stored in two tables:

Customer and Product. The relationships have already been built, so these data can be retrieved by including all tables in the relationship in the query. If you do not include all of the tables that make up the relationship, the result will be a Cartesian product where each row of the first table is joined with each row of the second table.

Creating a Cartesian product:

1. Verify that the **ac04KoryoKicks.mdb** database is open

2. Select the **Queries** object from the Database Window

3. Double-click the **Create Query in Design View**

4. Double-click the **Customer** table in the Show Table dialog box

5. Double-click the **Product** table in the Show Table dialog box. Notice that no relationship lines show between the Customer and Product tables

6. Close the Show Table dialog box

7. Double-click LastName and FirstName from the Customer table. Double-click ProductClass and ProductDescription from the Product table

8. Run the query and observe the resulting Cartesian product

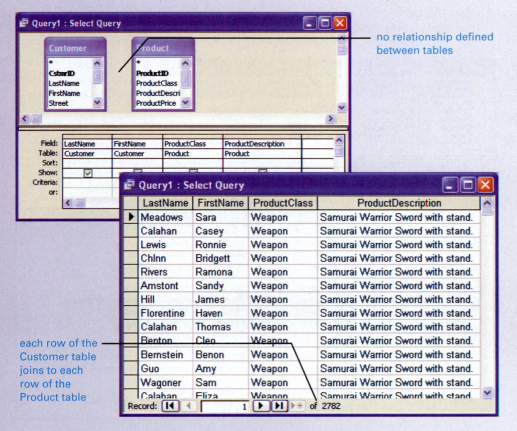

no relationship defined between tables

each row of the Customer table joins to each row of the Product table

FIGURE 4.10

Tables joined without a defined relationship create a Cartesian product

9. Close the query naming it **CartesianProduct**

The query just viewed created a Cartesian product because the relationships between the tables involved were not defined so every row of the first table was joined with every row of the second table. This is not usually the desired result. Remember that Missy and Micah wanted to know what products each customer ordered. The CartesianProduct query does not provide this information. To produce the desired output, you must include all of the tables that make up the relationship, whether or not any fields from those tables will be displayed. You will repair the query by adding the Order and OrderDetail tables that create the relationship between the Customer and Product tables.

Repairing a Cartesian product:

1. Verify that the **ac04KoryoKicks.mdb** database is open

2. Select the **Queries** object from the Database Window and open CartesianProduct in Design View

3. Click **File** and then **Save As**. Name the query **CustomerProducts**

4. Click the **Show Table** button on the toolbar. Add the **Order** and **OrderDetail** tables to the design grid and then close the Show Table dialog box

5. Use the Product table Title bar to drag it to the right of Order and OrderDetails. Observe the relationships

6. Run the query and note the difference from the Cartesian product created in the earlier steps

F I G U R E   4.11

CustomerProducts query

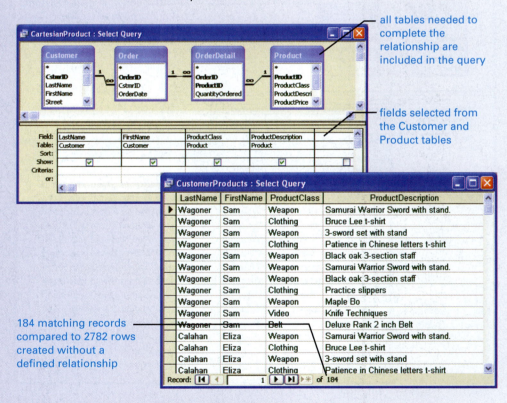

all tables needed to complete the relationship are included in the query

fields selected from the Customer and Product tables

184 matching records compared to 2782 rows created without a defined relationship

7. Close the query, saving your changes

This query will allow the twins to analyze the products that have been purchased by each customer. Any tables from the database can be used to create the desired query output as long as Access has a way to establish a relationship between the tables being used. Be sure to verify relationships and query output before using the results to make business decisions.

Analyzing Data Using Crosstab Queries

Select Queries retrieve specified data and create groups and calculations based on those data. Using this methodology, data can only be grouped vertically to create sums, averages, and other calculations. *Crosstab Queries* are used to calculate and organize data for easier analysis of more complex problems. Crosstab Queries perform calculations such as sum, average, or count and then group them by two types of information—one down the left side of the datasheet and another across the top.

Crosstab Queries can be created using the Crosstab Query Wizard or in Query Design View. Which field will be used as the column heading (across the top of the datasheet) and which field will be used as the row heading (down the left side of the datasheet) must be specified to let Access know how to group the data. The available aggregate functions include Sum, Avg, Count, Min, and Max.

KoryoKicks sells multiple products. Missy and Micah want to know which product sells best in each state. This query will list KoryoKicks products down the left side and states across the top. The Sum function will total each product by state. Since the Crosstab Query Wizard is the easiest way to create a Crosstab Query, you will start there.

---

task reference   Creating a Crosstab Query

- Click the **Queries** object in the Database Window, select **Create query by using wizard**, and then click **New**
- Select **Crosstab Query Wizard** from the New Query dialog box and then click **OK**
- Follow the Wizard's instructions to choose the data source, row heading, column heading, and aggregate functions for the query
- Name the query and then view the results

Analyzing sales with a Crosstab Query:

1. Verify that the ac04KoryoKicks.mdb database is open
2. Select the **Queries** object from the Database Window
3. Double-click the **CustomerStateJoin** query and review the result. Notice that many of the products have multiple rows for each state. The Crosstab Query will sum these into one value for each product and state
4. Close the CustomerStateJoin window
5. Click **New** to open the New Query dialog box
6. In the New Query dialog box, click **Crosstab Query Wizard** and select **OK**
7. Click the **Queries** option button and then select the **CustomerStateJoin** query and click **Next** (see Figure 4.12)
8. Select **ProductDescription** as the row heading and click **Next**
9. Select **State** as the column heading and then click **Next**

ACCESS

F I G U R E   4.12
Selecting a query for the
crosstab data source

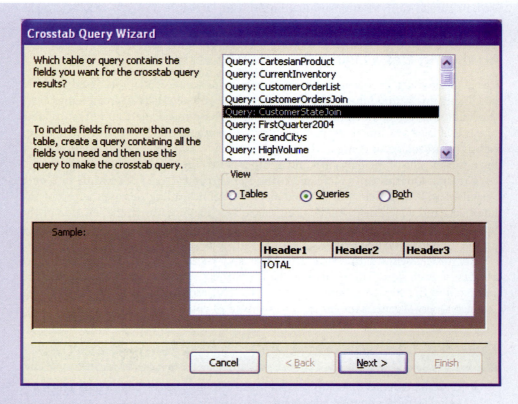

10. Select **QuantityOrdered** as the field and **Sum** as the function and then click **Next**

11. Name the query **ProductByStateCrosstab** and click **Finish**

F I G U R E   4.13
Crosstab results

ProductDescription	Total Of QuantityOrdered	CA	CO	IN	MI	OH
▶ 1001 Street Fighting Secrets	5		3		2	
3-sword set with stand	163	15	36	69	37	6
A Woman's QiGong Guide	10					10
Ancient Chinese Weapons	14	2	10		2	
Bag Gloves	17		15		2	
Balisong Butterfly Knive	10				10	
Bamboo Dragon Fighting Fan	5			1	4	
Bamboo Short Staff	16		6		10	
Black oak 3-section staff	33		22	1		10
Black V-neck Elastic Waist Uniform	6				6	
Bo Case	5		5			
Bruce Lee t-shirt	129		35	75	14	5
Chen Style Tai Chi Chuan	11		10	1		
Chest Protector	26		21		5	

ProductByStateCrosstab : Crosstab Query

Record: 1 of 74

grand total orders for Bruce Lee t-shirt ——

total Colorado orders for Bruce Lee t-shirt ——

12. Change to Design View (see Figure 4.14) to see the QBE grid for this query

13. Close the query

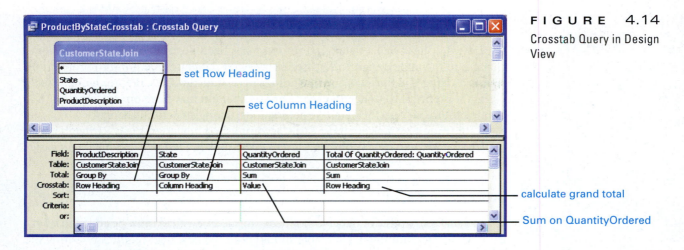

FIGURE 4.14
Crosstab Query in Design View

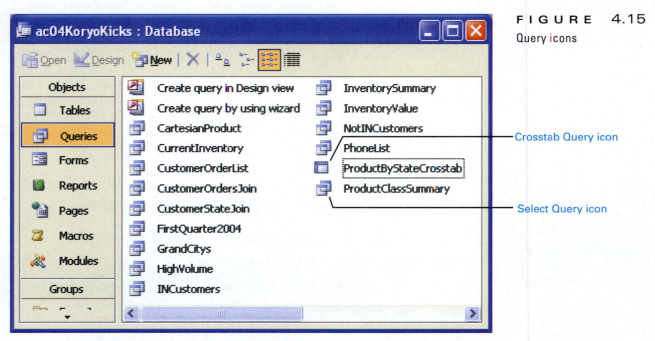

FIGURE 4.15
Query icons

This query will allow the twins to analyze the sales of each of their products by state. Notice that Access uses different icons for each type of query in the Database Window. Figure 4.15 shows Select and Crosstab Query icons.

As you add other types of queries to the database, more icons will display. The icons are representative of the query operation being performed.

making the grade

1. Describe the use of the Like operator.

2. What condition would return all Game (GME) software from tblSoftware?

3. What are the benefits of using Crosstab Queries?

4. How many conditions can be included in the Between operator?

5. How do you avoid creating a Cartesian product when querying two or more tables?

SESSION 4.2 MODIFYING TABLE DEFINITIONS

Regardless of how well a database prototype has been designed, it is likely that some changes to the table design will be necessary. After databases are put into production, required changes in business and technology necessitate updates. Before changing table design, it is critical to understand the impacts changes may have on existing data. It is always best to back up the database before undertaking structural changes.

Table modifications are most easily accomplished in Design View. Remember that the Undo and Redo operations store up to 20 actions in Design View, making it easier to correct errors.

Adding a Field

When a necessary piece of data has not been stored, a new field must be added to an existing table. Determining which table should hold the new field requires revisiting the design process. Once it is determined which table will hold the field, table Datasheet View can be used to add the new column using steps that are similar to those used when building a new table.

After reviewing and using the prototype of the KoryoKicks database, Missy and Micah decide that they would like to have a field in the Customer table that will hold notes. This field could be used to store information about contacts with customers who have not received their merchandise or who have not paid their bill. It could also hold notes about comments concerning students' rank, competitions, and preferences. Although there are several ways to provide this ability, you decide to try adding a Memo field to the Customer table.

Adding a Memo field to the Customer table:

1. If it is not already open, open the ac04KoryoKicks.mdb database

2. Activate the **Customer** table in Design View

3. Although the order of fields in a table is not critical, there is often logic in their placement. The twins would like the notes field at the end of the record, so click in the empty row after Phone and enter the data for a field named **Notes** with a **Memo** data type

4. No other fields are required for the table to be functional, but we will add a dummy field to be deleted in the next series of steps

5. Click on the **Notes** field that you just added, then select the **Rows** option of the **Insert** menu to add a new field between Phone and Notes

6. Type **Dummy** as the Field Name and leave the default Text data type

7. Click the **Datasheet View** 🔲 ▾ button on the Access toolbar to view the results (see Figure 4.16). You will be prompted to save your changes. Answer **Yes**

---

anotherway

. . . to Select the Data Type of a Field

When working with table designs, it can be time consuming to move from typing to selecting with the mouse. Access allows you to keep your hands on the keyboard. For example, when entering a new table field, type the Field Name and then press Tab to move to the data type. Type the first character of the data type (m for memo, n for number, and so on). Access will complete the entry and you can Tab to the next field

---

anotherword   **. . . on Adding Fields to Table Design**

When it makes sense to add a new table field between existing table fields, a new row is added to the design grid. To insert a row, select the row for the new field and select **Rows** from the Access **Insert** menu. Right-clicking the row to activate the shortcut menu also will provide an Insert Rows option

FIGURE 4.16

Notes and Dummy fields added to Customer table

		CstmrID	LastName	FirstName	Street	City	State	ZipCode	Phone	Dummy	Notes
▶	+	01	Wagoner	Sam	5480 Alpine Lane	Sterling	CO	88661	(303) 161-5545		
	+	02	Calahan	Eliza	2140 Edgewood Road	Grand Lake	CO	80446	(303) 886-6003		
	+	03	Lake	James	701 East Street	Grandby	MI	49571	(616) 562-4499		
	+	04	Meadows	Sara	Pond Hill Road	Monroe	IN	46161	(313) 792-3646		
	+	07	Calahan	Casey	82 Mix Rd. West	Bootjack	CO	89945	(303) 643-8321		
	+	21	Smith	Alto	114 Lexington Ave.	Granby	CO	49302	(303) 838-7111		
	+	22	Lewis	Ronnie	8408 E. Fletcher Road	Clare	MI	48617	(517) 936-8651		
	+	23	Chinn	Bridgett	400 Salmon Street	Ada	MI	49301	(616) 838-9827		
	+	25	Katz	Ben	56 Foursone Road	Detroit	MI	49505	(616) 315-7294		
	+	27	Gray	Monica	3915 Hawthorne Lane	Richmond	OH	43603	(419) 332-3681		
	+	28	Rivers	Ramona	37 Queue Highway	Lacota	MI	49063	(313) 329-5364		
	+	29	Amstont	Sandy	95 Bay Boulevard	Jenison	CO	80428	(616) 131-9148		
	+	31	Hill	James	5365 Bedford Trail	Eagle Point	CO	80031	(906) 395-2041		
	+	33	Florentine	Haven	874 Western Avenue	Drenthe	CA	49464	(616) 131-3260		
	+	35	Calahan	Thomas	840 Cascade Road	Coatesville	IN	80464	(316) 343-4635		
	+	36	Benton	Cleo	4090 Division St.	Borculo	OH	49464	(616) 838-2046		
	+	43	Pointe	Bryson	11 Marsh Rd	Shelbyville	IN	46344	(616) 379-5681		

Record: 1 of 26

It is essential to make design changes like adding a field as early in the life of a table as possible. When an empty field is added, it can be overwhelming to gather and enter the new data for the existing records.

Deleting a Field

Deleting a field from a table is as simple as deleting a record from a table, but the repercussions are much more involved. Deleting a field in a database that already contains data deletes all of the values held in the field. Delete operations can be undone as long as Design View is active but become permanent after changing views.

Deleting a field from the Customer table:

1. If it is not already open, open the ac04KoryoKicks.mdb database
2. Activate the **Customer** table in Design View
3. Select the **Dummy** field using the record selector
4. Press the **Delete** key on your keyboard and answer **Yes** to the prompt
5. Use the **Undo** button to undo the delete
6. Use the **Redo** button to delete the Dummy field again
7. Change to Datasheet View to review the results. Save the table design changes when prompted

The delete operation on the Dummy field is permanent because you changed views. As a precaution against destroying valuable data, it is strongly recommended that you back up tables in production databases before deleting fields from the table design.

Moving a Field

The order of fields in a table is not important to its overall functionality, so they can move without impacting data functionality. The field order set by the table definition is the default column order that displays when viewing data. Typically, the leftmost field(s) represents the table's primary key and other fields are in order by how they are used.

ACCESS

Moving a field in the Customer table:

1. If it is not already open, open the ac04KoryoKicks.mdb database

2. Activate the **Customer** table in Design View

3. Select the **Notes** field by clicking its record indicator

4. Click and drag to move the Notes field between CustomerID and LastName

tip: *During the drag process, a line across the record indicator and data grid represents where the field will be dropped. If you missed on the first drag attempt, repeat steps 3 and 4 until Notes is positioned properly*

5. Change to **Datasheet View** to review the results. Save the table design changes when prompted

6. Change back to **Design View** and restore Notes to its original position of the last field in the table

7. Close the Customer table, saving your changes

All database objects allow you to control the order of the fields displayed, thereby overriding the field order of the table design.

Changing Field Attributes

Of all the table design updates, changing field properties is the most likely to destroy needed data and/or invalidate other database objects. Changing the Field Name can produce invalid results in objects that refer to fields by name, including Queries, Forms, Reports, and Modules. Making a field smaller will truncate existing data if they exceed the new size. Altering the data type causes Access to perform a conversion from the original type to the new type that can result in loss of data. A message will display when Access detects conversion errors so the user can choose to cancel or continue the process. Access does not detect all conversion errors. Making fields larger or changing other field attributes has little impact on the validity of the database.

help yourself: *Use the Type a Question combo box to improve your understanding of how to update a field's data type by typing* **change field type**. *Review the contents of About changing a field's data type. Close the Help window when you are finished*

Changing field properties in the Product table:

1. If it is not already open, open the ac04KoryoKicks.mdb database

2. Activate the **Product** table in Design View

3. Select the **ProductDescription** field. When entering the Products data, the twins discovered that the ProductDescription field was not long enough for a full product description. They would like it expanded to 50 characters

4. Change the Field Size from 40 to **50**

5. Click the **Save** button on the Access toolbar to save your work

After making changes to table field attributes that might impact the validity of data held in the tables, it is recommended that the table be thoroughly tested and its data validated before placing it in production.

Building Lookup Fields

A *Lookup field* is a tool to ease data entry. Rather than requiring users to remember important values that identify customers, orders, or vendors, a Lookup field displays the list of possible values. Missy and Micah are having difficulty entering product vendors because they don't remember the VendorCode. They have asked for a Lookup field that will access valid VendorCodes in the Vendor table and reduce errors. The Lookup field will allow them to select from a list of vendors rather than type a VendorCode.

---

task reference   **Creating a Lookup Field**

- Remove any existing table relationships based on the Lookup fields. The most likely relationship is one-to-many where the child (many sides of the relationship) table will look up the key value of the parent table (one side of the relationship)

- Open the child table and change the Data Type of the foreign key field to Lookup Wizard

- Follow the Lookup Wizard instructions

Setting a Lookup field for vendors in the Product table:

1. If it is not already open, open the **ac04KoryoKicks.mdb** database

2. Activate the **Product** table in Design View

tip: *Lookup fields must be built between tables that do not already have a defined relationship. There is no defined relationship between the Product and Vendor tables*

3. Select the Data Type of VendorCode and change it to **Lookup Wizard**

4. The Lookup Wizard will prompt you through the rest of the process (see Figure 4.17). In the first Lookup Wizard screen, select **I want the lookup column to look up the values in a table or query** and then click **Next**

5. In the second Wizard screen choose the **Vendor** table as the source of your Lookup data and click **Next**

6. In the third Wizard screen select the **VendorCode** and **Name** fields using the field selector button (>) as shown in Figure 4.18. VendorCode must be selected because it is the shared column between the tables identifying the foreign key. Name is the identifying field that the twins can use to lookup the VendorCode. Click **Next**

7. The next Wizard screen allows you to sort by up to three fields. Sort by **Name** and click **Next**

8. In the next Wizard screen, verify that **Hide key column** is checked so that VendorCode does not display. Double-click on the right border of the Name field selector and adjust the column width to match the width of the data and click **Next**

FIGURE 4.17
Lookup Wizard opening
screen

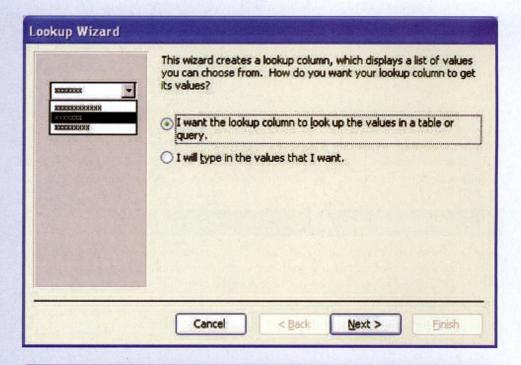

FIGURE 4.18
The third Lookup Wizard
screen

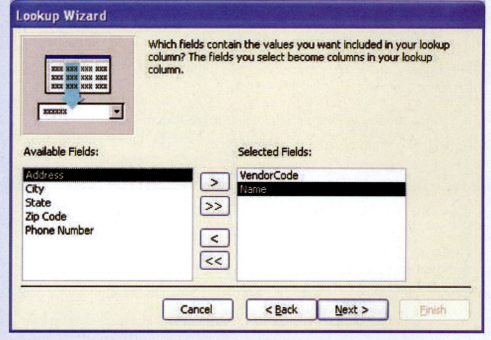

9. The final Wizard screen asks you to name the Lookup column. The default, VendorCode, is fine, so just click **Finish.** You will be prompted to save the table changes; choose **Yes**

10. Change to Datasheet View. The VendorCode field will now display the vendor's name, but store VendorCode (see Figure 4.19). When you enter a new record, a list of valid vendor names will be presented

11. Change the Vendor for product 9 to **Topview Martial Arts Supplies** using the Lookup field

12. Close the Product table

FIGURE 4.19

The Product table with VendorCode Lookup field

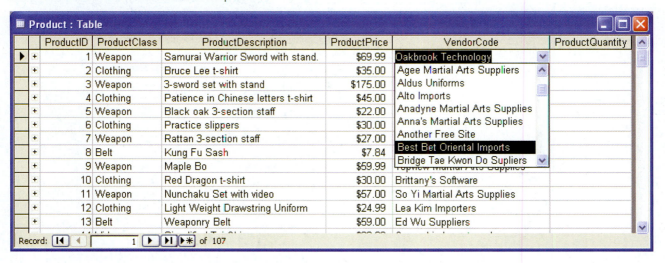

With the Lookup field set, each new product added to the Product table will automatically list the valid vendors from the Vendor table. You can also create Lookup lists that contain a fixed set of values. Lookup lists should only be used when the values are limited and don't change. For example, a Lookup list of salutations (Mr., Mrs., Ms.) would be appropriate.

Creating Input Masks

Field templates or *input masks* improve data entry for Text, Date, Number, and Currency field types. The input mask provides a pattern of input for the user to follow. For example, a 10-character Text field to store phone numbers would allow the user to enter any character from the keyboard and would not force the user to enter all 10 characters. Applying an Input Mask property would present the user with a template like (_____)_____-_____ and require that all 10 digits of the phone number be entered.

A string of characters is entered into the Input Mask property to tell Access what to display to the user as a template and what to accept as valid input. The syntax used to enter the mask is outlined in Figure 4.20. Literal values in the string, like the ( ) in the phone number example, are entered where you want them to appear. To use one of the mask characters like the # sign, precede it with a backslash (\#).

---

task reference   Creating an Input Mask

- Open a table in Design View

- Select the field for which you want to define an input mask

- From the General tab select the **Input Mask** property and either

- Click the **Build** button and follow the Input Mask Wizard instructions (Text and Date fields only)

  or

- Type the input mask definition (Numeric and Currency masks must be entered manually)

FIGURE 4.20

Input mask definition
characters

Character	Description
0	Required digit (0–9); no plus (+) or minus (−) sign
9	Optional digit; no plus (+) or minus (−) sign
#	Optional digit; plus (+) or minus (−) sign allowed
L	Required letter (A–Z)
?	Optional letter (A–Z)
A	Required letter or digit
a	Optional letter or digit
&	Required character or space
C	Optional character or space
.,:;-/	Placeholders and separators
<	Causes all characters that follow to be converted to lowercase
>	Causes all characters that follow to be converted to uppercase
!	Causes input mask to display from right to left
\	Used to display any of the characters in this table as a literal
Password	Creates a password entry text box with all entries displayed as *

Setting an input mask for the OrderDate field:

1. If it is not already open, open the ac04KoryoKicks.mdb database

2. Open the **Order** table in Design View

3. Click in the **OrderDate** field

4. In the General tab click the **Input Mask** text box and evaluate the existing input mask. Click the ellipsis to initiate the Input Mask Wizard (see Figure 4.21)

5. Select the **Medium Date** format and click **Next**

6. Review the input mask created and the placeholder characters. Without updating them, click **Next,** and then click **Finish**

7. Switch to Datasheet View, saving your changes (see Figure 4.22)

8. Enter a new record for Ronnie Lewis using today's date (i.e., 28-May-04). Notice that the template displayed by the input mask is replaced by the Format display when entry is complete

9. Try entering a day of 41 in Sheila Monarch's record. You will receive an error

10. Close the Order table

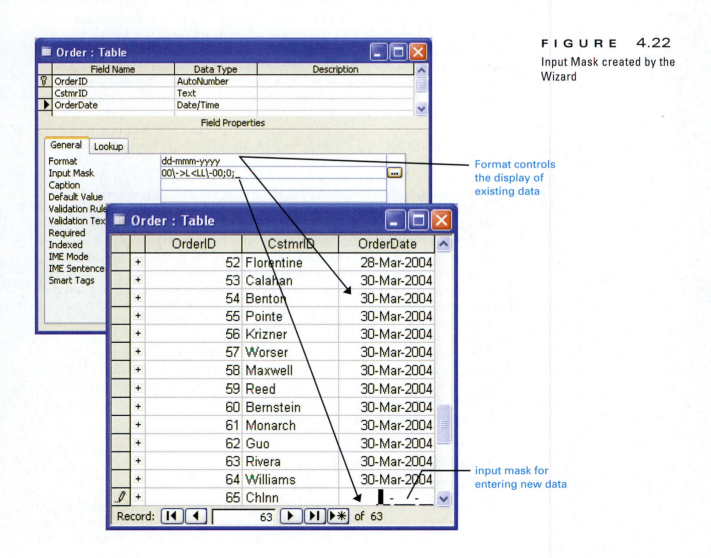

FIGURE 4.21
Input Mask Wizard

FIGURE 4.22
Input Mask created by the Wizard

Format controls the display of existing data

input mask for entering new data

---

*another*word   . . . on Input Masks and Formats

At first glance, input masks and formats are similar field properties, but really serve different purposes. A Format property controls how the data display to the user, but does not control how they are entered or stored. To control how data are entered, use an input mask. An input mask ensures that the data match the format and values you define. When both properties are defined for a field, Microsoft Access uses the input mask when you are adding or editing data and the format when data are displayed. It is important that the results of these settings don't conflict

---

The Input Mask Wizard supplies a list of standard input masks such as the Medium Date mask demonstrated in the steps. These masks provide a template for data entry and perform simple data validation tasks like testing for the entry of a valid month. When these masks are not sufficient, a custom mask is built using the definition characters outlined in Figure 4.20.

Compacting and Repairing a Database

As an Access database is used, it becomes larger. Each data item and database object added increases the file size. Deleting data records and database objects does not release the space that was occupied by that object.

Access combines the processes of compacting and repairing a database into a single operation. **Compacting** is the process of releasing unused space from a database. Access compacts the database by reorganizing all database objects so that they take the least amount of space possible. The process is similar to defragmenting your hard drive. Besides reducing the size of the database, compacting improves database performance because well-organized data can be read and written faster. This process is also referred to as *optimizing* a database.

Compacting an older version of a database in Access 2003 does not convert the database to the new file format. There is a separate utility for converting database files to other versions.

AutoNumber fields are not adjusted for deleted records during the compact process, unless the deletions occurred at the end of the table (the last AutoNumbers generated). So deletion of any record that is not the last table record does not impact AutoNumbers. Such deleted numbers will not be generated again. When deletions occur at the end of the table, the AutoNumber value is reset so that the next generated number will be one greater than the AutoNumber value of the last undeleted record.

When Access is able to detect a problem with a database, a prompt to *repair* the damage is issued. Normally, Access will detect file corruptions when trying to load a database. Since Access cannot detect all file corruptions, it is important to compact and repair databases regularly. In addition, if a file begins to behave unpredictably, compact and repair it manually.

Access can repair most of the errors introduced during normal operation, but cannot repair certain user errors. For example, Access can repair a table index that has become corrupted by deleted records, but Access cannot repair queries or forms that refer to a table or query that has been deleted by the user.

In general, Access can repair corruption in

- A table
- The structure of a database or table
- A form, report, or module

When Access shuts down unexpectedly, significant problems can be introduced to the database if maintenance operations were under way. For example, if you were in the process of changing a record but Access was unable to complete the process, the table or tables involved become corrupted. To remedy this situation, when Access restarts, it creates a copy of the file that was open when the shutdown occurred. The copy is named filename_Backup.mdb, where filename is the name of the database file that was open during the crash. Access then attempts to compact and repair the original file.

---

task reference   **Compact and Repair the Open Database**

- If the open database begins to behave erratically, on the **Tools** menu, point to **Database Utilities**, and then click **Compact and Repair Database**

Compacting and repairing the KoryoKicks database:

1. Verify that the ac04KoryoKicks.mdb database is open

2. On the **Tools** menu, point to **Database Utilities**, and then click **Compact and Repair Database**

FIGURE 4.23
Manually compact and repair the open database

3. If the process completed successfully, no messages will display. If the process was unsuccessful, a message will display and you will need to restore from your most recent database backup

4. Close ac04KoryoKicks.mdb

Compact and repair can also be used on a database that is not open. This method has the advantage of allowing the compacted database to be stored in another file, maintaining both the original and the compacted file.

---

task reference   Compact and Repair an Unopened Database

- Access must be running with no open database
- On the **Tools** menu, point to **Database Utilities**, and then click **Compact and Repair Database**
- In the **Database to Compact From** dialog box, specify the Access file you want to compact, and then click **Compact**
- In the **Compact Database Into** dialog box, specify a name, drive, and folder for the compacted Access file
- Click **Save**

Compacting and repairing the unopened KoryoKicks database:

1. Verify that Access is running with no open databases. If the ac04KoryoKicks.mdb or another database is still open, click the Close button on the Title bar of the Database Window to close it

2. On the **Tools** menu, point to **Database Utilities**, and then click **Compact and Repair Database** (see Figure 4.24)

3. In the **Database to Compact From** dialog box, click on **ac04KoryoKicks.mdb**, and then click **Compact**

4. In the **Compact Database Into** dialog box, specify a drive and folder for the compacted Access file. Name the file **ac04KoryoKicksCompacted.mdb**

tip: *If you use the same name, drive, and folder, and the Access database is compacted successfully, Microsoft Access replaces the original file with the compacted version*

5. If the process completed successfully, no messages will display. If the process was unsuccessful, a message will display and you will need to restore from your most recent database backup

6. Continue with your other database tasks

Compacting into another file is one way to create copies of a database that can be used to restore a damaged database after maintenance. The most common use is to create a current snapshot of the database just before performing tasks that could result in invalid data. For example, a query to adjust the pay rate of all employees could destroy the entire contents of the table if it contained an error. Creating a snapshot just before running the query will allow you to return to the prequery condition without much effort.

You also can create backups of individual database objects such as a table, query, or form by creating a blank database and then importing the backup objects from the original database. If only one table of the database could be damaged by the planned maintenance, this method would allow only that table to be backed up and restored. Restoring the damaged table is as simple as importing the backup copy.

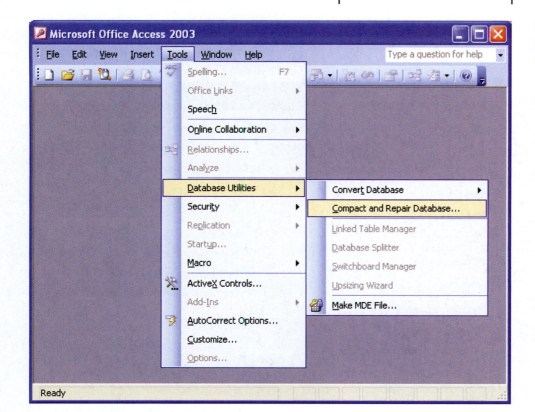

Compacting a Database Automatically

Since corrupted databases can lead to loss of data, queries, forms, and reports, it is important to compact and repair Access files regularly. Several generations of backup also should be maintained so that an unrepairable database can be restored to an earlier version. The most common user errors that cause database corruption are turning off the computer without closing Access or removing the disk (usually the A: or other removable disk) that Access is using before closing Access. Obviously avoiding these mistakes reduces the likelihood of database corruption.

Access automatically checks a file when it is being opened and will repair it if needed. You will not be prompted to compact the database if it is not performing optimally. Access also can be set to compact and repair the open Access file each time it is closed.

---

task reference — Setting Automatic Compact and Repair

- Open the Access database that you want to compact automatically
- On the **Tools** menu, click **Options**
- Click the **General** tab
- Select the **Compact on Close** check box

Setting the Automatic Compact and Repair option for KoryoKicks:

1. Open the ac04KoryoKicks.mdb database so that its Compact on Close property can be set

2. On the **Tools** menu, click **Options**

3. Click the **General** tab

FIGURE 4.25

Automatically compact
and repair databases

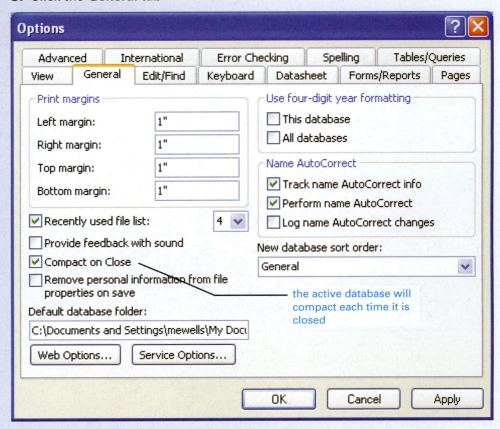

4. Click the **Compact on Close** option and click **OK**

5. ac04KoryoKicks.mdb will now compact and repair each time it is closed

tip: *You can stop the compact and repair process by pressing Ctrl+Break or Esc*

It is important to note that ***Compact on Close*** is a property of the database, not a property of Access. As such it must be set for each database for which you want to automate this process.

Automatically Repairing Office Programs

The same problems that can cause databases to corrupt also can damage Microsoft Office programs. All Office products later than 2000 offer a ***Detect and Repair*** facility that will notify the user when this happens and reinstall the affected software.

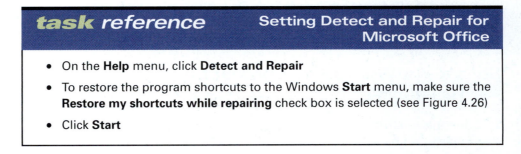

task reference   Setting Detect and Repair for
                               Microsoft Office

- On the **Help** menu, click **Detect and Repair**
- To restore the program shortcuts to the Windows **Start** menu, make sure the **Restore my shortcuts while repairing** check box is selected (see Figure 4.26)
- Click **Start**

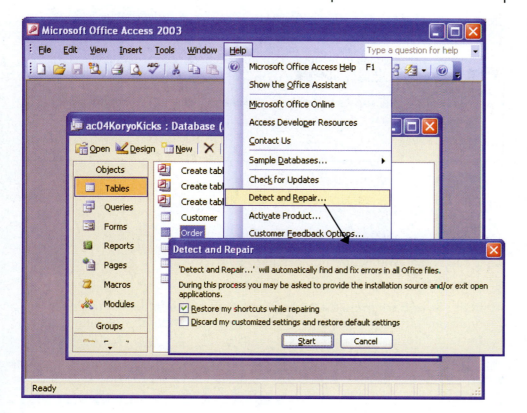

Microsoft Office Detect
and Repair

This procedure detects and repairs problems such as missing files and registry set-tings associated with all installed Microsoft Office programs. It will not repair personal files such as spreadsheets or documents. If the Detect and Repair command does not fix the problem, you might need to reinstall Microsoft Office.

Backing Up and Restoring a Database

Database backups are critical in organizations that rely on data for their operation. Besides creating backups before performing tasks that could destroy data, it is impor-tant to have regularly scheduled backups to protect against other types of loss.

Remember that data are valuable and should be protected against unforeseen events. The volume of updates to data determines how often database backups are needed. Any changes made to the database since the last backup will need to be reap-plied to make it current. The question you need to ask yourself is "How much mainte-nance am I willing to repeat?" Weekly backups are the most common, but daily backups are not at all unusual for critical data with a high maintenance volume.

It is important to note that documentation also must be maintained for backups to be effective. You must know what updates have been made to your database since the last backup so that these can be reapplied.

Catastrophes such as floods, fires, and other acts of nature are not frequent but also should be considered when creating a backup plan. The simplest way to protect against such devastating problems is to store backups at an offsite location. This can be as sim-ple as taking a copy of the backup home or sending it to another company site.

Backups of individual database objects can be accomplished using Copy and Paste to create a duplicate object in the database. Manual backups of the entire open database can be completed using the Back Up Database option of the File menu.

task reference   Database Backup with Access

- Open the database to be backed up. All database objects should be closed
- From the **File** menu select **Back Up Database**
- In the Save Backup As dialog box, indicate the drive, folder, and filename for the backup
- Click **Save**

Using Access to back up KoryoKicks:

1. Verify that ac04KoryoKicks.mdb is open

2. Close and save any open objects

3. On the **File** menu, click **Back Up Database**

4. In the Save Backup As dialog box, navigate to the folder for this chapter and review the default backup name (a combination of the filename and backup date)

FIGURE 4.27

Microsoft Access Save
Backup As dialog box

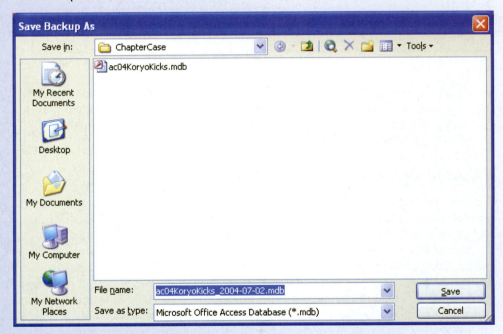

5. Click **Save**

To restore individual database objects from an Access backup, import them into the active database using the File menu. To restore the entire database, use Windows Explorer to delete the active database and then copy the backup to the active folder and rename it.

The demonstrated backup method requires the user to control the backup schedule, name, and process. For critical databases, it is advisable to use software tools such as Microsoft Windows XP Professional Backup and Recovery Tools. Such tools are designed to complete backups of multiple files on a scheduled basis, are optimized for restoring all or part of a particular backup, and can back up to multiple disks, CDs, and/or networked drives.

Converting Databases

Access cannot update database designs created in earlier versions of the product. When a database that was created in an earlier version of Access is opened, a notice that the database must be converted before making changes is issued (see Figure 4.28). The Enable the database option will open the database without converting it. Enabled databases allow users to view and change data and run existing forms, queries, and reports but not change the design of database objects. Since the database format has not been converted, the database will still function in the earlier version of Access.

If the database will be used only in the current version of Access, better database performance is achieved by converting it. If, however, there is still a need to use the database in an older version of Access, enable it in the current version by opening it without converting it. In this case, modifications to the design of database objects must be made in the original Access version. Once the database is open, it can still be converted using the Tools menu, as demonstrated in Figure 4.29.

Sometimes different parts of the same organization are using different Access versions, resulting in a need for multiple versions of the same database. Files created in the current version of Access can be converted to the file format of previous Access versions back to Access 97. Bear in mind that converting to a previous Access version will cause the database to lose all of the functionality that is specific to newer versions of Access.

F I G U R E   4.28

Conversion notification

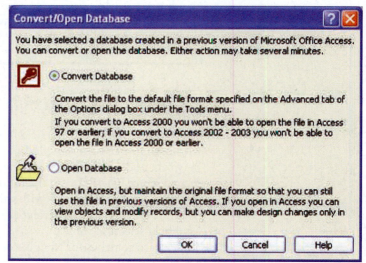

F I G U R E   4.29

Converting an open database to an older or newer Access version

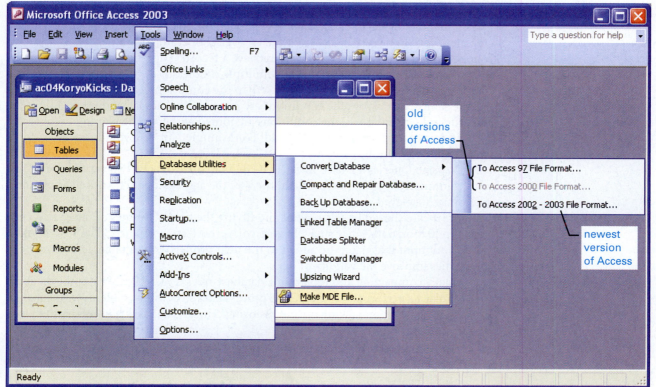

Knowing how and when to convert databases means that you can work on the same database with different versions of Access, making your work more portable.

making *the grade*

1. Why should you back up a database?

2. How do you decide when to convert a database to a newer version of Access?

3. What happens when you delete a field from a table structure?

4. What is the purpose of Detect and Repair?

5. What are some possible conversion issues when changing a field from single to integer?

SESSION 4.3 SUMMARY

Effective analysis of the data held in a relational database often requires creating queries with complex conditions. Multiple criteria can be applied to one field using the In, Between, and Like conditional operators. The In operator is used to submit a list of match values. The Between operator supplies an upper and lower limit for values that will be retrieved. All records with values between the upper and lower limit—including the limit values—will be retrieved. The Like operator is used to submit a pattern match for a field selection value.

Pattern matches for the Like operator make use of wildcards to state the criteria. The * wildcard is used to represent any number of characters, the ? wildcard is used to represent a single character, and the # wildcard is used to represent a single numeral. The Like operator is designed to work with Text fields and provides haphazard results with other field types.

The And and Or operators provide another way to enter compound conditions. When the And logical operator combines two conditions, both conditions must be true for the record to be retrieved. When the Or logical operator combines two conditions, one or both conditions can be true to retrieve a record. The words And and Or can be entered into Criteria for a field to state multiple conditions for that field or they can be used to join criteria for multiple fields. When the conditions are in different fields and on the same Criteria row, the conditions are joined with And. When the conditions are on different Criteria rows, the conditions are joined with Or. The Not logical operator is used to negate a condition for a field. For example Not =6 would retrieve records that do not contain the value 6.

Crosstab Queries are used to calculate and organize data by two variables. The row and column headings are defined and then set the aggregate function used to calculate the values displayed.

Great care should be taken when modifying the field attributes of tables that contain production data, since such changes could result in permanent data loss. Lookup fields and input masks can be added to the field properties of a table definition. Both properties improve the validity of data.

Finally compacting and repairing a database frees unused space from the database to optimize its performance. The repair process fixes structural problems with database objects. A strategy for backing up and restoring critical databases is necessary to reduce the risk of data loss.

Visit www.mhhe.com/i-series/ to explore related topics.

MICROSOFT OFFICE SPECIALIST OBJECTIVES SUMMARY

- Creating Lookup fields—MOS AC03S-1-3
- Changing field types—MOS AC03S-1-3
- Changing field properties to display input masks—MOS AC03S-1-4
- Modifying field properties for tables in Table Design View—MOS AC03S-1-4
- Creating Crosstab Queries—MOS AC03S-1-7
- Back up a database—MOS AC03S-4-5
- Using Compact and Repair—MOS AC03S-4-6

making the grade answers

SESSION 4.1

1. The Like operator allows you to use wildcards to set a pattern that retrieved data must match. The question mark (?) wildcard replaces one character. The asterisk (∗) wildcard replaces a group of characters. The pound sign (#) replaces one numeral. The Like operator is designed to work on Text fields.

2. Placing GME in the Criteria row of the Category field would produce the desired results.

3. Crosstab Queries allow you to perform aggregate functions using two controlling fields represented by the row and column header.

4. The Between operator has two arguments: an upper and lower limit. These arguments specify a range of values to be retrieved that can be any size.

5. A Cartesian product results when the relationship between tables is not defined in the query. To avoid this situation, place all tables involved in the relationship in the query, whether or not their fields will be included in the output.

SESSION 4.2

1. Databases need to be backed up to protect against data loss. Data loss can occur due to user errors like shutting off the computer without properly exiting Access, or computer errors like a drive failure.

2. A database should not be converted if there is still a need to use it in the older version of Access. Convert it if it won't be used in the older version.

3. All data stored in that field are also deleted.

4. Detect and Repair will detect problems with Office software and initiate the steps to repair the problem.

5. Integers store whole numbers that are smaller than Single formats and cannot keep decimals. Loss of any decimal values is certain. There is also a potential for loss of Single values that are larger than Integer format supports.

task reference summary

Task	Page #	Preferred Method
Creating a Crosstab Query	AC 4.13	• Click the **Queries** object in the Database Window, select **Create query by using wizard**, and then click **New** • Select **Crosstab Query Wizard** from the New Query dialog box and then click **OK** • Follow the Wizard's instructions to choose the data source, row heading, column heading, and aggregate functions for the query • Name the query and then view the results
Creating a Lookup field	AC 4.19	• Verify the relationship between the table that will have the Lookup field and the table where the field is being looked up. The most likely relationship is one-to-many, where the child (many sides of the relationship) table will look up the key value of the parent table (one side of the relationship) • Open the child table and change the data type to **Lookup Wizard** • Follow the Lookup Wizard instructions
Creating an input mask	AC 4.21	• Open a table in Design View • Select the field for which you want to define an input mask • From the General tab select the **Input Mask** property and either • Click the **Build** button and follow the Input Mask Wizard instructions (Text and Date fields only) or • Type the input mask definition (Numeric and Currency masks must be entered manually)
Compact and repair the open database	AC 4.25	• On the **Tools menu**, point to **Database Utilities**, and then click **Compact and Repair Database**
Compact and repair an unopened database	AC 4.26	• Access must be running with no open database • On the **Tools** menu, point to **Database Utilities**, and then click **Compact and Repair Database** • In the **Database to Compact From** dialog box, specify the Access file you want to compact, and then click **Compact** • In the **Compact Database Into** dialog box, specify a name, drive, and folder for the compacted Access file • **Click** Save
Setting Automatic Compact and Repair	AC 4.27	• Open the Access database that you want to compact automatically • On the **Tools** menu, click **Options** • Click the **General** tab • Select the **Compact on Close** check box
Setting Detect and Repair for Microsoft Office	AC 4.28	• On the **Help** menu, click **Detect and Repair** • To restore the program shortcuts to the Windows **Start** menu, make sure the **Restore my shortcuts while repairing** check box is selected • Click **Start**
Database backup with Access	AC 4.30	• Open the database to be backed up. All database objects should be closed • From the **File** menu select **Back Up Database** • In the Save Backup As dialog box, indicate the drive, folder, and filename for the backup • Click **Save**

TRUE/FALSE

1. Input masks control how data are displayed to the user after they are entered.

2. When a field is deleted from a table structure, the data it contained are stored in a backup table.

3. The Between operator selects values between an upper and lower limit, including the stated limits.

4. Double quotes are used to enclose selection values for Text data fields.

5. When both conditions need to be true to select records, the conditions are connected with *And*.

6. Crosstab Queries can only Sum data.

FILL-IN

1. The _____ operator would be used to select records containing the values Life, Love, and Death.

2. The value that appears across the top of a Crosstab Query is the _____.

3. The condition that would be used to select values Smith and Smyth is _____.

4. The oldest version of Access to which a current database can be converted is _____.

5. Compact on Close is a property of _____.

6. A _____ field retrieves valid values for a field from a related table.

7. In Datasheet View, data from related tables can be displayed in a _____ by clicking the plus sign before a record.

MULTIPLE CHOICE

1. The * wildcard is used to
   a. match any number of values in a numeric field.
   b. match values between stated limits.
   c. match any number of values in a Text field.
   d. all of the above.

2. The In operator
   a. uses a comma to separate match values.
   b. requires text values to be enclosed in double quotes.
   c. lists multiple values for selection.
   d. all of the above.

3. The condition *Not >= 20* could also be stated
   a. < 20.
   b. $>= 20$.
   c. Like *20.
   d. none of the above.

4. Tables and databases should be backed up
   a. before major design changes.
   b. on a scheduled basis.
   c. to reduce the risk of data loss.
   d. all of the above.

5. Changing a field's _____ property is one of the design updates that is most likely to destroy data.
   a. Size
   b. Data Type
   c. Default Value
   d. Lookup

review of concepts

REVIEW QUESTIONS

Each of the following topics should be addressed in one to three paragraphs.

1. What should you do if your database begins to behave erratically?

2. When should a snapshot backup be created?

3. What criteria would select records where the JobDescription is manager and the Salary is over 35000?

4. Why would you compact a database into another file?

5. How are Select Queries and Crosstab Queries the same?

6. When is the Table Design View Undo buffer cleared?

7. What are some possible conversion issues when changing a field from single to integer data type? Refer to Help Yourself on page 18 for the Number data type specifications.

CREATE THE QUESTION

For each of the following answers, create the question.

ANSWER	QUESTION
1. Like "C?ndy?"	_____
2. Clicking this allows a field to be used for selection criteria, but does not display in the result	_____
3. Between 7 And 9	_____
4. ?	_____
5. Shutting off your computer without closing Access properly	_____
6. &	_____
7. Both conditions must be true to retrieve records	_____

FACT OR FICTION

For each of the following, determine whether the statement is fact, fiction, or both and present your arguments for that conclusion.

1. It is not necessary to compact and repair a database each time it is used.

2. Not > 10 is the only way to enter this condition.

3. Like "5/##/01" will match all May values in a Date field.

4. Creating copies of databases using Windows Copy is an effective way to back up databases.

5. You should always convert databases to the newest version of Access.

6. AutoNumber fields are always reset when the database is compacted.

7. Changes made to a table's design have no impact on data already stored in the table.

8. Input masks improve data entry by displaying a template for user entry and restricting the type of data accepted in each input position.

practice

1. Merrill Middle School Software Tracking

Merrill Middle School maintains an inventory of its software in an Access database. To date no analysis of the data has been completed. There is no centralized purchasing and no one knows just exactly how much software they have, where it is stored, or what it cost. You have been asked to prepare some queries to help determine what policies should be set about software purchases.

1. Start Access and open the **ac04Merrill.mdb** database
2. Open the Software table and review the data to become familiar with them
3. Create a query in Design View that selects the English software that has been purchased from Learnit Software (LS)
   a. Enter **ENG** in the Criteria row of Category
   b. Enter **LS** in the Criteria row of Vendor (entering an And condition)
   c. Save the query as **LearnIt** (see Figure 4.30)
4. The administration has decided to begin by checking software that is valued at over $500. Since you believe that the bulk of software expense is in the business area, you will create a query for business software valued at over $500
   a. Open a new query in Design View
   b. Add the InventoryValue query to the query design grid and add all of its fields to the Field row of the query
   c. Place **BUS** and **>500** in the Criteria row of the appropriate columns to create an And condition
   d. Run the query
   e. Save the query as **BusOver500**
5. Since the school purchases up to five evaluation copies of each software title, you need to look at software in the other (nonbusiness) categories where there are more than five copies
   a. Open a new query in Design View
   b. Add the InventoryValue query to the query design grid and add all of its fields to the Field row of the query
   c. Place **ENG**, **MTH**, **SYS**, and **SCI** in separate rows of the Category column to create Or conditions
   d. **>5** needs to be entered in each of the corresponding Quantity rows to create an And condition for each Category value
   e. Run the query
   f. Save the query as **NonBus1**
6. There are often multiple ways to accomplish the same task. Here is a second and more efficient way to create the previous query
   a. Open a new query in Design View
   b. Add the InventoryValue query to the query design grid and place all of its fields in the Field row of the query
   c. Place **Not Bus** in the Criteria row of Category (see Figure 4.31)
   d. Place **>5** in the Criteria row of Quantity (creating an And condition with Not Bus)
   e. Run the query. The results should be the same as the previous query
   f. Save the query as **NonBus2**
7. Close the database and Access if you have competed your work

FIGURE 4.30

English software from Learnit

LearnIt : Select Query

Software Number	Name	Category	Quantity	Price	VendorCode
1693	Kid-Writer	ENG	22	$29.95	LS
5950	Easy English	ENG	10	$29.95	LS
			10	$0.00	

Record: 1 of 2

FIGURE 4.31

NonBus2 query

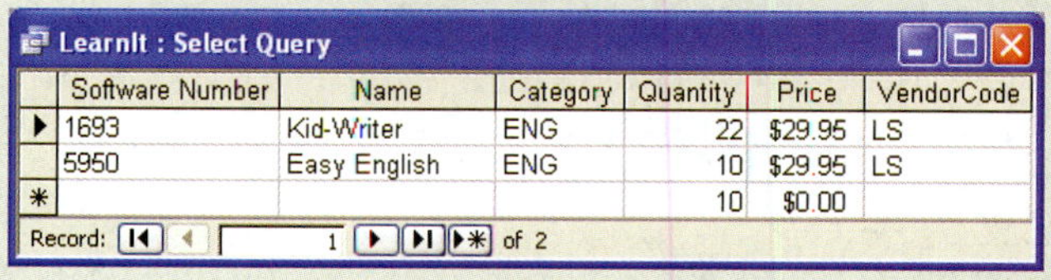

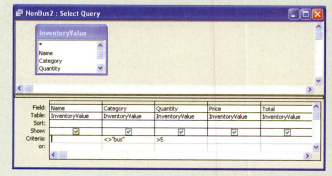

2. Using a Database for Sports Recruiting

Jon Zuccereli is the soccer coach at a small college in the eastern United States. Soccer is a new sport at the school and Jon is the third coach in three years. He believes that he must recruit and retain quality players to survive as a coach. Last year he was able to successfully recruit several players, and both the male and female teams have won more games than they have lost.

This year Jon has developed an Access database to improve his recruiting efforts. He has attended large tournaments across the United States and obtained data files used to track the entrants. The raw data files were imported into his database so that he had a list of all potential recruits. To be considered for admission, students must have a minimum GPA of 3.5. He has researched the players and eliminated all players who are not academically eligible from his database. You will help Jon evaluate the remaining players.

1. Start Access and open **ac04Recruiting.mdb**

2. Open the **Players** table in Datasheet View and review the data

3. Create a query in Design View that selects potential recruits from Michigan, Illinois, and Wisconsin for Jon's next recruiting trip. Include all table fields. Order the output by gender, last name, and first name. Place the sort columns to the left of the other columns. Name the query **NextTrip**

4. Jon saw a player at a midwestern tournament that he is particularly interested in recruiting. Her first name is Caitlin, but Jon is not sure whether it is spelled with a *C* or a *K*. Create a query using wildcards that will help Jon contact this person. Name the query **CaitlinSearch**

5. Jon would like to know how many candidates he has in each state by gender to help him decide where to recruit first. Create a Crosstab Query with Gender in the column headings and State in the row headings. Count ID. Name the query **GenderStateCrosstab** (see Figure 4.32)

6. Jon is paying existing team members to contact potential recruits. He needs several lists for this project. Each list should include the recruit's full name and address

   a. Create a list of female recruits from Michigan. Name the query **MichiganWomen**

   b. Create a list of male recruits from Michigan. Name the query **MichiganMen**

   c. Create a list of female recruits from Oklahoma. Name the query **OklahomaWomen**

7. Set this database to automatically compact and repair

8. If your work is complete, exit Access; otherwise, continue to the next assignment

FIGURE 4.32

GenderStateCrosstab

State	Total Of ID	F	M
CO	1		1
IA	145	69	76
IL	5	3	2
IN	1	1	
MI	312	128	184
MN	1		1
MO	2	1	1
NE	136	52	84
OH	1	1	
OK	266	139	127
WI	22	3	19

Record: ◄ ◄ 1 ► ►

challenge!

1. More Queries for Curbside Recycling

Curbside Recycling maintains a database of customers and their recyclable pickups. You have been asked to create some queries to help evaluate their business.

1. Start Access and open **ac04CurbsideRecycling.mdb**

2. Create a query in Design View that joins the Customer table to the Customer Records table. All fields from both tables should be included. Name the query **CustomerDetails**.

3. Run CustomerDetails to observe the resulting 53 records

4. Curbside is considering implementing a minimum pickup weight to improve its profit margin. Management would like to know how many customers have less than 10 pounds of each type of recyclable

   a. Open a new query in Design View using the CustomerDetails query. Include the name, street, address, and weight fields

   b. Add the criteria that will cause the query to retrieve records with less than 10 pounds in both recyclable categories

   c. Save the query as **LowVolumeBothCat**

   d. Alter LowVolumeBothCat to retrieve records with less than 10 pounds in either recyclable category. Save the query as **LowVolumeEitherCat**

5. Curbside employees are concerned about the impacts of repeatedly lifting the recyclables. You have been asked to determine how much each employee lifts per day

   a. Create a query called **TotalWeight** that lists the **CustID**, **SrvcDate**, **EmployeeID**, **WeightPaper**, **WeightOther**, and **TotalWeight:WeightPaper+WeightOther**

   b. Run the TotalWeight query to observe the result

   c. Use TotalWeight to create a new Crosstab Query with SrvcDate as the row headings and EmployeeID as the column heading. Sum TotalWeight. Save the query as **SumTotalWeightCrosstab** (see Figure 4.33)

   d. Run the SumTotalWeightCrosstab to observe the result

   e. Edit the SumTotalWeightCrosstab in Design View to find the Max value of TotalWeight. Use the **Save As** option of the **File** menu to save the modified query as **MaxTotalWeightCrosstab** (see Figure 4.34)

6. Close the database and Access if you have completed your work

F I G U R E   4.33
SumTotalWeightCrosstab

SrvcDate	Total Of TotalWeight	218	382
10/15/2002	13		13
11/22/2002	46	46	
10/14/2003	33	20	13
10/15/2003	422	60	362
11/4/2003	20	20	
11/7/2003	242	148	94
11/14/2003	20	20	
11/15/2003	116		116
11/22/2003	1310	762	548
12/4/2003	286	91	195

Record: 1 of 10

F I G U R E   4.34
MaxTotalWeightCrosstab

SrvcDate	Total Of TotalWeight	218	382
10/15/2002	13		13
11/22/2002	23	23	
10/14/2003	20	20	13
10/15/2003	117	20	117
11/4/2003	20	20	
11/7/2003	55	22	55
11/14/2003	20	20	
11/15/2003	58		58
11/22/2003	202	95	202
12/4/2003	39	34	39

Record: 1 of 10

2. Analyzing Texas Lacrosse Data

In Texas, like the rest of the United States, Lacrosse is growing in popularity. A new competitive league is being formed for players with the best skills. A Microsoft Access database table has been loaded with sample data from the three oldest age groups (under 30, under 19, and under 16). You will test the database by creating some useful queries.

1. Start Access and open **ac04Lacrosse.mdb**. Open the **Roster** table and review its contents

2. Coaches for each gender and age group need to be provided with lists of players who can be contacted to join their team. Each list should include full name, address, and phone number

   a. Create a list of potential under-30 players. Order the list by gender, last name, and first name. Name the query **U30**

   b. Create a list of potential male under-19 players. Order the list by last name and first name. Name the query **MU19**

   c. Create a list of potential female under-16 players. Order the list by last name and first name. Name the query **FU16**

3. Use the In operator to create a query that will retrieve potential players from **Irving**, **Ft Worth**, and **Dallas**. Include each person's full name, address, phone number, and gender. Order the output by gender, last name, and first name. Name the query **Area3Players**

4. To help determine the number of coaches and teams necessary, count the number of players grouped by gender and age group. Make gender the column heading and age group the row heading. Name the crosstab **AgeGenderSummary** (see Figure 4.35)

5. Create an input mask for the phone number field. The input display for entering new values should be ____-____-____. All 10 digits are required

6. Set this database to compact and repair automatically

7. If your work is complete, exit Access; otherwise, continue to the next assignment

FIGURE 4.35

AgeGenderSummary query

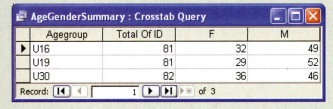

Agegroup	Total Of ID	F	M
U16	81	32	49
U19	81	29	52
U30	82	36	46

Record: ◄◄ ◄ 1 ► ►► ►* of 3

e-business

1. Tracking Photographs for SportsPix

SportsPix is a digital photography operation that specializes in taking pictures of youth sports teams. Ray Damask and Grace Bishop began photographing sports teams when their nephew was playing soccer at the local YMCA. They shoot individual and team pictures for baseball, softball, soccer, football, volleyball, tennis, and martial arts. Three other photographers pitch in during peak demand periods. On a busy day, they can shoot hundreds of children with their teams, resulting in over 10,000 customers in a year.

Tracking customer receipts is easy since all packages are paid for when the photographs are shot. Customers can preview their pictures on the Web and submit an order for the shots that they want included in their package. The biggest problem is keeping effective records on who is in each photograph, to which team they belong, when the photograph was shot, and where the photograph was shot. You have developed a prototype of a Photographs table that you believe will help Ray and Grace. You have selected some test data from the information that they provided and entered it into the table. Perform the following tests to ensure the effectiveness of this solution.

1. Make sure that you have access to the data from your data disk

2. Start Access and open the **ac04SportsPix.mdb** database from your Chapter 4 files

3. Open the **Photographs** table and add records for yourself and two of your friends. You should all be on the same team and have had your pictures taken at the same time and at the same location. Use Film ID **5443** and PhotographerID **1**

4. Create a query that will select all fields for photographs and the photographer's name from 8/14/2003 at 9 AM. Use Team as the primary sort and Subject Name as the secondary sort. Print the results and save the query as **DateTime**

5. Create a query that contains the Subject Name, Date, Film ID, and Photo #. Select records with Film ID values **5385**, **4638**, and **5443**. Sort the query datasheet by Subject Name and print the result (see Figure 4.36). Save the query as **FilmID**. Print the query datasheet

6. Create a query that lists the **Photographer's Name**, **Subject Name**, **Team**, and **Date Taken** where David Hough and Katharine O'Hara were the photographers. Name the query **PhotographersSubjects**

7. Create a query using the Like operator to select players from teams with *long* in the team name. Name the query **LongTeams**

8. Set the database to automatically compact and repair

9. Create a Crosstab Query to document the number of subjects photographed by date and time. Make Date the row header and Time the column header. Use the Count function on Subject Name (see Figure 3.36). Save the query as **DateTimeCrosstab**

10. If your work is complete, exit Access; otherwise, continue to the next assignment

FIGURE 4.36

FilmID query and DateTimeCrosstab Query

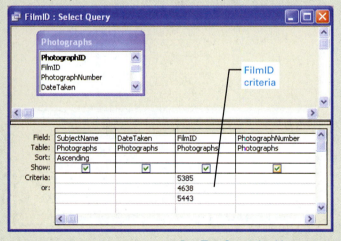

2. Analyzing United States Crops

The United States Department of Agriculture provides access to National Agricultural Statistics from its Web site at www.usda.gov. The available statistics include all crops raised in the United States from 1970 through 2001. Over 99,000 records have been downloaded from this site representing crop production for 1999 through 2001. The downloaded Excel files were edited and then imported into the Crops table. You will be analyzing this data.

1. Open Access and open **ac04USDA.mdb**

2. Open the **Crops** table and review the contents. Close the table

3. Create a query that will select records with the word *red* anywhere in the Practice field. Include all fields in the result. Name the query **RedCrops**

4. Select records from Illinois, Indiana, Ohio, and Michigan. Include all fields in the result. Name the query **InIlOhMiData**

5. Create a query that will select records with the word *dry* anywhere in the Practice field. Include all fields in the result. Name the query **DryCrops**

6. Create a Crosstab Query with State as the row heading and Year as the column heading. Sum the Production value (see Figure 4.37). Name the query **ProductionByStateAndYear**

7. Create a Crosstab Query that reports total Idaho production with Year as the column heading and County as the row heading. Name the query **IdahoCountiesProduction**

8. The data downloaded from the Web site contained formatting errors that caused blanks in the County field. Create a query to retrieve all fields of records with a blank value in County. (*Hint: Null* is the match value for blank fields.) Name the query **BadData**

9. Set this database to automatically compact and repair

10. Close the database and exit Access if your work is complete

FIGURE 4.37

IdahoCountiesProduction Crosstab Query

County	Total Of Production	2000	2001
	42096000		42096000
Ada	4027400	102000	3925400
Bannock	6593000		6593000
Bear Lake	1215000		1215000
Benewah	5615000		5615000
Bingham	68241800		68241800
Blaine	3226000		3226000
Bonner	8000		8000
Bonneville	31212100		31212100
Boundary	4537000		4537000
Butte	3686000		3686000
Camas	812000		812000
Canyon	18915300	371800	18543500
Caribou	16053000		16053000
Cassia	50467600	301200	50166400
Clark	4472000		4472000
Clearwater	2540600	28600	2512000

Record: |◄ ◄ | 1 | ► ►| ►* of 51

1. Toy Purchase Statistics by Internet Research Inc.

Internet Research Inc. (IRI) is a statistical evaluation organization specializing in Internet commerce that was introduced in Chapter 2. You are gathering data from the Internet on Web sites that sell toys and using Access to evaluate them.

1. Use a Shopping Bot like www.mysimon.com or a search engine to find at least two sites selling popular toys (www.eToys.com and www.ToysRUs.com are good sites, but there are many others). Select and compare bicycle prices
   a. Determine the price of a model of bike at the first site
   b. Find the price for the same model at the second site
   c. Repeat this process for another bike

2. Add your new research to the data that already exist in the ac04IRI.mdb database Toys table with ToyIDs **500–503**

   tip: *If you did this exercise in Chapter 3, use your updated copy of the database renamed ac04IRI.mdb*

3. Sometimes you want to convert data in a table to display with different row and column headings. This can be accomplished with a Crosstab Query

4. Create a new Crosstab Query with the Wizard
   a. Use the **Toys** table as the data source
   b. Make ToyName the row headings and Web site the column headings
   c. Display Price in the cells using the Sum function (since there is only one record per toy/Web site combination, the aggregate function will not do anything, but you must select one anyway)

   d. Click off the check box to include row sums so there is no Total column in the result
   e. Run the query. Your results should resemble those shown in Figure 4.38
   f. Save the Query as **PriceByToyAndSite**. Use the Report Wizard to create a report based on this query. Name the report **Crosstab Report**

5. Create a query in Design View that finds all products with Barbie in the ToyName. Sort the results by ToyName and Price. Save the query as **BarbieProducts**

6. Modify the query from step 5 to retrieve Barbie products that cost under $25. Save the query as **BarbieLT25**

7. Create a query to select toys without *Barbie* in the name at a price of less than $40.00. Name the query **LowPriceNotBarbie**

8. Set this database to automatically compact and repair

9. Close the database and exit Access if your work is complete

FIGURE 4.38

PriceByToyAndSite Crosstab Query

ToyName	www_etoys_com	www_toysrus_com
Barbie Airplane	$58.99	$59.99
Barbie Family House	$49.28	$58.92
bike1		
bike2		
Celebration Barbie	$37.99	$36.99
Cool Blading Barbie	$22.50	$22.12
Cool Clips Barbie	$15.28	$15.87
Ferrari Barbie	$42.28	$39.99
Game Boy Army Men	$29.95	$32.99
Game Boy Asteroids	$23.32	$24.87
Game Boy Mario Golf	$31.15	$31.99
Game Boy Perfect Dark	$32.50	$59.99
Generation Girl Barbie	$21.64	$21.88
Princess Bride Barbie	$23.38	$22.99

Record: 1 of 17

around the world

1. Tracking the World's Population

Brandon Pryor's middle school class is still working on ways to evaluate the population of the world's largest cities. The students have a pretty good idea of how large these cities are compared to their hometown, but now they need to understand how the cities are related to each other.

1. Open the **Cities** table of the **ac04Populations.mdb** database

tip: *If you did this exercise in Chapter 3, use your up-dated copy of the database renamed to ac04Populations.mdb*

2. Create a query in Design View that will select all records with Korea in the country name. Sort the results by City and save the query as **Korea**

3. Create a query that will select cities with populations between 15 and 35 million. Sort by descending population and name the query **35M**

4. The class is looking for a Middle East city but cannot remember the full name. They believe that it starts with al. Write a query that will help them find the correct city. Save the query as **MiddleEast**

5. Create a query that will select cities in South America (Argentina, Bolivia, Brazil, Chile, Ecuador, Peru, and Venezuela). Sort the results by Country and then City (see Figure 4.39). Save the query as **SouthAmerica**

tip: *The countries have both English and German names displayed, so you will need to match for both or use wildcards*

6. Modify the previous query to select only ABC Powers (Argentina, Brazil, and Chile). ABC Powers are the nations striving to maintain peace in South and Central America. The alliance was formed to protect against aggressive policies of the United States prior to World War II. Save the query as **ABCPowers**

7. Create a query that will select all cities in North America. Sort the result from largest to smallest city. Save the query as **NorthAmerica**

8. With the world's largest population, China also has the greatest number of large cities. Create a query that will select all cities in China and order them by decreasing population. Save the query as **China**

9. Since the database contains the German names for countries as well as the English names, the students decide to see how large the cities in Germany are. Create a query that will display German cities sorted by ascending population. Save the query as **Germany**

10. Set this database to automatically compact and repair

11. Close the database and Access if your work is complete

FIGURE 4.39

SouthAmerica Query

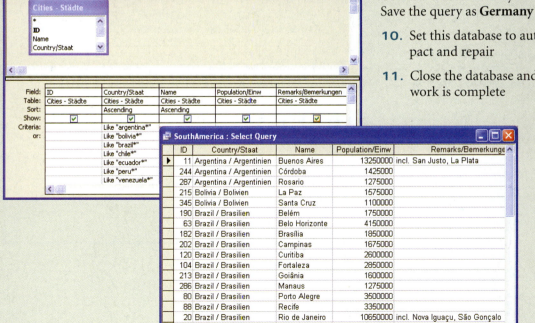

running project: tnt web design

More Analysis of TnT Table Data

The TnT database now consists of three related tables. The tblCustomers table holds the static data about the organization's customers. The CustomerSites table contains the URLs for the sites TnT has built. The CustomerSites table has a Lookup field for the customer name so that you do not have to remember CustomerID values when entering data. TnT's employees are listed in the Employees table. CustomerSites is related to both the Customers table and the Employees table. The employee listed in the CustomerSites table is the one who managed the Web site development project.

1. Start Access and open the **ac04TnT.mdb** database
2. Open each table and review the data
3. Create a query based on the Employees table that will list all of the employees who are either programmers or scripters. Order the data by JobClass, LastName, and FirstName. Save the query as **ContentDevelopers**
4. Modify the previous query to select programmers and scripters who live in Washington (WA) (see Figure 4.40). Save the query as **WAContentDevelopers**

5. There is an employee that you know as Jim, but you are not sure how he has been entered into the database. It could be Jim, Jimmy, or James. Create a query to search for this person. Save the query as **JimSearch**
6. The first six employees of TnT are the project managers. The site table lists the company, the URL, and the employee number of the project manager. Tori wants a table that outlines what companies each project manager has worked with. Create a Crosstab Query using the **CustomerSites** table that displays company name (CustID) as the row header, employee number as the column header, and counts the site number (so that it just displays that number). Do not display a totals column. Save the query as **ProjectManagersCrosstab**
7. Create a report with the previous query as the data source. Display the logo from ac04Tnt.tif in the report header. Save the report as **ProjectManagers**
8. Create a query using data from both Employees and CustomerSites tables. Include **LastName** and **FirstName** from Employees and **CustID** and **URI** from CustomerSites. Name the query **EmployeeSites**. Order the output by Employee Name
9. Set this database up to automatically compact on exit. Document the steps used to accomplish this

FIGURE 4.40
WAContentDevelopers Query

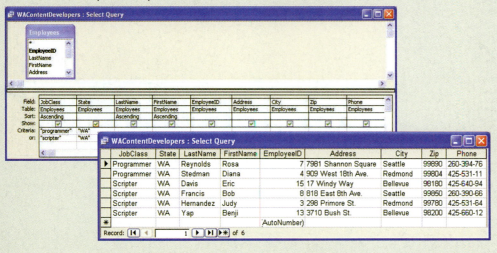

1. Tracking Travel Routes

In many countries public transportation is created by ride sharing rather than the buses, trains, trams, and vans used in the United States. Assume you are in a country where ride sharing is the norm and have decided to start a business that will coordinate ride-sharing activities. You will develop an Access database named **ac04Travel.mdb** to facilitate ride sharing.

The database will need to store information about drivers willing to accept riders such as the number of available seats, trip point of origin, destination, departure date, departure time, and so on. You will also need to store data on riders. Spend time designing this database and then develop the tables. Use destinations in South America or Africa to test your database. Add at least 10 routes with a minimum of two customers each. Build at least one multicondition query such as two or more seats available to a particular destination. Build a Crosstab Query that totals the number of rides available by destination and date.

2. Start a Database Charitable Organization

Design and develop a Microsoft Access database for a small charitable organization such as a local food bank or small church. The database should be named **ac04Charities.mdb** and include data to track services and clients. Include enough data to effectively create queries such as those demonstrated in the chapter. Be sure to document how your database will be used and include at least one query with multiple selection criteria and a Crosstab Query.

5

Customizing Forms and Reports

did you
know?

a *goldfish is the only animal that can see both infrared and ultraviolet light.*

there *are more than 50,000 earthquakes throughout the world each year.*

the *highest place people have settled in the United States is Climax, Colorado, at 11,360 feet above sea level.*

in *reality, electric lightbulbs existed 50 years prior to Thomas Edison's 1879 U.S. patent date.*

it *really can be too cold to snow! During very cold weather, the capacity of the air to contain moisture is reduced and most of the vapor is deposited as frost, resulting in extremely low humidity. In these conditions snow cannot form.*

to *find out what year mechanical engineering professor M. W. Thring said, "Within ten to twenty years' time we could have a robot that will completely eliminate all routine operations around the house and remove the drudgery from human life," visit www.mhhe.com/i-series.*

Chapter Objectives

- Build and modify a form in Design View—MOS AC03S-1-9 and MOS AC03S-3-2

- Understand the Form toolbox

- Create a report in Design View—MOS AC03S-3-3

- Summarize report data

- Preview and print reports

- Add and modify report control properties—MOS AC03S-1-11

- Sort records in forms—MOS AC03S-3-5

- Preview reports for print—MOS AC03S-4-2

KoryoKicks: Customizing Database Input and Output

Missy and Micah Hampton are in the midst of building a database to support their entrepreneurial business. The twins began the business to earn some extra spending money for college and have been very successful teaching self-defense classes and selling martial arts supplies on campus. As most small businesses do, they initially kept records manually but found that method ineffective as the data needed to efficiently make business decisions became increasingly complex.

Most entrepreneurs have a business idea and give little thought to data that must be stored, maintained, and analyzed for the business to thrive. The volume and complexity of these data increase with the success of the business as does the need to make more complex business decisions and appear professional to customers and suppliers. Finding effective ways to store and analyze business data is a critical factor in business success.

Since Missy and Micah were not familiar with database technology, they have had to learn a new technology while they were learning to run a successful business and going to school. They have worked with you for the past several months learning Microsoft Access 2003 and evaluating the data storage and reporting needs of KoryoKicks. The current database contains tables to track customers, products, orders, and vendors. There are a number of select queries to analyze sales, unpaid invoices, and product demand. A Crosstab Query to calculate total sales by month and state has let the twins know how their products sell in each state over time. Simple reports have been developed to document the status of sales and product orders.

While all of this is helpful, the twins need more complex analytical information, friendlier forms, and more professional reports. Since they will be hiring part-time help to load and maintain data, the database interface must be improved by adding custom forms developed using Form Design View. In addition, more powerful reporting features will improve data analysis, and the use of Report Design View to customize printed output will help the business project a more professional image (see Figure 5.1).

The twins know that no amount of information can guarantee the result of a decision, but timely and effective information can significantly improve the likelihood of a positive outcome. They expect to improve their decision-making ability by learning more ways to use Microsoft Access form and report facilities.

SESSION 5.1 MAINTAINING DATA WITH FORMS

The form object is used to create a custom screen interface used to enter and display database data. Forms also create user interfaces called *switchboards* that open other forms and reports in the database, and custom dialog boxes to accept user input and carry out an action based on the input.

Most forms are bound to one or more tables or queries referred to as the form's *record source*. All of the fields from the underlying tables and queries do not need to be included in the form.

Defining a Form in Form Design View

You already have created forms using form Wizards and modified the result by adding images. It's time to take a look at how forms work from the ground up. The design of a form stores all of the specifications for the appearance and function of the form including information about its underlying record source. Calculations are stored in the form's design and executed just before data are displayed to the user. The data displayed in the form (except calculations) are stored and/or retrieved from its underlying record source.

Form Design View

Forms are built using graphical objects called controls. Each control has a special purpose. A **Label** control is used to display descriptive text to the user. A **Text Box** control is used to enter and display data from the record source or execute and display a calculated value. These underlying controls were introduced in the previous chapter when Form Design View was used to add a graphic to the AutoForm Wizard form. Customizing an AutoForm is often the fastest way to develop a usable product.

When a new form is created in Design View (see Figure 5.2), you begin with an empty form and a toolbox containing the tools (controls) needed to create the form elements. Controls are added to the form to build the desired functionality. Since the developer is in complete control of the format, it is always best to have an idea of the operation and design of the end product before beginning.

To design a form, decide what fields need to be included. If the fields are from different tables, it is often better to create a query that joins the tables and selects the appropriate records. After documenting the fields to be included, organize a layout for those fields and any other necessary elements that are to be included such as a logo. Figure 5.3 shows a sample form design for KoryoKicks Customers input.

FIGURE 5.2

A new form in Design View

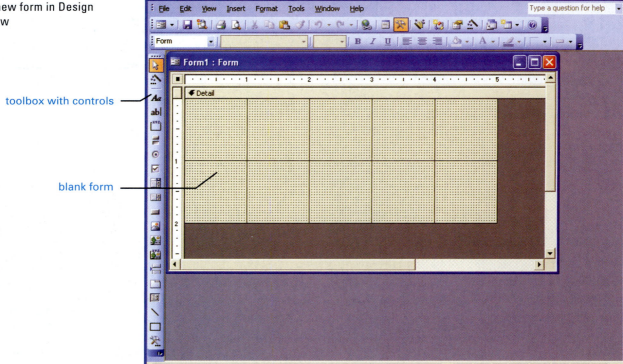

FIGURE 5.3

Customers Form Design

KoryoKicksLogo	Customers		
Cstmr ID: XXX			
Last Name: XXXXXXXXXXXXXXXXXX		First Name: XXXXXXXXXXXXXXXXXX	
Street: XXXXXXXXXXXXXXXXXX		City: XXXXXXXXXXXXXXXXXX	
State: XXX		Zip Code: XXXXXX	
Phone: XXXXXXXXXXXX			

The design reflects the complete layout of the form including titles, graphics, captions, and field length. In the design shown, the field captions appear as the twins want to see them on the form. Xs are used to indicate the placement and the length of the data display area. When the form is built, the captions will be in Label controls and the data values will be displayed in Text Box controls. The KoryoKicks logo will reside in an Image control and the form title will be entered in a Label control. Since you have a good idea of the data and its layout for the Customers form, it is time to start building it.

The Form Toolbox and Field List

The Form toolbox is a special toolbar with all of the controls that can be added to a form. If you forget what a Toolbox button is, display a Screen Tip by pausing the mouse pointer over it. Like all toolbars, the toolbox can be displayed or removed from display using the View menu. It also can be anchored or unanchored by dragging its Title bar.

When a control is placed on the form, its *properties* are set, to direct what it will display and how it will appear on the form. A few of the properties that can be set will alter a control's background color, foreground color, and font. Controls and their uses are outlined in Figure 5.4.

Form controls are classified as bound, unbound, or calculated. **Bound** controls display data from a record source and are said to be bound to a field in the underlying table or query. Bound controls are typically added using the Field List dialog box rather than the toolbox. **Unbound** controls are not linked to a record source and so display fixed data such as the title of a form, instructions, or labels for other form elements. A **calculated** control stores the instructions on how to complete the calculation using one or more fields of the record source and displays the calculated value.

The simplest way to create a bound control is to open the Field List dialog box for the record source using the Field List button of the Form Design toolbar. With the Field List dialog box open, select a field and drag it to the form surface. Repeat this process for each field that is to display on the form. Bound controls can be rearranged on the form by dragging until they are positioned where you would like.

Bound controls created in this fashion will consist of a text box to display the field value and a label to hold a caption. The Caption property of a Label displays the

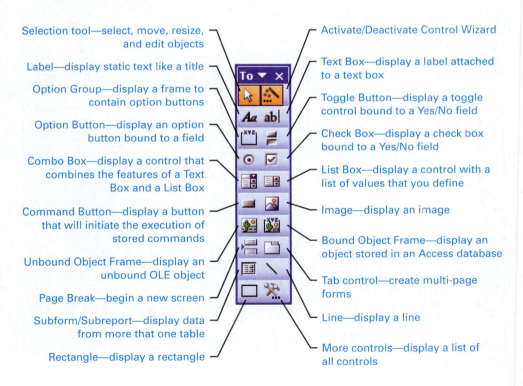

Selection tool—select, move, resize, and edit objects

Label—display static text like a title

Option Group—display a frame to contain option buttons

Option Button—display an option button bound to a field

Combo Box—display a control that combines the features of a Text Box and a List Box

Command Button—display a button that will initiate the execution of stored commands

Unbound Object Frame—display an unbound OLE object

Page Break—begin a new screen

Subform/Subreport—display data from more that one table

Rectangle—display a rectangle

Activate/Deactivate Control Wizard

Text Box—display a label attached to a text box

Toggle Button—display a toggle control bound to a Yes/No field

Check Box—display a check box bound to a Yes/No field

List Box—display a control with a list of values that you define

Image—display an image

Bound Object Frame—display an object stored in an Access database

Tab control—create multi-page forms

Line—display a line

More controls—display a list of all controls

F I G U R E 5.4

The Form toolbox

ACCESS

Caption value set for the field in the table design. The Field Name is the default Caption property value and will display in the label when no custom value is set.

Building a Form in Design View

Missy and Micah like using the Customer form to enter new customers, but they believe that the format could be improved. Rather than customize the existing form, you decide to rebuild it in Design View to get some practice with building forms from scratch.

---

task reference   Open a New Form in Design View

- In the Database Window of an open database, click the **Forms** object

- Click the **New** button on the Database Window toolbar

- In the New Form dialog box, click **Design View**

- Select the table or query that will be the record source for the form and click **OK**

Creating the Customer form in Design View:

1. Open the **ac05KoryoKicks.mdb** database

2. Select the **Forms** object from the Database Window

3. Click the **New** button on the Database Window toolbar

4. Verify that **Design View** is selected from the list of ways to create forms

5. Select **Customer** as the source of data for this form and click **OK**

F I G U R E 5.5

Customer form Design View

Form Design toolbox anchored to left window border

Customer table field list

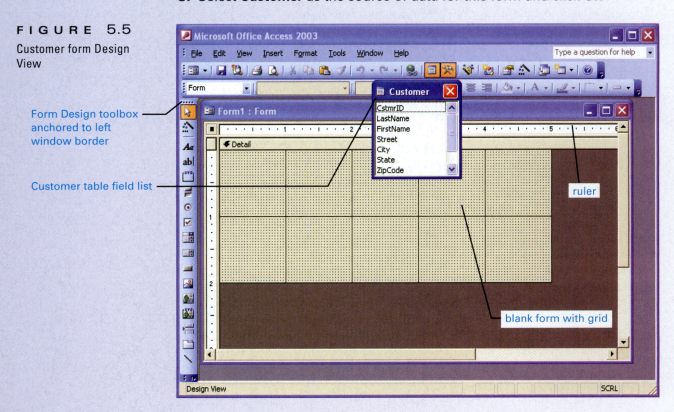

tip: *If your screen is missing the ruler, grid, or toolbox, use the View menu to add them. The toolbox may be floating or anchored without impacting functionality. Drag the toolbox Title bar to anchor or unanchor it*

6. Select all of the fields in the Field List dialog box by double-clicking its Title bar (see Figure 5.6)

tip: *If the field list is not displaying, click the Field List button on the Form Design toolbar*

7. Drag the selected fields to the form

tip: *Your form should generally match the appearance shown, but fields do not need to be positioned exactly since they will be moved to their final locations later*

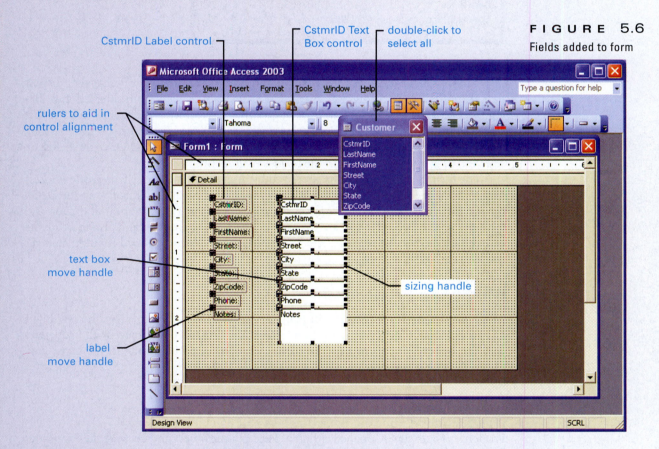

CstmrID Label control

CstmrID Text Box control

double-click to select all

rulers to aid in control alignment

text box move handle

label move handle

sizing handle

FIGURE 5.6

Fields added to form

8. The simplest edit in Design View is to delete a field. Click the form background to deselect all fields and then click the **Notes** field and press the **Del** key to remove it from the form (we will place it on a new form page later)

tip: *When you click on the Notes field, both the Label control and the Text Box control are selected*

9. Close the field list, since you won't need it for some time, by clicking the X in its Title bar

tip: *The field list has Customer in the Title bar*

10. Click the **Save** button and name the form **Customers**

FIGURE 5.7

Form Properties pages

Properties pages for the Detail form section

page tabs

properties and their settings

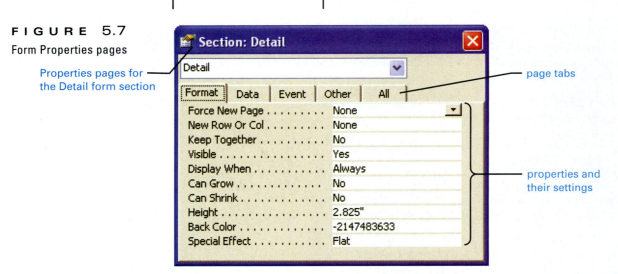

You now have created a blank form and added bound controls that will display data from the form's record source, the Customer table. Fields from the Field List dialog box can be added one at a time or in groups. To select multiple fields, click the first field and then hold down the Ctrl key as you click the other fields. As you experienced, double-clicking the Field List Title bar will select all fields in the list. Once the fields are selected, drag and drop them on the form Detail section.

The form Detail section can be resized by dragging its borders. This is often necessary to make the form fit the controls it will display. The grid that displays in the Detail section is to help position the controls effectively. The rulers that appear at the top and left sides of the Detail section are to assist in positioning controls and also indicate the actual dimensions of the form. The Undo button can always be used to undo changes made to the Detail section or a control.

Modifying Properties

All objects have *properties* that control behavior. In Form Design View, the developer has access to all object properties, providing full control. One object with properties that can be set is the form itself. In turn, each control added to the form can be customized using its properties.

Form Properties

Properties are set using the *Properties pages* for an object (see Figure 5.7). An object's Properties pages can be opened either by selecting the object and clicking the Properties button on the Form Design toolbar or by right-clicking the object and selecting Properties from the pop-up menu.

The properties that can be set are specific to each type of object, but the general layout of the Properties page is always the same. The object that owns the Properties pages is listed in the Title bar; the properties are divided by type on tabbed pages. The first Properties page to present is the Format page, which contains properties about how the object will display.

Changing form properties:

1. Verify that the **ac05KoryoKicks.mdb** database is open and that the **Customers** form created in the previous steps is in Design View

2. Right-click on a blank area of the form and select **Properties** from the pop-up menu

3. Click in the Back Color property in either the Format or All tab

4. Select the ellipse to the right of the current Back Color property

5. Click the sixth square on the third row (light blue) square and click **OK**

6. Close the Properties pages

The form is now light blue because the Back Color property was set in the Properties pages. Changing the size of the form by dragging its borders also sets the form properties related to size. This could be done manually in the Properties pages, but it is easier to drag the borders. You can change the properties of the controls on a form by moving them, changing their size, or setting other properties on the Properties pages.

Adjusting Controls on a Form

Both a Label and a Text Box control represent each field from the table. Since developers typically want to manipulate both at the same time, both are selected when either one is clicked. The square *handles* that appear on a selected control can be used to resize it. A selected control can be moved to a new position on the form using drag and drop. The Text Box and Label controls for a field move in concert unless a move handle is used. The largest square (top left) on a label or text box is called the *move handle* and will allow each component of the bound control to be moved independently.

Multiple controls on a form can be selected and operated on simultaneously. To select multiple controls, click and drag a selection box around the controls or click the first control and then hold down the Shift key while selecting subsequent controls. Once the controls are selected, resize, move, or set properties such as the background color.

---

task reference   Select and Move Form Controls

- Select the control to be operated on by clicking it. The Shift key can be used to select multiple controls

- Drag the control(s) to the new location. Use the large move handle to independently move components of a bound control

---

Repositioning Customers form controls:

1. Verify that the **ac05KoryoKicks.mdb** database is open and that the **Customers** form created in the previous steps is in Design View

2. First let's organize the work area. Click in the CstmrID text box to select the field and then drag it to the position shown in Figure 5.8

3. Click and drag a selection box around the remaining fields and position them as shown in Figure 5.8

4. Now let's put the fields where the twins want them. Select **FirstName** and drag it until it is on the same line and to the right of LastName

FIGURE 5.8
Repositioned Customers
controls

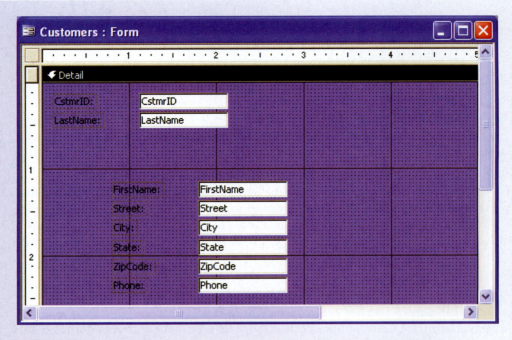

tip: *If something is selected that you don't want, deselect it by clicking on the form surface away from any control. The mouse pointer changes to a hand when you can drag the
selection*

   5. Select **Street** and move it up until it is under LastName

   6. Select **City** and move it to the right of Street, aligned with FirstName

   7. Select **State** and move it up until it is under Street

   8. Select **ZipCode** and move it to the right of State, aligned with City

   9. Select **Phone** and move it up until it is under State

   10. Drag the borders of the Detail pane to reduce its size, as shown in
       Figure 5.9

FIGURE 5.9
Customers Design View

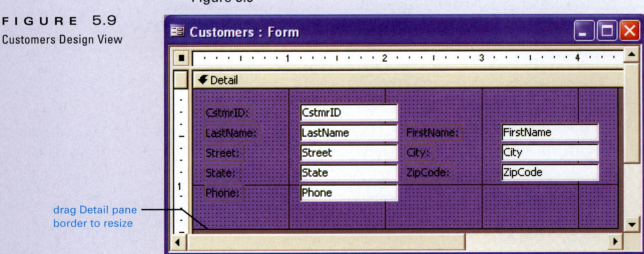

drag Detail pane
border to resize

   11. Click the **Form View** button to preview the results

       Click the **Design View** button and click the **Save** button to save
       the form

When moving fields it is important to notice the mouse pointer's shape. A hand with all of the fingers extended indicates that the selection can be moved to a new location. This will drag both the label and text box of a bound control. A pointing hand indicates that a move handle has been accessed to move the parts of a bound control independently. A two-headed arrow indicates that a *sizing handle* is being used to resize the control.

The field names from the table are usually picked for technical reasons and are often not what the user wants to see. To change the content of any label, set the Caption property of the field in Table Design. The benefit of setting this property is that its value is the default for any form or report created. A label can be directly edited, but this is effective for the current object only and will not be reflected in other forms or reports.

After previewing the form, the twins have decided they want spaces in the field labels. The fields need to be adjusted to match the size of the data that they will display. For example, the CstmrID, State, and ZipCode fields are much too large for their data. They would also like the labels to be right-justified and closer to the text boxes to make the relationship easier to view. These changes will require setting the properties of the Label controls.

---

task reference   **Set Control Properties**

- Right-click the control to open the pop-up menu
- Select **Properties** from the pop-up menu
- Select the appropriate Properties tab (usually Format)
- Navigate to the property and change its setting

---

help yourself *Use the Type a Question combo box to improve your understanding of setting control properties by typing* **control properties**. *Review the contents of* About customizing a control *and* About property sheets. *Close the Help window when you are finished*

Changing labels:

1. Verify that the **ac05KoryoKicks.mdb** database is open with the **Customers** form created in the previous steps in Design View

2. Click an insertion point in the CstmrID label and add a space between Cstmr and ID (see Figure 5.10)

tip: *With the label selected, use the I-beam to click an insertion point between the r and I. When this is successful, the label background becomes white and a blinking insertion point appears. This text edit area behaves like a little word processor*

3. Repeat this process for LastName, FirstName, and ZipCode

4. Now let's put the fields where the twins want them. Click and drag a selection box around the CstmrID, Last Name, Street, State, and Phone Labels (not text boxes)

   a. Right-click on a selected label and choose **Properties** from the pop-up menu
   b. Scroll down to Text Align on the All tab and choose **Right**
   c. Close the Multiple Selection dialog box
   d. From the **Format** menu choose **Align** and then **Right**

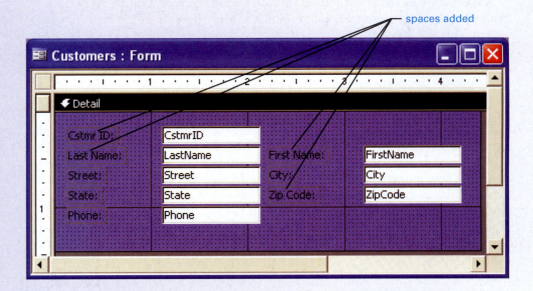

spaces added

tip: *All labels should be right-justified. If they are not, check your selection and try step 4b again*

5. Repeat step 4 for the right-column labels

6. Since the labels are in the correct position, you will move the text boxes to be closer to the labels. Select the CstmrID text box and use the move handle to reposition it until only one grid line shows between the label and the text box

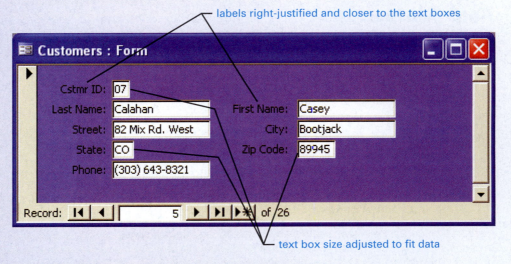

labels right-justified and closer to the text boxes

text box size adjusted to fit data

anotherway
...to Change Label Text

The text displayed in a Label control is a property of that control. All properties, including the displayed text, can be changed from the Properties pages. Right-click on the label to activate the shortcut menu and select Properties to open the Properties pages. Set the Caption property to control the displayed text

7. Repeat this process for all of the other labels

8. Select the text box for CstmrID and use the sizing handles to reduce its size to display about three characters

9. Check your results in Form View and adjust the field width as needed to properly display the data (see Figure 5.11)

tip: *You will need to move through the records and view the field with various data values to ensure that you have correctly modified the width*

10. Repeat this process for State and ZipCode

11. Move the right column controls close to the left column with four grid lines between them

12. Save your changes

The properties of multiple selected objects can be set simultaneously. When working on multiple objects, the selected objects must be of the same type (e.g., changing the alignment of all the labels in earlier steps). In the next steps you will simultaneously modify the properties of all the text boxes on the form, by changing their Back Color and Font.

Changing text boxes:

1. Verify that the **ac05KoryoKicks.mdb** database is open and that the **Customers** form created in the previous steps is in Design View

2. Select *all* of the text boxes on the form by holding down the Shift key as you click

3. Open the Properties pages by clicking the **Properties** button from the toolbar (the shortcut menu also can be used)

4. Click in the **Font Name** property and select **Batang**

tip: *You will need to scroll down to find the Font property in the Format tab. If you do not have Batang, select another font. All available properties are in alphabetical order on the All tab. Move the Properties pages by dragging the Title bar to see the results of your changes*

5. Click in the **Fore Color** property and then click the ellipse

6. In the Color dialog box select the **Define Custom Colors** button to create a custom color for the text box backgrounds

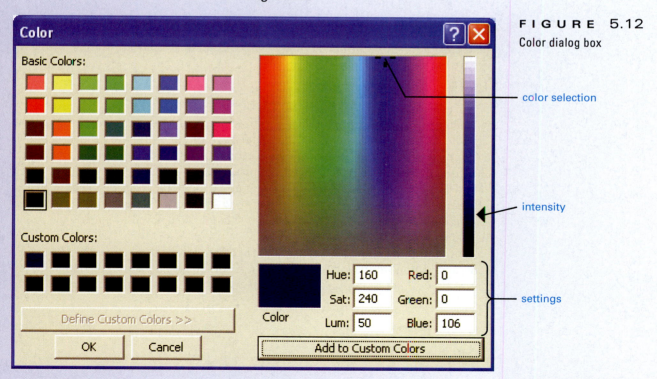

FIGURE 5.12
Color dialog box

color selection

intensity

settings

7. You can click to choose color and intensity or enter the settings manually. Set Hue, Sat, Lum, Red, Green, and Blue to match Figure 5.12; click **Add to Custom Colors**; and click **OK**

8. Set the **Special Effect** property to **Raised**

9. Set the Back Color property to Hue **120**, Sat **240**, Lum **216**, Red **204**, Green **255**, Blue **255**.

FIGURE 5.13

Modified text boxes

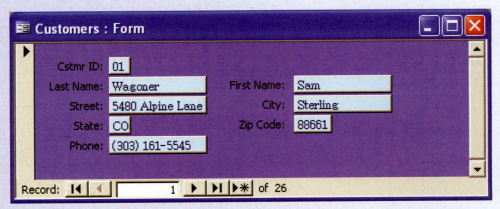

10. Close the Multiple Selection dialog box and use the Form View to preview your changes

11. Save the form

Although color adds interest and draws the eye, use color sparingly when creating forms that will be used frequently. Default colors are used throughout the Microsoft Office System Applications, and users understand how the various colors are normally applied. Using these defaults can make your application easier to learn. In addition, color viewed over time can increase eye fatigue, making the screen harder to read.

If you do use color, be consistent in its application. The same color should always mean the same thing. Make sure that the contrast between the background color and the text color is sufficient for easy readability. In general, pale backgrounds with dark text are the most effective.

Inserting Form Headers and Footers

So far in this chapter, form modifications have been made to the Detail section of the form. Recall that in an earlier chapter a graphic was inserted into the Header section of a form created using a Wizard. Each form section has a specific function and behavior. The *Form Detail section* of a form is typically used to display data from a record source. The *Form Header section* will appear at the top of the form when it is displayed in Form View and at the beginning of a printed selection of forms. The *Form Footer section* will appear at the bottom of a form when it is displayed in Form View and at the end of a printed selection of forms.

Form Header and Footer sections are characteristically used to add titles, instructions, and buttons to the top or bottom of a form. The header and footer contents are static—they do not change as the data displayed in the Detail section change.

task reference	Show Form Headers and Footers

- Open a form in Design View
- Select **Form Header/Footer** from the **View** menu

Adding Form Header/Footer:

1. Verify that the **ac05KoryoKicks.mdb** database is open and that the **Customers** form created in the previous steps is in Design View

2. On the **View** menu select **Form Header/Footer**

tip: *If both the Header and Footer sections do not display, drag the border of the Form Design Window and expand it until all three form sections display*

Section selectors   Section bars

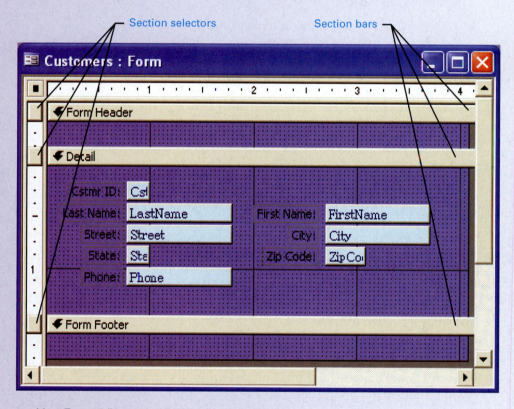

FIGURE 5.14

Customers form with Header and Footer sections

3. Use Form View to preview the changes

*another***word**	. . . on Form Headers and Footers

Headers and footers can only be added and removed together. If you don't want both a header and a footer, you can set the Visible property of the section that you don't want to No, or set its Height property to 0

Deselecting Form Header/Footer on the View menu will remove both sections from the form along with any controls they contain. Either the Section selectors or Section bars (see Figure 5.14) can be used to select a form section. Once a section is selected, it can be operated on by adding controls or setting its properties.

To complete the design of the Customers form, you need to add the logo and form title. These are unbound controls that will be placed in the form header. The logo will be placed in an Image control and the form title will be in a Label control. These controls are available from the toolbox.

---

task reference   Add Toolbox Controls to a Form

- Open a form in Design View

- If necessary, activate the toolbox using the **Toolbox** button on the Form Design toolbar

- Verify that the Toolbox **Control Wizards** button is depressed (a blue outline will show around it)

- Click the Toolbox control that is to be added to the form

- Click in the form section that will contain the control

- Set the control's properties by entering its contents, sizing, moving, and using the Properties pages

---

Adding content to the Form Header:

1. Verify that the **ac05KoryoKicks.mdb** database is open and that the **Customers** form created in the previous steps is in Design View

2. Select the **Image control** button from the toolbox and then click in the Form Header to activate the Control Wizard

   tip: *If the Wizard does not activate, delete the Image control, click the Control Wizard button in the toolbox to activate Wizards, and repeat step 2*

3. The Image Control Wizard will open the Insert Picture dialog box. Navigate to the data files for this chapter and select **ac05KoryoKicks.gif**. The logo shown in Figure 5.15 should display in the Image control

4. Click the **Label control** button in the toolbox and click in the Form Header next to the image

5. Type **Customers** (there is no Label Control Wizard)

6. Right-click on the Customers Label control and select **Properties** from the pop-up menu

7. Set the following properties

Back Style	**Normal**
Font Name	**Tahoma**
Font Size	**26**
Font Weight	**Extra bold**
Font Italic	**Yes**

anotherway

. . . to Change Label Text

The Formatting toolbar can be used to set the Font Name, Font Size, Italic, and Color properties of a control when you are using standard values. The Font Weight and custom color used in the Customers form are not available using this method

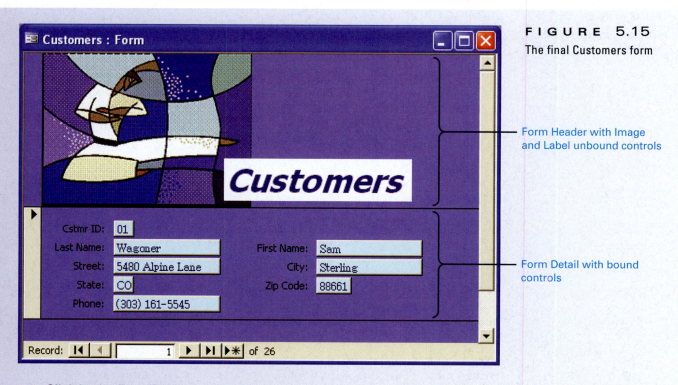

FIGURE 5.15
The final Customers form

Form Header with Image
and Label unbound controls

Form Detail with bound
controls

8. Click in the **Fore Color** property (to set the text color) and then click the **ellipse** to the right of the property

9. Click the **Define Custom Colors** button. Set Hue to **174**, Sat to **240**, Lum to **60**, Red to **44**, Green to **0**, and Blue to **128**; click **Add to Custom Colors**; and click **OK**

10. Close the Properties pages

11. Drag the Customer label until it is in the position shown. Resize as needed

12. Use Form View to preview the changes

13. Save the form

In the previous steps, adding an Image control to the form initiated the Image Control Wizard. The complex controls in the toolbox have *Control Wizards* designed to walk users through the process of building the control's content. The Control Wizards button on the toolbox will enable and disable these Wizards. Figure 5.16 indicates which controls have Wizards available.

As controls are added to a form, they are actually layered so that the most recently added control is on the top layer. This layering is called *z-order*. You may notice as you adjust the position and size of controls that one may be on top of another. For example, in the Customers Form Header, the label is in front of the image because it was added last. To change the z-order of a control, use cut and paste to remove this control from its current layer and paste it to the top layer.

Navigating Data with Forms

Besides using forms to page through data in the underlying record source (table or query), users need to be able to navigate directly to a specific record or records to perform maintenance. Forms already have been used to view data and print the current

FIGURE 5.16
Toolbox Control Wizards
availability

Button Name	Control Wizard?	Button Name	Control Wizard?
Bound Object Frame	Yes	Option Button	No
Check Box	No	Option Group	Yes
Combo Box	Yes	Page Break	No
Command Button	Yes	Rectangle	No
Control Wizards	No	Select Objects	No
Image	Yes	Subform/Subreport	Yes
Label	No	Tab Control	No
Line	No	Text Box	No
List Box	Yes	Toggle Button	Yes
More Controls	No	Unbound Object Frame	Yes

record, but it is also possible to use Find to navigate to a specific record and filters to create a subset of data to work on. Find and filters in Form View work in the same fashion as was covered in Datasheet View.

Finding Data with Forms

By default, a form displays all of the data in the underlying record source (table or query). When there are hundreds or even thousands of records, it can be an arduous task to find the ones that you want to work on without some helpful database tools.

Access provides a Find tool for locating and updating specific records. It can be used in many of the views of a database including the Form View. Click in the field containing the values to be searched, and then click the Find button on the toolbar. The Find and Replace dialog box is used to set the criteria for a search. Valid criteria are outlined in Figure 5.17.

When entering the Find What criteria, wildcards play an important role. A question mark (?) can be used to match any single character, and the asterisk (*) wildcard will replace any number of characters. The Find and Replace dialog box also can be used to replace values that have been found. It is best to test the Find and then add the Replace value so that data are not accidentally destroyed.

Finding form records:

1. Verify that the **ac05KoryoKicks.mdb** database is open and that the **Customers** form created in the previous steps is in Form View

2. Select the **LastName** field and click the **Find** button on the toolbar

3. Enter ***g*** in the Find What criteria to find all last names containing the letter g, and click **Find Next**

4. Repeat clicking **Find Next** until no more matches are found

tip: *Wagoner, Gray, and Guo should all be found*

5. Close the Find dialog box

FIGURE 5.17
Find and Replace dialog
box components

Critieria	Find and Replace Dialog Box	
	Action	
Find What	Sets the value that will be matched in the search	
Look In	Determines what will be searched. The default is the active column, but you also can choose to search the entire table.	
Match	Any Part of Field	Matches if the *Find What* value is anywhere in the field
	Whole Field	Matches if the Find What value is all that is in the field
	Start of Field	Matches if the Find What value is at the start of the field
Search	All	Searches for a match in the entire *Look In* area
	Up	Searches for a match above the cursor in the *Look In* area
	Down	Searches for a match below the cursor in the *Look In* area
Match Case	Matches the case of *Find What* when clicked on	

Filtering Form Records

Recall from the datasheet filtering discussion that there are four ways to apply filters. The first, Filter by Selection, returns records that match the value selected in the form. The second, Filter by Form, presents an empty version of the current form where match values can be typed. Filter for Input accepts a value or expression used to restrict the records, and the Advanced Filter/Sort window presents a design grid used to create criteria from scratch. Regardless of the type of filter being applied, the goal is to select only records that meet the stated criteria. Creating the criteria is slightly different for each type of filter.

Filtering form records:

1. Verify that the **ac05KoryoKicks.mdb** database is open and that the **Customers** form created in the previous steps is in Form View

2. Navigate to a record containing Wagoner and select the **g** (this is the same as *g*) and click **Filter By Selection** in the toolbar

3. Use the navigation buttons to explore the filtered records

4. Use the **Remove Filter** button to return to the entire record set

5. Click the **Filter By Form** button. Like "*g*" should display as the current criteria (see Figure 5.18)

6. Click the **OR** tab and add the condition **s*** (Access will convert this to Like "s*") as a Last Name criterion

7. Click the **Apply Filter** button (see Figure 5.19)

tip: *Gray, Guo, Smith, and Wagoner should all be found*

8. Click in Last Name and click the **Sort Ascending** button

F I G U R E 5.18

Filtered records by **g**

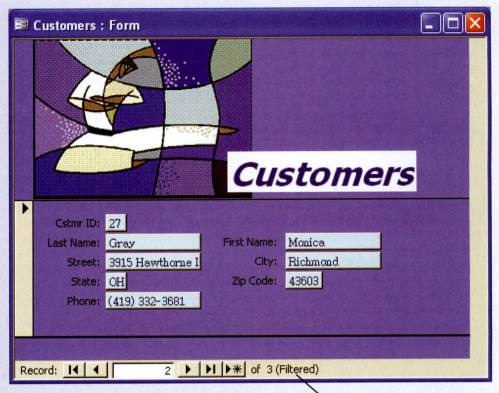

3 records met the filter criteria

F I G U R E 5.19

Filtered records by ***g*** **and s*** and then sorted by Last Name

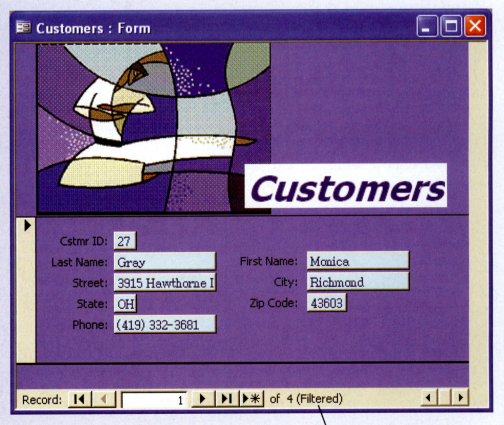

4 records of filtered data sorted by Last Name

9. Use the record navigation buttons to explore the filtered records

10. Return to Filter by Form and use the **Save As Query** button and name the query **LastNameFilter**

11. Use the **Remove Filter** 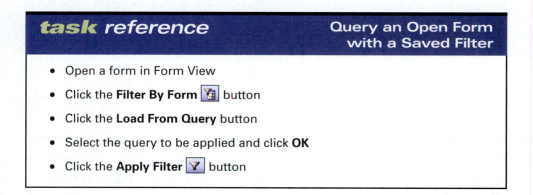 button to return to the entire record set

A filter can be saved as a query for reuse by clicking the Save As Query button on the Filter/Sort toolbar. Filter by Form and Filter for Input both can be used to filter by multiple criteria. Only Filter by Selection and Filter by Form were demonstrated, but Filter for Input and Advanced Filter/Sort can be accessed using the Filter option of the Records menu or the pop-up menu. Filters saved as queries also can be applied to an open form using the Filter by Form facility.

---

task reference   Query an Open Form with a Saved Filter

- Open a form in Form View
- Click the **Filter By Form** button
- Click the **Load From Query** button
- Select the query to be applied and click **OK**
- Click the **Apply Filter** button

Querying an open form:

1. Verify that the **ac05KoryoKicks.mdb** database is open and that the **Customers** form created in the previous steps is in Form View

2. Click the **Filter By Form** button

3. Click the **Load From Query** button

4. Choose **LastNameFilter** from the Applicable Filter dialog box and click **OK**

5. Click the **Apply Filter** button

6. Close the form

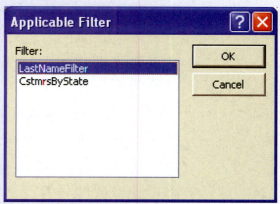

FIGURE 5.20

Applicable Filter dialog box

Using Forms to Maintain Data and Print Selected Records

Forms are built to display and maintain data. Besides creating a custom interface, forms allow control over the subset of data being operated on. Recall that the form itself is based on a record source, which is a table or query. If the record source is a table, all records from that table can initially be viewed, maintained, or printed in the form. If the record source is a query, only the records selected by the query are available to the form.

When a filter or query is applied to the record source, a subset of the data matching the criteria is returned. Until the query or filter is removed, all operations are processed against the subset of data, which impacts the data that are available for maintenance, printing, and other operations.

One of the simplest mistakes to make is to forget to remove a query or filter and then apply another criterion. For example, if a filter to select Ohio customers is applied and then a filter for orders over $100, the result will be Ohio customers who ordered over $100 of goods. If the intent was to give a discount to all orders over $100, customers who are not from Ohio would be missed.

Printing all of the records in the record source is accomplished using the Print button on the toolbar. When forms were first introduced, you learned to use the Print dialog box activated from the File menu to print the current record using the Selected Records option. To print a specific subset of the data such as customers who ordered replacement parts, filter for that subset and then use the Print button to print the selected records.

SESSION 5.1

making *the grade*

1. What would you do to change the alignment of all the labels on a form?

2. Describe the difference between bound and unbound controls.

3. What are object properties and why do you set them?

4. Why would you use Form Design View rather than a Wizard to create a form?

SESSION 5.2 CREATING COMPLEX REPORTS

The report object allows the creation of a custom hard copy output based on the data in one or more database tables. Printed output can be created using each of the database objects (forms, tables, and queries) that have already been explored, but the report object provides the greatest power and flexibility for creating printed output. Printed output from the other database objects is often used for internal analytical reporting, but when a report goes outside a department or organization, a formal report is usually created using the report object. Public reports, billing statements, and mailing labels are common organizational reports that could use the improved visual impact provided by custom reports.

Defining a Report in Report Design View

Creating a report in Design View provides complete control of all the report elements and their properties, making Design View much more powerful than using a Wizard. While the Report Design View is very similar to Form Design View, the process of building a report is more complex.

Report Sections

Reports can have up to seven types of sections (see Figure 5.21). The exact number of sections is determined by the report layout. The controls placed in the *Report Detail section* will appear once for each record in the underlying record source. The *Group Header/Footer sections* appear before and after each group of records. Group Header/Footer sections can be added individually or in pairs for each level of grouping in the report. The *Page Header/Footer sections* appear at the top and bottom of each report page. The *Report Header/Footer sections* are added in pairs and appear at the beginning and end of the report.

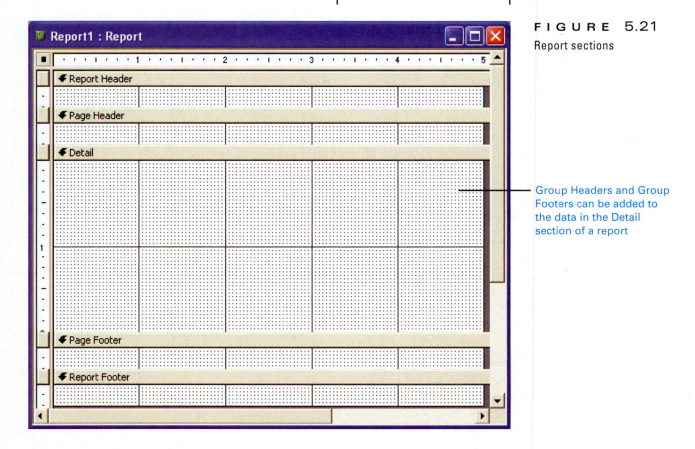

FIGURE 5.21
Report sections

Group Headers and Group Footers can be added to the data in the Detail section of a report

Each section has a **Selection bar** that can be adjusted to resize the section. Empty sections can have their size set to 0 or their Visible property set to No so that they do not display in the final report. If, for example, your report needs a Report Header but not a Report Footer, you could set the Report Footer size to 0.

The Report Header section normally contains the title of the report with the date and any other information that will print once at the beginning of the report. The Page Header contains information that should appear at the top of each page such as a page number, column headings for the report fields, and a reduced report title. The Group Header indicates the field or fields that will control data summaries.

The Group Footer section holds the summary that will be printed at the end of each detail group. For example, the order total would be printed each time the OrderNumber (group field) changes. The Page Footer section is used for page numbers and other information that needs to print at the bottom of every report page. If a report has both a Page Footer and a Report Footer, the print order of the last page is Report Footer and then Page Footer. The Report Footer section normally holds information that will be printed only once at the end of the report such as grand totals and report footnotes.

Since the Report Design View is complex, it is important to design a report before attempting to build it. One significant difference between designing forms and reports is that forms generally display one record per page in columns, while reports generally display several records of data per printed page in rows.

Start the report design with the Detail section by outlining where the rows of data will display. Decide what fields need to be included for each record. After documenting what fields are to be included, choose a layout for those fields and any other elements that are to be included such as a calculation or a graphic. The Detail section repeats for each record, so only one line of output needs to be specified. Figure 5.22 shows a sample form design for KoryoKicks Customers input.

FIGURE 5.22

Customers report design

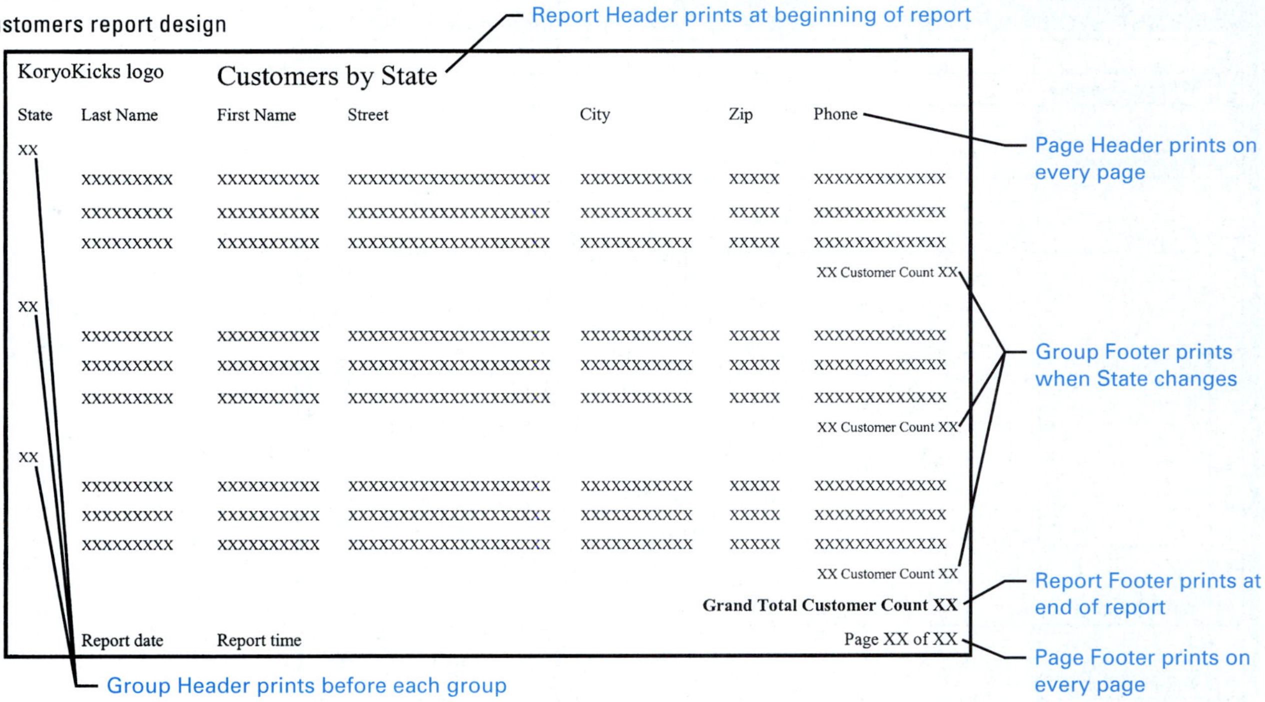

Report Header prints at beginning of report

KoryoKicks logo   Customers by State

Page Header prints on every page

Group Footer prints when State changes

Report Footer prints at end of report

Page Footer prints on every page

Group Header prints before each group

Headers are generally easier to design than footers, so let's look at those next. Most reports have a title. If your title is to appear only once at the beginning of the report, place it in the Report Header. If your title is to appear on every page, place it in the Page Header. Some reports place a large-font title in the Report Header and a small-font title in the Page Header so that the report is identified on every page without wasting page space.

Report and Page Headers can contain any other static data that your report requires. Candidates for these sections include page numbers, the report date, prepared by information, a report overview, and the company logo. The Page Header should contain the column labels that identify the data in the Detail section. Group Headers and Footers will be discussed in the Calculating and Summarizing Data topic. Place the remaining information in the header that prints with the desired frequency. When a report contains both a Report Header and a Page Header, the Report Header prints first on the initial report page.

Footers are pretty straightforward when there are no calculations involved. Place page numbers, explanatory text, legend of symbols, and preparation and use notes in the footer that prints with the frequency needed.

The design reflects the complete layout of the report including titles, graphics, captions, and field lengths. In the design shown, the field captions appear as the twins want to see them on the report and Xs are used to indicate where the data will display and the length of the data display area. The fields placed in the Detail section will print for each record in the record source and are depicted on the design as the repeated lines within each state group. The notations with the figure indicate the contents of the other report sections.

In Report Design View, field captions will be in Label controls and the field data will be displayed in Text Box controls. The data are grouped by state, and a count of customers in each state is displayed. The KoryoKicks logo will display in an Image control, and the form title will be entered in a Label.

Since a common development technique is to build a report using the AutoReport Wizard and then to customize it in Design View, it is important to understand how the

Wizard behaves. The Wizard places the title provided in the Report Header section. The date and page numbers are placed in the Page Footer. The field names are used as column headings and are placed in the Page Header when there is no grouping.

Whether the report is developed completely in Report Design View or was customized after the Wizard created the first cut, it is called a ***custom report***. Custom reports are more time consuming to create and maintain and should be used only when the Wizard cannot create the output that is needed.

The Report Toolbox and Field List

The toolbox used in Report Design View is the same as that used in Form Design View. Recall that the toolbox can be positioned anywhere on the screen and has Screen Tips that can be activated and deactivated using the View menu. The toolbar buttons are presented in Figure 5.4 if you need to review them.

When a control is placed in a report section, its properties direct what it will display and how it will appear. The Data properties of a bound control (those linked to a record source) are set to direct what field it will display. Data properties are set automatically when the record source field list is used to add the control to your report or when the first cut of the report is created with the Wizard. Control Wizards with step-by-step instructions are available for the more complex toolbox options. Figure 5.16 outlines the availability of Control Wizards.

Customizing an AutoReport Wizard Form

To become familiar with the Report Design View, we'll start with a simple report on the KoryoKicks Customer table that has been built for you. The Wizard was used to create a report that will display all of the Customer fields except Notes in order by customer name within state. The report was saved as AutoReportCustomer.

Customizing the Customer AutoReport:

1. Verify that the **ac05KoryoKicks.mdb** database is open

2. In the Database Window, select the **Reports** object and the **AutoReportCustomer** report, and click the **Design View** button

3. Explore the report design. Notice that some fields are too wide and some too narrow (Street and PhoneNumber do not completely display)

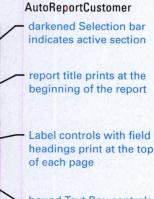

FIGURE 5.23

Updated AutoReportCustomer

— darkened Selection bar indicates active section

— report title prints at the beginning of the report

— Label controls with field headings print at the top of each page

— bound Text Box controls to display data

— expression to display today's date

— expression to display the word *Page*, the current page number, and total number of pages

4. Use the **Print Preview View** 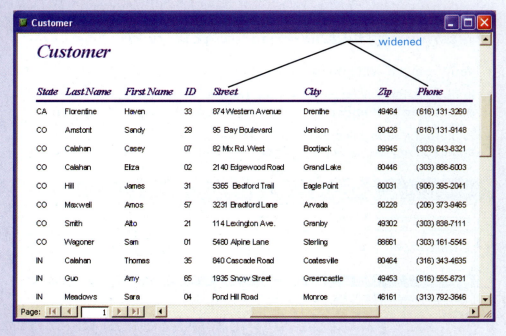 button to preview the report and then return to Design View

5. Modify the field labels as follows

   LastName   **Last Name**

   FirstName   **First Name**

   CstmrID   **ID**

   ZipCode   **Zip**

   tip: *Click an insertion point in the label and then make corrections*

6. Use the sizing handles to reduce the size of the Label and Text Box controls associated with State, Last Name, First Name, ID, City, and Zip

   tip: *Use the View and Design buttons to move between Report views and verify the validity of your results. Each field should display all of the heading and data without too much space left over*

7. Use the move handle to adjust the positions of Last Name, First Name, ID, and Street, removing the extra space between them caused by reducing field sizes

8. Use the sizing handles to increase the size of Street until all of its data display on every detail row of the report

9. Move City, Zip, and Phone to adjust for the resizing, as shown in Figure 5.24

FIGURE 5.24

Edited
AutoReportCustomer

10. Resize Phone so that it will display the complete phone number

11. Edit the title to read **Customers by State**

12. Preview your results and save your changes as **CustomerByState** when you are satisfied

In this process the contents of the Report Header, Page Header, and Detail sections of this simple report were edited. The Page Footer contains expressions that will be discussed later. The Report Footer has been set to a Height of 0 so that it will not display.

Building a Form in Design View

Let's build a Customers by State Report in Design View. The CstmrsByState query has already been prepared as the record source to simplify the process.

---

task reference   Create a Report in Design View

- In the Database Window click the **Reports** object and click the **New** button

- Click **Design View** as the way to develop the report, select the record source from the drop-down list, and click **OK**

Building the Customer report in Design View:

1. Verify that the **ac05KoryoKicks.mdb** database is open

2. In the Database Window, select the **Reports** object and click the **New** button

3. In the New Report dialog box, select **Design View**, select **CstmrsByState** as the record source, and click **OK**

4. Double-click on the Title bar of the field list to select all of the fields from the record source table, drag the fields to the Detail section of the report, and drop them

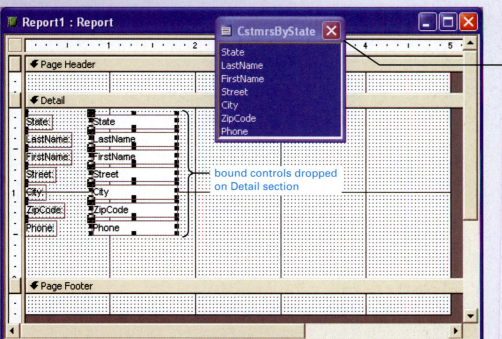

FIGURE 5.25

Customer fields placed in the Detail section

field list

bound controls dropped on Detail section

5. Click on the background to deselect the fields and then close the field list since it won't be used again

6. Use Shift to select all of the labels with field headings and use Cut to remove them from the Detail section

7. Click the **Page Header bar** and paste the labels there

8. With all of the labels selected, activate the Properties pages and change the Font Size to **10** points, Font Weight to **bold**, and Fore Color to the darkest custom blue previously developed

9. Organize and edit the labels in the Page Header and the text boxes in the Detail section as shown in Figure 5.26

FIGURE 5.26

Redesigned Page Header and Detail section

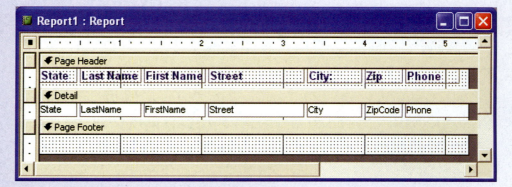

10. Reduce the size of the Page Header section by dragging the Detail bar up until there is just enough room for the labels

tip: *Remember to preview your results. Use move handles and size handles to adjust the position and size of controls. Get the labels and text boxes as close as you can to the positions shown. We'll work on exact alignment in the next set of steps*

11. Organize the text boxes in the Detail section to match Figure 5.26

12. Reduce the size of the Detail section by dragging the Page Footer Selection bar up until there is just enough room for the text boxes

13. Use the **View** 🔍▾ button to preview the results. Make any needed adjustments to column widths

14. Save the report as **CustomerByStateDesignView**

In Figure 5.26 the text displaying in the column headings has been changed to match the labels from the form design. You still need to apply those changes to your report. By default, a colon (:) is included after each field name. You will need to remove the colons, add spaces, and abbreviate headings that are too long.

Editing label Captions:

1. Verify that the **ac05KoryoKicks.mdb** database is open and that **CustomerByStateDesignView** is open in Design View

2. Click on the **State** label and use the **Properties** 📋 button to open its Properties pages

3. Remove the colon from the **Caption** property

4. Use the drop-down list at the top of the Properties pages to move to the next label (LastName)

tip: *The text box controls are represented by the field name of the data they will contain. Labels are numbered beginning with Label01*

5. Edit this label to remove the colon (:); add spaces between words

6. Repeat this process for FirstName, Street, City, State, and Phone

7. Use the drop-down list at the top of the Properties pages to select the **ZipCode**

8. Remove the colon from the **Caption** and edit it to read **Zip**

9. Preview and save your changes

You also could have clicked in each label and edited the Captions directly. Use whichever method you prefer. Working in the Properties pages can be easier when you are setting multiple properties or working on multiple controls. Editing in the report design is simpler when you are changing the Caption of a label or two.

The foundation of the final report is complete, but the controls need to be aligned exactly before moving on to the other report sections. Access provides an *Align* command that allows multiple controls to be selected and aligned to each other or to the grid. A row of objects can be aligned by their top edges (Align Top) or their bottom edges (Align Bottom). A column of objects can be aligned by their left edges (Align Left) or right edges (Align Right). Once the controls are aligned to each other, drag them as a unit to their exact report position.

For the Customer by State report to look professional, the rows need to be straight and the headings need to align exactly over the data. The Align command is the way to make that happen.

Aligning Customer report controls:

1. Verify that the **ac05KoryoKicks.mdb** database is open and that **CustomerByStateDesignView**, created in the previous steps, is open in Design View

2. Select all of the Label controls in the Page Header section by clicking the first control and then holding down the Shift key to select the remaining controls

3. Activate the **Format** menu, choose **Align**, and then click **Top** to align the tops of the selected controls (see Figure 5.27)

4. Now that the labels are aligned to each other, move them (they are already selected) to the top of the Header section

5. Repeat this process to align the Text Box controls and place them at the top of the Details section

6. Select the State label and hold down the Shift key and select the State text box

7. Activate the **Format** menu, choose **Align**, and then click **Left** to align the left sides of the controls

FIGURE 5.27

Aligning control tops

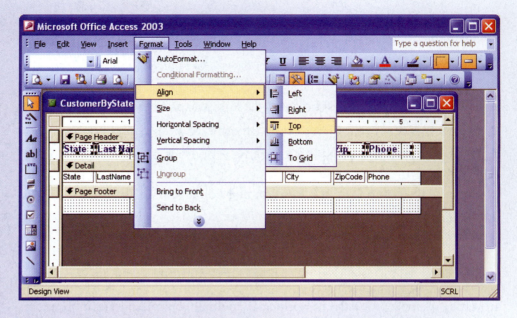

8. Adjust the position of both controls if necessary

9. Repeat steps 6 through 8 for the remaining Header/Detail pairs as needed to make your report look like Figure 5.28

FIGURE 5.28

Aligned report

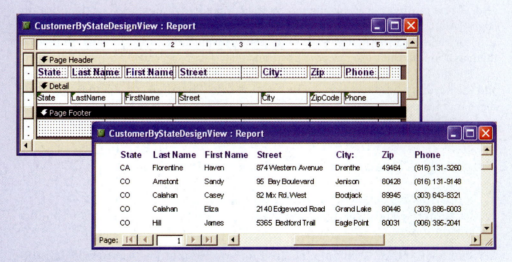

10. Preview and save the report

Now that the detail portion of the report is complete, it is time to add the contents of the Page Footer and the Report Header.

Adding and Modifying Unbound Controls

The remaining elements of the report are composed of unbound controls. Recall that unbound controls are not dependent on the values in the underlying record source. The Page Footer section is already on the form, so we will begin building it. The date and time are added using the =*Now()* function, a predefined calculation that returns the current date and time. All calculations begin with an equals sign (=). The format applied to the text box containing the =Now() controls how it will display.

Building the Page Footer

The Page Header was added to the form to contain the field labels. When the header was added, the Page Footer also was added since they are paired. The report displays the report date, time, and page number at the bottom of each page or in the Page Footer.

Adding the Customer report date and time:

1. Verify that the **ac05KoryoKicks.mdb** database is open and that **CustomerByStateDesignView**, created in the previous steps, is open in Design View

2. If the toolbox is not displaying, select the **Toolbox** button to activate it

3. Select the **Text Box** 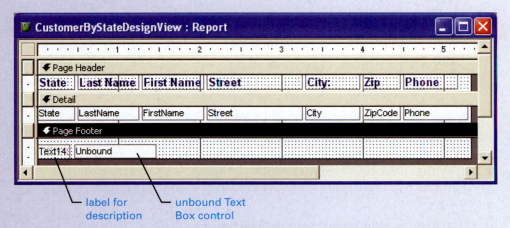 tool from the toolbox and click in the Page Footer

tip: *The label displays the word Text with a number. Your number may be different since it reflects what you have been doing in your session*

4. Select the label and press **Del** since the report doesn't need it

5. Select the text box (it says unbound) and use the move handle to move it to the left side of the report

6. Click in the text box and type **=Now()** and use the View button to preview your changes

label for description — unbound Text Box control

FIGURE 5.29
Text box with label added to Page Footer

tip: *You will need to scroll to the bottom of the report. Both the date and time should display in one text box until the format is changed*

7. Select the text box and use **Ctrl+C** to place it on the Clipboard

8. Select the Page Footer and use **Ctrl+V** to paste a second copy of the text box in the footer

9. Position the second copy to the right of the first

10. Click the leftmost text box, use the **Properties** button to activate the Properties pages, and set the Format property to **Long Date**

11. Set the Format property of the second text box to **Medium Time** and the Text Align property to **Left**

12. Use the View button to preview your changes and make any needed adjustments to the position and size of the text boxes (see Figure 5.30)

13. Save the report

F I G U R E 5.30
Date and time in Page
Footer

Two text boxes with the =Now() calculation were used to display the date and time so that they could be formatted the way the twins wanted them. Whenever this report is printed, the =Now() function will retrieve the current system date and time. The Text Box format will cause the first text box to display a long date and the second to display a medium date.

Page numbers are added to a report in a similar fashion with an unbound control and a function. The text box and function can be entered manually or from the Insert menu. Regardless of how the page function is added, it automatically places the correct page number on each page of the report.

anotherway
**. . . to Add the
Date and Time**

The Insert menu also has an option to insert the date and time. This method does not allow the formatting and placement options provided by building your own, but it is easy

---

task reference   Add Page Numbers to a
                                                 Report in Design View

- Display the report in Design View

- Choose **Page Numbers** from the **Insert** menu

- Select the formatting, position, and alignment options that you want and click **OK**

Adding page numbers to the Customer report:

1. Verify that the **ac05KoryoKicks.mdb** database is open and that **CustomerByStateDesignView**, created in the previous steps, is open in Design View

2. Choose **Page Numbers** from the **Insert** menu

3. Choose the following options:

   Page N of M

   Bottom of Page [Footer]

   Alignment—Right

   Show Number on First Page—Checked

4. Click **OK**

5. Use the View button to preview the results (see Figure 5.31)

6. Save the report

Any other information that is to print at the bottom of each report page can be added using the methods demonstrated.

F I G U R E 5.31
Page Numbers dialog box

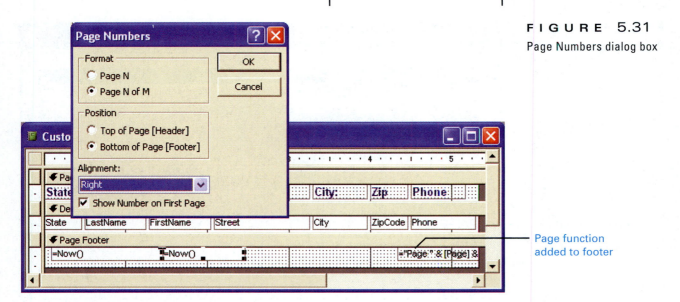

Page function
added to footer

Building the Report Header

To complete the basic report, the Report Header section will need to be added to hold the report title. Recall that a Report Header appears only once at the beginning of a report. The title will be entered in a Label and formatted with an increased font size and color.

Adding the Report Header to the Customer report:

1. Verify that the **ac05KoryoKicks.mdb** database is open and that **CustomerByStateDesignView**, created in the previous steps, is open in Design View

2. Click the **View** menu option and select **Report Header/Footer** to add the sections to the report

3. If the toolbox is not displaying, select the **Toolbox** button to activate it

4. Select the **Image** tool from the toolbox and click the Report Header

tip: *If the Image Control Wizard does not initiate, click the Control Wizards button in the toolbox*

5. Navigate to the files for this chapter and chose **ac05KoryoKicksLogo.gif** as the graphic to display

6. Select the **Label** tool from the toolbox and click in the Report Header to the right of the logo

7. Type **Customers by State**

8. Select the title label and open the Properties pages, set the Font Size to **26**, and the Fore Color to the custom dark blue (hue **174**, sat **240**, lum **60**, red **4**, green **0**, blue **128**) previously added to the palette

9. Choose **To Fit** from the **Size** option of the **Format** menu to expand the label. Position the label as shown in Figure 5.32

10. Use the View button to preview the results

11. Save the report

ACCESS

Report Header

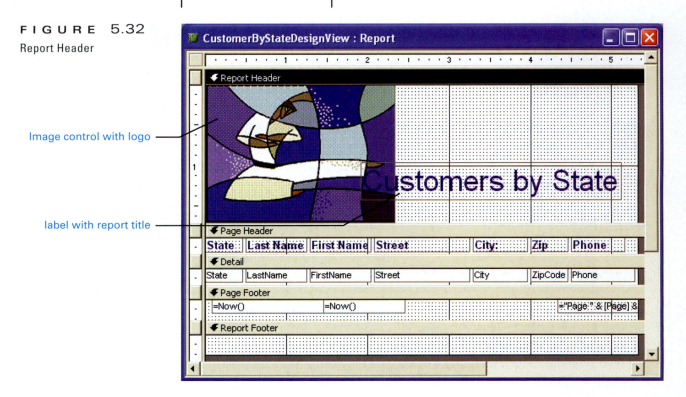

Image control with logo

label with report title

It should now be apparent that creating and using custom colors is easy when they are added to the palette. Custom colors can greatly enhance the professional look of any report.

Adding Separators

The AutoReport Wizard places lines to separate the data from the column headings and Page Footer. The Line control is used to add such separators to your report. Like other report objects, the properties of the line determine how it displays.

Adding separators to the Customer report:

1. Verify that the **ac05KoryoKicks.mdb** database is open and that **CustomerByStateDesignView**, created in the previous steps, is open in Design View

2. Use the Detail section border to expand the height of the Page Header section to make space for the line

3. Click the **Line** tool on the Drawing toolbar

4. Click in the Page Header section above the column headers, hold down the Shift key, and drag the line the full width of the report

tip: *Holding down the Shift key while dragging a line keeps the line straight. You can use this technique when resizing the line too*

5. Activate the Line's Properties pages
   a. Set the Border Color to the custom dark blue that you have developed
   b. Set the Border Width to 1 pt
   c. Close the Properties dialog box

6. Use the Report Footer border to expand the height of the Page Footer section making room for the line

7. Select the Line tool and hold down the Shift key while dragging a line above the Page Footer controls

8. Activate the Line's Properties 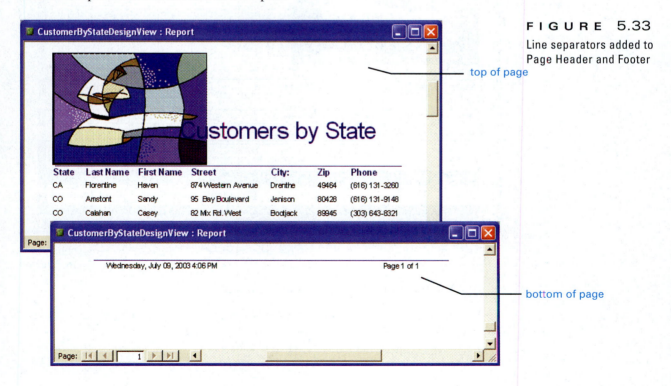 pages and set the Border Color to the custom dark blue that you have developed and the Border Width to 1 pt

9. Use the View button to preview the results and adjust the lines to match the left and right margins of the data (see Figure 5.33)

10. Save the report

   Missy and Micah would like the report to present the data in order by state and customer name. They also want the number of customers in each state counted.

Calculating and Summarizing Data

The Design View of Access reports can be used to sort, group, and calculate. The Sorting and Grouping button on the toolbar activates the Sorting and Grouping dialog box where field(s) can be selected or expressions built that will control the order of data presentation. These fields also can be used to group data, to keep records with the same value together, or to calculate subtotals.

Calculating Totals

The simplest calculations involve totaling or counting all of the values of a field. The *=Sum()* function is used to calculate the total of numeric fields. The *=Max()* and *=Min()* functions will return the maximum or minimum value of a numeric or date field. The *=Count()* function can be used to count the number of entries in either numeric or text fields. The Report Footer section is the most likely place for grand totals, since it prints once at the end of the report.

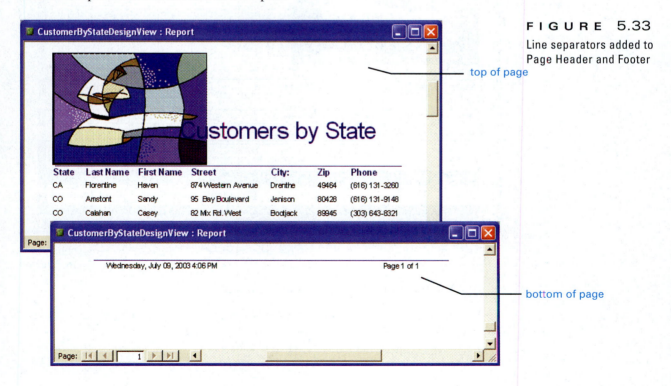

FIGURE 5.33
Line separators added to Page Header and Footer

ACCESS

For the KoryoKicks report, the twins want a total count of their customers so the =Count() function will be used. The equals (=) sign indicates that the text box will display a calculated value. Count is the name of the function that controls the calculation. A field name is included in the parenthesis to tell Access what to count. In this case, it is not terribly important which of the fields is counted, but we'll use =Count(LastName) to count the number of LastName entries in the table. The basic syntax for applying a function is =functionname(field) where field indicates what is to be operated on, like =Count(LastName).

Adding a report total (Count) to the Customer report:

1. Verify that the **ac05KoryoKicks.mdb** database is open and that **CustomerByStateDesignView**, created in the previous steps, is open in Design View

2. Click the **Text Box** abl tool

3. Click in the right half of the Report Footer to add a text box and its associated label

4. Click in the label and type **Grand Total Customer Count**

5. Click in the text box and type **=Count(LastName)**

FIGURE 5.34

Total count of customers

label describing
Text Box contents

text box with
Count function

6. Use the View button to preview the results

tip: *The Report Footer will appear after the last record but before the Page Footer on the last page of the report*

7. Save the report

One text box is added to the Report Footer for each Grand Total calculation being specified. In a report calculating customer charges, possible calculations include the grand total charge (=Sum), the minimum charge (=Min), and the maximum charge (=Max). Including all three calculations would require adding three text boxes with the appropriate expression in each.

Sorting and Grouping Data

The ability to sort and group data was introduced with the Report Wizard. As expected, sorting controls the order that data are presented in the report. Grouping controls what groups of data are used for page breaks or subtotals. For example, to create a count of customers in each state, the records will be grouped by state. When grouping is applied to a field or fields, the records also must be sorted by those field(s) so that the data to be grouped always present together in the report.

The Sorting and Grouping dialog box allows the selection of a field or fields that will control the presentation order of the report. Each field selected can be further specified to control its sort order and grouping properties. If Grouping Properties are not specified for a selected field, a sort on that field is created. If Grouping Properties are set, either a Group Header, a Group Footer, or both are added to the report design. The contents of the Group Header and Footer must be specified using the techniques covered for other components of the report design.

---

task reference   Control Sorting and Grouping in a Report

- Display the report in Design View

- Click the **Sorting and Grouping** button on the toolbar

- Use the Field/Expression drop-down list box to select each field that you want to use to sort or group data. Each selected Field/Expression will be on a different line of the grid

- Select the Sort order for each Field/Expression listed. The order of multiple fields determines their priority in the sort

- Select the grouping option(s) for each field

- Close the Sorting and Grouping dialog box

- Add the necessary controls and content to any Group Headers and Footers created

---

help yourself *Use the Type a Question combo box to improve your understanding of grouping data by typing* **grouping records**. *Review the contents of* About grouping records *and* Change sorting and grouping levels. *Close the Help window when you are finished*

Adding Sorting and Grouping to the Customer report:

1. Verify that the **ac05KoryoKicks.mdb** database is open and that **CustomerByStateDesignView**, created in the previous steps, is open in Design View

2. Click the **Sorting and Grouping** ⟦≣⟧ button on the toolbar

3. Use the drop-down list box to select **State** as the first sort field, **LastName** as the second, and **FirstName** as the third

FIGURE 5.35

Sorting and Grouping dialog box

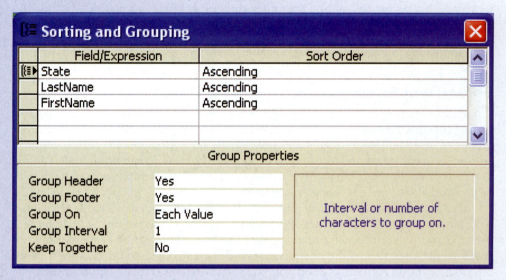

4. Set both the Group Header and Group Footer properties of *State* to **Yes**

tip: *State Header and Footer sections should be added to the report. If you set other fields for grouping, they will add the additional headers and/or footers you specify to the report*

5. Close the Sorting and Grouping dialog box

6. Save the report

Now both the Group Header and Group Footer sections for State need to have their contents defined. A Group Header usually contains the field that identifies the group, in this case State. Since the header prints at the beginning of each new group, placing State in the Group Header section will cause it to print once at the beginning of each new state, rather than repeating the state on every detail line.

The Group Footer usually contains the calculations for the group and any group-specific text. For the KoryoKicks report, the Group Footer will contain the count of customers in a state. This is the same calculation as was entered in the Report Footer section, but in the Group Footer it will be printed at the end of each state and zeroed to begin counting the next state.

Adding State Header and Footer content:

1. Verify that the **ac05KoryoKicks.mdb** database is open and that **CustomerByStateDesignView**, created in the previous steps, is open in Design View

2. Click the **State** field in the Detail section and use the **Cut** button to place it on the Clipboard

3. Click the **State Header** bar and use the **Paste** button to place the State field in this section

4. Click the **Text Box** 🔲 tool and then click in the **State Footer** to the right of center

5. Delete the label, leaving only the text box (it contains the text "unbound")

6. Type **=State & " Customer Count " & Count(LastName)**

tip: *Be sure to type the space before and after Customer Count. You can expand the text box using the sizing handles so that you can see the entire expression. Access will convert the statement to =[State]&"CustomerCount"&Count([LastName])*

7. Using the Formatting toolbar, set the State Footer text box properties to **Bold** and **Align Right**

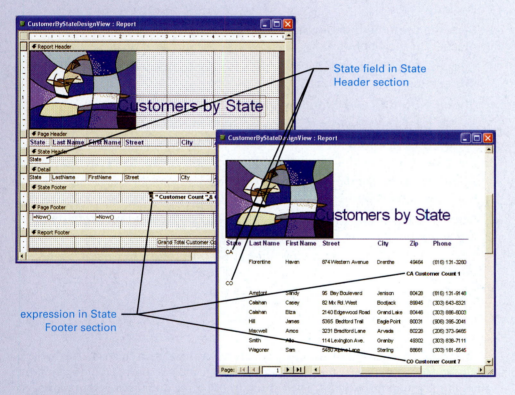

State field in State Header section

expression in State Footer section

FIGURE 5.36

Completed Customer by State report

8. Use the View button to preview the report and return to Design View

9. Save the report

Add one text box to the Group Footer for each group calculation that is being specified. The ampersand (&) operator is used to *concatenate* different parts of an expression. When double quotes (") are included in an expression, the values between the double quotes will display exactly as entered, including spaces. There are no double quotes around field names because they will be replaced with the current field value. For example, `=LastName&", "&FirstName` would cause the value of LastName, a comma and a space, and the value of FirstName to display in a text box.

The expression used in the report created in the previous steps was `=State&"Customer Count" &Count(LastName)`. This expression causes the current value of State to print, followed by a space, the text Customer Count, another space, and the result of the expression Count(LastName).

Hiding Duplicate Report Values

After previewing the report, the twins decide they don't want State in the Group Header section taking up a whole line of the report. They would like State displayed on the first line of each group. To accomplish this, you will need to put State back in the Detail section of the report, remove the State Header, and format State so that duplicate values do not display.

Hiding duplicate State values:

1. Verify that the **ac05KoryoKicks.mdb** database is open and that **CustomerByStateDesignView**, created in the previous steps, is open in Design View

2. Click the **State** field in the State Header section and use the **Cut** button to place it on the Clipboard

3. Click the **Detail** bar and use the **Paste** button to place the State field in this section

4. Click the **Sorting and Grouping** button
   a. Set the Group Header property of State to **No**
   b. Close the Sorting and Grouping dialog box

5. Click **State** and use the **Properties** button to activate its Properties pages
   a. Set the Hide Duplicates property to **Yes**
   b. Close the Properties dialog box

6. Using the Formatting toolbar, set the State Footer text box property to the custom dark blue Fore Color

7. Use the View button to preview the report and return to Design View (see Figure 5.37)

8. Save the report

Two final versions of the CustomersByState report have been created. One that uses the Group Header to display the group identification and a second that hides duplicate values in the group field (State). The advantage of hiding duplicates is that more data display on a report page. The advantage of using the Group Header is that it can make the beginning of a group easier to identify.

Lines, boxes, and other formatting can be added to make the groups on your report more clear. Formatting is a matter of preference, but in general keep it simple. Don't use too many colors, lines, or unnecessary indents that can detract from the purpose of the report.

Previewing and Printing Reports

The Print Preview View button on the toolbar has been used throughout the steps to evaluate design changes in a WYSIWYG (what you see is what you get) environment. Print Preview is also used to set up the printer before printing. The Setup button opens

FIGURE 5.37
Updated Customer by
State report

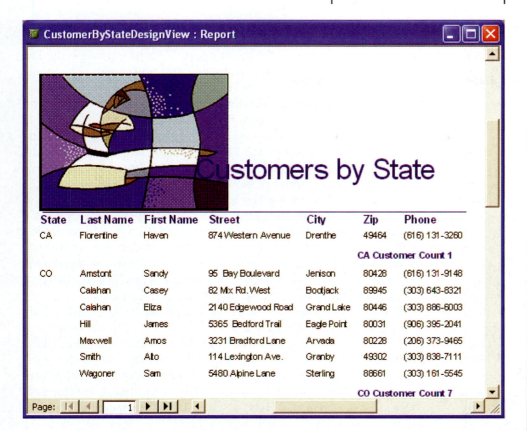

a dialog box with settings for page margins, page orientation, alternate printers, paper source, and other printer-specific options. The settings available from Setup are specific to your software configuration and printer installation, so the options beyond setting margins and page orientation will vary from computer to computer.

Both the magnifier glass and the percent drop-down list box control the zoom of your preview. The three buttons between the zoom controls set the view to one page, two pages, or multiple pages of the report. When uncertain about the function of a button, pause the cursor over it to view Screen Tips. The OfficeLinks button is used to send the report design to other Office products such as Word and Excel. The Print button will send the report directly to the printer without any further options.

Reports have a third view, Layout Preview, that also can be used to view the impact of design changes. A Layout Preview shows only a few sample records to evaluate the overall impact of design updates without reviewing multiple pages of output.

making the grade

SESSION 5.2

1. Describe the function of the Detail section of a report.

2. How do you decide whether to place a calculation in the Report Footer or a Group Footer?

3. What is the difference between a control's sizing handle and its move handles?

4. How do you determine what control to use when building a report?

ACCESS

SESSION 5.3 SUMMARY

Access form and report objects are designed to support different output needs. The form object is used to create screen output used to view and update data. The report object is used to create formal printed output. The output from all Access objects can be printed, but the report object is specifically designed to format printed output. Both forms and reports are bound to a record source such as a table or query.

Controls are the building blocks used to build both forms and reports. The toolbox is a special toolbar that contains controls. The Field List dialog box displays all of the fields from the record source. Bound controls are those that display data from the record source fields. Unbound controls are those that display data not bound to the record source such as report titles, logos, and lines.

The Design Views used to develop both custom forms and reports are very similar. The main design area is called the Detail section. Controls added to the Detail section most commonly display data from the underlying record source. Text Box controls are used to display fields and calculations. Label controls are used to display text that doesn't change such as the report title or field headings. A Line control is used to draw lines on a form or report. The Image control will display a variety of image formats.

The easiest way to add a bound control is to drag fields from the field list. The bulk of bound controls are placed in the Detail section of a form or report. Unbound controls are added to a form or report by clicking the tool in the toolbox and then clicking the surface where the control is to display. For simple controls such as a Label, use the Properties button to activate the Properties pages. The properties of an object control what and how it displays. More complex controls such as the Image control have Control Wizards for step-by-step instructions on setting control properties.

Visit www.mhhe.com/i-series/ to explore related topics.

MICROSOFT OFFICE SPECIALIST OBJECTIVES SUMMARY

- Modifying form properties—MOS AC03S-1-9
- Adding calculated controls to a report section—MOS AC03S-1-11
- Showing and hiding headers and footers—MOS AC03S-3-2
- Aligning, resizing, and spacing controls—MOS AC03S-3-3
- Changing margins and page orientation—MOS AC03S-3-3
- Previewing for print—MOS AC03S-4-2

making the grade *answers*

SESSION 5.1

1. Open the form in Design View. Select all of the labels to be adjusted by holding down the Shift key while you click. Use either the justification buttons on the toolbar or the Properties pages to change the alignment.

2. Bound controls display data from a table or query and are bound to the field that the control will display. The contents of a bound control change as the user moves through records. An unbound control is not attached to a record source and displays static data.

3. Object properties are set using Properties pages, by resizing the object, by moving the object, or by formatting the object. Properties are settings that control how an object appears or behaves. They are set to change such things as the background color, font, or format of an object.

4. Form Design View allows the developer to have full control over the alignment, layout, and properties of form elements. Often forms developed using a Wizard are customized in Design View.

SESSION 5.2

1. The Detail section of a report is used to define the fields that will be displayed for each row of data in the record source.

2. The frequency of the calculation determines where you place the calculation. If the calculation is to print summary information about the groups on the report, the calculation needs to be in the Group Footer. If the calculation is to summarize all of the records in the record source, place it in the Report Footer.

3. Sizing handles are smaller and used to resize the control. The large handle at the top left of a control will move joined controls independently.

4. Controls are chosen by what they are to display. Labels hold text that doesn't change such as the title of a report. Text boxes hold calculations and display values from record source fields. Images hold graphics such as a logo.

task reference *summary*

Task	Page #	Preferred Method
Open a new form in Design View	AC 5.6	• In the Database Window of an open database, click the **Forms** object • Click the **New** button on the Database Window toolbar • In the New Form dialog box, click **Design View** • Select the table or query that will be the record source for the form and click **OK**
Select and move form controls	AC 5.9	• Select the control to be operated on by clicking it. The Shift key can be used to select multiple controls • Drag the control(s) to the new location. Use the large move handle to independently move components of a bound control
Set control properties	AC 5.11	• Right-click the control to open the pop-up menu • Select **Properties** from the pop-up menu • Select the appropriate Properties tab (usually Format) • Navigate to the property and change its setting
Show Form Headers and Footers	AC 5.15	• Open a form in Design View • Select **Form Header/Footer** from the **View** menu

ACCESS

task reference *summary*

Task	Page #	Preferred Method
Add Toolbox controls to a design	AC 5.16	• Open a form or report in Design View • If necessary, activate the toolbox using the **Toolbox** button on the Form Design toolbar • Verify that the Toolbox **Control Wizards** button is depressed (a blue outline will show around it) • Click the Toolbox control that is to be added to the form • Click in the Form section that will contain the control • Set the control's properties using the Properties pages activated with the Properties button
Query an open form with a saved filter	AC 5.21	• Open a form in Form View • Click the **Filter By Form** button • Click the **Load From Query** button • Select the query to be applied and click **OK** • Click the **Apply Filter** button
Create a report in Design View	AC 5.27	• In the Database Window click the **Reports** object and click the **New** button • Click **Design View** as the way to develop the report, select the record source from the drop-down list, and click **OK**
Add page numbers to a report in Design View	AC 5.32	• Display the report in Design View • Choose **Page Numbers** from the **Insert** menu • Select the formatting, position, and alignment options that you want and click **OK**
Control Sorting and Grouping in a report	AC 5.37	• Display the report in Design View • Click the **Sorting and Grouping** button on the toolbar • Use the Field/Expression drop-down list box to select each field that you want to use to sort or group data. Each selected Field/Expression will be on a different line of the grid • Select the Sort order for each Field/Expression listed. The order of multiple fields determines their priority in the sort • Select the grouping option(s) for each field • Close the Sorting and Grouping dialog box • Add the necessary controls and content to any Group Headers and Footers created

TRUE/FALSE

1. A Label control must always be added to a form with an associated Text Box control.

2. You must be in Form Design View to adjust the properties of a Form control.

3. The Align option of the Format menu operates to align selected controls to each other.

4. The largest handle of a selected control can be used to resize it.

5. Control properties can only be updated from the Properties pages.

6. In Report Design View, the field list contains all database fields in the record source that can be added to the design.

FILL-IN

1. Use the _____ key to select multiple controls on a form or report.

2. The _____ property controls the font color of text.

3. The squares that allow you to resize and move controls are called _____.

4. Sections are added to report or form design using the _____ menu.

5. Use _____ to remove controls from a section so that they can be pasted into a new section.

6. An _____ control is not linked to the data in a record source.

7. Use the _____ key when dragging a line to keep it straight.

MULTIPLE CHOICE

1. The _____ control is used to create separators in a report.
   a. Text
   b. Line
   c. Bound Object
   d. all of the above

2. Report page numbers are inserted in Report Design View from the _____ menu.
   a. Tools
   b. Format
   c. Insert
   d. View

3. Calculated report values _____.
   a. are added using an unbound control
   b. must begin with =
   c. are recalculated each time the report is run
   d. all of the above

4. Report content to appear once at the end of the report should be placed in the _____ section.
   a. Report Footer
   b. Report Header
   c. Detail
   d. Page Footer

5. Objects added to a form are layered in what is called _____.
   a. z-order
   b. stack order
   c. control order
   d. none of the above

REVIEW QUESTIONS

Each of the following topics should be addressed in one to three paragraphs.

1. When setting properties for multiple controls, what governs the controls that you can choose?

2. Why should you add a custom color to the palette?

3. Explain the use of grouping in reports.

4. Discuss all of the ways that you can control what records print from a form.

5. Explain why both the form and report objects are needed in Access.

CREATE THE QUESTION

For each of the following answers, create the question.

ANSWER	QUESTION
1. Click the Wizard button on the toolbar	_____
2. Controls	_____
3. Sections, controls, toolbox, grid, and ruler, to name a few	_____
4. Caption, Fore Color, Font Name, Font Weight, and Font Size, to name a few	_____
5. The most efficient way is to use the field list	_____
6. Sorting and Grouping	_____
7. Label control	_____

FACT OR FICTION

For each of the following, determine whether the statement is fact, fiction, or both and present your arguments for that conclusion.

1. You must set properties for every control added to a report or form.

2. Only calculations can be included in the expression for a calculated control.

3. A calculated control stores the instructions on how to calculate a value, not a precise value.

4. The toolbox must always appear anchored to the left of the Design Window.

5. The only way to align controls on a form or report is to use the ruler and grid.

6. A Text Box control added to a form or report in Design View is always accompanied by a Label control.

7. When modifying a form or report in Design View, a pointing hand indicates that a control or controls are being resized.

1. Forms and Reports for Cyberia Coffee Shop

Cyberia Coffee Shop is a Barona, California, neighborhood coffee shop. Besides serving gourmet coffee, Cyberia dishes up sandwiches and desserts. Local bands, Internet connections, and floor-to-ceiling books on every wall provide entertainment. Li Houng, the proprietor, has decided that a database would be helpful in the acquisition of new books. Although customers rarely buy books, they do disappear or fall apart from use. Li needs a way to keep track of what books he has so that he doesn't pick up duplicates. You will use the Wizards and then Design View to create a custom form and report.

1. Start Access and open **ac05Cyberia.mdb**
2. Select the **Form** object and double-click on **Create form by using wizard**
3. Select the **Books** table, move all fields to the Selected fields list, and click **Next**
4. Select **Columnar** and click **Next**
5. Select **Sumi Painting** and click **Next**
6. Click **Finish** and then use the **View** 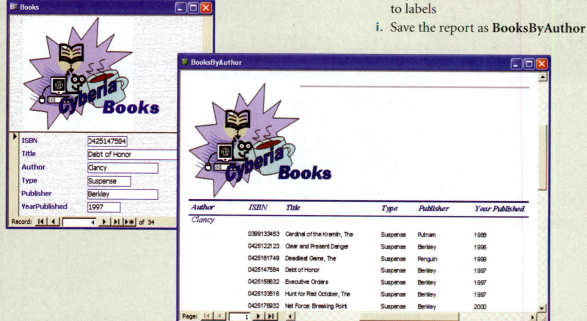 button to change to Design View
7. Use the Detail Selector bar to expand the height of the form header

FIGURE 5.38

Books form and report

8. Click the **Image** control and then click in the Form Header
9. Navigate to the files for this chapter and select **ac05Cyberia.tif**
10. Position the logo in the top left corner and adjust the size of the Form Header to the logo size
11. Add a Label Control to the Form Header section. Place the text **Books** in it, set it to **26** point **Franklin Gothic Heavy** (or another heavy font), and position it as shown in Figure 5.38
12. Save the form as **Books**
13. Create a report that groups the records by author
    a. Select the **Report** object and double-click on **Create report by using wizard**
    b. Move all of the fields to the Selected fields list Group by Author and click **Finish**
    c. Click the **View** button to switch to Design View
    d. Select the Books label and move it to the right
    e. Click the **Image** tool, click in the Report Header, navigate to the files for this chapter, and select **ac05Cyberia.tif**
    f. Move the label Books until it is positioned overlapping the logo. Format it to match step 11. Set Back Style to **Transparent**
    g. Use **Cut** and **Paste** to move the label to the foreground
    h. Adjust columns to match data and add spaces to labels
    i. Save the report as **BooksByAuthor**

2. Using a Database to Store Student Grades

Prairie Valley College is implementing a centralized gradebook for all faculty members. Currently each faculty member maintains a paper or Microsoft Excel gradebook. The goal of a centralized repository for grades is to improve the record keeping of individual faculty members, allow students to review their own course grades throughout the semester in an automated format, and provide management with necessary grade reports. Test data have been added to the table, and you will be creating a custom form and report for teachers to use.

1. Start Access and open **ac05Gradebook.mdb**

2. Open the **Gradebook** table and review the data. There is one record for each student assignment in each course

3. Use the Form Wizard to create the default columnar form with all fields for the Gradebook table. Use the SumiPainting style and name the form **GradebookUpdate**

4. Use Form Design View to customize the form. Refer to Figure 5.39

   a. Reorganize the fields to match the figure

   b. Adjust the field labels so that all text displays and contains spaces. Delete unnecessary labels

   c. Adjust the size of text boxes to better fit the data

   d. Add a line to separate course data from student data

   e. Add the graphic **ac05GradebookLogo.gif** to the heading section of the form

   f. Add a Label control to the Heading section of the form and place the text **Gradebook Pilot** in it. Make the text 28 point

   g. Preview your results and make any necessary adjustments before saving and closing the form

5. Use the Report Wizard to build and customize the **GradebookReport** with the following features

   a. Create the basic report with the Report Wizard using all the fields from the GradebookQuery. Set the report to Group By Course ID and StudentName. Use the Summary Options to Sum Score. Sort by Assignment. Use the **Align Left 2** layout and the **Formal** style. Use the default name

   b. In Form Design View add a space to the Gradebook Report title

   c. Add the graphic **ac05GradebookLogo.gif** to the heading section of the form

   d. Adjust the position of the Header contents to match the figure

6. If your work is complete, exit Access; otherwise, continue to the next assignment

FIGURE 5.39

GradebookUpdate form and GradebookReport

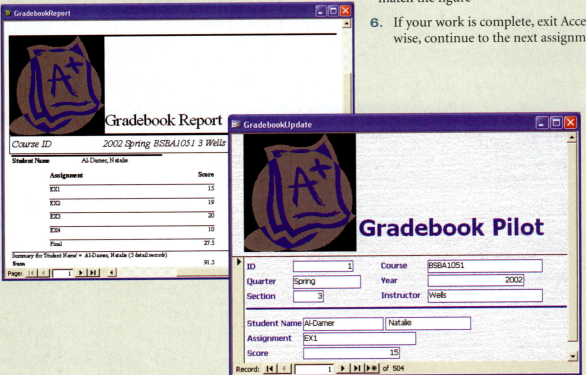

challenge!

1. Sorting and Grouping for Cyberia Coffee Shop

Cyberia Coffee Shop was introduced in the Practice exercise for this chapter. You have developed a form and simple report to help Li Houng track his book purchases. Now he would like reports that his customers can use to find books by a specific author or in a particular category.

1. Start Access and open **ac05CyberiaChallenge.mdb**

2. Open a new blank report on the books table in Design View

3. Use the field list to place all of the Books fields into the Detail section of the report and close the field list

4. Select all of the labels and cut them out of the Detail section; select the Page Header section and paste them there

5. Edit the labels to remove the colons (:) and make them all dark blue

6. Order the labels Author, Title, Type, Publisher, YearPublished, ISBN, and make the Page Header just tall enough for the labels

7. Align the text boxes in the detail section to match the Page Header. Use Report View to make sure field sizes are appropriate. Make the Detail section just tall enough for the text boxes

8. Add the Report Header/Footer sections and use the Image control to place **ac05Cyberia.tif** in the top left corner of the Report Header

9. Add a label with the properties that cause the text Report Title to display in Times New Roman, 28 point, italic, and dark blue

10. Size the label appropriately

11. Save the report as **BooksByAuthor** and make the following adjustments to the design
    a. Change the title to Books By Author and adjust the size of the label
    b. Use the Sorting and Grouping dialog box to sort by Author and then Title. Display a Group Footer for Author
    c. Use the Properties of the Author control to hide duplicate values
    d. Add a calculated control to the Author Footer that displays an appropriate message and the count of books by each author
    e. Save the report

12. Return to the GroupByTemplate and make the following changes
    a. Save the report as **BooksByCategory**
    b. Change the report title and field order (Type, Title, Author, YearPublished, Publisher, ISBN)
    c. Count the number of reports in each category
    d. Use the Properties of the Type control to hide duplicate values

FIGURE 5.40

Books GroupByTemplate and BooksByAuthor report

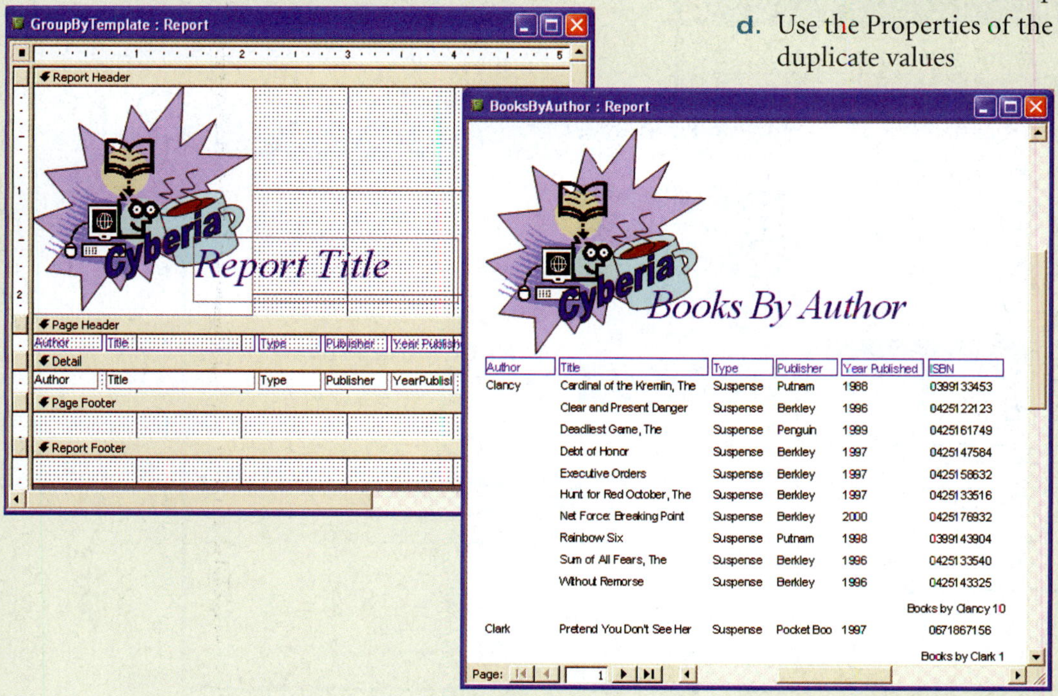

2. Sorting and Grouping Gradebook Data

Prairie Valley College is implementing a centralized gradebook for all faculty members. Testing of the prototype began in a Practice exercise for this chapter. You will continue testing the prototype by building a custom report to list the courses that each student has taken.

1. Start Access and open **ac05GradebookChallenge.mdb**. Review the existing table

2. Open a new blank report on the **SelectDistinct** query in Design View. Add all fields to the report

3. Use the AutoFormat button to add the Corporate style to the report

4. Add a Report Header section and refer to Figure 5.41 as you complete the following

   a. Use a label to add the text **Student Courses Report**. Make the text 22-point extra bold and be sure that all characters display in Report View

   b. Add the graphic **ac05GradebookLogo.gif**

   c. Use the Insert menu to add report run Date and Time. Use the format 6/6/2004 9:36AM. The text boxes will load over the graphic. Arrange the header contents to match Figure 5.41

FIGURE 5.41

Student Courses Report

5. Add page numbers with the format Page N as a centered Page Footer. Show the number on the first page

6. Use the Sorting and Grouping dialog box to sort by an expression that combines student last and first names (=[StudentLast] & "," & [StudentFirst])

   a. Set the Group Header to **Yes**

   b. Set Keep Together to **Whole Group**

   c. Move StudentLast and StudentFirst text boxes into the left side of the Group Header. Set them to 11-point font

   d. Delete the StudentFirst label in the Page Header and make the StudentLast label read **Student**

   e. Place the controls for Course, Quarter, Year, and Instructor in the Detail section. Cut the labels and paste them into the Group Header. Arrange the labels above the corresponding Text Box controls. Refer to Figure 5.41

7. Edit the Label controls so that they do not contain a colon(:). Draw a line under the labels

8. In the Detail section

   a. Adjust the height to fit the controls

   b. Draw a line under the Text Box controls in the Detail section. Make it the same length as the one drawn in step 7

9. Compare your results to Figure 5.41 and make any necessary adjustments

10. Save the report as **StudentCoursesReport**

11. If your work is complete, exit Access; otherwise, continue to the next assignment

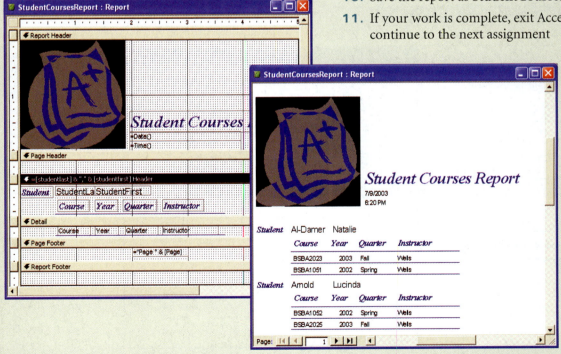

1. Previewing SportsPix Photographs on the Web

SportsPix is a digital photography operation that specializes in taking pictures of youth sports teams. Ray Damask and Grace Bishop began photographing sports teams when their nephew was playing soccer at the local YMCA. They shoot individual and team pictures for baseball, softball, soccer, football, volleyball, tennis, and martial arts. You have developed a prototype of a Photographs table that you believe will help Ray and Grace. You have selected some test data from the information that they provided and entered it into the table. Create the form and report outlined to ensure the effectiveness of this solution.

1. Start Access and open the **ac05SportsPix.mdb** database

2. Use Design View to create the form depicted in Figure 5.42 for the **Photographs** table
   a. The logo is **ac05Sportspix.tif**. Do not use a Header section
   b. Set the form properties to make the background light blue
   c. Set the Border Style property of all the text boxes to Solid and the Border Color to a complementary darker blue
   d. Align all controls
   e. Adjust the size of all controls and form sections to fit the data
   f. Remove the colons (:) from Labels
   g. Save the form as **PhotoInput**

3. Open the **Photographs** form and add records for yourself and two of your friends. You should all be on the same team and have had your pictures taken at the same time and at the same location. Use Film Id 5443

4. Create the report shown in Figure 5.42 for the **Photographs** table. This report will become a Web page that will allow photographs to be previewed and purchased
   a. Add the logo (**ac05Sportspix.tif**), lines, and colors shown
   b. Add a Group Header for Location and a Group Footer for Team
      i. Set the properties of both Location and Team to suppress duplicate values
      ii. Count the Subjects for each team in the Group Footer
   c. Format Time to ShortTime and ensure that the text box is large enough to display all of the date
   d. Place the report date and Page XX of XX in the Page Footer
   e. Save the report as **PhotosByLocationAndTeam**

5. If your work is complete, exit Access; otherwise, continue to the next assignment

FIGURE 5.42

Photographs form and report

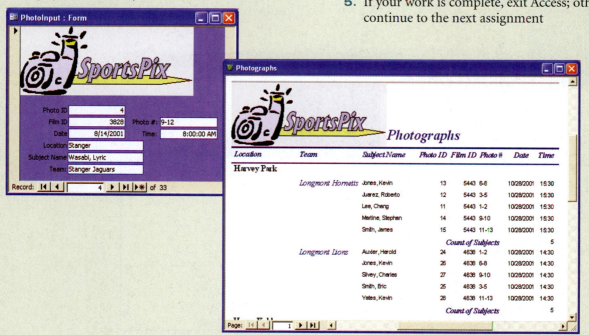

2. Custom Output for NMO Energy

NMO Energy supplies products to consumer energy companies across the United States. NMO maintains a list of current customers for potential clients to review. Some of these companies have agreed to provide references and referrals. This reference list is maintained in Microsoft Access and placed on the company's Web site. You will create a custom form that will be used to update this list and the custom report that will be posted to the Web.

1. Open Access and open **ac05NMOEnergy.mdb**

2. Open the **References** table and review the contents. Close the table

3. Use the Wizard to create the default columnar form for the References table. Name the form **ReferencesUpdate**. Customize the form as follows

    a. Add spaces to separate the words in each field name

    b. Change the color of the text box text to dark blue. Set the Back Style to **Transparent** and Special Effect to **Raised**

    c. Add the logo **ac05NMOLogo.gif** to the Header section

    d. Add a label to the Header with the text **NMO Customer References**. Change the text color to black, the back color to dark blue, and set the font size to 14

4. Test the form by adding a new record for **Excel Energy** with an internal ID of **EXEN**

5. Use the Wizard to create the report that will be available from NMO's Web site. Name the report **CustomerReferences**. The completed report should have the following attributes

    a. Include only the CompanyName field sorted in ascending order

    b. Use the Tabular layout and Corporate style

    c. Add spaces between the words in the title and field name

    d. Add the logo **ac05NMOLogo.gif** to the Header section. Set the title text box back color to dark blue and the fore color to black. Arrange the header objects as shown in Figure 5.43

    e. Add the bullet **aco5DiamondBullett.emf** to the left of the customer name in the Detail section

    f. Extend the line in the Page Header section to match the width of the page

    g. Format the Date to Medium Date. Adjust the size to fit the data

    h. Add a Label control to the right of the date and cause it to display the current time in the Medium Time format. Delete the label. Adjust the size and position of these two controls so that they appear side-by-side on the left of the Page Footer

    i. Add a label to the center of the Page Footer section and place your name in it

6. Close the database and exit Access if your work is complete

FIGURE 5.43

NMO Custom form and report

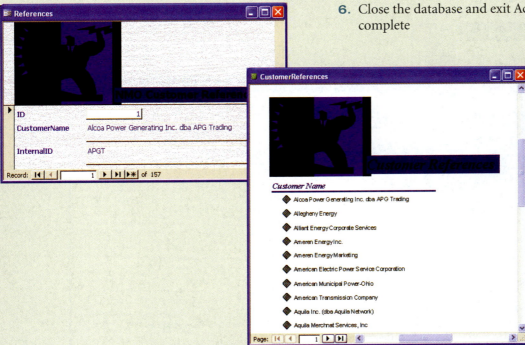

1. Terra Patrimonium Agricultural Chemicals Customer Analysis

Terra Patrimonium (Latin for "land of our fathers") is a company that provides agricultural chemicals, supplies, and services to farmers. Vaughn Michaels, the president and founder, is experienced at using Excel and accounting software but has asked you to help create the database forms and reports needed to support the organization.

1. To prepare for this exercise, use a search engine to find three farm pictures that are representative of healthy corn, barley, soy bean, or sorghum crops

2. Start Access and open **ac05TerraPatrimonium.mdb**

3. Create a new form in Design View to display healthy crops using Terra Patrimonium chemicals. The form will be placed on the Web later

   a. Use an Image control to display the image **ac05TerraPatrimonium.tif** at the top left of the form

   b. Use a Label control to insert **Bountiful Terra Patrimonium Crops** as a title below the logo. Set the font color to brown and the font size to 18 points

   c. Use the Expedition Auto Format

   d. Use Image controls to insert and arrange your pictures

   e. Save the form as **Bounty**

4. Create the form shown in Figure 5.44, save it as **CstmrInput**, and use the form to add the following data starting with CstmrNmbr **150**

Greg Mendenhall	2481 W. State Rd 1000, Monrovia, IA 55738
Kerry Preston	68888 S State Rd 115, Red Oak, IA 51828
Lonnie McCammack	14486 E IA265, Creston, IA 51828
George McCammack	20281 E IA265, Creston, IA 51828
Gordon Foss	74589 South IA 71, Morton Mills, IA 51826
Randy Knetzer	RR 12, Box 217, Osceola, IA 53871
Michael Knudson	2829 Hwy 2 East, Mount Ayr, IA 51627
Bob Kalahari	RR 2 Box 105, Knoxville, IA 51726
Joseph Kabassa	RR 2 Box 162, Knoxville, IA 51726
Jason Van Horne	RR 12 Box 189, Osceola, IA 53871
Dominic Black	RR 1, Box 98, Osceola, IA 53871

5. Make up a phone number for each customer added in 4 and set First Contact to today's date

6. Use Design View to create the report shown in Figure 5.44 and save it as **PhoneList**

7. Use the Sorting and Grouping dialog box to Group by State. Put the State text box in the State Header and suppress duplicates. Add Last Name and First Name sorts

8. Set Last Name to hide duplicates

9. Close the TerraPatrimonium database and exit Access if your work is complete

FIGURE 5.44

CstmrInput form and PhoneListByState report

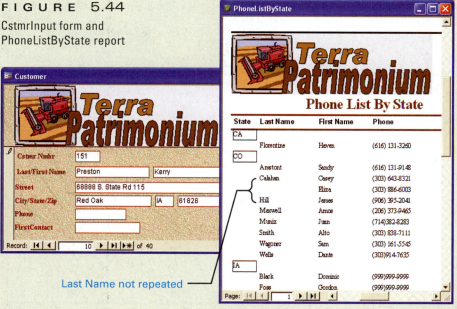

Last Name not repeated

hands-on projects

around the world

1. TechRocks Seminars Forms and Reports

TechRocks Seminars is an organization of independent seminar facilitators who provide onsite technical training to large businesses around the world. The facilitators build curriculum that is marketed by TechRocks. TechRocks books the seminars, arranges facilities, enrolls participants, and collects the money. While the facilitators are not employees of TechRocks, they provide the service that is marketed and their skills and schedules need to be available to all TechRocks offices.

Aisha Jackson has been charged with tracking facilitators and their classification. She has asked you to help develop the reports that will be placed on the company's Web site for use by all of the organization's offices in scheduling seminars.

1. Start Access and open the **ac05Seminars.mdb** database

2. Create a data entry form for the Facilitators table in Design View
   a. Add the **ac05TechRocks.tif** logo to the Form Header
   b. Set the form background color to a blue that complements the logo
   c. Organize and align all controls for effective use and full data display
   d. Save the form as **FacilitatorsInput**

3. Use the Enrollment table to create a report listing the students currently enrolled in each seminar
   a. The field order is Seminar ID, Last Name, First Name, Phone Number, and Student Number
   b. Adjust all controls to display all of their contents
   c. Adjust the color and content of the column headings as shown in Figure 5.45
   d. Align all controls
   e. Add a blue line below the column headings. Create two copies of the line. Place one above the image and one above the heading
   f. Use Sorting and Grouping to sort by Seminar ID, Last Name, and First Name. Add a Group Footer for Seminar ID
   g. Suppress the display of duplicate Seminar ID values

   h. Add a text box with the expression **=[Seminar ID] & " students " & Count([Last Name])** to the Seminar ID Footer

tip: *Make sure to include the spaces. In this table the field names have spaces and so must be enclosed in square brackets []. The spaces before and after students in " students " prints the spaces after the Seminar ID and before the student count*

   i. Place the report date, time, and Page XX of XX in the Page Footer. Format the date and time to long format
   j. Set the Visible property of the Report Footer to **No**
   k. Place **ac05TechRocks.tif** in the Report Header and add the three labels (one for each word)
   l. Set the position and color of the title labels as shown
   m. Save the report as **StudentsBySeminar**

4. If your work is complete, exit Access; otherwise, continue to the next assignment

FIGURE 5.45

Students by Seminar report

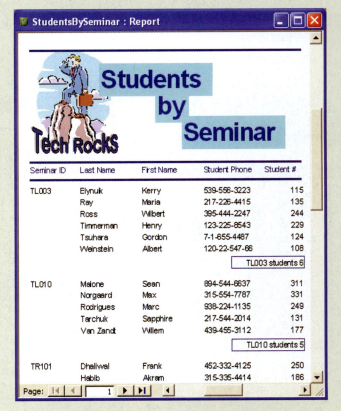

running project: tnt web design

Custom Forms and Reports for TnT

As TnT grows, so does the complexity of its database. Tori and Tonya now have over 65 employees and several hundred customers, so it is becoming critical to have simple data entry and reporting.

1. Start Access and open the **ac05TnT.mdb** database. Familiarize yourself with each table

2. Create a custom form for the Employees table
   a. Use the format shown in Figure 5.46

   tip: *You will need to add Label controls for the Name and Address headers in the Detail section*

   b. Use the **Rectangle** tool to group the data as shown. The Border Width is **Hairline** and the Border Color is a medium blue
   c. Set the Visible property of the Form Footer to **No**
   d. Add the TnT logo from **ac05TnT.tif**
   e. Use two separate labels to add the form title. Make each label 28 point, bold, italic, and dark blue
   f. Save the form as **EmployeeUpdate**

3. Create a custom report for the Employees table
   a. The Detail line contains Job Class, Last Name, First Name, State, and Phone
   b. Adjust the headings, align and size all controls, and set the headings to dark blue
   c. Use Sorting and Grouping to sort the data by JobClass, LastName, and FirstName

   d. Set the Properties of JobClass to Hide Duplicates
   e. Create a Report Header containing the TnT logo and three labels (one for each word) with the report title
      Employees is 28 point, bold, italic, and dark blue. By is 24 point, italic, and dark blue. **Job Classification** is 18 point, italic, and dark blue
   f. Create a Page Footer with the report date (mm/dd/yyyy), military time at the left margin, Page XX of XX at the right margin, and a blue line above it
   g. Set the Visible property of the Report Footer to **No**
   h. Save the report as **EmployeesByJobClass**

FIGURE 5.47

Employees by Job Classification report

FIGURE 5.46

Employee Update form

1. Create a Personal Database

A previous Analysis problem in Chapter 1 asked you to evaluate your personal needs and select an area such as classes, grades, or belongings that could benefit from a database. The instructions asked that a new blank database named ac01<yourname>.mdb be created and Wizards used to create table(s) in the database. At least one table should be populated with 10 or more records and then use the Wizards to create an update form and simple report for the populated table.

If you did not compete this assignment earlier, complete it now naming the file **ac05PersonalDatabase.mdb**. If you have already completed this assignment, use Microsoft Windows to rename your file as indicated. Use the skills from this chapter to customize the form and report. Add a graphic to each. Align the controls. Create more effective labels. Add calculations. If necessary, create a new report that uses Sorting and Grouping.

2. Start a Personal Business

The second Analysis problem in Chapter 1 asked you to assume that you were starting a personal services business such as mowing lawns or tutoring and then to create a new blank database named ac01<yourname>Business.mdb. Wizards were used to create table(s) in the database and at least one table was populated with 10 or more records. Wizards were also used to create an update form and simple report for the populated table.

If you did not complete this assignment earlier, complete it now naming the file **ac05PersonalBusiness.mdb**. If you have already completed this assignment, use Microsoft Windows to rename your file as indicated. Use the skills from this chapter to customize the form and report. Add a graphic to each. Align the controls. Create more effective labels. Add calculations. If necessary, create a new report that uses Sorting and Grouping.

6

Defining Table Relationships

did you know?

the *average person takes seven minutes to fall asleep.*

the *dial tone of a normal telephone is in the key of F.*

"live *so that you wouldn't mind selling your pet parrot to the town gossip."—Will Rogers*

cutting *an onion releases a passive sulfur compound created by propanethiol S-oxide gas and enzymes contained in the onion. When this upwardly mobile gas encounters the water produced by the tear ducts in our eyelids, it produces sulfuric acid.*

quicksand *is buoyant. Anything or anyone who steps into it can float much higher than is possible in water alone.*

to *find out who predicted that "No flying machine will ever fly from New York to Paris," in 1908, visit* www.mhhe.com/i-series.

Chapter Objectives

- **Review the types of table relationships**
- **Build table relationships in the Relationships window— MOS AC03S-1-5**
- **Change the properties of table relationships including join type and referential integrity—MOS AC03S-1-6**
- **Query multiple tables**
- **Create and use multitable custom forms including subdatasheets and subforms**
- **Create multitable custom reports**
- **Identify object dependencies—MOS AC03S-4-1**

KoryoKicks: Relating and Indexing Tables

The data, forms, and reports for KoryoKicks are shaping up nicely. Missy and Micah are very comfortable entering data, running queries, and printing reports. They have enjoyed learning about the Design View of reports and forms and even like manipulating the controls and properties to get exactly the look and performance they want. Missy and Micah are accomplished users of the database that you have set up, but they want to be able to develop their own databases so that they are no longer dependent on outside expertise.

Although the twins were very involved in every stage of developing the current database and even built some of the components with your help, they do not understand how to set up tables, relationships, queries, forms, and reports without assistance. They still have lots of questions about how database objects really work such as:

- What records are retrieved when multiple tables are involved in a Select Query?
- How can the data from all KoryoKicks tables be maintained from one form?
- Why can't an order be added before Customer data is placed in the Customer table?
- What is the point of indexing a field or group of fields? How can you tell if indexing has done any good?
- Why use a query to build a form or report instead of just going directly to the tables involved?
- What is stopping us from modifying and deleting records for customers that have been entered with errors?
- We keep hearing that SQL is the language of relational databases. We haven't see any SQL yet, so where is it?

You and the twins sit down and develop a plan to address their questions and improve their comfort level with the inner workings of Microsoft Access. Since the twins are very comfortable with the use of single tables to create queries, forms, and reports, you will start with table relationships and how they impact output. Figure 6.1 displays some of the components that will be used in this process.

FIGURE 6.1

Relating and indexing
KoryoKicks tables

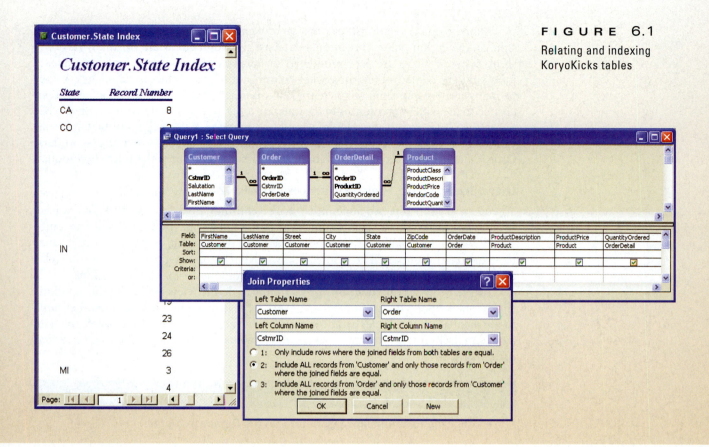

SESSION 6.1 RELATING TABLES

Chapter 1 introduced the concepts and terminology of relational database management systems. Subsequent chapters presented methods of using these database objects (tables, queries, forms, and reports) to view and manipulate the data held in a single table.

Chapter 2 discussed how to properly design relational databases using a common-sense version of the more formal normalization rules. Data are placed in multiple tables to reduce redundancy and increase integrity. Defining common table fields (foreign keys) so that data from multiple tables could be joined using queries was presented as an integral component of effective design.

The focus of this chapter is learning to build and use table relationships. It is not enough to create table designs with common fields in related tables. Like all other database objects, relationships have properties. The properties of each relationship must be correctly defined for the relationship to behave as expected.

Understanding Types of Relationships

Table relationships fall into one of three general categories: one-to-one (1:1), one-to-many (1:∞), or many-to-many (∞:∞). This notation identifies how many records in the first table are related to how many records in the second table. Thus, the one-to-many notation means that one record from the *primary table* is related to many records in the *related table*. In the KoryoKicks database, one customer can place many orders, so the relationship between the Customer and Orders tables is one-to-many.

AC 6.3

Many-to-many relationships must be broken into multiple one-to-many relationships in the design phase of relational database development. Many-to-many relationships between tables are accommodated in databases by adding a junction table. A junction table contains the primary key columns of the two tables to be related. A one-to-many relationship from the primary key columns of each of those two tables is then created to the matching columns in the junction table. In KoryoKicks the relationship between the Order and Product tables would be a many-to-many relationship. One order can involve multiple products and one product can appear on multiple orders. OrderDetail is a junction table containing the primary key from both Order and Product.

Introducing the Relationships Window

To build a relationship, two tables must share a common field, but the fields do not have to carry the same name. The fields must carry the same Data Type and Field Size. Since all many-to-many relationships are broken down at design time, only one-to-one or one-to-many relationships will be defined in an active relational database. One-to-one relationships are less common, so we will concentrate on one-to-many relationships.

Access provides the ***Relationships window*** to define, view, and edit table relationships. In a properly designed database, every table is related to at least one other table in the database. Some tables can be related to multiple tables. It is also possible to relate a table to itself. It is important to know which table is the primary table when building relationships.

---

task reference   **View Table Relationships**

- Click the **Relationships** button on the Database toolbar

- If relationships exist, they will be displayed. If there are no current relationships, you can add tables and build relationships between them

---

Viewing KoryoKicks relationships:

1. Verify that the **ac06KoryoKicks.mdb** database is open (see Figure 6.2)
2. Click the **Relationships** button on the Database toolbar

tip: It does not matter what database object is active during this process

3. Leave the Relationships window open so that you can refer to it as it is being discussed

---

The Relationships window for KoryoKicks (see Figure 6.2) shows a field list for each table with relationship lines depicting how the tables are related to each other. The notation on the relationship line indicates the type of relationship and which table is primary in the relationship. For example, the Customer.CstmrID (CstmrID field of the Customer table) field defines a one-to-many relationship with the Order.CstmrID (CstmrID field of the Order table). The Customer table is primary in this relationship since it is on the one side, meaning that each Customer.CstmrID record can link to multiple Order.CstmrID records.

The Customer table is related to one other database table, Order. The Order table, however, is related to both the Customer and the OrderDetail tables. Order is the related table in the Customer/Order relationship and the primary table in the Order/OrderDetail relationship. When speaking of related table pairs, it is customary to list the primary table first.

FIGURE 6.2

KoryoKicks table
relationships

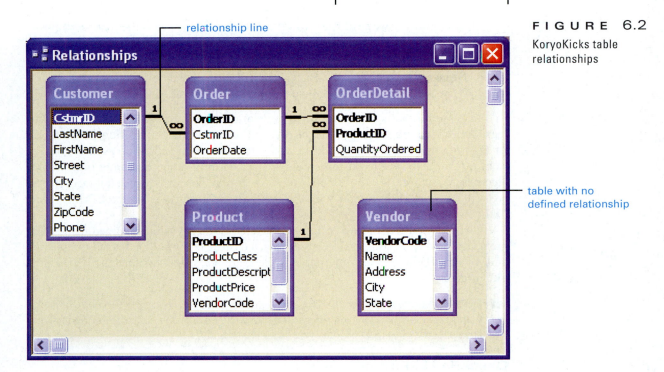

Think about invoices or bills that you have received. They contain your name, address, an order or invoice number, and each product that you ordered with a description and a quantity. Take a look at the KoryoKicks relationships and find all of the components needed for an invoice. It should be clear by now that without the ability to join tables, users would be restricted to working with the data from each table independently. In such an environment, KoryoKicks would not be able to combine data from the Customer, Order, and Product tables to create an invoice since the Customer table holds the customer's name and address, the Order table contains the order date, the Order Detail table holds the quantity ordered, and the Product table holds descriptions of each product.

The KoryoKicks invoice needs fields from each of the tables. Let's look at the relationships from a business perspective to understand what they mean in practice. Here are the KoryoKicks relationships from left to right in the Relationships window:

- One customer can place multiple orders
- One order can have multiple details (products and quantities)
- One product can appear on multiple order details

Ideally relationships are defined before any data are placed in the related table, but there is nothing in Access to prevent adding or editing relationships in an active database. Adding or changing the properties of relationships is governed by the rules of referential integrity. Your efforts to add or edit relationships also will be governed by these rules.

Referential Integrity

The rules of referential integrity govern table relationships and are sometimes referred to as parent/child rules. These rules prevent "orphans" such as an OrderDetail for a product that is not in the Products table or an order for a CstmrID that is not in the Customer table. For a relationship to be valid,

- The primary record must exist before a secondary record of that foreign key can be added to the related table (parent key must exist before the child can use that key)

- Changing the value of the primary table field that governs the relationship is not allowed if there are related records (the parent cannot be removed while it still has children)
- Deleting the record in the primary table is not allowed if there are related records (the parent cannot be deleted while it still has children)

Take another look at the KoryoKicks Relationships window. What referential integrity means in practice is that the record on the one side of the relationship must exist before any related records can be added on the many side. For example, in the KoryoKicks database, the Customer table record defining a new customer must be created before an Order can be added for that customer. For an OrderDetail record to be created, both the OrderID must exist in the Order table and the ProductID must exist in the Product table.

Further, the parent record cannot be deleted or its key value changed while there are still related child records. In KoryoKicks, a customer cannot be deleted or assigned a new CstmrID in the Customer table while there are orders for that CstmrID in the Order table.

help yourself *Use the Type a Question combo box to improve your understanding of table relationships by typing* **referential integrity**. *Review the contents of* About table relationships. *Close the Help window when you are finished*

Cascade Update and Delete

Double-clicking on a relationship line will open the Edit Relationships dialog box, which displays the properties of that relationship. When table relationships are defined, an option is provided to not enforce referential integrity (a very bad idea for data integrity). When referential integrity is enforced, there are options on how it is enforced.

The referential integrity options are check boxes shown in Figure 6.3 that are labeled:

- Enforce Referential Integrity, which should always be checked
- Cascade Update Related Fields
- Cascade Delete Related Records

When *Cascade Update Related Fields* is checked, any changes made to the key value of the primary table also will be applied to records in the related table. With this option, if you need to change a CstmrID for some reason, making the change in the Customer table would also update the CstmrID of related child records in the Order table.

Selecting the *Cascade Delete Related Records* check box will cause related records to be deleted when the primary record is deleted. In KoryoKicks, deleting a customer from the Customer table will also delete all orders for that customer. Cascade deletes are not always a good idea since it would allow a customer and all of the customer's orders to be deleted without verifying each delete.

---

task reference   **View Relationship Properties**

- Click the **Relationships** button on the Database toolbar
- If relationships exist, they will be displayed. If there are no current relationships, you can add tables and build relationships between them
- Double-click the relationship line that you would like to view
- The Edit Relationships dialog box displays the properties of that relationship

primary table and field(s)
defining the relationship

related table and field(s)
defining the relationship

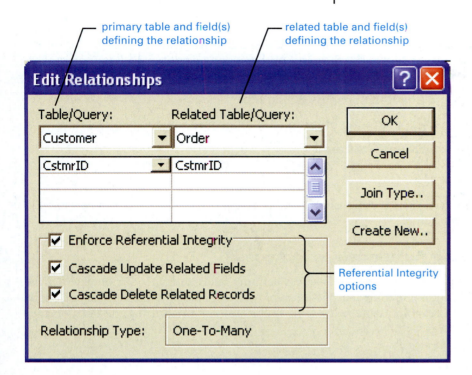

Viewing KoryoKicks relationship properties:

1. Verify that the **ac06KoryoKicks.mdb** database is open

2. If you are not currently viewing the Relationships window, click the
   Relationships 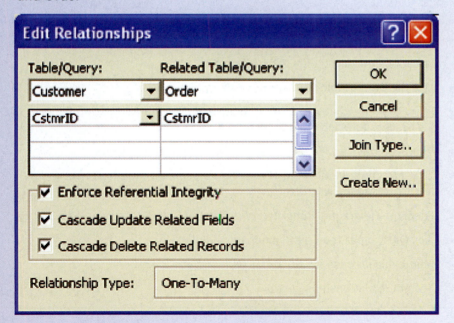 button on the Database toolbar

3. Double-click the one-to-many relationship line between Customer
   and Order

F I G U R E   6.4
Customer/Order Edit
Relationships dialog box

4. Notice that the common field is named CstmrID in both tables, the referential integrity is enforced, and both cascade updates and deletes are activated

5. Close the Edit Relationships dialog box

6. Double-click one of the other relationships and review its properties

7. Close **ac06KoryoKicks.mdb**

Now that existing relationships have been explored, let's take a look at how to build new relationships.

Creating Relationships in Access

Building a new database table involves defining fields and their attributes. After the table definitions are complete, relationships between tables in the same database can be built using common table fields. This task is accomplished using the Relationships window.

One-to-One

One-to-one relationships exist when one record in the primary table is related to no more than one record in the related table. Normally the data in the related table would be part of the primary table, so these relationships are not common. They are created when the data in the related tables are used infrequently or when the primary table size exceeds the Access limit, causing the table to be split.

Both tables in a one-to-one relationship have the same primary key. When a relationship is created from the primary key of one table to the primary key of another table, a one-to-one relationship is defined. We'll demonstrate this by creating a relationship between the KoryoKicks Customer table and a dummy table created for this purpose, CustomerPart2.

---

task reference   **Create a Relationship**

- Click the **Relationships** button on the Database toolbar

- If relationships exist, they will be displayed

- Click the **Show Table** button on the toolbar

- Select the table that you want to relate and click the **Add** button. Repeat this process for each table to be related

- When you have added all of the necessary tables, click **Close**

- Click the primary table field of the relationship and drag to the secondary field to initiate the relationship

- Select the Referential Integrity options in the Edit Relationships dialog box

- Click **OK** to close the Edit Relationships dialog box

- Repeat this process for any other relationships to be built

- Close the Relationships window

Building a one-to-one relationship:

1. Verify that the **ac06KoryoKicks.mdb** database is open

2. Use the **Relationships** button from the toolbar to activate the Relationships window (see Figure 6.5)

3. Click the **Show Tables** button from the toolbar to display the list of tables that can be related

4. Select the **CustomerPart2** table and click the **Add** button to add the second table of customer data

5. **Close** the Show Table dialog box

6. Click **Customer.CstmrID** and drag to **CustomerPart2.CstmrID** to open the Edit Relationships dialog box for this relationship

tip: *Recall that the notation Customer.CstmrID identifies the table.field*

7. Click on all of the referential integrity options to enforce referential integrity and activate cascade updates and deletes

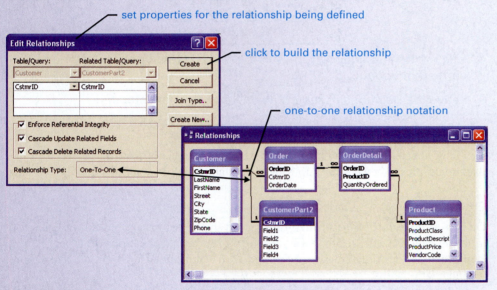

FIGURE 6.5
One-to-one relationship

8. Click **Create**

9. Close the Relationships window and click **Yes** to save your changes

This relationship was created for demonstration purposes and is not functional for KoryoKicks. A relationship sometimes needs to be deleted from a production database because it was created in error, or is no longer needed. Delete a relationship in the Relationships window by clicking the relationship line and then pressing the Del key.

Since the CustomerPart2 table is not needed, both the table and the relationship just built will be deleted. Deleting either table in the relationship also deletes the relationship. A table can be deleted from the Tables object list in the Database Window or from the Relationships window. Deleting the table from the Database Window permanently removes it from the database.

Deleting a table and its associated relationships:

1. Verify that the **ac06KoryoKicks.mdb** database is open

2. In the Database Window, click on the **Tables** object

3. Select the **CustomerPart2** table and click **Del**; respond **Yes** to both delete prompts

FIGURE 6.6

Deleting a table and its relationships

4. Use the **Relationships** button to open the Relationships window and verify that update

5. Leave the Relationships window open for the next steps

Table deletes cannot be undone, so execute them with caution. Using Windows Backup utilities to create a backup copy of a database before deleting tables is advisable.

One-to-Many

One-to-many relationships, when one record in the primary table can be related to multiple records in the related table, are the most common relationship type. Creating a one-to-many relationship is very similar to the technique just reviewed to create one-to-one relationships.

Both tables in a one-to-many relationship have the same field or foreign key. This shared field *cannot* be the primary key of the related (second) table although it may be one field in a composite primary key. Clicking the field in the primary table and dragging it to the related field in the second table opens the Edit Relationships window. Set the relationship properties, most importantly referential integrity, and click Create to build the relationship.

Building a one-to-many relationship:

1. Verify that the **ac06KoryoKicks.mdb** database is open

2. Click the **Show Tables** button on the toolbar to display the list of tables that can be related

3. Add the table **Vendor** to the Relationships window. Close the Show Tables dialog box

tip: *You can drag the Title bar of a table to move it in the Relationships window*

4. Click and drag a relationship from **Vendor.VendorCode** to **Product.VendorCode**

tip: *If you miss and build the relationship between the wrong fields, select the relationship line and press **Del***

5. Check only Enforce Referential Integrity and click **Create**

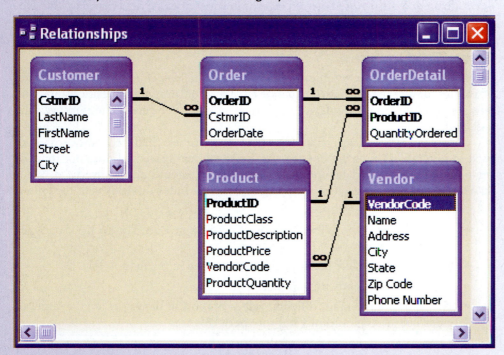

FIGURE 6.7

KoryoKicks table relationships

6. Compare your results with Figure 6.7 and make any necessary changes

7. Close the Relationships window

Although the type of relationship is not directly specified, the fields used and the direction of the drag-and-drop operation control how the relationship is built. The field at the starting point of the drag operation should always be the primary (one side) of the relationship even though the relationships often will be built correctly if the direction is reversed.

Dragging from the primary key field of one table to the primary key field of another table will create a one-to-one relationship, reflecting the fact that key fields can contain only one occurrence of each value. Dragging from the primary key field of one table to a nonkey field in another table builds a one-to-many relationship with the key field's table as primary since it can contain only one occurrence of each key value. When dragging from a nonkey field to a nonkey field, the direction of the drag operation determines which table is primary in the relationship.

The KoryoKicks OrderDetail table has a compound key using both OrderID and ProductID. Since the relationships built with the Order and Product tables only use part of the compound key, they are one-to-many.

Any attempt to create a relationship between tables that already contain data will fail if the existing data violate the referential integrity rules selected. For example, trying to relate the Customer and Order tables would fail if there were orders in the Order table for a customer that was not in the Customer table. When all violations are repaired in the existing data, the relationships can be edited to enforce referential integrity rules for all new data entry.

Building and Using Indexes

Microsoft Access uses indexes to find and sort records faster. Access uses indexes in a table as you use an index in a book: to find data, it looks up the location of the data in the index. Indexes can be based on a single field or on multiple fields. Multiple-field indexes are used to distinguish between records in which the first field may have the same value such as LastName and FirstName.

Single-Field Indexes

Access automatically creates indexes on primary key fields defined in the Design View of a table. Foreign key fields used to define table relationships in the Relationships window are also automatically indexed. Additional indexes can be created to improve database performance.

Consider indexing large tables with fields that are searched frequently, sorted, or used to join tables. Indexing does require extra storage space and does not improve the performance of all database operations, so they should not be overused. When database performance needs to be improved, consider indexing fields with the following qualities:

- The field's data type is Text, Number, Currency, or Date/Time (OLE data types can't be indexed)
- Frequent searches are executed for values stored in the field
- The field is frequently used to sort
- The field contains many different values (if most of the values are the same, an index does not significantly improve performance)

When two or more fields are used frequently in combination such as LastName and FirstName, it makes sense to create a multiple-field index containing both fields. Such an index can provide dramatic performance improvements for large tables. Up to 10 fields can be included in a multiple-field index.

In the KoryoKicks database, the most frequent searches will involve the Customer table. Several Customer table forms, queries, and reports use the State field to order the results, so State is a prime candidate for indexing. Normally, database performance would be tracked before creating an index to determine whether or not indexing produced the desired results. An index should improve the search, sort, and query performance or be removed and other ways to improve performance evaluated.

One way to track performance is to ask users to document response times and their satisfaction with specific operations such as a query or report. This is a subjective measure, but can be effective. Microsoft Access provides a tool to analyze database performance that will be covered in a later session. The Performance Analyzer suggests updates that could improve database performance with no indication of the degree of improvement likely. Third-party vendors provide the most comprehensive performance tools that can be used to verify execution and response times before and after indexing.

Creating an index actually creates an index table, similar to Figure 6.8, telling Access which records in the table belong to each index value. When an operation is performed using the index, Access is able to look up values in the index and then move directly to the associated table records. Figure 6.8 shows a portion of the index for the State field of the Customer table. In a query that retrieves CA records, Access will use the index to retrieve only record 14 of the Customer table. This is much faster than searching every record in the Customer table for a match.

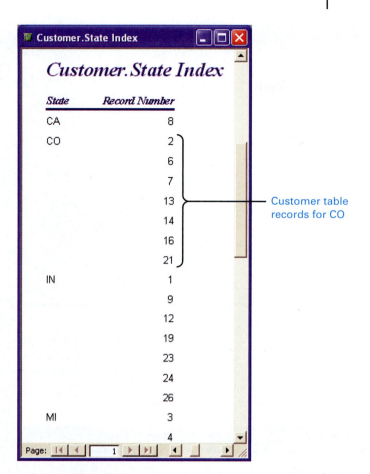

FIGURE 6.8
A portion of the
Customer.State Index

task reference   Index a Table Field

- Open the table in Design View
- Select the field to be indexed from the Field Name column
- Set the Indexed field property to **Yes (Duplicates OK)** or **Yes (No Duplicates)**
- Close the table design and save the changes

Indexing Customer.State:

1. Verify that the **ac06KoryoKicks.mdb** database is open

2. Open the Design View of the Customer table

3. Select CstmrID and notice the Indexed property setting

4. Select the **State** field

5. Set the Indexed property of State to **Yes (Duplicates OK)** as shown in Figure 6.9

tip: *Yes (No Duplicates) would be used if there were no records in the table with the same index value. The primary key of a table would have an Indexed value of Yes (No Duplicates)*

6. Close the Design View and save your changes

ACCESS

FIGURE 6.9

Customer.State Indexed
property

active field

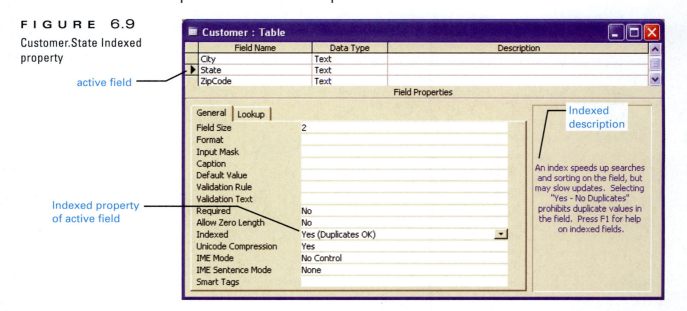

Indexed property
of active field

anotherway
**. . . to Set and
Delete Indexes**

Indexes also can be
created, updated,
and deleted using
the Indexes 📝
button from the
Design View of a
table. Since this is
the only way to set
multifield indexes, it
is covered in that
topic

Indexes created automatically, such as the primary key index, cannot be deleted. Deleting other indexes simply requires setting the Indexed property of the field to No. Since the data held in each database are unique, there is no standard increase in performance gained from indexing. Additionally, an index that does not improve performance with the current data may be beneficial as more data are stored.

---

task reference   **Delete an Index**

- Open the table in **Design View**
- Select the field whose index is to be removed from the Field Name column
- Set the Indexed field property to **No** (this does not impact the field or its data)
- Close the table design and save the changes

There are two disadvantages to adding indexes. Since creating an index actually adds a new table to a database, it enlarges the size of the database. Second, when values are added or changed in an indexed field, the index also must be updated, slowing the overall update process. Indexes should be monitored and retained only if they improve sort, select, and query performance.

Multiple-Field Indexes

As was mentioned, *multiple-field indexes* are created when fields are used in combination to sort or search a table. The most common example of LastName and FirstName exists in the KoryoKicks Customer table. Multifield indexes cannot be set in the table design, but are set in the Indexes dialog box that can only be accessed from the Design View of a table.

---

task reference   **View the Indexes of a Table**

- Open the table in **Design View**
- Click the **Indexes** 📝 button of the toolbar
- Click an index to review its properties

Viewing Customer table indexes:

1. Verify that the **ac06KoryoKicks.mdb** database is open
2. Open the Design View of the Customer table
3. Click the **Indexes** button on the toolbar
4. Click on each index to review its properties

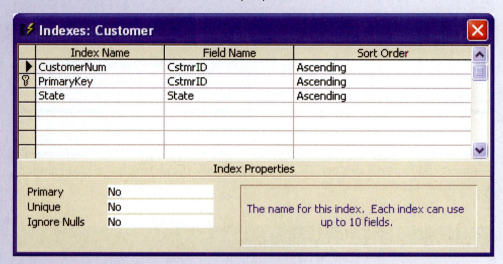

FIGURE 6.10
Customer table indexes

The Customer table should have three indexes. The PrimaryKey index was created by Access when CstmrID was set as the primary key field. The CustomerNum index also was created by Access to be used as a foreign key when linking to other tables. The State index was built in the previous steps. Selecting an index in the Indexes dialog box and pressing the Del key will delete that index from the database.

Setting a multifield Customer table index:

1. Verify that the **ac06KoryoKicks.mdb** database is open
2. If necessary, open the Design View of the Customer table and then click the **Indexes** button on the toolbar
3. In the first empty Index Name type **WholeName**

tip: *Index names can be anything that you want, but something reflecting the field(s) involved usually works best*

4. In the Field Name column, click the arrow and select **LastName**, the first field for the index
5. In the Field Name column of the next row, click the arrow and select **FirstName**, the second field for the index

tip: *This step can be repeated to add up to 10 fields to the index*

6. Select the sort order for each index field. Ascending, the default, is correct for this index (see Figure 6.11)
7. Close the Indexes window
8. Close the Customer table Design View, saving your changes

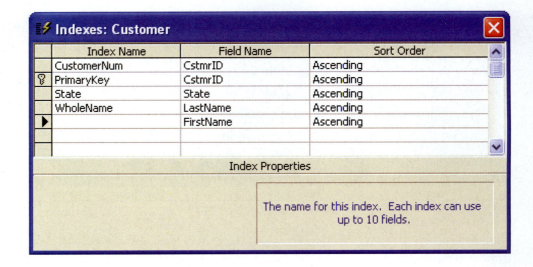

Remember that indexing is only one way to improve database performance; Compact and Repair is another. The only way to know if indexing has made operations more efficient is to monitor those operations.

S E S S I O N   6 . 1

making *the grade*

1. How would you view existing table relationships?

2. What is the relevance of the direction of the drag operation that creates a new relationship?

3. Why is referential integrity important?

4. Why are indexes important?

SESSION 6.2 CREATING OUTPUT WITH RELATED TABLES

You have been using data in related tables without an understanding of how these operations are really accomplished. When table relationships are properly defined, creating a query, form, or report using data from multiple tables is simply a matter of selecting the fields and arranging them as you would like.

Constructing Multitable Queries

Combining the data from two or more tables is usually accomplished using a query and is called joining the tables. Access supports three types of joins. The most common join is called an inner join and is the default join operation.

Inner Join

Joining the data from multiple tables can be accomplished by matching records with a common value. Typically the values being matched are in fields with defined relationships. For example, matching OrderDetail.ProductID to Product.ProductID would allow retrieval of the Product.ProductDescription using a defined relationship. Existing relationships are displayed as join lines in the query grid and display the one-to-many notation when referential integrity is enforced. Even if no relationships have been defined between the tables selected for a query, Microsoft Access will infer a relationship if they contain fields with the same name.

Sometimes data from unrelated tables are needed. In this case, there is no field that will connect the data in one table to another table, so one or more extra tables must be added to the query as a bridge between the two unrelated tables. Data from the bridge tables need not be displayed in the query result. For example, to retrieve fields from the KoryoKicks Customer and OrderDetail tables, the Order table would be included as a bridge because it is related to each of the tables containing the desired data.

Records that don't have matching join field values can be either included or excluded from the query result. An ***inner join*** specifies that a row is created in the query result only when the join values of both tables match. For example, joining the KoryoKicks Customer and Order table using the default inner join will return rows only for customers who have placed orders. If any customers have not placed orders, they will not be included in the inner join query results.

As an example, you will create the query that will join all of the tables in the KoryoKicks database using the relationships built in the previous session. The result will contain only customers who have placed orders and will be used to create invoices in the Multitable Report topic.

Creating a multitable query, InvoiceJoin:

1. Verify that the **ac06KoryoKicks.mdb** database is open

2. Select the **Queries** object and click **New**

3. Select Design View from the New Query dialog box and click **OK**

4. Add **Customer, Order, OrderDetail,** and **Product** tables to the query design

tip: *Although the position of the tables in the Design Window is not important, the order shown is the most effective way to view the relationships. If needed, drag the tables to the positions shown*

5. Close the Show Table dialog box

6. From the Customer table add **FirstName, LastName, Street, City, State,** and **ZipCode** to the QBE grid

7. From the Order table, add **OrderDate**

8. From the Product table add **ProductDescription** and **ProductPrice**

9. From the OrderDetail table add **QuantityOrdered**

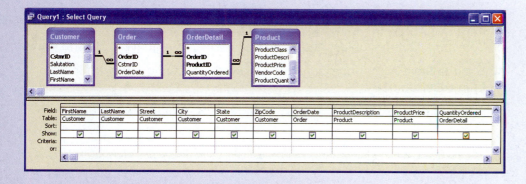

FIGURE 6.12

Select Query joining most of the KoryoKicks tables

10. Click the **Run** button to view the query results

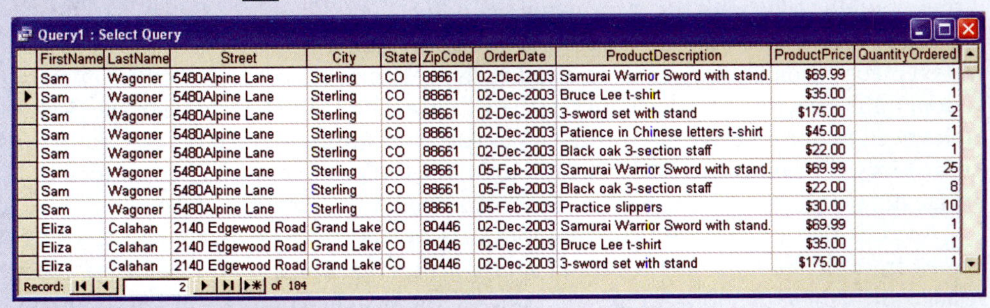

FirstName	LastName	Street	City	State	ZipCode	OrderDate	ProductDescription	ProductPrice	QuantityOrdered
Sam	Wagoner	5480Alpine Lane	Sterling	CO	88661	02-Dec-2003	Samurai Warrior Sword with stand.	$69.99	1
Sam	Wagoner	5480Alpine Lane	Sterling	CO	88661	02-Dec-2003	Bruce Lee t-shirt	$35.00	1
Sam	Wagoner	5480Alpine Lane	Sterling	CO	88661	02-Dec-2003	3-sword set with stand	$175.00	2
Sam	Wagoner	5480Alpine Lane	Sterling	CO	88661	02-Dec-2003	Patience in Chinese letters t-shirt	$45.00	1
Sam	Wagoner	5480Alpine Lane	Sterling	CO	88661	02-Dec-2003	Black oak 3-section staff	$22.00	1
Sam	Wagoner	5480Alpine Lane	Sterling	CO	88661	05-Feb-2003	Samurai Warrior Sword with stand.	$69.99	25
Sam	Wagoner	5480Alpine Lane	Sterling	CO	88661	05-Feb-2003	Black oak 3-section staff	$22.00	8
Sam	Wagoner	5480Alpine Lane	Sterling	CO	88661	05-Feb-2003	Practice slippers	$30.00	10
Eliza	Calahan	2140 Edgewood Road	Grand Lake	CO	80446	02-Dec-2003	Samurai Warrior Sword with stand.	$69.99	1
Eliza	Calahan	2140 Edgewood Road	Grand Lake	CO	80446	02-Dec-2003	Bruce Lee t-shirt	$35.00	1
Eliza	Calahan	2140 Edgewood Road	Grand Lake	CO	80446	02-Dec-2003	3-sword set with stand	$175.00	1

FIGURE 6.13
Inner join results

11. Save the Query as **InvoiceJoin**

Inner joins are also called equi-joins because the values of the join fields must match for a row to be created in the query result. Remember that when there is a Customer table record with no orders, there will be no entry in the query result. To verify this, Judy Johnson is CstmrID 105 in the Customer table. Since there is no order for this customer in OrderDetail, her record does not appear in the result of InvoiceJoin.

Outer Join

There are two types of outer joins. The ***left outer join*** selects all of the records from the first (left) table and joins them to values that match the other table. A left outer join would display all of the records from the previous inner join example, plus Judy Johnson's record since it is in the left table.

help yourself *Use the Type a Question combo box to improve your understanding of joining tables by typing* ***join types****. Review the contents of* About joining tables or queries in a query *and* Modify a join in a query. *Close the Help window when you are finished*

The ***right outer join*** selects all of the records from the right (second) table and only those with matching values from the left table. For example, in the Customer/Order join, a right outer join would show all orders whether or not they are associated with a customer. This relationship can't be demonstrated with KoryoKicks because the referential integrity rules selected when the table relationships were built preclude this type of entry.

Creating a KoryoKicks left outer join query:

1. Verify that the **ac06KoryoKicks.mdb** database is open
2. Select the **Queries** object and open the **InvoiceJoin** query in Design View
3. Use the **Save As** option of the **File** menu to save the query with the name **InvoiceLeftJoin**
4. Delete the OrderDetail and Product tables from the top of the query design

tip: *This action automatically removes the fields from the design grid previously selected from these tables*

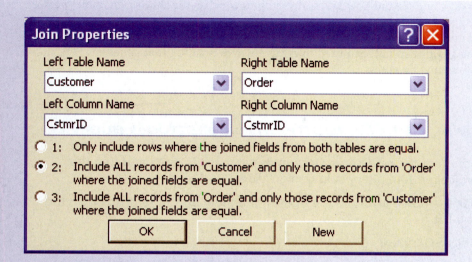

FIGURE 6.14

Setting join properties

5. Double-click the relationship line between the Customer and Order tables to open the Join Properties dialog box (see Figure 6.14)

6. Select option button **2: Include ALL records from 'Customer' and only those records from 'Order' where the joined fields are equal** and click **OK**

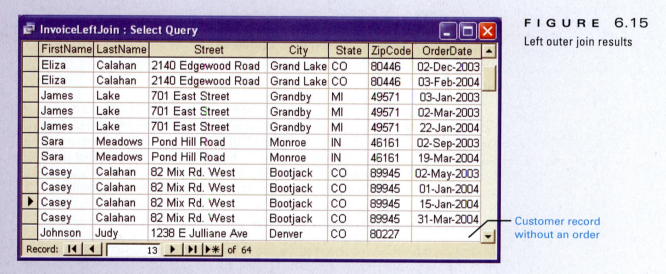

FIGURE 6.15

Left outer join results

7. Run the query to view the results (see Figure 6.15)

tip: *If your results do not show the record for Judy Johnson, return to Design View and repeat steps 5–7*

8. Leave the query open in Design View for the next series of steps

Left and right outer joins can involve only two tables, so the OrderDetail and Product tables were removed from the previous example. If other tables need to be included in the final result, a second query joining the InvoiceLeftJoin query results to other tables would be built. As was demonstrated, the results of the query can differ depending on the type of join and the order in which the joins are performed.

To fully understand how Access determines which is the left or right table, we need to take a look at the underlying SQL. Recall that SQL (Structured Query Language) is the standard language used to query relational databases. The QBE (Query by Example) grid that has been used to create queries is a GUI that generates SQL statements executed by Access.

Viewing the SQL for the InvoiceLeftJoin query:

1. Verify that the **ac06KoryoKicks.mdb** database is open and that the **InvoiceLeftJoin** query is in Design View

2. Click the down arrow to the right of the View button to drop down the view list

3. Select **SQL View**

FIGURE   6.16

SQL View of
InvoiceLeftJoin

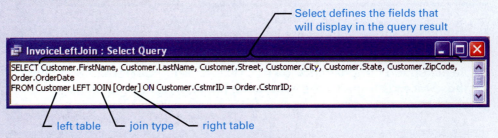

Select defines the fields that will display in the query result

InvoiceLeftJoin : Select Query

SELECT Customer.FirstName, Customer.LastName, Customer.Street, Customer.City, Customer.State, Customer.ZipCode, Order.OrderDate
FROM Customer LEFT JOIN [Order] ON Customer.CstmrID = Order.CstmrID;

left table   join type   right table

4. Close the SQL View saving your updates

The order in which tables are added to the design pane of the QBE grid determines their order in the resulting SQL statement. Since tables can be moved in the design grid, the order in which they appear is not always indicative of which was added first. When a left or right outer join is specified, it will be based on the order in which the tables were added to the query and to the order in which they appear in the SQL statement in the SQL pane. It is always best to check the SQL to be sure of the query results.

Developing Multitable Forms

To create a multitable form, a relationship between the tables must be defined first. Since the relationships in the KoryoKicks database have already been set, it is ready for multitable operations.

Creating a Lookup Field

The Lookup Wizard data type has already been used to create a Lookup field in the Order table. When table relationships are set, a Lookup field provides a list of valid values used when entering data. This makes data entry easier and ensures the consistency of the data in that field.

The relationship defined between the Customer and the Order tables forces the user to enter the CstmrID for a customer that is already in the primary (Customer) table. In Chapter 4, a Lookup field was created to retrieve the customer's last and first name from the Customer table and display it in a drop-down list for the user. A Lookup field can get its list of values from a table or query, or from a fixed set of values provided when it is created.

FIGURE 6.17

CstmrID Lookup field and query

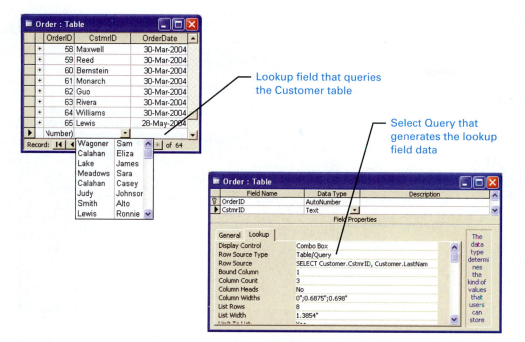

Figure 6.17 shows the Order table in both Datasheet and Design Views. In Datasheet View, the user sees the result of the Lookup field. In Design View, the query developed by the Wizard to look up the CstmrID is visible.

Lookup fields also can display a fixed list of possible values. This is effective when there is a limited set of valid values for a field. A good example would be the salutation used for customers in correspondence. A Salutation field with values of Ms., Mrs., and Mr. would be an effective way to add these data to a table. Other uses for such a Lookup field would be the departments of an organization, sales regions, or book classifications. In other words, any field with limited values should use a Lookup field to improve data integrity.

Creating a fixed-list Customer Lookup field:

1. Verify that the **ac06KoryoKicks.mdb** database is open

2. Open the Customer table in Design View

3. Insert a row in the field design after CstmrID and before LastName

4. Name the new field **Salutation** and make its data type **Lookup Wizard**

5. Select **I will type in the values that I want** from the Lookup Wizard dialog box and click **Next**

tip: *The other option, I want the Lookup column to look up the values in a table or query, was used to create the list of customers from the Customer table when you click in the CstmrID field of the Order table*

6. Type **Mr.** as a value in the cell of the Lookup column

7. Type **Ms.** in the next cell, **Mrs.** in the third cell, and click **Next**

8. Click **Finish** and set the Field Size to **5**

9. Select **Salutation** and then click the **Lookup** tab in the bottom portion of the screen to view the Lookup criteria created by the Wizard (see Figure 6.18)

FIGURE 6.18

Fixed value Lookup field

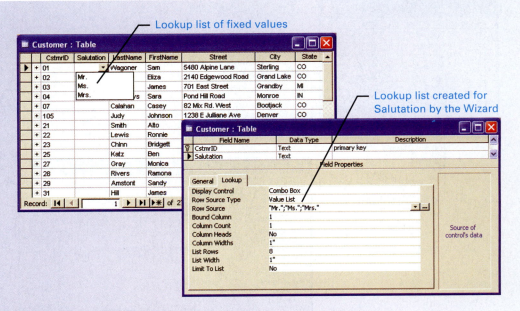

10. Click the **Datasheet** View button and save your changes

11. Click in the **Salutation** field to drop down the Lookup list. Assign an appropriate value to each record

12. Close the Customer table

Of course, a Lookup list can be created by typing the values in the Row Source property of the Lookup tab using the format shown. Alternatively SQL can be used to compose queries that will pull data from related tables such as the Customer table previously demonstrated. The Lookup Wizard simply ensures the validity of the syntax.

Lookup fields can be very powerful in improving data integrity and increasing data entry efficiency. Consider the time that is saved by the phone number Lookup employed by pizza delivery organizations. The customer provides a phone number, which is used to look up an address and in some cases an order history. All the person taking the order has to enter are a phone number and any changes to the current order. This saves typing and greatly reduces errors. Another example is entering a zip code in an Internet form that is used to look up the correct city and state. The rule of thumb is, if the data exist or can be derived, don't have the user reenter them.

Displaying Related Data in a Subdatasheet

When the relationships between tables are set in a database, the related table data can be viewed from the primary table. Again the KoryoKicks Customer table provides a good example. The Customer table is the primary table in the relationship between the Customer and the Order tables. Clicking the plus (+) sign in a Customer record will display the related Order records (see Figure 6.19). Further, the Order table is primary in the relationship between the Order and the OrderDetail tables, so the associated OrderDetail can be viewed by clicking the plus (+) sign in the Order record. The final relationship in the chain, the Product table, cannot be viewed because OrderDetail is the related (not the primary) table in this relationship.

To view related records in this fashion, nothing beyond setting up the table relationships was required. The KoryoKicks database has had this ability since relationships between the tables were built.

FIGURE 6.19

Customer table
subdatasheets

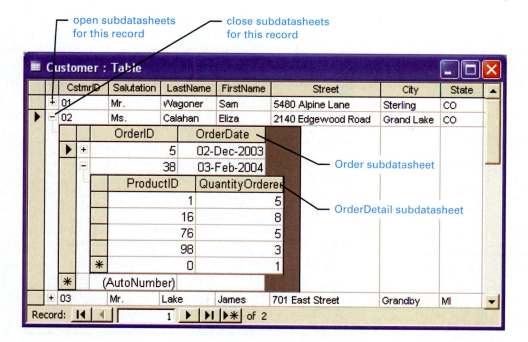

open subdatasheets
for this record

close subdatasheets
for this record

Order subdatasheet

OrderDetail subdatasheet

Creating a Main Form and SubForm

While subdatasheets are a fast and effective way to view related data, they are busy and sometimes confusing. Forms that show only a single record from the primary table and all of the related records provide better clarity. One way to accomplish this is to use a **main form** to display the primary table data with a synchronized **subform** to display the related data from the second table. The subform is inserted into the main form to display data from a related table (see Figure 6.19). Form/subform combinations also can be referred to as hierarchical forms, master/detail forms, or parent/child forms.

The Form Wizard is a fast way to create main form/subform combinations. As you know, forms and reports created using Wizards can be customized in Design View to improve their appearance and effectiveness. When using the Wizard to select data for the form, the primary table fields are selected first and then the related table fields. If the form is to be used to maintain table data, each table should appear in its own form or subform.

Creating a KoryoKicks main form/subform:

1. Verify that the **ac06KoryoKicks.mdb** database is open

2. Select the **Forms** object and click **New**

3. Select **Form Wizard**, choose **Customer** as the record source for the form, and click **OK**

4. Select **all fields** from the Customer table

5. Select the **Order** table from the drop-down list

6. Select **all fields** from the Order table and click **Next**

7. Select **by Customer** as the way to view data and click **Next**

8. Select **Tabular** as the layout for your subform and click **Next**

9. Choose **Ricepaper** as the style and click **Next**

ACCESS

10. Title the form **Customer Order** and click **Finish**

FIGURE 6.20

Customer form with a subform

Customer table data ──

related data from Order table ──

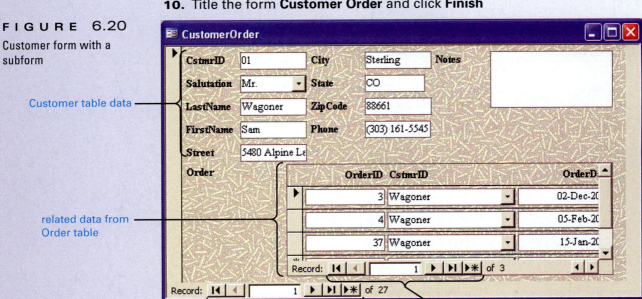

navigate Customer records   navigate Order records

11. Practice navigating the main form and the subform

This form could obviously benefit from customization. At a minimum, the size and alignment of existing fields should be adjusted to fit the data.

Customizing the KoryoKicks main form/subform:

1. Verify that the **ac06KoryoKicks.mdb** database is open with the **Customer Order** form in Design View

2. Use the **Size** option of the **Format** menu to adjust the size of each Label to fit its contents. Add spaces between words

tip: *You can select all of the Label controls by holding down the Shift button*

3. Delete Notes. Move each text box closer to its associated label and arrange them as shown in Figure 6.21.

4. Adjust the position of the subform. Add spaces to the labels

tip: *When you click the subform Label, the label and subform each displays a move handle since they are linked (like a bound text box and its label)*

5. Use the Line tool to draw a line that separates the areas of the form

6. Adjust the headings and compress the field width for the three subform columns as shown in Figure 6.21

7. Use the **Form View** 🔲 button to preview your changes

tip: *You will be prompted to save both the form and the subform*

8. Close the form and save your changes (see Figure 6.22)

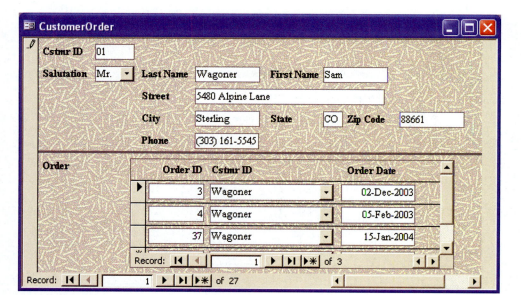

Customized
CustomerOrder form

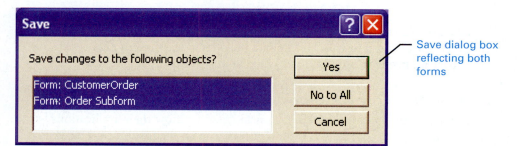

F I G U R E   6.22
Main form/subform save

Save dialog box
reflecting both
forms

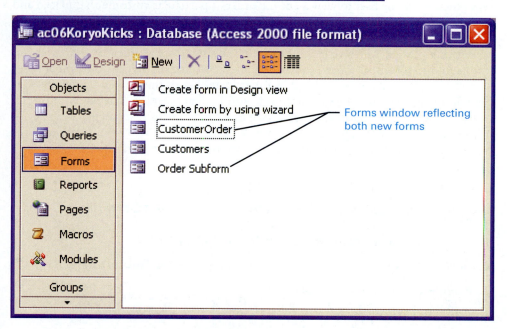

Forms window reflecting
both new forms

When a main form/subform pair is built, it is actually creating two forms, both of which are listed in the Forms object window. Figure 6.22 shows the save prompt reflecting the two forms and the Forms object window after the save is complete. The Order Subform is in reality a form that has been embedded into the Customer form. Double-click Order Subform, and it will open independently. The subform also can be viewed and edited in Design View without the Customer form being open.

FIGURE 6.23

Customer filtered by
Grand

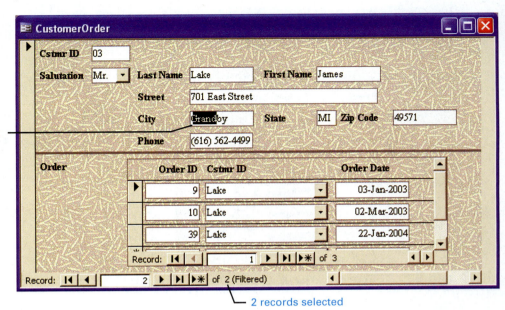

select filter value and click
Filter By Selection button

2 records selected

When the Customer form is opened, both this form and the embedded subform display. Forms are used to view and update the data in the underlying record source. Since this form involves four tables, we will demonstrate its update capabilities.

Using a Main Form/Subform

Users typically don't care about the technical details of how their applications work; they just want them to be effective. The Customer main form/subform just created is very efficient for the user to view all of the orders a particular customer has placed and is visually more appealing than the default subdatasheet.

All of the techniques used to order and find data on a single table form can be used on the multiple tables involved in this form. The default display order for data in a main form/subform is controlled by the primary table, Customer in this case. If no other order is specified, data will display ordered by the primary key of the primary table. The user can select a field and use the sort buttons to sort by that selection. The Find button can be used to search for a particular value, such as a LastName of Rivera. Filters can be applied to retrieve and manipulate a subset of the data (see Figure 6.23) and new records can be created. Remember to remove any applied filters before proceeding.

Using the KoryoKicks main form/subform:

1. Verify that the **ac06KoryoKicks.mdb** database is open

2. Select the **Forms** object and double-click the **Order Subform**

3. Navigate through the orders

4. Add a new order for **Thomas Calahan** with today's date

tip: *OrderID is an AutoNumber field and will be generated. The date format is dd-mmm-yyyy, for example, 10-Oct-2003*

5. **Close** the Orders Subform

6. Open the **CustomerOrder** form

7. Navigate through the customers using the lower navigation buttons

8. Add yourself as a customer with CstmrID **328**

9. Add two orders for yourself

10. **Close** the form

Multitable forms can be used to update data only when they represent one-to-many relationships. The main form is the primary side of the relationship and the subform is the related table. When forms are nested, each subform must be nested in its primary table's form (see Figure 6.24).

It is usually most effective to have one subform for each table involved. The main form can have as many subforms as are needed to represent the data. Subforms also can contain subforms—up to seven layers deep. Figure 6.24 shows three levels of nested subforms. The outer form is the Customer table data, which contains the Order table subform, which in turn contains the OrderDetail table subform.

Specifying Multitable Reports

Unlike forms, which are built to interact with the data, multitable reports retrieve data and report on them without further interaction. Because of this, reports are typically based on queries that retrieve the required data so that the report is only responsible for formatting.

Selecting Data from Multiple Tables

Although queries are commonly the foundation for reports, the Report Wizard can help create a report without first creating a query. As with other "automatic" things that we have looked at, a SQL query is being built and submitted behind the scenes.

To demonstrate the use of queries, an invoice report will be created without using a query as its data source and then the same report will be created with a query. The restriction of not using a query is that the report will display all of the data returned by

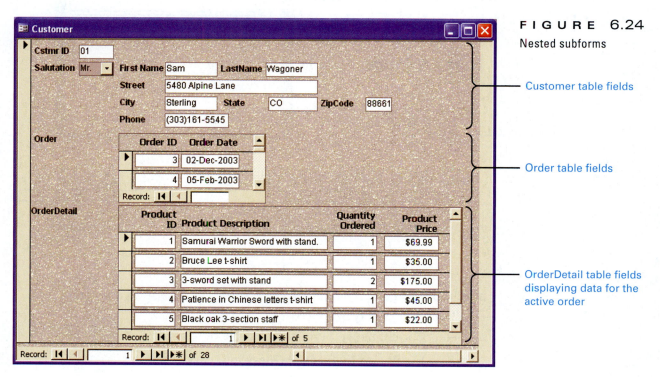

FIGURE 6.24
Nested subforms

— Customer table fields

— Order table fields

— OrderDetail table fields displaying data for the active order

ACCESS

joining the tables—a subset cannot be specified. When a query is used, a subset of the data can be retrieved for the report. For example, only invoices for customers who have made purchases in the last month could be printed. The invoices query would select those records and make them available to the invoice report for formatting.

Building the KoryoKicks Invoice report without a user-defined query:

1. Verify that the **ac06KoryoKicks.mdb** database is open

2. Click the **Reports** object and select **New**

3. Choose **Report Wizard** and click **OK**

4. Add all of the fields from the **Customer**, **Order**, **OrderDetail**, and **Product** tables to the Selected Fields list and click **Next**

5. The default by Customer is appropriate for this report, but explore the other options and then return the selection to **by Customer**

6. Add two levels of grouping, **Customer.CstmrID** and **Order.OrderID**, and click **Next**

FIGURE 6.25

Invoice report grouping

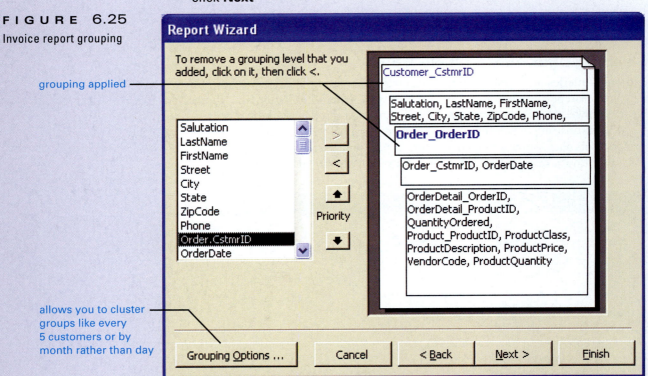

grouping applied

allows you to cluster groups like every 5 customers or by month rather than day

7. Select **OrderDetail_ProductID** as the only sort field and click **Next**

tip: *No summary options are applied, because there is no detail line item total to sum since we did not use a query as the record source*

8. Choose **Align Left 1** as the Layout style, **Landscape** as the page Orientation, and click **Next**

9. Select **Formal** as the Style and click **Next**

10. Name the Report **InvoicesNoQuery** and click **Finish**

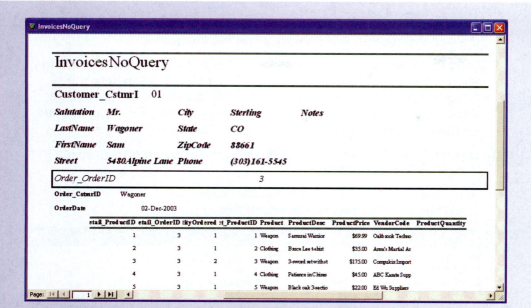

FIGURE 6.26
InvoicesNoQuery report

11. Close the report

The report created in the previous steps is a very effective first cut at invoices, but it needs considerable customization. The company logo needs to be added, the alignment of the labels and text boxes adjusted, and page breaks added between each invoice. Additionally, the calculations to total each detail line item and provide an invoice total and a grand total would need to be added manually.

Sorting, Grouping, and Calculating Report Data

Obviously the Report Wizard provides the ability to sort, group, and calculate data in the record source. Queries also provide the ability to sort, group, and calculate. The question then is "How do I know where to sort, group, and calculate when using a query as the record source for a report?"

There are probably as many answers to this question as there are people working with databases. There are no absolutes, and many approaches are effective. For many the best approach is the one that will minimize the customization needs of the report. With that in mind, a good rule of thumb is to sort and place calculations that display with each row of data, such as a detail line total, in the query. That leaves grouping and summary calculations, such as invoice total and report total, to be added in the report.

To try this reporting approach, the InvoiceJoin query created earlier will be modified to include sorting and the detail line calculation. This updated query will be used as the data source for the Report Wizard.

Modifying the InvoiceJoin query:

1. Verify that the **ac06KoryoKicks.mdb** database is open

2. Click the **Queries** object

3. Choose **InvoiceJoin** and click the **Design** View button

4. Double-click on **Customer.CstmrID** and **Order.OrderID** to add them to the query since they will be needed on the invoice

5. Drag the fields to the order that will be used in the invoice by clicking the bar above each Field Name to select a column. Then drag the selected column to the correct position. The final field order should be OrderID, OrderDate, CstmrID, FirstName, LastName, Street, City, State, ZipCode, QuantityOrdered, ProductDescription, and ProductPrice

6. Use the **Save As** option of the **File** menu to save your changes with the name **InvoiceJoinWithCalc**

7. In the first empty column add the expression **ItemTotal:QuantityOrdered*ProductPrice**

FIGURE 6.27

InvoiceJoinWithCalc expression

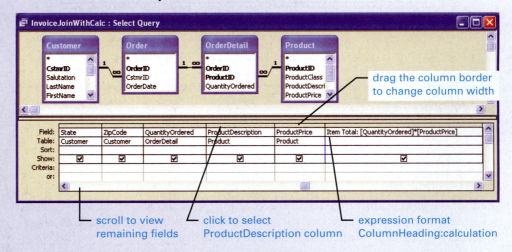

anotherway

... to Create InvoiceJoinWithCalc

If you prefer working with lists of table fields rather than the QBE grid, it might be easier to create a new query rather than extensively editing the InvoiceJoin query. You could use the Query Wizard to select and order the fields from the related tables and then use the QBE grid to add the calculation

8. Add the **Between #7/1/2003# And #7/31/2003#** selection criteria to OrderDate so that only orders for July of 2003 will be invoiced

tip: *Access will add the # signs if you do not type them*

9. Use the **Run** ![ ] button to view the query results. Verify the column order, the calculation, and the selection

10. Close the query saving your updates

Besides simplifying the customization that will need to be done on the invoice report, creating the InvoiceJoinWithCalc query also allows the organization, calculation, and selection of data to be verified prior to report generation. It is helpful to know that the correct data are going into your report since that directly impacts the validity of the report result.

InvoiceJoinWithCalc report:

1. Verify that the **ac06KoryoKicks.mdb** database is open

2. Select the **Reports** object and Click **New**

3. Select **Report Wizard**, and **InvoiceJoinWithCalc** as the data source, and click **OK**

tip: *If an empty report opens in Design View, close it and repeat steps 2 and 3, being sure to select the Report Wizard*

4. Move all of the fields of InvoiceJoinWithCalc to the Selected Fields box and click **Next**

5. Add grouping for **OrderID** and **CustmrID** and click **Next**

F I G U R E   6.28

Grouping added to InvoiceJoinWithCalc report

6. Sort by **ProductDescription** and click **Summary Options**

7. Check the **Sum** calculation for QuantityOrdered and ItemTotal to calculate group totals on these fields

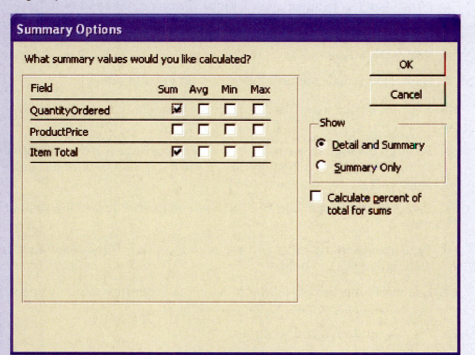

F I G U R E   6.29

Adding group calculations to InvoiceJoinWithCalc report

8. Click **OK** and then **Next**

9. Select **Align Left 1** as the layout and **Landscape** as the page orientation, and click **Next**

10. Choose **Formal** as the report style and click **Next**

11. Click **Finish** to preview the report

This report is very similar to the one created without the query, but it has the advantage of already having the calculations in place. Customizing this report is a matter of adding a logo and title, reorganizing the fields to the correct report section, and then adding the page break.

To print on each invoice page, the logo and report title need to be in the Page Header section of the report. The GrandTotal of all invoices would print on the last invoice page, so it will be deleted. The simplest way to accomplish this is to remove the Report Header/Footer sections, which also will remove all controls they contain.

Creating a logo and title for the InvoiceJoinWithCalc report:

1. Verify that the **ac06KoryoKicks.mdb** database is open with the **InvoiceJoinWithCalc** report open in Design View

2. Select **Report Header/Footer** from the **View** menu to remove those sections of the report

3. Answer **Yes** to the prompt informing you that this operation is not reversible

4. If the Field List is open, close it since it won't be needed

5. Use the CstmrID Header bar to expand the space in the Page Header

6. Select the **Image** tool from the toolbox and click in the Page Header

7. Navigate to the **ac06KoryoKicksLogo.gif** file and select it

tip: *You may need to change the Type of File in the Open dialog box to Tag Image File Format or All Files*

8. Position the logo in the top left corner of the Page Header and use the CstmrID Header to adjust the size of the Page Header until it is just large enough to hold the logo

9. Select the **Label** tool and click in the Page Header just to the right of the logo

10. Type **Invoice** in the Label and set its properties to Times New Roman, 48 point, italic, and bold

11. Use the **Properties** button to open the Properties window and set the Fore Color property to the darkest blue

12. Preview and save your changes

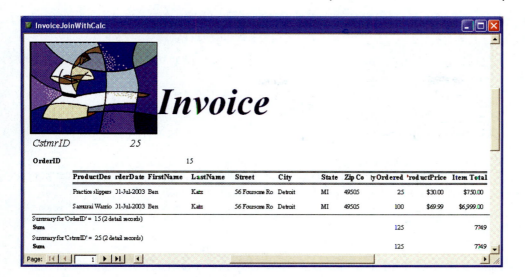

F I G U R E 6.30
KoryoKicks logo and
report title

The most arduous reorganization tasks involve moving fields the Wizard placed in the Detail portion of the report. The first field that we'll address is OrderDate. The OrderDate only needs to appear once per order and most reasonably should be in the OrderID Group Header.

Modify the OrderID Header of the InvoiceJoinWithCalc report:

1. Verify that the **ac06KoryoKicks.mdb** database is open with the **InvoiceJoinWithCalc** report open in Design View

2. Adjust the size of the OrderID label and text box to match the data. Add a space between the words in the label

3. Select the **OrderDate** label and drag it to the right of the OrderID text box

4. Select the **OrderDate** text box in the Detail section, click the **Cut** button on the toolbar, click the **OrderID Header**, and click the **Paste** button on the toolbar

5. Click the **OrderID** label, click the **Format Painter** button on the toolbar, and click the **OrderDate** text box to transfer the format to it

tip: *Double-clicking the Format Painter allows you to paint the format of the current object to multiple other objects. Clicking the Format Painter again turns it off*

6. Resize the OrderDate controls and position them as shown in Figure 6.31

7. Hold down the **Shift** key while using the **Line** tool to draw a line above the fields of the OrderID Header

8. Preview and save your updates

FIGURE 6.31

KoryoKicks headers

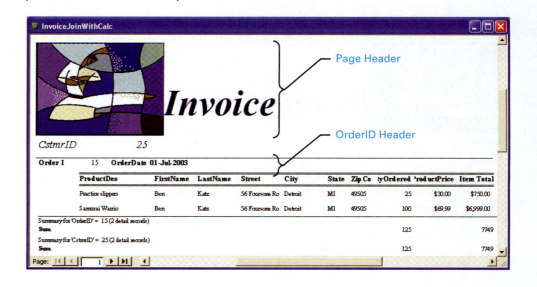

The customer name and address needs to appear only once per invoice and belongs in the CstmrID Group Header. The process of moving and formatting them is very similar to that just performed to modify the OrderID; however, both the text boxes and labels need to be moved since neither are currently in the CstmrID Group Header.

Modify the CstmrID Header of the InvoiceJoinWithCalc report:

1. Verify that the **ac06KoryoKicks.mdb** database is open with the **InvoiceJoinWithCalc** report open in Design View

2. Drag the OrderID Header section border to increase the height of the CstmrID Header section

3. Select the labels for FirstName, LastName, Street, City, State, and Zip by holding down the Shift key as you click

4. Cut the selection and paste it into the CstmrID Header section

5. Repeat the Cut and Paste process for the text boxes

6. Arrange the FirstName, LastName, Street, City, State, and ZipCode labels as shown in Figure 6.32. Arrange the text boxes below the labels

7. Edit the ZipCode caption to read Zip and add spaces to the Captions of the other labels

8. Adjust the size and position the CstmrID label and text box. Add a space to the label

9. Set all of the Text Box controls to display 10 point

10. Preview the report and adjust the size of the controls to display all of the data

11. Use the Format menu to finalize control alignment in the CstmrID Header section

12. Preview and save your updates

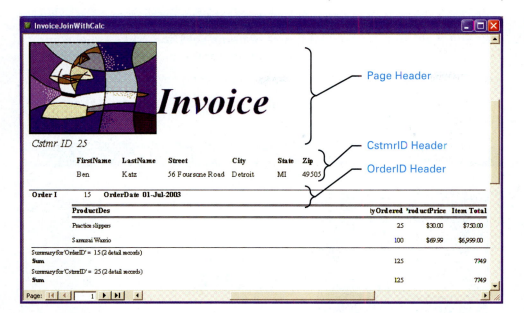

FIGURE 6.32
KoryoKicks headers

The Wizard added a Group Footer section for both OrderID and CstmrID. Both footers contain the same information unless a customer has placed multiple orders in the time period selected, so the CstmrID Footer needs to be eliminated. After this footer is removed and the Detail section sized and aligned, the Page Break tool will be used to print one invoice per page.

Modify the Detail and Footer sections of the InvoiceJoinWithCalc report:

1. Verify that the **ac06KoryoKicks.mdb** database is open with the **InvoiceJoinWithCalc** report open in Design View

2. Select the Text Box controls in the Detail section and set them to 10 point. Adjust the text box width to match its data

3. Select Quantity, ProductPrice, and ItemTotal text boxes and select Right Alignment so that the numbers will line up. Add spaces to labels and adjust label width

4. Align the Text Box controls in the Detail section with their corresponding Label controls in the CstmrID Header section

tip: *The numeric fields need to right-align and the text fields need to left-align*

5. Click the Sorting and Grouping button, select the CstmrID row, and set the Group Footer value to **No**

6. Respond **Yes** to the prompt and close the Sorting and Grouping dialog box

7. Delete the text box in the OrderID footer containing = "Summary for " & . . .

8. In the OrderID Footer, select the the two labels and set them to 10-point bold. Set the two text boxes to 10-point

ACCESS

9. Edit the Sum label to read **Count of items sold** and add a Label control for the other text box containing **Order Total**

10. Set the Format for the sum of ItemTotal to **currency**

11. Add a line above the Footer contents and organize them as shown in Figure 6.33

F I G U R E 6.33

KoryoKicks invoice

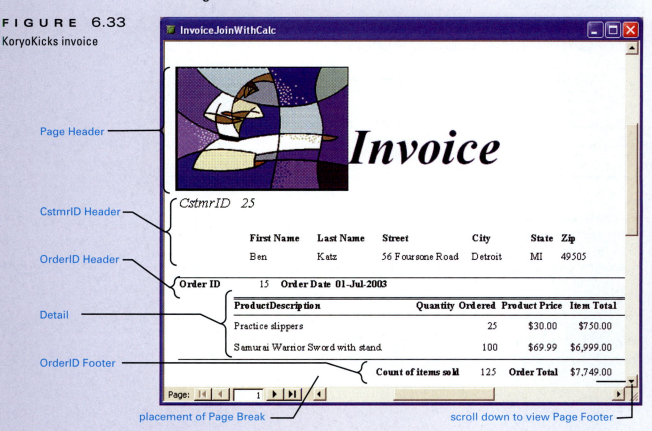

Page Header

CstmrID Header

OrderID Header

Detail

OrderID Footer

placement of Page Break

scroll down to view Page Footer

12. Click the Page Break tool and click below the contents of the OrderID Footer

tip: *The page break appears as six dots (. . . . . .) on the report*

13. Preview the report and adjust as needed

14. Save and close the report

---

anotherword   . . . on Modifying Database Objects

In this chapter you have modified queries, forms, and reports. Sometimes the modification was to improve the functionality. Sometimes it was to improve the visual impact. Regardless of why you are modifying an object, it is always wise to keep the original object as a backup. When making large numbers of changes, you should create intermediate backups also. A copy of the original design can be made using copy and paste in the Objects list before opening the object. You can use the Save As option of the File menu to save intermediate work under different names. Attaching sequential letters or numbers to the file-name works well (InvoicesNoQuery1, InvoicesNoQuery2, and so on). Rename the final file and delete all unneeded files when you are done

The KoryoKicks Invoice is a complex report involving four tables, two levels of grouping, detail line calculations, and summary calculations. No matter how this report is approached, it will be time consuming to develop, but once it is completed it can be used over and over again. The way this report is implemented, the twins will need to edit the selection criteria of the query before each report run. A more efficient methodology using Parameter queries will be introduced in later chapters.

Viewing Object Dependencies

Databases are storehouses of related data and objects. For example, each form or report is tied to a record source and each query is based on a table or tables. One common way to introduce errors into a database is to delete an object such as a table that removes the record source of another object that is still useful. In this situation, the useful object will generate a missing data source error because the data on which it is based are no longer available.

It is almost impossible to remember all interdependencies in a production database. Before deleting or maintaining a database object, it is valuable to know how it interacts with other database objects so you can make effective maintenance choices. Fortunately, Access 2003 provides a simple way to view table, query, form, and report dependencies, thereby reducing the likelihood of introducing errors through maintenance on these objects. Dependency data are not available for Data Access Pages, macros, or modules.

---

task reference   Viewing Object Dependencies

- Open the task pane and use the drop-down arrow to select **Object Dependencies**

- In the dependency pane

  - Review the list of objects that use the selected object

  - To view the list of objects that are being used by the selected object, click **Objects that I depend on** at the top of the pane

  - To view dependency information for an object listed in the pane, simply click on the expand icon (+) next to it

---

Viewing KoryoKicks object dependencies:

1. Verify that the **ac06KoryoKicks.mdb** database is open with no open objects

2. Select the **Tables** object and the **Customer** table

3. Open the task pane and use the drop-down arrow to select **Object Dependencies**

tip: *Click the New button on the toolbar to open the task pane*

4. Review the *Things that cause dependencies* link

5. Review the list of tables, queries, forms, and reports that could be impacted by changing or deleting the Customer table

FIGURE 6.34

The Customer table object dependencies

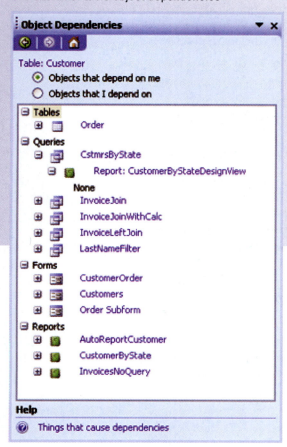

6. Click the + to the left of the CstmrsByState query to see the second-level dependencies for the Customer table (objects that are dependent on CstmrsByState and so could be impacted by changes to the Customer table)

7. Click the + to the left of the Report: CustomerByStateDesignView to view the third-level dependencies for the Customer table (objects that are dependent on the CstmrsByState query and so could be impacted by changes to the Customer table)

8. Click the **Objects that I depend on** option button and review the objects that could impact the Customer table

Database objects are dependent on each other anytime they share a defined relationship, a Lookup field, or use a data source. It is a good idea to review object dependencies before deleting or changing the design of any database object to avoid causing database errors through maintenance.

SESSION 6.2

making *the grade*

1. How would you decide whether to use an inner join or one of the outer join queries?

2. Why would you want to see the SQL generated by a query that you create in the QBE grid?

3. How do you know which table to open when you want to view related data in a subdatasheet?

4. Why would you consider adding indexes to your database tables?

5. Why would you use a query as the record source for a form?

SESSION 6.3 SUMMARY

To reduce data redundancy and increase data validity, database data are stored in multiple tables. Multiple tables reduce data redundancy because data that are common to multiple records are stored only once and then joined to each related row using a query. Data validity is improved because there is only one place to add or update each piece of data.

Only one-to-one and one-to-many relationships can be defined in a relational database. Many-to-many relationships use a junction table containing the key fields of both original tables, so that a one-to-many relationship is built from each of the original tables to the junction table.

While properly designed multiple-table databases greatly enhance the reliability of the data, it is necessary to understand and define appropriate relationships between the tables to control updates, deletions, and joins for output. Each defined relationship has properties that control its behavior. Referential integrity rules control how data in related tables can be entered and updated. Referential integrity rules can be turned off, enforced, or partially enforced. Double-click a relationship line in the Relationships window to set these options. In general, database data are more reliable when all referential rules are enforced.

When creating a multitable query, the relationship lines can be double-clicked to set the join properties. The default, inner join, returns records when the join field values of both tables match. A left outer join returns all of the rows from the left table and rows from the right table with a matching foreign key value. A right outer join returns all of the rows from the right table and rows from the left table with a matching foreign key value.

Data from multiple tables can be updated using the default primary datasheet and related subdatasheets. To open a subdatasheet, click the plus sign in the primary datasheet row. Related table data also can be displayed in a main form/subform combination. Data from the primary table are displayed in the main form and those from the related table are displayed in the subform.

Visit www.mhhe.com/i-series/ to explore related topics.

MICROSOFT OFFICE SPECIALIST OBJECTIVES SUMMARY

- Create and modify one-to-many relationships—MOS AC03S-1-5
- Enforce referential integrity—MOS AC03S-1-6
- Identify object dependencies—MOS AC03S-4-1

making the grade answers

SESSION 6.1

1. With the database open, click the Relationships button to activate the Relationships window. The properties of each relationship can be viewed by double-clicking the relationship line.

2. The drag operation is from the primary field to the related field.

3. Referential integrity rules govern how data are entered and deleted in related tables. They prevent orphans by requiring that the parent record exist before child records can be added to the related table, and that the parent can't be removed while it still has active children.

4. Access uses indexes to speed sort and search operations. An index is a table that can be used to look up index values and then move directly to the fields containing that value.

SESSION 6.2

1. Inner join queries are used when you want only rows of data where both tables have the same join field value. Use one of the outer joins when you want all of the data in one or the other table, regardless of whether there is a matching value in the other table.

2. You might want to see the SQL to verify which table is the left and which is the right table in the defined relationship. It could also help you learn SQL so that you could type your own queries for operations like Lookup fields.

3. Open the primary table. A plus sign displays in front of each record that will allow you to open the related table records.

4. Indexes improve search and sort operations. Candidates for indexing include fields that are frequently used in these operations, are not automatically indexed (like primary and foreign key values), and contain a wide range of values.

5. Queries allow you to verify the validity of data selection and calculations before applying formatting in the form.

task reference summary

Task	Page #	Preferred Method
View table relationships	AC 6.4	• Click the **Relationships** button on the Database toolbar • If relationships exist, they will be displayed. If there are no current relationships, you can add tables and build relationships between them
View relationship properties	AC 6.6	• Click the **Relationships** button on the Database toolbar • If relationships exist, they will be displayed. If there are no current relationships, you can add tables and build relationships between them • Double-click the relationship line that you would like to view • The Edit Relationships dialog box displays the properties of that relationship
Create a relationship	AC 6.8	• Click the **Relationships** button on the Database toolbar • If relationships exist, they will be displayed • Click the **Show Table** button on the toolbar • Select the table that you want to relate and click the **Add** button. Repeat this process for each table to be related • When you have added all of the necessary tables, click **Close** • Click the primary table field of the relationship and drag to the secondary field to initiate the relationship • Select the Referential Integrity options in the Edit Relationships dialog box • Click **OK** to close the Edit Relationships dialog box • Repeat this process for any other relationships to be built • Close the Relationships window

task reference *summary*

Task	Page #	Preferred Method
Index a table field	AC 6.13	• Open the table in **Design View** • Select the field to be indexed from the Field Name column • Set the Indexed field property to **Yes (Duplicates OK)** or **Yes (No Duplicates)** • Close the table design and save the changes
Delete an index	AC 6.14	• Open the table in **Design View** • Select the field whose index is to be removed from the Field Name column • Set the Indexed field property to **No** (this does not impact the field or its data) • Close the table design and save the changes
View the indexes of a table	AC 6.14	• Open the table in **Design View** • Click the **Indexes** button of the toolbar • Click an index to review its properties
Viewing object dependencies	AC 6.37	• Open the task pane and use the drop-down arrow to select **Object Dependencies** • In the dependency pane • Review the list of objects that use the selected object • To view the list of objects that are being used by the selected object, click **Objects that I depend on** at the top of the pane • To view dependency information for an object listed in the pane, simply click on the expand icon (+) next to it

TRUE/FALSE

1. A many-to-many relationship must be broken up into two one-to-many relationships before it can be implemented in Microsoft Access.

2. A left outer join query retrieves all records from the right table and only matching records from the left table.

3. The only way to tell whether or not indexing works is to monitor performance before and after an index is applied.

4. A key value in the primary table cannot be changed while there are records with that key value in the related table unless Cascade Update Related Fields is checked for that relationship.

5. When ∞ appears next to a table on a relationship line, data must be added to that table before related (same key value) records can be added to the table on the one side of the relationship.

6. The table on the one side of a relationship is also called the parent or primary table.

FILL-IN

1. Indexing is accomplished in _____ View.

2. A _____ retrieves all of the records in the second table, but only rows of the second table with matching foreign key values.

3. The _____ menu option is used to align multiple selected controls.

4. The _____ menu option causes a Label control Caption text to right-justify.

5. The _____ table is on the many side of a one-to-many relationship.

6. When a primary record is deleted, all related secondary records (those with the same key value) will automatically delete when _____ is set.

7. To build a one-to-one relationship, both tables must have the same _____.

MULTIPLE CHOICE

1. In a one-to-many relationship the primary key of the primary table _____ match exactly the primary key of the related table.
   a. must
   b. should
   c. cannot
   d. all of the above

2. The Referential Integrity setting that automatically updates the key field of related records when the primary key of the primary table is altered is _____.
   a. Cascade Update Related Fields
   b. Enforce Referential Integrity
   c. Cascade Delete Related Records
   d. AutoUpdate Related Records

3. An index created on more than one field is referred to as a _____.
   a. compound index
   b. complex index
   c. multiple-field index
   d. none of the above

4. When relationships have been set, related data can be viewed in Datasheet View by _____.
   a. running a query
   b. clicking the plus (+) sign
   c. clicking the Subdatasheet button
   d. all of the above

5. When a query selects all records in the first (left) table and only matching records from the second (right) table, the join is a _____.
   a. left inner join
   b. right inner join
   c. right outer join
   d. left outer join

review of concepts

REVIEW QUESTIONS

Each of the following topics should be addressed in one to three paragraphs.

1. Give an example of a one-to-many relationship between tables and explain how it might be used.

2. Describe the relationship line notations in the Relationships window and how they can impact the construction of a main form/subform.

3. How are many-to-many relationships handled?

4. How would you delete a relationship that was built in error or is no longer needed?

5. What is the importance of cascade updates and deletes?

CREATE THE QUESTION

For each of the following answers, create the question.

ANSWER	QUESTION
1. Yes (No Duplicates)	_____
2. SQL View button	_____
3. Lookup fields	_____
4. The report or form section and all of the controls it contains are permanently deleted	_____
5. The Sorting and Grouping dialog box	_____
6. Double-click the relationship line in the Relationships window	_____
7. Drag the large box in the upper left-hand corner of a control selected in Form Design View	_____

FACT OR FICTION

For each of the following, determine whether the statement is fact, fiction, or both and present your arguments for that conclusion.

1. Calculations must always be completed in a query before creating a report.

2. Both a Group Header and a Group Footer must exist on a report for each defined group.

3. For the best database performance, index every field in a table.

4. To create a new relationship, you must drag from the primary table to the related table.

5. You can drag and drop controls from one form section to another.

6. Often the same report can be built using either table(s) or a query as the data source.

7. A logo placed in the Report Header section of a report will print on each page.

1. Altamonte High School Booster Club Donation Tracking—Part I: Setting Table Relationships

Altamonte High School Booster Club is an organization of students, teachers, parents, and community members who sponsor high school activities. The Boosters are using an Access database to track donations.

1. Start Access and open **ac06AltamonteBoosters.mdb**

2. Use Figure 6.35 to create and populate the **DonationClass** table depicted in the figure

3. Close the DonationClass table and use the **Relationships** button to open the Relationships window

4. Add the **Boosters** and **DonationClass** tables to the Relationships window

5. Drag a relationship from **DonationClass.Class** (Class in the DonationClass table) to **Boosters.DonationClass** (DonationClass in the Boosters table)

6. Close the Relationships window, saving your updates

7. Open the Donations table in Design View

8. Use the Lookup Wizard to create a Lookup field for Booster that retrieves the Name field from the Boosters table. Sort the Lookup by Name and do not display ID

tip: To test the Lookup field, open the Donations table in Datasheet View. A drop-down list of names should be available in the Booster column

9. Open the Relationships window and add the Donations table

tip: You may need to use the **Show Table** button to display the Show Tables dialog box

10. Adding the Lookup field created a relationship between the Donations table and the Boosters table without any attributes (no notation on the lines)

11. Double-click the Donations/Boosters relationship line

12. Click on all of the Referential Integrity options and click **OK**

13. Open the Boosters/DonationClass relationship, click on Enforce Referential Integrity, and then click **OK**. Do not check any other Referential Integrity options

14. Verify your table relationships using Figure 6.36

15. Close the Edit Relationships dialog box saving your changes

16. Open the Boosters table in Datasheet View

17. Add yourself as a booster in Class 1

18. Use the subdatasheets to add two donations for yourself dated last month and this month for $15 and $25, respectively

19. Close the AltamonteBoosters database and exit Access if your work is complete

FIGURE 6.35
DonationClass table

FIGURE 6.36
AltamonteBoosters table relationships

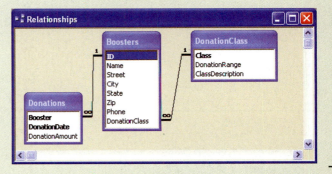

2. Building Table Relationships for NMO Energy

NMO Energy supplies products to consumer energy companies across the United States. NMO has a large sales force with offices in various locations. Each company that does business with NMO has an assigned salesperson. Each salesperson supports multiple companies. Two tables are in the Microsoft Access database for NMO, Salesforce and Customer. You will build a Lookup field from Customer to Salesforce to simplify updates.

1. Start Access and open **ac06NMOEnergy.mdb**

2. Open the Customer table in Design View

   a. Use the Lookup Wizard to create a Lookup field for SalesID that retrieves the LastName and FirstName of the Salesperson from the Salesforce table

   b. Do not display the SalesID in the Lookup

3. Use the Relationships button on the toolbar to open the Relationships window

   a. Double-click the relationship between the Salesforce and Customer table to open the relationship created by the Lookup field

   b. Verify that the relationship between Salesforce.SalesID and Customer.SalesID is one-to-many

   c. Enforce Referential Integrity

   d. Do not Cascade Update or Cascade Delete Related Records

   e. Close the Relationships window saving your changes

4. Test the Lookup field

   a. Open the Salesforce table and add yourself as a salesperson

   b. Close the Salesforce table

   c. Open the Customer table

   d. Use the Lookup field to make yourself the salesperson for customers 71, 81, and 93

   e. Close the Customer table

5. Test the relationship

   a. Open the Salesforce table

   b. Use the subdatasheet to add **Mississippi Power and Light** as a new company for Ramona Amstont. Use MPLI as the InternalCode

   c. Use the subdatasheet to add the local power company to your customer list. Select an appropriate InternalCode

6. If your work is complete, exit Access; otherwise, continue to the next assignment

FIGURE 6.37

Salesforce Lookup field

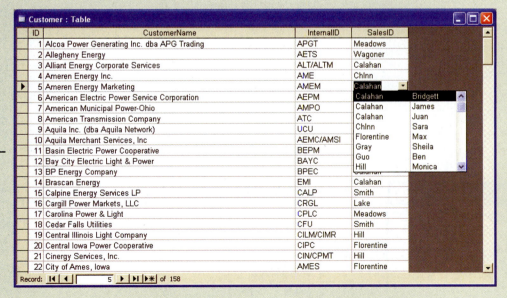

1. Altamonte High School Booster Club—Part II: Using Related Tables

1. Start Access and the **ac06AltamonteBoosters.mdb** database

tip: *If you did not complete the Practice assignment, you will need to do so now*

2. Use the Form Wizard to create a main form/subform
   a. The main form should display all of the Boosters table fields
   b. The subform should display all of the Donations table fields
   c. Set the data to be viewed **by Boosters**
   d. Use the **Tabular** layout for the subform
   e. Use the **Blueprint** style
   f. Name the form **BoostersDonations**
   g. Refer to Figure 6.38 and customize the main form and subform so that all the labels display and the field sizes are appropriate

3. Use the form to add another donation for Matthew Hoff for the current date and **$700**. Change his DonationClass to **6**

4. Close the form, saving your changes

5. Create a query that
   a. Selects **Boosters.DonationClass**, **Boosters.Name**, **Donations.DonationDate**, and **Donations.DonationAmount**
   b. Selects all of the donations for October 2003

6. Save the query as **Oct03Donations**

7. Use the Report Wizard to create a report using **Oct03Donations** as the record source
   a. List data by Donation
   b. Group the data by DonationClass
   c. Sort the data by **Name** and **DonationDate**
   d. Total **DonationAmount**
   e. Use **Block** format and **Casual** style, and name it **BoostersOct03Donations**

8. Customize the report using Figure 6.39 as a guide
   a. Change title to **Altamonte HS Boosters**
   b. Add a Label control under the report title with a Caption property of **October 2003 Donations Report**, teal color, bold, and a point size of 14
   c. Adjust the labels and text boxes so that all of the data display
   d. Adjust the first group Summary label so that it is indented
   e. Delete the Group Footer Sum label
   f. Align the = Sum text box in the Amount column to the right of the Summary label
   g. Align the Grand Total = Sum text box in the Amount column

9. Close the AltamonteBoosters database and exit Access if your work is complete

FIGURE 6.39

Customized October 2003 Donations Report

FIGURE 6.38

BoostersDonations form

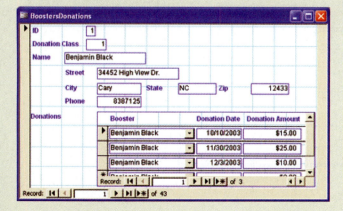

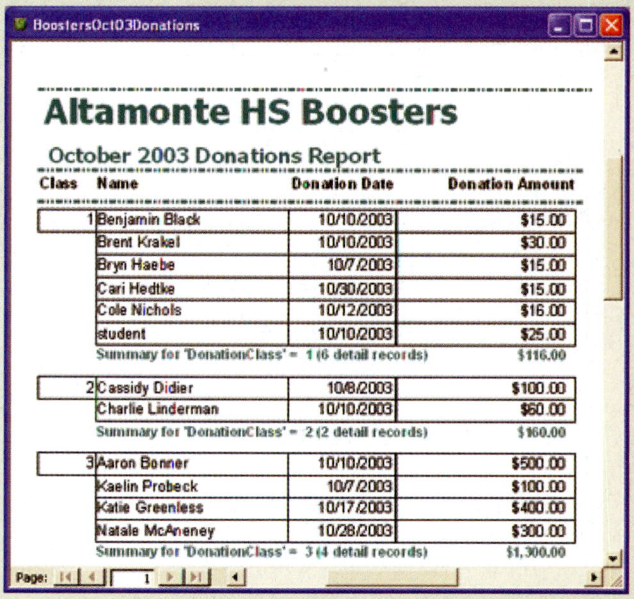

2. Multitable Operations for NMO Energy

NMO Energy supplies products to consumer energy companies across the United States. NMO has a large sales force with offices in various locations. Two tables are in the Microsoft Access database for NMO, Salesforce and Customer. In the Practice exercise for this chapter, a Lookup field was built and properties for the relationship assigned.

1. Start Access and open **ac06NMOEnergy.mdb**

2. If you have not already completed steps 1 through 3 from the second Practice exercise in this chapter, do so now

3. Use the Form Wizard to create a main form/sub-form pair

   a. The Salesforce form should be the main form

   b. The Customer form should be the subform

   c. All fields of both tables should display

   d. Use the **Tabular** layout for the subform

   e. Use the **SumiPainting** style

   f. Name the form **SalesforceCustomers**

   g. Customize the form to match Figure 6.40. You will need to adjust both the height and width of text boxes

4. Use the Report Wizard to create a report showing customers grouped by employee

   a. Include **SalesID**, **LastName**, **FirstName**, and **Phone** from the Salesforce table

   b. Include all fields from the Customer table

   c. View the data by Salesforce

   d. Group by SalesID

   e. Sort by CustomerName

   f. Use the **Align Left 1** layout and the **Soft Gray** style

   g. Name the report **SalesforceCustomers**

   h. Customize the report so that all labels have spaces and table names are not included

   i. Make the report title **Customers by Salesperson**

   j. Adjust the size of the LastName and FirstName control and place them on the same row. Move PhoneNumber up directly under FirstName. Move the row labels up until it is just under PhoneNumber and adjust the height of the Salesforce_SalesID Header to be just tall enough for the revised design

5. If your work is complete, exit Access; otherwise, continue to the next assignment

FIGURE 6.40

NMOEnergy SalesforceCustomers form

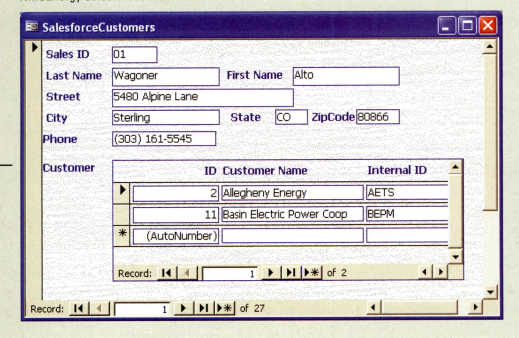

1. Curbside Recycling

Curbside Recycling is enhancing its Web presence so customers can view their current account status and the profit position of the organization.

1. Open the **ac06CurbsideRecycling.mdb** database
2. Open the Relationships window and review the relationship between the Customer and the CustomerRecords tables
3. Open the Edit Relationships dialog box and click on all of the referential integrity options
4. Close the Edit Relationships dialog box and the Relationships window, saving your changes
5. Users have reported significant delays when searching by LastName and FirstName. Create a multicolumn index called **Name** to try to address this issue
6. Use the Form Wizard to create a main form/subform for maintaining table data
   a. Include all fields from both tables
   b. View the data **by Customer**
   c. Use the Datasheet View for the subform
   d. Select the **Standard** style
   e. Name the form **CustomerRecordsUpdate**

FIGURE 6.41
Updating table relationships

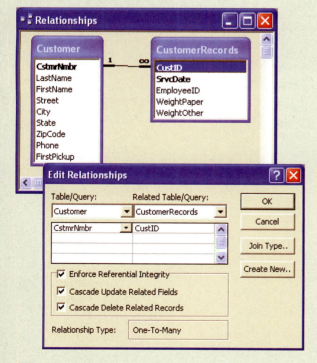

7. Customize the form to improve its functionality
   a. Narrow the subform to about 4 inches
   b. Add spaces to the form and subform labels
   c. Change to Form View and drag the subform column widths to display the column headings and data

tip: *You cannot change the width in Design View because you have chosen a Datasheet for the subform*

8. Use the Report Wizard to create a report
   a. Select **CstmrNmbr**, **LastName**, and **FirstName** from the Customer table
   b. Select **SrvcDate**, **WeightPaper**, and **WeightOther** from the CustomerRecords table
   c. View the data by **Customer**
   d. Sort the data by **SrvcDate**
   e. Sum both weight fields
   f. Use **Block** format
   g. Use **Compact** style
   h. Name the report **CustomerPickups**

9. Customize the report
   a. Add spaces to the labels
   b. Adjust the field widths to fit the size of the column headings and labels
   c. Change the label for the sum to **Total Weight** and put the totals under the correct column
   d. Preview and save your changes

10. If your work is complete, exit Access; otherwise, continue to the next assignment

FIGURE 6.42
Customized CustomerRecordsUpdate form

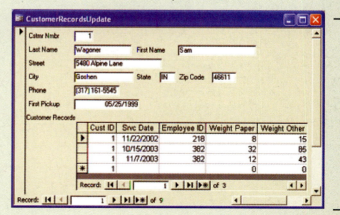

2. Using Multiple Tables to Track Employee Skills

Community Hospital, like most hospitals nationwide, is feeling the crunch of insufficient medical staff. To effectively treat patients, it has had to change the way it does business. One of these changes is to try to match staff to patients' needs rather than try to staff to cover any possible need. In order to schedule staff, the Scheduling Department needed a way to track and report each employee's current set of skills. You will create a custom report that will be posted to the Web to allow the nurses in charge of a unit to assign patients to nurses based on the patient's needs and the nurse's skills.

There are a number of tables in the **ac06Community Hospital.mdb** database, and this report requires an understanding of three of them. The Employee table holds general data about each employee being tracked. The Competency table holds data about each measurable competency needed by the hospital. The Competency Assignment table uses EmployeeID and CompetencyID to assign competencies to individual employees who have met those requirements. You will create a list of employees and their skills organized by Unit. This report will be posted to the hospital intranet so that all charge nurses have access to it for patient assignment.

FIGURE 6.43

NursingSkills report

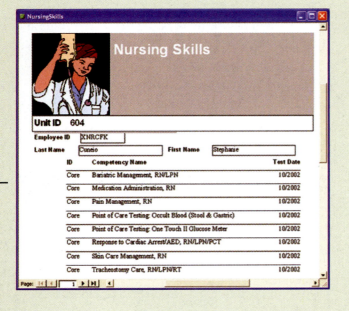

1. Open Access and open **ac06CommunityHospital.mdb**

2. Review the data in the tables that will be used for this report. Close the tables when done

3. Open the Relationships window. Build relationships from Employee to Competency Assignment and Employee to Unit. Enforce referential integrity

4. Use the Report Wizard to create the report shown in Figure 6.43 that will be available from the hospital's Web site. Name the report **NursingSkills**. The completed report should have the following attributes

   a. Include only **EmployeeID**, **LastName**, **FirstName**, and **UnitID** from the Employee table

   b. Include **CompetencyID** and **TestDate** from the CompetencyAssignment table

   c. Include **CompetencyName** from the Competency table

   d. List the Data by Employee grouped by Unit

   e. Order the Data by CompetencyID and CompetencyName

   f. Use the **Align Left 2** layout and the **Soft Gray** style

   g. Add the image **ac06Nurse.gif** to the Header section

   h. Change the CompetencyId heading to ID. Edit the remaining report controls so that the title and headings have spaces. Change the widths of the ID and CompetencyName columns to match the size of the data. Move LastName and FirstName to the same row and move the competency headings to the row where FirstName was

5. Close the database and exit Access if your work is complete

on the web

1. Academic Software Multitable Relationships and Reports

Academic Software, as the name implies, is a clearinghouse for educational software. You are improving its existing Access database.

1. Use a search engine to find at least three academic software titles and prices for the K–12 environment. Find at least three free download titles

2. Open the **ac06Software.mdb** database

3. Open the Relationships window and review the relationship between tblVendor and tblSoftware

4. Open the Edit Relationships dialog box and click on Cascade Updates and Deletes

5. Close the Edit Relationships dialog box and the Relationships window

6. Users have reported significant delays when searching by tblSoftware.Category. Index this field to try to address these issues

7. Open tblVendor and use the subdatasheet to add the three software titles that you found to the Edusoft Inc. vendor with Software Numbers 7000–7002. Add a new vendor named **Web Downloads** with a VendorCode of **WD**

8. Open a new query in Design View and put both tables on the QBE grid
   a. From tblSoftware add **Category**, **Name**, **Quantity**, **Price**, and **VendorCode**
   b. From tblVendor add **Name**, **Address**, **City**, **State**, **ZipCode**, and **Phone Number** (see Figure 6.44)
   c. Run the query (see Figure 6.45)
   d. Save the query as **SoftwareByCategory**

9. With the Report Wizard, create a report using the SoftwareByCategory query
   a. Use the **by tblSoftware** option
   b. Group by **Category**
   c. Sort by **tblSoftware.Name**
   d. Select the **Landscape** page orientation and **Stepped** layout
   e. Choose the **Soft Gray** style
   f. Name the report **SoftwareByCategory**

10. Customize the report using Figure 6.46 as a guide

FIGURE 6.44

SoftwareByCategory query

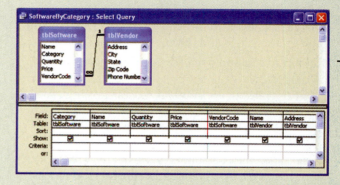

FIGURE 6.45

SoftwareByCategory report

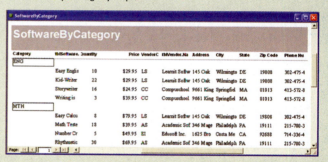

FIGURE 6.46

Customized SoftwareByCategory report

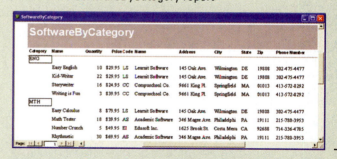

around the world

1. TechRocks Seminars Forms and Reports

TechRocks Seminars provides onsite technical training to large businesses around the world. You will build the Table relationships and test the multitable abilities.

1. Start Access and open the **ac06Seminars.mdb** database

2. Open the Relationships window
   a. Use the **Show Tables** button to add the Facilitators table to the Relationships window
   b. Open the Facilitators/Seminars relationship and enforce all referential integrity rules
   c. Open the Seminars/Enrollment relationship and enforce all referential integrity rules
   d. Use Figure 6.47 to verify your relationships and then close the Relationships window

3. Create a mulitable query in Design View
   a. From the Seminars table select **Seminar ID**, **Description**, **Date**, **Time**, **Hours**, and **Place**
   b. From the Facilitators table select **LastName**, **FirstName**, and **Phone**
   c. From the Enrollment table select **Student Number**, **Last Name**, **First Name**, and **Student Phone**
   d. Save the query as **StudentListing**

4. Use the StudentListing query to create a report listing the students currently enrolled in each seminar
   a. Initiate the Report Wizard
   b. Select the **StudentListing** query as the data source
   c. Select all of the fields from the query
   d. Select **by Seminars** as the way to view the report
   e. No additional grouping is necessary
   f. Select **Align Left1** as the layout
   g. Select the **Bold** style
   h. Name the report **StudentListingBySeminar**

5. Customize the StudentsBySeminar report. Refer to Figure 6.48
   a. Change the title and column headings as shown
   b. Adjust the size of labels and text boxes
   c. Rearrange the Seminar ID Header fields as shown. Be careful to adjust the *Facilitator* name fields not the enrollment name fields
   d. Adjust the length of the lines above and below the header (there are two above and two below even though it looks like one line each)
   e. Activate the Sorting and Grouping dialog box and add a Group Footer for Seminar ID
   f. Insert a Page Break in the Seminar ID Footer section
   g. Preview and save your work

FIGURE 6.47

Seminars table relationships

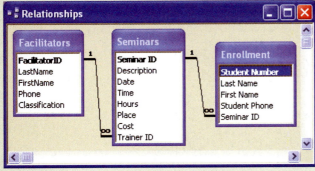

FIGURE 6.48

Customized StudentListingBySeminar report

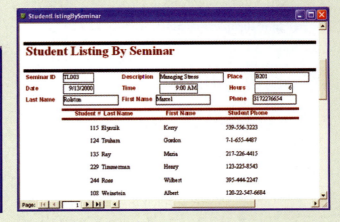

running project: tnt web design

Custom Forms and Reports for TnT

As TnT grows, so does the complexity of its database. Tori and Tonya now have over 65 employees and several hundred customers. Employees and projects are spread across the United States, so it is becoming critical to have simple data entry and reporting.

1. Start Access and open the **ac06TnT.mdb** database. Familiarize yourself with each table if necessary
2. Open the Relationships window
   a. Edit the tblCustomers/CustomerSites relationship
   b. Enforce all referential integrity rules
   c. Close the Relationships window and save your changes
3. Use the Query Wizard to create a query listing fields from each table
   a. From the tblCustomers select **cusName** and **cusAddress**
   b. From CustomerSites select **URL**
   c. From Employees select **LastName** and **FirstName**
   d. Save the query as **CustomerWebSites**

4. Use the Report Wizard to create a report with all of the fields of the CustomerWebSites query
   a. No additional sorting or grouping is needed
   b. Choose **Stepped** layout
   c. Select **Soft Gray** style
   d. Save the report as **CustomerWebSite**
5. Customize the CustomerWebSite report
   a. Put spaces in the report title
   b. Remove the "cus" prefix from the Customer table fields
   c. Change the LastName label to **Development Manager**
   d. Delete the FirstName label
   e. Expand the URL label and text box
   f. Adjust the position of controls to match Figure 6.49
6. If your work is complete, exit Access; otherwise continue to the next assignment

FIGURE 6.49
TnT Relationships

FIGURE 6.50
CustomerWebSites report

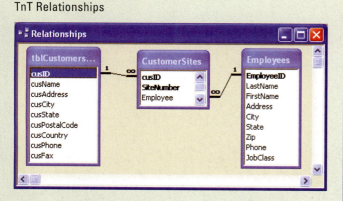

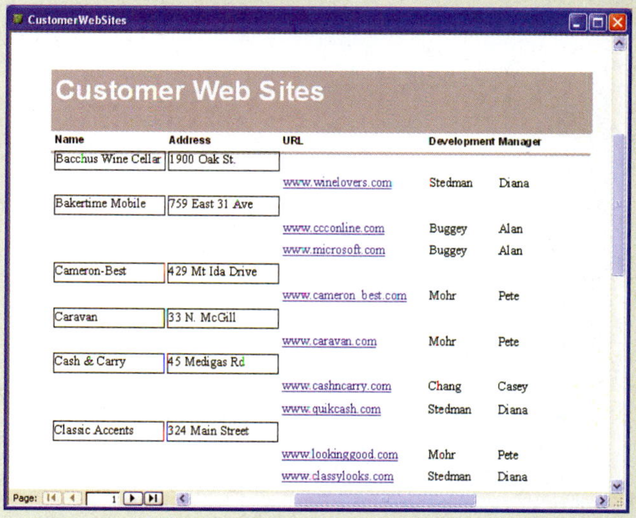

1. Create a Multitable Database to Invoice Customers

Create a new database named **ac06CustomersMultiTableDatabase.mdb**. Select a small business that is of interest to you such as selling skateboard products, a clothing boutique, or a bakery and create a database to support billing customers. The database must store data about customers, products, prices, and orders. Build all necessary table relationships. Include data for at least 10 customers and 10 orders. Create an invoice report using a query to join the table data. Name the query **InvoiceQuery** and the report **InvoiceWithQuery**. Create a second invoice without using a query. Name this report **InvoiceNoQuery**. Customize both reports to align report headings, include a line item calculation, and include an invoice total calculation.

2. Create a Multitable Database to Track Employees

Create a new database named **ac06Employees MultiTableDatabase.mdb**. Select a local or Internet business that you frequent and create a database that can be used to track their employees. The database must contain tables for employees, benefits, and departments. The Department table should have a DepartmentID, DepartmentDescription, and DepartmentManager at a minimum. All employees must belong to a department and have benefits. Build all necessary table relationships. Include data for at least 10 employees and 3 departments. Create a query named **EmployeesByDepartmentQuery** that will list the department, manager, and all employees for that department. Use the query to create an **EmployeesByDepartmentReport**. Group the data by department and manager. List all employees. Add a calculated field with an appropriate label that will count the number of employees in each department.

did you know?

playing *cards were originally invented by the Chinese.*

the *average human has over 1,500 dreams every year.*

"for *every complex problem, there is a solution that is simple, neat, and wrong."—Henry L. Mencken*

Victoria *Woodhall became the first woman to run for president of the United States in 1872.*

the *largest nerve in the human body is the sciatic nerve, which is about 2 cm wide and runs from the spinal cord down the back of each leg.*

corporations *and government agencies report that the average cost to investigate, repair, and secure computer systems that have been hacked is $1 million per intrusion.*

to *find out how many times a day the average person laughs, visit* www.mhhe.com/i-series.

Chapter Objectives

- Use data validation criteria to ensure data accuracy
- Create and modify custom input masks—MOS AC03S-1-4
- Add user permissions to a database
- Set database passwords
- Use database replication to synchronize multiple copies of a database
- Apply database encryption to secure data
- Use the Database Splitter to protect databases from modification and to create a front and back end

KoryoKicks: Database Design Review

Missy and Micah have been using the KoryoKicks database for several months and believe that it is time to reevaluate its design. When the database was built, KoryoKicks was a simple organization. Missy and Micah, the only employees, taught a few martial arts and self-defense classes and sold martial arts supplies to their students. The twins handled all of the deliveries, kept track of the money, and taught all classes.

Because their products were successful, the twins recruited two additional instructors allowing them to offer four times as many classes. They also began to use the Internet and a local mall kiosk to market martial arts supplies. The mall kiosk is managed by a friend and most deliveries are handled by still another. A bookkeeper has been hired to manage Internet product orders, bill customers, and book money received. In short, KoryoKicks is a more complex business handling more than four times the initial product volume and supporting seven employees (including Missy and Micah) operating from multiple locations.

Because employees are now responsible for a specialized group of tasks, the current single database with a single set of reports is not effective. The twins have built additional queries, forms, and reports to try to address these evolving needs, but the database has become cumbersome. There are too many database objects, which slows overall performance. Since multiple people are using the database, more data entry errors are cropping up caused by individual style differences and varying user skill levels. There is a real need to share the database using a network, the Internet, or specialized data subsets.

A design review is the process used to evaluate the effectiveness of an operational database, evaluate necessary changes, and develop a plan to implement changes. The first step of a design review is to gather known issues and problems with each database object. Missy and Micah documented their own concerns and then talked to each of the other users. These issues can be as minor as "I don't like the date format on this screen" or more critical such as "I have to adjust the tax on every invoice because the tax rate changed and the database has not been updated." Some of the current issues include

- Data entry errors need to be reduced
- The Phone input mask is confusing users and therefore does not provide the expected result of simplifying data entry
- Consistency in the capitalization of data would improve the data's value
- Sharing the database on one computer in one location is cumbersome and results in data not being entered for an extended period of time, and sometimes completely lost

- Many fields could benefit from default quantities

- Some of the fields that are now blank should not allow blank values

- Security has become an issue since there are so many database users and the database is physically on a computer in a shared area

Since issues with the current performance of the database have been identified, the next logical step is to evaluate the various ways that Access can be used to address each issue. Missy and Micah have asked you to help in this process because they are unfamiliar with these features.

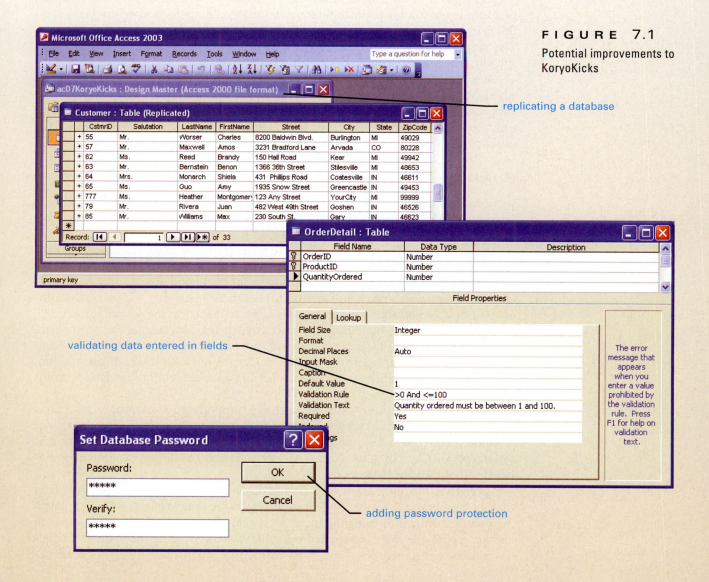

FIGURE 7.1

Potential improvements to KoryoKicks

AC 7.3

ACCESS

SESSION 7.1 REFINING TABLE DESIGN

The design of any database needs to be reviewed periodically to ensure that the user's needs are being appropriately met and that it is optimized for performance. Databases are designed to fit the needs of their users at a given point in time. Over time these needs change for a number of reasons. Change is fundamental to the growth and success of any organization or business, so over time data and data analysis needs can change dramatically. It is also true that the more people use a database, the more they want from the database. Users become more familiar with their data over time and recognize additional touches that would improve the usability of the database.

Add to the mix that you get better at designing, developing, and supporting databases, and it is easy to see that leaving a database alone is dooming it to failure. On the system optimization side, databases that are not optimized become slow and hog system resources. Disk space and seek time are wasted by storing records that could be archived because they are never accessed in the active database. Besides impacting other applications on the system by not sharing resources, these issues also can impact user satisfaction.

Don't panic. If the original database design was sound, most of these concerns can be addressed by adding tables to hold the new data, adding fields to existing tables, refining indexes, archiving unused records, and building new queries, forms, and reports. The more heavily a database is used, the more critical this review is. This is where spending the time up front to design sound tables pays off.

It is sometimes difficult to see the need for maintenance on a functioning system. Think about what it would cost the organization if this database failed. How much happier and more efficient could the users be with an optimized database? Maintaining a database is like changing the oil or tuning up your car. It significantly decreases the likelihood of a major disaster.

Building Custom Input Masks

Input masks were introduced in Chapter 2 as a way to improve data entry by providing a template like (_____)_____–_____ for the user to follow when entering data. Input masks are field properties and can be set for Text, Date, Number, and Currency field types. Input masks make what needs to be entered clear to users and reduces their keystrokes.

Reducing input keystrokes always improves the likelihood of valid data. In the case of a phone number, using an input mask cuts out three keystrokes ((,), and -) that otherwise would be necessary for the phone number to display in the desired format.

Consider building input masks for any table data that have a repetitive component. Repetitive components include punctuation such as parentheses, dashes, periods (decimal places), slashes, at signs (@), and so on. Cutting out a keystroke or two may not seem like much, but remember that keystrokes add up when multiple fields and records are considered.

When using an input mask with repetitive components, mask properties control whether or not those fixed values are stored with the data. Typically they are not, since it would require extra disk space, and the Format property allows control over how stored data display. Using the Format property, it is easy to display repetitive components without storing them.

In general, the Input Mask property and display Format property should match on the data entry forms because it is less confusing to the user. When they do not match, the user enters the data using the Input Mask template and when he or she moves to another record, the entry is displayed using the format. Avoiding such visual ambiguities will lead to happier users. Remember that setting the Format property of the field's text box on a form or report can control the display format for that output. Output formats are covered in the next topic.

To create an input mask, provide Access with a string outlining what is to be presented to the user, what will be accepted as valid input, and what will be stored. Figure 7.2 lists the valid mask characters. Any character not listed in Figure 7.2 becomes a literal when included in an input mask. Characters in the list must be preceded by a backslash to literally appear in the mask.

The Input Mask Wizard is great for creating default masks, but like most Wizards it lacks the flexibility to effectively create complex or uncommon masks. Figure 7.3 depicts some of the masks that could be applied to a 15-character field with an explanation of their results.

In the KoryoKicks Customer table, the Input Mask property of the Phone field was set in Chapter 2 with the Wizard for a standard phone number. Users often do not like this mask because it makes it difficult to *not* enter the area code. Even though the area code does not have to be entered, the user must space by the first three characters of the input mask. If your data always include the area code, this setup is satisfactory. If, however, your data do not include the area code a significant amount of the time, the area code should be split into another field that the user could tab past.

Missy and Micah are not happy with the Phone input mask for KoryoKicks data so it has been removed. They have noticed that they are inconsistent in capitalizing customer's names and decide that a mask for the Name fields is in order. State and Zip Code also need input masks to reduce entry errors.

Character	Description
0	Required digit (0–9), no plus (+) or minus (−) sign
9	Optional digit, no plus (+) or minus (−) sign
#	Optional digit, plus (+) or minus (−) sign allowed
L	Required letter (A–Z)
?	Optional letter (A–Z)
A	Required letter or digit
a	Optional letter or digit
&	Required character or space
C	Optional character or space
.,:;-/	Placeholders and separators
<	Causes all characters that follow to be converted to lowercase
>	Causes all characters that follow to be converted to uppercase
!	Causes input mask to display from right to left
\	Used to display any of the characters in this table as a literal
Password	Creates a password entry text box with all entries displayed as *

FIGURE 7.2
Input mask definition characters

ACCESS

Input Mask	Sample Display	Explanation
00000-999;;_	_____-____	Zip Code mask created by the Wizard. 0s are required positions, 9s are optional positions. Both require digits for valid data. The dash is a literal that will not be stored due to the;; notation. The _ notation sets that as the character that displays to the user.
000-00-0000;;_	___-__-____	SSN mask created by the Wizard. All 0s represent required digits. The dashes display as literals and ;;_ causes the literal characters (-) not to be stored. The _ notation sets that as the character that displays to the user.
!(999) 000-0000;;_	(___) ___-____	Phone Number mask created by the Wizard. 0s are required digits, 9s are optional digits, the dashes and parentheses are literals that will not be stored due to the ;;_ notation. The ! causes the field to display from right to left. The _ notation sets that as the character that displays to the user.
>L<?????????		The first letter entered will be converted to uppercase before it is stored. The remaining nine characters are optional but, if entered, will be converted to lowercase before being stored.

Customizing the Customer table input masks:

1. Start Access and open **ac07KoryoKicks.mdb**

2. Open the **Customer** table in Design View

3. Select the **LastName** field. This is a 30-character text field that should always begin with a capital letter, followed by up to 29 lowercase letters

4. Click the **Input Mask** property of LastName and type **>L<?????????????????????????????**

tip: > L< followed by 29 question marks

5. Click the **FirstName** field. This is a 30-character text field that should always begin with a capital letter, followed by up to 29 lowercase letters

6. Click the **Input Mask** property of FirstName and type **>L<?????????????????????????????**

tip: > L< followed by 29 question marks

7. Click the State field. This is a 2-character text field that should always contain two uppercase letters

8. Click the **Input Mask** property of State and type **>LL** to force the entry of two uppercase letters

9. Click in the ZipCode field. This is a 5-digit required field

10. Click the **Input Mask** property of ZipCode and type **00000**

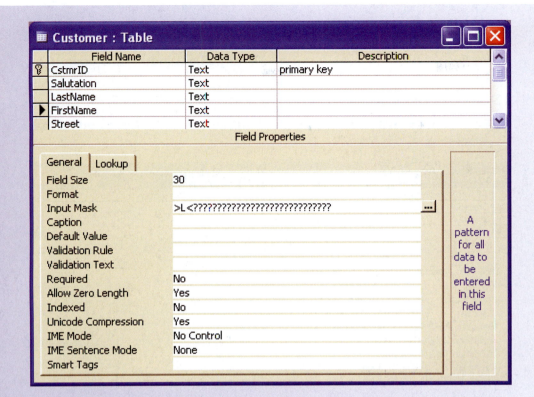

FIGURE 7.4

FirstName input mask

11. Switch to Datasheet View, saving your changes

12. Make up the data for two new customers. Use CstmrID 100 and 101. Enter the first record in all lowercase and observe the result. Enter the second record in all uppercase and observe the result

Input masks are a simple way to improve data validity and user satisfaction without negatively impacting performance. It is important to be sure that the masks don't get in the user's way (like the phone number example). Adding, editing, or deleting an input mask has no impact on existing table data, since the template is only activated on input. Input masks do impact editing existing data because newly entered data must meet the mask criteria.

Defining Custom Output Formats

Output formats were introduced in Chapter 2 as the way to control how a value displays. Output formatting is controlled by the Format property of a field. The Format property set in table design becomes the default format of that field in queries, forms, and reports. As was mentioned in the input mask discussion, the Format property set in table design should match the Input Mask property.

The twins are not satisfied with the Order.OrderDate (OrderDate field of the Order table) input mask/format combination. It works great for data entry when the input mask ____ / ____ / ____ is displayed. The problem arises when editing an existing date. The Format property is set as dd-mmm-yyyy, so when a portion of a date (such as the dd component) is selected and a new value entered, the input mask generates an error because it doesn't know what to do with the dashes generated by the Format property. Since the twins will be satisfied with a dd/mm/yyyy format, you will update the table.

Customizing the Order.OrderDate field format:

1. Verify that Access is running with **ac07KoryoKicks.mdb** as the open database

2. Open the **Order** table in Design View

3. Select the **OrderDate** field and review the current Input Mask and Format properties

FIGURE 7.5

Order.OrderDate
properties

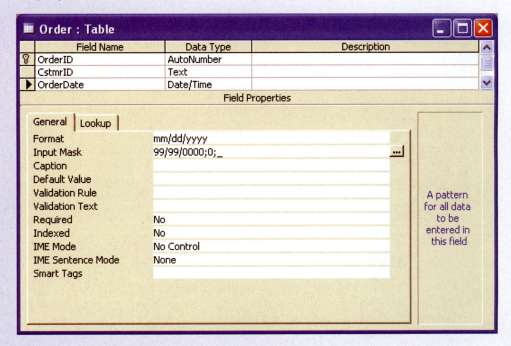

4. Click the **Format** property of OrderDate and type **mm/dd/yyyy** and change the input mask to match the figure (see Figure 7.5)

5. Move to Datasheet View, saving your changes

6. Add orders for Sara Meadows and Juan Rivera with today's date (OrderID is an AutoNumber field and will be generated) to observe the effectiveness of your changes

7. Edit the day on each of these new records to yesterday's date

tip: *If the change has been correctly applied, you should be able to select and change the day portion of the date successfully*

When custom forms and reports are created, Design View is used to set the Format property of the Text Box control displaying the field. This action does not impact the field and what it stores, or change the Format set in table design, but simply applies a template altering how a field is displayed on that particular form or report. The Text Box Format property overrides the Format property set in table design and is applied only to that text box. In both form and report design, the *Format Painter* is available to copy formats from one control to another.

When setting a Format property, selections can be made from a list of predefined formats for AutoNumber, Number, Currency, Date/Time, and Yes/No data types or a custom format can be defined. Text data types do not have any predefined formatting. Formats cannot be applied to OLE Object data types.

Number and date data types have predefined formats displayed in a drop-down list. To improve consistency among applications, the regional settings from Microsoft Windows Control Panel are used for the predefined Number and Date/Time formats. Changing the Windows format does change the display but does not perform conversions. This can cause problems when moving between computers with different regional settings. For example, the value 5.47 displayed with currency format would result in $5.47 in the United States and 5,47kr on a computer set for Denmark. One or both of the displayed currency values would be inaccurate since no conversion was performed. In such cases, a custom format should be entered representing the true currency of the data. Custom formats override the Windows settings.

Using Data Validation

Data validation is another area that can often improve the usability and validity of database data. Validation settings are used to check the accuracy of data entered by the user. Several of the field properties that can be set in table design to validate data are covered in the following topics.

Default Value Field Property

Each field in a Microsoft Access table has a Default Value property that can be set to the most common value for that field. This value will display in that field for new records. The user can accept this entry by tabbing past it or can stop and type a new entry to override the default. Default values are beneficial because they reduce typing and improve data integrity.

The twins have determined that most of their remote customers are in Michigan and they would like MI to be the default state value. Since most orders are for the current date, they would also like that default added to the Order table. The default order quantity was set to 1 when the table was developed and is working well.

Adding default values to the KoryoKicks database:

1. Verify that **ac07KoryoKicks.mdb** database is open

2. Open the **Customer** table in Design View

3. Select the **State** field

4. Click the **Default Value** property of State and type **MI**

tip: *Access will add double quotes around this string value, resulting in "MI"*

help yourself *Use the Type a Question combo box to improve your understanding of how to validate data by typing* **data validation**. *Review the contents of* About restricting or validating data *and* Validate or restrict data entry in a table. *Close the Help window when you are finished*

5. Change to Datasheet View and test the default value by adding records for two classmates. Use CstmrIDs 106 and 107. For the first record accept the default value. For the second record set the State to NM

6. Close the Customer table

7. Open the **Order** table in Design View

8. Click in the **OrderDate** field and type **=Now** in the Default Value property (see Figure 7.6)

FIGURE 7.6

Adding a default value for
OrderDate

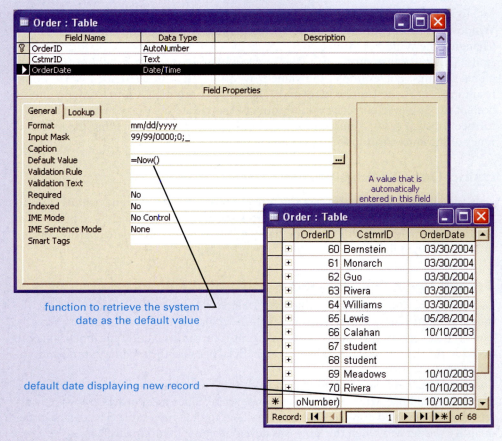

function to retrieve the system
date as the default value

default date displaying new record

tip: *Access will convert it to =Now() since the parentheses are required for correct function syntax*

9. Switch to Datasheet View and add an order for each of the two classmates added earlier. Accept the default of today's date for your order. Set the date from your friend's order to tomorrow

Default values are not limited to fixed quantities such as 1 or "MI" but can also use expressions like =Now(). An expression can be either typed, as was done in the steps, or built using the Expression Builder. An ellipsis (. . .) will appear to the right of the Default Value property after it is clicked. Clicking the ellipsis will activate the Expression Builder.

Required and Allow Zero Length Field Properties

The Required and Allow Zero Length field properties work together to control the types of blank values allowed in a field. Microsoft Access differentiates between **null** values and *zero-length strings*. A null value indicates missing or unknown data. A field is null when nothing has been entered. A zero-length string can be used to indicate that no data are supposed to be in a field. The user creates a zero-length string by typing two double quotes with nothing between them ("").

Sometimes it is important to differentiate between when a data value is not known and when it does not exist. For example, if a fax number field was added to the customer table, a null value could indicate that the fax number is not currently known, while a zero-length string would indicate that the customer does not have a fax. While there is nothing visual to differentiate these values, queries searching for nulls will not return zero-length strings and vice versa.

FIGURE 7.7

Combinations of Required
and Allow Zero Length
values

Required	Allow Zero Length	Result
No	No	Allows blank values when you don't need to distinguish blank values that indicate unknown data from blank values that indicate you know there's no value
Yes	No	Prevents users from leaving a field blank
Yes	Yes	Allows blank values in a field only when you know that there are no data. In this case, the only way to leave a field blank is to type double quotation marks with no space between them, or press the Spacebar to enter a zero-length string
No	Yes	Allows both types of blank values so that you can distinguish blank values that indicate unknown data from blank values that indicate you know there are no data

The Required property of a field determines whether it can be left blank during data entry, resulting in a null value. The Allow Zero Length property determines whether a zero-length string ("") can be entered in a field. Allow Zero Length property is only valid for Text, Memo, or Hyperlink fields. (See Figure 7.7.)

In the KoryoKicks tables, the OrderDetail table needs to require the user to enter a product and a quantity. In the Order table, the OrderDate needs to be required. In the Customer table, everything but notes and phone should be required. There is no need to differentiate between types of blank values, so the Allow Zero Length value will remain No.

---

task reference   Controlling Blank Data Values

- Open the table in Design View

- Click the field whose blank values you would like to control

- Set Required to **Yes** to disallow blank values (Allow Zero Length should be set to No)

Requiring fields in the KoryoKicks database:

1. Verify that **ac07KoryoKicks.mdb** database is open

2. Open the **Customer** table in Design View

3. Click in **LastName** and double-click the **Required** property to change it to **Yes**

4. Repeat this process for **FirstName**, **Street**, **City**, **State**, and **ZipCode**

5. Close the Design View of Customer, saving your changes and validating existing data (see Figure 7.8)

FIGURE 7.8

Checking existing data for missing values

6. Open **OrderDetail** in Design View and set the Required property of **QuantityOrdered** to **Yes**

tip: *ProductID does not have to be set to Required because as a key field it is already required*

7. Close the Design View of OrderDetail

8. Open **Order** in Design View and set the CstmrID and OrderDate fields to Required

9. Close the Design View of Order

The Required property of a field can only be set in Design View, but it is applied throughout all database objects (datasheets, forms, and reports). When the table design is saved after updating a Required property, Access presents the option of checking existing records for compliance. Entry can be required in future records whether or not there are currently blank fields.

Validation Rules and Validation Text Field Properties

The Validation Rule and Validation Text properties work together to help verify the data values entered by users. Validation rules are based on expected data values. For example, when accepting credit card payments, expired cards are not valid. In such a case, the validation rule would be >=(=now()). Recall that =now() is a function that will return the current system date and time. The function is enclosed in parentheses to separate it from the relational operator, >=. The expression >=(=now()) says that the date entered must be greater than or equal to today's date.

Validation text contains the message that will display to the user when the data entered do not meet the validation rule. Continuing with the credit card expiration date example, the Validation text might be *Expired Credit Card. Check the expiration date or choose another card* (see Figure 7.9). If, for example, an expiration date of 1/03 is entered, the Validation text would be displayed and the user must either enter data that pass the validation or abandon his or her changes. Validation rules cannot be overridden, so be very sure of the rules created.

FIGURE 7.9
Validation text displaying

Validation rules and their associated Validation text are most effectively added to the field properties of table design. Like other field properties, validation rules can be set in a form or report, but it is ineffective to validate data entry only on specific forms. Validation rules and text can be added to table field properties at any time, and then the rules will be enforced by all controls for that field (even those created before the rule).

Validation rules follow the syntax rules of expressions. String data are enclosed in double quotes (""), Date data are enclosed in pound signs (##), and numeric data are not enclosed in any character. All relational operators can be used (>, <, >=, <=, <>). Compound conditions can be connected with *And* or *Or*. Use *And* when both conditions must be true for the data entered to be valid. Use *Or* when only one condition must be true for the data to be valid. For example, >=#1/1/2003# And <#1/1/2004# would accept any date in the year 2003, but the Validation Text dialog box would be issued for any date outside this range.

Figure 7.10 contains validation expressions for text, number, and date data types with the appropriate delimiters. The use of And and Or to create compound conditions for validation is demonstrated, as is the use of wildcards. The wildcards ?, *, and # can be used to create match values for data validation in the same fashion that they were used to create filter and query criteria.

FIGURE 7.10

Sample validation rules

Sample Validation Rule	Sample Validation Text	Result
<>0	Please enter a non-zero value	Validation text will display when a non-zero value is entered
0 Or >25	Please enter zero or a number greater than 25	Validation text will display when values 1 through 24 or a negative number is entered
<=Now()	Date must be earlier than today	Validation text will display when dates equal to or later than the current system date are entered
>100 And <1,000	Please enter a number between 100 and 1,000	Validation text will display when a value of 100 or less is entered or a value of 1,000 or greater is entered
Like "X???"	Please enter a 4-character string beginning with X	Validation text will display when X is not the first character or the text entered is not 4 characters
"M" Or "F"	Please enter M for male or F for female	Validation text will display for any value not equal to M or F. This text is case sensitive
>#10/1/01# And <#10/31/01#	Please enter an October date	Validation text will display for values not between the dates in the condition

Missy and Micah have determined that their KoryoKicks customers always need to order 100 or fewer units of each invoice item. KoryoKicks can't deliver larger volumes and current distributors can't handle them either. OrderDates also need to be the current date or later (backdating is not allowed). Adding these validation rules will help reduce errors in orders and improve customer satisfaction.

---

task reference   Defining Field Validation Rules

- Open the table in Design View

- Click the field that will be monitored by the validation rule

- Select the **Validation Rule** property for that field

- Type the validation expression or use the Expression Builder by clicking the ellipsis to the right of the Validation Rule text box

- Click the Validation Text property box for the same field and enter the text that is to display when the validation rule is broken

- Save the table update

  - If the validation rule has been set for a field that already contains data, Access will ask if you want to apply the new rule to existing data

  - If there are no existing data in the field, there will be no prompt

---

Adding field validation to the KoryoKicks database:

1. Verify that **ac07KoryoKicks.mdb** is open

2. Open the **OrderDetail** table in Design View

3. Click the **QuantityOrdered** field

   a. Click the **Validation Rule** property and type **>0 And <=100**
   b. Click the **Validation Text** property and type **Quantity ordered must be between 1 and 100.** (see Figure 7.11)

4. Switch to Datasheet View, saving your changes and answering **Yes** to the data integrity prompt

5. Enter an order detail that violates the rule

tip: *Closing the OrderDetail in the next step will allow you to abandon this record*

6. Close OrderDetail

7. Open the **Order** table in Design View

8. Click the **OrderDate** field

   a. Set the **Validation Rule** property and type **>=Now()**
   b. Set the **Validation Text** property and type **The date must be greater than or equal to today.**

9. Switch to Datasheet View, saving your changes and answering **Yes** to the data integrity prompt. Read and close the data violations notification

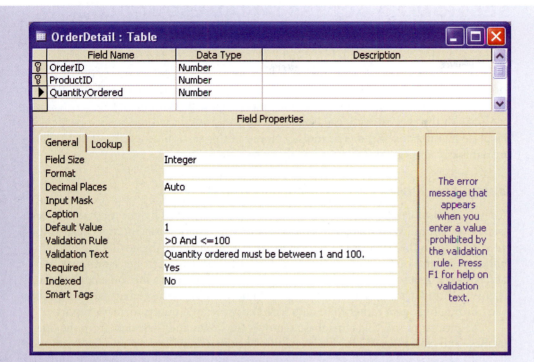

FIGURE 7.11

OrderDetails validation rule and validation text

10. Enter a record that violates the rule, move to another record to view the validation text, and then respond **OK**

11. Close the Order table to abandon the erroneous record

Although validation rules and text can be added to tables at any time, difficulty can arise when testing these rules. The only way to check the rules that have been added is to add both valid and invalid data.

When testing validation rules, it is best to use a trait to mark the records so that they can be deleted when testing is complete. For example, customers named Dummy1, Dummy2, and so on could be added to the Customer table, along with Order and OrderDetail records added for those records. When testing is complete, deleting the Dummy records would remove all of the test data.

Validation rules and text are the simplest tools for validating data, but they lack flexibility and cannot compare data from field to field or across records. Users cannot override the rule and there is no check to ensure that values are internally consistent. For example, a man's medical records should not include pregnancy data, but validation rules cannot check for that condition. Record validation, macros, and Visual Basic code provide the power to perform more extensive validation.

SESSION 7.1

making the grade

1. How can you determine whether or not a field should have an input mask?

2. How are Input Mask and Format properties of a field different?

3. How would you determine the default value of a field?

4. Why use validation rules for table fields?

SESSION 7.2 ACCESS DATABASE TOOLS

The Tools menu in Microsoft Access contains a variety of facilities to help maintain and optimize databases. These tools can help to analyze the design and performance of your database, convert to other versions of Access, secure data, and so on. Some of these tools already have been introduced. Convert Database and Compact and Repair Database are examples of tools that already have been explored.

As with the tools already used, each Access tool is designed to satisfy a particular database maintenance need. The tools explored in this session generally relate to sharing databases among several users and securing data.

Using the Database Splitter Wizard

Access databases can be stored on a network drive and shared by authorized network users. One approach to sharing a database is to separate the user interface, called the *front-end*, from the data, or the *back-end*. This approach has the advantage of maintaining one data source while allowing each user to control his or her front-end interface. A single data source means that users always have access to the most current data because all updates are made to the same tables. It also reduces network traffic by transmitting only data rather than data with the associated query, form, or report.

The process of splitting a database removes the tables and their data from the open database and places them in the back-end file. The open database becomes the front-end file, with arrow icons in front of the table names to indicate the link to the back-end.

---

task reference   **Splitting a Database**

- Back up the database

- On the **Tools** menu, point to **Database Utilities**, and then click **Database Splitter**

- Follow the Database Splitter Wizard instructions

Splitting the KoryoKicks database:

1. Verify that **ac07KoryoKicks.mdb** is open

2. Select **File** and then **Backup Database** and place a copy of ac07KoryoKicks.mdb in your homework folder

3. Open the copy of **ac07KoryoKicks.mdb**

4. On the **Tools** menu, point to **Database Utilities**, and then click **Database Splitter**

5. Click **Split Database**

6. Select your homework folder as the location, accept the default name for the back-end, and click **Split**

tip: *By default _be is included in the back-end filename and the front-end name is not changed. The back-end holding the tables would normally be on a shared network drive*

7. Notice the icons in front of each table name indicating that you are now working in a front-end file

8. Save the front-end

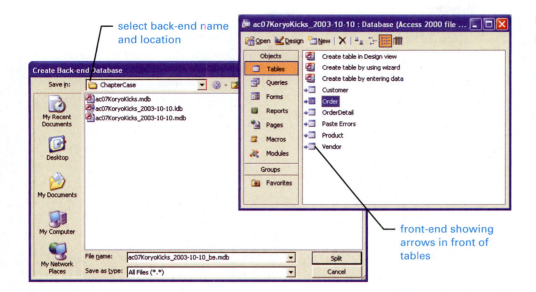

select back-end name and location

front-end showing arrows in front of tables

FIGURE 7.12

Creating the back-end

The front-end file contains all of the queries, forms, and reports. Each user can store a copy of this file on his or her computer and customize it for his or her needs. One copy of the back-end file containing the data is stored on a shared network drive.

Commercial software developers split databases so that they can implement interface changes without impacting the data stored by clients. Each copy of the front-end has access to the data stored in the back-end, but cannot change table design. Opening the back-end database will allow table design changes to be specified.

Exploring the split KoryoKicks database:

1. Open the front-end copy of **ac07KoryoKicks.mdb** if it is not open from the previous steps

2. Select the **Customer** table and then click **Design**

tip: Click the Tables object in the Database Window, then click Customer, and then Design. A dialog box notice that this is a linked file will display

3. Click **Yes** to open the table in Design View. You can review table design but not modify it

FIGURE 7.13

Viewing the design of a linked table

4. Close the Customer table Design View. Close the database

5. Open the back-end file

6. Select the **Customer** table and then click **Design**. You have complete access to modify table design in the back-end database

7. Close

Once a database has been split, there is no facility for rejoining it. If the back-end file moves to a new drive or folder, the links in all of the front-ends must be adjusted using the Linked Table Manager (Tools/Database Utilities, Linked Table Manager).

Using the Database performance Analyzer

The Database Performance Analyzer is a tool that reviews database objects and suggests improvements. The goal is to optimize database performance, but the performance of Access itself or the computer running Access cannot be evaluated in this manner. When the Performance Analyzer starts, a dialog box used to select database objects for evaluation is displayed. The Analyzer will review the specified objects and recommend changes that could benefit performance.

The proposed changes are classified by their potential benefit (Recommendation, Suggestion, Idea, and Fixed). Items classified as Fixed have already been repaired. Recommendations have the most potential benefit, while Ideas have the least. It is important to carefully review each proposed change in light of the database design and utilization.

---

task reference   **Optimizing Database Objects**

- Open the database to be optimized

- Click the **Tools** menu, then **Analyze**, and then **Performance**

- Select the tab for the database object (table, query, report, form, etc.) that you would like to analyze

- Click the check box of each object to be evaluated or click Select All to select all objects in the list

- Select objects from other tabs if desired

- Click **OK**

- Review and apply results as needed

Optimizing KoryoKicks database objects:

1. Open the original copy of **ac07KoryoKicks.mdb**

2. Click the **Tools** menu, then **Analyze**, and then **Performance**

3. Select the **Tables** tab and check each table (see Figure 7.14)

tip: *The check box in front of each table must be checked—selecting a table does not check the check box*

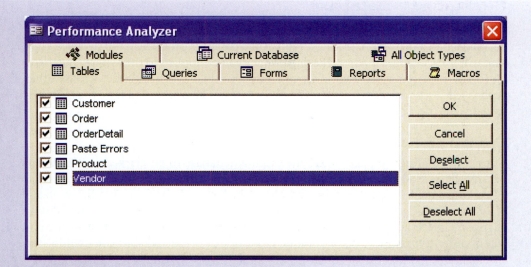

FIGURE 7.14
Selecting objects to be analyzed

4. Click **OK**

5. Review the suggestions by clicking each and reading the Analysis Notes. None of the suggestions are consistent with the design in this case, so don't apply them

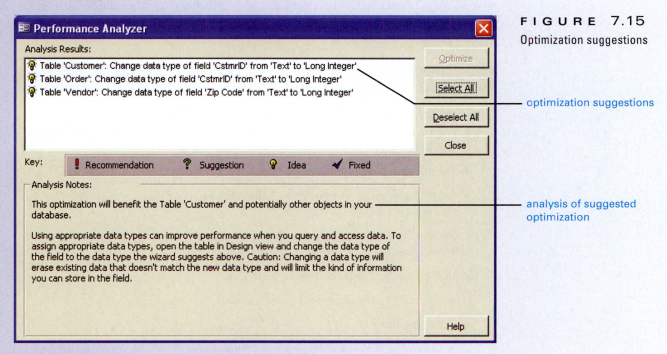

FIGURE 7.15
Optimization suggestions

optimization suggestions

analysis of suggested optimization

6. Click **Close**

After reviewing the Analysis Notes, you can elect to have Access perform Recommendation and Suggestions optimizations for you. Click the Recommendation or Suggestion optimizations to be performed and then click the Optimize button. Idea optimizations must be completed manually by following the instructions in the Analysis Notes.

Replicating a Database

Replication is a way of sharing database data between computers that may or may not be attached to a network. Creating a *replica* of a database produces a full database copy that will track changes made to the data so they can be applied to the original database. Normally each replica is used independently and then synchronized with the other replicas on a scheduled basis. Users of replicas are not guaranteed to have the most up-to-date data, because data can be modified in each replica.

Creating a Replica

The act of creating a replica causes the original database to be marked as the *Design Master*. The Design Master and all of its replicas are called the *replica set*. The design of existing database objects can be updated in the Design Master, but not in a replica.

Special tables in both the Design Master and replica databases keep track of data changes. The Design Master also tracks changes made to the design of any database object in order to pass these updates to the replicas. These special tables are used in *synchronization*, the process of updating the Design Master and its replicas so that all copies reflect the same status.

Each replica created has a priority assigned to using a number between 0 (lowest) and 100 (highest). When conflicting updates are made to different replicas of the database, the priority is used to resolve them. The Design Master has a priority of 100. The default priority of a replica is 90, but any valid priority can be assigned. Changes made to the Design Master always have precedence over those made to a replica. During synchronization, the priority setting of each replica is evaluated and the record with the highest priority wins in any conflicts.

---

task reference   Replicating a Database

- Open the database to be replicated

- Remove any password protection (covered later in this session) and ensure that the database is not open by any other users

- On the **Tools** menu, point to **Replication**, and then click **Create Replica**

- Click **Yes** when prompted with: The database must be closed before you can create a replica

- Answer **Yes** when prompted with: Converting a database into a Design Master results in changes . . .

- In the Location of New Replica dialog box

  - Navigate to the location for the replica

  - Set the **Priority**

  - Check the **Prevent deletes** check box to prevent record deletions in the replica

  - In the Save as type box, select the replica Visibility

  - Click **OK**

Replicating KoryoKicks:

1. Verify that the original copy of **ac07KoryoKicks.mdb** is open

2. On the **Tools** menu, point to **Replication**, and then click **Create Replica**

tip: *You will not have enough space on the A: drive to create a replica set, so you will need to use another drive like C:*

3. Click **Yes** to close the database

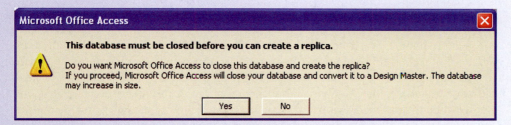

FIGURE 7.16

Create a replica

4. Click **Yes** when prompted with: Converting a database into a Design Master results in changes . . .

5. Click **OK** in the Location of New Replica dialog box to accept the default location, name, priority, and deletion settings

6. Click **OK** to complete the replication process in the dialog box reading Microsoft Access has converted . . .

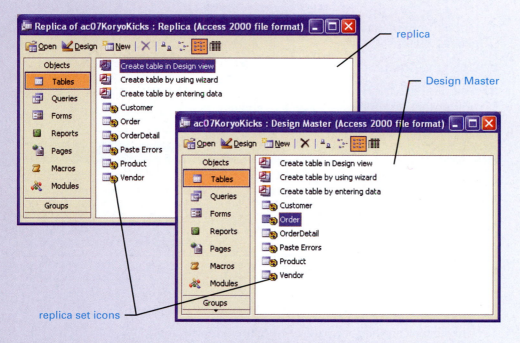

FIGURE 7.17

Design Master and replica

7. Notice that the Title bar now says Design Master and the icons to the left of each database object (table, query, form, and report) indicate that this database belongs to a replica set

8. Close the Design Master

9. Open the Replica

10. Notice the word *Replica* in the Title bar and the icons to the left of each database object (table, query, form, and report) indicate that this database belongs to a replica set

ACCESS

> ## another**word**　　　　　　　　. . . on Creating Replicas
>
> Single-copy replicas can be created using My Briefcase. When you want to work on files using another computer, drag the file(s) to My Briefcase and then copy My Briefcase to a floppy disk or link the computers and transfer the files. Use the Update All feature of the briefcase to synchronize the files. This is an ideal way to create a copy of a personal database for use on your laptop while you are away from the office

When a database is replicated, the Design Master and each replica contain all of the database objects (tables, queries, forms, reports, and so on). Significant changes are made to the database during the replication process. Fields are added to each table, tables are added to the database, and the database properties are changed. Any AutoNumber fields that previously generated sequential numbers will generate random numbers to reduce synchronization conflicts caused by users adding two different records using the same AutoNumber. The overall result is a larger database.

The backup created in the replication process has a .bak file extension. It can be used to create an emergency replica set. It will not be possible to synchronize replicas made from the backup with replicas made from the original.

Updating KoryoKicks replica data:

1. Open the **Replica of ac07KoryoKicks.mdb** if it is not still open from the previous steps

2. Open the **Customer** table

3. Add a record for **Heather Montgomery** with a CstmrID of 777 (make up the remaining data)

FIGURE 7.18

Adding a new customer to the replica

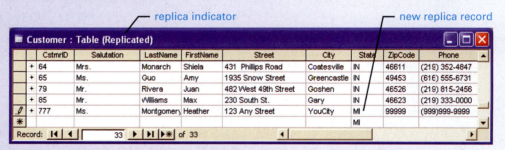

4. Close the Customer table

The new record has been added to the replica but does not exist in the Design Master. As you can imagine, multiple users with replicas can make a significant number of updates to each copy of the database. Changes also can be made in the Design Master that need to be synchronized with the replicas. When multiple copies of a database have high-volume updates, replication may not be the most successful method of sharing data for users who need current information. It can be very effective, however, if synchronization is performed frequently, or if the various users typically update and use different data.

Synchronization

Once replicas have been generated, each database can be updated independently of the others. Exchanging updated records between two or more members of a replica set is called *synchronization*. Two replica set members are synchronized, or in sync, when the changes made individually in each have been applied to the other.

---

task reference — Synchronizing Replicated Databases

- Open the replica to be synchronized

- On the **Tools** menu, point to **Replication**, and then click **Synchronize Now**

- Select the other replica set member to be synchronized from the Directly with Replica drop-down list box

- Click **OK**

- Respond **Yes** when prompted to close the database for synchronization

- Respond **OK** when notified that the process has been completed

---

The previous steps created one replica and a Design Master for the KoryoKicks database. The new record added to the replica needs to be applied to the Design Master so that the databases are synchronized again.

Synchronizing KoryoKicks:

1. Open the **Replica of ac07KoryoKicks.mdb** if it is not still open from the previous steps

2. On the **Tools** menu, point to **Replication**, and then click **Synchronize Now**

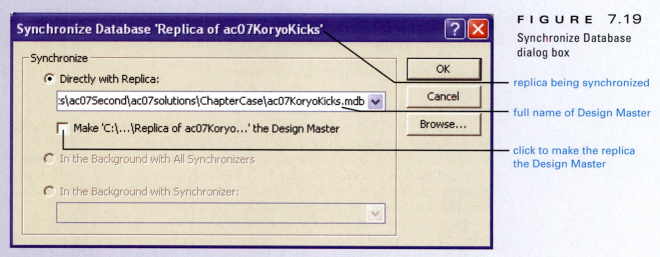

FIGURE 7.19
Synchronize Database dialog box

— replica being synchronized

— full name of Design Master

— click to make the replica the Design Master

3. Select the Design Master name from the drop-down list

tip: *If the Design Master name does not display, use the Browse button to locate it*

4. Click **OK**

5. Respond **Yes** when prompted to close the database for synchronization

6. Respond **OK** when notified that the process has been completed

7. Close the replica and open **ac07KoryoKicks.mdb**—the Design Master

8. Open the Customer table and locate record 777

FIGURE 7.20

Replica record added to the Design Master by synchronization

Design Master indicator

Table Replication indicator

record added to replica and synchronized into the Design Master

9. Close the Customer table

This was a very simple example of adding one record to the replica and then using synchronization to update the Design Master with the same record. Normally synchronization is completed at regular intervals, like the close of business each day or Friday at 4:00 P.M.

The synchronization method demonstrated is called *direct synchronization* and is effective for replica sets that are stored on the same computer or in shared folders of a network. The alternate Indirect and Internet synchronization methods can be applied when it is necessary to synchronize using a dial-up connection or the Internet. Both methods are well documented in Access Help.

Resolving Synchronization Conflicts

Synchronization of replicas can result in conflicts created by unrestricted updates to the various copies of the database. Access uses the priority of the replica (set when it was created) to resolve as many conflicting updates as it can. The update from the replica with the highest priority is applied and all other updates are discarded. Conflicts that cannot be resolved by Access are stored and the user is prompted to resolve them manually the next time the database is opened.

Manual conflict resolution is accomplished using the *Conflict Viewer.* The Conflict Viewer can be opened from the Tools menu (see Figure 7.21) or from the unresolved conflicts prompt that displays when a database containing conflicts is opened. When using the Tools menu, you will be notified when there are no conflicts and the Conflict Viewer will not open. If there are conflicts, possible resolutions will be presented in a selection list.

The most common conflict is a simultaneous update conflict that occurs if changes have been made to the same record in more than one replica set member. Conflicts also can be caused by two or more replicas adding a new record with the same key or applying updates that impact referential integrity. Remember that referential integrity stops parent records from being deleted when there are still child records. If one database deletes a parent and all of its children while another adds a new child, a referential

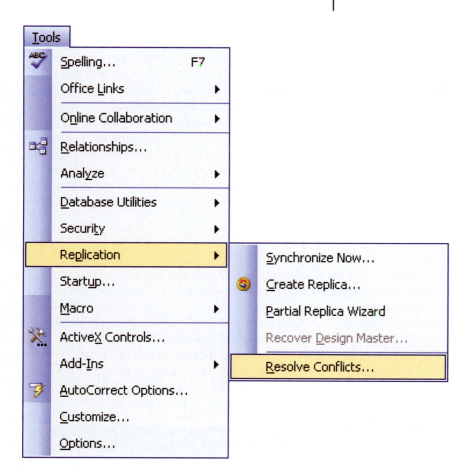

FIGURE 7.21

Initiating the Conflict Viewer

integrity conflict would result. Regardless of the source of synchronization conflicts, it is important to review and resolve them each time synchronization is performed.

Retaining and Deleting Replicas

Each replica that is created has a retention period that controls the number of days non-synchronized records are kept. The default retention period is 60 days, but any period between 5 and 32,000 days is valid. Set a long retention period if the replicas do not synchronize frequently and a short retention period for frequently synchronized replicas. Shorter retention periods keep replica sizes smaller and improve database performance.

The Design Master and replica must be synchronized within the retention period. If synchronization is not accomplished before the replica expires, the replica will be removed from the replica set when synchronization is attempted. Synchronization must occur whether or not any updates have been made.

Mechanically deleting a replica is the same as deleting any other file in the Microsoft Windows environment. Use Windows Explorer, select the file, and press the Delete key. A Yes response will place the replica in the Recycle Bin until it is emptied. A word of caution, however: deleting a replica without synchronizing will lose any changes that it contains. Deleting the Design Master removes the controlling database of the replica set. The other members of the set cannot be synchronized until a new Design Master is assigned.

It is best not to delete a Design Master, but replicas can be deleted with no impact when they are no longer needed. The Design Master retains all of its attributes and continues to track updates for synchronization whether or not there are any current replicas. New replicas can be created as the need arises.

Securing an Access Database

All data stored for business or operational purposes are valuable and need to be protected from theft, loss, misuse, and unwanted updates. Whether the breech is accidental, mischievous, or malicious, the result of unauthorized database access is usually damaged or destroyed data. Protecting data from unauthorized access requires careful planning. The level of security should match the importance of the data.

Microsoft Access data files can be read by a number of utility and word-processor programs, meaning that data can be viewed outside the environment in which they were created. Access supports several methods of controlling access to a database and its objects. These methods range from simple to complex. The simpler methods are less costly and less secure, but are adequate for restricting access to nonessential data. More time and care should be taken with critical data.

Hiding Files

One of the simplest protections is to hide your sensitive files from the casual observer. Microsoft Windows assigns properties to each file that is saved including the Hidden property. A hidden file does not display in a standard file listing like that provided by Windows Explorer. Setting the Hidden property is accomplished by right-clicking on the file, selecting Properties, and clicking Hidden. Even though the file is not visible, it can be manipulated using its name. For example, a hidden file can be opened with the standard Open dialog box by typing its name rather than clicking a name in the file list. Viewing hidden files is also easy; set the folder's properties to Show Hidden Files.

task reference	Hiding a Database
• Open Windows Explorer • Navigate to the file to be hidden • Right-click on the file to be hidden • Click the **Properties** option • Click the **Hidden** attribute • Click **OK**	

Hiding the KoryoKicks backup:

1. Close the open Access database

2. Use the Start menu to open Windows Explorer

tip: *Usually Start/AllPrograms/Accessories/Windows Explorer*

3. Navigate to the backup of KoryoKicks created during replication, **ac07KoryoKicks.bak**

4. Right-click on ac07KoryoKicks.bak

5. Choose **Properties**

6. Select the **Hidden** check box and click **OK** (see Figure 7.22)

7. Click **OK**

8. Press **F5** to refresh Windows Explorer

tip: *ac07KoryoKicks.bak should be grayed out or not listed because it is hidden. If the file does display, the folder options on your computer (steps 9–11) have already been set and you will need to reverse them to see how a hidden file behaves*

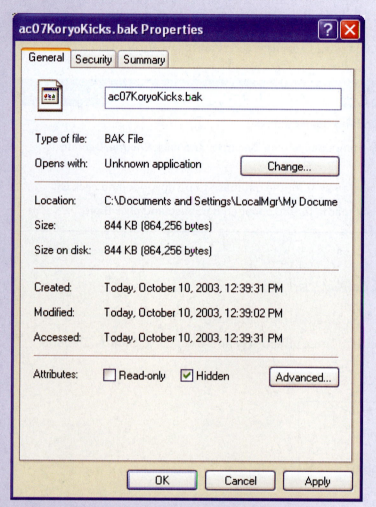

FIGURE 7.22
File Properties dialog box

9. Click **Tools** and select **Folder Options**

10. Click the **View** tab

11. Click **Show Hidden Files and Folders** and click **OK**

tip: *If ac07KoryoKicks.bak is not visible, press F5*

Setting a folder's Show Hidden Files and Folders properties causes all hidden files and folders to display in the current folder. Selecting the Like Current Folder button, rather than OK, will cause all folders to display hidden files. Since hidden files can be so readily displayed, hiding the file only keeps it out of the hands of people who don't really know how to look.

Encoding Data

Encoding is a simple method of securing a database. Encoding a database ensures that it is indecipherable to utility and word-processor programs. This method is most effective for a database that is being transported on a storage medium or digitally transmitted. Since the process of opening an encoded database in Access decodes it, this is not an effective way to stop Access users from viewing and updating the database.

An important component of security is that only specific users can apply and remove database security measures. The person who created a database is its *owner* and has full security rights to it. When multiple users or user groups have been defined for a database, the users who have full rights are members of the administrator group called Admins. Only the owner or a member of the Admins group can open the database exclusively so that no other users have access and can set security.

---

task reference   **Encoding a Database**

- Open Access with no open database

- Open the **Tools** menu, pause over **Security**, and click **Encode/Decode Database . . .**

- Enter a folder and a name for the database to be encoded and click **OK**

- Enter a folder and name for the encoded database and click **Save**

Encoding KoryoKicks:

1. Open Access and close any open database

2. On the **Tools** menu, point to **Security**, and then click **Encode/Decode Database . . .**

F I G U R E 7.23

Encoding menu selections

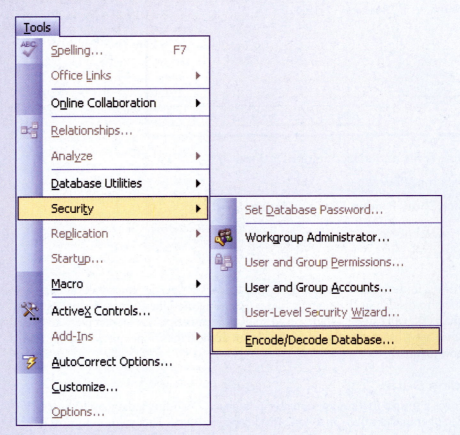

3. Navigate to the folder containing your files and select
   ac07KoryoKicks.mdb as the database to encode

4. Click **OK**

5. Name the encoded database **Encodedac07KoryoKicks.mdb**

6. Click **Save**

When naming the encoded file, one option is to use the same name as the original file. If the encoding operation is successful, the database is replaced with the encoded version. If the encoding operation fails, the original file is retained. Data added to an encoded file are encoded before they are stored. Data are decoded by Access before they are displayed to the user. Decoding a database is the reverse of encoding.

Continually encoding and decoding the data as the database is used can slow database performance. It is best to encode the database for transport and decode it for use.

help yourself *Use the Type a Question combo box to improve your understanding of the options available for securing an Access database by typing* **security**. *Review the contents of* Overview of Access security. *Close the Help window when you are finished*

Setting Password Protection

Missy and Micah would like to add a password to the KoryoKicks database to control who has access to the data. Adding a *password* or passwords to a database is the simplest way to prevent unauthorized access to the data and other objects it contains. Users will have to provide the password before they are able to open the file. The Password dialog box displays asterisks as the user enters the password to keep others from viewing it.

Opening an Access database in the usual fashion allows *shared* access. Shared access means that two or more users can open the same database simultaneously. *Exclusive* access is required while setting a password to prevent other users from entering the database.

---

task reference   Password Protecting a Database

- Open Access with no open database
- Click the **Open** button on the Database toolbar
- Navigate to the folder and select the file to be password protected
- Click the Open button's list arrow and select **Open Exclusive**
- Open the **Tools** menu, pause over **Security**, and then click **Set Database Password**
- Type the password in the Password text box, repeat the same password in the Verify text box, and then press **Enter**

Adding a password to KoryoKicks:

1. Use Windows Explorer to create a copy of **ac07KoryoKicks.bak** and rename the copy **ac07KoryoKicksPassword.mdb**

2. Open Access and close any open databases

3. Click the **Open** button

4. Locate **ac07KoryoKicksPassword.mdb** and click it

5. Click the list arrow on the Open button

FIGURE 7.24

Open button options

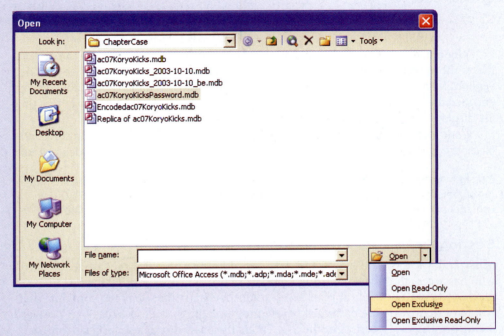

6. Select **Open Exclusive**

7. Select **Tools**, pause over **Security**, and then click **Set Database Password**

tip: *If Set Database Password is grayed out, the database is not exclusively opened. Close it and repeat steps 2 through 5*

FIGURE 7.25

Set Database Password
dialog box

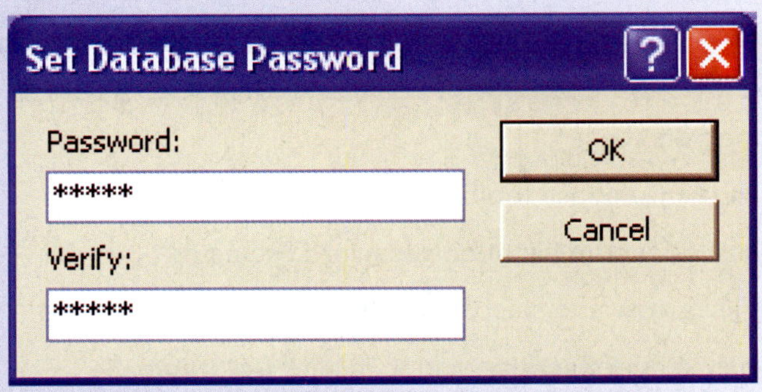

8. Type **gizmo** in the Password text box

9. Type **gizmo** in the Verify text box

10. Click **OK**

11. Close ac07KoryoKicks.mdb leaving Access open

Figure 7.24 displays all of the available open modes. As previously discussed, choosing Open results in shared access and choosing Open Exclusive locks the database so that no other users have access. The *Open Read-Only* option allows shared access for reading database objects. Read access allows all actions that do not update any database objects. Examples of allowable read-only operations include printing reports and running queries. The *Open Exclusive Read-Only* option locks out other users and allows you read access.

A new password must be entered twice to prevent typing errors in the password. Access passwords are case sensitive, so be very careful when entering them. Pick a password that is easy to remember since opening the database is not possible without the password. Replicated databases should not be password protected, since the password halts the synchronization process. Testing the password is accomplished by trying to open the database.

Testing the KoryoKicks password:

1. Click the Open button

2. Locate **ac07KoryoKicksPassword.mdb** and click it

3. Click the **Open** button

4. Type **GIZMO** and click **OK**

tip: *Passwords are case sensitive, so GIZMO will not work*

5. Respond OK to the prompt that you have entered an invalid password

6. Type **gizmo** and click **OK**

FIGURE 7.26

Password dialog box

Passwords are unencrypted so that they can be viewed by other users from the password file. This can be handy for forgotten passwords, but does not provide the most effective password protection. Encrypted passwords can be set with user-level security.

Removing the KoryoKicks password:

1. Verify that Access is running and that **ac07KoryoKicks.mdb** is open

2. Click the **Tools menu**, then **Security**, and then **Unset Database Password** (see Figure 7.27)

3. Type **gizmo** and click **OK**

Removing a password from a file is accomplished with the file open. With the Security option of the Tools menu displaying, select Unset Database Password and enter the correct password when prompted. Successfully entering the password will remove it from the file.

User-Level Security

In a multiuser database **user-level security** settings can allow some users to have full access to the database while others have restricted access. Restricted access might keep certain users from replicating the database, changing the database design, creating new tables, changing the database password, or almost any other operation.

F I G U R E 7.27

Removing a password

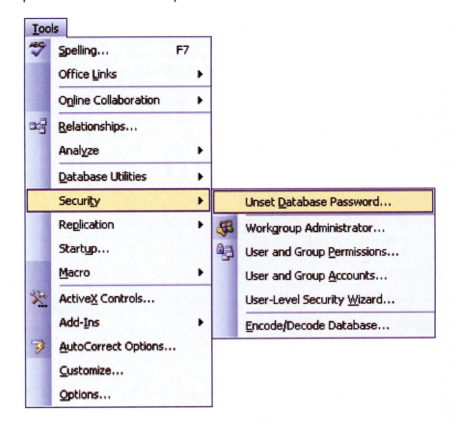

User-level security provides the most comprehensive security available for an Access database. When user-level security is applied, the user must type a password to enter the database. The password used is matched against a list of users to establish a level of access to each database object called **permissions**.

Each user has a set of permissions that determine what operations they can perform on each table, query, form, report, and macro. Permissions are either explicit or implicit. **Explicit permissions** are granted directly to each user by setting a user account. **Implicit permissions** are granted to a user group and inherited by the users belonging to that group.

Permissions can be changed for a database object by

- Members of the Admins group
- The owner of the object
- Any user who has Administer permission for the object

The user who creates a table, query, form, report, or macro is the owner of that object. Additionally, the group of users that can change permissions in the database also can change the ownership of these objects, or they can re-create these objects, which is another way to change ownership of the objects. Access provides the User-Level Security Wizard to aid in implementing common security schemes.

---

task reference   Setting User-Level Security

- Open the Access database to be secured

- On the **Tools** menu, pause over **Security** and then click **User-Level Security Wizard**

- Follow the Wizard instructions

Setting KoryoKicks user-level security:

1. Verify that Access is running and that **ac07KoryoKicksPassword.mdb** is open

2. Open the **Tools** menu and pause over **Security** and then click **User-Level Security Wizard**

3. Click **Next** to create a new workgroup information file

4. Read and accept the defaults on this Wizard page by clicking **Next**

5. Accept the default of securing all database objects by clicking **Next**

6. Create user groups

   a. Check **Full Permissions** and read the Group Permissions description

   b. Check **Full Data Users** and read the Group Permissions description

tip: *You are creating two unique and encrypted user groups with different permissions. The Administrator group is created by default*

7. Click **Next**

8. Accept the default of not assigning Users group permissions by clicking **Next**

9. Add users and passwords

   a. Add **user1** with a password of **user1** and then click **Add This User to the List**

   b. Add **user2** with a password of **user2** and then click **Add This User to the List**

   c. Click **Next**

10. Add users to the groups (see Figure 7.28)

    a. Select **user1** from the drop-down list and click **Full Permissions**

    b. Select user2 from the drop-down list and click **Full Data Users**

11. Click **Next**

12. Name the backup **KoryoKicksUserSecurityBak** and click **Finish**

13. Print the Security report and save it

The KoryoKicks database now has three users with unique passwords. The username and password used to open the database determine the operations that can be performed.

Testing KoryoKicks user-level security:

1. Close Access and reopen it using the ac07KoryoKicksPassword.mdb icon placed on your desktop by the previous steps

2. Log on as user2 and try to change the database design

The Administrator user name and password will allow full access to the database including altering security settings. Logging on as user1 will allow full access to the database except assigning permissions to other users while user2 will allow data editing, but no updates to database objects.

Setting user-level security

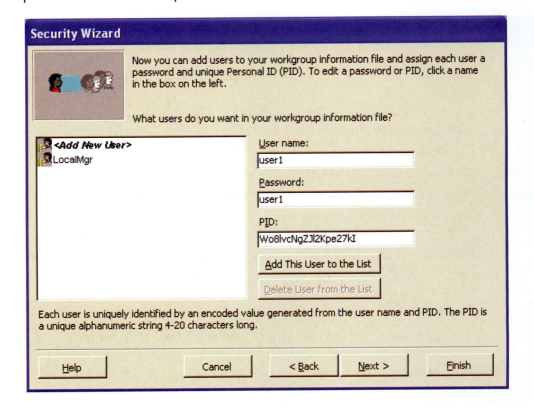

SESSION 7.2

making *the grade*

1. What is the purpose of splitting a database?

2. What tool will suggest changes to improve database performance?

3. How is replicating a database different from splitting a database?

4. When should you consider securing an Access database?

SESSION 7.3 SUMMARY

Every database requires periodic maintenance to repair known problems regardless of how well it was designed. Preventive maintenance or design reviews are performed to reduce the likelihood of a serious system failure. The frequency of preventive maintenance is determined by how critical the data are to the operation of the organization.

Periodic maintenance starts with the users evaluating the system and suggesting modifications that would improve usability and performance. User issues typically involve ease of data entry, validity of data, and reporting. Input masks, formats, default values, data validation, and other field properties are usually the way to address such issues. Access also provides the Database Performance Analyzer for monitoring database performance and suggesting areas for object design improvement.

Often design changes are necessary because the organization using the data or the business operations supported by the data have changed. New tables, fields, and reports can be created to support business changes, but organizational changes are more complex. When multiple users need access to the same data, effective methods of sharing must be employed. One alternative for sharing is to create replicas of a database that must be synchronized so that all replicas reflect the same data.

The method chosen for sharing data is determined by whether or not the organization is networked and the level of access needed by each user. Another sharing method splits the database into a front-end and back-end. Each user maintains unique front-end (queries, forms, and reports) with access to the data held in the back-end.

When a database is exposed to risk of violation, it is wise to implement security measures. Security is also needed when there are multiple users with differing levels of responsibility. Encoding can be used to secure a database being transported. A simple password can ensure that only authorized users access the data. End-user security uses permissions to determine exactly what operations a user can perform on each database object.

MICROSOFT OFFICE SPECIALIST OBJECTIVES SUMMARY

- Modify field properties for tables in Design View—AC03S-1-4

making the grade answers

SESSION 7.1

1. Input masks speed data entry by reducing keystrokes. They also improve reliability by not requiring users to enter repetitive data. Any field containing data with a repetitive component such as punctuation should be considered for an input mask.

2. Both the Input Mask and Format properties are similar since they use the same definition characters. The input mask displays a pattern for the user to enter data, such as (___)___-___. You can choose whether or not the punctuation is stored with the data. If the punctuation is not stored with the data, it will need to be added before displaying data from the field to the user. The Format property is used to add repeating characters to data retrieved from a table.

3. The default value assigned to a field should be the most common data value for the field.

4. Validation rules are designed to improve data validity by ensuring that data entered into a field are appropriate for that field.

SESSION 7.2

1. Splitting a database separates the data from the queries, forms, and reports that use it. This is normally done in a networked environment to share the data while allowing users to have their own custom queries, forms, and reports.

2. Database Performance Analyzer

3. When a database is replicated, there are multiple full copies of the database that have to be synchronized with each other. A split database maintains only one copy of the data in a central location that is shared by all users. With a split database, each user has his or her own front-end (queries, forms, and reports) based on the centralized data.

4. Databases should be secured whenever there is risk of theft, inappropriate use, or unwanted data altering.

task reference *summary*

Task	Page #	Preferred Method
Controlling blank data values	AC 7.11	• Open the table in Design View • Click the field whose blank values you would like to control • Set Required to **Yes** to disallow blank values (Allow Zero Length should be set to No)
Defining field validation rules	AC 7.14	• Open the table in Design View • Click the field that will be monitored by the validation rule • Select the **Validation Rule** property for that field • Type the validation expression or use the Expression Builder by clicking the ellipsis to the right of the Validation Rule text box • Click the Validation Text property box for the same field and enter the text that is to display when the validation rule is broken • Save the table update • If the validation rule has been set for a field that already contains data, Access will ask if you want to apply the new rule to existing data • If there are no existing data in the field, there will be no prompt
Splitting a database	AC 7.16	• Back up the database • On the **Tools** menu, point to **Database Utilities**, and then click **Database Splitter** • Follow the Database Splitter Wizard instructions
Optimizing database objects	AC 7.18	• Open the database to be optimized • Click the **Tools** menu, then **Analyze**, and then **Performance** • Select the tab for the database object (table, query, report, form, etc.) that you would like to analyze • Click the check box of each object to be evaluated or click Select All to select all objects in the list • Select objects from other tabs if desired • Click **OK** • Review and apply results as needed
Replicating a database	AC 7.20	• Open the database to be replicated • Remove any password protection and ensure that the database is not open by any other users • On the **Tools** menu, point to **Replication**, and then click **Create Replica** • Click **Yes** when prompted with: The database must be closed before you can create a replica • Answer **Yes** when prompted with: Converting a database into a Design Master results in changes . . . • In the Location of New Replica dialog box • Navigate to the location for the replica • Set the **Priority** • Check the **Prevent deletes** check box to prevent record deletions in the replica • In the Save as type box, select the replica visibility • Click **OK**
Synchronizing replicated databases	AC 7.23	• Open the replica to be synchronized • On the **Tools** menu, point to **Replication**, and then click **Synchronize Now** • Select the other replica set member to be synchronized from the Directly with Replica drop-down list box • Click **OK** • Respond **Yes** when prompted to close the database for synchronization • Respond **OK** when notified that the process has been completed

task reference *summary*

Task	Page #	Preferred Method
Hiding a database	AC 7.26	• Open Windows Explorer • Navigate to the file to be hidden • Right-click on the file to be hidden • Click the **Properties** option • Click the **Hidden** attribute • Click **OK**
Encoding a database	AC 7.28	• Open Access with no open database • Open the **Tools** menu, pause over **Security**, and click **Encode/Decode Database . . .** • Enter a folder and a name for the database to be encoded and click **OK** • Enter a folder and name for the encoded database and click **Save**
Password protecting a database	AC 7.29	• Open Access with no open database • Click the **Open** button on the Database toolbar • Navigate to the folder and select the file to be password protected • Click the Open button's list arrow and select **Open Exclusive** • Open the **Tools** menu, pause over **Security**, and then click **Set Database Password** • Type the password in the Password text box, repeat the same password in the Verify text box, and then press **Enter**
Setting user-level security	AC 7.32	• Open the Access database to be secured • On the **Tools** menu, pause over **Security** and then click **User-Level Security Wizard** • Follow the Wizard instructions

ACCESS

TRUE/FALSE

1. Microsoft Access will *not* allow an output format to be selected that does not match the input mask display.

2. The Input Mask property **0L** indicates that data entered in this field must consist of a required number followed by a required letter.

3. The Validation Text property of a field contains the validation rule that data being entered in this field must follow.

4. A field with a validation rule of *"Mr" Or "Ms" Or "Mrs"* will only accept one of the three listed values.

5. When both the Required and Allow Zero Length properties of a field are set to No, the field will accept blank values.

6. A front-end and back-end version of a database are created through database replication.

FILL-IN

1. Passwords protect a database from _____ access.

2. The least effective method of securing a database discussed is _____.

3. Administrators and owners can grant _____ to database objects.

4. Encoding is not effective in protecting against people who own _____ software.

5. One of the easiest ways to improve the validity of database data is to reduce _____.

6. The _____ input mask character causes all text that follows to be converted to lowercase.

7. The _____ can be used to copy formatting from one control to another control in both Form and Report Design Views.

MULTIPLE CHOICE

1. A security permission granted to a specific user is called a(n) _____ permission.
   a. implied
   b. explicit
   c. implicit
   d. personal

2. To set passwords the database must be opened using the _____ option of the Open button.
   a. Open
   b. Open Single User
   c. Open Read-Only
   d. Open Exclusive

3. _____ causes the data in an Access database to be indecipherable to utility and word-processing programs.
   a. Hiding
   b. Scanning
   c. Encoding
   d. None of the above

4. The act of updating the Design Master of a replicate set with data from a replica is called _____.
   a. synchronization
   b. master update
   c. harmonizing
   d. all of the above

5. The Database Performance Analyzer automatically repairs items classified as _____.
   a. Critical
   b. Fixed
   c. Auto
   d. Idea

review of concepts

REVIEW QUESTIONS

Each of the following topics should be addressed in one to three paragraphs.

1. Consider the data that your college or university stores about you and suggest some validation rules that would be effective for improving data validity with that type of data.

2. Explain the relationship between validation rules and validation text.

3. Assume that you have created a database that will track service calls for billing purposes. The minimum service call is 30 minutes. How would you set up and verify the performance of data entry restrictions on the ServiceTime field?

4. Why is it important for split databases to be on a network?

5. If your database resides on a desktop computer and you are taking a business trip with a laptop, what is the most effective way to take your database with you?

CREATE THE QUESTION

For each of the following answers, create the question.

ANSWER	QUESTION
1. _____–_____–_____	_____
2. The Text Box format overrides the format set in the table definition	_____
3. When you can identify a value that is most often entered in a field	_____
4. Please enter a value between 1 and 100	_____
5. The back-end	_____
6. The front-end	_____
7. It indicates missing or unknown data	_____

FACT OR FICTION

For each of the following, determine whether the statement is fact, fiction, or both and present your arguments for that conclusion.

1. The queries, forms, and reports contained in the front-end file of a split database cannot be updated.

2. You should always follow the suggestions of the Database Performance Analyzer.

3. When you add a record to a replica, the other members of the replica set are automatically updated.

4. Synchronization conflicts that cannot be resolved with the priority must be handled manually with the Conflict Viewer.

5. Deleting a replica does not impact the Design Master or the remaining replicas.

6. The Format property set in table design can be overridden for the Text Box control displaying the field in Form Design View.

7. Well-designed Microsoft Access databases will not require periodic design reviews.

1. Altamonte High School Booster Club Donation Tracking—Part III: Database Design Review

The Altamonte Boosters have been using their database for several months and are encountering some problems. Since there are no input masks or validation rules, and multiple users, the data are not at all consistent. The capitalization of names is an issue and incomplete data entry occurs too frequently. A database design review has been completed uncovering the need for the updates outlined below.

1. Start Access and open **ac07AltamonteBoosters.mdb**

tip: *You cannot use your copy of the database from the previous chapter, since there have been modifications for this chapter*

2. Open the **Boosters** table

   a. Make each field required by setting the Required property to **Yes**

   b. Correct the Field Size property of Name to **25**

   c. Change the Data Type of Phone to **Text**. Set Size to 13 and use the ellipsis (. . .) to set the input mask to **Phone Number**. Do not store the symbols

   d. Edit the Phone Input Mask property to be **!(000)000-0000** since the area code in Altamonte is required

   e. Change the Data Type of Zip to **Text** with a size of 5 and set an input mask of **00000**

   f. Since all of the boosters are in-state, the zip code should begin with 27. Enter the validation rule **Like "27???"**

   g. Enter the validation text **Booster's Zip Code must begin with 27**

   h. Since most of the boosters are in the **27234** zip code, set that as the default value of Zip

   i. Set the Default property of the State field to **NC**

3. Save your changes to the Boosters table and respond yes to the prompt informing you that validation rules have changed

4. To test your updates, change to Datasheet View

   a. Create a new booster record for **Mark Funk** and try to move to another record

   tip: *You should receive a validation message for the missing street address*

   b. Add a Street address for Mark Funk in **Cary, NC**

   c. Leave the Zip blank and try to move to another record

   d. Enter a Zip of **33228** and try to move to another record (see Figure 7.29)

   e. Change the Zip to **27228** and try to move to another record

   f. Enter a Phone of **3174382851** and try to move to another record

   g. Set DonationClass to **1** and move to another record

   tip: *Now you have tested and corrected each modification to the database and the record should be accepted for update*

5. Close the Boosters table

6. Exit Access if your work is complete

FIGURE 7.29

Testing Boosters design changes

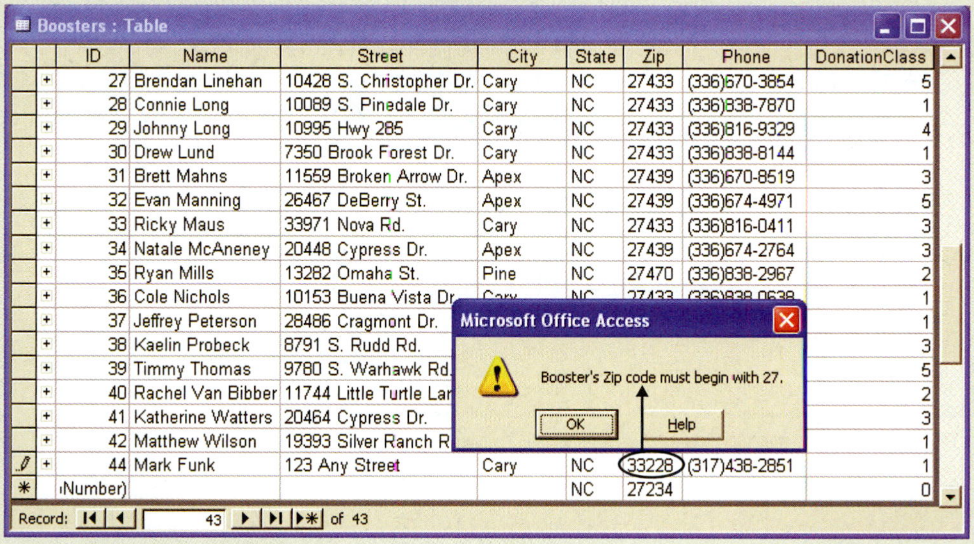

AC 7.41

2. BBs Shoes Database Design Review

BBs is a family-owned shoe store specializing in athletic shoes. The store is owned by Roberto (Berto) and Benita Lopez, who developed their own Microsoft Access database to track the shoe inventory. Since Berto and Benita are new to Access databases, they have asked you to help them complete a design review.

1. Start Access and open **ac07BBsShoes.mdb**

2. Familiarize yourself with the database
   a. Open the Inventory table in Design View and review the current table design
   b. Switch to Datasheet View and review the sample data Berto and Benita have provided
   c. Take a look at the existing form and report

3. The biggest problems that Berto and Benita have identified are data entry errors. They would like you to add some validation rules to improve the integrity of their data
   a. Create a validation rule that will accept ShoePrice values between 50 and 250. Make the validation text **Valid shoe prices are between 50 and 250 inclusive.**
   b. Create a validation rule that will accept QtyOnHand values between 0 and 100. Make the validation text **Valid quantities are between 0 and 100 inclusive.**

4. Create an input mask for the Location field that will require the user to enter an uppercase letter followed by at least one digit. Refer to Figures 7.2 and 7.3

5. Set the default QtyOnHand value to **12**, since that is the most common order quantity and therefore the most common quantity on hand value

6. Another problem area for BBs Shoes is missing data. None of the Inventory table's fields should be blank. Set the Required property to **Yes** and the Allow Zero Length property to **No** for each nonkey field in the table

7. Switch to Datasheet View, save your changes, and answer **Yes** to the data integrity prompt

8. Verify your design changes using data for your favorite athletic shoes using a StockNbr value of **TX99999**
   a. Enter a price that violates the validation rule and document the result
   b. Enter a QtyOnHand that violates the validation rule and document the result (see Figure 7.30)
   c. Enter a Location of 7A and document the result
   d. Try to leave each nonkey field blank and document the result

9. After making any needed adjustments to the table design, enter the shoes with a valid ShoeDescription and Price. Make the QtyOnHand **15** and the Location **B4**

10. If your work is complete, exit Access; otherwise, continue to the next assignment

FIGURE 7.30

Testing BBs Shoes design changes

challenge!

1. Altamonte High School Booster Club Donation Tracking—Part IV: Exploring Alternatives for Sharing the Database

The Altamonte Boosters are preparing for a fund-raising drive and believe that it would be more effective to have a way for multiple members to update the database. Since the computers holding the databases will not be networked, replication will provide the most effective way to share database access. At this point they think that there should be three users: the club president, vice president, and fund-raising chair.

1. If you did not complete the Altamonte Practice project in this chapter, do so now

2. Open **ac07AltamonteBoosters.mdb**

tip: *You can use your copy of the database from the Practice project in this chapter. You cannot use your copy of the database from the previous chapter since there have been modifications for this chapter*

3. Use the Performance Analyzer to evaluate the performance of all tables in the AlatamonteBoosters database. Document the Analysis Results and outline whether or not the results should be acted on

4. Create a replica set for the three users. The Design Master will be retained by the club president and each of the other users will need a replica (see Figure 7.31)

FIGURE 7.31

AltamonteBoosters Design Master and replicas

a. Use the Tools menu to create the first replica with the following attributes:
   i. Create a backup and close the open database when prompted
   ii. Name the replica **ReplicaAltamonte1** and save it in a folder named **ReplicaAltamonte**
   iii. Click on the **Prevent Deletes** check box so that this replica can't delete existing records
b. Use the Tools menu to create the second replica, named **ReplicaAltamonte2**, with the same attributes as ReplicaAltamonte1

tip: *You will not be prompted to create a backup in subsequent replications*

5. Passwords cannot be applied to replicated databases, so each user will have to be responsible for securing his or her computer and folders to protect the database. For added security, use Windows Explorer to
   a. Create a folder in ReplicaAtlamonte database for each user named **VPres** and **Chair**
   b. Move ReplicaAltamonte1 to Vpres, and ReplicaAltamonte2 to Chair
   c. Hide the VPres and Chair folders

6. Open the Design Master and initiate synchronization on Altamonte1. Since it has been moved, you will need to browse to the hidden folder

7. Exit Access if your work is complete

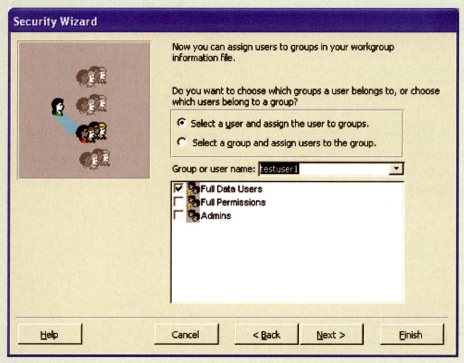

2. HealthCare2Go Design Review

HealthCare2Go is a temporary services agency providing short-term employees to the medical community. Riki Lee has built a database that is functioning fairly well, but she believes the design can be improved to increase data reliability. Additionally, new users are being added to the system and security needs to be developed to protect against unauthorized updates to the data.

1. Start Access and open **ac07HealthCare2Go.mdb**

2. Open the TempEmployees table in Datasheet View and review the existing data

3. Switch to Design View and review the table's field definitions

4. Set the Required and Allow Zero Length properties so that LastName, FirstName, Phone, and JobClass must have values entered and will not accept ""

5. Set Formats to obtain the following results
   a. Always display the State value in uppercase
   b. Ensure that the first letter of both LastName and FirstName is always uppercase
   c. Display Phone as (___)___-_____
   d. Display the SocialSecNmbr with dashes

6. Set input masks to obtain the following results
   a. Ensure that 9 numbers are entered in the SocialSecNmbr field
   b. Ensure that 5 numbers are entered in the Zip field

7. Set a default value of WA for the State field

8. Add a new record testing each required field, format, and input mask

9. Use the User-Level Security Wizard to create a new workgroup for this database
   a. Check both **Full Data Users** and **Full Permissions**
   b. Do not assign the additional User group permissions
   c. Create three users and their associated passwords (see Figure 7.32)
      i. testuser1/test1 as a Full Data Users group member
      ii. testuser2/test2 as a Full Permissions group member
      iii. <yourlastname>/<yourlastname> as an Admins group member
   d. Name the backup **ac07HealthCare2GoBak.mdb**
   e. Print the security report and save it
   f. Repeatedly close the database using the icon on your desktop and test each password
   g. Place a copy of your desktop icon in your homework folder

10. If your work is complete, exit Access; otherwise, continue to the next assignment

FIGURE 7.32

HealthCare2Go group assignments

1. Curbside Recycling

A design review for the Curbside Recycling Access database has been completed and a list of updates compiled. The updates include adding input masks and default values and replicating the database.

1. Start Access and open **ac07CurbsideRecycling.mdb**

tip: *You cannot use your copy of the database from the previous chapter since there have been modifications for this chapter*

2. Open the Customer table
   a. Make each field required by setting the Required property to **Yes**

tip: *CstmrNmbr is the key field and so is already required*

   b. Create a Phone input mask that requires the area code to be entered
   c. Create an input mask for ZipCode that requires all five digits to be entered
   d. Create an input mask for State that requires both characters to be entered
   e. Apply a Short Date input mask to FirstPickup
   f. Based on the current data, set appropriate default values for City, State, and Zip
   g. Test these updates with **Connor McKinsey, 838 E. Jay St., Indianapolis, IN, 46121, 7518300848.** Use the current date for FirstPickup
   h. Close the Customer table

3. Use the **Replication** option of the **Tools** menu to create replicas (see Figure 7.33)
   a. Create a new folder for the replicas named **CurbsideReplicas**
   b. Set the appropriate properties to stop the replica from deleting records and name the replica **Curbside1**
   c. Create a second replica that cannot delete records, **Curbside2**, in the same folder

4. You are in the Design Master where changes to database design should be made
   a. Open the Customer table in Design View
   b. Set an input mask for First Name that causes the first letter to be capitalized
   c. Set an input mask for Last Name that causes the first letter to be capitalized

5. Open Curbside1
   a. Open the Customer table in Design View
   b. Verify that the input masks for First and Last Names do not exist yet in the replica
   c. On the **Tools** menu, point to **Replication** and select **Synchronize Now**
      i. Respond **Yes** to closing open objects
      ii. Select the **Design Master** for synchronization and click **OK**
   d. Open the Customer table in Design View and verify that the input masks for First and Last Names now exist

6. Exit Access if your work is complete

FIGURE 7.33

Curbside replicas

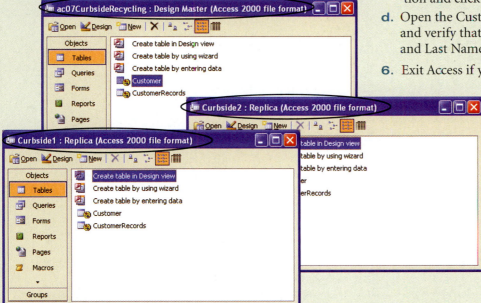

2. SportBabies.com Design Review

SportBabies.com is an online storefront selling replica sports uniforms for babies and toddlers. A Microsoft Access database to support this Web site was developed by an employee who has moved on to another position. The database has not been implemented and currently contains a small number of test records. You have inherited the database development project and need to evaluate its design before updating it to meet current business needs.

1. Open Access and open **ac07SportBabies.mdb**

2. Open the ProductList table in Datasheet View and review the existing data

3. Switch to Design View and review the table's field definitions

4. Run the Database Performance Analyzer and document the results. Be sure to include the form and report in your evaluation

5. You have determined that knowing that a product is in stock would benefit potential customers and improve sales. Add a new field, **QtyOnHand** before the Price column. Make this field an **Integer** data type

6. Set the following default values
   a. MatchingCap, HomeJersey, and AwayJersey should each default to Yes (checked)
   b. Price should default to 42.38

FIGURE 7.34

SportBabies.com passwords

7. Create a validation rule to ensure that the price entered is between 25 and 200 inclusive. Be sure to include appropriate validation text

8. Make League, Team, Player, and Price required fields that will not allow a zero-length value

9. Use a new product to test each of your design updates. Print the table design

10. Use the User-Level Security Wizard to create a new user group for this database
    a. Check both **Full Data Users** and **Full Permissions**
    b. Do not assign the additional User group permissions (see Figure 7.34)
    c. Create three users and their associated passwords
       i. testuser1/test1 as a member of Full Data Users
       ii. testuser2/test2 as a member of Full Permissions
       iii. <yourlastname>/<yourlastname> as a member of Admins
    d. Print the security report and save it
    e. Repeatedly close and open the database using the icon on your desktop to test each password
    f. Place a copy of your desktop icon in your homework folder

11. Close the database and exit Access if your work is complete

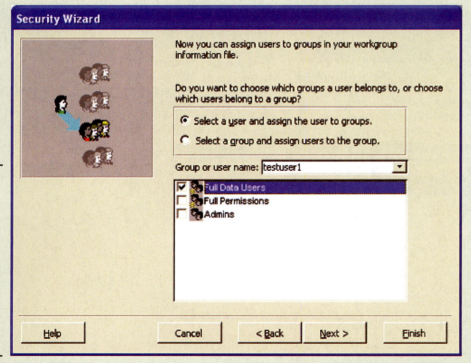

1. Academic Software

The design review for the Access database used by Academic Software has been completed and a list of updates compiled. Additionally, Academic has installed a network and plans to split the database so that the various users can customize their front-end components.

1. Use your favorite search engine to find an Academic software title for the study of chemistry

2. Start Access and open **ac07Software.mdb**

tip: *You cannot use your copy of the database from the previous chapter since there have been modifications for this chapter*

3. Open tblVendor

   a. Make each field required by setting the Required property to **Yes**

   b. Use Find and Replace to remove the dashes from the current phone numbers

   c. Use the ellipsis (. . .) to set the input mask to **Phone Number.** Do not store the symbols

   d. Edit the Phone input mask to require the area code to be entered

   e. Create an input mask for Zip that requires all five digits to be entered

   f. Create an input mask for State that requires both characters to be entered

FIGURE 7.35

Front-end of Software.mdb

g. Test these updates with **RS, Ricks Software, 838 E. Jay St., Indianapolis, IN, 46121, 7518300848**

h. Close ac07Software.mdb

4. Use the File menu to create a backup of the database named **ac07SoftwareBak.mdb** before splitting it

5. Use the **Database Utilities** option of the **Tools** menu to activate the Database Splitter Wizard

   a. Name the back-end file **ac07Software_be.mdb**

tip: *This file would normally be placed on a shared network disk so that all of the front-ends would have access to it. The front-end can be copied to any number of computers*

   b. Select **tblSoftware** and click **Design** (see Figure 7.35)

tip: *A message will warn you that this is a linked table, which means that the data are stored in the back-end and you are in the front-end*

   c. Use the Query Wizard to create a query, **tblSoftwareQuery**, displaying Name, Category, and Vendor Code

6. Open **ac07Software_be.mdb**

   a. Open **tblSoftware** and add the validation rule "MTH" Or "ENG" Or "SCI" to the Category field

   b. Add appropriate validation text for the Category field

7. Open **ac07Software.mdb** and add a record to the Software for **NewsNow** with a SoftwareNumber of **6060**, Category of **Che**, and VendorCode of **LS**

tip: *You should receive the message from the validation rule added to the back-end*

8. Change Che to **SCI** and move to another record to save the change

9. Add a record for the software title that you located on the Internet with a VendorCode of **CC**

10. Exit Access if your work is complete

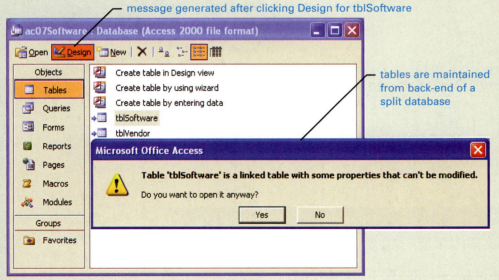

message generated after clicking Design for tblSoftware

tables are maintained from back-end of a split database

hands-on projects

around the world

1. TechRocks Seminars

The design review for the TechRocks Access database used to track seminars, facilitators, and enrollment has been completed. Several design updates to improve usability have been approved. Additionally, TechRocks enrollment will now be handled from multiple locations around the world, so users in various offices must have access to the data. Since the offices are not networked, replicated databases using Internet synchronization is the planned approach.

1. Start Access and open **ac07SSeminars.mdb**

tip: *You cannot use your copy of the database from the previous chapter since there have been modifications for this chapter*

2. Open the **Seminars** table in Design View

   a. Make SeminarID, Date, Time, and Hours required by setting the Required property to **Yes**

   b. Set an input mask for SeminarID that requires the entry of 5 characters (letters or digits)

   c. Set an input mask for SeminarTime of **Medium Time**

   d. Set the default seminar cost to 250

   e. Set a data validation rule to ensure that the Cost entered is between $50 and $2,500. Do not set validation text; the default message is sufficient

tip: *Use the Between comparison operator*

   f. Set a data validation rule to ensure that Hours is between 16 and 80 (see Figure 7.36)

   g. Use the Datasheet View to test these updates with a new seminar **XX134** and Trainer **5**. Be sure to enter invalid values for each field before settling on valid values

   h. Close Seminars

3. Activate the **Tools** menu, pause over **Replication**, and select **Create Replica**

   a. Create a folder **ReplicaSeminars**

   b. Name this replica **ParisSeminars.mdb**

   c. Create a second replica called **LondonSeminars.mdb** with a priority of **70**. Store this replica in the same folder

4. Open **ParisSeminars.mdb**

   a. Open the **Enrollment** table

   b. Locate record one for student 114 and change the student's name to **Edna**

5. Open **LondonSeminars.mdb**

   a. Open the **Enrollment** table

   b. Locate record 114 and change the student's name to **Evan**

   c. Open the **Tools** menu, point to **Replication**, select **Synchronize Now**, and select **ParisSeminars.mdb** as the database to synchronize with

tip: *You may need to manually resolve the conflict in favor of the Paris changes, but they should resolve themselves if the priorities were set correctly*

   d. Open the Enrollment table to verify that the Paris change (Edna) was used to resolve the conflict

6. Open the Enrollment table of ac07ParisSeminars.mdb to verify that it still holds the value Edna for student 114

7. Exit Access if your work is complete

FIGURE 7.36

Validation rule violation message

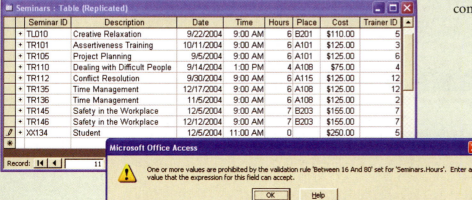

running project: tnt web design

Database Maintenance and Security

TnT has continued to grow and the database is out of control. In a recent design review, inactive records were archived and a plan for refining table design outlined. Since there are a large number of users who need to be able to view and report on data, but only a few users who need to be able to update data, two user groups will be created.

1. Start Access and open **ac07TnT.mdb**

tip: *You cannot use your copy of the database from the previous chapter since there have been modifications for this chapter*

2. Open the **Employees** table in Design View
   a. Make each field required by setting the Required property to **Yes**
   b. Create an input mask for First Name that will cause the first letter to always be uppercase and subsequent letters lowercase
   c. Create an input mask for Last Name that will cause the first letter to always be uppercase and subsequent letters lowercase
   d. Create an input mask for State that requires both characters to be entered
   e. Use the ellipsis (. . .) to set the input mask to **Phone**. Do not store the symbols.
   f. Edit the Phone input mask to require the area code to be entered

F I G U R E   7.37

Creating a Read-Only Users Group

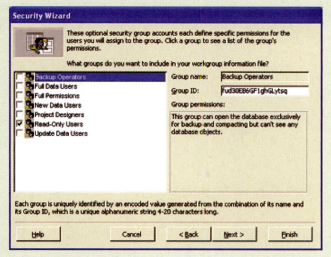

g. Create an input mask for Zip that requires all five digits to be entered
h. Test these updates with a record for **Bob Willson** with a JobClass of **QA**
i. Close Employees
3. Activate the **Tools** menu, point to **Security**, and select **User-Level Security Wizard**
   a. Click **Next** on the first panel
   b. Click **Next** again to accept the default names
   c. Click **Next** again to secure all database objects
   d. Check **Read-Only Users** to create a group for the users who can't update the database

tip: *The Administrators group has full rights to the database and is created automatically*

   e. Click **Next**
   f. Click **Next** to bypass setting permissions for users
   g. Create users
      i. **Tori**, with password **purple**
      ii. **Tonya**, with password **yellow**
      iii. **Readers**, with password of **seeit**
   h. Click **Next**
4. Assign permissions to the users you added
   a. Select **Tori** from the drop-down list and click **Admins**
   b. Repeat this process for **Tonya**
   c. Select **Readers** from the drop-down list and click **Read-Only Users**
   d. Click **Finish**
   e. Print the report and save it
5. Use the icon on your desktop to test each password
6. Exit Access if your work is complete

1. Design Review of a Multitable Database to Invoice Customers

Locate your copy of the database named **ac06CustomersMultiTableDatabase.mdb** created in the Analysis assignment from Chapter 6. Use Microsoft Windows Explorer to create a copy of the file named **ac07CustomersMultiTableDatabase.mdb** and then open the copy in Microsoft Access. Take a look at the data and forecast issues that would most likely be uncovered by questioning users in a design review. Be sure to evaluate

- Default values
- Fields that are required but might be left blank
- Fields that need input masks and formats
- Fields that could benefit from default values
- Fields that need validation rules

Update your database design with at least five items from your list. Use the Database Splitter Wizard to create a front-end and back-end from your updated database.

2. Design Review of a Multitable Database to Track Employees

Locate your copy of the database named **ac06EmployeesMultiTableDatabase.mdb** created in the Analysis assignment from Chapter 6. Use Microsoft Windows Explorer to create a copy of the file named **ac07EmployeesMultiTableDatabase.mdb** and then open the copy in Microsoft Access. Take a look at the data and forecast issues that would most likely be uncovered by questioning users in a design review. Be sure to evaluate

- Default values
- Fields that are required but might be left blank
- Fields that need input masks and formats
- Fields that could benefit from default values
- Fields that need validation rules

Update your database design with at least five items from your list. Use the Database Splitter Wizard to create a front-end and back-end from your updated database.

Integrating with Other Applications

did you know?

most *landfilled trash retains its original weight, volume, and form for 40 years.*

a *"jiffy" is an actual unit of time for 1/100th of a second.*

there *are more insects in one square mile of rural land than there are human beings on the entire earth.*

a *chameleon's tongue is twice the length of its body.*

the *Neanderthal's brain was bigger than yours is.*

any *month that starts on a Sunday will have a Friday the 13th in it.*

to *find out what the most popular first name in the world is, visit* www.mhhe.com/i-series.

Chapter Objectives

- **Use Microsoft Graph to chart data in tables or queries**
- **Import data to Access—MOS AC03S-2-3**
- **Export data from Access—MOS AC03S-4-4**
- **Create a Data Access Page using the Page Wizard— MOS AC03S-1-12**
- **Use Design View to modify a Data Access Page**

KoryoKicks: Interactive Web Reporting

KoryoKicks, like most successful businesses, has outgrown its current physical environment, distribution channels, and organization structure. Products are being back-ordered because the existing production facilities can't meet the demand. Orders are not being processed in a timely manner because the volume is more than the current staff can handle. Adding employees and products is a reasonable step, but that will mean an added need for space and money.

Missy and Micah have enlisted the help of a marketing research firm to determine the real potential of their market and to create a diversification plan to help protect against business losses. Until now the business has been low-risk because the only real investment was the cost to secure and ship products that had already been paid for. Employees have also been paid using money already collected. To support growth, the twins must consider hiring full-time employees, acquiring facilities, and securing a business loan. The overall business risk is increasing making the need for planning and reporting more critical.

The twins are attending college in Colorado and don't plan to leave until they graduate. Current research indicates that most of their products are shipped to Indiana, Ohio, and Michigan. Placing facilities close to the largest demand can reduce overhead, so they are considering facilities in Indiana. Their aunt is a CPA who lives in Indianapolis and is willing to champion KoryoKicks in that area.

Accepting orders, shipping products, and billing customers from two sites will require new data sharing and communication methods. The twins believe that the Web will provide the necessary communication channels. The KoryoKicks database can be replicated and the Internet used for synchronization. In addition, Data Access Pages can be used for shared reporting.

Before finalizing a plan, the twins need to create a sales forecast that will be used to determine how many employees and how much space are needed at each location. They will need to learn about the charting utility, Microsoft Graph, in order to analyze the history of sales trends and then forecast them into the future. Existing documents from Word and Excel will need to be incorporated to appropriately present their business. The resulting forecast will be the foundation of the business plan they will present to lenders in order to secure the loan necessary to accomplish the goals outlined.

The twins do not want to build the data storage, reporting, and sharing infrastructure until they are further along in their business plan. However, they do want to see exactly how the necessary components work before they commit to a design that will support their expanding business.

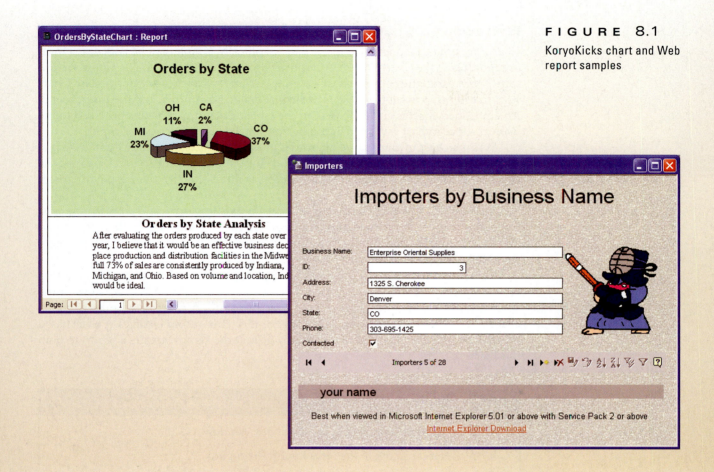

SESSION 8.1 OFFICE INTEGRATION

A basic tenet of computing is not to re-create anything that already exists. Office System products are designed to integrate with each other to avoid re-creating documents, data, and formatting when another form of output is needed. Microsoft Office System applications are able to import and export multiple Office file formats to facilitate sharing documents across software platforms. The formats of other common documents such as Paradox, DBase, and Lotus 1-2-3 also can be accessed.

Importing and exporting are made possible through the features of **OLE (object linking and embedding)**. Most programs designed for the Microsoft operating system support some level of OLE. Programs designed for other operating systems typically don't support OLE.

Adding a Chart to a Form or Report

Sometimes it is not necessary to import or export data to obtain alternative formatting. Office products include an array of applets that provide commonly needed features. WordArt is an example of a small application that is available in all office applications that use the Drawing toolbar. Similarly, the Microsoft Graph is a small application available in Access, Excel, and PowerPoint to create charts and graphs based on table data.

Embedding a Chart in a Report

Charts are used to represent numeric data graphically. Graphs can be added to a form or report using the Chart Wizard or imported from Microsoft Excel. The *Chart Wizard* steps users through the process of defining a *chart* on an Access report. The Chart Wizard can be accessed from the New Report dialog box or by using the Insert menu. An embedded chart is created based on the table data and parameters provided to the Wizard. Once a chart is created, it can be customized using *Microsoft Graph*.

When a chart involves large quantities of data that do not already exist in Access, when there are complex calculations, or when the data are already in Excel, creating the chart in Excel and then importing it to Access is more effective than using Microsoft Graph.

The twins believe that charts can enhance the existing forms and reports by graphically displaying data relationships. For example, the Customers by State report could use a chart to show the number of customers from each state, or the Orders report could display a chart of orders by state.

Using the Chart Wizard, the fields to be plotted can be selected from any existing table or query. The chart can be based on all of the data in the table using sums or the chart can depict only the data from the current record. A chart based on a record is called a *record-bound chart* and will change as the active record changes. A chart based on all of the data is called a *global chart*. By default the Wizard creates a report to hold the chart.

---

task reference   **Create a Microsoft Graph**

- Click the **Reports** object in the Database Window

- Click **New** to activate the New Report dialog box

- Select **Chart Wizard**, use the drop-down list to select the query or table containing the data to be charted, and then click **OK** to initiate the Chart Wizard

- Follow the instructions to select the field(s) with the data to be charted, select the chart type, specify the layout, and add a chart title

---

Creating a report with a chart:

1. Verify that Access is running with **ac08KoryoKicks.mdb** open

2. Click the **Reports** object in the Database Window

3. Click **New** to open the New Report dialog box

4. Click **Chart Wizard**, select **CustomerStateJoin** from the drop-down list, and choose **OK** (see Figure 8.2)

5. Move the **State** and **QuantityOrdered** fields to the Fields for Chart list box and click **Next**

6. Review the available chart types, then select **3-D Pie Chart**, and click **Next** (see Figure 8.3)

7. Use the **Preview Chart** button to see a sample of the chart that you are building

tip: *Microsoft Graph displays dummy data for the design process*

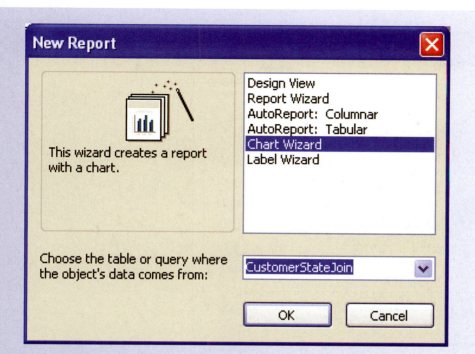

FIGURE 8.2

Initiating the Chart Wizard

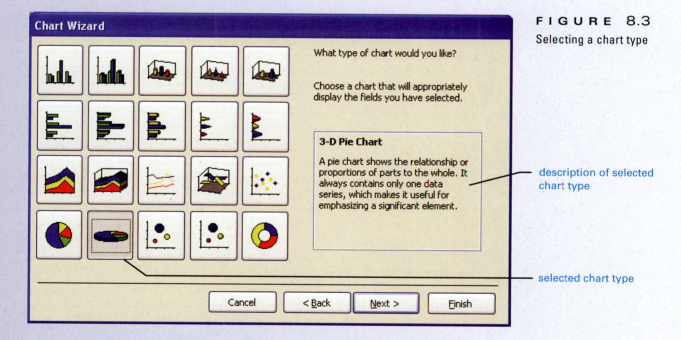

FIGURE 8.3

Selecting a chart type

description of selected chart type

selected chart type

8. Double-click on the value being plotted, **SumOfQuantityOrdered**, to see the other summary options available. Click **Cancel** when you have completed your review

9. Click **Next**

10. Enter **Orders by State** as the Chart Title and click **Finish** (see Figure 8.4)

11. Use the toolbar Zoom button to preview the chart

12. Change to Design View

13. Click **Save** and name the report **OrdersByStateChart**

FIGURE 8.4

The OrdersByStateChart
report

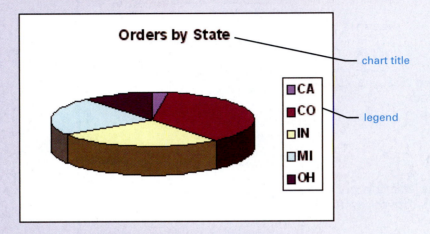

The OrdersByStateChart is a global chart created using the Chart Wizard and based on data from an Access query. The chart is placed in the Detail section of a standard Access report. Changing the data in the underlying tables will change the display of this chart. The Chart Wizard presented 20 chart types for your selection. These represent the most commonly used chart types available from Microsoft Graph. It is important to select a chart type that best suits the data being plotted and the report audience. When plotting one data series to emphasize how each value in the series relates to the total of all values, a pie or stacked column chart is appropriate. Area and line charts work best to display data movement across time or categories such as a sales trend. Bar and column charts effectively show the relationships between categories of values.

The chart being developed is an object that has been embedded in an Access report. **Embedded** objects retain a connection to the program that developed them, called the *source* program. The application holding the object, in this case Microsoft Graph, is called the *destination*. Double-clicking an embedded object will open the source program in edit mode.

Editing a Chart

Editing a chart involves either altering the look of the chart or changing the data used to create it. Changes to the data need to be made in the table(s) on which a chart is based. The simplest visual change is to adjust the size of the chart on the form or report, which is accomplished by dragging the object borders. Other changes are accomplished by double-clicking the chart to activate Microsoft Graph.

Because Graph is the source program, it has greater functionality than that provided by the Wizard. For example, the Wizard presented 20 chart types while Graph organizes the charts into 14 chart types with at least 2 subtypes each, providing many more options. Chart types include pie, line, column, and bar. Subtypes define formatting within a type. For example, a pie chart has flat and 3-D subtypes.

When Microsoft Graph is active, its menus and toolbars display. The Graph menu and toolbar are designed for manipulating and formatting the chart. For example, the Chart menu contains options for changing the chart type, setting chart options that control how the data are charted, and controlling the 3-D view.

Editing a chart also involves moving and formatting the various components of the chart. For example, a legend can be moved, a wedge of a pie exploded, the color of a data series changed, and chart titles adjusted. Those familiar with Microsoft Graph from other Office applications will recognize the datasheet and data that display when editing. In other applications, the datasheet is used to enter the data to be plotted. Since Access holds data in tables, the datasheet is not used and any changes that are made there will not be reflected in the chart. That being the case, closing the datasheet frees screen space and avoids confusion about the chart data source.

Missy and Micah would like the OrdersByStateChart to have a background consistent with the KoryoKicks color scheme. They also want each wedge of the pie labeled with the state and the legend eliminated.

Modifying the OrdersByStateChart:

1. Verify that Access is running with **ac08KoryoKicks.mdb** open with the OrdersByStateChart report open in Design View

tip: *The Orders By State chart should be in the Detail section of the report*

2. Click the chart object to select it and then use the bottom-right sizing handle to expand its height and width until it is the width of the report page

3. Double-click on the chart to open Microsoft Graph (see Figure 8.5)

4. Close the Datasheet Window since it is not useful in Access

5. Right-click on the chart background and click **Format Chart Area**

6. Choose the light blue color square and click **OK**

7. Right-click on the chart background, click **Chart Options**, click the **Legend** tab, and uncheck **Show legend**

tip: *The Office Assistant provides information about these options if it is active*

8. Click the **Data Labels** tab, click **Category name** and **Percentage**, and then click **OK**

9. Click off the chart area to leave **Microsoft Graph**

10. Click the **Print Preview** button on the toolbar (see Figure 8.6)

tip: *Your chart (rather than the default chart) will display as it will print*

11. Close and save

The twins believe that the pie chart is probably the most effective way to present these data but would like to see some alternatives. It is usually helpful to review charting alternatives before settling on the chart type that best presents the data.

F I G U R E   8.5
Microsoft Graph window

Microsoft Graph menus
and toolbar

chart based on default
data—used for formatting

datasheet with default
data

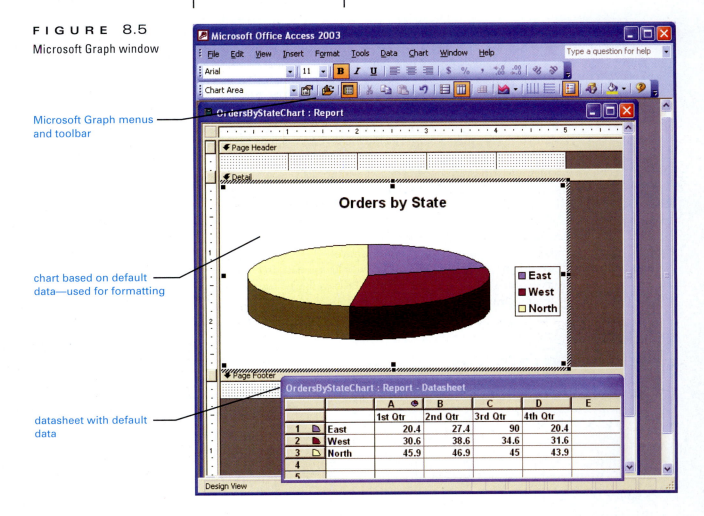

F I G U R E   8.6
OrdersByStateChart with
formatting

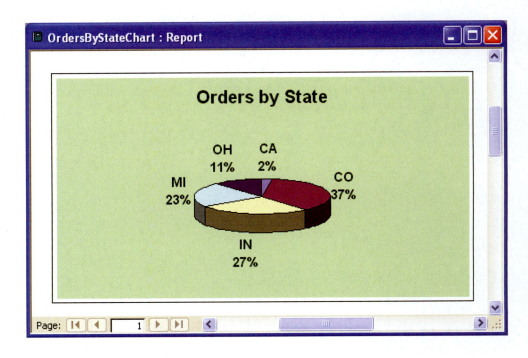

Exploring chart types and subtypes for OrderByStateChart:

1. Verify that Access is running with **ac08KoryoKicks.mdb** open with the OrdersByStateChart report in Design View

2. Double-click on the chart to open Microsoft Graph and close the datasheet

3. Select **Chart Type** from the **Chart** menu

4. Review the current chart type and subtype

5. Select the first subtype for a Column chart and press and hold the button to view the sample

6. Select the **Line** chart type and preview the result

7. Experiment with other chart types and subtypes

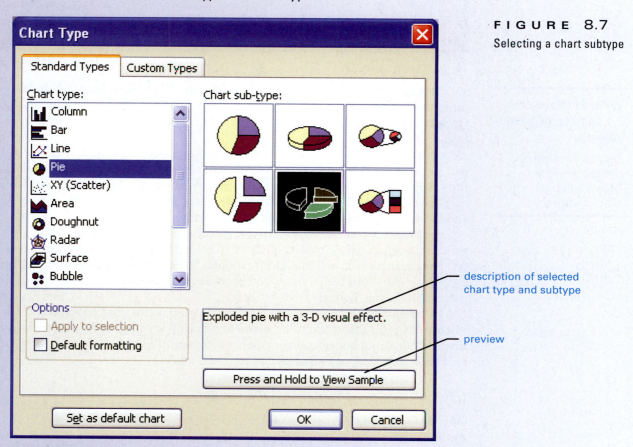

FIGURE 8.7
Selecting a chart subtype

8. Select **Pie** chart type, **Exploded 3-D** subtype, and click **OK**

9. Click off the chart to close Microsoft Graph

10. Use Print Preview to review the changes (see Figure 8.8)

11. Save the OrdersByStateChart

FIGURE 8.8
Exploded Pie chart

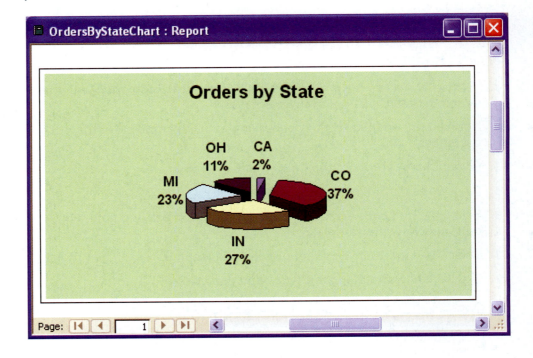

*another***way**
**. . . to Select Chart
Objects**

Double-clicking on
almost any chart
object will open it to
edit its attributes

Because a pie chart is being used, there is no need for X- or Y-axis labels. Bar, column, and line charts all use axes that typically need to be labeled using the Chart Options selection of the Chart menu. This option also can be used to modify the chart title.

Chart options allow control of the titles, axes, gridlines, legend, data labels, and data table display. The gridlines behind the chart can be turned off or made finer using the Gridlines tab. The chart legend can be turned off or placed in a new location with the Legend tab. Data labels can be added to the chart displaying the value plotted and the datasheet can be displayed in the slide with the chart.

Each chart object can be selected and modified. Font, size, and orientation can be set for text objects. Shape objects can have fill colors, border colors, and shapes options set. The chart consists of a plot area that holds the graph and a chart area that holds everything else. Both the plot area and chart area can be set to a custom color, fill, or pattern. By default, both are transparent.

In addition to all of the standard chart components that have been covered, Microsoft Graph allows text to be added to a chart by typing. Additional text may be needed to draw out information or emphasize a point. Typing opens a text box that can be moved, modified, or formatted like any other object.

Importing and Linking Objects

Oftentimes the data in one or more Access tables will need to be combined with objects stored in an external format such as HTML, Excel, Word, or another Access database. When this occurs, the external objects can be brought into Access using the import facilities. Besides graphics and text, other database file formats such as Fox Pro and dBase can be imported.

An *imported* object displays in an Access container such as a table or unbound object on a form or report. For example, an Excel spreadsheet can be converted to an Access table or text from Word can be placed in an unbound object on a report through importing.

During the import process, settings determine how the Access object is related to the original file. When an imported object is just a picture of the contents of a file, it is said to be *linked*. Linked files cannot be updated from Access. Double-clicking a linked object will open the source application where edits can be applied. Link the object if it is important to retain one copy of the file with a connection to the source application.

The other option for importing an object is to embed it. Embedding an object places a complete copy of the object in the Access container. An embedded object is a full copy completely separate from the original file and can be updated without impacting the source file.

Adding Objects to a Form or Report

The simplest imports are used to place objects on an Access form or report. You already have used this method to add graphics to both forms and reports.

---

task reference   Importing with an Unbound Object Frame on a Form or Report

- Open the Design View of the form or report to contain the imported object

- Click the **Unbound Object Frame** tool in the toolbox

- Click and drag the area on the form or report that will contain the object

- In the Microsoft Access dialog box

  - Click **Create From File**

  - Browse to the file for import

  - Click the Link check box to create a linked object or leave it unchecked to create an embedded object

  - Click **OK**

Linking a Word document to the OrdersByStateChart report:

1. Verify that Access is running with **ac08KoryoKicks.mdb** open with the OrdersByStateChart report in Design View

2. Expand the report Detail section by dragging the Detail border up and the Page Footer border down

3. Click the **Unbound Object Frame** 🖼 tool in the toolbox and then click and drag the area in the Detail section of the report that will hold the Word object (see Figure 8.9)

4. Click **Create from File**, use the Browse button to navigate to **ac08OrdersAnalysis.doc**, check the **Link** check box, and click **OK**

5. Size and reposition the object to resemble if needed

6. Double-click the object to open Word

7. In Word

   a. Select all of the text
   b. Use the ruler to adjust the margins for the Access object as shown in Figure 8.10
   c. Save the changes and close Word

FIGURE 8.9

Linking a Word document

path and filename of your import file

description of Link— unclick Link to see embedded description

area for object

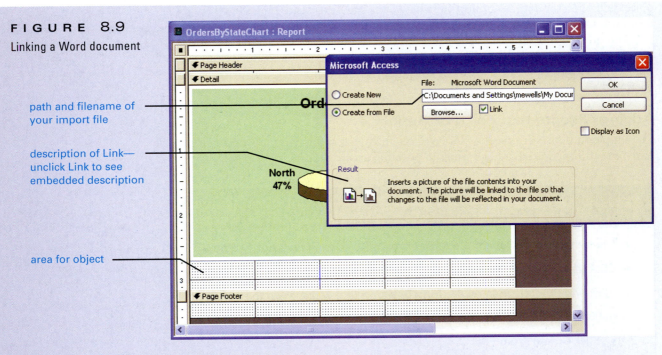

8. If your report does not reflect the margin changes, close and reopen Design View to update the link

9. Activate Print Preview to review your changes (see Figure 8.11)

10. Save

FIGURE 8.10

Adjusting margins with the Word ruler

drag box to adjust left margin of selection

drag to adjust right margin of selection

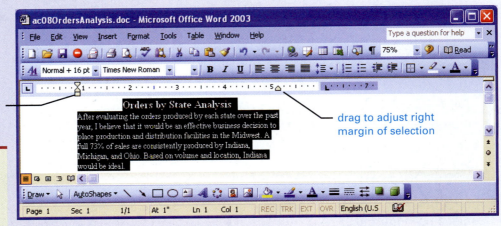

another**way**
. . . to Update Linked Objects

Linked objects do not maintain continual contact with the source document. Once a report or form is open and displaying a linked object, the object won't change until the link is updated. You can manually update the link using the OLE/DDE Links option of the Edit menu. The dialog box allows you to select a link or links to update and then click the Update Now button

Because the Linked check box was used in the import process, the Access report holds only a picture of the Word document. Updates to the document are made using Word and are reflected in the Access copy each time the link is updated. By default, the Update option of a linked object is set to Automatic, which will refresh the object each time it is opened.

Of course, if the Linked check box had been left unchecked, the Word document would have been embedded in the Access report. Embedding is the best option when the Access copy of the document needs to be manipulated independently of the Word version of the document. To experience the difference between manipulating a linked and an embedded object, the linked Word document will be deleted and reimported as an embedded object.

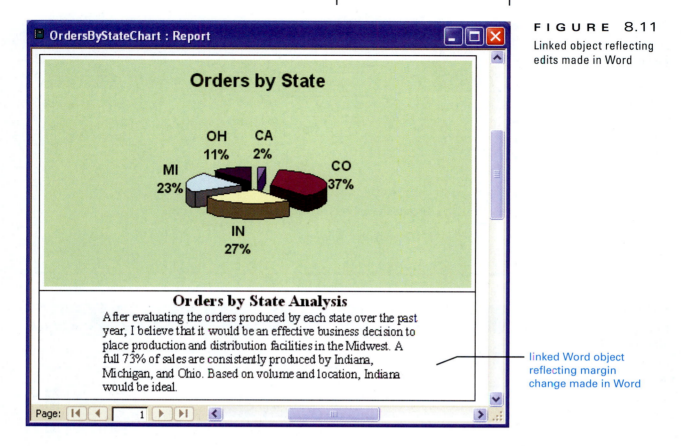

FIGURE 8.11
Linked object reflecting
edits made in Word

linked Word object
reflecting margin
change made in Word

Embedding a Word document in the OrdersByStateChart report:

1. Verify that Access is running with **ac08KoryoKicks.mdb** open with the OrdersByStateChart report in Design View

2. Click the Unbound Object Frame containing the Word document and press the Delete key

3. Select the **Unbound Object Frame** tool from the toolbox and then click and drag the area to contain the Word document

4. Click **Create from File**, navigate to **ac08OrdersAnalysis.doc**, uncheck the **Link** check box, and click **OK** (see Figure 8.12)

5. Size and reposition the object to resemble Figure 8.13 if needed

6. Double-click the object to initiate editing

7. Click the cursor after the period in the last line of text and press **Enter**

8. Type your full name and then use the toolbar to center the text

9. Click outside of the Unbound Object Frame object to end editing and save your changes

10. Save the report changes

ACCESS

FIGURE 8.12

Embedding a Word document

file type to be embedded

Link unchecked to embed

description of embed operation

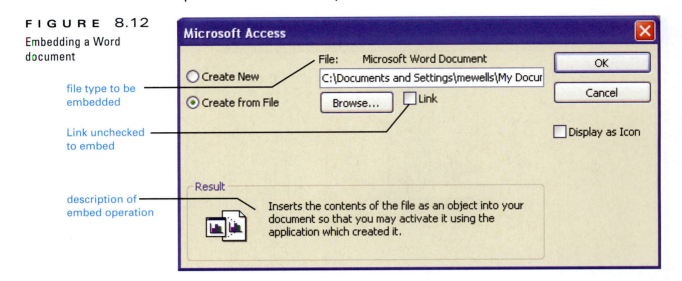

FIGURE 8.13

Editing an embedded Word document

border indicating that the object is being edited

ruler from Word

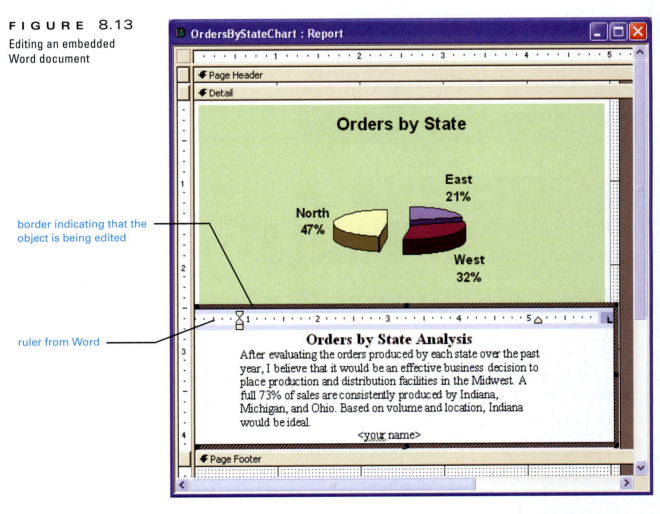

In the previous steps a *linked* Word document was edited using a full version of Word, indicating that there is only one copy of the document controlled by Word. In this set of steps, edits were performed on the same Word document that had been *embedded*. An Edit Window provided the same features as Word but indicated that this copy of the document is independently updated by Access. Let's take a look at the Word document to verify that the changes made to the embedded document did not impact it.

Verifying the status of the source Word document:

1. Click the **Start** button on the Taskbar, point to **Programs**, and select **Microsoft Word**

2. Use the Open button on the toolbar to open **ac08OrdersAnalysis.doc**

3. Notice that the margin changes applied to the linked document are saved. Your name, which was added to the embedded version of the document, is not part of the source but is retained in the OrdersByStateChart report

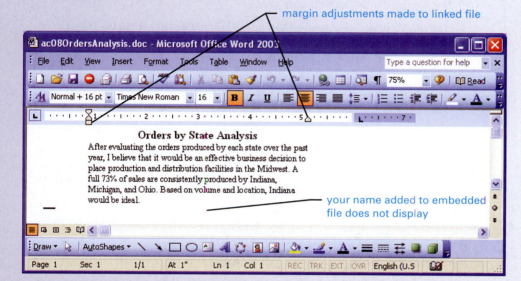

margin adjustments made to linked file

your name added to embedded file does not display

F I G U R E 8.14

ac08OrdersAnalysis.doc

4. Close Word

The same linking and embedding procedures demonstrated can be used to place objects on Access forms. Any OLE-compliant application can be imported. All of the Microsoft Office products support OLE, as do most applications developed by other vendors for the Windows environment.

Using Data from Another Access Database

Sometimes due to a design flaw or change in business practice, it is desirable to use data that are stored in multiple Access database files or in files maintained by another database program. In such cases the data tables can be imported into Access and treated like any other Access table, or linked so that they retain the properties of the original database and can be maintained in the source. The process is very similar to importing application objects, but the result is data that can be used like any native Access table.

Missy and Micah have created a NewCustomerContacts database used to create form letters in Microsoft Word. These letters introduced KoryoKicks products and services to new audiences with the goal of signing up new customers. The twins would like the table to be incorporated in the KoryoKicks database so they only have to worry about sharing one database file.

task reference — Import or Link to Another Access Database

- Open the Access database that is to contain the imported data
- Open the **File** menu, point to **Get External Data**, and then do one of the following:
  - Click **Import** to create Access tables from the external data
  - Click **Link Tables** to create links to tables that remain in the source location
- In the Import or Link dialog box
  - Use the Files of Type drop-down list to select **Microsoft Office Access (*.mdb, *.mda, *.mde)** as the type of file to be linked or imported
  - Use the Look in box to select the drive, folder, and filename of the file to be imported or linked
  - Select the import tables and click **Import**

Importing ac08NewCustomerContacts.mdb:

1. Verify that Access is open with the **ac08KoryoKicks.mdb** database open and no active object (table, query, form, report, etc.)

2. Activate the **File** menu, point to **Get External Data**, and click **Import**

3. From the Import dialog box select **ac08NewCustomerContacts.mdb** and click **Import**

tip: *Verify that the Files of type box will display Microsoft Access files for you to select from*

4. On the Tables tab of the Import Objects dialog box, select **Contacts** and click **OK**

F I G U R E 8.15

Import Objects options

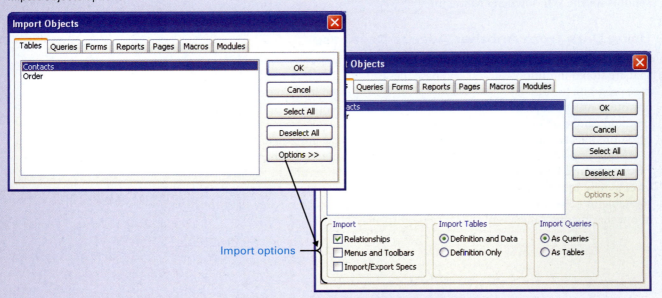

Import options

5. Open the **Contacts** table in Datasheet View to preview the data

6. Switch to Design View

7. Close the view

When importing data from another Access database, either both the table and its contents or just the definition can be imported, using the options shown in Figure 8.15. The Contacts table now belongs to the KoryoKicks database and you have full control over its design and contents. The original ac08NewCustomerContacts.mdb is not impacted by changes made in KoryoKicks.

The procedure for linking data is very similar to that used to import data. The twins want to evaluate the difference between embedding and linking the Contacts table so a linked copy needs to be created.

Linking ac08NewCustomerContacts.mdb:

1. Verify that Access is open with the **ac08KoryoKicks.mdb** database active with no open objects (tables, queries, forms, reports, etc.)

2. Activate the **File** menu, point to **Get External Data**, and click **Link Tables**

3. From the Link dialog box select **ac08NewCustomerContacts.mdb** and click **Link**

4. On the Tables tab of the Link Tables dialog box, select **Contacts** and click **OK**

5. Right-click on the linked copy and rename it **ContactsLinked**

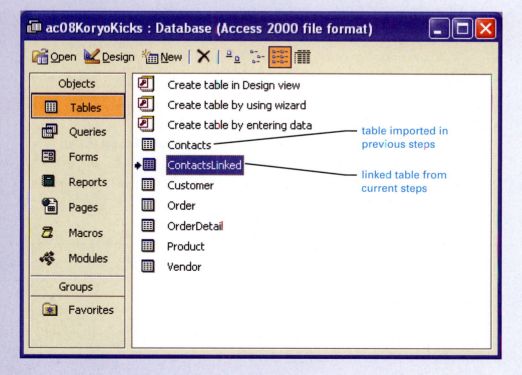

FIGURE 8.16

Imported and Linked Contacts tables

ACCESS

6. Open the ContactsLinked table in Datasheet View to preview the data

7. Switch to Design View

tip: *You will be notified that this is a linked table*

8. Close the view

For the most part, linked tables behave the same as any other Microsoft Access table. The icon to the left of the table name indicates that the table is linked and a dialog box is a reminder that much of the table design can't be modified outside the original database. Linked tables can be used to create queries, forms, and reports. No changes can be made to the design, but properties can be set to control local behavior.

Importing Data from Excel

Since Microsoft Excel is designed to store and analyze data, many users already have a great deal of valuable data stored in spreadsheet format before learning to use an Access database. The data stored in Excel do not need to be reentered because they can be imported and stored in a table for use in Access.

Imported Excel data can be either linked or embedded. Before beginning the process, it is important to make sure that the data in the spreadsheet are arranged appropriately into fields (columns) and records (rows). The twins have been trying to recruit new businesses to distribute for KoryoKicks products. They have been tracking these contacts in an Excel spreadsheet that should be incorporated in the KoryoKicks database.

task reference   Import or Link to an
                                      Excel Spreadsheet

- Open the Access database that is to contain the imported data

- Open the **File** menu, point to **Get External Data**, and then click **Import**

  - Click **Import** to create Access tables from the external data

  - Click **Link Tables** to create links to tables that remain in the source location

- In the Import or Link dialog box

  - Use the Files of Type drop-down list to select **Microsoft Excel (*.xls)** as the type of file to be linked or imported

  - Use the Look in box to select the drive, folder, and filename of the file to be imported or linked

  - Follow the Import Spreadsheet Wizard instructions

Importing ac08Importers.xls:

1. Verify that Access is open with the **ac08KoryoKicks.mdb** database active

2. Activate the **File** menu, point to **Get External Data**, and click **Import**

3. In the Import dialog box

   a. Use the Look in drop-down list to navigate to the folder containing your files

   b. Set Files of type to **Microsoft Excel (*.xls)**

   c. Select **ac08Importers.xls** and click **Import**

4. Verify that the Import Spreadsheet Wizard selections match those shown in Figure 8.17 and click **Next**

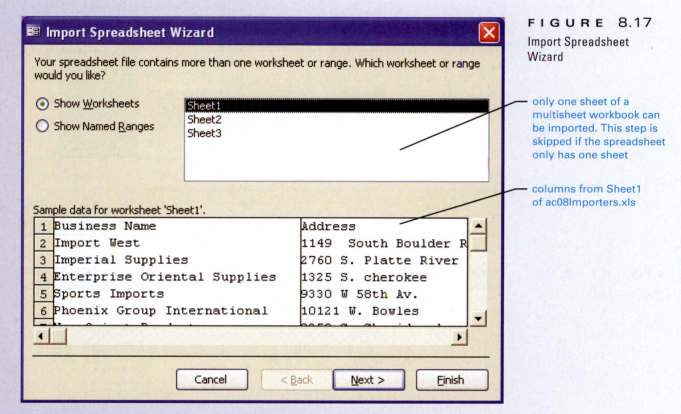

FIGURE 8.17

Import Spreadsheet Wizard

only one sheet of a multisheet workbook can be imported. This step is skipped if the spreadsheet only has one sheet

columns from Sheet1 of ac08Importers.xls

5. Check the **First Row Contains Column Headings** check box so that the Excel column headings will be used as Access field names and click **Next**

6. Verify that **In a New Table** is selected and click **Next**

7. Explore selecting fields to set their properties. Do not set any properties and click **Next** (see Figure 8.18)

8. Verify that **Let Access Add Primary Key** is selected so that Access will add an AutoNumber field to the table for a key and click **Next**

9. Name the table **Importers** and click **Finish**

10. Click **OK** in the Finished Importing message dialog box

11. Open Importers in Design View and change the data type of Contacted to **Yes/No** (see Figure 8.19)

12. Switch to Datasheet View, saving your changes. Close the datasheet when your review is complete

FIGURE 8.18
Setting Import Field Options

Options for selected field

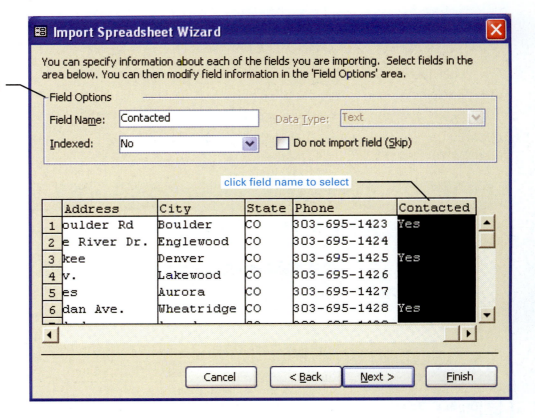

FIGURE 8.19
Importers table

Importers : Table

ID	Business Name	Address	City	State	Phone	Contacted
1	Import West	1149 South Boulder Rd	Boulder	CO	303-695-1423	☑
2	Imperial Supplies	2760 S. Platte River Dr.	Englewood	CO	303-695-1424	☐
3	Enterprise Oriental Supplies	1325 S. Cherokee	Denver	CO	303-695-1425	☑
4	Sports Imports	9330 W 58th Av.	Lakewood	CO	303-695-1426	☐
5	Phoenix Group International	10121 W. Bowles	Aurora	CO	303-695-1427	☐
6	New Orient Products	9359 S. Sheridan Ave.	Wheatridge	CO	303-695-1428	☑
7	Ready International Products	3224 Lowell Blvd.	Arvada	CO	303-695-1429	☐
8	Rocky Mountain Marketers	5083 E. Colfax Blvd.	Boulder	CO	303-695-1430	☑
9	Sequal Imports	1006 Wadsworth Blvd.	Englewood	CO	303-695-1431	☐
10	Tailor Made International	4943 W 72 Ave.	Denver	CO	303-695-1432	☑
11	United Wholesale Network	270348 E. Iliff Ave.	Lakewood	CO	303-708-8060	☑

Record: 15 of 28

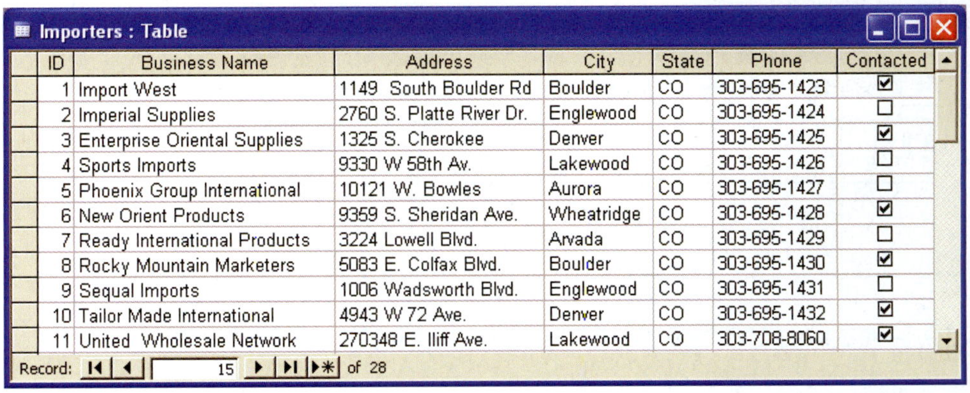

The import options control whether all of the data from a spreadsheet are retrieved or only data in a named range of cells. Spreadsheet data can be used to create a new table or append to the data already in an existing table. To successfully append the data to an existing table, the spreadsheet column headings must match the Access field names exactly.

Access assigns data types to the import fields based on their content. It is important to review data types and other field properties before using the imported table.

Retrieving Data from Other Applications

Besides being able to import data from most other Office System products, Microsoft Access can accept a variety of other file formats including Lotus 1-2-3, Text files, HTML, Paradox, XML, and dBase. The process to import or link these file types is the same as that used for Excel since each file type can be selected from the Look in box of the Import or Link dialog box. Each file format has a Wizard to provide instruction on the conversion process. Paradox and dBase require special drivers that are provided by Microsoft Technical Support if the native software is not locally installed.

If data to be imported are not in one of the supported file formats, try to use the source application to save it in a supported file format. Almost every database and spreadsheet has the ability to save comma delimited text files that can then be imported by Access. For example, a Microsoft Works database cannot be directly imported into Microsoft Access. Works can save the database as a comma delimited text file that can be imported.

Regardless of the file type being imported, the data must be stored in a format that can be recognized as fields and records. For example, HTML tables can be effectively imported, but lists are less successful. Access Help has extensive information on importing from supported file types that will be helpful if you ever need to perform these tasks.

Exporting Data

Access also has the ability to export database objects to other file formats. While Access has powerful data storage and retrieval capabilities, other applications provide better analytical and formatting capabilities. For example, Access is the ideal tool for gathering sales data, but Excel would be a better choice for using those data to create a model used to forecast future sales.

help yourself *Use the Type a Question combo box to improve your understanding of how to export data by typing* **export**. *Review the contents of* About exporting data and database objects *and* Export data or database objects. *Close the Help window when you are finished*

Organizations often use different database programs that may need to share data. The different programs can be the result of varying needs across the organization or simply a matter of preference. Regardless of why data for the same organization are stored in multiple formats, Access's import and export capabilities usually can facilitate sharing data. Most other database software packages support similar import and export features.

Sharing Access Data with Word-Processing Applications

Although Microsoft Access data can be shared with virtually any word-processing application, this discussion will focus on Microsoft Word since it provides the simplest and cleanest integration.

Data from a Microsoft Access table can be used in conjunction with Word Mail Merge to create form letters based on data stored in a table or query. This process can use an existing Word document, or create a new merge document if it does not exist.

The second sharing method uses the formatting and publishing capabilities of Word to enhance Access output. The output of any Access datasheet, form, or report can be exported in Rich Text Format (.rtf) that can then be opened and manipulated with Word or any word processor supporting the format. The Rich Text Format preserves fonts, styles, and other formatting.

The twins would like to use the ProductByState Crosstab Query results as a table in a Word document that they are preparing. You will export it for them.

<table>
<tr><td colspan="2">task reference</td><td align="right">Export an Access Object
to Microsoft Word</td></tr>
</table>

- Open the Access database with the object to be exported
- Select the object to be exported in the Database Window (it is best to preview the object before exporting)
- Open the **Tools** menu, point to **Office Links**, and then either
  - Select **Merge It with Microsoft Word** to use an Access table or query as the data source for a Word merge document
  or
  - Select **Publish It with Microsoft Word** to create an .rtf file in the default database folder (usually C:\My Documents or the folder containing the database) with the same name as the exported object

Exporting ProductByStateCrosstab.rtf:

1. Verify that Access is open with the **ac08KoryoKicks.mdb** database active

2. In the Database Window select the **Queries** object and open **ProductByStateCrosstab**

3. Activate the **Tools** menu, point to **Office Links**, and click **Publish It with Microsoft Word**

FIGURE 8.20

ProductByStateCrosstab.rtf

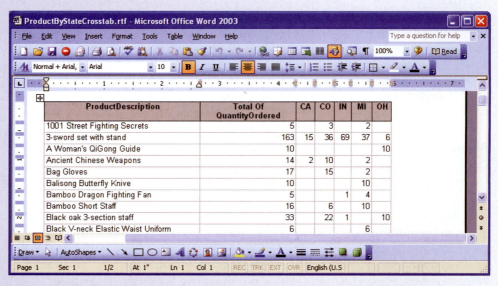

4. Add your name to the Word document as a centered header and save it to your homework folder.

tip: *Use the Header and Footer selection from the View menu*

5. Close Word

When the Office Tools option of the Tools menu is used to export an Access object, Word automatically opens with the exported file displaying. With the document open,

Word has full access to it with formatting capabilities that are far superior to those provided by Access. Word supports multicolumn reporting, drop cap text formatting, borders, graphics, and sectioning to apply differing formats to various report components. Word also can be used to create a report based on multiple Access outputs by combining exported data into one document.

Finally, to output a .txt file or control the folder and name of the file, use the Export option of the File menu. The Export To dialog box contains options used to select a folder, filename, and output format for the object being exported. Both .rtf and .txt files can be opened by most word-processing applications. An .rtf file retains formatting while a .txt file does not.

Exporting Access Data to Spreadsheet Applications

Microsoft Access database objects also can be exported to a number of spreadsheet file formats. Spreadsheets enhance datasheet formatting options and provide greater analytical capabilities than Access. Microsoft Excel or any of the other supported spreadsheet file formats can provide modeling, forecasting, what-if analysis, and charting capabilities that greatly exceed those available in Access.

The simplest way to apply Excel features to an Access object is to use the Office Links option of the Tools menu just demonstrated to export a word-processing file. Missy and Micah would like to perform what-if analysis on the orders data generated by the OrderData query.

---

task reference　　　　Export an Access Object
　　　　　　　　　　　　　to an Excel Spreadsheet

- Open the Access database that contains the data to be exported

- Select the object to be exported in the Database Window (it is best to preview the object before exporting)

- Open the **Tools** menu, point to **Office Links**, and then click **Analyze It with Microsoft Excel**

Exporting OrderData.xls:

1. Verify that Access is open with the **ac08KoryoKicks.mdb** database active

2. In the Database Window select the **Queries** object and open **OrderData**

3. Activate the **Tools** menu, point to **Office Links**, and click **Analyze It with Microsoft Excel** (see Figure 8.21)

4. Add your name to the Excel worksheet in cell F1 and save it in your homework folder

---

When the Office Tools option of the Tools menu is used to export an Access object to Excel, Excel automatically opens with the exported file displaying. The exported file will normally be saved in either C:\My Documents or the folder containing the database. The name of the exported object is used as the filename. The OrderData.xls file can now be modified like any native Excel file. The .xls file is not linked to Access and will not reflect database updates.

FIGURE 8.21

OrderData.xls

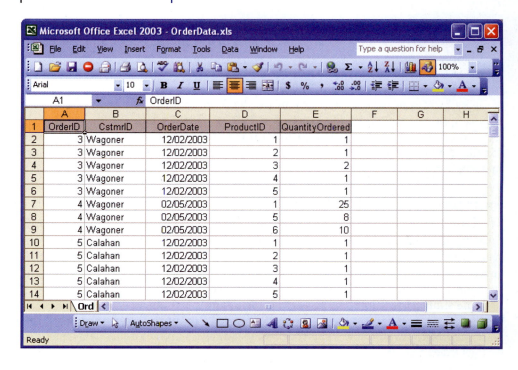

To output a spreadsheet format other than Excel or control the folder and name of the file, use the Export option of the File menu. The Export To dialog box provides options to select a folder, filename, and output format for the object being exported. Older versions of Excel, Lotus 1-2-3, dBase, and Paradox selections are available from the Save As type drop-down list. The non-Excel options require conversion software that is not included in the typical Access install.

SESSION 8.1

making *the grade*

1. How are the Chart Wizard and Microsoft Graph related?

2. What is a source application?

3. How do you determine whether to link or embed an object?

4. Why is a chart type important?

SESSION 8.2 WEB PUBLICATION

Access Web technology tools are designed for sharing data, queries, forms, and reports generated from Access using an intranet or the Internet. Access provides an array of Web publication methodologies to meet the differing needs of organizations.

Reviewing Web Technologies

The *World Wide Web (WWW)*, or simply the Web, is an international network of linked documents that share a common computer network called the *Internet*. Each computer on the network can be located by a unique address called a *Uniform Resource Locator (URL)*. These computers are called *Web Servers* because they run server software that allows a web of linked documents to be viewed using a *Web browser*. Web pages also can be delivered over private networks called *intranets* to share documents within an organization or using both Internet and intranet technology called an *extranet*.

F I G U R E 8.22

An HTML example

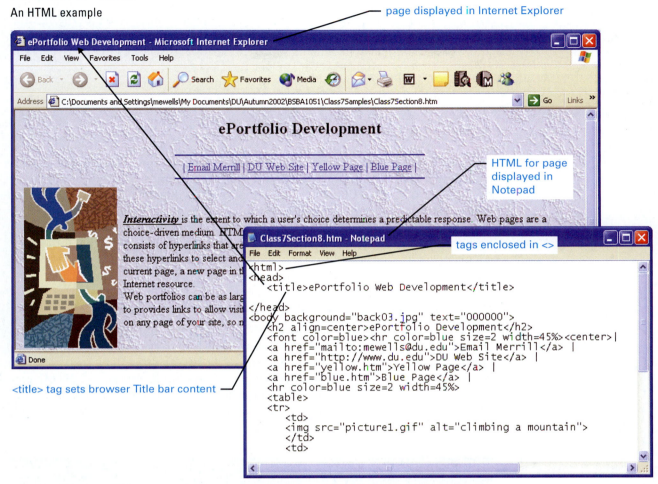

People who use the Web from work are typically provided continual access through a local server. Most home users who use the Web are not continuously connected to the Internet but, typically, a phone or other type of cable is used to connect to an **Internet Service Provider**, a company that sells the use of its Internet Servers to individuals and businesses.

Regardless of whether the documents are on the Internet, an intranet, or an extranet, they can be viewed using a Web browser such as Microsoft Internet Explorer or Netscape Navigator. **Hypertext Markup Language (HTML)** is used to provide instructions to the Web browser outlining how to deliver the page content. HTML instructions are enclosed in <> and are called **tags**. As its name implies, HTML was developed to deliver text but it has been expanded to deliver graphics and multimedia content as well. HTML tags set fonts, colors, position, and other formatting characteristics of text. Tags also control what graphic file displays and what other document is opened when a **hyperlink** is clicked. Hyperlinks define the paths between Web documents and typically display in a different color than nonlinked text. (See Figure 8.22.)

Figure 8.22 shows an example of a Web page documenting a physics lab assignment created with Office products. The table of data and chart were created in Excel and exported to Word, where the explanatory text was added, and then the page was saved as Filtered HTML (filtering removes Office-specific tags added by the generator). The document was submitted for grading by placing it on the school's intranet. Notice the tags enclosed in <> brackets and the relationship between the <title> tag and the Internet Explorer Title bar. While this type of conversion is fast and relatively painless, it may not provide the most efficient HTML code or fastest Web page load times.

Building HTML Pages

The preferred method of creating HTML pages with new content is to type the tags and text of a page into a basic text editor like Notepad and save the file with an .htm (or .html) extension. When the content for a page already exists, it can be converted by any Office application and many other applications.

Most Web pages are static; that is, their content does not change. Dynamic Web pages contain data that are updated to reflect the current status of something such as the price of a stock. Microsoft Access has the ability to create both *static Web pages* and *dynamic Web pages* based on database objects.

Static Web pages created from an Access object cannot be updated from a browser, and changes made to the data after the static page was generated are not reflected. The content of a dynamic Web page is updated each time that page is viewed so that it reflects the current status of the object. Certain types of dynamic Web pages will allow users to update the Access database object using a Web browser.

KoryoKicks will need both static and dynamic Web pages to support sharing information between geographically dispersed locations. Objects from the KoryoKicks database will be converted to HTML and stored on a Web server where they can be viewed and sometimes updated using a Web browser.

Creating a Static HTML Document

The simplest Web pages to generate are static—those that do not update as the data change and cannot be modified by Web users. Static Web pages can be generated from tables, queries, forms, or reports in an existing Access database. Tables, queries, and forms will display as datasheets on the Web page. Reports will appear with HTML versions of the page formatting, which does not always provide ideal conversions. Static Web pages can be viewed using any current Web browser and are best for data that change infrequently.

---

task *reference*   Export an Access Object
                                          to a Static HTML Page

- Open the Access database that contains the data to be exported
- Select the object to be exported in the Database Window (it is best to preview the object before exporting)
- Open the **File** menu and click **Export**
- In the Export To dialog box
  - Use the Save In box to select the drive and folder for the Web page
  - Set the Save As Type to **HTML Documents (*.html; *.htm)**
  - In the File Name box, enter the name for the Web page (it is best not to use spaces in these names)
  - **Save Formatted** should be clicked to retain the formatting applied to the datasheet in Access and activate the next two options
    - Check **AutoStart** to display the page in your default browser
    - In the HTML Output Options dialog box
    - Apply an HTML template to standardize formatting (Optional)
    - Click **OK**

Exporting Importers.html:

1. Verify that Access is open with the **ac08KoryoKicks.mdb** database active

2. In the Database Window select the **Tables** object and open **Importers**

3. Activate the **File** menu and click **Export**

4. In the Export Table Importers To dialog box

   a. Set the Save In drive and folder
   b. Set the Save As box to **HTML Documents (*.html; *.htm)**
   c. Check **Save Formatted**, **AutoStart**, and then click **Export All**

5. In the HTML Output Options dialog box click **OK** (see Figure 8.23)

the display of Netscape and
other browsers will vary slightly

F I G U R E 8.23

Importers.html displayed
in Internet Explorer

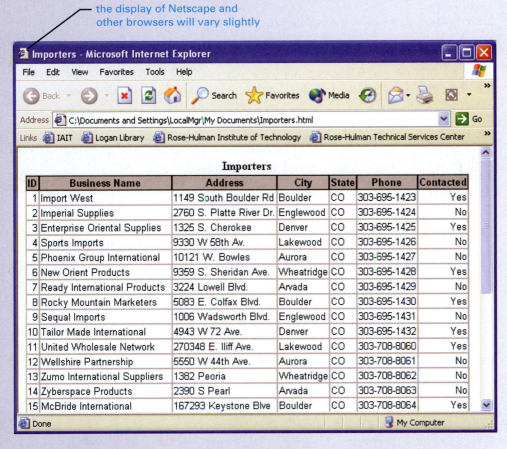

6. If your browser is Internet Explorer, click **View** and **Source** to review the HTML code for the generated page

7. Close Notepad

8. Close the browser window

Once a static Web page is built, it can be edited outside of Access using Notepad or any other text editor to add links, create additional content, or modify the design. Most browsers have an option on the File menu that will allow a local drive file to be opened so changes can be reviewed.

To make manual changes, update the HTML code in the editor software, save the file, and then refresh the browser screen to see the impact. When the page is complete, it can be loaded into a folder on a Web server where it can be accessed via the Internet. The URL used to retrieve a Web page that has been placed on a Web server is the WebServerAddress+ path+filename.

The process for creating static HTML pages from queries, forms, and reports is the same, but the result is slightly different. An Access report creates one HTML file for each printed page of the report numbered sequentially. The CustomersByState-Chart report would create CustomersByState-Chart.html, CustomersByState-ChartPage2.html, CustomersByState-ChartPage3.html, and so on. OLE objects stored in a database, including most graphics, do not display on the HTML page but they can be added manually or using a template file.

Using Access to View and Update an HTML Page

Microsoft Access Web tools integrate well with those of other Microsoft products. The Access Web toolbar is very similar to the Microsoft Internet Explorer toolbar and allows users to modify and view Access-based Web pages without leaving the Access interface. If Microsoft Internet Explorer is not the default browser, you will not be able to complete these steps.

---

task reference   **Use Internet Explorer to View a Static HTML Page**

- Open Access
- From the **View** menu, pause over **Toolbars** and then click **Web**
- On the Web toolbar, drop down the **Go** list and select **Open Hyperlink**
- Click the **Browse** button in the Open Internet Address dialog box
- Use the Browse dialog box to navigate to the file to be viewed
- Select the file and click **Open**
- Click **OK**

Using the Access Web toolbar to view Importers.html:

1. Verify that Access is open

2. Open the **View** menu, point to **Toolbars**, and select **Web**

3. Drop down the **Go** list on the Web toolbar and click **Open Hyperlink**

4. Click the **Browse** button in the Open Internet Address dialog box (see Figure 8.24)

5. Use the Browse dialog box to select the drive and folder containing Importers.html and double-click **Importers.html**

6. Click **OK**

browse to the drive and path for your files

FIGURE 8.24
Open Internet Address
dialog box

7. The page opens in its own browser window. Click **View** and **Source** to review the HTML code for the generated page

8. In the first few lines find the <CAPTION><B>Importers</B></CAPTION> and edit it to be **Importers - your name** (see Figure 8.25)

tip: *Be sure to edit only text between <CAPTION><B> and <\B></CAPTION>*

9. Use the File menu to Save and then close Notepad

10. Use the Refresh button of Internet Explorer to update the browser view

FIGURE 8.25
Importers.html edited

11. Close the browser window and the Importers table

Static HTML pages must be reexported to display updated data. Each time a page is regenerated, any customizations such as added text, graphics, or navigation will need to be reapplied. Because recustomizing is tedious and prone to error, it is a good idea to create HTML templates. An HTML template is a file that contains HTML instructions for creating a Web page and can include text, graphics, and navigation. When a template is applied, Access will place its content based on the instructions, and the remainder of the page is not impacted. In the Export process the HTML Output Options dialog box has an option to specify a template.

Creating Data Access Pages

Data Access Pages are built using Dynamic HTML and can be viewed only in browsers supporting that technology (Internet Explorer 5.0 and above). Data Access Pages consist of an exported HTML page and a new database object that links the HTML file to a database object. Because this connection is maintained, Data Access Pages can be used to view, edit, update, delete, filter, group, and sort live data in the database using a Web browser. Data Access Pages also can contain components from spreadsheets, Pivot tables, or charts.

help yourself *Use the Type a Question combo box to improve your understanding of the Web page options available from Access database by typing* **about web pages**. *Review the contents of* About data access pages. *Close the Help window when you are finished*

Displaying Data and Reports

To make Data Access Pages available from the Internet, publish the HTML pages to a Web server. The Access database supporting the pages also must be made available to page users. The best security is provided by placing the HTML pages and the database on the same server. It is a good idea to place the database on a shared server before you create Data Access Pages. Moving the database after pages are created will cause the connection between the database and the HTML page to be interrupted.

task reference   Use the Page Wizard to Create a Data Access Page

- Open the database containing the data for the Data Access Page
- Click the **Pages** object in the Database Window
- Double-click **Create data access page by using wizard**
- Follow the Wizard instructions

Using the Page Wizard to create ImportersDataAccess.htm:

1. Verify that Access is running with **ac08KoryoKicks.mdb** open
2. Click the **Pages** object in the Database Window
3. Double-click **Create data access page by using wizard**
4. Select the **Importers** table and move all of the fields to the Selected Fields list and click **Next** (see Figure 8.26)
5. Click **Next** without setting any grouping
6. Choose **BusinessName** for the ascending sort and click **Next**
7. Click **Finish** (see Figure 8.27)
8. Click in the Title placeholder and type **Importers by Business Name**

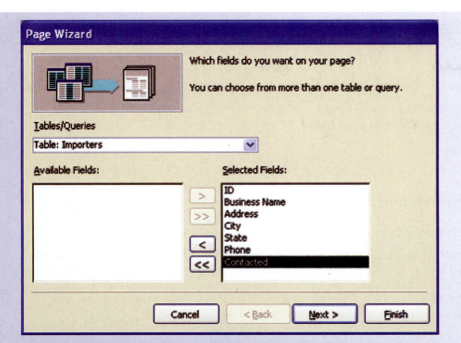

FIGURE 8.26
The Page Wizard

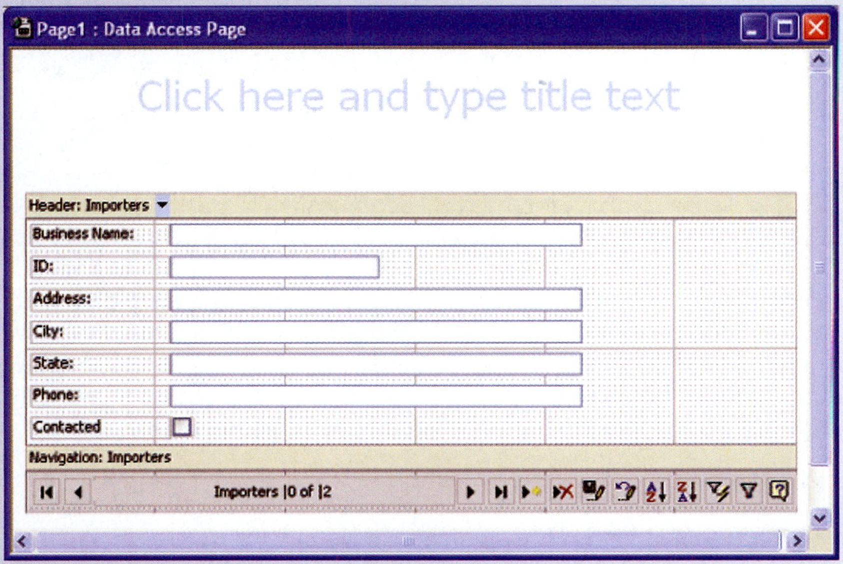

FIGURE 8.27
Data Access Page Design View

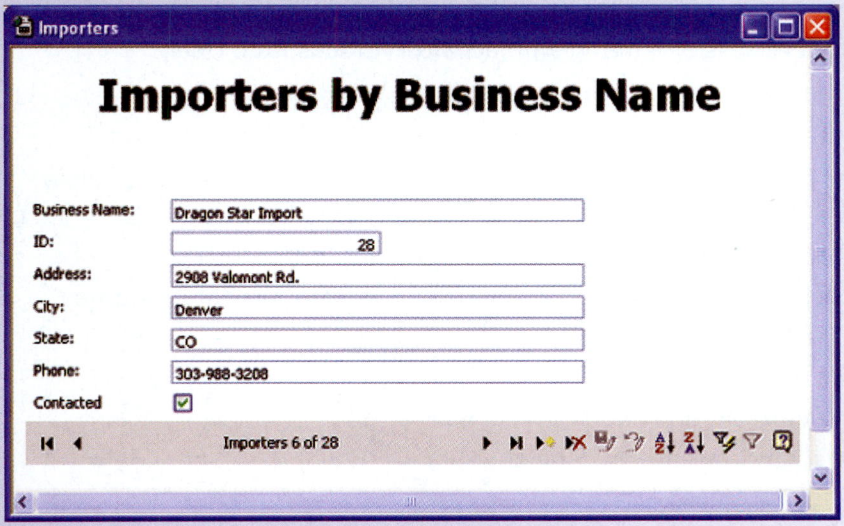

FIGURE 8.28
Data Access Page in the browser

tip: *If the Title placeholder is not visible, click in the header area*

9. Click the View [⊞ ▾] button

10. Use the navigation bar to move through the records (see Figure 8.28)

11. Close the browser window, saving the page as
    ImportersDataAccess.htm

12. Click **OK**

---

*another*way

. . . to Create a Data Access Page

Access provides several options for creating a Data Access Page. The steps have
covered using the Page Wizard, but a page also can be created from scratch in
Design View, created from an existing page, or created in a columnar format.
Select the Pages object in the Database Window and click New to activate the
New Access Data Page with all of the page creation options.

* Design View—Create a new page without using a Wizard

* Existing Web Page—Use an existing Web page to create a Data Access Page

* Page Wizard—Automatically generate a page based on your field selections.
  You also can specify grouping and sorting options

* AutoPage—Columnar—Creates a default page based on your table or query
  selection.

You cannot specify fields, grouping, or sorting

The Importers Data Access Page has an appearance similar to a form displaying
one record at a time. In the browser, the ***Record Navigation toolbar*** is used to move
from record to record, add new records, delete records, edit records, and sort and filter
data. Most of the buttons should be familiar because they appear on other Access toolbars. Screen tips will display for each button when the cursor pauses over it.

Adding scrolling text to
ImportersDataAccess.html:

1. Verify that Access is running with **ac08KoryoKicks.mdb** open

2. Select the **Pages** object from the Database Window

3. Select the **ImportedDataAccess** Page and click the **Design** button

4. Click the **Scrolling Text** [▦] tool in the toolbox and drag the area below
   the Record Navigation toolbar on the Data Access Page (see Figure 8.29)

5. Select the default Marquee text and type your name

6. Right-click on the Scrolling Text object and select Element Properties

   a. Set Background Color to silver
   b. Close the Properties dialog box

7. Click the **View** button (see Figure 8.30)

8. Close the window and save the changes

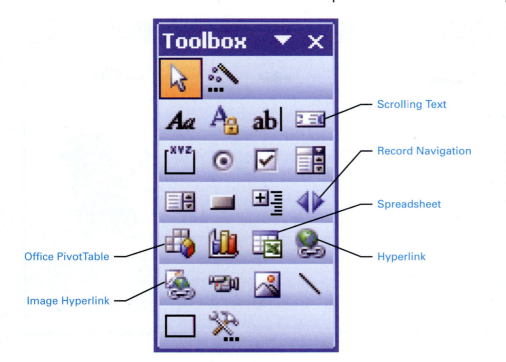

FIGURE 8.29
Data Access Page Design
View toolbox

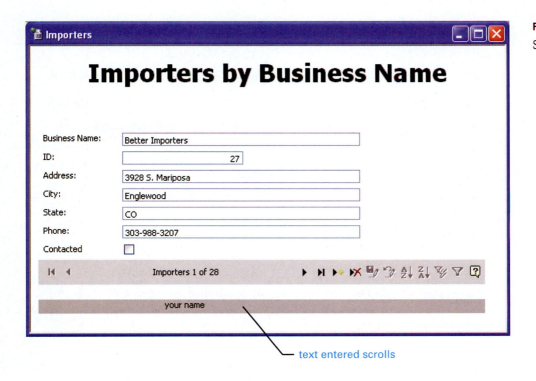

FIGURE 8.30
Scrolling text

Making edits in the Design View of a Data Access Page is very similar to updating a form or report. Notice that some of the toolbox buttons are specific to Data Access Pages. The most important differences are noted in Figure 8.29.

ACCESS

FIGURE 8.31

Adding an image to a Data Access Page

Importers

Importers by Business Name

ac08Warrior.gif added to an Image control

Business Name:	Better Importers
ID:	27
Address:	3928 S. Mariposa
City:	Englewood
State:	CO
Phone:	303-988-3207
Contacted	☐

Importers 1 of 28

your name

Adding an Image to ImportersDataAccess.htm:

1. Verify that Access is running with **ac08KoryoKicks.mdb** open

2. Select the **Pages** object from the Database Window

3. Select the **ImportersDataAccess** Page and click the **Design** button

4. Click the **Image** tool in the toolbox and drag the area shown in Figure 8.31

5. Navigate to the files for this chapter and select **ac08Warrior.gif**

6. Click the **View** button

7. Close the window and save the changes

8. Use Windows Explorer to view the files in the ImportersDataAccess_Files folder

9. Close Windows Explorer

Access provides artistic themes that can be applied to pages for visual impact. Themes are available from the Format menu and can be changed at any time without impacting the presentation.

Applying a Theme to ImportersDataAccess.htm:

1. Verify that Access is running with **ac08KoryoKicks.mdb** open

2. Select the **Pages** object from the Database Window

3. Select the **ImportersDataAccess** Page and click the **Design** button

4. Open the **Format** menu and select **Theme**

5. Click through the available themes to preview them

6. Select **Sandstone** and click **OK** (see Figure 8.32)

7. Click the **View** button to see the page results

8. Click the Save button and then close the window

FIGURE 8.32

Applying a theme

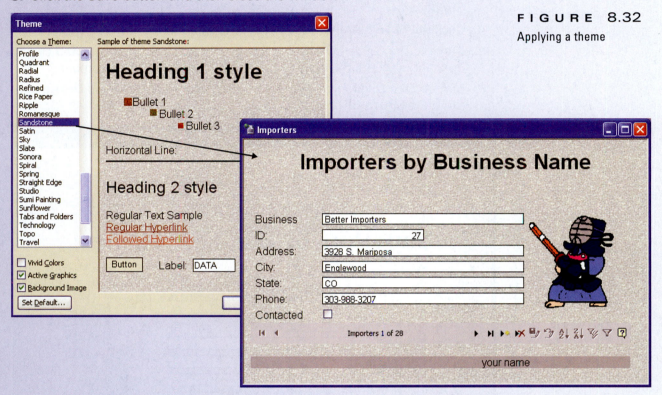

Any bullets, backgrounds, or graphics displayed in a Data Access Page are stored in a folder that must be moved with the Data Access Page. The folder will carry the name of your page with an underscore and the word Files. So the supporting files for ImportersDataAccess are stored in a folder named ImportersDataAccess_Files. The folder should contain an .xml file with references to the other objects on the page and the .gif file containing the image. The remaining files were generated by the theme applied.

Allowing Database Access

When Data Access Pages, the supporting files, and the database have been properly loaded on a shared server, live database data can be updated. The process is similar to using a form to update data in an open Access database, but is accomplished from a browser.

Updating the database using ImportersDataAccess.htm:

1. Close Access if it is open

2. Use Windows Explorer to navigate to the **ImportersDataAccess.htm** file and double-click to open it

ACCESS

tip: *The icon for this file incorporates both the Web page and Access icons. If Internet Explorer is not your default browser, you will need to open IE and use the File menu to open ImportersDataAccess.htm. You cannot accomplish these steps with a browser that doesn't support Data Access technology*

3. Move to record 2 and edit the business name to read **Tao Asian Supplies**

4. Click the **Save** button on the Record Navigation toolbar

5. Move to the Golden Orient Products record, check the **Contacted** check box, and click the **Save** button on the Record Navigation toolbar

6. Move to the Diversified Women's Center record and use the **Delete** button on the Record Navigation toolbar to delete it

FIGURE 8.33
Saving edits

7. Answer **Yes** when notified that the delete cannot be undone

8. Use the New button on the Record Navigation toolbar to add a new importer to the list named **<yourname>Imports**. Make up the remaining data. Do not leave any fields blank

9. Use the Save button or move to the previous record to save the change

10. Close Internet Explorer

11. Open **ac08KoryoKicks.mdb** and review the updates that have been applied to the Importers table

For demonstration purposes, the steps in this topic are using local files that are not stored on a shared server. Using a Web browser to update a database through a Data Access Page will work the same way from an intranet or the Internet as it did with these local files.

Because Data Access Pages are based on live data, sorts and filters can be used to control the order of records and what records display. These features work from the Record Navigation toolbar when viewing a page in the browser.

Sorting and filtering ImportersDataAccess.htm:

1. Close Access if it is open

2. Use Windows Explorer to navigate to the **ImportersDataAccess.htm** file and double-click to open it

tip: *If your default browser is not Internet Explorer, you will need to open IE and use the File menu to open this file*

3. Click in the **City** field and then click the **Sort Descending** button on the Record Navigation toolbar

4. Move through the records to verify the sort

5. Click in the **Business Name** field and then click **Sort Ascending** button on the Record Navigation toolbar to return those data to their original order

6. Select the city **Englewood** and then click the **Filter By Selection** button on the Record Navigation toolbar

FIGURE 8.34

Filter by Selection

5 records with Englewood filter applied

Filter by Selection button

Filter Toggle button—removes/applies current filter

7. Use the **Filter Toggle button** on the Record Navigation toolbar to remove and then reapply the filter

8. Close the Internet Explorer Window

Filter by Selection is the only filtering methodology available from a browser. Remember that Filter by Selection supports partial-field filtering but not multiple-field filtering. Selecting the first character of a field retrieves all records starting with that character. Selecting any other character in a field will return all records containing that character.

Repairing Links to Data Access Pages

Data Access Pages allow access to the live database data by maintaining a link between the Data Access Web page and the database. Moving or renaming either the database or the Data Access Web page can cause this link to be invalid. Moving the Data Access Web page without its associated data folder (pagename-field) can also damage this link.

To avoid Data Access Pages that are no longer connected to an active database, place the database on the shared intranet or Internet server before creating the pages. For the most consistent results, the Data Access Pages should be placed on the same server as the database. When the link between a database and its Data Access Pages is destroyed, follow the instructions in the next Task Reference to repair it.

---

task reference   Repair Broken Data
                                       Access Page Links

- Open the Data Access Page with a broken database link in Design View
- Click **Update Link** in the informational dialog box
  - Navigate to the network folder containing the Data Access Page
  - Select the page and click **OK**
  - Click **OK** in the dialog box explaining that the connection needs to be repaired
- On the right-hand side of the Data Access Page Design View, click the **Page connection properties** option in the Field List Window
  - On the Connection tab, click the ellipsis (…) and update the database name
  - Click **Open**
  - Click the **Test Connection** button
  - When the test works, click **OK**
  - Click **OK** again to end the update

Importing an HTML Document as an Access Table

A fundamental concept of database storage is that data should be entered and validated only once. After valid data are stored, they should always be used from that validated source. This principle reduces errors and is more efficient than reentering data each time a new data storage or evaluation technology is needed.

Building an Access Table from a Web Page

To support this concept, Access can use and incorporate data from sources outside itself. Since the World Wide Web is a great informational resource, one of the formats that Access can interpret is HTML. When Web page data are compiled as a table or list, they can be directly converted to an Access table.

Missy and Micah have used Web search utilities to locate Web merchants selling martial arts supplies. Their goal is to research and contact these companies as potential distributors of KoryoKicks products. After the page resulting from the search was saved, it was edited in Notepad to remove the unneeded page components such as the search engine and logo. Now the data retrieved can be loaded directly into an Access table.

task reference	Importing an HTML Document as an Access Table

- Open the database to hold the imported table
- Verify that the layout of the data to be imported is either a list or a table
- On the **File** menu, point to **Get External Data**, and then click **Import**
- Select the HTML file for import and click **Import** (be sure to set the Files of Type to HTML documents)
- Complete the Wizard dialog boxes

Importing WebImporters.htm as an Access table:

1. Verify that Access is running with **ac08KoryoKicks.mdb** open
2. Use Internet Explorer to preview ac08WebImporters.htm

tip: On the Web toolbar in Access click **Go**, then **Open Hyperlink**, and then **Browse**

3. Close the Internet Explorer window
4. On the Access **File** menu, point to **Get External Data**, and then click **Import**
5. In the Import dialog box
   a. Set Files of Type to **HTML Documents (*.html; .htm)**
   b. Navigate to the drive and folder containing files for this chapter, select **ac08WebImporters.htm**, and click **Import**
6. In the Import Wizard (see Figure 8.35)
   a. Click **First Row Contains Column Headings** and then click **Next**
   b. Click **Next** to save the HTML import in a new table
   c. Change the Merchants data type to **Hyperlink** and the Description data type to **Memo**, and click **Next**

tip: You may need to scroll to find these fields

   d. Click **Next** to let Access assign a primary key
   e. Type **WebImporters** in the Import to Table box and click **Finish**
7. Click **OK** to the Import Complete message

The WebImporters table has successfully been created from the modified HTML document. You should also see an _ImportError table. This table contains a record for each improperly imported row that Access detected. The most common import problem occurs when the data are longer than the field can hold and are truncated in the import process.

FIGURE 8.35

The Import HTML Wizard

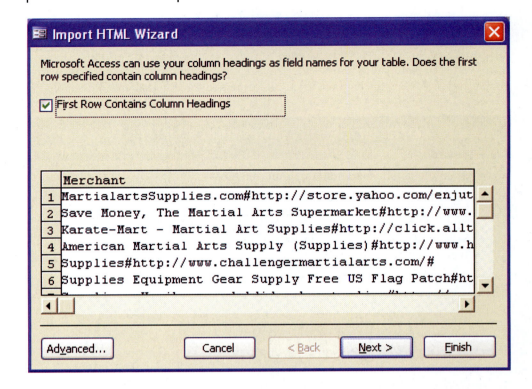

Confirming the import:

1. Verify that Access is running with **ac08KoryoKicks.mdb** open

2. Click the **Tables** object in the Database Window

3. Double-click the **WebImporters** table to open it and confirm the import

4. Double-click the column button border for each field to adjust its width

FIGURE 8.36

WebImporters table

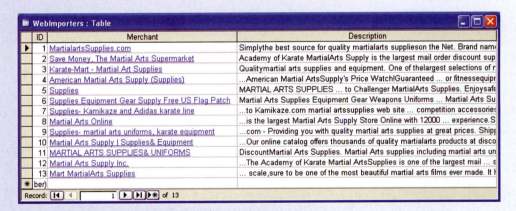

5. Close the window and save your changes

6. Double-click **Martial Arts Supplies ImportError** to evaluate any import issues (see Figure 8.37)

7. Review the errors and close the window

The import errors encountered in this case are in the second field, the hyperlink to the importers. The links that were truncated will need to be repaired. Additionally, the text in the memo field has some spacing problems, but overall the conversion is good.

Martial arts supplies
__ImportErrors table

	Error	Field	Row
▶	Field Truncation	F1	4
	Field Truncation	F2	5
	Field Truncation	F2	6
	Field Truncation	F2	7
	Field Truncation	F2	8
	Field Truncation	F2	9
	Field Truncation	F2	10
	Field Truncation	F2	11
	Field Truncation	F2	12
	Field Truncation	F2	13
	Field Truncation	F2	14
*			

Record: |◀ ◀   1   ▶ ▶|

F I G U R E 8.38

Hyperlink address

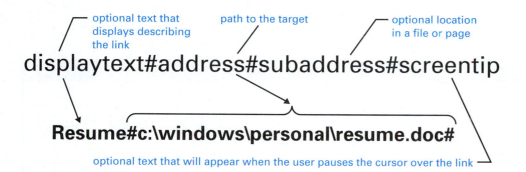

optional text that displays describing the link

path to the target

optional location in a file or page

displaytext#address#subaddress#screentip

Resume#c:\windows\personal\resume.doc#

optional text that will appear when the user pauses the cursor over the link

Constructing World Wide Web Hyperlinks

Most people associate hyperlinks with Web pages, but since they are really pointers from one object to another object, they can be used to link to pictures, e-mail addresses, or files. The hyperlink itself can display as text or a clickable image.

Hyperlinks can be used to navigate to another file, open another Web page, send an e-mail message, or start a file transfer (FTP). When pointing to text or a picture that contains a hyperlink, the pointer becomes a hand, indicating that it is something that can be clicked. When a hyperlink is clicked, the destination is displayed, opened, or run, depending on the type of destination. For example, a hyperlink to a sound file opens the file in a media player, and a hyperlink to a Web page displays the page in the Web browser.

Access provides a dialog box with the component parts of a hyperlink address (see Figure 8.38). Each address can have up to four parts separated by the number sign (#), but only the address is required.

In an Access table setting the data type of a field to hyperlink allows users to enter any type of a link into the field. When the user enters more than the required address component of a hyperlink, only the display text is visible. This is also true of a text box that is formatted to display hyperlinks. In either case, to see the rest of the entry, click in a cell and press F2.

The error table for WebImporters indicates that there are potential problems with the hyperlink for record and several Description field truncations. We will ignore Description truncations but test and repair each hyperlink. To review and repair these

ACCESS

links, the correct URL for the pages must be known. The twins have returned to the Internet and retrieved the correct addresses so that this import can be completed.

Entering and repairing a hyperlink in WebImporters:

1. Verify that Access is running with **ac08KoryoKicks.mdb** open

2. Click the **Tables** object in the Database Window and open **WebImporters** in Design View

3. Confirm that the Merchant field has a Data Type property of Hyperlink

4. Use the View button to switch to Datasheet View and pause the cursor over each hyperlink to preview its URL

5. For records 2, 3, and 6
   a. Right-click on the hyperlink, point to **Hyperlink**, and click **Edit Hyperlink**
   b. Review and edit the links
      i.   Record 2 does not need to be changed
      ii. Record 3 needs to have the address changed to www.Karate-mart.com (Access will add the protocol http://)
      iii. Record 6 needs an address of www.allblackbelt.com

FIGURE 8.39

Editing Hyperlinks

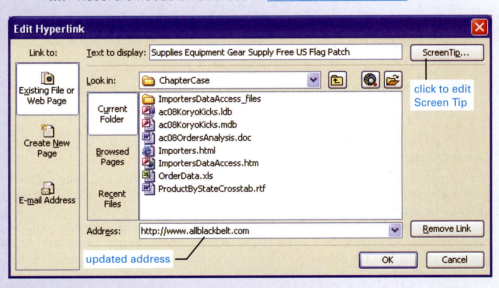

6. Click in the Merchant column of the new record row and click the **Insert Hyperlink** button on the Standard toolbar

7. In the Insert Hyperlink dialog box: (see Figure 8.40)
   a. Enter **KoryoKicks** as the Display text
   b. Click the ScreenTip button, enter **KoryoKicks**, and click **OK**
   c. Navigate to **ac08KoryoKicksHome.html**, select it, and click **OK**

tip: *This file is with the other files for this chapter, not on the Internet*

8. Click the KoryoKicks link—it should open the skeleton of a new home page

9. Add text describing KoryoKicks to the Description field and close the view

The address to a destination object can be either absolute or relative. An **absolute address** is said to be fully qualified because it includes all of the information needed to find an object including the protocol (http, ftp, …), the server address, the path, and the filename. A **relative address** omits some of the address components. When components are omitted, they default to the values of the source object (the object containing the hyperlink). For example if the source document http://www.microsoft.com/index/htm contains a link samples.htm, the source protocol (http) and address (www.microsoft.com) are used to determine the full address of the destination, http://www.microsoft.com/samples.htm.

Absolute addresses do not function when files are moved to a new location. Relative addresses will function after files are moved, as long as they are still in the same relative locations (the folders and filenames remain the same).

FIGURE 8.40

Adding the KoryoKicks hyperlink

Adding a hyperlink to ImportersDataAccess:

1. Verify that Access is running with **ac08KoryoKicks.mdb** open

2. Click the **Pages** object in the Database Window and Open **ImportersDataAccess** in Design View

3. Click the **Label** 🔤 tool in the toolbox

   a. Click and drag the area shown in Figure 8.41 below the name marquee

FIGURE 8.41

Hyperlink added to ImportersDataAccess

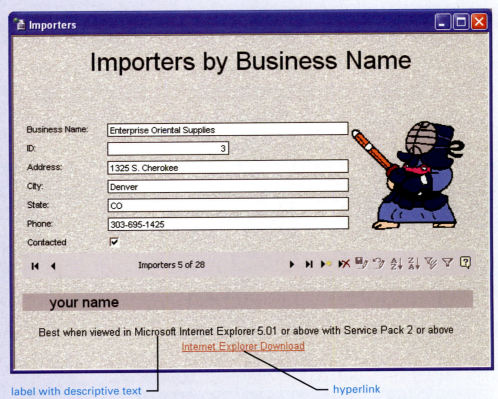

label with descriptive text ┘   └ hyperlink

   b. Click in the label and type **Best when viewed in Microsoft Internet Explorer 5.01 with Service Pack 2 or above**

4. Click the **Hyperlink** 🖼 tool in the toolbox

   a. Click and drag the area shown in Figure 8.41 below the label just created, making it the width of the page
   b. In the Text to display box type **Internet Explorer Download**
   c. Click the ScreenTip button, type **Newest IE Version!**, and click **OK**
   d. In the address type www.microsoft.com
   e. Click **OK**

5. Change the label and Hyperlink text to 10-point and center align both

6. Click the View button to preview the page

7. Close the window, saving the changes

When adding a hyperlink to a Data Access Page, a special Hyperlink control is used. Forms and reports do not have a Hyperlink control, but use labels with the hyperlink information entered into the properties of the label. To test the hyperlink on the ImportersDataAccess Page, you switched to Page View and clicked the link. When testing a hyperlink stored in a label on a form or report, right-click the label, point to Hyperlink, and then click Open.

Take another look at the Insert Hyperlink dialog box (Figure 8.40) and note the similarities to a standard Open dialog box. Notice also that it contains items specific to locating a file for a hyperlink. The Link to options are used to define the type of link Access should create. We have created links using Existing File or Web Page, but there are also options to link to a Page in This Database, Create New Page, and E-mail Address. The HTML syntax for each of these options is unique, but the process to create them in Access is the same.

The Look In options are used to search the Current Folder, which works like a standard Open File dialog box. Browsed Pages, which will list Internet Explorer's browsing history, also can be used to select a Web address, or Recent Files can be used to easily link to a file that was recently opened.

The twins are now satisfied that they understand the import, export, and Web capabilities of Access. They believe that they will help immensely in managing and sharing data in a distributed organization. They will evaluate and begin implementing these features when their business plan is complete.

---

making *the grade*

1. What is the difference between a static HTML page and a Data Access Page?

2. Why are relative and absolute addresses important?

3. How is the data content of a static Web page updated?

4. What is the Record Navigation toolbar?

SESSION 8.3 SUMMARY

Sharing data is important in reducing data entry and saving time. Allowing multiple applications to have access to the same data allows users to apply the best formatting and analytical tools available in every situation. Access can import data from external sources such as Word, Excel, or another database. Embedded objects belong to the Access database while linked objects remain under the control of their source program.

The Chart Wizard uses Microsoft Graph to create graphs based on numeric data stored in a table. There are a number of chart types that can be created including bar, pie, column, and line. A global chart reflects summaries from all of the table data, while a record-bound chart is based on a single record. Once created, charts can be modified to display other chart types, contain explanatory text, and customize each chart component.

The Access Tools menu contains an Office Links option that automates data sharing with Microsoft Word and Excel. The Export option of the File menu can be used to export other file types such as .txt, HTML, or Paradox. HTML pages created from using the Export menu are static.

Dynamic Web pages called Data Access Pages are created using the Pages object in the Database Window. An HTML page that can be used to interact with live data is created along with a database object that maintains the connection between the database and the HTML page. Creating and editing a Data Access Page is very similar to the Design View of an Access form or report. The Data Access Design toolbar contains controls specifically designed for creating Web pages such as the Scrolling Text control and the Hyperlink control. Data Access Pages work best with Microsoft Internet Explorer 5.01 with Service Pack 2 or above.

MICROSOFT OFFICE SPECIALIST OBJECTIVES SUMMARY

- Create a Data Access Page—AC03S-1-12
- Import data to Access—AC03S-2-3
- Export data from Access—AC03S-4-4

making the grade *answers*

SESSION 8.1

1. The Chart Wizard walks you through creating a chart using Microsoft Graph. Microsoft Graph is used to edit an existing chart.

2. The source application is the software that originated a linked or embedded object.

3. Embedded objects are a copy of the original that can be edited independently. Linked objects are just a picture and should be used when you want only one copy of a file.

4. The chart type controls how the data are plotted. Chart types include bar, pie, column, and radial.

SESSION 8.2

1. Static HTML pages cannot be used to update a database and so are not browser specific. Data Access Pages allow database updates and require specific browser technology.

2. Hyperlinks use addresses to point to another object. Absolute addresses contain all of the components while relative addresses omit some components. The missing components are assigned the values of the current page.

3. Static Web pages do not maintain any connection to the original data and so must be reexported to display updated data.

4. The Record Navigation toolbar displays on a Data Access Page and is used to edit, filter, and move through displayed records.

task reference *summary*

Task	Page #	Preferred Method
Create a Microsoft Graph	AC 8.4	• Click the **Reports** object in the Database Window • Click **New** to activate the New Report dialog box • Select **Chart Wizard**, use the drop-down list to select the query or table containing the data to be charted, and then click **OK** to initiate the Chart Wizard • Follow the instructions to select the field(s) with the data to be charted, select the chart type, specify the layout, and add a chart title

Importing with an unbound object frame on a form or report	AC 8.11	• Open the Design View of the form or report to contain the imported object
		• Click the **Unbound Object Frame** tool in the toolbox
		• Click and drag the area on the form or report that will contain the object
		• In the Microsoft Access dialog box
		  • Click **Create From File**
		  • Browse to the file for import
		  • Click the Link check box to create a linked object or leave it unclicked to create an embedded object
		  • Click **OK**

task reference summary

Task	Page #	Preferred Method
Import or link to another Access database	AC 8.16	• Open the Access database that is to contain the imported data • Open the **File** menu, point to **Get External Data**, and then do one of the following: • Click **Import** to create Access tables from the external data • Click **Link Tables** to create links to tables that remain in the source location • In the Import or Link dialog box • Use the Files of Type drop-down list to select **Microsoft Office Access (*.mdb, *.mda, *.mde)** as the type of file to be linked or imported • Use the Look in box to select the drive, folder, and filename of the file to be imported or linked • Select the import tables and click **Import**
Import or link to an Excel spreadsheet	AC 8.18	• Open the Access database that is to contain the imported data • Open the **File** menu, point to **Get External Data**, and then click **Import** • Click **Import** to create Access tables from the external data • Click **Link Tables** to create links to tables that remain in the source location • In the Import or Link dialog box • Use the Files of Type drop-down list to select **Microsoft Excel (*.xls)** as the type of file to be linked or imported • Use the Look in box to select the drive, folder, and filename of the file to be imported or linked • Follow the Import Spreadsheet Wizard instructions
Export an Access object to Microsoft Word	AC 8.22	• Open the Access database with the object to be exported • Select the object to be exported in the Database Window (it is best to preview the object before exporting) • Open the **Tools** menu, point to **Office Links**, and then either • Select **Merge It with Microsoft Word** to use an Access table or query as the data source for a Word merge document or • Select **Publish It with Microsoft Word** to create an .rtf file in the default database folder (usually C:\ My Documents or the folder containing the database) with the same name as the exported object
Export an Access object to an Excel spreadsheet	AC 8.23	• Open the Access database that contains the data to be exported • Select the object to be exported in the Database Window (it is best to preview the object before exporting) • Open the **Tools** menu, point to **Office Links**, and then click **Analyze It with Microsoft Excel**
Export an Access object to a static HTML page	AC 8.26	• Open the Access database that contains the data to be exported • Select the object to be exported in the Database Window (it is best to preview the object before exporting) • Open the **File** menu and click **Export** • In the Export To dialog box • Use the Save In box to select the drive and folder for the Web page • Set the Save As Type to **HTML Documents (*.html; *.htm)** • In the File Name box, enter the name for the Web page (it is best not to use spaces in these names) • **Save Formatted** should be clicked to retain the formatting applied to the datasheet in Access and activate the next two options • Check **AutoStart** to display the page in your default browser • In the HTML Output Options dialog box • Apply an HTML template to standardize formatting (Optional) • Click **OK**
Use Internet Explorer to view a static HTML page	AC 8.28	• Open Access • From the **View** menu, pause over **Toolbars** and then click **Web** • On the Web toolbar, drop down the **Go** list and select **Open Hyperlink**

ACCESS

task reference *summary*

Task	Page #	Preferred Method
		• Click the **Browse** button in the Open Internet Address dialog box • Use the Browse dialog box to navigate to the file to be viewed • Select the file and click **Open** • Click **OK**
Use the Page Wizard to create a Data Access Page	AC 8.30	• Open the database containing the data for the Data Access Page • Click the **Pages** object in the Database Window • Double-click **Create data access page by using wizard** • Follow the Wizard instructions
Repair broken Data Access Page links	AC 8.38	• Open the Data Access Page with a broken database link in Design View • Click **Update Link** in the informational dialog box • Navigate to the network folder containing the Data Access Page • Select the page and click **OK** • Click **OK** in the dialog box explaining that the connection needs to be repaired • On the right-hand side of the Data Access Page Design View, click the **Page connection properties** option in the Field List Window • On the Connection tab, click the ellipsis (…) and update the database name • Click **Open** • Click the **Test Connection** button • When the test works, click **OK** • Click **OK** again to end the update
Importing an HTML document as an Access table	AC 8.39	• Open the database to hold the imported table • Verify that the layout of the data to be imported is either a list or a table • On the **File** menu, point to **Get External Data**, and then click **Import** • Select the HTML file for import and click **Import** (be sure to set the Files of Type to HTML documents) • Complete the Wizard dialog boxes
Construct a Web page or file hyperlink	AC 8.43	• Open the form, report, or Data Access Page in Design View • Click the Insert Hyperlink 🖳 button in the toolbox and drag the display area on the form, report, or Data Access Page • In the Insert Hyperlink dialog box • Select the type of object to **Link to** (Existing File or Web Page, Object in This Database, Create New Page, or E-Mail Address) • Enter the **Text to display** for the hyperlink (if this is blank, the URL will display) • Enter the **Screen Tip text** (if this is blank, the URL displays when the user pauses the cursor over the link) • In the Address box, type or browse to the path of a file or a URL • Click **OK**

TRUE/FALSE

1. A chart based on all the data in a table is called a record-bound chart.

2. A pie chart is best suited for showing how several series of data change over time.

3. Linked data must be edited in the application that created it.

4. Data imported from Microsoft Excel cannot contain column headings in the first row of the worksheet.

5. HTML tags instruct the Web browser on how to format page content and are enclosed in {}.

6. A URL is a pointer to an object such as a Web page, e-mail address, or other file.

FILL-IN

1. An _____ combines the technologies of an intranet and the Internet.

2. A company that sells the use of its Internet connection is a(n) _____.

3. _____ allow a database table to be updated from a Web browser.

4. HTML instructions are called _____.

5. An HTML _____ can be imported into Access as a table.

6. A Web page with content that doesn't change or link to the database is a(n) _____ Web page.

7. Saving Microsoft Access data to a format that can be used by another application such as Microsoft Word is called _____.

MULTIPLE CHOICE

1. When a Data Access Page is moved or renamed, the _____ to its Microsoft Access database must be updated.
   a. implied connection
   b. explicit connection
   c. relation
   d. link

2. Which of the following can be specified when creating a hyperlink in Microsoft Access?
   a. display text
   b. Screen Tip
   c. Web page address
   d. all of the above

3. Built-in artistic templates that can be applied to Data Access Pages are called _____.
   a. Themes
   b. Formats
   c. Encrypting
   d. none of the above

4. Data Access Pages allow database data to be viewed and updated using a(n) _____.
   a. plug in
   b. Microsoft Access player
   c. Web browser
   d. all of the above

5. A(n) _____ Web page does not change to reflect updates to the data stored in the associated Microsoft Access database.
   a. fixed
   b. static
   c. auto
   d. printed

REVIEW QUESTIONS

Each of the following topics should be addressed in one to three paragraphs.

1. Why would you use a template when creating Web pages from Access objects?

2. Why is the Access Web toolbar important?

3. Discuss the components of a hyperlink.

4. The address provided in a hyperlink specifies a protocol. What is this?

5. Why are the toolbox tools different for Data Access Pages and Reports?

CREATE THE QUESTION

For each of the following answers, create the question.

ANSWER	QUESTION
1. Import Wizard	_____
2. A column chart	_____
3. The legend	_____
4. Unbound Object Frame	_____
5. The linked check box	_____
6. OLE	_____
7. Destination application	_____

FACT OR FICTION

For each of the following, determine whether the statement is fact, fiction, or both and present your arguments for that conclusion.

1. Embedding an object is always the best option when you want to maintain only one copy of the object.

2. Object linking and embedding can be used to import and export all file formats.

3. Imported Excel data can be placed in an Access table or an Unbound Object Frame.

4. The Office Links feature is a simple way to share features of other Office products.

5. The Internet is the only way to share Access forms, reports, and data.

6. Once created and placed on a Data Access Page, the formatting of a chart cannot be updated.

7. A Record Navigation toolbar is used to allow users to move from record to record in a Data Access Page.

practice

1. Altamonte High School Booster Club Donation Tracking—Part V: Sharing Database Data

The Altamonte Boosters database has been successfully secured and data validation added to ensure data integrity. Now it is time to look at options for sharing data that do not impact security and integrity. The leadership believes that importing and exporting appropriate file formats will allow them to share data using e-mail attachments. The organization has a secured area on the school's Web server that can be used to share Web documents with authorized members.

1. Start Access and open **ac08AltamonteBoosters.mdb**

tip: *You cannot use your copy of the database from the previous chapter since there have been modifications for this chapter*

2. Use the Query Wizard to create a query that totals the donations made for each class of donor. These data will be charted
   a. From the **Boosters** table move the **DonationClass** field to the Selected Fields list
   b. From the **Donations** table move the **DonationAmount** field to the Selected Fields list
   c. From the **DonationClass** table move the **ClassDescription** field to the Selected Fields list
   d. Click **Next**

FIGURE 8.42

DonationsByClassChart

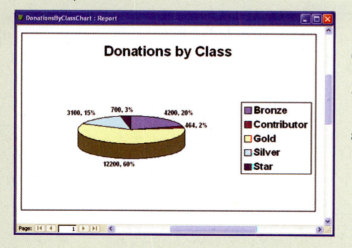

e. Select the **Summary** Option button and then use the Summary Options button to **Sum** DonationAmount
   f. Click **Next**
   g. Name the query **DonationsByClass** and click **Finish**
   h. Close the Query window after verifying the result

3. Select the Reports object from the Database Window
   a. Click the **New** button
   b. Select the **Chart Wizard**, select **DonationsByClass** as the data source, and click **OK**

4. In the Chart Wizard
   a. Select **ClassDescription** and **Sum of DonationAmount** as the fields for the chart and click **Next**
   b. Select **3-D Pie** as the chart type and then click **Next**
   c. Preview the chart and then click **Next**
   d. Title the chart **Donations by Class** and click **Finish** (see Figure 8.42)
   e. Double-click on the chart in Design View to open Microsoft Graph
      i. Right-click in the chart area (not on the pie itself) and select **Chart Options**
      ii. On the Data Labels tab check **Values** and **Percentage**
      iii. Click **OK**
   f. Enlarge the chart area by dragging a sizing handle to be 5 inches wide by 4 inches tall

5. Close and save the form, naming it **DonationsByClassChart**

6. Open the DonationsByClassChart in Report View to preview your work and then close it

7. Save the DonationsByClassChart as a static HTML page

8. Exit Access if your work is complete

2. ScaleModels.com—Part I: Charting Database Data

ScaleModels.com uses the Internet to sell scale models of classic cars. The storefront deals largely with American classics scaled to 1/18, 1/24, 1/42, or 1/64 actual size. Currently the Web site is being manually maintained, but since a product list is being developed in Microsoft Access, you have been asked to create prototype Data Access Pages that could be used instead. Owner Rico Juarez believes that Data Access Pages will improve customer service by allowing them to see what is actually in inventory and reduce the current overhead required to continually update static Web pages.

1. Start Access and open **ac08ScaleModels.mdb**

2. Use the Query Wizard to create a query that totals QtyOnHand by Make. These data will be charted

   a. Select **Make** and **QtyOnHand** from the Catalog table

   b. Click **Next**

   c. Select the **Summary** Option button and then use the Summary Options button to sum QtyOnHand and click **OK**

   d. Click **Next**

   e. Name the query **QtyOnHandByMake**

3. Select the Reports object from the Database Window

   a. Click the **New** button

   b. Select the Chart Wizard, select **QtyOnHandByMake** as the data source, and click **OK**

4. In the Chart Wizard

   a. Select all QtyOnHandByMake fields to be in the chart and click **Next**

   b. Select **3-D Pie** as the chart type and click **Next**

   c. Preview the chart and click **Next**

   d. Accept the default chart name by clicking Finish

5. Change to Report Design View and double-click on the chart to open Microsoft Graph

   a. Right-click in the chart area (not on the pie itself) and select **Chart Options**

   b. Edit the Chart Title to **Quantity on hand by Make**

   c. Use the Legend tab to turn off the legend display

   d. Use the Data Labels tab to display both the category name and value on each pie wedge

   e. Click **OK**

   f. Use the sizing handles to make the chart 5 inches wide by 3 inches tall

6. Click outside of the chart area to close Microsoft Graph and change to Report View to evaluate the results obtained

7. Return to Report Design View and double-click the chart to edit it

   a. Enlarge the chart area to 6.5 inches wide by 4 inches tall

   b. Double-click one of the data labels to open the Format Data Labels dialog box, and change the font size to 10-point

   c. Verify your updates in Report View (see Figure 8.43)

   d. Close the report saving it as **QtyOnHandByMake**

8. If your work is complete, exit Access; otherwise, continue to the next assignment

FIGURE 8.43

Quantity on Hand by Make chart

challenge!

1. Altamonte High School Booster Club Donation Tracking—Part VI: Exploring Alternatives for Sharing the Database

The Altamonte Boosters' fund-raising drive is complete and it is time to publish the results for the next meeting.

1. If you did not complete the Practice project for this chapter, start Access and open **ac08AltamonteBoosters.mdb** and complete it

tip: *You can use your copy of the database from the Practice project in this chapter. You cannot use your copy of the database from the previous chapter since there have been modifications for this chapter*

2. Review the chart created in the Practice steps and then open Microsoft Word and write a brief (3–4 line) summary of what the chart presents. Save the document as **ac08AltamonteSummary.doc**

3. Open the DonationsByClassChart report in Design View

   a. Enlarge the report by dragging the Detail and Page Footer borders

   b. Use an Unbound Object control to import (embed) ac08AltamonteSummary.doc and position it below the chart

   c. Double-click on the unbound object to enter edit mode and adjust the margins to the size of your form (see Figure 8.44)

tip: *You may need to enlarge the form to adjust the right margin and then reduce the size again*

   d. Preview your work, update as needed, and save

4. From the Pages object of the Database Window

   a. Use the Page Wizard to create a Data Access Page based on the Boosters table named **AltamonteBoosters**

   b. Include all fields from the Boosters table

   c. Sort by Name

   d. Make the title **Altamonte H. S. Boosters**

   e. Use the View button to preview the page (see Figure 8.45)

tip: *Select a DonationClass, then click the + to the left to view the boosters for that DonationClass*

   f. Use the AltamonteBoosters Data Access Page to add a record for **Pierre Verrizen** in DonationClass **3**. Supply the remaining data

5. Exit Access if your work is complete

FIGURE 8.44

Fund-raising chart and description from Word

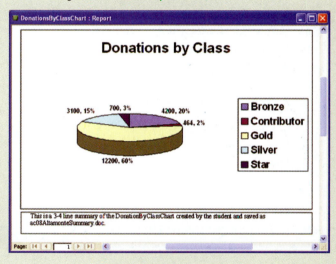

FIGURE 8.45

AltamonteBoosters Data Access Page

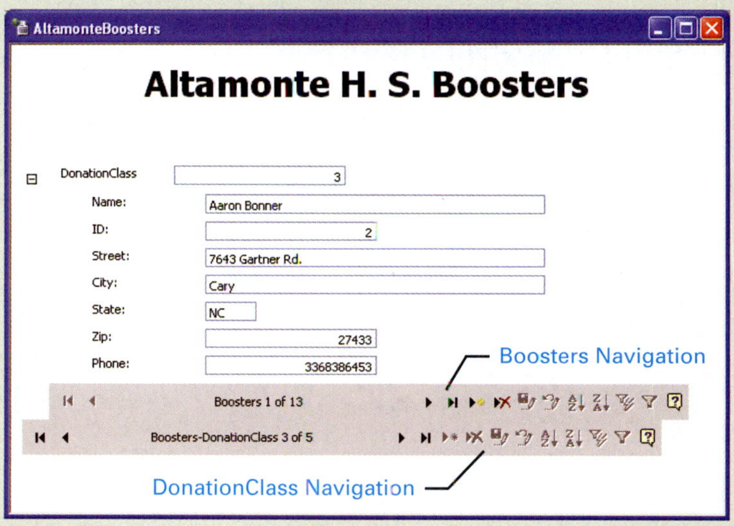

2. ScaleModels.com—Part II: Data Access Pages

Design of the ScaleModels.com database is complete, and it is time to evaluate the use of Data Access Pages to create interactive Web pages based on live data.

1. Start Access and open your copy of **ac08ScaleModels.mdb.** If you did not complete the ScaleModels.com Practice exercise for this chapter, do so now

2. Review the chart created in the Practice steps and then open Microsoft Word

   a. In Microsoft Word, write a brief description (3–4 lines) of what the chart represents

   b. Close Microsoft Word and save the document as **ac08ScaleModelSummary.doc**

3. In Microsoft Access, open the QtyOnHandByMake report in Design View

   a. Use an Unbound Object control to import (embed) ac08ScaleModelSummary.doc

   b. Double-click on the unbound object to enter edit mode and adjust the margins to the size of the form

   c. Preview your work, update as needed, and save

4. From the Pages object of the Database Window

   a. Use the Page Wizard to create a Data Access Page based on the Catalog table

   b. Include all fields for the Catalog table

   c. Group by Make and sort by Model

   d. Name the page **Catalog**

5. From the Design View of the Catalog Data Access Page

   a. Add a page title of **Scale Model Catalog**

   b. Use an Image control to insert **ac08ScaleModel.gif** to the left of the title

   c. Adjust the image size so that the title fits on one line

   d. Switch to Page View and test the Data Access Page by adding your favorite car to the table (see Figure 8.46)

6. From the Pages object of the Database Window

   a. Use the Page Wizard to create a Data Access Page based on the QtyOnHandByMake query

   b. Include all fields

   c. Group by Make

   d. Accept the default page name

   e. Add a title and the ac08ScaleModel.GIF image

   f. Switch between Page View and Design View making any necessary adjustments

   g. Close and save

7. If your work is complete, exit Access; otherwise, continue to the next assignment

FIGURE 8.46

Scale Model Catalog Data Access Page

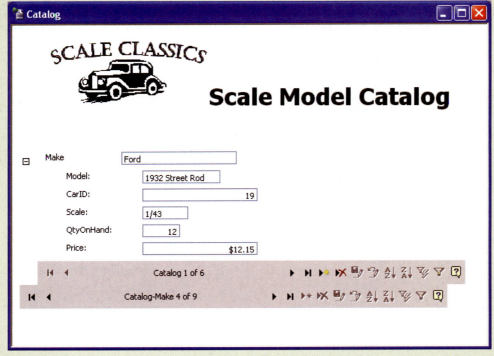

1. Curbside Recycling

Earth First, the parent company of Curbside Recycling, is sponsoring a recycling competition between the cities that it serves. The status of the competition will be posted on the Web site and the city that recycles the most will receive a donation earmarked for park renovation.

1. Start Access and open **ac08CurbsideRecycling.mdb**

tip: *You cannot use your copy of the database from the previous chapter since there have been modifications for this chapter*

2. Use the **Get External Data** option of the **File** menu to import **ac08Competition.xls**

tip: *Use Excel to preview this file before import*

   a. There are no headings in the file

   b. Import to a new table

   c. Name Field1 **City** and Field2 **TonsRecycled**

   d. Let Access set the key

   e. Name the table **Competition**

   f. Open Competition to verify the import and then close it

3. Create a Data Access Page with a chart based on the Competition table

   a. Click the **Pages** object in the database Window and open a new page in Design View

   b. Set the title to **Earth First Recycling Competition**

   c. Click the Office Chart tool in the toolbox and then click an area on the page surface that covers the width of the page

   d. Click the Office Chart to open the Commands and Options dialog box if necessary

   e. In the Commands and Options dialog box

      i. Click **Data from the following Web page item** and then click **DataSource Details** button

      ii. Select **Competition** from the Data member table, view, or cube name drop-down list

tip: *If you lose the Commands and Options dialog box, right-click on the chart*

      iii. Click the **Type** tab and select **Bar** and **3-D clustered**

      iv. Close the Commands and Options dialog box

   f. Use the Field List button on the Standard toolbar if you do not have a field list displaying

      i. Open the Competition field list using the +

      ii. Drag **City** to the Drop Category Field area of the chart

      iii. Drag **TonsRecycled** to the Drop Data Fields Here area of the chart

      iv. Save the Data Access page as **Competition**

   g. Adjust the chart height and width for readability

4. Open Competition in Internet Explorer

   a. Drop down the City list and uncheck one to see the chart result (see Figure 8.47)

   b. You can change the data in the Drop areas too

5. Exit Access if your work is complete

FIGURE 8.47

Internet Explorer with Competition Data Access Page

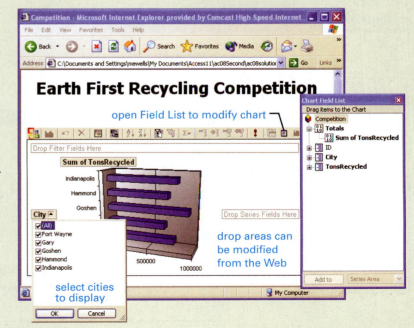

2. Sharing xXtreMeSportz.com Data

Casey Lewis, Evan Roach, and Wei Wong are extreme sports enthusiasts. They play hockey, skateboard, and snowboard. After discussing it with many of their friends the three decided to create a cooperative organization for extreme sports aficionados. The main goal of the co-op would be to act as a clearinghouse for equipment and events so that members would be able to purchase supplies, clothing, and event tickets at a bulk reduced rate.

After enlisting over 300 local members, the partners launched the www.xXtreMeSportz.com Web site to communicate their services and recruit additional members. Keeping the Web site updated with new services has become too time-consuming, so the partners have agreed to use Data Access Pages from a Microsoft Access database.

1. Open Access and then open **ac08xXtreMeSportz.mdb**

2. Current services are maintained in a Microsoft Excel spreadsheet named ac08xXtreMeSportzLinks.xls

   a. Use Excel to view the contents of this file

   b. Use the **Get External Data** option of the **File** menu to import the contents of this file into the **Links** table. The first row of the spreadsheet contains the Column Headings

   c. Verify the validity of the import

3. Use the Report Wizard to create a report based on the Links table

   a. Include all fields from the table except LinkID and Group by LinkCategory

   b. Customize the report to ensure that all Link data display. Set the Can Grow property of the Description text box to **Yes**

   c. Make the title **xXtreMeSportz.com Links**

   d. When you are satisfied, export the report as a static HTML page named **xXtreMeSportzLinks**

4. Use the Page Wizard to create a Data Access Page based on the Links table

   a. Include all table fields

   b. Group the data by LinkCategory

   c. Name the page **LinkUpdatePage**

5. Customize the LinkUpdatePage in Design View

   a. Set the title to **xXtreMeSportz Links Update**

   b. Use an Image control to insert a **ac08xXtreMeSportz.gif** to the left of the title

   c. Adjust the title and image so they display on one line

   d. Add the **Blends** theme

   e. Review your changes in Page View and make any needed updates (see Figure 8.48)

6. Close the database and exit Access if your work is complete

FIGURE 8.48

xXtreMeSportz.com Web pages

on the web

1. Academic Software

Academic Software is a fairly large organization with diverse data needs. In the past users have created the data that they needed to complete each job. Now that a functioning database is available, the goal is to use import, export, and Web capabilities to avoid re-creating data.

1. Use your favorite search engine to locate two foreign language software titles suitable for academic language study. Be sure to note the prices too

2. Start Access and open **ac08Software.mdb**

tip: *You cannot use your copy of the database from the previous chapter since there have been modifications for this chapter*

3. Several users have been tracking new software titles in an Excel spreadsheet. Use the import capabilities of Access to add these data to tblSoftware

   a. Open tblSoftware to view the existing 12 records

   b. Close tblSoftware

   c. Import **ac08SoftwareTitles.xls**

tip: *Open it in Excel first to review the content*

   i. The file does have column headings in the first row

   ii. Proceed with the import even if there are warnings

FIGURE 8.49

Software Data Access Page

d. Open tblSoftware to verify the addition of 12 records

tip: *Only 10 of the 12 records from Excel were imported because the other 2 records violate the validation rule set for Category (="MTH" Or ="ENG" Or ="SCI")*

   e. Add "LNG" to the validation rule and repeat the import

tip: *Duplicate key violations will keep the 10 records that imported the first time from being duplicated*

   f. Open tblSoftware, verify that the two LNG software titles have been added, and close the table

4. From the Pages object of the Database Window

   a. Use the Page Wizard to create a Data Access Page based on the tblSoftware table named **Software TitlesbyVendor**

   b. Include all fields from the tblSoftware table

   c. Sort by Name

   d. Make the title **Software Titles by Vendor**

   e. Apply the Technology theme

   f. Use the View button to preview the page (see Figure 8.49)

tip: *Select a VendorCode, then click the + to the left to view the titles for that vendor*

   g. Use the Software Data Access Page to add a record for the software titles located on the Internet. Add them to VendorCode **EI** with a Category of **LNG**

5. Exit Access if your work is complete

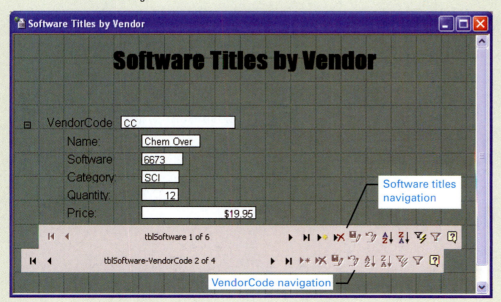

AC 8.57

hands-on projects

around the world

1. TechRocks Seminars

TechRocks Seminars is a worldwide organization with requirements to share data, analysis, and update capabilities. Management has decided to try using Data Access Pages to allow all of the sites to enter students into a class.

1. Start Access and open **ac08Seminars.mdb**

tip: *You cannot use your copy of the database from the previous chapter since there have been modifications for this chapter*

2. Activate the **Pages** object in the Database Window
   a. Activate the Page Wizard
   b. Set the **Enrollment** table as the data source and move all of its fields to the field list
   c. Group the data by **SeminarID**
   d. Sort by LastName and FirstName
   e. Name the page **Enrollment**

3. In the Design View of the Enrollment Data Access Page
   a. Make the page title **Seminar Enrollment**
   b. Use an Image control to add **ac08Seminars.gif** positioned as shown in Figure 8.50
   c. Add a scrolling text box the width of the page and below the data area with the text **New Class! Data Access Pages. Limited Enrollment**, and set the Font size to **Medium**

tip: *Right-click on the marquee and select* **Element Properties**

   d. Add the **Corporate** theme
   e. Adjust the height, width, and position of the contents to match Figure 8.50 and fully display the data

4. Open **Enrollment**
   a. Move to seminar TR105
   b. Move through the records and then add two new records for **Kate Whittey** and **Thomas Elliott**. Make up the remaining data

5. Create a Data Access Page from the StudentListing query
   a. Activate the Page Wizard and select **StudentListing** as the data source
   b. Use all of the StudentListing fields
   c. Group by **SeminarID**
   d. Sort by LastName and FirstName

6. Use Design View to customize the page
   a. Apply the **Corporate** theme
   b. Add spaces between words in labels
   c. Add the title **StudentListing** with **ac08Seminars.gif**
   d. Move Description, LastName, FirstName, Place, Phone, Date, Time, and Hours to the Student Listing-SeminarID header

7. Exit Access if your work is complete

FIGURE 8.50

Enrollment Data Access Page

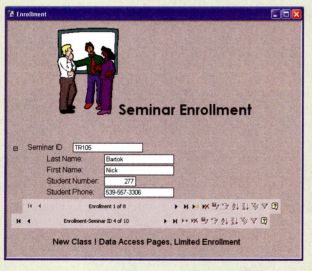

running project: tnt web design

Web Publishing from Access

TnT is continuing in its use of Access to gather and analyze data. It is time to develop the interfaces from the database to the Web site to provide current and accurate data and improve data sharing.

1. Start Access and open **ac08TnT.mdb**

tip: *You cannot use your copy of the database from the previous chapter since there have been modifications for this chapter*

2. Open the CustomerSites table and use the Hyperlink button on the Standard toolbar to update the following hyperlinks:
   a. MMB Holdings Site 1—Set the display text and Screen Tip to **MMB Holdings, Inc**. Remove the comma from the display text, and add the Address
   b. MMB Holdings Site 2—Set the display text and Screen Tip to **Your Holdings!** and add the address
   c. Omega Distributions—Set the display text and Screen Tip to **Omega Distributions** and add the address

tip: *While this process should be repeated for all of the links, for brevity we will just pretend that they are all displaying descriptive text and have addresses*

3. Export the CustomerSites table as a static Web page and then use Internet Explorer to review it. You should notice that the improperly entered hyperlinks display as text not links. The properly entered hyperlinks would work if the Web pages actually existed. This export has other problems we will not address (see Figure 8.51)

4. Export the EmployeesByJobClass report as a static Web page and then use Internet Explorer to review it. Notice that two HTML pages are created and that the navigation is automatically added to the bottom of each page. This is the public version of the report that cannot be updated

5. Create a Data Access Page based on the Employees table that will reside in a secure area of the intranet to update the Employees table
   a. Use all fields from the table
   b. Group by **JobClass** and sort by **LastName** and **FirstName**
   c. Check the **Apply theme** check box and then apply **Edge**
   d. Set the title to **Employees by Job Classification**
   e. Preview the result

6. Close Access if your work is complete

FIGURE 8.51

CustomerSites.html

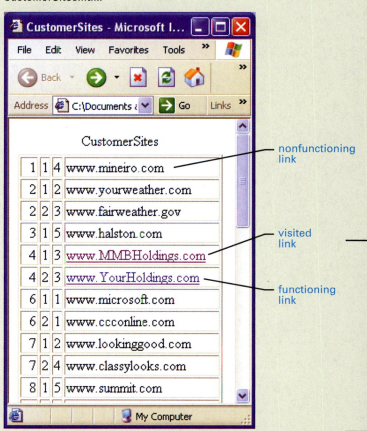

nonfunctioning link

visited link

functioning link

1. Sharing a Multitable Database to Invoice Customers

Locate your copy of the database named **ac07CustomersMultiTableDatabase.mdb** created in the Chapter 7 Analysis assignment. Use Microsoft Windows Explorer to create a copy of the file named **ac08CustomersMultiTableDatabase.mdb** and open the copy in Microsoft Access. Take a look at your current database objects and determine how to implement each of the following:

- Create a graph on a report page. Customize the graph to include a title and appropriate labels
- Embed data from either Microsoft Excel or Microsoft Word in the report
- Create a static HTML document from the report
- Create a Data Access Page with a title and image for at least one of your tables
- Include a hyperlink on your Data Access Page and apply a theme

2. Sharing a Multitable Database to Track Employees

Locate your copy of the database named **ac07EmployeesMultiTableDatabase.mdb** created in the Chapter 7 Analysis assignment. Use Microsoft Windows Explorer to create a copy of the file named **ac08EmployeesMultiTableDatabase.mdb** and open the copy in Microsoft Access. Take a look at your current database objects and determine how to implement each of the following:

- Create a graph on a report page. Customize the graph to include a title and appropriate labels
- Embed data from either Microsoft Excel or Microsoft Word in the report
- Create a static HTML document from the report
- Create a Data Access Page with a title and image for at least one of your tables
- Include a hyperlink on your Data Access Page and apply a theme

CHAPTER

nine

9

Using Queries to Analyze and Maintain Data

did you
know?

about *11 percent of murders in the United States are the result of domestic violence.*

an *adult elephant eats between 155 and 300 pounds of food each day.*

more *water flows over Niagara Falls every year than over any other falls on earth.*

anything *described as "saurian" is much like a lizard.*

the *first Rolls-Royce sold for $600.00 in 1906.*

to *find out how many grooves are on the edge of a quarter, visit* www.mhhe.com/i-series.

Chapter Objectives

- **Create and run parameter queries**
- **Create and run action queries**
- **Use Aggregate functions in queries**
- **Use SQL (Structured Query Language) to create and run simple queries to select records, join tables, and sort**
- **Build Find Duplicates and Find Unmatched queries to improve data integrity—MOS AC03S-1-7**
- **Construct a Self-join query to display data based on relationships within a table**

KoryoKicks: Data Analysis with SQL Queries

Like many first-time business owners, Missy and Micah Hampton had a marketable idea and launched their business without much thought about data storage and retrieval needs. As their business has grown, so too has their need for reliable and timely data. When there are only a few records in each database table, data are easily evaluated and maintained; but after several years of gathering data on products, suppliers, orders, payments, inventory, and every other aspect of business, databases become unwieldy. The KoryoKicks database contains three years of business data that need to be tailored to meet current business needs.

Storing table records that are not active slows the processing of records that are active. Although inactive records could be deleted, it is usually better to create an inactive or history table to hold such data. KoryoKicks' inactive customers should be placed in a CustomerHistory table to speed processing of the Customer table without losing valuable data. The twins will need to use an Append Query to select inactive records and add them to the history table.

To support changing business practices, data about products, suppliers, shippers, and other business relationships must be maintained. As the volume of data grows, simple data updates like raising product prices or changing a supplier can be very time-consuming and prone to error when each record must have the same change applied manually. Action queries are used to apply the

FIGURE 9.1

Using SQL to query KoryoKicks

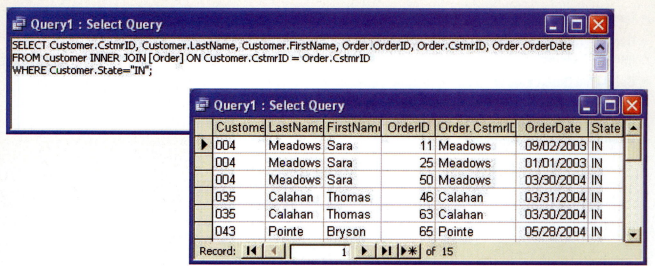

same change to multiple table rows simultaneously. The applied change can be to replace existing data with a new value (a new supplier of a class of raw material comprised of 30 inventoried items), update the existing value with an expression (raise prices for one product line by 5 percent), place data in a new table, or delete unused data. Action queries will be added to KoryoKicks to improve the likelihood that these mass changes are applied to all affected records.

The twins are looking into ways to improve the performance and consistency of data in the KoryoKicks database. Find Duplicate, Find Unmatched, and Top Values queries can all be used to evaluate the quality of the data contained in a database. Ensuring quality data is critical to effective business decisions. Finally, Missy and Micah want to understand how to use SQL to improve processing and save time maintaining existing queries.

SESSION 9.1 DESIGNING ADVANCED QUERIES

Select Queries, used to select and summarize data, provide the foundation for understanding and creating advanced queries. Advanced queries enhance the functionality and analytical capabilities provided by simple Select Queries. Crosstab Queries provide multidimensional calculations, *parameter queries* allow the user to enter unique select criteria each time the query is run, and *action queries* update multiple data selections simultaneously.

Developing a Crosstab Query

Crosstab Queries were introduced in Chapter 4 as a way to analyze data by restructuring them into groups based on two data fields. The values of one field are listed across the top of the query result, while the values of the second field are listed down the left-hand side. Retrieved data are summarized into the cells created by these two values using an aggregate function, such as Sum, Average, or Count.

Designing a Crosstab Query

Uncovering trends in vast quantities of data is one of the significant ways that businesses serve their customers better and gain a competitive edge. Figure 9.2 shows KoryoKicks data organized by product and state. This organization allows easy analysis of product performance in each state, which is valuable since consumer preferences vary across geographic regions. Such data could be used to determine which products to warehouse in a given state, what products salespeople should carry for demonstration purposes, or even where new facilities should be located.

Queries begin as a business problem. When a user outlines a business problem as a question, it is usually apparent how table data can be combined and organized to answer the question. For example, the question "What product sells best in each state?" tells the query designer that sales data must be organized by product and state using a Crosstab Query. Knowing that, the next step is to determine what data should appear across the top and down the left-hand side of the crosstab result. It is often a matter of

FIGURE 9.2

Crosstab Query example

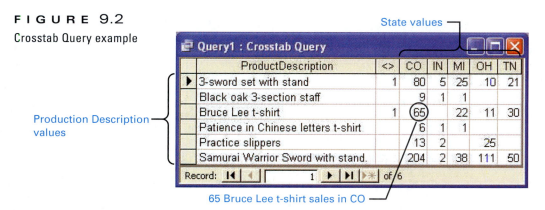

Production Description values

State values

65 Bruce Lee t-shirt sales in CO

user preference, but typically the table field with the fewest or narrowest data values is placed across the top of the crosstab result.

Finally, the appropriate summary function must be determined. It is not always obvious which summary function will best answer the question posed. In this case, Sum, Average, and Count could each be appropriate depending on how the user wants to measure sales and how the result will be applied. Sum of QuantityOrdered will outline the total number of each product ordered in each state that would be appropriate for determining how much product to produce. An average might be more appropriate to determine how much product to warehouse, while counting the number of orders would help determine how many people are needed to process orders in each state. Since Missy and Micah are evaluating alternative locations for facilities, an average is appropriate for the KoryoKicks data.

Once the layout of the query has been determined, it can be built using the Crosstab Query Wizard or from scratch in the query design grid. Both methods will be demonstrated.

Using the Crosstab Query Wizard:

1. Open the **ac09KoryoKicks.mdb** database

2. Select the **Queries** object from the Database Window

3. Click **New** to open the New Query dialog box

4. In the New Query dialog box, click **Crosstab Query Wizard** and select **OK**

5. Click the **Queries** option button, select the **CustomerStateJoin** query, and then click **Next**

6. Move **ProductDescription** to the Selected Fields category as the row heading and click **Next**

7. Select **State** as the column heading and then click **Next**

8. Select **QuantityOrdered** as the field, **Avg** as the function, uncheck **Yes, include row sums.**, and then click **Next**

9. Name the query **ProductByStateAvgCrosstab** and click **Finish**

10. Change to Design View to see the design grid for this query

11. Close the query

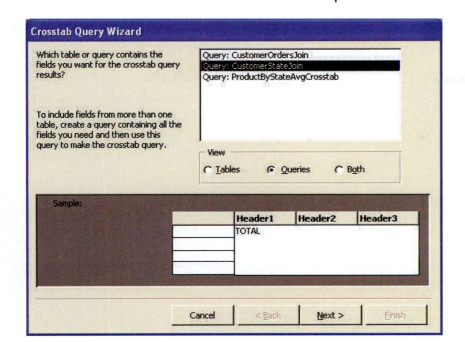

FIGURE 9.3
Selecting a query for the
Crosstab data source

The Query Wizard is an efficient way to develop Crosstab Queries when the developer knows how the data are to be organized and when the crosstab result will be based on all of the data held in a table or retrieved by a query. Creating a query in Design View allows data to be retrieved using criteria and reorganized in one query.

Building a Crosstab Query in Design View

All advanced queries use a Select Query as their foundation. Before any analysis or action is performed, the Select Query should be run and verified. Once correct data selection is verified, actions and analytical operations are added to create the final result.

Missy and Micah would like to forecast future customer behavior based on 2002 purchases, since they are the most complete data available. Using Query Design View will allow the Crosstab Query organizing data by state and products to also select sales of a specified year.

---

task reference **Create a Crosstab Query in Design View**

- Create a Select Query to retrieve the rows and columns to be cross-tabulated

- Open the Select Query in Design View and use the **Query Type** button on the toolbar to select **Crosstab**

- Set the Crosstab property of the field to appear across the query answer set to **Column Heading** and the Total property of this field to **Group by**

- Set the Crosstab property of the field to appear down the left-hand side of the query answer set to **Row Heading** and the Total property of this field to **Group by**

- Set the Crosstab property of the field to be cross-tabulated to **Value** and select an appropriate aggregate function for the Total property

- Move to Datasheet View to verify the query answer set

Creating a Crosstab Query in Design View:

1. Verify that the **ac09KoryoKicks.mdb** database is open

2. Select the **Queries** object from the Database Window

3. Double-click on **Create Query in Design View**

4. Add Customer, Product, Order Detail, and Order tables to the query and close the Show Table window

5. Place **Customer.State, Product.ProductDescription, OrderDetail.QuantityOrdered**, and **Order.OrderDate** into the Field row of the design grid

6. Place **Between #1/1/2003# And #12/31/2003#** in the Criteria row of OrderDate and run the query to test the selection

7. Return to Design View

8. Use the **Query Type** 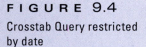 button of the Query Design toolbar to specify a **Crosstab** Query type

tip: *A new line labeled Crosstab should be added to the design grid*

9. Set the Crosstab value of the
   a. State field to **Column Heading**
   b. ProductDescription to **Row Heading**
   c. QuantityOrdered to **Value**

tip: *This field will be used to determine the values displayed in each cell of the cross-tabulation grid. Only one field can be set to Value*

   d. OrderDate to **(not shown)**

FIGURE 9.4

Crosstab Query restricted by date

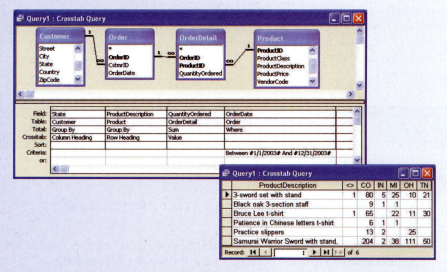

10. Set the Total row of QuantityOrdered to **Sum** and OrderDate to **Where**

tip: *Any aggregate function can be applied to the Value field. The Row and Column headings must have Group by as the Total row value. Fields used to select data before aggregation must have Where as the Total row value*

11. Change to Design View to evaluate the query results

12. Save the query as **DesignViewCrosstab**

The previous steps demonstrated building and testing a Select Query that is converted to a Crosstab Query. It is always best to build complex queries in stages so that the result of each stage can be verified before proceeding. Notice that nothing in the query result indicates that the crosstab reflects only data for 2003. The query name should reflect any selection criteria used. Notice also that the Crosstab Query icon displays next to the query name in the Database Window. Each query type displays a unique icon.

It is also possible to set query criteria to limit the Column headings that display in the query answer set. The twins are only considering Indiana and Michigan for new facilities. The Crosstab Query can be limited to a display of those locations so their values can easily be compared.

Restricting crosstab column headings:

1. Verify that **ac09KoryoKicks.mdb** database is open

2. Select the **Queries** object from the Database Window and open the **DesignViewCrosstab** Query created in the previous steps in Design View

3. Use the Save As option of the File menu to save a copy of this query as **DesignViewCrosstabRestricted**

4. Click the button above the OrderDate column to select it and click **Delete**

5. In the Criteria row of State type **"IN"**

tip: *The double quotes must be typed around IN because IN is also a logical operator used to define a list of valid criteria*

6. In the Or row of State type **"MI"**

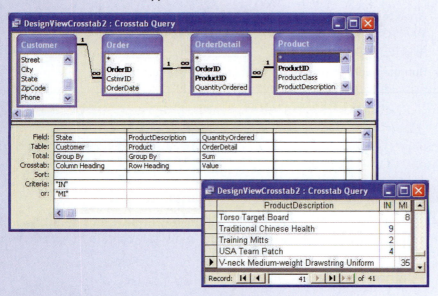

FIGURE 9.5
Crosstab Query with restricted column heading

7. Change to Datasheet View to evaluate the query results

8. Save the query

ACCESS

By default, the column headings of a Crosstab Query are sorted alphabetically or numerically. Setting the Sort property of this field will override the default. The same techniques are effective at restricting and sorting the row heading field(s).

Generating Parameter Queries

Parameter queries are used to allow new query criteria values to be entered each time the query is run. This is useful when the same type of query is run frequently against different subsets of the data. For example, a query that archives old records could prompt the user for an archive date and then archive records older than the date provided. In a similar fashion, a query to retrieve customer account information could prompt the user for an account number or customer name and then use the data provided to retrieve the correct account.

Prompting Users for Parameters

Parameter queries are frequently used to retrieve appropriate data for forms, reports, and data access pages. When a Parameter query is run, a dialog box displays prompting the user for one or more values. After the user enters the requested value(s), they are used to retrieve data that are displayed in the form, report, or Data Access Page.

The CustomerOrdersJoin query was created to display all customer orders. This functioning Select Query will be modified to allow the user to enter date parameters. By entering beginning and ending dates, the user can control the time period of the orders being retrieved.

---

task reference   Create a Parameter Query

- Create and test a Select Query with static criteria to retrieve the desired rows and columns

- Open the Select Query in Design View and type prompt(s) contained in square brackets in the Criteria row of field(s) that will prompt the user for data retrieval criteria

- Run the query to test the prompts and parameters

Adding parameters to the CustomerOrderJoin query:

1. Verify that the **ac09KoryoKicks.mdb** database is open

2. Select the **Queries** object from the Database Window and open the **CustomerOrderJoin** query in Datasheet View to evaluate its performance without parameters

tip: *206 records should be retrieved*

3. In the OrderDate Design View Criteria row type **Between [Type beginning date:] And [Type ending date:]**

4. Run the query

5. Enter **10/1/03** in the Type beginning date: dialog box and **12/31/03** in the Type ending date: dialog box pressing **OK** for each

6. Evaluate the query results

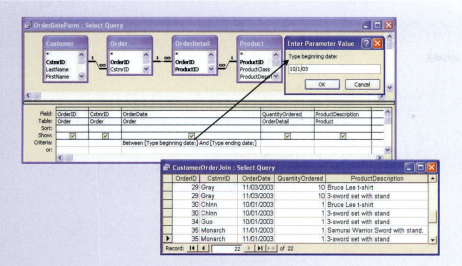

FIGURE 9.6
Parameter query

tip: *Orders for the fourth quarter of 2003 should be displayed*

7. Save the query as **OrderDateParm**

8. Close the query Design View and notice that parameter queries do not have an identifying icon in the Database Window

Parameters can be included in any condition row of a Select or Crosstab Query. As with a fully stated condition, it is important to place multiple parameters on the same criteria row to create an And condition or on a unique criteria row to create an Or condition. The Access default is to present the user with one dialog box for each parameter of a query, however; custom forms or dialog boxes can be created to prompt the user for all parameters at once.

Creating a Custom Parameter Form

Forms to accept values entered by users for query parameters are built using controls in Form Design View. Unlike creating a form that can be directly attached to an existing table or query, a parameter form must be manually attached to the query field(s).

KoryoKicks often receives customer inquiries. The process of locating customer data would be simplified by a parameter query to retrieve records based on the customer's name. Missy and Micah would like a custom form so that color can be used to draw the user's attention.

Creating a custom form for customer retrieval:

1. Verify that the **ac09KoryoKicks.mdb** database is open

2. Select the **Forms** object from the Database Window

3. Double-click **Create form in Design view**

4. Right-click on the form, select **Properties**, and set the Back Color property to custom color Hue **140**, Sat **240**, Lum **184**, Red **136**, Green **196**, Blue **255**

5. Use Figure 9.7 to add a Label control and a Text Box control (with an associated label) to the form. Set their properties

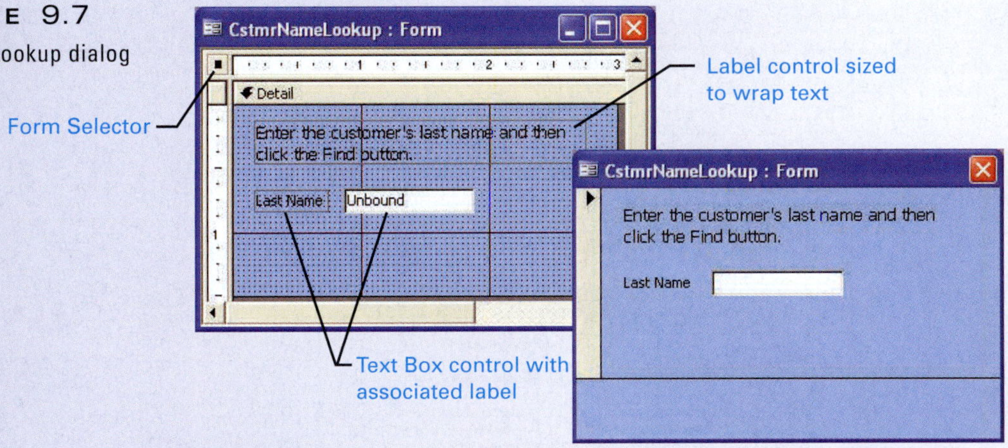

FIGURE 9.7

CstmrNameLookup dialog box form

Form Selector

Label control sized to wrap text

Text Box control with associated label

a. Right-click on the Label control, select **Properties**, change the Font Size property to **10**, and set the Caption property to **Enter the customer's last name and then click the Find button**
b. Click the label associated with the Text Box control and change the caption to **Last Name**
c. Click the text box portion of this control and set the Name property to **txtCstmrLastName**

tip: *The Name property of the text box is used to pass the contents of the control to a query*

d. Resize and align the controls as needed
e. Use Form View to evaluate the form and return to Design View

6. Double-click the form selector to open the Form properties dialog box

tip: *In Form Design View, the form selector is the square joining the horizontal and vertical rulers*

a. Set the Modal property to **Yes**
b. Set the Pop Up property to **Yes**
c. Set the Scroll Bars property to **Neither**
d. Set the Border Style property to **Dialog**
e. Set the Navigation Buttons property to **No**
f. Set the Min Max Buttons property to **None**

7. Save the form as **CstmrNameLookup**

The form properties are used to control form behavior. When the Pop Up property is set to Yes, the form will remain on top of any other open Access Windows. A Modal property of Yes will not allow the user to switch to other open windows. Modal forms must be closed to access other objects. The Scroll Bars property controls which scroll bars, if any, display. Since this is a fixed-size form, scroll bars have no function and the property was set to None (Figure 9.7). The Navigation Buttons property controls whether or not the record navigation toolbar displays on the form. Since this form is not bound to a table or query, there is no need for record navigation and the property was set to No. The Min Max Buttons property controls whether or not the minimize and maximize buttons display in the form's toolbar. A setting of none causes only the Close button to display in the toolbar (Figure 9.7).

At this point, the CstmrNameLookup form contains explanatory labels and a text box for the user to enter data, but the text box data don't go anywhere. Before the form can be instructed to send the data, the query that will select data based on user input must be built. A simple Select Query with a criterion based on the text box name is used to link the form and query objects.

Creating the CstmrNameLookup query:

1. Verify that the **ac09KoryoKicks.mdb** database is open

2. Select the **Queries** object and double-click the **Create query in Design View** option

3. Add the Customer, Order, and OrderDetail tables to the query design grid and then close the Show Table dialog box

4. Place the fields shown in Figure 9.8 into the query grid

5. Enter **[Forms]![CstmrNameLookup]![txtCstmrLastName]** as the Criteria for LastName

tip: *Double-check your entry. The query cannot be tested and the syntax must be exact*

6. Save the query as **CstmrNameLookup**

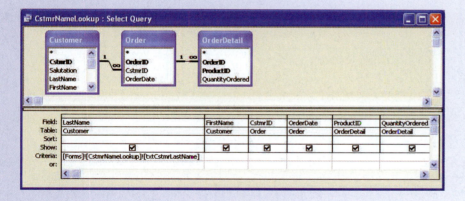

FIGURE 9.8
CstmrNameLookup query

The LastName criterion entered in step 5 provides the link from the CstmrNameLookup form built in the previous steps to the CstmrNameLookup query built in these steps. The entry follows the basic syntax of [Object Class]![Object Name]![Control Name]. Square braces are used to enclose each element of the argument, and exclamation points are used as separators. The syntax of the argument, [Forms]![CstmrNameLookup]![txtCstmrLastName], tells Access to look in the Forms object list for CstmrNameLookup and then use the contents of the txtCstmrLastName control as the LastName criterion.

The LastName criterion creates the pathway for data entered in the form to be used by the query. The final step in this process is to add a way to initiate the transfer of data from the form to the query. A **procedure** consisting of stored instructions is required to control this process. Command buttons are frequently used to initiate procedures. The Command Button Wizard will be used to walk through the process of creating the necessary procedure.

ACCESS

Adding a Command button to the CstmrNameLookup form:

1. Verify that **ac09KoryoKicks.mdb** database is open with the **CstmrNameLookup** form created in the previous step in Design View

2. Add a Command Button control to the bottom right of the form and move through the Wizard dialog boxes as follows

   a. Click the **Miscellaneous** Category, then the **Run Query** Action, and then click **Next**
   b. Select **CstmrNameLookup** and then **Next**
   c. Click the **Text** Option button, change the text to **Find**, and then click **Next**
   d. Name the button **cmdRunQuery** and click **Finish**

F I G U R E 9.9

Find command button

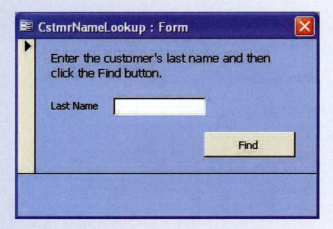

CstmrNameLookup : Form

Enter the customer's last name and then click the Find button.

Last Name [   ]

Find

3. Save the form

4. Switch to Form View, enter **Calahan**, and click **Find**

tip: *36 Calahan records should display. If this does not work, return to the steps to create the form and verify that each step from that point was completed. You will not be able to switch windows without closing the dialog box because it was set to modal*

5. Close the form and the Query window

6. Reopen the form, enter **Williams**, and click **Find**

7. Close the form

   The Command Button Wizard automatically created a stored procedure that is initiated each time the Find button is clicked. This procedure is stored in the On Click Event of the button's properties and causes the CstmrNameLookup query to run each time the button is clicked. Creating and editing procedures will be covered in greater detail in a later chapter.

*another*word . . . on Parameter Queries Using Wildcards

Parameter queries can also be created using wildcards on text and memo fields. Remember that ? can be used to match a single character in a string, * can match any number of characters, and # can be used to match a number. For example, the Like operator can be used with wildcards to find records beginning with the character entered by the user. To search for entries beginning with a character, enter *Like [Enter the first character to search by:] & "*"*. To search for a character anywhere in the string, use *Like "*" & [Enter a search character:] & "*"*

Understanding Action Queries

Select and Crosstab Queries retrieve and organize data held in database tables while action queries are used to update table data. There are four basic types of action queries: delete, update, append, and make-table.

A ***Delete Query*** is used to remove a group of records from one or more tables based on a criterion. An ***Update Query*** makes the same change to a group of records. An ***Append Query*** adds a group of records from a table or tables to the end of another table. A ***Make-Table Query*** creates a new table from all or part of the records in existing tables.

Append Query

An Append Query is used to add records to the end of a table. The source records can be stored in one or more existing tables and can be appended to an existing table based on criteria. If the fields in the source and destination tables do not match, an Append Query will add the matching data and ignore the rest.

The KoryoKicks sales personnel have been responsible for maintaining their own customer lists and contact information. The twins would like this data centralized in the KoryoKicks Customer table whether or not orders have been placed. The append process will be tested with a table, BenCustomers, which has been imported from Ben's copy of the KoryoKicks database.

task reference — Create an Append Query

- Create and test a Select Query with the data to be appended to another table
- In Query Design View, click the **Query Type** button on the toolbar and select **Append**
- In the Append dialog box
  - Enter the name of the table where records are to be appended
  - Select the database location
  - Click **OK**
- Use the **View** button to preview the records that will be appended
- Use the **Run** button to execute the query responding **Yes** to the prompt indicating the number of rows that will be updated

Creating an Append Query to add Ben's customer records:

1. Verify that the **ac09KoryoKicks.mdb** database is open

2. Select the **Queries** object and double-click **Create query in Design view**

3. Place the **BenCustomer** table in the query design grid and then close the Show Table dialog box

4. Place all of the fields from BenCustomer in the query design grid

5. Click the **Query Type** button and select **Append Query**

6. In the Append To dialog box

   a. Select **Customer** as the Table Name

   b. Verify that Current Database is selected

   c. Click **OK**

tip: *The Append To row is automatically completed because the fields of the two tables have the same field names*

7. Use the **View** button to preview the records that will be appended

8. Use the **Run** button to execute the query responding **Yes** to the prompt that 54 rows will be updated

9. Close the query saving it as **BenAppend**

10. Open the Customer table and verify the update

FIGURE 9.10

Appended Customer records

CstmrID	LastName	FirstName	Street	City	State	Country	ZipCode	Phone
001	Wagoner	Sam	5480 Alpine Lane	Sterling	CO		88661	(303) 161-5545
002	Calahan	Eliza	2140 Edgewood Road	Grand Lake	CO		80446	(303) 886-6003
003	Lake	James	701 East Street	Grandby	MI		49571	(616) 562-4499
004	Meadows	Sara	Pond Hill Road	Monroe	IN		46161	(313) 792-3646
007	Calahan	Casey	82 Mix Rd. West	Bootjack	CO		89945	(303) 643-8321
008	Zundel	Barbara	7836 E Mississippi Ave	Memphis	TN		28732	5093892893
010	Morey	Mitch	4731 S Meadow Creek	Netherland	MI		75843	8613891928
021	Smith	Alto	114 Lexington Ave.	Granby	CO		49302	(303) 838-7111
022	Lewis	Ronnie	8408 E. Fletcher Road	Clare	MI		48617	(517) 936-8651
023	Chinn	Bridgett	400 Salmon Street	Ada	MI		49301	(616) 838-9827
025	Katz	Ben	56 Foursone Road	Detroit	MI		49505	(616) 315-7294
027	Gray	Monica	3915 Hawthorne Lane	Richmond	OH		43603	(419) 332-3681
028	Rivers	Ramona	37 Queue Highway	Lacota	MI		49063	(313) 329-5364
029	Amstont	Sandy	95 Bay Boulevard	Jenison	CO		80428	(616) 131-9148
031	Hill	James	5365 Bedford Trail	Eagle Point	CO		80031	(906) 395-2041
033	Florentine	Haven	874 Western Avenue	Drenthe	CA		49464	(616) 131-3260
035	Calahan	Thomas	840 Cascade Road	Coatesville	IN		80464	(316) 343-4635
036	Benton	Cleo	4090 Division St.	Borculo	OH		49464	(616) 838-2046
043	Pointe	Bryson	11 Marsh Rd	Shelbyville	IN		46344	(616) 379-5681
047	Krizner	Jean	44 Tower Lane	Mattawan	MI		49071	(517) 630-4431
055	Worser	Charles	8200 Baldwin Blvd.	Burlington	MI		49029	(517) 317-9855
057	Maxwell	Amos	3231 Bradford Lane	Arvada	CO		80228	(206) 373-9465
062	Reed	Brandy	150 Hall Road	Kear	MI		49942	(206) 324-1824
063	Bernstein	Benon	1366 36th Street	Stilesville	MI		48653	(517) 392-8040
064	Monarch	Shiela	431 Phillips Road	Coatesville	IN		46611	(219) 352-4847

Record: 1 of 84

84 Customer records after append

11. Close the Customer table

In this example the field names in the source and destination tables matched exactly. Because of this, the append would have worked equally as well using the asterisk (*) field selection from BenCustomer table. When the field names do not match, each field must be placed in the query grid and the Append To value must be manually selected for each field. Criteria can be specified to select rows to append. When no criteria are specified, all rows are appended.

Most businesses maintain historical copies of inactive data in *history tables*. For example, inactive customers could be stored in a history table to speed processing of active customers. Sometimes storing history is driven by business needs and other times it is to meet legal requirements. Records of employees who no longer work for an organization are kept for legal reasons. Sales data are often kept for later trend analysis. Whatever the reason for storing inactive data, an Append Query is an easy way to copy data from the active table to the history table.

Updating Multiple Rows

When the same change needs to be applied to multiple records, use an Update Query. For example, the price of all products in a specific category could be raised by 5 percent to cover increased processing costs. When building an Update Query, construct a Select Query that retrieves the records to be updated, change the query type to Update Query, and then add the Update To value to the query design grid.

The KoryoKicks Customer table does not contain any country values for U.S. customers. All addresses outside the United States have a country value entered. Missy and Micah have decided that there is no benefit to this blank status and would like to use an Update Query to store a value of U.S.A.

---

task reference   Create an Update Query

- Back up the data to be updated to protect against update errors
- Create and test a Select Query with criteria to retrieve the desired data
- Verify the Select Query
- Use the **Query Type** button to change the query to an Update Query
- Place the update expression in the Update To row of the Query Design grid
- Run the query responding **Yes** to the update prompt notifying you of the number of records to be updated
- Verify the update

Creating an Update Query to add U.S.A.:

1. Verify that the **ac09KoryoKicks.mdb** database is open

2. With the Tables object selected, use copy and paste to create a backup of the Customer table named **CustomerBak**

3. Select the **Queries** object and double-click **Create query in Design view**

4. Add the **Customer** table to the Query Design grid and close the Show Table dialog box

5. Add **CstmrID, LastName, State**, and **Country** to the design grid

6. Enter **Null** as the criteria for Country and run the query

tip: *Only records with no Country value should be retrieved*

ACCESS

7. Return to Design View and use the **Query Type** 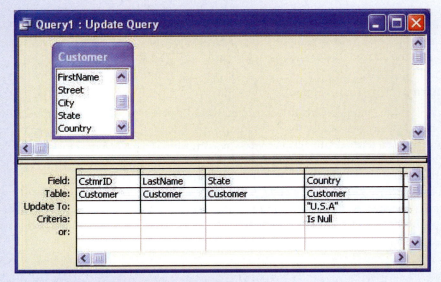 button to change the query type to **Update Query**

8. Enter **"U.S.A."** in the Update To row of Country. The double quotes are required since this is a string value

FIGURE 9.11
U.S.A. Update Query

	Query1 : Update Query				

Customer
FirstName
Street
City
State
Country

Field:	CstmrID	LastName	State	Country	
Table:	Customer	Customer	Customer	Customer	
Update To:				"U.S.A"	
Criteria:				Is Null	
or:					

9. Run the query and respond **Yes** to the prompt informing you that 82 rows will be updated

10. Close the query saving it as **USAUpdate**

11. Open the Customer table to view the updates

12. Close the Customer table

It is important to stringently verify Update Queries before executing them because their actions cannot be undone. For critical data, creating a backup of the table before updating is also advisable. The steps demonstrated creating a backup copy of the table in the same database. If the data being updated are critical, backing up the entire database may be preferable.

Although the only field needed to complete this update process was Country, other fields were included in the query to improve the ability to visually check the validity of record selection. The most important check field in this example was State because only records for states in the United States should be selected.

Expressions can also be used to update selected records. If, for example, a supplier raises prices by a fixed amount, all records for that supplier can be selected and the fixed amount added to the current price. The Products table from the Northwind database that ships with Microsoft Access has been imported to KoryoKicks and will be used to demonstrate updating selected records with an expression. In addition to the product price, this products table contains data about the number of each product on hand, units on order, and when each product should be reordered. Let's assume that the price of all products in Category 3 needs to be increased by 8 percent.

Creating an Update Query using an expression:

1. Verify that the **ac09KoryoKicks.mdb** database is open

2. With the Tables object selected, use copy and paste to create a backup of the NorthwindProducts table named **NorthwindProductsBak**

3. Open the NorthwindProducts table and review the data

4. Select the **Queries** object and double-click **Create query in Design view**

5. Add the **NorthwindProducts** table to the design grid and close the Show Table dialog box

6. Add **ProductID**, **ProductName**, **CategoryID**, and **UnitPrice** to the design grid

7. Add the criteria to select **CategoryID** values of 3 only and run the query to test the selection

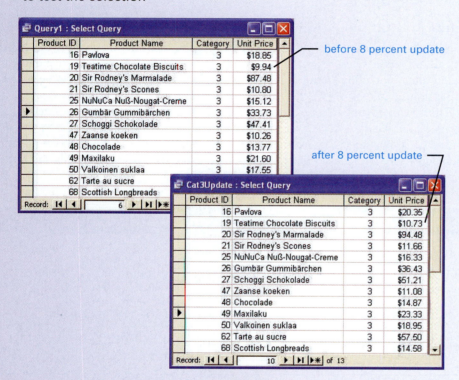

FIGURE 9.12

NorthwindProducts before and after update values

tip: *Be sure to note the pre-update UnitPrice values*

8. Return to Design View and use the **Query Type** button to change the query type to **Update Query**

9. Enter **[UnitPrice]*1.08** in the Update To row of UnitPrice

tip: *The square braces are required so that Access knows that an expression is being entered and does not treat your entry as a string*

10. Run the query and respond **Yes** to the prompt informing you that 13 rows will be updated

11. Save the query as **Cat3Update** without closing it

12. Change the Query Type to **Select** and run it to verify the changes and then close the query without saving changes

---

***another*word**   . . . on Update Queries

A common mistake with Update Queries is to run the same update multiple times. In the UnitPrice update example, each time the Update Query is run UnitPrice will be increased by 8 percent. To avoid destroying data, use a Select Query to verify the updates and do not save Update Queries that will not be used again. Saving an unneeded Update Query risks accidentally running it again

---

Saved Update Queries retain only fields with Criteria or Update To entries. Any valid expression can be used to update field values. It is important to note that the update value must be consistent with the data type of the field being updated. In the first example, the string "U.S.A." was used to update a text field, while the second example used the expression [UnitPrice]*1.08 to update a currency field.

Deleting Multiple Rows

A Delete Query permanently removes a group of records from one or more tables. For example, all records before a specified date could be deleted from the active database (usually after appending them to a history table). Only complete records can be deleted; there is no way to remove only selected fields within records.

The period of time that records are retained is governed by business practice and law. When there are no laws governing record retention, individual businesses can determine their own needs. There are no laws specifying a retention period for product orders, and the twins have determined that KoryoKicks no longer needs the Order records from the year 2002.

***task* reference**   Create a Delete Query

- Create and test a Select Query to retrieve the data to be deleted
- In Query Design View, click the **Query Type** [icon] button and select **Delete Query**
- Use the **View** [icon] button to preview the records that will be deleted
- Use the **Run** [icon] button to execute the query responding **Yes** to the prompt indicating the number of rows that will be deleted

---

Deleting Order records for the year 2002:

1. Verify that the **ac09KoryoKicks.mdb** database is open

2. Select the Tables object and double-click on **Order**

   a. Sort the records by OrderDate

   b. Click a few of the plus (+) signs of the 2002 records to view the OrderDetail for the order

   c. Close the Order table saving your changes

3. Select the **Queries** object and double-click **Create query in Design view**

4. Place the **Order** table in the query design grid and then close the Show Table dialog box

5. Place the **OrderDate** field in the query design grid

6. Enter a criterion of **Between 1/1/2002 and 12/31/2002,** run the query to verify the selection and then return to Design View

   tip: *Access may change the entry to Between #01/01/2002# and #12/31/2002#*

7. Click the **Query Type** button and select **Delete Query**

8. Use the **View** button to preview the records that will be deleted

9. Use the **Run** button to execute the query responding **Yes** to the prompt that 10 rows will be deleted

10. Close the query saving it as **Delete2002**

11. Open the Order table and verify the deletion. Close the Order table

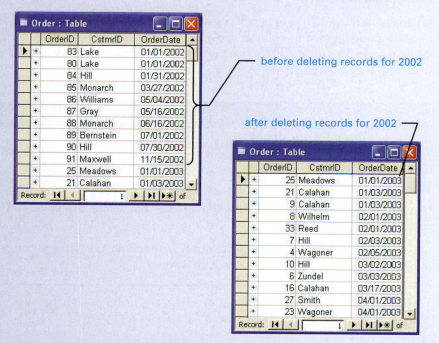

FIGURE 9.13

Order before and after records for the year 2002 delete

12. Open the OrderDetail table and look for records matching those deleted in the Order table

tip: *Refer to Figure 9.13 for OrderId values*

Like the result of other action queries, deletes cannot be undone. Backing up the table(s) that will be impacted is strongly recommended. As was demonstrated, a Delete Query can delete records in related tables that are not included in the query. Deleting Order records for the year 2002 also deleted all OrderDetails for those orders. Deleting a record on the one side of a one-to-many relationship with cascading deletes enabled deletes all related records on the many side of the relationship. Cascade settings are properties of a table relationship set from the Edit Relationships dialog box. If cascading deletes are not enabled, the records on the one side of the relationship cannot be deleted until related records on the many side of the relationship are removed.

help yourself *Use the Type a Question combo box to improve your understanding of queries by typing **query types**. Review the contents of About types of queries. Close the Help window when you are finished*

Make-Table Query

Make-Table Queries are used to create a new table from all or part of the data contained in existing tables. Make-Table Queries are useful for:

- Creating a table of data to export to another database or application
- Creating a *snapshot table* that preserves the status of data as of a specific point in time. For example, data as of the close of each quarter could be stored in a table for later evaluation and comparison
- Automatically creating backups by running the query periodically using a macro or stored procedure
- Creating a table of old records
- Improving the performance of forms, reports, and Data Access Pages based on multiple queries

Missy and Micah would like to create periodic snapshots of order data. They believe these data could be used to evaluate order processing and verify accounting figures. Tables created with a Make-Table Query are rarely updated and should be deleted when they are no longer valuable.

---

task reference   Create a Make-Table Query

- Create and test a Select Query to retrieve the data to be moved
- In Query Design View, click the **Query Type** button and select **Make-Table Query**
- Use the **View** button to preview the records that will be copied to a new table
- Use the **Run** button to execute the query responding **Yes** to the prompt indicating the number of rows that will be deleted

---

Making a new table for 2003 orders:

1. Verify that **ac09KoryoKicks.mdb** database is open

2. Select the **Queries** object and double-click **Create query in Design view**

3. Place the **Order** and **OrderDetail** tables in the design grid and then close the Show Table dialog box

4. Place all fields from both tables in the design grid

5. Enter an OrderDate criterion of **<1/1/2004**, run the query to verify the selection, and then return to Design View

tip: *Access will change the entry to <#1/1/2004#*

6. Click the **Query Type** button and select **Make-Table Query**

7. In the Make-Table dialog box
   a. Set the table name to **OrderHistorySnapshot**
   b. Verify that Current Database is selected
   c. Click **OK**

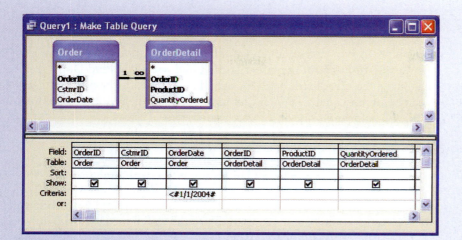

FIGURE 9.14
OrderHistorySnapshot
query

8. Use the **View** [□ ▾] button to preview the records that will be deleted

tip: *Three 2003 records should be displayed for OrderID 16. All of the 2002 records would also be placed in the history table if they had not already been deleted*

9. Use the **Run** [!] button to execute the query responding **Yes** to the prompt that 72 rows will be pasted

10. Close the query saving it as **OrderHistorySnapshotQuery**

11. Open the OrderHistorySnapshot table and verify the move for OrderId 16

12. Open the Order table and look for OrderId 16. Use the plus (+) sign to view the three OrderDetail records for this order

The field properties of the original table are not inherited by the new table created with a Make-Table Query. For example, there is no primary key set in the OrderHistorySnapshot table. As you observed in step 11, a Make-Table Query does not delete the records that are placed in a new table. A Delete Query must be created for that.

Make-Table Queries are largely used to create snapshots of data at a particular point in time, but they are also useful in combination with other action queries. Rerunning a Make-Table Query will delete any existing table before copying currently selected data.

making *the grade*

SESSION 9.1

1. How are Select Queries and action queries different?

2. What indicates a parameter in the query design grid?

3. How are Command buttons used on forms?

4. How would you know whether to use a Make-Table Query or an Append Query?

5. How is data type important in an Update Query?

ACCESS

SESSION 9.2 IMPROVING DATA INTEGRITY WITH QUERIES

Besides their many uses to analyze and answer business questions, queries can also be used to answer questions about the integrity of stored data. The Find Duplicates and Find Unmatched queries are used to test for data that fall outside the norms. Aggregate functions can be used to analyze values that have been stored, and understanding the basics of SQL will help you locate and correct data retrieval errors.

Using the Find Duplicates Query Wizard

Well-designed databases set key, data validation, and other field properties to avoid duplicating data. Unfortunately there are still ways to enter duplicate data values. For example, two employees could enter the same customer with different CstmrID values. Or the same customer could be entered with their full legal name (Victoria) and their nickname (Tori). The *Find Duplicates query* is used to locate and evaluate data that could be in error.

Since each KoryoKicks salesperson maintained an independent customer list and those lists have been combined into the Customer table, duplicate customers are possible. To avoid duplicate CustID values, each salesperson was assigned a range of values. Ben used CustIDs between 200 and 400 while Micah used CustIDs less than 200 and Missy used numbers over 400. Since CustID is the key of the Customer table, no duplicate values are allowed. Duplicate customers would be indicated by multiple records with the same values for all of the other fields (LastName, FirstName, and so on). The twins would like to test for duplicate customers and remove any unwanted records.

---

task reference   Create a Find Duplicates Query

- Select the **Queries** object in the Database Window

- Click the **New** button in the Database Window

- Select **Find Duplicates Query Wizard** and click **OK**

- Follow the instructions provided by the Find Duplicates Query Wizard

---

Locating duplicate records in the Customer table:

1. Verify that the **ac09KoryoKicks.mdb** database is open

2. Select the **Queries** object in the Database Window

3. Click **New** in the Database Window

4. Select **Find Duplicates Query Wizard** and click **OK**

5. In the Find Duplicates Query Wizard screens

   a. Select **Table: Customer** and click **Next**

FIGURE 9.15

Find Duplicates query result

	LastName	FirstName	CstmrID	Street	City	State	Country	ZipCode	Phone
▶	Morey	Mitch	202	4731 S Meadow Creek	Netherland	MI	U.S.A.	75843	8713891928
	Morey	Mitch	010	4731 S Meadow Creek	Netherland	MI	U.S.A.	75843	8613891928
	Zundel	Barbara	215	7836 E Mississippi Ave	Memphis	TN	U.S.A.	28732	5093892893
	Zundel	Barbara	008	7836 E Mississippi Ave	Memphis	TN	U.S.A.	28732	5093892893
*						MI			

DuplicateCustomers : Select Query

Record: 1 of 4

   b. Make **LastName** and **FirstName** the Duplicate-value fields and click
      Next
   c. Place the remaining fields in Additional query fields and click **Next**
   d. Name the query **DuplicateCustomers** and click **Finish**

6. Evaluate the records returned by the query to determine if they are in-
   deed duplicates

7. Delete the rows for CustID 202 and 215 and close the datasheet

The Find Duplicates query presents duplicate records in a datasheet so that they
can be evaluated. There is no facility for automatically deleting duplicate records, so
their disposition is controlled by the reviewer.

Using the Unmatched Query Wizard

The *Unmatched Query Wizard* is used to create a query that will find rows in one table
with no matching rows in another table. For example, a college could locate all students
who have not declared a major and are currently enrolled in classes. The twins want to
send promotional materials to individuals in the Customer table who have not purchased any products. This situation is represented by customers who have no Order
records.

---

task reference   Create an Unmatched Query

- Select the **Queries** object in the Database Window

- Click the **New** button in the Database Window

- Select **Find Unmatched Query Wizard** and click **OK**

- Follow the instructions provided by the Find Unmatched Query Wizard

---

Locating customers without orders:

1. Verify that the **ac09KoryoKicks.mdb** database is open

2. Select the **Queries** object in the Database Window

3. Click **New** in the Database Window

4. Select **Find Unmatched Query Wizard** and click **OK**

5. In the Find Unmatched Query Wizard screens
   a. Select **Table: Customer** as the table whose results will be in the
      datasheet and click **Next**
   b. Select **Table: Order** as the related table and click **Next**
   c. Verify the CstmrID is selected as the field that relates the tables and
      click **Next**
   d. Select all of the fields for the query result and click **Next**
   e. Name the query **NoOrderCustomers** and click **Finish**

6. Evaluate the records returned by the query and close the datasheet

FIGURE 9.16

Unmatched query results

The twins now have a list of customers who need to be sent follow-up materials. The datasheet resulting from this query can be used to create mailing labels, provide fields for a mail merge document, or can simply be printed.

Creating Top Values Queries

The *Top Values property* box on the Query Design toolbar is used to cause an Append, Make-Table, or Select Query to return a specific number of values or a percent of records. This can be particularly useful when there are many records and the goal is to review a representative few. For example, the Top Values box can be used to display the top 10 sales record values or 25 percent of customer orders. It can also be used to test for data above or below the normal range of values.

---

task reference   **Create a Top Values Query**

- Create a Select, Make-Table, or Append **Query** that returns all records meeting the desired criteria

- In Query Design View, enter the number or percent of records to be selected in the Top Values text box on the Query Design toolbar

- Run the query

Displaying the top five Quantity values:

1. Verify that the **ac09KoryoKicks.mdb** database is open

2. Open the **CustomerOrderJoin** Select Query in Datasheet View, review the results, and then switch to Design View

3. Set an **Ascending** sort for Quantity ordered and select 25 from the Top Values drop-down list (it says All by default)

4. Run the query and evaluate the result

tip: *The query returns 65 rows rather than 25 because all 65 rows have the same Quantity*

5. Return to Design View, set the Quantity sort to **Descending**, and run the query

tip: *The query returns 30 rows rather than 25 because the value of 15 appears in multiple rows*

6. Close the datasheet without saving changes to the query

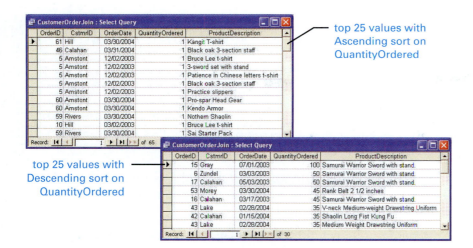

FIGURE 9.17
Top Value query results

top 25 values with Ascending sort on QuantityOrdered

top 25 values with Descending sort on QuantityOrdered

The Top Values property is set using a Combo box that behaves as both a text box and a list box. In the steps, a value was selected from the drop-down list. Typing a value in the text box is also effective. When typing a value, an integer can be entered alone or with a percent sign. For example, an entry of 15 would return 15 values while 15% would return 15 percent of the records. As the steps demonstrated, the number of records returned is not exact with a Top Values query. When there are multiple records with the same selected value, they are all returned.

The Top Values property works in conjunction with the sort fields set for a query. The direction of the sort (Ascending or Descending) determines what values are at the top of the datasheet and therefore what records will be selected. When there is no sort field, the key field is used to determine top values. When there are multiple sort fields, the leftmost field is used to determine top values.

Creating a Self-Join

A Self-join query is one that uses two copies of the same table. When two or more fields in the same table are related, a self-join can be used to retrieve data based on that relationship. For example, a ReferredBy field has been added to the KoryoKicks Customer table. When a customer is referred by an existing customer, the existing customer's CStmrID is stored in the ReferredBy field. Missy and Micah would like to send thank-you notes to customers who refer new business. To accomplish this, the Customer table will be joined to itself. The first or left copy of the table will report customer data, while the right table will retrieve data about who referred the customer.

task reference   Create a Self-Join Query

- Select the **Queries** object and double-click **Create query in Design view**
- Add two copies of the self-join table to the design grid and close the Show Table dialog box
- Define the relationship between the two copies of the self-join table by clicking and dragging from the one side of the relationship to the many side of the relationship
- Right-click on the relationship line and set the join properties
- Select the query fields, define the selection criteria, and run the query

ACCESS

Locating customers who referred other customers:

1. Verify that the **ac09KoryoKicks.mdb** database is open

2. Select the **Queries** object and double-click **Create query in Design view**

3. Add two copies of the Customer table to the design and close the Show Table dialog box

4. Drag a relationship from Customer_1.CstmrID to Customer.ReferredBy. Double-click the join line to review properties. Close the Join Properties dialog box without making any changes

5. From the Customer table, add **CstmrID**, **LastName**, **FirstName**, and **ReferredBy** to the Query Design grid

6. From the Customer_1 table, add **LastName**, **FirstName**, **Street**, **City**, **State**, and **ZipCode**

7. Run the query

8. Save the query as **CstmrReferrals**

FIGURE 9.18

Customer Referrals Self-join query results

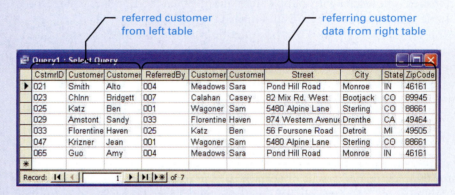

referred customer from left table

referring customer data from right table

In this example, CstmrID is contained in two fields of the Customer table. The field labeled CstmrID is the key table field used to uniquely identify each customer. When a new customer is referred by an existing customer, the existing customer's CstmrID is placed in the ReferredBy field of the new customer. Using two copies of the Customer table in a self-join, the data such as name and address for both the new customer and referring customer can be displayed side-by-side.

Using Aggregate Functions in Queries

You have practiced many types of query calculations. For example, the quantity field value can be multiplied by the price field value to determine how much a customer owes for a product purchased. This type of custom calculation is performed on each record and is specified using mathematical operators and field names.

Aggregate functions are used to summarize or "total" data in a single field. For example, the quantity on hand values of all products in inventory can be summed to determine the total number of items in inventory. Aggregate functions include sum, average, count, minimum, maximum, standard deviation, or variance. These calculations can be based on all records to create a grand total, or on groups of records to create subtotals.

The Query Wizard can be used to calculate some types of totals and subtotals, but the Query Design grid provides the broadest array of options. Entering criteria in the Query Design grid allows you to limit

- Groups before performing group calculations
- Data displayed after group calculations are completed
- Records before they are grouped and calculated

Aggregate queries display only summary data. The available aggregate functions are described in Figure 9.19. The *Group by* setting determines the number of rows a query will return. When no Group by options are set, one row of data displays summarizing all selected data. When a Group by field is set, one row of summary displays for each unique value of that field. For example, grouping by city would display one summary row for each city value in the data.

One use of aggregate functions for KoryoKicks is to determine the number of orders from each state. These data could be used to better organize processing and distribution of products. Other uses would be to determine the average number of times a business customer orders in a year or the average number of items in inventory each month.

FIGURE 9.19
Query Design grid Total row options

Function	Use to
Sum	Total the values in a Number, Currency, Date/Time, or AutoNumber field
Avg	Average the values of a Number, Currency, Date/Time, or AutoNumber field
Max	Display the highest value in a Text, Number, Currency, Date/Time, or AutoNumber field
Min	Display the lowest value in a Text, Number, Currency, Date/Time, or AutoNumber field
Count	Display the number of non-null values in a Text, Memo, Number, Currency, Date/Time, AutoNumber, Yes/No, or OLE Object field
StDev	Display the standard deviation of the values in a Number, Currency, Date/Time, or AutoNumber field
Var	Display the variance of the values in a Number, Currency, or AutoNumber field
First	Display the first chronological record in the group you are performing calculations on. This function is based on when the record was created and is not impacted by sorting
Last	Display the last chronological record in the group you are performing calculations on. This function is based on when the record was created and is not impacted by sorting
Expression	Calculate using multiple functions
Where	Specify criteria used to select records to be grouped
Group By	Define groups for subtotals. For example, Group By State would create subtotals for each state

---

task reference   Create an Aggregate Query

- Select the **Queries** object and double-click **Create query in Design view**
- Add the needed table(s) to the design grid and close the Show Table dialog box
- Add the fields to the design grid (only fields that will be used to aggregate or select should be added)
- Click the **Totals** Σ button on the Query Design toolbar
- Set the Total row option for each field in the grid

Aggregating state data:

1. Verify that the **ac09KoryoKicks.mdb** database is open
2. Select the **Queries** object and double-click **Create query in Design view**
3. Add the **NorthwindProducts** table to the Query Design grid and close the Show Table dialog box
4. Add the **CategoryID** and **UnitsInStock** field to the design grid
5. Click the **Totals** Σ button on the Query Design toolbar
6. To determine the total units in stock for each inventory category, set the Total row of CategoryID to **Group By** and UnitsInStock to **Sum**
7. Run the query

FIGURE 9.20

NorthwindProducts aggregate examples

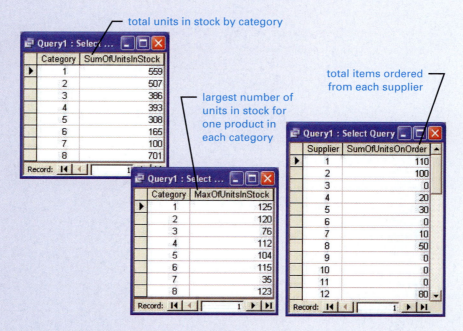

total units in stock by category

largest number of units in stock for one product in each category

total items ordered from each supplier

8. Return to Design View. Change the Total value of UnitsInStock to **Max** to determine the largest number of units in stock for one product in each category
9. Run the query

10. Return to Design View. Change the first field to **SupplierID** with a Total value of **Group By**. Change the second field to **UnitsOnOrder** with a Total value of **Sum** to determine the total number of units ordered from each supplier

11. Run the query

12. Close the window saving the query as **TotalUnitsBySupplier**

Aggregate functions ignore null values in fields when calculating. So for example, a Min function will not report blank values in a column and the Count function will not count blank records. To include null values in Count function results, use the asterisk (*) wildcard character. For other aggregate functions, use the **Nz** (null zero) function to convert null values to zero for inclusion in the calculation.

Introducing SQL

SQL (Structured Query Language) is the standard language used to query relational databases. Although there is a standard for SQL syntax, each relational DBMS uses a slightly different version. In spite of these differences, it is still relatively easy to move from one version of SQL to another.

Using SQL to Select Data

Each Access query that you have created using the Query Design grid was submitted to the database for processing as a series of SQL statements. Based on your entries, Access constructed the SQL statements. Each query is actually saved as a series of SQL statements. Queries can be created, viewed, and edited in SQL View or in Query Design View. Some queries, called SQL-specific queries, must be created and maintained in SQL View. Although SQL-specific queries are beyond the scope of this book, there are many places in Access where it is helpful to understand the basics of SQL syntax.

The most common SQL clauses are Select, From, and Where. The *Select* clause lists the field(s) of data to be retrieved. The *From* clause defines the table(s) containing the fields to be retrieved. The *Where* clause contains the criteria for data retrieval.

---

task reference   Create a Query Using SQL

- Select the **Queries** object and double-click **Create query in Design view**

- Without adding fields to the design grid, close the Show Table dialog box

- Click the **SQL View** [SQL ▾] button on the Query Design toolbar (you may need to drop down the View list for this selection to be visible)

- Enter SQL statements and run the query

Selecting Indiana Customer data:

1. Verify that the **ac09KoryoKicks.mdb** database is open

2. Select the **Queries** object and double-click **Create query in Design view**

3. Without adding fields to the design grid, close the Show Table dialog box

4. Click the **SQL View** 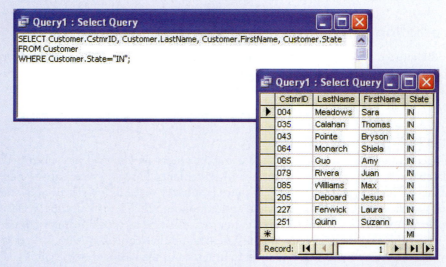 button on the Query Design toolbar

tip: *You may need to drop down the View list for this selection to be visible*

5. Type **SELECT Customer.CstmrID, Customer.LastName,**

   Customer.FirstName, Customer.State

   FROM Customer WHERE Customer.State=“IN”;

tip: *Pressing Enter has no impact on the validity of the SQL statements. New lines make SQL easier to read and debug*

6. Run the query

FIGURE 9.21

Indiana customers selected with SQL statements

7. Change to Design View and notice what has been entered into the Query Design grid from the SQL entered

8. Save the query as **IndySQL**

Although it would have been simpler to create this query in Query Design View, it was an easy place to start with SQL. Many developers create the core components of a Query in Design View and then switch to SQL View for customization. SQL is not case sensitive, but it is customary to capitalize keywords like SELECT, FROM, and WHERE as was done in this example. It is also not necessary to move to a new line for each statement, but the code is easier to read and debug when each keyword is on a new line.

Many of the syntax rules that have been discussed for entering queries in Design View are really SQL syntax rules. Some of the syntax rules are:

- Field names with spaces must be enclosed in square brackets
- Precede field names with the table name and a period
- End the statement with a semicolon
- Separate field names and table names in a list with commas
- Use appropriate delimiters when stating conditions. Use quotes for text fields, pound signs for date fields, and nothing for numeric fields

help yourself *Use the Type a Question combo box to improve your understanding of Access SQL by typing* **SQL query**. *Review the contents of* About SQL queries. *Close the Help window when you are finished*

SQL can be used almost anywhere in Access that accepts the name of a table, query, or field. Many times Access will construct the SQL statements for you by providing a Wizard or builder. In each case, alternatives to using the Wizard include typing SQL into the correct object property or using the Query Design grid to build a query whose name is stored in the correct object property. For example, each of the following can contain SQL statements created by a Wizard, specified in Design View, or typed in SQL View:

- The Row Source value of a Lookup field whose value tells Access what field(s) to retrieve and display in the lookup
- The RecordSource property of the form or report that tells Access what data to select and display in the form or report
- The RowSource property of a List Box control or Combo Box control tells Access what data to display when the box is dropped down

The KoryoKicks Order table was set to look up CstmrID in the Customer table using a Wizard. This lookup eases data entry because users can use the customer's name to retrieve CstmrID.

Viewing the Row Source value of the CstmrID lookup:

1. Verify that the **ac09KoryoKicks.mdb** database is open

2. Select the **Tables** object and open **Order** in Datasheet View. Click the drop-down list of a CstmrID field and recall that the lookup displays customer first and last names for data entry rather than CstmrIDs like 057 because they are easier to remember

3. Change to Design View

4. Click in the CstmrID field and select the Lookup tab

5. Review the Row Source Type property and the SQL in the Row Source property

Lookup tab properties for selected field

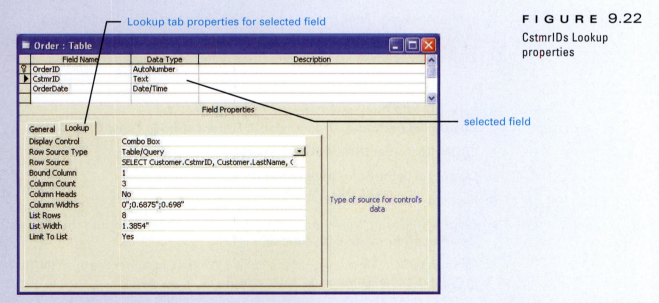

selected field

FIGURE 9.22

CstmrIDs Lookup properties

ACCESS

tip: *Click in the Row Source property and use the right arrow to scroll through all of the SQL code*

6. Click in the Row Source property and drop down the list of fields that can be displayed in this lookup

7. With the Row Source property active, click the build (ellipse) button and review the query grid for this lookup

8. Close the Query Design View

9. Close the Table Design View without saving changes

The SQL for the Order table CstmrID lookup field was created using the Lookup Wizard, but any of the methods explored could have been used. It is often easier to use the Design View or SQL View to correct or maintain Wizard-generated SQL.

Using SQL to Join Related Tables

Now that you are familiar with the use of SQL to retrieve data from one table, let's take a look at SQL in multitable queries. Chapter 6 discussed the various ways that tables can be joined to accomplish multitable queries. The most common join type is the inner join where a row is created in the query result only when the join values of both tables match. For example, joining the KoryoKicks Customer and Order tables using the default inner join on the CstmrID field will only return rows for customers who have placed orders. If any customers have not placed orders, they will not be included in the inner join query results.

As with most query properties, SQL provides keywords that define what tables to join and the join type. The INNER JOIN keyword defines the join type, while the ON clause tells Access what fields and conditions are used to join the tables.

Using SQL to join Customer and Order tables:

1. Verify that the **ac09KoryoKicks.mdb** database is open

2. Select the **Queries** object and double-click **Create query in Design view**

3. Without adding fields to the design grid, close the Show Table dialog box

4. Click the **SQL View** [SQL ▾] button on the Query Design toolbar

tip: *You may need to drop down the View list for this selection to be visible*

5. Type **SELECT Customer.CstmrID, Customer.LastName, Customer.FirstName, Order.OrderID, Order.CstmrID, Order.OrderDate**

   FROM Customer INNER JOIN [Order] ON

   Customer.CstmrID = Order.CstmrID;

6. Run the query

7. Change to Design View and notice what has been entered into the Query Design grid from the SQL entered

8. Change to SQL View and add the clause **Where Customer.State = "IN"** to the end of the existing SQL statement

F I G U R E 9.23

Indiana orders with
OrderDetails selected with
SQL statements

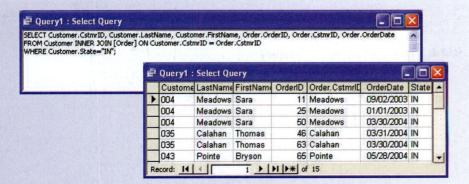

tip: *Be sure to add the new clause before the ; ending the SQL*

9. Run the query

10. Return to SQL View

11. Save the query as **IndyOrdersSQL** while remaining in SQL View

The FROM statement in the IndyOrdersSQL query contains two new keywords:
INNER JOIN and ON. The *FROM Customer INNER JOIN Order* portion of the statement tells Access the tables and join type for this query. The *ON Customer.CstmrID =
Order.CstmrID* portion of the statement tells Access which fields to match from each
table. Taken as a whole, the FROM statement tells Access to place rows in the answerset
when the CstmrID value of the Customer table matches the CstmrID value in the
Orders table.

Using SQL to change IndyOrdersSQL output order:

1. Verify that the **ac09KoryoKicks.mdb** database is open with
IndyOrdersSQL open in SQL View

2. Add the phrase **ORDER BY Customer.LastName, Customer.FirstName** to
the end of the existing SQL statements

tip: *Be sure to add the new clause before the ; ending the SQL*

3. Run the query

4. Change to Design View and notice the Ascending Sort values entered
into the Query Design grid from the SQL entered

5. Change to SQL View and edit the clause to **ORDER BY
Customer.LastName DESC, Customer.FirstName DESC**

6. Run the query

7. Change to Design View and notice the Descending Sort values in the
Query Design grid

8. Close the query saving your changes

FIGURE 9.24

Descending FirstName
and LastName sort

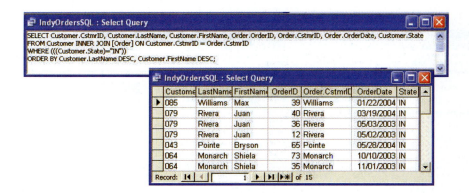

The ORDER BY statement is used to control the order of the data returned by a query. The default sort order is ascending. Adding the keyword DESC to an ORDER BY statement causes a descending sort.

The aggregate functions covered earlier in this session also have keywords used to outline requirements in SQL. Each aggregate function follows the format of FunctionName(arguments). So SUM(OrderDetail. QuantityOrdered) will sum all of the values in the QuantityOrdered field of the OrderDetail table.

Using SQL to total OrderDetail rows:

1. Verify that the **ac09KoryoKicks.mdb** database is open

2. Select the Queries object and double-click **Create query in Design view**

3. Without adding fields to the design grid, close the Show Table dialog box

4. Click the **SQL View** [sql] button on the Query Design toolbar

tip: *You may need to drop down the View list for this selection to be visible*

5. Type **SELECT Sum(OrderDetail.QuantityOrdered) AS [Total Items Ordered] FROM OrderDetail;**

6. Run the query

tip: *The result should be one number representing the total number of items ordered*

7. Change to SQL View and edit the SQL statement to read **SELECT Avg(OrderDetail.QuantityOrdered) AS [Average Items Ordered] FROM OrderDetail;**

8. Run the query

tip: *The result should be one number representing the average of all QuantityOrdered values*

9. Change to SQL View and edit the SQL statement to read

   SELECT OrderDetail.OrderID,
   Sum(OrderDetail.QuantityOrdered)
   AS [Total Items Ordered]
   FROM OrderDetail
   GROUP BY OrderDetail.OrderID;

10. Run the query

11. Close the query saving it as **SumOrderDetailsSQL**

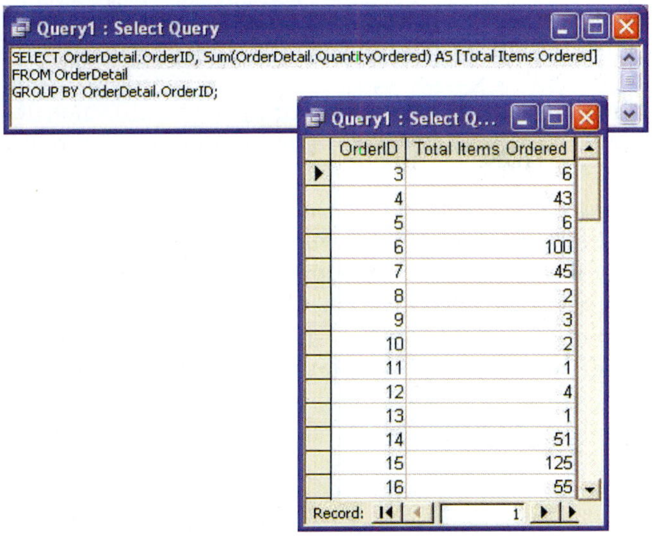

FIGURE 9.25
Subtotaling OrderDetails

The field(s) to be aggregated is listed with the appropriate function in the SQL SELECT statement. The AS clause can be paired with any member of the SELECT list to specify a column heading for a field. In the steps *AS [Total Items Ordered]* changed the default column heading, SumOfQuantityOrdered, to Total Items Ordered. The new heading must be enclosed in square brackets because it contains spaces.

How the field(s) is aggregated is determined by the GROUP BY clause. When no GROUP BY clause is used, the function will be applied to compile a grand total of all values for a field as in the total of QuantityOrdered from step 6. Adding a GROUP BY clause defines groups of records to be subtotaled. The final query created in the steps presented a total quantity of items ordered for each OrderID.

SESSION 9.2

making *the grade*

1. Is it imperative to understand SQL to effectively use Access databases?

2. How does storing duplicate records for the same person corrupt database data and what tool can be used to locate such data?

3. When is it appropriate to join a table to itself?

4. What SQL keyword is used to control sorting?

SESSION 9.3 SUMMARY

As database data are collected over time, inconsistencies and anomalies are introduced that can cause skewed reports. Cleaning up old data and repairing irregularities are critical to a well-functioning database. A standard maintenance task is to place inactive records to a history table using an Append Query. A Delete Query can then be used to remove the history records from the active table. Fewer records to process speeds queries, forms, and reports based on the data and decreases the likelihood of accidentally reporting inactive data and skewing results.

Find Duplicates, Find Unmatched, and Top Values queries are all used to evaluate the validity of data by comparing them to other stored records. After the data returned are evaluated, they can be updated as necessary.

ACCESS

As an organization matures, its business practices change. Prices increase, new suppliers replace older ones, and so on. Such business adjustments lead to the same change being applied to multiple records. Update queries are used to select rows of data and then apply the same changes to a value or values. The change can be a fixed value like the name of a new supplier for a class of goods or an expression like raising all product prices by 3 percent.

Parameter queries are used when there are frequent queries against the same data using the same criteria fields. For example, a monthly sales parameter query would prompt the user for the month and then generate the report based on the user's entry. Without this capability, a new query would need to be created for each month.

A self-join is used when two or more fields of the same table are related, such as when one customer refers another customer. In this case, the record contains the customer number with his or her data and the customer number of the referring person. A self-join allows the name and address of both the referred and referring customer to be displayed.

Although knowledge of SQL is not required to query databases, it can be very helpful. The most common SQL clauses are Select, From, and Where. Other keywords such as Group By and Order By are added to these statements to control what records are selected and how they are displayed.

Visit www.mhhe.com/i-series/ to explore related topics.

MICROSOFT OFFICE SPECIALIST OBJECTIVES SUMMARY

- Creating and modifying Crosstab, Unmatched, and Duplicates queries—MOS AC03S-1-7

making the grade *answers*

SESSION 9.1

1. Select Queries are used to retrieve and organize data while action queries update data.

2. Square brackets enclose the text that will prompt the user.

3. Command buttons are used to initiate commands or instructions stored in a macro or procedure. The Command Button Wizard will walk the developer through the creation of a simple stored procedure. More complex procedures must be developed using Visual Basic.

4. Evaluating the operations that need to be performed will indicate which type of query is appropriate. A Make-Table Query is appropriate for creating a snapshot of data at a specific point in time in a new table. This can be used to speed other processing or create backups. An Append Query adds selected data to an existing table. This could be useful for placing records in a history table before deleting them.

5. The data type of the field being updated determines how the update expression is formatted. Numeric data types do not use any special punctuation. Text data types use double quote delimiters, and date data types use pound signs.

SESSION 9.2

1. Yes and no. Basic operations databases are all possible without understanding SQL since it is generated for you. Knowing SQL does improve a user's understanding of Access operations and is essential for advanced processes.

2. Duplicate records for the same person leads to the retrieval of incomplete information in queries, forms, and reports. Data can also appear lost. For example, when data are stored under both Rick Wilmington and Ricky Wilmington and orders by customer are retrieved, it appears that there are two distinct customers, which is misleading. If Rick calls for the status of his order, it could appear to be missing if records for Rick Wilmington were pulled and the order was placed for Ricky Wilmington. The Find Duplicates query can be used to find records with duplicate values in one or more fields so that they can be evaluated for validity and combined or deleted as necessary.

3. When the same values are being used in two fields for multiple purposes, a self-join will display data related to both fields. For example, each customer is assigned a unique customer number. The same number can be used to represent the customer who referred this customer. When this happens, there are two customer numbers in the same table row. The row of data is for the current or referred customer. A self-join can be used to retrieve the name and other pertinent information for the referring customer.

4. ORDER BY

task reference *summary*

Task	Page #	Preferred Method
Create a Crosstab Query in Design View	AC 9.5	• Create a Select Query to retrieve the rows and columns to be cross-tabulated • Open the Select Query in Design View and use the **Query Type** [ ] button on the toolbar to select **Crosstab** • Set the Crosstab property of the field to appear across the query answer set to **Column Heading** and the Total property of this field to **Group by** • Set the Crosstab property of the field to appear down the left-hand side of the query answer set to **Row Heading** and the Total property of this field to **Group by** • Set the Crosstab property of the field to be cross-tabulated to **Value** and select an appropriate aggregate function for the Total property • Move to Datasheet View to verify the query answer set
Create a parameter query	AC 9.8	• Create and test a Select Query with static criteria to retrieve the desired rows and columns • Open the Select Query in Design View and type prompt(s) contained in square brackets in the Criteria row of field(s) that will prompt the user for data retrieval criteria • Run the query to test the prompts and parameters
Create an Append Query	AC 9.13	• Create and test a Select Query with the data to be appended to another table • In Query Design View, click the **Query Type** [ ] button and select **Append** • In the Append dialog box • Enter the name of the table where records are to be appended • Select the database location • Click **OK** • Use the **View** [ ] button to preview the records that will be appended • Use the **Run** [!] button to execute the query responding **Yes** to the prompt indicating the number of rows that will be updated
Create an Update Query	AC 9.15	• Back up the data to be updated to protect against update errors • Create and test a Select Query with criteria to retrieve the desired data • Verify the Select Query • Use the **Query Type** [ ] button to change the query to an Update Query • Place the update expression in the Update To row of the Query Design grid • Run the query responding **Yes** to the update prompt notifying you of the number of records to be updated • Verify the update
Create a Delete Query	AC 9.18	• Create and test a Select Query to retrieve the data to be deleted • In Query Design View, click the **Query Type** [ ] button and select **Delete Query** • Use the **View** [ ] button to preview the records that will be deleted • Use the **Run** [!] button to execute the query responding **Yes** to the prompt indicating the number of rows that will be deleted
Create a Make-Table Query	AC 9.20	• Create and test a Select Query to retrieve the data to be moved • In Query Design View, click the **Query Type** [ ] button and select **Make-Table Query** • Use the **View** [ ] button to preview the records that will be copied to a new table • Use the **Run** [!] button to execute the query responding **Yes** to the prompt indicating the number of rows that will be deleted
Create a Find Duplicates Query	AC 9.22	• Select the **Queries** object in the Database Window • Click the **New** button in the Database Window • Select **Find Duplicates Query Wizard** and click **OK** • Follow the instructions provided by the Find Duplicates Query Wizard

task reference *summary*

Task	Page #	Preferred Method
Create an Unmatched Query	AC 9.23	• Select the **Queries** object in the Database Window • Click the **New** button in the Database Window • Select **Find Duplicates Query Wizard** and click **OK** • Follow the instructions provided by the Find Unmatched Query Wizard
Create a Top Values Query	AC 9.24	• Create a Select, Make-Table, or Append **Query** that returns all records meeting the desired criteria • In Query Design View, enter the number of percent of records to be selected in the Top Values text box on the Query Design toolbar • Run the query
Create a Self-Join Query	AC 9.25	• Select the **Queries** object and double-click **Create query in Design view** • Add two copies of the self-join table to the design grid and close the Show Table dialog box • Define the relationship between the two copies of the self-join table by clicking and dragging from the one side of the relationship to the many side of the relationship • Right-click on the relationship line and set the join properties • Select the query fields, define the selection criteria, and run the query
Create an Aggregate Query	AC 9.28	• Select the **Queries** object and double-click **Create query in Design view** • Add the needed table(s) to the design grid and close the Show Table dialog box • Add the fields to the design grid (only fields that will be used to aggregate or select should be added) • Click the **Totals** Σ button on the Query Design toolbar • Set the Total row option for each field in the grid
Create a query using SQL	AC 9.29	• Select the **Queries** object and double-click **Create query in Design view** • Without adding fields to the design grid, close the Show Table dialog box • Click the **SQL View** button on the Query Design toolbar (you may need to drop down the View list for this selection to be visible) • Enter SQL statements and run the query

TRUE/FALSE

1. An Update Query applies the same change to all selected records.

2. A Crosstab Query must always present the first table column across the top of the grid.

3. A Make-Table Query deletes any existing data in the table being made before saving selected records there.

4. A Top Values Query set to 5 will always display five rows of data.

5. The Where clause of an Aggregate query determines the groups used for subtotals.

6. In SQL Select is the keyword used to outline what columns of data a query should retrieve.

FILL-IN

1. The _____ delimiter is used to specify criteria for date fields.

2. The _____ query is the foundation for all action queries.

3. Parameters are enclosed in _____.

4. A form that must be closed to access other windows is said to be _____.

5. Selecting _____ in the Top Values box of a Select Query will cause the query to return all rows with the top five values of the sorted field.

6. In a SQL query, the default column heading of Quantity can be changed to *Qty On Hand* by adding the clause _____.

7. The Aggregate function used to determine the lowest value in a group is _____.

MULTIPLE CHOICE

1. The SQL keyword(s) that causes a row in the query result to be created only when the join values for both tables match is _____.
   a. SELECT
   b. OUTER JOIN
   c. INNER JOIN
   d. WHERE

2. Changes made to a SQL query in SQL View are also reflected in the _____.
   a. Wizard
   b. Query Screen Tip
   c. Query Design grid
   d. all of the above

3. Aggregate functions are added to the Query Design grid using the _____.
   a. Totals button
   b. Aggregate button
   c. Insert menu
   d. none of the above

4. Which of the following are valid entries for the Top Values combo box?
   a. 8
   b. 12%
   c. 1
   d. all of the above

5. When two copies of the same table are used in a query, it is called a(n) _____.
   a. dual-join
   b. plural-join
   c. auto-join
   d. self-join

review of concepts

REVIEW QUESTIONS

Each of the following topics should be addressed in one to three paragraphs.

1. What is the advantage of building a Crosstab Query in Design View?

2. Explain how to construct a parameter query that allows the user to enter a company name as a criterion of the CompanyName field when the query is run.

3. Write the SQL to retrieve PetName, Breed, Age, and Weight from the Pets table sorted by Breed.

4. Explain the term *self-join*.

5. Describe how Group By values impact Aggregate functions in a query.

CREATE THE QUESTION

For each of the following answers, create the question.

ANSWER	QUESTION
1. Data are summarized into cells specified by one field value across the top of the grid and a second field value down the left-hand column	_____
2. Append	_____
3. Creates a new table from selected rows	_____
4. They are used to store inactive records	_____
5. [Shipping]+2	_____
6. Avg	_____
7. Unmatched Query Wizard	_____

FACT OR FICTION

For each of the following, determine whether the statement is fact, fiction, or both and present your arguments for that conclusion.

1. Aggregate functions such as Sum, Average, and Max include blank cells as zero values.

2. A Command Button Wizard is the only way to create a procedure.

3. Deleted records can be reinstated using the Undo button.

4. SQL View is reached from the Design View of a query.

5. A Find Duplicates query is used to find duplicate key field values.

6. It is impossible to enter duplicate data in a properly designed database.

7. The Undo button can be used to reverse the actions of a Delete Query.

practice

The Little White School House

Samuel Mink is the director of The Little White School House, a small private mountain community school. There are 142 students from preschool through grade 6. The staff consists of eight teachers, the director, a secretary, and community volunteers. In earlier assignments, the records for the school were converted from an Excel spreadsheet to an Access database. Samuel would like to evaluate the data that have been converted and learn to perform mass updates.

1. Use the Crosstab Query Wizard to build a query based on the Students table of **ac09LWSH.mdb**. Teachers should be listed in the left-hand column, Bus should be listed across the top, and the Count function should be used to display the number of students for each teacher and bus in the resulting cells. Name the query **TeacherBusCrosstab**

2. Use Design View to restrict the bus columns to those starting with W1 and ending with any number. W10, W12, W13, W15, and W16 should display

3. Delete the Total Of StdntName Column, review the results, and save

4. Build a parameter query based on the Employees table that will prompt the user for a Function field value. The prompt should read **Teacher or Administration?** The query should be named **EmployeesParameter**. Test the query using both Function values

5. Use the Unmatched Query Wizard to find records in the Student table whose Teacher value does not match the last name of a teacher in the Employees table. Display student ID, name, and teacher in the answerset. Name the query **StudentsWithoutTeachers**. In the Students table, change Evens to **Evans** and the other unmatched teachers to **Gibbs**

6. In the Employee table, change the 2nd grade teacher's name to **Madonna Ballay** and run the StudentsWithoutTeachers query again to review the students who need to be assigned a new teacher

7. Use an Update Query to change the students Teacher value from Gibbs to **Ballay**. Name the query **TeacherUpdate**. Run the StudentsWithoutTeachers query to verify that no student records have an invalid value in Teacher

FIGURE 9.26

TeacherUpdate query design

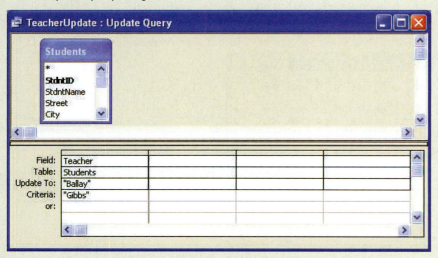

2. xXtreMeSportz.com—Part I: Event Sponsors Advanced Queries

xXtreMeSportz.com is organizing a snowboarding competition in Utah. Part of organizing an extreme event is to solicit the funds that will be used to pay for the event venue, participants, and awards for the winners. A new database has been created to track the fund-raising for this event. There are three tables of interest to this project. tblSponsors contains the list of customers who are willing to be solicited to contribute to events. tblEventOrganizers contains the list of xXtreMeSportz employees who are contacting customers to solicit contributions. tblContributions links employees to their assigned customers and tracks the dollar amount of contributions received.

1. Start Access and open **ac09xXtreMeSponsors.mdb**

   a. Open tblSponsors and review its contents

   b. Open tblEventOrganizers and review its data

   c. Open tblContributions and review its records

2. Use the Query Wizard to create a Select Query that joins all three tables

   a. Include all table data with only the column from the parent table for each foreign key field (CustomerID, for example, should appear only once)

   b. Name the query **EventJoinQuery**

3. Management would like to evaluate the contributions event organizers have obtained in each state. Use the EventJoinQuery to create a Crosstab Query

   a. Make tblSponsors_State the row heading

   b. Make EventOrganizerID the column heading

   c. Sum Contribution

   d. Name the Query **ContributionsByStateAndOrganizer**

   e. Change to SQL View and change the heading [Sum Of Contribution] to [**State Total**]

   f. Return to Datasheet View to verify the result

   g. From Design View restrict the data to reflect only contributions from Colorado (CO), California (CA), New York (NY), or Pennsylvania (PA)

   h. Return to Datasheet View to verify the result

   i. Close the query

4. Create a copy of ContributionsByStateAndOrganizer named **AvgContributionsByStateAndOrganizer**

   a. Use Design View to change the summary function to Avg and delete the State Total column

   b. Verify your updates in Datasheet View

5. If your work is complete, exit Access; otherwise, continue to the next assignment

FIGURE 9.27

ContributionsByStateAndOrganizer

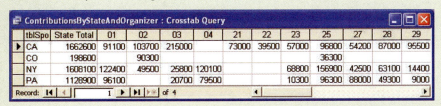

tblSpo	State Total	01	02	03	04	21	22	23	25	27	28	29
CA	1662600	91100	103700	215000		73000	39500	57000	96800	54200	87000	95500
CO	198600		90300						36300			
NY	1608100	122400	49500	25800	120100			68800	156900	42500	63100	14400
PA	1128900	96100		20700	79500			10300	96300	88000	49300	9000

Record: |◄| ◄ | 1 | ► | ►| | ►* | of 4

1. Success Training Inc.

Success Training Inc. is a loosely organized training group of management trainers. Trainers produce and schedule their own course materials. Success Training generates and distributes advertising, schedules class-rooms, enrolls students, and collects money. You have been asked to create queries to help manage the sched-uling process.

1. Open **ac09SuccessTraining.mdb**

2. In the past, trainers have inadvertently double-booked themselves. Create a Crosstab Query based on the Schedule table that will display the number of seminars with Date as the Row Heading and Trainer ID as the Column Heading. A value greater than one in any cell will indicate a double-booked trainer. Accept the default query name

3. Create a Select Query to retrieve the fields neces-sary to produce the Crosstab Query from step 2 displaying Trainer LastName from the Trainers table and Seminar ID and Date from the Schedule table. Name the query **CrosstabSelect**

4. Create a Crosstab Query based on the CrosstabSelect Query that will display the number of seminars with Date as the Row Heading and LastName as the Column Heading.Count SeminarID. Name the query **TrainerUtilizationCrosstab**

5. Build a Crosstab Query that will show when a room has been double-booked. Name the query **RoomsUtilizationCrosstab**

6. Build a parameter query that will prompt the user for a trainer's last name and then list the data for all seminars being offered by that trainer. Test the query with Anderson and Chang. Name the query **SeminarsByLastName**

7. It is time to evaluate inactive trainers in the Trainers table. Use the Unmatched Query Wizard to list trainers with nothing scheduled. Name the query **InactiveTrainers**

8. Create a copy of the InactiveTrainers query named MakeInactiveTrainersTable. Convert **MakeInactiveTrainersTable** to a Make-Table Query and run it to create the **Inactive** table. Be sure to open the Inactive table to verify its content

9. Use SQL View to create a query that will count the number of seminars offered by each trainer. Display the facilitator ID, last name, first name, and count the seminar ID. Label the aggregate field **Seminars** and save the query as **SeminarsCount**

FIGURE 9.28

Trainer Utilization Crosstab and Count of seminars offered by each facilitator

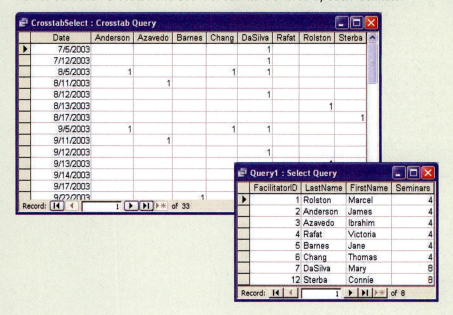

Date	Anderson	Azavedo	Barnes	Chang	DaSilva	Rafat	Rolston	Sterba
7/5/2003					1			
7/12/2003					1			
8/5/2003	1			1	1			
8/11/2003		1						
8/12/2003					1			
8/13/2003							1	
8/17/2003								1
9/5/2003	1			1	1			
9/11/2003		1						
9/12/2003					1			
9/13/2003								
9/14/2003								
9/17/2003								
9/22/2003				1				

Record: 1 of 33

Query1 : Select Query

FacilitatorID	LastName	FirstName	Seminars
1	Rolston	Marcel	4
2	Anderson	James	4
3	Azavedo	Ibrahim	4
4	Rafat	Victoria	4
5	Barnes	Jane	4
6	Chang	Thomas	4
7	DaSilva	Mary	8
12	Sterba	Connie	8

Record: 1 of 8

2. xXtreMeSportz.com—Part II: Event Sponsors Data Analysis Queries

xXtreMeSponsors.mdb was introduced in this chapter's Practice exercise. Please return to the Practice exercise and review the table descriptions. xXtreMe Sponsors.mdb is a database that was created for this special project using data from the company's normal business database. Before proceeding, it is important to ensure that the selection and assignment processes produced valid data. You will be using queries to guarantee that nothing has been missed.

1. Start Access and open your copy of **ac09xXtreMeSponsors.mdb**. If you did not complete the xXtreMeSportz.com practice exercise for this chapter, do so now

2. Management is concerned that some of the potential contributors may have been missed when event organizers were assigned. Create a Find Unmatched query using tblContributions and tblEventOrganizers. Display only the CustomerId for customers who have not been assigned an event organizer. Name the query **UnassignedSponsors**

3. Management is also concerned that some event organizers have not been assigned any sponsors to contact. Create a Find Unmatched query using tblEventOrganizers and tblContributions. Display only the EventOrganizerID, LastName, FirstName, and Phone. Name the query **UnassignedOrganizers**

4. Create an Update Query that assigns the event organizer identified in step 3 to the unassigned sponsors identified in step 2. Name the query **AssignSponsor**. Run the queries from both steps 3 and 4 again to confirm the update

5. A thank-you letter needs to be sent to those sponsors who have already contributed. Microsoft Word will be used to create a form letter that will use data from an Access table for the name, address, and contribution amount. Use a Make-Table Query Named **MakeContributorThankYou** to create the data source for Microsoft Word to use

    a. From tblContributions select **Contribution**. From tblSponsors select **Contact**, **CompanyName**, **Address**, **City**, **State**, and **ZipCode**

    b. Use **Not Null** as the Contribution selection criteria

    c. Name the table created **ContributorThankYou**

    d. Open the ContributorThankYou table and verify your results

6. If your work is complete, exit Access; otherwise, continue to the next assignment

F I G U R E 9.29

AssignSponsor Update Query

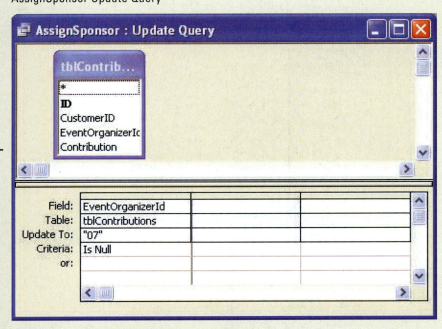

e-business

1. LumberOnline

A large nationwide distributor of construction products has decided to accept orders from contractors via the Internet using the company name LumberOnline. The orders will be processed within 24 hours of receipt. All Internet orders will be delivered to the job site the business day before the requested date listed on the order. An additional charge applies to orders that must be delivered in three days or less. The existing sales force will continue to support current walk-in and phone customers. A new salesperson will be responsible for Internet orders

1. Open **ac09LumberOnline.mdb**

2. To simplify looking up products, create a query based on the Products table to display a crosstab of products

   a. Make **Category**, **Species**, and **Size** the row headings

   b. Make **Grade** the column headings

   c. Sum **QuantityOnHand**

   d. Name the query **ProductsCrosstab**

   e. Change the heading of the Total of QtyOnHand column to **Total On Hand**

3. Earle Peake, the sales representative for territory 4, has been promoted. Erika Martinez has been hired to replace him. Earle's customers must be assigned to Erika before moving Earle's record to the his-

tory table; otherwise, deleting Earle's record would delete his clients using referential integrity rules

   a. Add Erika Martinez to the SalesReps table as SalesRep MA2 for the 4th territory and a phone number of 317-484-9348

   b. Create an Update Query named **ModifySalesRep** that will change the SalesRep value of Earle's customers from PE1 to **MA2**, Erika's identifier

   c. Create an Append Query named **EmployeeHistoryAppend** to copy Earle Peake's Sales Rep record to the end of the EmployeesHistory table

   d. Create a parameter query named **EmployeeDelete** to prompt the user for a last name and then delete the indicated record. Use the query to remove Earle Peake's record

4. Mitzi Becker has been hired to manage Internet sales. Create an Update Query, **InternetSalesRep**, that will select Internet sales and assign her identifier, **BK1**

5. Build a Find Unmatched query that will list any customers that have not been assigned a SalesRep. Name the query **MissingSalesRep**

6. Create a copy of the Missing Sales Rep query named **Update Sales Rep**. Add yourself to the Sales Reps table as Sales Rep **XXX**. Use this query to assign unassigned customers to you

FIGURE 9.30

ProductsCrosstab Query results

	Category	Species	Size	Total On Hand	2+	3+	Cab_	Constr_	Standard	Ungraded	Utility
▶	Board	DFIR	1 X 4	123984						123984	
	Board	DFIR	1 X 6	134976						134976	
	Board	SPF	1 X 4	626286						626286	
	Board	SPF	1 X 6	47346						47346	
	Board	SPF	1 X 8	564738						564738	
	Board	WPINE	1 X 10	958346							958346
	Board	WPINE	1 X 3								
	Board	WPINE	1 X 4	423743							423743
	Board	WPINE	1 X 6	2434687							2434687
	Board	WPINE	1 X 8	167348							167348
	Dim.	DFIR	2 X 10	59317					59317		
	Dim.	DFIR	2 X 4	1611534	573972				953890		83672
	Dim.	DFIR	2 X 6	64820					64820		
	Dim.	DFIR	2 X 8	1348908					1348908		

Record: |◀| ◀ | 1 | ▶ | ▶| | ▶* | of 34

2. xXtreMeSportz.com—Part III: Event Sponsors Parameter and SQL Queries

xXtreMeSponsors.mdb was introduced in this chapter's Practice exercise and further explored in the Challenge assignment. Please turn to the Practice exercise and review the table descriptions. Although it is helpful to complete all three parts of this project, it is not necessary since they are not interdependent

1. Open Access and a copy of **ac09xXtreMeSponsors.mdb**. If you have completed other parts of this project, use your updated database; otherwise, use the database from the files for this chapter

2. Build a parameter query that will list the sponsors assigned to one event organizer

   a. Prompt the user to enter their last and first names, but do not display these in the query answer set

   b. Display sponsor's **Contact**, **CompanyName**, and **PhoneNumber**

   c. Name the query **EventOrganizersParameter**

   d. Test your query with Haven Krizner

3. Create a custom form in Design View

   a. Set the following form properties

      i. Back Color property to **white**

      ii. Scroll Bars property to **Neither**

      iii. Border Style property to **Dialog**

      iv. Navigation Buttons property to **No**

      v. Min Max Buttons property to **None**

   b. Add a label control with the text **Enter your name to look up your Sponsors**

   c. Add a Text Box control

      i. Set the Label Caption property to **Last Name**

      ii. Set the Text Box Name property to **Last**

   d. Add a Text Box control

      i. Set the Label Caption property to **First Name**

      ii. Set the Text Box Name property to **First**

   e. Name the form **LookupSponsors**

4. Create a copy of the EventOrganizersParameter query named **EventOrganizersCustomForm**

   a. Open EventOrganizersCustomForm in Design View and then move directly to SQL View

   b. In the Where clause change [Enter your Last Name] to [Forms]![LookupSponsors]![Last]

   c. Similarly update the first name prompt

5. Add a command button to the LookupSponsors form that will run the EventOrganizersCustomForm query

   a. Label the button **Lookup**

   b. Test the form using **Ronnie Smith**

6. Close the database and exit Access if your work is complete

F I G U R E 9.31

LookupSponsors form and query

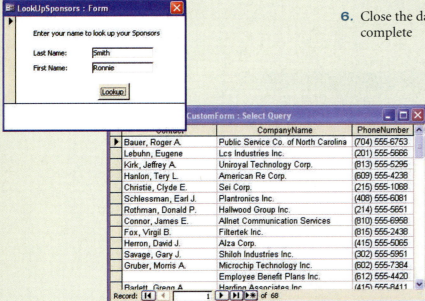

1. Internet Café

The management of a local coffee shop has decided to update their image by providing Internet access for their customers. The goal is to accommodate people who bring their own laptops as well as those who do not have a computer. For laptop users, each table will be cabled to a network providing high-speed Internet access and other services such as printing. Desktop computers will be available at a few selected tables.

The current selection of books and magazines shelved at the café does not address technological topics. To augment the transition to an Internet café, you have been asked to compile a list of useful books for management to purchase.

1. Use Web search tools to locate and document at least 10 helpful books on technology. Document the author, ISBN, title, publisher, and year published. Don't select any titles over two years old

2. Add your findings to the Books table of the **ac09InternetCafe.mdb** file with a Category of **Technology**

3. You have also been asked to evaluate the need for newer books in each category. Create a Crosstab Query with date across the top and category down the left-hand side. Sum the quantity values and name the query **CategoryYearCrosstab**

   a. Change the heading Total of Quantity to **Total**

   b. Close and save

4. Multiple employees have entered data into the Books table. Create a Find Duplicates query that will locate entries that have been duplicated based on their author, title, and publisher. Name the query **DuplicateBooks**

5. The correct ISBN for *Hunt for Red October* is 0425133516. Delete the other entry. The correct ISBN for *Net Force: Breaking Point* is 0425176932. Delete the other entry

6. Build a Delete Query with a parameter that will remove all books that were published before a date entered by the user from the Books table. Name the query **DeleteBooksByDate**. Use the query to remove all books published before 1990

7. Use the Wizard to create a query that displays the total number of books in each category sorted by category. Use SQL View to make the calculated column heading **Copies Available**. Name the query **CopiesAvailableByCategory**

8. Patrons have expressed an interest in being able to search specialty tables. Use a Make-Table Query to place books with a Category of Women or Spiritual in a table named **WomensTopicsMaketable**

FIGURE 9.32

Books crosstab without Technology

Category	Total	1982	1988	1993	1994	1995	1996	1997	1998	1999	2000	2001	2002
Fiction	3												3
Novel	22			4	3	1	4	5	3	2			
Spiritual	2				2								
Suspense	51	1	4	3	2		6	18	7	7	3		
Women	3											3	

FIGURE 9.33

DuplicateBooks query results

Author Field	Title Field	Publisher Field	NumberOfDups
Clancy	Hunt for Red October, The	Berkley	2
Clancy	Net Force: Breaking Point	Berkley	2

LEVEL **THREE**

CHAPTER NINE

around the world

1. Projecting the World's Population

Government agencies throughout the world tabulate census data on a regular basis. No two organizations are on the same cycle, so many of the numeric values used to determine world populations are actually projections based on an earlier census and historical growth patterns. You have been asked to build queries that will convert 2002 census numbers to 2003 population projections. The largest 378 cities from the 2002 census are stored in the Largest2002Cities. The GrowthClass column indicates the historical growth rate for the cities. Class 1 cities are projected to grow 8 percent, class 2 cities are projected to grow 6 percent, and class 3 cities are projected to grow 4 percent.

1. Open **ac09WorldPopulations.mdb**

2. Make a copy of the Largest2002Cities table and name it **Cities2003Projections**

3. Create and apply an Update Query named **UpdateClass1** to increase class 1 cities by 8%. 88 rows should be updated

4. Create and apply an Update Query named **UpdateClass2** to increase those cities by 6%. 192 rows should be updated

5. Create and apply an Update Query named **UpdateClass3** to increase those cities by 4%. 98 rows should be updated

6. Use several values from the Largest2002Citites table to verify the updates

7. Sort the Cities2003Projections table by descending population and then create a query to select the top 100 values using the Top Values drop-down on the Query Design toolbar. Name the query **Top100Query**

8. Create a copy of the Top 100 query named **Top100Maketable**. Update this query to create a table named **Top 100**

9. Create a Make-Table Query that will prompt the user for a value and then store Cities2003Projections records for populations less than that value in the **ExtraCities** table. Use the value 1200000 to test the query. Name the Query **MakeExtraCities**

10. Build another Make-Table Query to save the values greater than or equal to 1200000 in the **Top2003Projections** table. Name the query **MakeTop2003Projections**

11. Create a Delete Query named **DeleteCities** to remove the ExtraCities records

12. Create a query that sums the population values in Cities2003Projection by country. Use SQL View to change the heading SumOfPopulation to Population. Sort by descending population. Save the query as **PopulationsByCountry**

FIGURE 9.34

PopulationsByCountry

running project: tnt web design

Analyzing TnT Data

TnT Web Design, like all organizations, needs to periodically verify the validity of their data. Queries need to be created to uncover duplicate data and maintain the integrity of the data.

1. Start Access and open the copy of **ac09TnT.mdb** in the files for this chapter (You cannot use your copy of the database from the previous chapter, since there have been modifications for this chapter)
2. Create a Find Duplicates query to locate duplicate customers by matching custName and custState. Display all tblCustomers data and name the query **DuplicateCustomers**
3. The record containing custID 34 is erroneous. Delete it
4. The job classification Graphics has been changed to Designer. Create an Update Query that will modify the appropriate values in the tblEmployees table. Name the query **UpdateJobClass**
5. Use SQL View to develop a query to count the number of employees in each job class. Title the summary column Count and name the query **EmployeesByClass**
6. Use SQL View to develop a query to count the number of employees in each state. Title the summary column Count and name the query **EmployeesByState**

7. Pete Mohr has moved to another company. Jack Hunt has been hired to replace him. Add Jack Hunt to tblEmployee. Use 387 S Harlan Ln., Seattle, WA 99900 as the address, 425-535-1233 as the phone number, and Designer as the Job Class
8. Create an Update Query that will assign Jack all of Pete's sites in tblCustomerSites. Save the query as **ChangeEmployee** (This step must be completed before deleting Pete's record so that his sites are not deleted too)
9. Create a Delete Query to remove records from tblEmployee. Prompt the user with **Enter the last name of the employee to delete**. Save the query as **DeleteEmployee**. Use the query to delete **Davis**

F I G U R E 9.35

EmployeesByClass and EmployeesByState

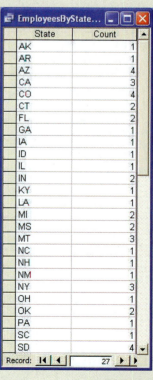

1. Advanced Queries for Community Hospital

Locate your copy of the database named **ac09CommunityHospital.mdb**. This database is used to track the skills of Community Hospital's critical medical staff. Open the relationships view so that you can see how the tables are related. Open each table and review the data; then determine how to implement each of the following

- Create a Crosstab Query comparing skills by unit. Include a selection criterion so that only two units are compared. Document how it would be used
- Create a parameter query with a custom form that will accept the unit and employee's last name and then display the skills for that employee
- Create a Delete, Update, Append, or Make-Table Query and document how it would be used
- Use SQL to create a query that joins two tables and aggregates data

2. Advanced Queries for your Multitable Database

Locate any multitable database that you have worked with during the course of this class. Take a look at your current database objects and determine how to implement each of the following

- Create a Crosstab Query with a selection criterion. Document how it would be used
- Create a parameter query with a custom form
- Create a Delete, Update, Append, or Make-Table Query and document how it would be used
- Use SQL to create a query that joins two tables and aggregates data

10

Automating Database Tasks

did you know?

Saturn *is named after the Roman god of seedtime and harvest.*

unopened *coconuts can be stored at room temperature for up to six months.*

in *1995 the potato became the first vegetable to be grown in space.*

seven *of the first ten domain names registered went to universities.*

logizomechanophobia *is the fear of computers.*

to *find out how fast the frigate bird can fly visit* www.mhhe.com/i-series.

Chapter Objectives

- **Create and edit macros**
- **Create, test, and run macro groups**
- **Debug a macro by single stepping**
- **Run a macro by attaching it to a command button**
- **Create a switchboard using the Switchboard Manager**
- **Set database startup options**

KoryoKicks: Building an End-User Interface

Professionally developed and distributed Access databases include icon-based user interfaces. A user interface provides familiar point-and-click ways to accomplish the most common database tasks and protects the structure of the database from becoming corrupted. Users of other Microsoft Windows applications are comfortable with the familiar menus, icons, and toolbars, and so learn the new application rapidly.

Database applications developed locally to support business operations should also be enhanced with a user interface consistent with the Microsoft Windows environment. Missy and Micah have been evaluating financial software to support the accounting needs of KoryoKicks. They have noticed the use of common interface features such as command buttons that would be appropriate for the KoryoKicks database.

The twins envision an environment where end users would be able to maintain and report on database data but would not be able to view or update the design of database tables, queries, forms,

or reports. They believe that a well-designed user interface will allow new employees to learn the applications in less time and with the certainty that database objects could not be accidentally damaged. The interface would also provide consistent access methods across all computers.

Their research indicates that macros can be used to create most of the automation for KoryoKicks and that the Switchboard Manager will allow the creation of point-and-click menus called switchboards. Database startup options are used to hide Access's normal toolbars and restrict the application's menu options to operations needed to maintain and report on data. Figure 10.1 depicts the opening form and end-user environment that the twins would like to build.

Both Missy and Micah have used the Microsoft Access Ask a Question feature to gather as much background on the processes as they can. They are ready to begin the development of the macros that will become the foundation of the user interface they have designed.

FIGURE 10.1

KoryoKicks end-user interface

restricted menu with no development options

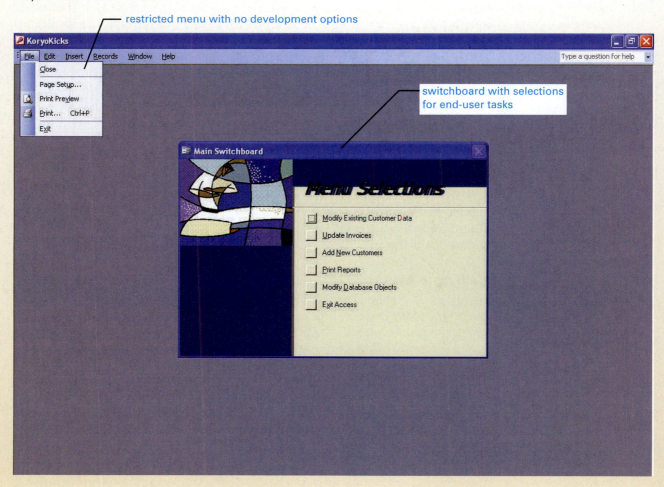

switchboard with selections for end-user tasks

SESSION 10.1 USING MACROS TO STORE ACTIONS

Most databases have a number of repetitive queries, forms, and reports. If the user normally opens the same form after opening a database, the task can be simplified by automatically opening the form when the database is launched. Macros provide the simplest way to automate such recurring tasks.

Choosing an Automation Method

The Access development interface where you have been working provides full entrée and control of all database functions, but is often too complex for users. Even those very familiar with the interface will agree that automation should be used to make repetitive tasks more straightforward. In Access, automated tasks can be created using *macros* or with *Microsoft Visual Basic for Applications (VBA)*. The automation method applied is dependent on the complexity of the task(s) to be performed.

AC 10.3

ACCESS

Macros are generally a better choice for simple tasks like running reports, opening forms, finding records, and closing open objects. Macros do not require an understanding of syntax, but are built by selecting actions such as OpenQuery or FindRecord from the Macro design grid. Once an action has been selected, arguments for that action can be specified in an environment similar to Table and Query Design Views.

Microsoft Visual Basic for Applications (VBA) is developed in a code window similar to SQL View. Like SQL, Visual Basic has keywords that must be memorized and a syntax that must be followed. While Visual Basic is more difficult to learn, it provides many more options than a macro, provides better error handling, makes an application easier to update, and often executes more efficiently. VBA will be covered in the next chapter.

Using Macros to Automate Tasks

Macros are created using the Macro object of the Database Window. Each macro can perform a series of specified actions. Macros are typically attached to a Command Button control on a form, report, or toolbar so that users can click to initiate the stored actions. For example, a command button could be added to a report that will print the report when clicked.

Building a Macro

The first step to building a macro is to decide what database task(s) need to be automated. One of the available actions must be used for each step of the automation. An *action* is an Access instruction to perform an operation like opening a form, copying an object, deleting an object, or displaying a query answerset. *Action arguments* are specified for each action outlining the object involved and how the action is to be executed.

In the preceding chapters, you have built Table, Query, Form, Report, and Page objects for KoryoKicks. Each of these objects is a candidate for automation. Multistep operations like backing up a table and then running an Update, Append, or Make-Table Query are ideal for macros. Missy and Micah want to start with something simple, so they ask you to show them how to run and print a query.

---

task reference   **Create a Macro**

- In the Database Window, click **Macros**

- Click the **New** button on the Database Window toolbar

- Add an action to the macro using the drop-down list in the Action column of the Macro design grid

- Use the lower part of the design grid to set the arguments for the action

- Add additional actions and set their arguments as needed

- Close, save, and name the macro

Creating a macro to run and print the CustomerOrdersJoin query:

1. Open the **ac10KoryoKicks.mdb** database

2. Select the **Macros** object from the Database Window

3. Click **New** on the Database Window toolbar to open the Macro design grid

4. Select the **OpenQuery** action from the Action drop-down list in the first row

tip: *Click in the first Action cell and the drop-down arrow will appear*

5. With the cursor still in the OpenQuery row
   a. Select **CustomerOrderJoin** from the Query Name drop-down list
   b. Select **Print Preview** from the View drop-down list
   c. Select **Read Only** from the Data Mode drop-down list

6. Move to the second row of the query and select **PrintOut** from the Action drop-down list. Review the arguments for this action, but do not change them

7. Move to the third row of the query and select **Close** from the Action drop-down list
   a. Set the Object Type argument to **Query**
   b. Set the Object Name argument to **CustomerOrderJoin**
   c. Set the Save argument to **No**

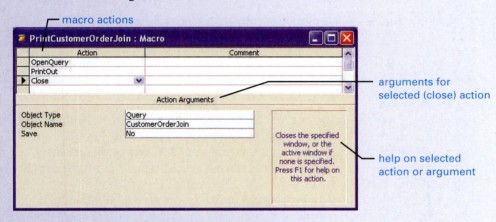

FIGURE 10.2

Print CustomerOrderJoin macro

8. Save the macro as **PrintCustomerOrderJoin**

9. Use the **Run** button of the Macro Design toolbar to execute the macro and observe the result

    The key to creating macros is to select the needed action and then set appropriate arguments. Comments can be added to any Action by clicking and typing in the Comments column of the appropriate row. Any comment entered is documentation only and has no impact on the associated action. The action arguments are set in the lower portion of the Macro window and are different for each action. These arguments provide additional information on how to carry out the selected action. When setting action arguments:

- Set arguments in the order listed since settings are often interdependent
- Object arguments can be set by dragging an object from the Database Window to the Macro design grid. Arguments are automatically set after such a drag
- Many arguments will accept an expression beginning with an equals sign (=)

    On occasion, you may want to perform an action or a series of actions only if a particular condition exists. For example, you may want to print the results of a query only if there are records to print. Or you may want to display one message when a retrieved

FIGURE 10.3

Sample conditional expressions

Use This Expression	To Carry Out the Action If
[City]="Paris"	Paris is the City value in the field on the form from which the macro was run
DCount("[OrderID]", "Orders")>35	There are more than 35 entries in the OrderID field of the Orders table
[ShippedDate] Between #2-Feb-2002# And #2-Mar-2002#	The value of the ShippedDate field on the form from which the macro is run is no earlier than 2-Feb-2002 and no later than 2-Mar-2002
Forms![Products]![Units InStock]<5	The value of the UnitsInStock field on the Products form is less than five
IsNull([FirstName])	The FirstName value on the form from which the macro is run is Null (has no value)
[Country] In ("France", "Italy", "Spain") And Len ([Postal Code])<>5	The value in the Country field on the form from which the macro is run is France, Italy, or Spain, and the postal code isn't five characters long
MsgBox("Confirm changes?",1)=1	You click **OK** in a dialog box in which the **MsgBox** function displays "Confirm changes?". If you click **Cancel** in the dialog box, Microsoft Access ignores the action

value is above a specific limit and another message when it is not. A conditional expression that evaluates to True/False (Yes/No) can be used to state the provision so that the macro will follow different paths based on the result of evaluating the statement.

The twins would like the ability to evaluate and edit query results before they are printed using a macro. A message box (*MsgBox*) will be used to implement this feature. The message box will contain instructions and two buttons: OK and Cancel. If the user clicks the OK button, the expression will evaluate to true and the datasheet contents will print. If the user clicks the Cancel button, no print will be submitted.

---

task reference

Adding Conditional Operations to a Macro

- In the Database Window, click **Macros**

- Click the **New** button to open a new macro or select the macro and click **Design** to open an existing macro

- Add the actions and arguments to be performed in the macro

- Click the **Conditions** 🔳 button on the Macro toolbar

- Enter a condition in the Condition column of the Action row to be conditionally executed

- Close, save, and name the macro

Creating a macro to conditionally print CustomersByState:

1. Verify that the **ac10KoryoKicks.mdb** database is open

2. Select the **Macros** object from the Database Window

3. Click **New** to open the Macro design grid

4. Select the **OpenQuery** action from the Action drop-down list in the first row
   a. Set the Query Name Action argument to **CstmrsByState**
   b. Set the View Action argument to **Datasheet**
   c. Set the Data Mode Action argument to **Read Only**

5. In line two of the Action column, select the Action **PrintOut**. The default Action Arguments need not be changed

6. In line three of the Action column, select the Action **Close**
   a. Set the Object Type Action Argument to **Query**
   b. Set the Object Name Action Argument to **CstmrsByState**
   c. Set the Save Action Argument to **No**

7. Click the **Conditions** button on the Macro toolbar

8. Enter **MsgBox("Click OK to print. Click Cancel not to print.",1)=1** in the Condition column of the PrintOut Action

tip: *There can be spaces in the text between the double quotes (" ") but not elsewhere in the statement. A column can be widened by dragging the right border of the gray button above it*

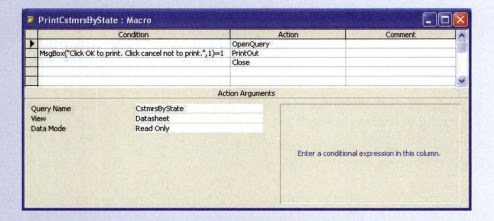

FIGURE 10.4
PrintCstmrsByState macro

9. Save the macro as **PrintCstmrsByState**

10. Use the **Run** button on the Macro Design toolbar to execute the macro. Click **OK** to print the query result.

11. Run the macro again. Click **Cancel** to abort the print

Microsoft Access executes macro actions without conditions from top to bottom. When a condition is added to the Macro design grid, the actions before the condition are performed in sequence, the condition statement is evaluated, the conditional action is executed only if the evaluation is true, and any remaining actions are completed in sequence.

Multiple conditions can be entered in the Condition column to create more complex macros, and an ellipsis (…) can be placed in the Condition column below an expression to make more than one action dependent on a condition. When the conditional requirements are more complex than this, Code Modules using Microsoft Visual Basic for Applications are probably a better solution.

Editing Macro Steps

Existing macros can be updated to improve functionality, repair processing errors, add features, or create new macros. The simplest edit is to change the action arguments of an existing action. Although macros will often work with multiple action argument settings, it is important that the settings match macro functionality. For example, the PrintCstmrsByState macro will run with any Data Mode argument for the OpenQuery action, but since data edits will not be completed while the macro is running, ReadOnly is the best setting. New arguments can be selected and saved applying the same techniques used to obtain the original settings.

New actions can be added to the end of an existing macro by moving to the first blank row of the Macro design grid, selecting the action, and setting the action arguments. To insert an action between two existing actions, move to the row below the row that will contain the new action, click the Insert Row button on the Macro Design toolbar, select the action from the drop-down action list, and set the action arguments.

Missy and Micah like being prompted before printing in the PrintCstmrsByState macro and would like other macros to mirror this behavior. The PrintCustomer OrderJoin will be updated by adding a condition to the print action.

Editing the PrintCustomerOrderJoin macro:

1. Verify that the **ac10KoryoKicks.mdb** database is open

2. Select the **Macros** object from the Database Window

3. Select **PrintCustomerOrderJoin** from the list of macros and click **Design**

4. Click the **Conditions** 🔧 button on the Macro Design toolbar

5. Enter **MsgBox("Click OK to print. Click Cancel not to print.",1)=1** in the Condition column of the PrintOut Action

6. Save and run the macro

The steps of an existing macro can also be reordered. Click the row selector (the small gray box to the left of a row that selects the entire row) of the action to be moved and then click and drag the selector to the new row position.

help yourself *Use the Type a Question combo box to improve your understanding of macros and macro groups by typing* **macro group**. *Review the contents of About macros or macro groups and Create a macro or macro group. Close the Help window when you are finished*

Building Macro Groups

Macros can be built and stored individually as demonstrated in the previous topic, or similar macros can be stored in a macro group. A *macro group* allows related macros to be stored and managed as a unit. When macros are stored in a group, they can be run as a unit or individually.

Grouping Macros

To group macros, the Macro Name column is added to the Macro design grid. The column contains a name for each new macro in the group. Saving and naming a macro grid with multiple macros creates a macro group. There is no absolute limit to the number of macros that can be placed in a group, but in general they should be related in some way. For example, the twins would like to create a point-and-click user interface to print reports using macros. It makes sense to place all of the macros to print reports into the same macro group.

---

task reference   **Creating a Macro Group**

- In the Database Window, click **Macros**

- Click the **New** button on the Database Window toolbar

- If the Macro Name column is not visible in the Macro design grid, click the **Macro Names** button on the Macro Design toolbar

- Type the name for the first macro and then enter the conditions, actions, and action arguments for that macro

- On the line under the last action of the first macro, enter the second macro name, and then enter the conditions, actions, and action arguments associated with this macro

- Continue adding macro names, conditions, actions, and action arguments to complete all of the macros in the group

- Close and name the macro group

Specifying the PrintReports macro group:

1. Verify that the **ac10KoryoKicks.mdb** database is open

2. Select the **Macros** object from the Database Window and click **New**

3. If the Macro Name column is not visible in the Macro design grid, click the **Macro Names** button on the Macro Design toolbar

4. In the first Macro design grid row
   a. Type **PrintCustomersByState** in the Macro Name column
   b. Select **OpenReport** as the Action and set the Action arguments to open the **CustomersByState** report in **Print Preview** View

5. In the second Macro design grid row, select **PrintOut** as the Action. Accept the default attributes

6. In the third Macro design grid row, select **MsgBox** as the Action and set the Message Argument by typing **CustomersByState has been printed**

7. In the Fourth Macro design grid row, select **Close** as the Action, set the Object Type to **Report**, the Object Name to **CustomersByState**, and Save to **No**

8. In the next blank row, type the Macro Name **PrintOrdersByOrderID**, select the **OpenReport** action and set it to open the **OrdersByOrderID** report in **Print Preview** View

9. In the next blank row, select **PrintOut** as the Action and accept the default Action Arguments

10. In the next blank row, select **MsgBox** as the Action and set the Message argument by typing **OrdersByOrderID has been printed**

11. In the next blank row, select **Close** as the Action, set the Object Type to **Report**, the Object Name to **OrdersByOrderID**, and Save to **No**

12. After the PrintOrdersByOrderID macro, create a **PrintOrdersByStateChart** macro containing the same actions as the first two macros built in these steps

FIGURE 10.5

PrintReports macro group

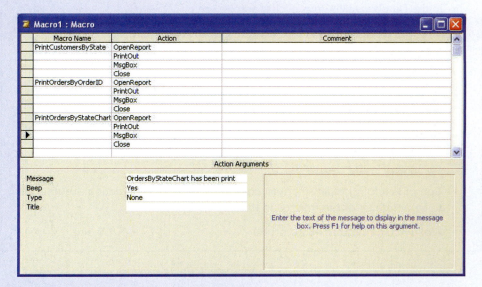

13. Save the macro group as **PrintReportsGroup**

Macro group names are listed with other macro objects in the Database Window. There is no special icon to identify macro groups, so it is a good idea for the name to indicate that multiple macros are stored under one name. For each new macro in the group, a name is placed in the Macro Name column. The Macro Name column is left blank when adding more actions to the same macro.

Individual macros in a group are referenced using the macro group name, a period, and the macro name. For example, *PrintReportsGroup.PrintOrdersByStateChart* refers to the last macro created in the previous steps. Macro names must be unique within a group. When a macro in a group is run, Access executes the first action of the macro and continues executing until either a new macro name or a StopMacro action is encountered.

Setting Macro Defaults

The macro development interface can be customized to better suit your needs. By default, the Macro design grid contains the Action and Comments columns, which are all that is necessary when developing single queries with no conditions. Within an individual query, the Macro Names and Conditions buttons on the toolbar can be used to display the additional columns as needed. When most macros developed will contain conditions or be macro groups, the interface can be customized to show those columns when a new macro is opened.

---

task reference — **Displaying Macro Name and Condition Columns by Default**

- On the Tools menu, click **Options**
- Select the **View** tab
- In the Show in Macro Design section of the View tab, check the **Names column** and/or the **Conditions column** check boxes

---

Steps are not included for changing the Macro design grid defaults because it is not necessary to complete chapter content. If displaying the Names and Conditions columns in the Macro design grid is the current setting, unchecking the boxes will remove them from all default displays.

Running and Debugging Macros

Macros can be executed a number of different ways. How you choose to run a macro depends on your preferences and what you are trying to accomplish. When a macro contains several steps and does not produce the desired results, macro debug features can be used to locate and repair the problem.

Executing a Macro

During development, macros can be run from the Macro design window by clicking the Run (exclamation point) button on the toolbar. When development is completed, single macros can be run from the Database Window, using the Tools menu, or in response to an event like opening a database or clicking a button. Individual macros in a macro group can be run from the Tools menu or in response to an event.

---

task reference — **Executing a Macro**

Do one of the following

- From the Macro window, click the **Run** button on the toolbar to run a stand-alone macro or the first macro in a macro group
- From the Database Window, select the **Macros** object and then double-click a macro name to run a stand-alone macro or the first macro in a macro group
- On the **Tools** menu, point to **Macro**, click **Run Macro**, and then select the macro from the Macro Name list to run any individual macro

---

Running KoryoKicks macros:

1. Verify that the **ac10KoryoKicks.mdb** database is open
2. Select the **Macros** object, click **PrintReportsGroup** and click **Design**
   a. Click the **Run** button

tip: *Only the first macro, PrintCustomersByState, should execute because macros only run until another macro is encountered*

b. Close the Macro window

3. With the Macros object still selected, double-click **PrintReportsGroup**

tip: *As before, only the first macro, PrintCustomersByState, should execute because macros only run until another macro is encountered*

4. With any object selected

a. Click the **Tools** menu, point to **Macro**, click **Run Macro**, then select **PrintReportsGroup.PrintCustomersByState** from the Macro Name list

FIGURE 10.6

Run Macro dialog box

b. Click **OK**

The method demonstrated in step 4 should be used when developing, editing, or testing macro groups since it can be used to run any member of the group.

Auto-Executing a Macro

On occasion there may be a macro that is run each time a database is opened. For example, you may need to print new orders each time the database is opened. Any macro named ***AutoExec*** will begin automatically running the next time the database is opened. Holding down the Shift key while a database is opening will suspend startup processing including the execution of the AutoExec macro.

Stepping through a Macro

When simply looking at the macro actions and arguments is not effective for diagnosing problems, ***single stepping*** allows you to directly observe the flow of the macro. In Single Step mode, you initiate each macro action and then directly observe the result.

---

task reference   **Single Stepping a Macro**

- Open the macro to be diagnosed in Design View
- Click the **Single Step** ![icon] button on the Macro Design toolbar
- Click the **Run** ![icon] button on the Macro Design toolbar
- Click **Step** to carry out an action and evaluate its result
- Click **Halt** to stop the macro and close the Macro Single Step dialog box

Single stepping the PrintCstmrsByState macro:

1. Verify that the **ac10KoryoKicks.mdb** database is open

2. Select the **Macros** object, click **PrintCstmrsByState**, and click **Design**

3. Click the **Single Step** button on the Macro Design toolbar

4. Click the **Run** button on the Macro Design toolbar

    a. Evaluate the action and action attributes displayed for the first macro action and then click **Step**

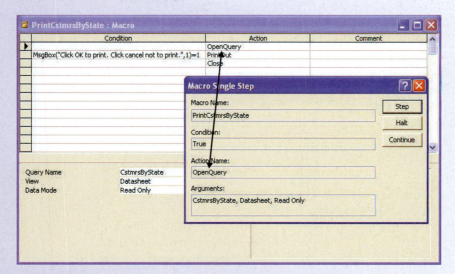

FIGURE 10.7
Stepping through the first action of PrintCstmrsByState

    b. Respond **OK** to the dialog box generated by the second action

    c. Review the Condition, Action Name, and Arguments for the second macro action and then click **Step**

    d. Review the Condition, Action Name, and Arguments for the third macro action and then click **Step**

5. Close the Macro window

Although the macro just stepped through was not in need of repair, it did demonstrate the evaluation features of stepping through a macro. Single stepping is ideal for locating errors in the order of actions, inappropriate actions, unneeded actions, and errant arguments.

Attaching a Macro to a Command Button

Although macros can be run from Macro Design View or from the Tools menu, it is not reasonable to expect users to avail themselves of stored actions that are so tedious to initiate. A simple solution is to attach the macro to a Command Button control that can simply be clicked by the user. The command button can be placed on any form, including built-in or custom toolbars.

Events

Microsoft Windows and all applications designed for the Windows environment make use of *events* to trigger programmatic actions. Not all events rely on a user, but user events are easier to see and understand. For example, when a user clicks the New Blank Document button on the Standard toolbar of any Microsoft application, a new document opens. In this case, clicking the button is an event that triggers the *event procedure* containing stored instructions on how to open a new document. Other examples of user events are double-clicking, scrolling, dragging, dropping, right-clicking, and triple-clicking.

The instructions executed in response to an event can be specified using macro actions, Visual Basic for Applications, or another programming language. Regardless of the method used to outline the actions, they are saved and given a name. The name is then used to activate the procedure.

Each object is designed to respond to specific events using *event properties*. Figure 10.8 shows some of the event properties available for command buttons. Command buttons use the On Click event property to determine what happens when the user clicks the button. The On Dbl Click property outlines the button's responses to double-clicking. By default, event properties are unset so that nothing happens in response to that event. For example, when a Command Button control is initially placed on a form, it will not respond to any events since all of its event properties are empty.

Running a Macro from a Command Button

It is common for users to seek more convenient ways to accomplish frequently repeated tasks. One way to accommodate this need is to attach macros to clickable objects like command buttons. The KoryoKicks employees would like a simple way to print data that are currently being viewed. A PrintObject macro will be created and then attached to a command button.

FIGURE 10.8

Command button event properties

---

task reference   Setting the On Click
                                       Event Procedure

- With a form or report open in Design View, right-click on the object that will respond to a click and select **Properties**

- Click the **Event** tab

- Click in the text box to the right of the On Click event property

- Either select a macro name from the drop-down list or use the Build (. . .) button to create an expression or event procedure

Attaching the PrintObject macro to a command button:

1. Verify that the **ac10KoryoKicks.mdb** database is open

2. Create the PrintObject macro
   a. Select the **Macros** object in the Database Window and click **New**
   b. Select **PrintOut** as the Action and set the Print Range argument to **Selection**
   c. Close the Macro Design Window and save the macro as **PrintObject**

3. Select the **Forms** object from the Database Window
   a. Click the **UpdateCustomers** object and click **Design**
   b. If necessary, deactivate the Control Wizard by clicking the **Control Wizard** button in the toolbox
   c. Click the **Command** button from the toolbox
   d. Click the form to position the command button as shown in Figure 10.9

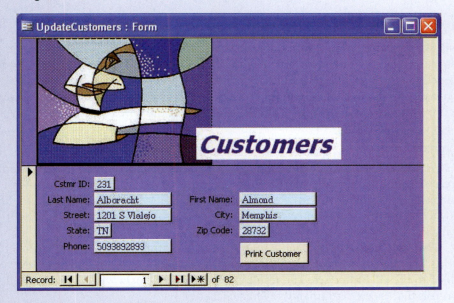

FIGURE 10.9
Print Customer button

tip: *If the Control Wizard initiates, cancel it*

4. Right-click on the new command button and select **Properties**
   a. On the Format tab, type **Print Customer** as the Caption property
   b. On the Event tab, use the drop-down list for the On Click event property to select **PrintObject**
   c. Close the Properties dialog box

5. Change to Form view and test the Print Customer button

Placing the name of a macro in an event property causes the macro to execute in response to the event. While any object that responds to events can be used to activate a macro, command buttons are most common.

making the grade

1. Compare and contrast macros and Microsoft Visual Basic for Applications.

2. What indicates that stepping through a macro could be helpful?

3. How are conditional actions specified in a macro?

4. What is the advantage of using the Tools menu to run a macro?

SESSION 10.2 CREATING A USER INTERFACE WITH SWITCHBOARDS

A *graphical user interface* (GUI; pronounced "gooey") provides the point-and-click environment most personal computer users have come to expect when interacting with software applications. While the Access development environment is perfect for creating database objects, it can be daunting for users. Macros and special forms called switchboards are used to construct a *user interface* using familiar Windows components like icons, dialog boxes, and pull-down menus.

Creating a Graphical User Interface (GUI)

Using common Windows components to build a GUI interface for a database simplifies the environment for end users. The familiar environment reduces the learning time needed to effectively use the database, improves productivity, decreases mistakes, and increases user satisfaction. Another benefit provided by a GUI is to protect database objects from inadvertent update by locking users out of the development environment.

Switchboards

A *switchboard* is a special form used to present a customized user environment to Access database users. Typically the switchboard is set to automatically open with the database so that the users can select from options designed to fulfill their needs. Since a switchboard is a custom interface, the designer has complete control over the options available and how they are presented to the user.

The *Switchboard Manager* is used to create, customize, and delete Switchboard forms. It is similar to a Wizard in that you can specify the commands and text to be added to the GUI interface. The result is a Switchboard form with Command Button controls that execute command(s) when clicked.

Adding a switchboard to a database creates two new objects in a database that should not be manually deleted: the Switchboard form and the Switchboard Items table. The Switchboard form object is the visual interface that will be presented to the user. The Switchboard Items table is used to track the items and their arguments that make the switchboard operational. Editing either of these objects outside the Switchboard Manager can cause the graphical user interface to malfunction.

The KoryoKicks switchboard should allow the user to access all forms, reports, and queries. The macros developed in the first session of this chapter will be used by the switchboard to print reports.

task reference   Creating a Switchboard

- Open the database to contain the switchboard
- On the Tools menu, point to **Database Utilities**, and then click **Switchboard Manager**
- Respond **Yes** if prompted to create a new switchboard
- The default Switchboard page named Main Switchboard is created
  - Click **Edit** to add items to the switchboard. This will open the Edit Switchboard dialog box
  - Click **New** on the Edit Switchboard Page dialog box to add a new item to Main Switchboard. This will open the Edit Switchboard Item dialog box
    - Enter the text to display on the switchboard
    - Select the command to execute when this item is activated from the drop-down Command list
    - Select any arguments needed for the selected command
    - Click **OK**
  - Repeat the previous step to add additional items to the switchboard. When all items have been added, click **Close**
- **Close** the Switchboard Manager

Beginning the KoryoKicks switchboard:

1. Verify that the **ac10KoryoKicks.mdb** database is open

2. On the Tools menu, point to **Database Utilities**, and then click **Switchboard Manager**

3. Respond **Yes** if prompted to create a new switchboard

4. In the Switchboard Manager dialog box with Main Switchboard (Default) selected, click **Edit** to modify the content of the main page

   a. In the Edit Switchboard Page dialog box click **New** to add the first switchboard item

      i. Type **Modify Existing Customer Data** for Text
      ii. Select **Open Form in Edit Mode** from the Command drop-down list
      iii. Select **UpdateCustomers** from the Form drop-down list
      iv. Click **OK**

   b. In the Edit Switchboard Page dialog box, click **New** to add a second switchboard item

      i. Type **Add New Customers** for Text
      ii. Select **Open Form in Add Mode** from the Command drop-down list
      iii. Select **UpdateCustomers** from the Form drop-down list
      iv. Click **OK**

   c. In the Edit Switchboard Page dialog box, click **New** to add a third switchboard item

      i. Type **View and Edit Invoices** for Text

      ii. Select **Open Form in Edit Mode** from the Command drop-down list

      iii. Select **Invoice** from the Form drop-down list

      iv. Click **OK**

   d. Click **Close** in the Edit Switchboard Page dialog box

5. Click **Close** in the Switchboard Manager dialog box

6. Click **Forms** in the Database Window and double-click on **Switchboard** to open that object

FIGURE 10.10

The Initial KoryoKicks switchboard

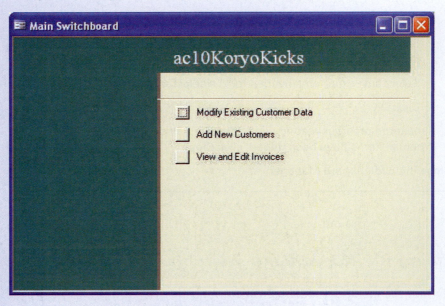

7. Click each of the switchboard buttons and observe the result

tip: *The switchboard will be behind any window that opens by clicking a switchboard button. Close the open window to return to the switchboard*

8. Close the switchboard and any windows opened from the switchboard

The switchboard developed in the preceding steps demonstrates the default Microsoft Access layout. Main Switchboard (see Figure 10.10 Title bar) is the normal name for the opening menu page, and the title is derived from the database name. Each item added to the switchboard page from the Switchboard Manager is represented as a command button with descriptive text. When the Switchboard form is activated, the command buttons can be clicked to execute the command outlined during switchboard development.

Although it is functional, this switchboard is not visually appealing and lacks the complexity needed for a viable interface. Cosmetic changes can be made to the switchboard in Form Design View, but it is important not to edit or delete buttons added from the Switchboard Manager. Additional elements that can be added to a switchboard include:

- *Shortcut* or *hot keys*. A shortcut key allows access to interface options from the keyboard. In Windows interfaces, the shortcut key is underlined and can be combined with the Alt key to activate an option

- Text boxes, pictures, and other elements to improve visual impact
- Links to other switchboard pages and/or custom dialog boxes
- Restricted access to tool and menu bars

Beautifying a Switchboard

Cosmetic changes are made to the switchboard using Form Design View. Changes impacting the functionality of the switchboard must be made from the Switchboard Manager. The twins would like the KoryoKicks logo and colors to appear on the switchboard to build a consistent image.

Beautifying the KoryoKicks switchboard:

1. Verify that the **ac10KoryoKicks.mdb** database is open

2. In the Database Window, select the **Forms** object, select the **Switchboard** form, and then click the **Design view** button

3. Right-click on the leftmost teal rectangle and select **Properties**
   a. Click the **Format** tab
   b. Locate the Back Color property and click the . . . (ellipsis) to the right of its value
   c. Select the blue color in the third row fifth column and then click **OK**
   d. Close the Image: Picture dialog box

4. Repeat step 3 to format the other teal rectangle

tip: *The Format Painter can be used to copy the format to the other rectangle*

5. Click **Insert**, **Picture**, navigate to the folder containing the data files for this chapter, select **ac10KoryoKicksLogo.gif**, and click **OK**

6. Adjust the position and size of the logo to match Figure 10.11

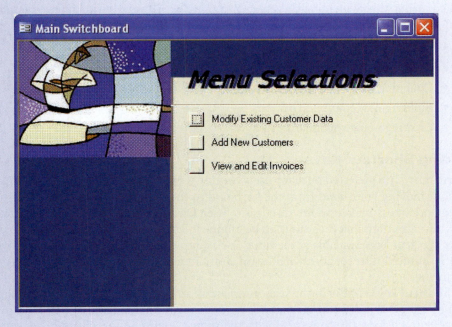

FIGURE 10.11

The beautified KoryoKicks switchboard

7. Right-click the ac10KoryoKicks text and choose **Properties**
   a. Change the Caption property to **Menu Selections**

    b. Set the Fore Color property to **Black**

    c. Set the Font Name property to **Tahoma**

    d. Set the Font Size property to **22**

    e. Set the Font Italic property to **Yes**

    f. Set the Font Weight property to **Semi-bold**

8. Use the Object drop-down list in the Properties dialog box to select the **Label2** control

tip: *It is the shadow behind the text edited in step 7*

    a. Set the Caption property to **Menu Selections**

    b. Set the Fore Color property to match the rectangles

    c. Set the Font Name property to **Tahoma**

    d. Set the Font Size property to **22**

    e. Set the Font Italic property to **Yes**

    f. Set the Font Weight property to **Semi-bold**

9. Close the dialog box

10. Use the Form View button to evaluate the modifications

11. Close the switchboard and any windows opened from the switchboard

The Format properties of any object on the Switchboard form can be modified in Design View without impacting switchboard functionality. For example, Command Buttons controls can have an image, text, and color added. The form itself is also an object with modifiable properties.

Modifying Switchboard Functionality

Modifications to the functionality of a switchboard can only be successfully accomplished using the Switchboard Manager. Examples of such switchboard updates include:

- Adding shortcut keys to menu option text
- Reordering the menu options
- Changing the menu option text
- Building new command buttons
- Creating new switchboard pages

Adding Shortcut Keys

Shortcut keys are preferred by many users because they allow commands to be executed without moving your hand from the keyboard to the mouse. Less motion and faster command access make the interface more user friendly. When developing shortcut keys, it is important that each shortcut be unique in its context. The context includes all other shortcut keys available at the time. For example, if the Standard menu is active, Alt+F should not be set as a switchboard shortcut key because it is already set as the File menu shortcut.

    Shortcut keys appear in the user interface as an underlined letter. Users familiar with Microsoft Windows know that Alt combined with the underlined letter is an alternative to clicking the command with the mouse. Defining the shortcut key is accomplished by adding an & (ampersand) before the shortcut letter in the text associated with a command.

task reference   Defining Shortcut Keys
                                                in a Switchboard

- On the Tools menu, point to **Database Utilities**, and then click **Switchboard Manager**
- Select the switchboard page and click **Edit**
- Select the Item and click **Edit**
- Insert an **&** (ampersand) before the shortcut character in the Text field
- Click **OK** on the Edit Switchboard Item dialog box
- **Close** the Edit Switchboard Page dialog box
- **Close** the Switchboard Manager

Adding shortcuts to the KoryoKicks switchboard:

1. Verify that the **ac10KoryoKicks.mdb** database is open

2. On the Tools menu, point to **Database Utilities**, and then click **Switchboard Manager**

3. With Main Switchboard (Default) selected, click **Edit**

4. With Modify Existing Customer Data selected, click **Edit**
   a. Place an **&** before the M in Modify
   b. Click **OK**

5. Select **Add New Customers** and click **Edit**
   a. Place an **&** before the N in New
   b. Click **OK**

6. Select **View and Edit Invoices** and click **Edit**

   a. Change View and Edit to **&Update**

tip: *If the menu is not hidden from the user, Edit and View are standard menu options making Alt+E and Alt+V inappropriate shortcuts for this switchboard item. Changing the text produced a viable shortcut key*

   b. Click **OK**

7. **Close** the Edit Switchboard Page dialog box

8. **Close** the Switchboard Manager dialog box

9. In the Database Window, select the **Forms** object, and double-click on **Switchboard**

10. Test the shortcut keys by holding down the Alt key and pressing an underlined letter

11. Close the switchboard and any windows opened from the switchboard

Most users prefer that the shortcut key be the first letter of the text, but that is not always possible. If the first letter is not chosen, use another prominent letter in the text

FIGURE 10.12
KoryoKicks shortcuts

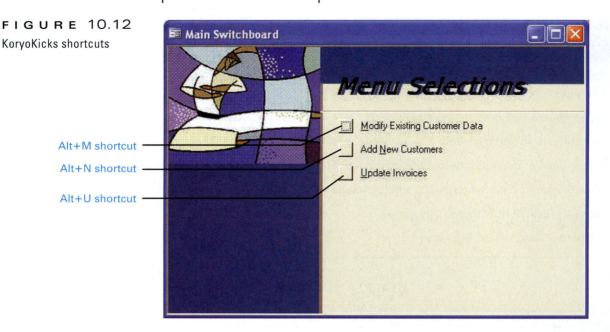

Alt+M shortcut

Alt+N shortcut

Alt+U shortcut

like the first letter of the second word or syllable. Sometimes changing the text associated with a command is necessary to produce a viable shortcut key.

Reordering Switchboard Items

The order of switchboard options is altered using the Switchboard Manager. The Move Up, Move Down, and Delete buttons on the Edit Switchboard Page dialog box are used to adjust item position.

---

task *reference*   Reordering Switchboard Items

- On the Tools menu, point to **Database Utilities**, and then click **Switchboard Manager**

- Select the switchboard page and click **Edit**

- Select the item to be moved or deleted

- Use the appropriate (Move Up, Move Down, or Delete) button to modify the item

- Click **Close** to close the Edit Switchboard Page dialog box

- Click **Close** to close the Switchboard Manager dialog box

---

Reordering items on the KoryoKicks switchboard:

1. Verify that the **ac10KoryoKicks.mdb** database is open

2. On the Tools menu, point to **Database Utilities**, and then click **Switchboard Manager**

3. With Main Switchboard (Default) selected, click **Edit**

4. With &Update Invoices selected, click **Move Up**

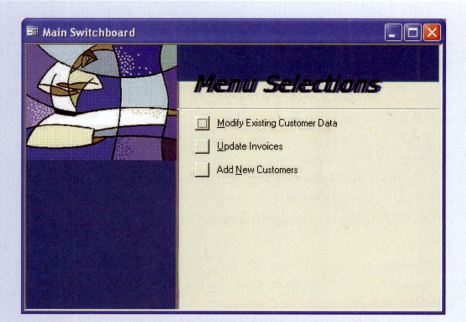

FIGURE 10.13
Reordered KoryoKicks
switchboard

5. **Close** the Edit Switchboard Page dialog box

6. **Close** the Switchboard Manager dialog box

7. In the Database Window, select the **Forms** object, then double-click on **Switchboard** and review the modification

8. Close the switchboard and any windows opened from the switchboard

When creating a user interface, it is customary to place the most frequently used items near the top. Items can also be grouped by type of task or table operated on. Regardless of how the items are organized, they should be easily recognized and accessed by the user.

Adding a New Switchboard Page

Often it is most effective to develop multiple switchboard pages. The main switchboard page can contain the most frequently accessed items or be a menu of switchboard pages. One way to organize KoryoKicks switchboards is by database object, developing a page for forms, a page for queries, and a page for reports. A new switchboard page will be developed to allow report printing. The macro group created in the previous session will provide automation for the print process.

Building the Print Reports switchboard:

1. Verify that the **ac10KoryoKicks.mdb** database is open

2. On the Tools menu, point to **Database Utilities**, and then click **Switchboard Manager**

3. In the Switchboard Manager, click **New**

4. Set the Switchboard Page Name to **Print Reports** and click **OK**

5. Select **Print Reports** from the list and click **Edit**

6. Click **New** to create a new switchboard item for the Print Reports Switchboard Page
   a. Type **Print Customers By State** as the Text
   b. Select **Run Macro** as the Command
   c. Select **PrintReportsGroup.PrintCustomersByState** as the Macro
   d. Click **OK**

7. Click **New** to create the second switchboard item for the Print Reports Switchboard Page
   a. Type **Print Orders By Order ID** as the Text
   b. Select **Run Macro** as the Command
   c. Select **PrintReportsGroup.PrintOrdersByOrderID** as the Macro
   d. Click **OK**

8. Click **New** to create a third switchboard item
   a. Type **Print Orders By State Chart** as the Text
   b. Select **Run Macro** as the Command
   c. Select **PrintReportsGroup.PrintOrdersByStateChart** as the Macro
   d. Click **OK**

9. Click **New** to create a fourth switchboard item
   a. Type **Return to &Main Switchboard** as the Text
   b. Select **Go to Switchboard** as the Command
   c. Select **Main Switchboard** as the Switchboard
   d. Click **OK**

10. Click **Close** to close the Edit Switchboard Page dialog box

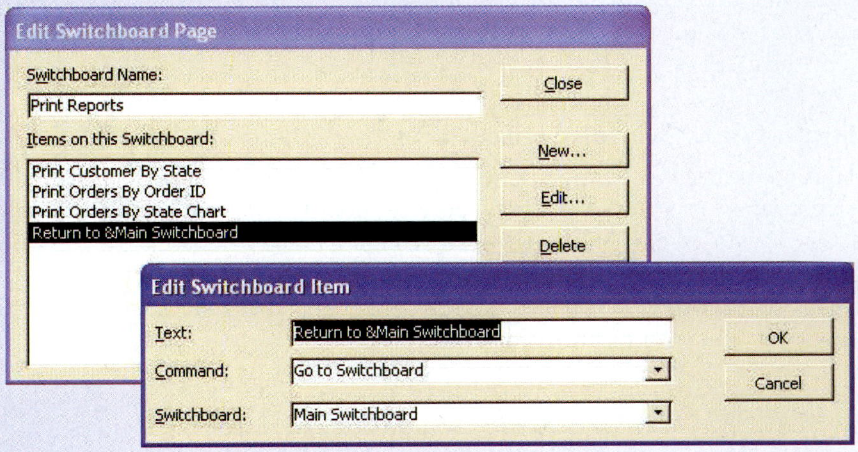

FIGURE 10.14

Building a second
switchboard page

The Print Reports switchboard page has options to print three KoryoKicks reports using macros from the PrintReportsGroup macro group. The fourth button will return the user to the Main Switchboard page. Now the link from the Main Switchboard page to the Print Reports page needs to be built and then the new interface options will be tested.

Adding a new button to the Main Switchboard page:

1. Verify that the **ac10KoryoKicks.mdb** database is open with the Switchboard Manager active

2. In the Switchboard Manager, Select **Main Switchboard (Default)** and click **Edit**

3. Select **Add &New Customers** and click **New**
   a. Type **&Print Reports** as the Text
   b. Select **Go to Switchboard** as the Command
   c. Select **Print Reports** as the Switchboard
   d. Click **OK**

4. **Close** the Edit Switchboard Page dialog box

5. **Close** the Switchboard Manager dialog box

6. In the Database Window, select the **Forms** object, then double-click on **Switchboard** and review the modification

7. Click the **Print Reports** button and test printing the reports

8. Click **Return to Main Switchboard**

9. Close the switchboard and any windows opened from the switchboard

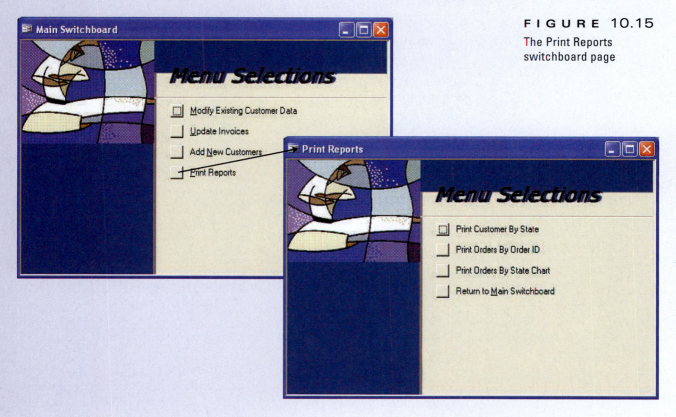

F I G U R E 10.15

The Print Reports switchboard page

*another***word**   . . . on Switchboards

By default, the Main Switchboard page opens first. To make another switchboard page open first, select it in the Switchboard Manager and then click Make Default

There is no limit to the number of switchboard pages that can be created, or on how those pages are interconnected. It is important to plan and organize the options that will be available to the user. When a switchboard page is created in error or is no longer needed, it can be deleted from the Switchboard Manager using the Delete button.

Finalizing the Graphical User Interface

Once the switchboard pages and interactions are set, it is time to finalize switchboard properties. The properties are used to control form behaviors such as whether or not a close button displays in the Title bar. When the form properties preclude the use of normal methods of closing it, buttons must be added to exit the interface.

Customizing Switchboard Properties

Like all forms, switchboards have properties that control their appearance and behavior. When a new switchboard is created, default properties are assigned that will allow the user to close, resize, and move the switchboard. In a controlled user environment, switchboard properties need to prevent the user from changing or closing the form. Missy and Micah would like the KoryoKicks switchboard to have a fixed size and position.

Setting switchboard properties:

1. Verify that the **ac10KoryoKicks.mdb** database is open

2. Select **Forms** in the Database Window, select the **Switchboard** form, and then click **Design**

3. Double-click the Form selector (the square in the top-left corner of the rulers) to open the Form Properties

   a. Set AutoResize to **No**

   tip: *You may need to adjust form size to match the content*

   b. Set Border Style to **Dialog**

   c. Set Max Min Buttons to **None**

   d. Set Close button to **No**

   e. Set Moveable to **No**

4. **Close** the Form properties dialog box

5. Change to Form View and notice the modifications to the Title bar. Try to move the switchboard (see Figure 10.16)

6. Change to Design View

Compare the switchboard Title bar in Figure 10.16 to that shown in Figure 10.15. Notice that after the form properties are set, the Minimize and Maximize buttons do not appear. Additionally, the Close button is disabled. Since the Access toolbar is still active, it can be used to return to Design View. When the user is to be blocked from design updates, this toolbar is typically hidden or disabled.

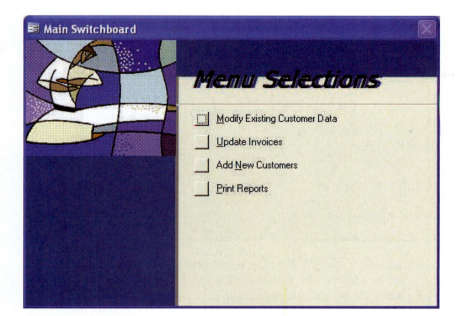

Exiting the Graphical User Interface

Most switchboards should include an option to close Microsoft Access. If users are to be allowed to make changes in the Access development environment, the switchboard should also close leaving the Database Window open. Both capabilities will be added to the KoryoKicks switchboard.

To enter the Access development environment, a macro is necessary. Switchboard commands do not include the ability to close open objects. This being the case, a macro will be created to close the switchboard form and added to the switchboard.

Building the CloseSwitchboard macro:

1. Verify that the **ac10KoryoKicks.mdb** database is open

2. Select the **Macros** object in the Database Window and click **New**

3. If necessary, activate the Names column using the **Macro Names** button

4. In the first row, type **Close** as the Name

   a. Set the Action to **Close**

   b. Set the Object Type to **Form**

   c. Set the Object Name to **Switchboard**

   d. Set Save to **No**

5. In the second row, type **Quit** as the Name and set the Action to **Quit**

6. Save the macro as **CloseSwitchboard** (see Figure 10.17)

7. **Close** the Macro design window

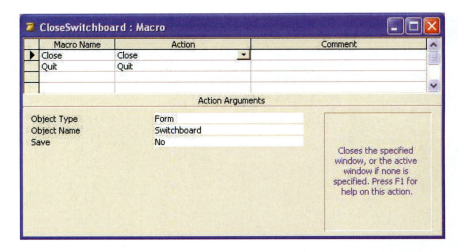

The CloseSwitchboard macro will be activated using the Switchboard Manager. Two new buttons will be added to the Main Switchboard. The first button will allow the user to exit to the development environment using the CloseSwitchboard macro, while the second will close Access.

Adding exits to the Main Switchboard page:

1. Verify that the **ac10KoryoKicks.mdb** database is open

2. Open the **Switchboard Manager**

3. In the Switchboard Manager, Select **Main Switchboard (Default)** and click **Edit**

4. Select **&Print Reports** and click **New** to add a Switchboard page

   a. Type **Modify &Database Objects** as the Text

   b. Select **Run Macro** as the Command

   c. Select **CloseSwitchboard.Close** as the Macro

   d. Click **OK**

5. Select **Modify &Database** Objects and click **New** to add another Switchboard page

   a. Type **E&xit Access** as the Text

   b. Select **Run Macro** as the Command

   c. Select **CloseSwitchboard.Quit** as the Macro

   d. Click **OK**

6. **Close** the Edit Switchboard Page dialog box

7. **Close** the Switchboard Manager dialog box

8. In the Database Window, select the **Forms** object, then double-click on **Switchboard** and review the new buttons (see Figure 10.18)

tip: *You will need to reopen the switchboard after testing the Modify Database Objects button and restart Access after testing the Exit Access button*

Keep the users' needs and security in mind when developing switchboard exits. If modifications to database objects will not be completed by the users, no option to close the switchboard (Modify Database Objects button) is needed. Additional options can be added to the switchboard as needed.

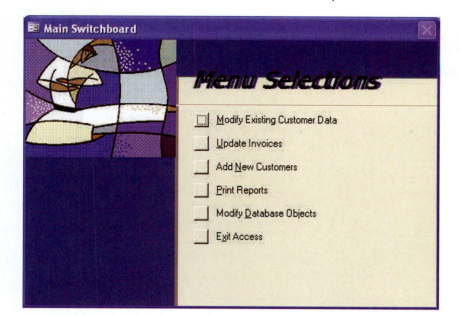

FIGURE 10.18
Exits added to the
KoryoKicks switchboard

help yourself *Use the Type a Question combo box to improve your understanding of Access switchboard operations by typing* **switchboard**. *Review the contents of* Create, customize, *and* delete a switchboard form. *Close the Help window when you are finished*

Setting Database Startup Options

Each Access database has startup option settings that control how the database behaves as it opens. These *startup options* include what form to display, whether toolbars can be customized, and whether shortcut menus are available. Remember that in addition to these options, an AutoExec macro can be created with tasks that will execute each time the database opens.

Startup options should help the user and protect database data and objects. Remove any options that should not be available to the user. Although it is probably not necessary for the KoryoKicks database to be completely secured since there are so few users, a closed user environment will be created for demonstration purposes.

---

task reference   **Setting Startup Options**

- On the Tools menu, click **Startup**

- Select the options or enter the desired settings

Setting KoryoKicks startup options:

1. Verify that the **ac10KoryoKicks.mdb** database is open

2. On the Tools menu, click **Startup**

3. Select **Switchboard** from the Display Form/Page drop-down list

4. Set the remaining options to match Figure 10.19

5. Click **OK**

F I G U R E 10.19

Setting startup options

F I G U R E 10.19

Setting startup options

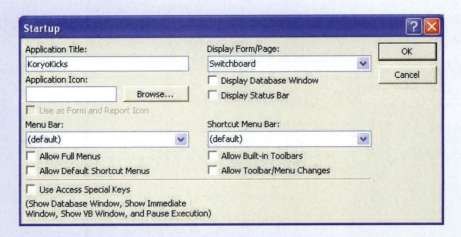

6. **Close** the Database Window to close the KoryoKicks database

7. Use the Open option of the File menu to reopen **ac10KoryoKicks.mdb**

F I G U R E 10.20

The KoryoKicks user interface

application name

switchboard displays at startup

no Database Window or toolbars

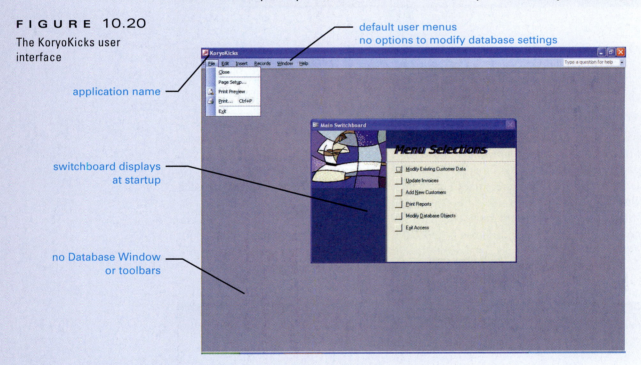

default user menus
no options to modify database settings

8. Explore the user interface

Changes made to the startup options do not take effect until the next time the database is opened. The previous steps created a user interface with no ability to reach the Access development environment. The settings disabled the normal database menus, toolbars, shortcuts, status bar, access keys, and Database Window. The settings are:

- Application Title—the text to appear in the Title bar
- Display Form/Page—the active form (usually the switchboard)
- Application Icon—the icon in the Title bar
- Display Database Window—when checked, the Database Window will display behind the Display Form/Page object

- Display Status Bar—when checked, the status bar will display
- Menu Bar—allows custom menus developed for the application to be displayed
- Allow Full Menus—when checked, the user will have full use of all Access menus
- Allow Default Shortcut menus—when checked, the user will have full use of Access shortcut menus
- Allow Built-in Toolbars—when checked, the user will have full use of all Access toolbars
- Allow Toolbar/Menu Changes—when checked, the user will be able to customize menus and toolbars
- Use Access Special Keys—when checked, the user will be able to enter the development environment using keystrokes such as F11 to open the Database Window

It may have occurred to you that the current KoryoKicks settings leave no way for you, the developer, to modify database objects and settings from the end-user environment. While this is true, the startup processes can be bypassed by holding down the Shift key while the database loads.

task reference — **Bypassing Startup Options**

- Open Access with no active database
- Click the **Open** button
- Navigate to the file and click to select it
- Hold the **Shift** key while clicking the **Open** button (or double-click a selected file)
- Release the Shift key when the load process is complete

Bypassing the KoryoKicks startup options:

1. Verify that Access is running with no database open
2. Click the **Open** button
3. Navigate to **ac10KoryoKicks.mdb** and click to select it
4. Hold the **Shift** key while clicking the **Open** button
5. Release the Shift key when the database load has completed
6. Explore the development interface

Missy and Micah are pleased with the KoryoKicks user interface. The switchboard now allows access to the most commonly used database items and can be modified to allow use of other objects as they are needed.

ACCESS

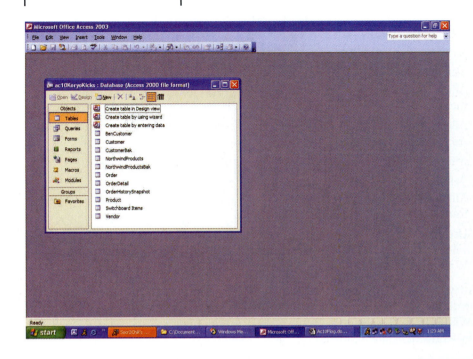

SESSION 10.2

making *the grade*

1. What are the benefits of building a GUI for an Access database?

2. How is the Switchboard Manager used to create a GUI?

3. How are shortcut or hot keys important to a GUI?

4. What modifications can be made to a switchboard in Form Design View?

SESSION 10.3 SUMMARY

Database development is not complete when all of the tables, forms, reports, and queries needed to support the user have been put into production. While these database objects provide all of the functionality necessary to complete user tasks, the Access development environment does not make these items easy to locate and use.

A complete database application automates common user tasks so that they are available in a point-and-click graphical user interface (GUI). The simplest automation method is to create macros for common tasks. Using Microsoft Visual Basic for Applications to automate tasks will be covered in a later chapter. Macros are simple to create because they are comprised of actions selected from a drop-down list. An action is an operation such as opening or copying an object. The action arguments specify the object to be acted upon and any parameters for that action. When all of the needed actions are added to the macro, it is saved with a name that will be used to run the actions.

When several macros are related in some way, they can be stored under the same name as a macro group. An individual macro from a macro group is run using the *GroupName.MacroName*. In addition to the Name column needed to create macro groups, the Macro Development grid can have a Condition column. The Condition column is used to conditionally execute a macro action.

The Switchboard Manager is used to create a point-and-click graphical user interface (GUI). A switchboard is a form with buttons for common user tasks such as opening a form or running a query. Some commands are available directly from the Switchboard Manager, but it is more common to use macros or event procedures to provide the automation behind the buttons. Multiple switchboard pages can be created so that all user options are organized and easily available. Switchboard formatting changes can be made from Form Design View, but functional changes must be made in the Switchboard Manager.

Visit www.mhhe.com/i-series/ to explore related topics.

MICROSOFT OFFICE SPECIALIST OBJECTIVES SUMMARY

- No specific MOS objectives were addressed in this chapter

making the grade answers

SESSION 10.1

1. Both macros and VBA are used to automate tasks. Macros can be developed for simple operations without understanding syntax. More complex operations require the use of VBA, which entails learning keywords and syntax.

2. When a macro is producing erroneous results and a review of the actions and action attributes doesn't uncover the problem, try stepping through the macros.

3. The Condition column must be added to the macro using the toolbar button and then a condition can be entered into the column before the action to be provisionally executed. Conditions are expressions that evaluate to either True or False. If the condition evaluates to True the action will be completed. If the condition evaluates to False, the action will not be completed.

4. The Tools menu allows any macro in a macro group to be executed.

SESSION 10.2

1. A GUI provides a familiar controlled environment for an end-user to interact with the database. All of the options needed for the users to complete their tasks should be available in an easy-to-learn point-and-click environment. Additionally, the application looks more professional.

2. The Switchboard Manager is used to create and maintain the switchboard, which provides the application's menus. It must be used to add, move, or delete switchboard buttons. It is also used to create new switchboard pages and to attach actions to each added button.

3. Shortcut or hot keys provide a way for the user to interact with the interface from the keyboard. Shortcuts are faster for experienced users and require less hand motion to complete tasks.

4. Formatting or beautification updates can be made to a switchboard in Form Design View without impacting functionality. Such updates include adding images, changing colors, and modifying the various font settings. Changes that impact the functionality of the switchboard must be made in the Switchboard Manager.

task reference *summary*

Task	Page #	Preferred Method
Create a macro	AC 10.4	• In the Database Window, click **Macros** • Click the **New** button on the Database Window toolbar • Add an action to the macro using the drop-down list in the Action column of the Macro design grid • Use the lower part of the design grid to set the arguments for the action • Add additional actions and set their arguments as needed • Close, save, and name the macro
Adding conditional operations to a macro	AC 10.6	• In the Database Window, click **Macros** • Click the **New** button to open a new macro or select the macro and click **Design** to open an existing macro • Add the actions and arguments to be performed in the macro • Click the **Conditions** [icon] button on the Macro toolbar • Enter a condition in the Condition column of the Action row to be conditionally executed • Close, save, and name the macro
Creating a macro group	AC 10.9	• In the Database Window, click **Macros** • Click the **New** button on the Database Window toolbar • If the Names column is not visible in the Macro design grid, click the **Macro Names** [icon] button on the Macro Design toolbar • Type the name for the first macro and then enter the conditions, actions, and action arguments for that macro • On the line under the last action of the first macro, enter the second macro name, and then enter the conditions, actions, and action arguments with this macro • Continue adding macro names, conditions, actions, and action arguments to complete all of the macros in the group • Close, save, and name the macro group
Displaying Macro Name and Condition columns by default	AC 10.11	• On the Tools menu, click **Options** • Select the **View** tab • In the Show in Macro Design section of the View tab, check the **Names column** and/or the **Conditions column** check boxes
Executing a macro	AC 10.11	Do one of the following • From the Macro Window, click the **Run** [icon] button on the Macro Design toolbar to run a stand-alone macro or the first macro in a macro group • From the Database Window, select the **Macros** object and then double-click macro name to run a stand-alone macro or the first macro in a macro group • On the **Tools** menu, point to **Macro**, click **Run Macro**, and then select the macro from the Macro Name list to run any individual macro
Single stepping a macro	AC 10.12	• Open the macro to be diagnosed in Design View • Click the **Single Step** [icon] button on the Macro Design toolbar • Click the **Run** [icon] button on the toolbar • Click **Step** to carry out an action and evaluate its result • Click **Halt** to stop the macro and close the Macro Single Step dialog box
Setting the On Click event procedure	AC 10.14	• With a form or report open in Design View, right-click on the object that will respond to a click and select **Properties** • Click the **Event** tab • Click in the text box to the right of the On Click event property • Either select a macro name from the drop-down list or use the Build (…) button to create an expression or event procedure

task reference summary

Task	Page #	Preferred Method
Creating a switchboard	AC 10.17	• Open the database to contain the switchboard • On the Tools menu, point to **Database Utilities**, and then click **Switchboard Manager** • Respond **Yes** if prompted to create a new switchboard • The default Switchboard page named Main Switchboard is created • Click **Edit** to add items to the switchboard. This will open the Edit Switchboard dialog box • Click **New** on the Edit Switchboard Page dialog box to add a new item to Main Switchboard. This will open the Edit Switchboard Item dialog box • Enter the text to display on the switchboard • Select the command to execute when this item is activated from the drop-down Command list • Select any arguments needed for the command • Click **OK** • Repeat the previous step to add additional items to the switchboard. When all items have been added, click **Close** • **Close** the Switchboard Manager
Defining shortcut keys in a switchboard	AC 10.21	• On the Tools menu, point to **Database Utilities**, and then click **Switchboard Manager** • Select the switchboard page and click **Edit** • Select the item and click **Edit** • Insert an **&** (ampersand) before the shortcut character in the Text field • Click **OK** on the Edit Switchboard Item dialog box • **Close** the Edit Switchboard Page dialog box • **Close** the Switchboard Manager
Reordering switchboard items	AC 10.22	• On the Tools menu, point to **Database Utilities**, and then click **Switchboard Manager** • Select the switchboard page and click **Edit** • Select the item to be moved or deleted • Use the appropriate (Move Up, Move Down, or Delete) button to modify the item • Click **Close** to close the Switchboard Item dialog box • Click **Close** to close the Switchboard Manager dialog box
Setting startup options	AC 10.29	• On the Tools menu, click **Startup** • Select the options or enter the desired settings
Bypassing startup options	AC 10.31	• Open Access with no active database • Click the **Open** button • Navigate to the file and click to select it • Hold the **Shift** key while clicking the **Open** button • Release the Shift key when the database load has completed • Explore the development interface

TRUE/FALSE

1. A macro can be used to automate any repetitive database task.

2. Access switchboards can contain a maximum of three pages.

3. Switchboard properties control whether or not the Switchboard Window can be closed, maximized, minimized, or resized.

4. In a macro with a condition statement, the actions associated with the condition will execute only if the condition is true.

5. User events such as clicking a button trigger event procedures containing stored instructions on how to complete a task.

6. A switchboard is a specialized Microsoft Access report.

FILL-IN

1. _____ are constructed by selecting Actions.

2. The Condition column is added to the Macro design grid by _____.

3. A _____ is used to display a message to the user and allow the user to select a course of action.

4. _____ are/is used to see the result of each macro action to evaluate and repair execution problems.

5. _____ are/is used to attach a macro to a command button or other object.

6. The _____ is used to add and edit the functionality of switchboard options.

7. A(n) _____ before a letter in the text of a switchboard item creates a shortcut that can be used to initiate that action.

MULTIPLE CHOICE

1. _____ changes to a switchboard can be made in Form Design View.
   a. Simple
   b. Functional
   c. Cosmetic
   d. All of the above

2. Shortcut or hot keys allow the user to make selections _____.
   a. without taking their hands off the keyboard
   b. using a mouse click
   c. by touching the screen
   d. all of the above

3. Creating a new switchboard builds _____.
   a. a form only
   b. a form and table
   c. a form, a table, and a report
   d. none of the above

4. A new switchboard page is created by _____.
   a. copying and pasting a new command button in Form Design View
   b. selecting a new command from the Switchboard Manager
   c. running a macro from Form Design View
   d. clicking the New button in the Switchboard Manager

5. A database's _____ control what processes are executed as the database opens (before the user can interact with the database).
   a. load options
   b. startup options
   c. AutoExec
   d. default properties

REVIEW QUESTIONS

Each of the following topics should be addressed in one to three paragraphs.

1. How do you cause a macro to run automatically each time the database is opened?

2. How is an individual macro in a macro group executed?

3. Explain the difference between an event property and an event procedure.

4. Why must the functionality of a switchboard be maintained using the Switchboard Manager?

5. How do you determine what character to use as a shortcut key?

CREATE THE QUESTION

For each of the following answers, create the question.

ANSWER	QUESTION
1. Make Default button	_____
2. Right-click the object and select Properties	_____
3. Hold down the Shift key while the database loads	_____
4. The next time the database is opened	_____
5. action arguments	_____
6. Click Tools|Database Utilities|Switchboard Manager	_____
7. On Click event procedure	_____

FACT OR FICTION

For each of the following, determine whether the statement is fact, fiction, or both and present your arguments for that conclusion.

1. All switchboards should contain multiple pages.

2. The switchboard page named Main Switchboard must always be the first page to open.

3. Placing an & before a character in the text of a switchboard item creates a shortcut key.

4. Macros are easier than Microsoft Visual Basic for Applications.

5. Each macro in a macro group must have a unique name.

6. Event procedure and event property are synonyms.

7. Stepping through or single stepping a macro causes it to execute one line at a time so that the result of each line can be observed and evaluated.

1. Completing the KoryoKicks Switchboard

The main pages of the KoryoKicks switchboard were developed in the chapter but do not provide user access to tables and queries. In these steps, you will create an additional switchboard page for these remaining objects with navigation to and from the Main Switchboard page. Tables and queries cannot be opened directly using Switchboard Commands, so macros must be created for each switchboard button.

1. Create a macro group named **TablesAndQueries**

   a. Build a macro named **OpenVendor** that will open the Vendor table to be edited in Datasheet View

   b. Build a macro named **OpenProduct** that will open the Product table to be edited in Datasheet View

   c. Build a macro named **OpenHighVolume** that will open the HighVolume query to be read-only in Datasheet View

   d. Build a macro named **OpenProductByState** that will open the ProductsByStateCrosstab Query to be read-only in Datasheet View

F I G U R E 10.22

The new KoryoKicks switchboard page

2. Open the Switchboard Manager

3. Create a new switchboard page named **Tables and Queries**

4. Edit the Tables and Queries switchboard page

   a. Create a new item, **&Vendor Table**, that runs the **TablesAndQueries.OpenVendor** macro

   b. Create a new item, **&Products Table**, that runs the **TablesAndQueries.OpenProducts** macro

   c. Create a new item, **&High Volume Query**, that runs the **TablesAndQueries.OpenHighVolume** macro

   d. Create a new item, **Products By State &Crosstab**, that runs the **TablesAndQueries.OpenProductsByState** macro

   e. Create a new item, **Return to &Main Switchboard**, that returns to the Main Switchboard page

5. Close the Edit Switchboard Page dialog box

6. Edit the Main Switchboard (Default) page to include **&Tables and Queries** after &Print Reports. Set the item to open the Tables and Queries switchboard page

7. Close the Edit Switchboard Page dialog box

8. Close the Switchboard Manager and test the interface updates

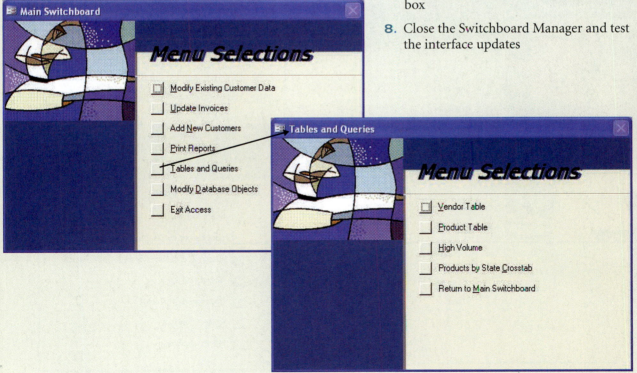

2. xXtreMeSportz.com—Part IV: Switchboard

xXtreMeSportz.com is organizing a snowboarding competition in Utah. The tables and queries to support this process were developed in Chapter 9 Practice, Challenge, and e-Business projects. This project will create switchboard access to new forms that you will build and whatever features you developed in Chapter 9.

1. Use Microsoft Windows to create a copy of your ac09xXtreMeSponsors.mdb file named **ac10xXtreMeSponsors.mdb**

2. Start Access and open **ac10xXtreMeSponsors.mdb**

3. Use the Forms Wizard to build a form with all of the fields from tblSponsors and ID and Contribution from tblContributions

   a. View the data in subforms by tblSponsors

   b. Use the **Tabular** layout and **Ricepaper** style

   c. Name the form **Contributions**

4. Create a macro group named **SwitchboardMacros**

   a. Build a macro named **OpenEventJoinQuery** that will open the EventJoinQuery query to be edited in Datasheet View

   b. Build a macro named **OpenContributionsByStateAndOrganizer** that will open the ContributionsByStateAndOrganizer query to be edited in Datasheet View

   c. Build a macro named **OpenAvgContributionsByStateAndOrganizer** that will open the AvgContributionsByStateAndOrganizer query to be edited in Datasheet View

   d. Build a macro named **ExitAccess** that will exit Access

5. Open the Switchboard Manager

   a. Create a new switchboard page named **Queries**

   b. The Main Switchboard page should contain options to open the **&Contributions** form, open the **&Queries** page, and **E&xit Access**

   c. The Queries page should use the macros from step 4 to run each query. Include shortcut keys and an option to return to the main page

6. Add the graphic **ac10xXtreMeSportz.gif** to the switchboard. Modify the rectangle colors to complement the logo

7. If you completed the Chapter 9 Challenge project, use macros to add switchboard buttons for the UnassignedSponsors, UnassignedOrganizers, and AssignSponsor queries to the Queries page

8. If you completed the Chapter 9 e-Business project, add options to open both the LookupSponsors and EventOrganizersParameter forms in Edit mode on the Main Switchboard page

9. If your work is complete, exit Access; otherwise, continue to the next assignment

FIGURE 10.23

xXtreMeSportz.com switchboard

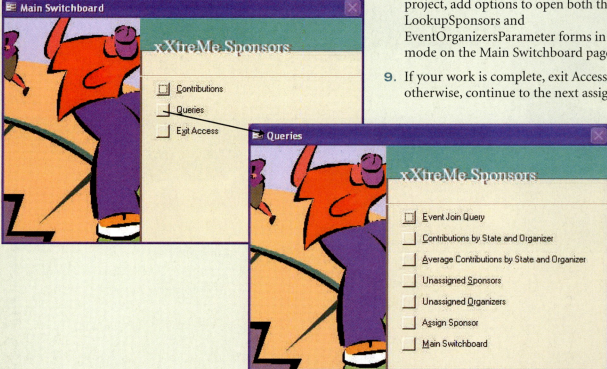

1. Rose University GUI

Rose University is a prestigious midwestern university specializing in math, science, and engineering. You have been asked to create a graphical user interface for the database that tracks professors, courses offered, and student enrollment.

1. Open **ac10RoseUniversity.mdb**

2. Create a macro named **PrintCurrentObject** that will print the current object. Attach the macro to a command button labeled Print on the main **EnrollStudent** form. The macro should verify that the user wants to print using a message box. Test the command button by printing CSI230

3. Create a macro named **PrintClassRosters** to display the ClassRosters report in Print Preview. Use a message box to verify that the user wants to print the displayed report and then close the report

4. Create a macro named **PrintInstructors** to display the Instructors report in Print Preview. Use a message box to verify that the user wants to print the displayed report and then close the report

5. Create a macro named **PrintStudentSchedule** to display the StudentSchedule report in Print Preview. Use a message box to verify that the user wants to print the displayed report and then close the report

6. Develop a Switchboard interface for the Rose University database

   a. The Main Switchboard page should contain options to open each form (EnrollStudent, MaintainCourses, MaintainProfessors, and MaintainStudents) in Edit mode, the Queries Switchboard page, the Reports Switchboard page, Perform Development Tasks, and Exit Access

   b. Use Figure 10.24 to set hot keys

   c. Use macros to close the switchboard (perform development tasks) and exit Access

   d. The Queries page should use macros to open each query and contain a link back to the Main Switchboard

   e. The Reports page should use the macros developed to open each report and contain a link back to the Main Switchboard page

7. Add the **ac10RoseGraphic.wmf** image to the switchboard

8. Set the Switchboard properties so that it cannot be resized, closed, moved, maximized, or minimized

9. Set the database startup options to open the Main Switchboard without the Database Window when the database is opened

10. Test the interface updates

FIGURE 10.24
Rose University switchboard

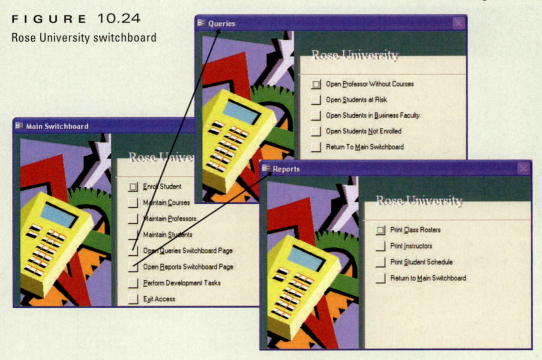

2. TechRocks Seminars Switchboard

TechRocks Seminars is an organization that markets seminars. You will improve their database by using Wizards to build simple forms and reports, building automation macros, and then using the Switchboard Manager to create a GUI for the Success Training database

1. Start Access and open your copy of **ac10TechRocks.mdb**

2. Use the Forms Wizard to build a form with all of the fields from Schedule and all nonduplicate fields from Enrollment
   a. View the data in subforms by Schedule
   b. Use the **Tabular** layout and **Ricepaper** style
   c. Name the form **Enrollment**

3. Use the Report Wizard to create **TrainerClassListing**
   a. Include all of the fields from Schedule, the Last and First names from Trainer, and Student Number, Last Name, First Name, and Student Phone from Enrollment
   b. Display the data by Trainer
   c. Group by Student Number, sort by LastName and FirstName
   d. Use the Formal format

FIGURE 10.25
Success Training Inc. switchboard

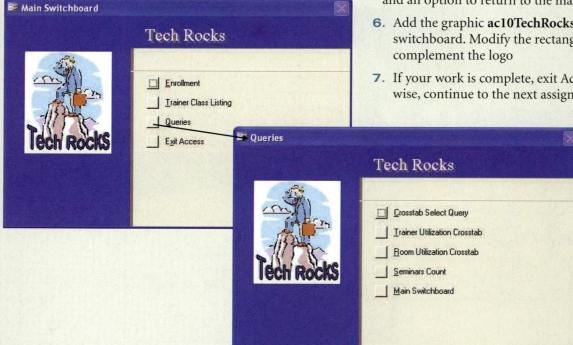

4. Create a macro group named **SwitchboardMacros**
   a. Build a macro named **OpenCrosstabSelectQuery** that will open the CrosstabSelect Query to be edited in Datasheet View
   b. Build a macro named **OpenTrainerUtilizationCrosstab** that will open the TrainerUtilizationCrosstab Query to be edited in Datasheet View
   c. Build a macro named **OpenRoomsUtilizationCrosstab** that will open the RoomsUtilizationCrosstab Query to be edited in Datasheet View
   d. Build a macro named **OpenSeminarsCount** that will open the SeminarsCount query to be edited in Datasheet View
   e. Build a macro named **OpenTrainerClassListing** that will open the TrainerClassListing report in Print Preview. Use a message box to verify that the user wants to print the report
   f. Build a macro named **ExitAccess** that will exit Access

5. Open the Switchboard Manager
   a. Create a new switchboard page named **Queries**
   b. The Main Switchboard page should contain options to open the **&Enrollment** form, open the **&TrainerClassListing** report, open the **&Queries** page, and **E&xit Access**
   c. The Queries page should use the macros from step 4 to run each query. Include shortcut keys and an option to return to the main page

6. Add the graphic **ac10TechRocks.tif** to the switchboard. Modify the rectangle colors to complement the logo

7. If your work is complete, exit Access; otherwise, continue to the next assignment

e-business

1. LumberOnline GUI

LumberOnline is a large distributor of construction products. The supporting database is accessed by many different users throughout a normal business day so it is critical to develop an intuitive graphical user interface.

1. Open **ac10LumberOnline.mdb** (Do not use a file from a previous chapter)

2. Create a macro named **PrintCustomersList** to display the CustomersList report in Print Preview. Use a message box to verify that the user wants to print the displayed report and then close the report

3. Create a macro named **PrintProductsBySpeciesList** to display the ProductsBySpeciesList report in Print Preview. Use a message box to verify that the user wants to print the displayed report and then close the report

4. Create a macro group named **RunQueries** containing a macro to open each of the queries, MissingSalesRep and ProductsCrosstab

5. Develop a Switchboard interface for the LumberOnline database
   a. The Main Switchboard page should contain options to

   i. Open each database form in Edit Mode
   ii. Run queries
   iii. Print reports
   iv. Perform development tasks (build a macro to accomplish this task)
   v. Exit Access (build a macro to accomplish this task)

   b. Use Figure 10.26 to set hot keys
   c. The Print Reports page should use the macros created in previous steps to display reports and have an option to return to the Main Switchboard
   d. The Run Queries should use macros from the macro group created in previous steps to display query results and have an option to return to the Main Switchboard

6. Add the **ac10OnlineLumber.wmf** image to the switchboard and change the color of the rectangle objects to complement it

7. Set the Switchboard properties so that the Switchboard cannot be resized, closed, moved, maximized, or minimized

8. Set the database startup options to open the Main Switchboard without the Database Window when the database is opened

F I G U R E 10.26

OnlineLumber switchboard

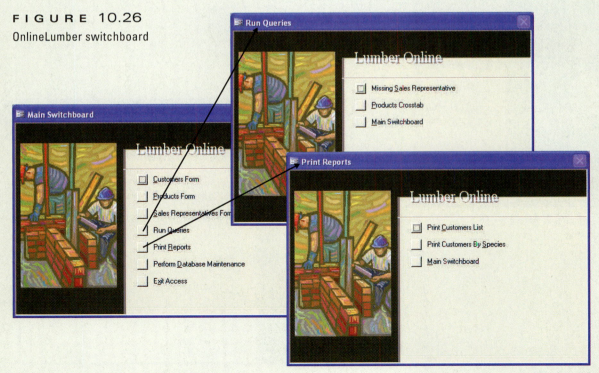

2. Everything Cheesecake Graphical User Interface

Everything Cheesecake is a bakery specializing in restaurant desserts. Orders are accepted from an Internet Web site. For processing, the data are loaded into a Microsoft Access database. Although this database is working well, it needs improved user access through forms, reports, and a graphical user interface.

1. Open **ac10Cheesecake.mdb**. Peruse the current tables and queries

2. Create a macro group named **SwitchboardMacros**
   a. Build a macro named **OpenCustomerProductCrosstabQuery** that will open the CustomerProductCrosstab Query to be edited in Datasheet View
   b. Build a macro named **OpenCustomerDateCrosstab** that will open the CustomerDateCrosstab Query to be edited in Datasheet View
   c. Build a macro named **OpenRecipeCountQuery** that will open the RecipeCount query to be edited in Datasheet View

d. Build a macro named **OpenCustomerOrderCount** that will open the CustomerOrderCount query to be edited in Datasheet View

e. Build a macro named **SalesSummaryListing** that will open the SalesSummaryListing report in Print Preview. Use a message box to verify that the user wants to print the report

f. Build a macro named **ExitAccess** that will exit Access

3. Open the Switchboard Manager
   a. Create a new switchboard page named **Queries**
   b. The Main Switchboard page should contain options to open the &CustomerOrder form, open the **&SalesSummary** report, open the **&Queries** page, and **E&xit Access**
   c. The Queries page should use the macros from step 2 to run each query. Include shortcut keys and an option to return to the main page

4. Add the graphic **ac10Cheesecake.gif** to the switchboard. Modify the rectangle colors to complement the logo

5. Close the database and exit Access if your work is complete

FIGURE 10.27

Cheesecake switchboard

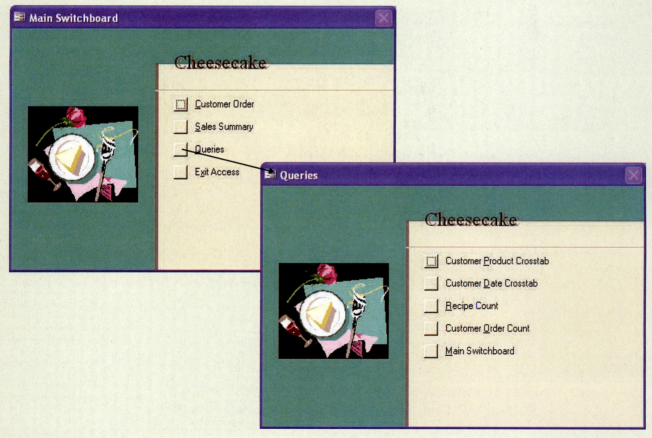

on the web

1. Internet Café GUI

Internet Café is a local coffee shop providing Internet access for their customers. You have been asked to create a graphical user interface for the database that will allow users to view and print queries and reports, but not update the Books table.

1. Use Web search tools to locate and document at least 10 helpful books on technology. Document the author, ISBN, title, publisher, and year published

2. Open **ac10InternetCafe.mdb** (You cannot use your copy of the database from Chapter 9 because changes have been applied for this chapter)

3. Create a macro named **PrintBooksByPublisher** to display the BooksByPublisher report in Print Preview. Use a message box to verify that the user wants to print the displayed report and then close the report

4. Create a macro named **PrintBooksByTitle** to display the BooksByTitle report in Print Preview. Use a message box to verify that the user wants to print the displayed report and then close the report

5. Create a macro group named **RunQueries** containing a macro to open each of the three queries, CategoryYearCrosstab, CopiesAvailableByCategory, and DuplicateBooks in Datasheet View

6. Develop a Switchboard interface for the Internet Café database

   a. The Main Switchboard page should contain options to Run Queries, Print Reports, and Exit Access (build a macro to accomplish this task)

   b. Use Figure 10.28 to set hot keys

   c. The Print Reports page should use the macros created in previous steps to display reports and have an option to return to the Main Switchboard

   d. The Run Queries page should use macros from the macro group created in previous steps to display query results and have an option to return to the Main Switchboard

7. Add the **ac10InternetCafe.wmf** image to the switchboard and change the color of the rectangle objects to complement it

8. Set the Switchboard properties so that it cannot be resized, closed, moved, maximized, or minimized

9. Set the startup options to open the Main Switchboard without the Database Window

10. Add the books you found on the Internet to the Books table with a Category of **Technology** (you will need to bypass startup processing)

FIGURE 10.28
Internet Café switchboard

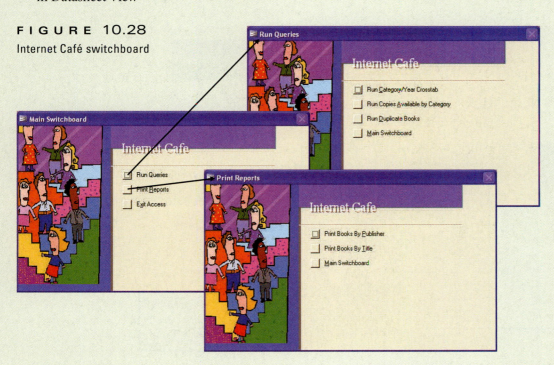

around the world

1. A GUI Interface for Projecting the World's Population

The ac10WorldPopulations database uses 2002 census figures to forecast 2003 populations. This is a shared database that needs a graphical user interface to reduce the learning time for new users.

1. Open **ac10WorldPopulations.mdb** (Do not use a file from a previous chapter)

2. Create a macro named **PrintAvgCity2003** to display the AvgCityByCountry1999 report in Print Preview. Use a message box to verify that the user wants to print the displayed report and then close the report

3. Create a macro named **PrintPopulationByCountry2001** to display the PopulationsByCountry2001 report in Print Preview. Use a message box to verify that the user wants to print the displayed report and then close the report

4. Create a macro group named **RunQueries** containing a macro to open each of the queries, PopulationByCountry2001 and PopulationsByCountry1999

5. Develop a Switchboard interface for the WorldPopulations database

   a. The Main Switchboard page should contain options to

      i. Open each database form in Edit mode
      ii. Run queries
      iii. Print reports
      iv. Perform development tasks (build a macro to accomplish this task)
      v. Exit Access (build a macro to accomplish this task)

   b. Use Figure 10.29 to set hot keys

   c. The Print Reports page should use the macros created in previous steps to display reports and have an option to return to the Main Switchboard. Some parameter values will be requested when testing reports based on parameter queries. You may leave the values blank and simply click **OK**

   d. The Run Queries page should use macros created in previous steps to display query results and have an option to return to the Main Switchboard

6. Add the **ac10WorldPopulations.wmf** image to the switchboard and change the color of the rectangle objects to complement it

7. Set the Switchboard properties so that it cannot be resized, closed, moved, maximized, or minimized

8. Set the database startup options to open the Main Switchboard without the Database Window

FIGURE 10.29

WorldPopulations switchboard

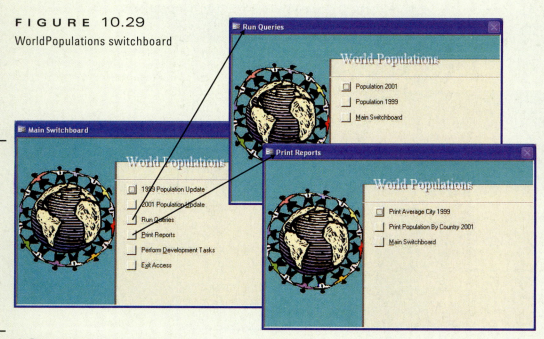

running project: TnT web design

Creating the TnT GUI Interface

The TnTdatabase contains the tables, queries, forms, reports, and pages that have been built to support the day-to-day operations of the business. Tori has asked you to complete a GUI for the database.

1. Open **ac10Tnt.mdb** (Do not use your previous file; changes have been made for this chapter)
2. Create a macro group named
   TnTSwitchboard
   a. Create a macro named
      PrintCustomerWebSites to display the CustomerWebSites report in Print Preview. Use a message box to verify that the user wants to print the displayed report and then close the report
   b. Create a macro named
      PrintEmployeesByJobClass to display the EmployeesByJobClass report in Print Preview. Use a message box to verify that the user wants to print the displayed report and then close the report
   c. Add named macros to open the CustomerWebSites, EmployeesByState, and EmployeesByClass queries
   d. Add a named macro to exit Access

3. Develop a Switchboard interface for the TnT database
   a. The Main Switchboard page should contain options to
      i. Open each database form in Edit Mode
      ii. Run queries
      iii. Print reports
      iv. Perform development tasks (build a macro in TnTSwitchboard to accomplish this task after the Switchboard is started)
      v. Exit Access
   b. Use Figure 10.30 to set hot keys
   c. The Print Reports page should use the macros created in previous steps to display reports and have an option to return to the Main Switchboard. Some parameter values will be requested when testing
   d. The Run Queries page should use macros from the macro group created in previous steps to display query results and have an option to return to the Main Switchboard

4. Add the **ac10TnT.tif** image to the switchboard and change the color of the rectangle objects to complement it

5. Set the Switchboard properties so that the Switchboard cannot be resized, closed, moved, maximized, or minimized

6. Set the database startup options to open the Main Switchboard without the Database Window when the database is opened

FIGURE 10.30

TnT switchboard

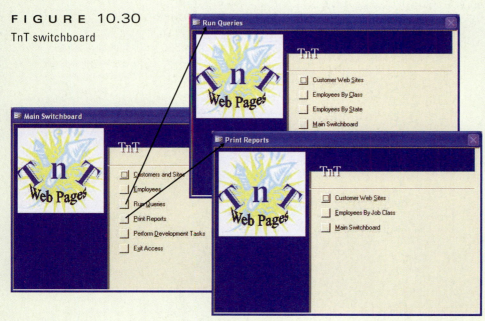

1. Switchboard for Presbyterian Hospital

Open the database named **ac10PresbyterianHospital .mdb**. This database is used to track the various hospital operations. Review each existing database object and design a switchboard that will allow users to run all of the queries and reports. The switchboard should

- Open the EmployeeSkillsUpdate form from the Main Switchboard page
- Consist of a minimum of three pages
- Include an appropriate graphic
- Include an option to exit Access on the Main Switchboard page
- Include navigation from all subpages back to the main page
- Have functional shortcuts
- Use a macro with a condition to print report(s)

2. Switchboard for Your Multitable Database

Locate any multitable database that you have worked with during the course of this class. The database should include at least two queries and at least two reports. Take a look at your current database objects and determine how to organize a switchboard that will allow users to use all of the available database objects. The switchboard should

- Consist of a minimum of three pages
- Include an appropriate graphic
- Include an option to exit Access on the main page
- Include navigation from all subpages back to the main page
- Have functional shortcuts
- Use a macro with a condition to print report(s)

Using Visual Basic for Applications

did you know?

there *is no real difference between doves and pigeons.*

oak *trees are struck by lightning more often than any other species of tree.*

the *first domain name, Symbolics.com, was registered March 15, 1985.*

the *technology contained in a single Game Boy unit in the year 2000 exceeded that used to put the first man on the moon.*

researchers *at the Kinsey Institute for Sex Research at Indiana University found lower sperm counts during hot weather.*

to *find out the number of movie theaters in New York City in 1913 (more than any current city), visit* www.mhhe.com/i-series.

Chapter Objectives

- **Create Microsoft Access modules**
- **Create an MDE file from a Microsoft Access database**
- **Understand the difference between sub procedures and Function procedures**
- **Code, test, and debug Event procedures**
- **Code, test, and debug Function procedures**
- **Add subreport controls to Access reports**

KoryoKicks: VBA Automation

It is rare to create a complete Microsoft Access application without hitting the limitations of Access's switchboards and macros. While switchboards and macros provide a great start to creating a user-friendly interface, they are based on tasks that are common to all databases. There are plenty of off-the-shelf solutions for common database tasks, and it is always less expensive to use existing applications than it is to create a new one.

When the business function being supported is unique, new database development is the only way to provide full operational capabilities. In such cases, the uniqueness of the application is more likely to require the development of custom components.

Fortunately, Microsoft products use the same full-featured programming language, Visual Basic for Applications (VBA), to create custom features for Office applications. VBA is both event driven and object oriented, so it can be used to create unique programmatic responses to user actions and to manipulate the objects (tables, queries, forms, and reports) already contained in your database. In Access, VBA code can be used to adjust the behavior of any control, complete complex calculations, validate data by comparing values from

FIGURE 11.1

Print Preview of the completed Customer Invoice report

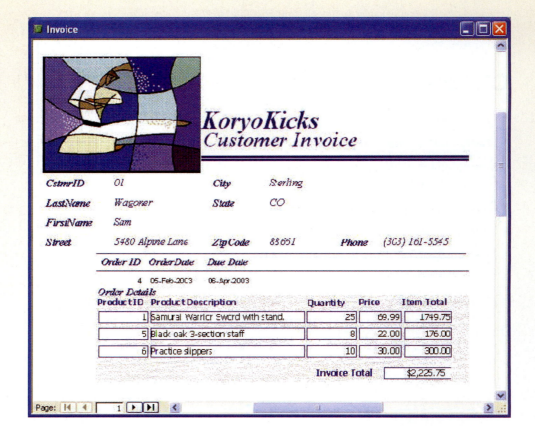

various fields and tables, and issue messages that are more user friendly than the default system messages.

Missy and Micah have a list of custom features that would improve user satisfaction and simplify use of the KoryoKicks database. Since the user interface has been significantly modified, the twins would like the application to open with a message about the change and who to contact with issues.

Second, the users have requested faster access to the most commonly used queries, forms, and reports that cannot be provided by the switchboard menu system. For example, a button on the UpdateCustom form that will open any orders for the current customer would allow users to move more readily to needed information when they are on the phone with a customer.

Finally, the twins have realized that due dates are needed on several forms and reports. A calcu-lation could be completed for each of these, but this creates a maintenance problem. If the method of determining the due date changes, each object, property, function, and procedure that used its own calculation would have to be updated. A better solution is to create a Function procedure for the calculation that can be called by each object that needs it. This methodology provides one place (the Function procedure) to change the code. Since all objects use the same code, they are automatically updated when the procedure is updated.

VBA code modules can also be compiled (converted to machine language), so that they execute more rapidly than macros. In addition, the source code is removed from the project, providing secure user environment that can only be modified by developers. Missy and Micah believe that compilation will significantly improve the usability of the KoryoKicks database.

SESSION 11.1 UNDERSTANDING VBA PROCEDURES

Microsoft Visual Basic for Applications (VBA) is a complex programming language that can be used to develop custom features for Microsoft Office products. Such customizations are often referred to as Office Applications. VBA is sometimes called VB but is really a subset of the Visual Basic (VB) programming language designed for the creation of Office applications. The most notable use for VBA in an Access database is to create custom expressions that can be applied to multiple database objects. For example, a procedure to convert data to uppercase can be applied to any control on any form. Additionally, VBA can be used to validate data, customize the behavior of any control, and process errors, circumventing Access-generated error messages that can be confusing to users.

CHAPTER OUTLINE

AC 11.3

ACCESS

Identifying Procedures

Microsoft Visual Basic code statements are grouped into units called procedures. A *procedure* contains all of the VB statements needed to complete one task such as calculating a value or updating object properties. A code *statement* is normally one line of a procedure containing one instruction needed to complete the procedure's task. Code statements follow rigid *syntax* rules using keywords, arguments, and punctuation. The process of adding code statements to a procedure is called *coding*. Two types of errors emerge during coding: syntax errors and logic errors. *Syntax errors* are caused by statements that do not follow the rules of the language. *Logic errors* are the result of statements that do not create the desired result because the statement is misplaced, misused, or misapplied.

There are two basic types of procedures: sub procedures and Function procedures. A *sub procedure* contains code that can accept data and perform operations. For example, turning the form blue when a button is clicked or verifying data when the cursor moves to a new text box. A *Function procedure* contains code that is designed to accept data, perform operations, and return a value. For example, a dollar amount could be passed to a conversion function that would return the equivalent yen value. Functions are typically *call*ed from other procedures or used in expressions. Access provides a substantial number of precoded functions. Some of the precoded functions that you are already familiar with are Sum, Count, Avg, Max, and Min.

Exploring Events

Event procedures are special sub procedures that run in response to an event such as the user clicking a command button. Most VBA statements can be members of an Event procedure and so the language is said to be *event-driven*. Additionally, VBA is used to create and manipulate objects such as tables, reports, and controls, and so is *object-oriented*. Macros are also event driven and object oriented.

Events can be initiated by the user, the system, or programmatically. User initiated events include clicking, double-clicking, and issuing keyboard commands. Often there are actually several events that happen in response to one user action. For example, when a user opens a form, the system initiates a series of form events:

Open ⇒ **Load** ⇒ **Resize** ⇒ **Activate** ⇒ **Current**

These events are run in the sequence shown. Although we will not discuss the specifics of each form event, it is important to note that each has a special purpose and each can trigger an Event procedure. If there is no macro, expression, or Event procedure for the event, nothing special happens. If there is a macro, expression, or Event procedure for the event, it is run before proceeding to the next event. Choosing the correct event for your Event procedure is as important as using valid code statements.

---

task *reference*   Viewing an Object's
                                                          Event Properties

- In Design View, right-click on the object

- Select **Properties** from the pop-up menu

- Click the **Events** tab and explore the available event properties

Viewing UpdateCustomers event properties:

1. Open the **ac11KoryoKicks.mdb** database
2. Select the **Forms** object from the Database Window
3. Select **UpdateCustomers** and click the **Design** button
4. Right-click on the LastName text box and click **Properties**
5. Click the **Event** tab and scroll through the event properties for this text box

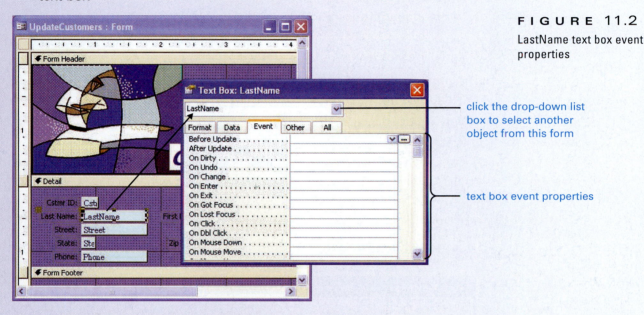

FIGURE 11.2
LastName text box event properties

click the drop-down list box to select another object from this form

text box event properties

6. Click the object drop-down list and select the **CstmrID** text box

tip: All text box objects will have the same event properties, but different object classes such as labels or images will have different event properties

7. Drop down the object list in the Properties dialog box and select the image object

tip: It will be named Image?? where ?? is the number of the object. For example, Image14

8. Explore the event properties available for an image
9. Use the **X** in the Title bar to close the Properties dialog box
10. Close the form

The Event tab of an object's Properties dialog box will reveal that object's event properties. In the last chapter, a macro name was placed in an event property's list box to run the macro in response to the event. VBA procedures can be run in response to an event by clicking the ellipsis to the right of the event drop-down list and coding an Event procedure.

ACCESS

Viewing Existing Event Procedures

Not all Event procedures are built by coding. Often, selections made from the menu or an Access dialog box will generate code for a specific Event procedure. For example, setting the startup page of a Switchboard form automatically creates a Form_Open Event procedure for the switchboard. Each time the switchboard is opened, this procedures runs.

Viewing the Switchboard Form_Open Event procedure:

1. Verify that **ac11KoryoKicks.mdb** is open

2. Select the **Forms** object from the Database Window, click **Switchboard**, and click the **Design** button

3. Right-click on the form selector (the square in the top-left corner of the rulers) and choose **Properties**

4. Verify that Form is the object in the drop-down list box of the Properties dialog box and that the Event tab is selected

5. Click the **On Open** event and then click the ellipsis (...) to the right of its text box

tip: *The Microsoft Visual Basic Editor will open showing the code for Private Sub Form_Open*

6. Click the **Procedure View** button (see Figure 11.3)

FIGURE 11.3

Private Sub Form_Open
Event procedure

Procedure view to see
one procedure at a time

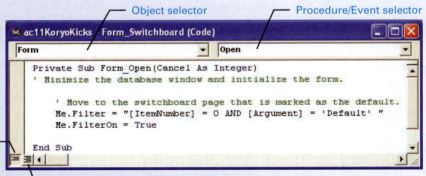

7. Click the Procedure drop-down list to view the other events available for the Form object

tip: *The current event should be bolded in the Procedure drop-down list because it already contains code. This code has also been automatically created by switchboard setup*

8. Click the Object drop-down list to view the other objects on this form

9. Maximize the code window

10. Click the Full Module View button and use the code window scrollbar to scroll through the existing procedures (see Figure 11.4)

tip: *Procedures start with Sub and terminate with End Sub. In Full Module view, there is a horizontal line separating procedures in the code window*

11. Use the **X** in the Microsoft Visual Basic Title bar to close the Visual Basic Editor

The **Visual Basic Editor** is a separate application that opens in its own window with the tools needed to view, code, debug, and maintain Visual Basic procedures. The **Code window** is used to enter and debug VB statements. The drop-down list boxes at the top of the Code window are used to select the Object (left list box) and Event (right list box) of the procedure being viewed or developed.

The Code window can be set to Procedure view, displaying a single procedure, or Full Module view to show all procedures in the current module (see Figure 11.3). When set to display multiple modules, a thin horizontal line visually separates the procedures. Closing the Visual Basic Editor exits the code development environment leaving the Database Window open.

The Visual Basic Editor uses color to help the developer understand and evaluate VB statements. Lines that begin with a single quote (') are comment or documentation lines not executed by the computer. These lines are shown in green. Statements executed by the computer to produce the desired outcomes are listed in black, and VB keywords are listed in blue. Syntax errors are listed in red and accompanied by a dialog box describing the syntax problem.

Investigating Modules

Figure 11.4 shows some of the procedures that are currently stored for the Switchboard form. Related procedures like these are stored as a **module**. Each procedure in the Switchboard form module begins with the keywords **Private Sub**, meaning that it is a private **sub**-procedure of the Switchboard form. These procedures can only be accessed from the Switchboard form. Each form or report in the database can have a module with private procedures used only by that object.

A **Standard module** can be created as a database object using the Modules object of the Database Window. A Standard module is a separate object not related to any other database object. Procedures stored in a Standard module typically begin with **Public Sub** and can therefore be accessed from other modules and database objects. You can think of the code stored in Standard modules as being in a shared library.

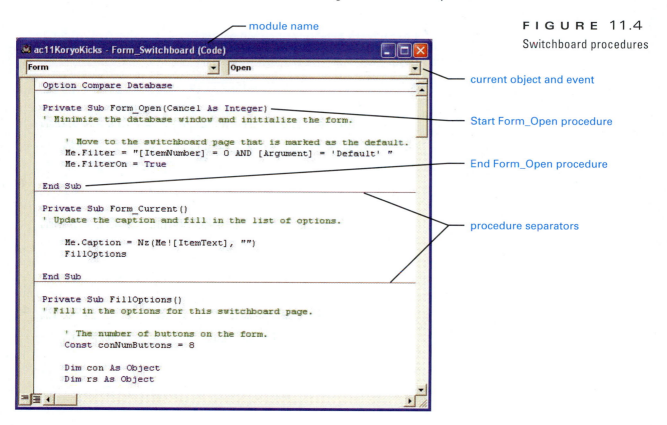

FIGURE 11.4

Switchboard procedures

Typically a module begins with a series of statements in the General Declarations section. Statements in this section apply to all procedures in the module. For example, an Option Explicit statement can be included to force all variables used in the module to be declared (named and defined). Without this statement, VB will dynamically create variables as they are needed. Variables used by multiple procedures are also declared in the General Declarations section.

The General Declarations section is followed by all of the procedures contained in the module. Procedures are listed in alphabetical order by their name. The procedure name follows Sub and precedes the parenthesis (). For example, in the statement *Private Sub Form_Open(Cancel As Integer)*, the procedure name is Form_Open.

Getting Visual Basic Help

The Visual Basic Editor is a complex development environment that takes practice to use effectively. The complete documentation for the Visual Basic language is larger than all the documentation provided for Microsoft Access, and books over an inch thick are required to teach the introductory programming level. Successful VBA programmers must become familiar with the resources available for building statements, built-in functions, Event properties, object properties, and built-in procedures. The task of selecting and properly applying VB statements can be daunting.

One source of assistance is the Northwind sample database that ships with Microsoft Access. For example, the Northwind database contains a variety of custom procedures. Microsoft encourages using sample procedures to learn and use VBA more rapidly.

Viewing a Northwind.mdb Standard module:

1. Click **Help** on the menu, point to **Sample Databases**, and select **Northwind Sample Database**

2. Select **Modules** from the Database Window

3. Select **Startup** and click the **Design** button

4. Drop down the Objects (left) list box (see Figure 11.5)

tip: *There is only a General object because Startup is a Standard module. Standard modules contain public code that can be called from other modules, but do not contain Event procedures or code for specific objects*

5. Drop down the Procedures (right) list box (see Figure 11.5)

tip: *The names of the coded procedures display*

6. Explore the procedures by reading the comment (green) statements

Microsoft also provides a comprehensive set of Help topics that can be accessed while the Visual Basic Editor is active. Context-sensitive Help is available by pressing F1, and topical Help can be obtained using the Ask a Question box on the menu bar. Both methods provide links to sample code and related topics.

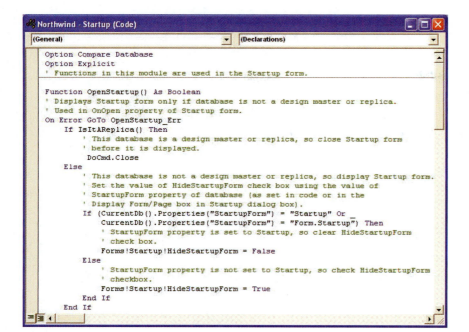

FIGURE 11.5

Northwind database
Startup module

Using Help from the Code window:

1. Verify that the Microsoft Visual Basic Code window from the previous steps is still open

tip: *Help can be activated from the Code window of any Visual Basic module*

2. Select the **IF** keyword of the function OpenStartup procedure and press **F1**

3. Explore the help available for the Visual Basic If statement (see Figure 11.6)

4. Type **End** in the What would you like to do? box of the Answer Wizard tab and click the **Search** button
   a. Read the End statement topic
   b. Click the **Example** link to see how End is used
   c. Click the left-pointing (Back) arrow to return to the End Statement topic
   d. Click the **See also** link to view related topics
   e. Close Microsoft Visual Basic Help

5. Close the Visual Basic Editor

The Visual Basic Editor is a separate application with its own Help facilities using the familiar Microsoft Help interface. Context-sensitive Help is available by selecting any keyword in a statement in the Code window and clicking F1. Help on specific topics can be obtained using the Ask a question box in the menu bar or by typing search words into the Answer Wizard tab of the Help dialog box. Take the time to become comfortable with finding and understanding Help topics.

ACCESS

related topics and examples

If statement syntax

description of the statement parts

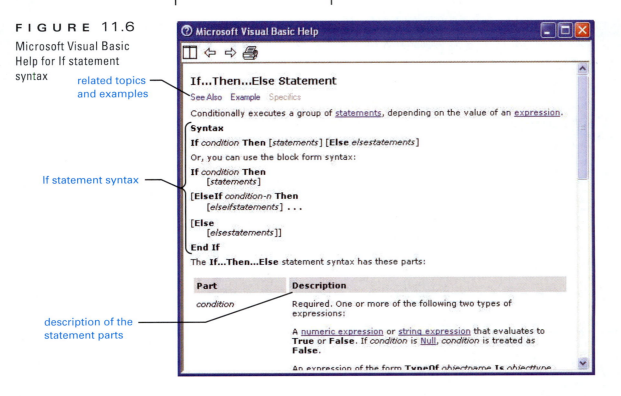

Building a New Event Procedure

An Event procedure is a special type of sub procedure that is triggered by a specific event, such as clicking a button. Event procedures are most often added to an existing Form module or Report module to customize the behavior of a control in response to an event. Form and Report modules hold code related to all objects contained on a specific form or report.

Missy and Micah have asked that a dialog box be displayed before the KoryoKicks switchboard opens. The purpose of the dialog box is to let users know that the interface has changed and who to contact with any technical problems. To accomplish this, you will use the Switchboard module's built-in Event procedure template.

Creating a New Procedure

Event procedure names use the format Object_Event. For example, when the option button named Option2 is clicked, the Option2_Click procedure statements execute. Before creating a new procedure, it is important to determine which object and event should trigger your procedure. The twins want the dialog box to display before the Switchboard form is visible to the user, which means that the object for this event is the Switchboard form.

Recall from our earlier discussion that a form triggers several events (**Open** $\Rightarrow$ **Load** $\Rightarrow$ **Resize** $\Rightarrow$ **Activate** $\Rightarrow$ **Current**) in the process of becoming visible to the user. The Form_Open Event procedure contains the code generated by Access that was reviewed in an earlier set of steps. The Form_Load event will execute after the Form_Open event as the form is loaded into memory, but before it is visible to the user. Since Form_Load will accomplish the twins' goal, it will be used for this procedure.

Creating the Switchboard Form_Load procedure:

1. Verify that **ac11KoryoKicks.mdb** is open

2. Click the **Forms** object in the Database Window

3. Select the **Switchboard** form and click **Design**

4. Right-click the Form selector (the square between the horizontal and vertical rulers) and click **Properties**

5. If necessary, click the **Event** tab

6. Verify that Form is the current object in the drop-down box

7. Scroll to the **On Load** event property and click in its text box

8. Click the **Build (...)** button to the right of the text box

9. Select the **Code Builder** and click **OK**

10. If multiple procedures are displayed, click the **Procedure view** button in the bottom-left corner of the code window

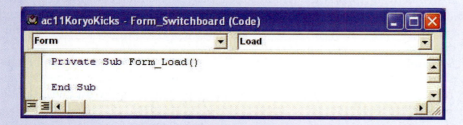

FIGURE 11.7

The Form_Load Event procedure template

The Form_Load Event procedure template has been added to the Switchboard form module. Code entered into this procedure will be executed each time the switchboard is loaded into memory.

Introducing VBA Syntax

Microsoft Visual Basic for Applications is a complex language that uses keywords, operators, variables, constants, and punctuation in very specific ways. VB statements fall into one of three categories discussed in the following paragraphs.

Declaration statements name and define procedures, variables, and other program structures. Procedures contain code statements to accomplish a task, and *variables* are RAM storage locations for values that can change during program processing. Declarations can include the *scope* or visibility of the object being declared and the *data type* of each structure. For example, a variable declared with a scope of *Public* is available to all procedures in all modules, while one declared as *Private* is available only to procedures of the current module. The Sub statement is used to declare procedures, while the Dim statement is used to declare variables.

The data type of a variable determines what type of data it can store, how much storage space is allocated, and how the data can be processed. For example, an Integer variable can store whole numbers between −32,768 and 32,767, requires two bytes of storage, and supports mathematical processing. Visual Basic uses a Variant data type when no other type is specified. Although it is tempting for beginning programmers to use Variant data types, they provide much less control over data and significantly increase program processing time. The other available data types are Byte, Boolean, Integer, Long, Single, Double, Currency, Decimal, Date, Object, and String. This chapter is limited in scope and will introduce only a few of these types.

help yourself *Use the Type a Question combo box in the Microsoft Visual Basic window to improve your understanding of VBA data types by typing* **data type summary**. *Review the contents of* Data Type Summary. *Close the Help window when you are finished*

Procedures and variables are named as they are declared. Proper names should be descriptive and must adhere to the following rules:

- Can be up to 255 characters long
- Must begin with a letter
- Can include letters, numbers, or underscore characters (_)
- Can't include punctuation characters or spaces
- Can't be a Visual Basic keyword. A keyword is a word that Visual Basic uses as part of its language such as Dim, If, Loop, Min, Max, Len, and Abs
- Must be unique within their context

Assignment statements are used to store a value in a variable. As shown in Figure 11.8, the variable (X) should be declared (Dim X as Integer) before it is assigned, and the assignment value must be consistent with the data type (X=5.9). The general format of an assignment statement is *variable=value*.

Executable statements are used to perform program actions. Actions can be simple, such as displaying a message (*MsgBox "All done!"*), or involve multiple lines of complex code. For a more in-depth discussion of this subject, visit the Writing Visual Basic Statements Help topic.

Coding the Form_Load Event Procedure

Event procedures are automatically named object_*event* (for the object and event that will trigger the code), or in this case Form_Load when they are created. The Switchboard Form_Load Event procedure will issue a time-sensitive (Good Morning or Good Afternoon) greeting, let the user know that the interface has changed, and provide a contact point for technical questions. Like all procedures, Form_Load will begin with a declaration (Sub) statement and terminate with an End Sub statement. The keyword Private precedes the Sub statement indicating that this procedure belongs to the current module (Switchboard). These opening and closing statements are provided by the template as "bookends" in which to enter the working statements of the procedure.

FIGURE 11.8
Declaring and assigning variables

Code	Result
Dim X As Integer	Creates a variable named X that can store whole numbers between −32,768 and 32,767
X=5.9	Stores 6 in X when it has been declared as an Integer
X=32768	Produces an error when X is declared as an Integer
Dim Y As Currency	Creates a variable named Y that can store values between 922,337,203,685,477.5808 and 922,337,203,685,477.5807
Y=74982.37	Stores the value 74982.37 in Y

Creating the Switchboard Form_Load procedure:

1. Verify that the **Private Sub Form_Load()** template created in the previous set of steps is open

2. Click the blank line between the Private Sub Form_Load() and End Sub statements

3. Type the statements shown in Figure 11.9

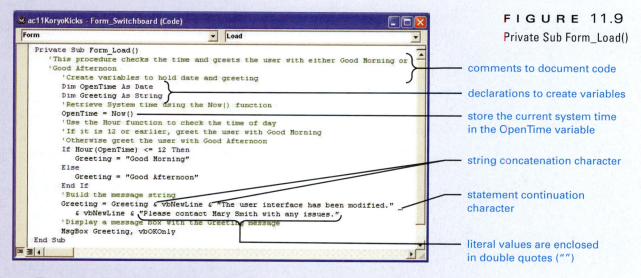

FIGURE 11.9

Private Sub Form_Load()

— comments to document code

— declarations to create variables

— store the current system time in the OpenTime variable

— string concatenation character

— statement continuation character

— literal values are enclosed in double quotes ("")

   a. The green statements beginning with a single quote (') are comments that document the procedure. Comments are not executed. Read them to help understand the executed lines of code
   b. The Visual Basic Editor displays key words in blue
   c. Visual Basic Constants such as vbNewLine and vbOKOnly have a set value and meaning and can be used in any procedure
   d. The proper use and syntax of the executable statements will be discussed after the steps

4. Click the **Save** button on the Standard toolbar and minimize the Visual Basic Editor

tip: *The Design View of the KoryoKicks switchboard should be visible*

5. If necessary, close the Properties dialog box

6. Click the **Form View** button on the Formatting (Form/Report) toolbar

tip: *The Form_Load procedure should display the new message box before the form displays. If no message box displays, return to step 3 and verify the code*

FIGURE 11.10

Private Sub Form_Load() message box

ACCESS

7. Click **OK** to proceed to the Switchboard

8. Return to Form Design View

9. Maximize the Visual Basic Editor

10. Replace Mary Smith with your name and repeat steps 4 through 7 to verify the update

The message box created in the Form_Load procedure will display each time the Switchboard form is opened. As you experienced, the text of the message displayed can be easily edited to meet new needs. The general order of statements in a procedure is

- Declare variable(s)
- Executable statement(s) to obtain output values
- Format and display output

The Dim statements of this module create two local (available only in this module) variables, OpenTime and Greeting. OpenTime is a Date data type because it will hold the current system date and time. Greeting is a String data type because it will store text.

The *OpenTime=Now()* assignment statement uses a Visual Basic function to retrieve the current system date and time. Recall that functions always return a value. Visual Basic has a vast library of precoded functions or you can create custom functions to complete unique operations. In this case, the Now() function retrieves the current system date and time and stores it in the function name, Now. Since OpenTime is set to Now, OpenTime also holds the current system date and time.

The If statement is used to conditionally execute code and usually includes several lines of code. If statements use conditions to determine which lines of code to execute. When the stated condition is true, the lines before the Else are executed. When the stated condition is false, the lines after the Else are executed. The general syntax of the If statement is

> **If** condition **Then**
>   true statements
> **ElseIF** condition **Then**
>   true statements
> **Else**
>   false statements
> **End If**

Any number of ElseIf clauses (including 0) can be included in an If statement. Regardless of the number of clauses, only one clause of the statement will execute. The Else branch executes if no previous branch has executed.

The Form_Load If statement is checking the time of day to display a time-sensitive greeting. Computers use a 24-hour clock, so the hour for 2 P.M. is 14. If the hour obtained using the Hour() Visual Basic function on the OpenTime variable is before 12, "Good Morning" will display. "Good Afternoon" will display for any other hours.

Now that the appropriate time-of-day greeting has been determined, the rest of the message must be constructed. The process of combining multiple string values is accomplished with the ampersand (&) operator and is called ***concatenation***. To concatenate multiple string (text) values, an assignment statement is used. In the Form_Load code, the Greeting variable will be concatenated to the static portion of the message and then displayed in a message box.

In VBA code, literal string (text) values are always enclosed in double quotes ("") to distinguish them from variables, constants, and keywords. Take another look at the Greeting assignment statement. The variable and literal components on the right of the = sign are concatenated and then stored in the original variable, Greeting.

```
Greeting =Greeting & vbNewLine & "The user interface has been modified."
    & vbNewLine & "Please contact <yourname> with any issues"
```

Visual Basic provides a vast collection of constants that can be used from any program and are identifiable because they all start with vb. vbNewLine is a constant that is used to add a new line to a string. Note that the message box text wraps to a new line for each vbNewLine constant concatenated in Greeting.

The last statement of the procedure displays the output created by the executable statements in a message box. The MsgBox statement displays the final value of the Greeting variable in a dialog box with an OK button (vbOKOnly) for the user to click to close the message box.

Designing an Event Procedure

Beginning programmers often try to code procedures without designing them. While this can be successful, it usually requires more time and can lead to unnecessary confusion. Taking the time to design the solution on paper improves your understanding of the problem and significantly increases the likelihood of success.

Designing an Event procedure is similar to solving a complex story problem in math class. Typically you know what you want to produce and have some of the components needed to produce it, but other components are unavailable (you must solve for them). That being the case, the first design task is to completely understand the output to be produced. Document the components of that output that already exist and the components you will need to build. The list of components to be built outlines the tasks that must be completed in the executable statements of a procedure.

For Form_Load, the desired output is a message box containing a time-sensitive greeting (Good Morning or Good Afternoon). The literal component of that message is known, but the time-sensitive greeting is unknown; therefore, the procedure's executable statements must determine whether it is morning or afternoon, assign the correct greeting, and then add the static portion of the message.

Now that you know what must be accomplished, the next step is to decide what Visual Basic statements to use to complete each task. Experience is very helpful in determining statements, but not critical. When experience is lacking, Microsoft Visual Basic Help and code samples that accomplish similar tasks often provide the best assistance.

In the Form_Load procedure, the first task is to determine whether or not it is morning. This entails getting the system date and time with the Now() function, stripping the hour from that time using the Hour() function, and then using an If statement to assign the correct time-of-day greeting. The final tasks are to assemble the full text of the message and display it to the user in a message box.

The variables used in a procedure are somewhat a matter of programmer style. In the example, one Date variable, OpenTime, was used to store the system date and time, and a String variable, Greeting, was used to assemble the various message components. This procedure could have been written with no variables or more variables without impacting the output. In general, the code produced is easier to follow and debug when variables are used to store data on which the output is dependent (OpenTime) and the component(s) that is being constructed (Greeting).

This simple methodology of working backward from the desired output allows you to concentrate on one thing at a time and can be used to design a solution for any programming problem. With a documented solution, it is faster and easier to code syntactically correct Visual Basic statements that will accomplish the desired results.

Compiling Modules

The computer's native language, low-level or machine language, consists entirely of zeroes and ones. In the electronic world, a 1 represents the on state of a tiny electronic switch inside a computer; a 0 represents the off state. High-level languages like VBA are used by programmers to simplify the process of writing program instructions. The process of converting program code, like VBA, into machine language that can be executed by a computer is called *compiling*.

The VBA code contained in Access projects must be compiled before it can be executed. Each time a user action initiates a procedure, it is compiled and then executed. One way to speed processing is to compile all of the modules in a database and compact the database by creating an *MDE file*. Using MDE files eliminates the need to compile procedures each time they are executed, because only compiled code is stored. MDE files will operate to store, maintain, and report on data, but database objects (forms, reports, queries, and VB code) cannot be viewed or modified.

task reference   Saving an Access Database as an MDE File

- Close all open copies of the database
- Create a backup copy of the database using Windows Explorer
- On the Tools menu, point to **Database Utilities**, and then click **Make MDE File**
- In the Database To Save As MDE dialog box, select the drive, folder, and filename of the Access database to be converted
- Click **Make MDE**
- In the Save MDE As dialog box, specify the drive, folder, and filename of the MDE file

Saving KoryoKicks as an MDE file:

1. Close any open copies of the KoryoKicks database leaving Access running
2. Use Windows Explorer to create a backup copy of ac11KoryoKicks.mdb named **ac11KoryoKicksBac.mdb**
3. On the Tools menu, point to **Database Utilities**, and then click **Make MDE File**
4. In the Database To Save As MDE dialog box, select the drive, folder, and **ac11KoryoKicks.mdb** and then click **Make MDE** (see Figure 11.11)
5. Click the **Save** button in the Save MDE As dialog box to accept ac11KoryoKicks.mde as the filename
6. Open the new MDE file and explore the tables, queries, forms, and reports
7. Close ac11KoryoKicks.mde

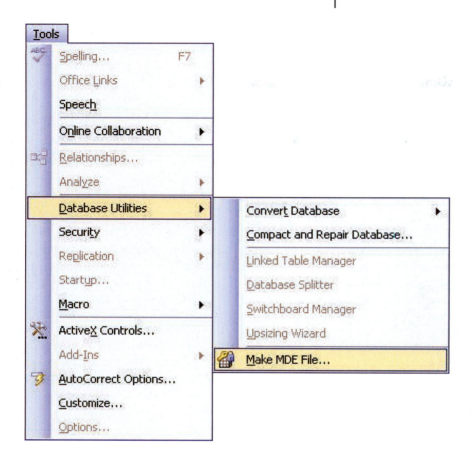

F I G U R E 11.11

Creating an MDE file from
an Access database

> **another word** .... **. . . on Creating MDE Files**
>
> When multiple copies of a database are being used, creating an MDE file can
> cause complications in reconciling the different versions of the data. Due to this
> restriction, replicated databases should not be converted to MDE files and in
> front-end/back-end applications, only the front-end should be converted to an
> MDE file

When a user opens the MDE copy of a database, all data maintenance and reporting operations are available, but the database objects cannot be updated. The MDE
Access icon contains a padlock to indicate that MDE files cannot be used to change
database objects (forms, tables, reports, VBA code, and so on). Updates to database objects should be made in the backup mdb file and then the MDE file must be re-created.

---

making the grade

SESSION 11.1

1. Explain the difference between a sub procedure and an Event procedure.

2. How do you determine which event to select from the Properties dialog box
   for your VBA code?

3. Write an If statement that sets the variable Message to *5 Vacation Days* when
   YearsOfService is less than or equal to 5 and *10 Vacation Days* otherwise.

4. How do you display a single procedure of a VBA module displayed in the
   Visual Basic Editor?

ACCESS

SESSION 11.2 UNDERSTANDING VBA FUNCTIONS

Function procedures and sub procedures are very similar because they both contain the VBA statements needed to perform a specific task; however, functions return a value while sub procedures do not. This small difference allows functions to be used in assignment statements.

To solidify our understanding of VBA code and procedure structure, we'll take another look at building an Event procedure before developing a function. Recall that an Event procedure is a special type of sub procedure that is executed in response to an event.

Building a Command Button Event Procedure

Providing menus to allow users to open various database objects such as forms, reports, and queries is a good start on creating a user-friendly interface but often requires the user to return to a menu between tasks. For example, with the KoryoKicks user environment, if the user has the UpdateCustomers form open to maintain customer data, the only way to view invoices for the current customer is to go to the Main Switchboard, open the Invoice form, and then find the desired customer.

Missy and Micah would like to provide shortcut access to the most frequently used database objects to reduce the number of steps between objects. The UpdateCustomers form already has a command button that can be used to print the current customer's data. The twins would like a second command button added that will open the Invoice form with data for the current customer active.

Creating the cmdOpenInvoice_Click event:

1. Open **ac11KoryoKicks.mdb**

tip: *Be sure to hold down the Shift key while the database is opening so that you will have access to the development environment*

2. Open the **UpdateCustomers** form in Design View

3. Use the Command Button tool to click a new command button below the existing Print Customer button. Size and align the new button to match the existing button

tip: *You may need to enlarge the Detail section of the form by dragging the Form Footer divider downward. If the Command Button Wizard activates, cancel it*

4. Right-click on the new button, select **Properties**, and click the **All** tab
   a. Set the Name to **cmdOpenInvoice**
   b. Set the Caption to **Open Invoice**
   c. Scroll down to the On Click event, select **[Event Procedure]** from the text box drop-down list, and click the ellipsis (...) button to the right of the text box to open the Visual Basic Code Editor with the cmdOpenInvoice_Click procedure visible

5. Enter the code shown in Figure 11.13. Remember that comments are documentation to help you understand the code. Since they are not executed, they do not impact the program

tip: *Maximizing the Visual Basic Code Editor window may make this task easier*

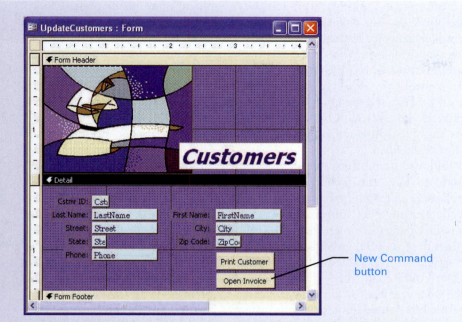

FIGURE 11.12
The revised
UpdateCustomers form

New Command button

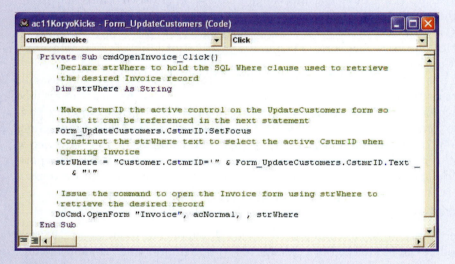

FIGURE 11.13
cmdOpenInvoice_Click
code

```
Private Sub cmdOpenInvoice_Click()
    'Declare strWhere to hold the SQL Where clause used to retrieve
    'the desired Invoice record
    Dim strWhere As String

    'Make CstmrID the active control on the UpdateCustomers form so
    'that it can be referenced in the next statement
    Form_UpdateCustomers.CstmrID.SetFocus
    'Construct the strWhere text to select the active CstmrID when
    'opening Invoice
    strWhere = "Customer.CstmrID='" & Form_UpdateCustomers.CstmrID.Text _
        & "'"

    'Issue the command to open the Invoice form using strWhere to
    'retrieve the desired record
    DoCmd.OpenForm "Invoice", acNormal, , strWhere
End Sub
```

6. Save your code and then minimize the Visual Basic Editor window

7. Test the code

   a. Open the **UpdateCustomers** form in Form View

   b. Move to Customer (CstmrID 02)

   c. Click the **Open Invoice** button

tip: *The Invoice form should open with CstmrID 02 active. If this does not happen, return to the Visual Basic Editor and check the syntax of your code*

8. Close the Invoice form

9. Move to another Customer record in the UpdateCustomers form, click the **Open Invoice** button, and verify that the records for the correct customer are active

10. Close the Invoice form

11. Close the UpdateCustomer form, saving the changes

ACCESS

It is customary in Windows applications development to use name prefixes to indicate the object type or data type. In the previous steps, the command button was named cmdOpenInvoice because *cmd* is the usual prefix for a command button. In the VBA code the variable strWhere used the *str* prefix to indicate that it is a String data type. Prefixing also avoids confusion when it is logical to use the same name for a variable and a control.

Like all procedures, the cmdOpenInvoice_Click Event procedure begins with a Sub statement and ends with the End Sub statement. The Private declaration indicates that this procedure can only be accessed within the current module for the UpdateCustomers form.

In Windows applications the active control, for example the CstmrID text box, is said to have the *focus*. To programmatically reference the data held in a control on a form, the control must have the focus. The statement Form_UpdateCustomers.CstmrID.SetFocus makes the CstmrID text box the active control on the UpdateCustomers form. The value of CstmrID on the UpdateCustomers form is then used to build an SQL Where clause that will be used to retrieve records with the same CstmrID value on the Invoice form. Remember that ampersands (&) are used to concatenate the various components of the Where clause. In SQL, text match values are enclosed in double quotes (""). String data in VBA code also need to be enclosed in double quotes (""). In instances where double quotes are required inside a string being built like this, single quotes (') are used inside the string. Notice the single quotes inside double quotes in the strWhere assignment statement. When CstrmID 003 is active on the UpdateCustomers form the strWhere = "Customer.CstmrID='" & Form_UpdateCustomers.CstmrID.Text & "'" statement results in Customer.CstmrID="003" being stored in strWhere.

The final statement, DoCmd.OpenForm "Invoice", acNormal, , strWhere, uses the strWhere clause to open the Invoice form in Normal view. The DoCmd object is used to run Access actions from Visual Basic. The **arguments** of the DoCmd object are positional, so commas are used as placeholders for unused arguments. **Methods** are actions that can be completed by an object. The OpenForm method of the DoCmd object is used in this procedure, but other DoCmd methods provide the ability to open reports and queries, print various objects, move to specific records, and many other actions.

Understanding Functions

Like Event procedures, Function procedures are stored in code modules. Recall that a code module can be attached to a form or report or a stand-alone Standard module. Functions that are stored in a form or report module are typically private and available only in that module. Functions stored in a Standard module are public and available to all project objects and modules.

Exploring Function Execution

Functions are distinct from Event procedures because they do not respond to events, but must be specifically executed or called. Additionally, functions always return a value. Common programmatic operations like converting Fahrenheit temperatures to Celsius, changing lowercase values to uppercase, or converting dollars to yen are ideally placed in a custom Function procedure where they can be accessed publicly.

Public functions are not just available in program modules, but can be used anywhere in Access that an expression can be specified. For example, a calculated control on a form or report can reference both built-in and custom functions and both built-in and custom functions can be referenced in VBA code. Regardless of whether a built-in or custom function is being used, the function call and evaluation processes follow the pattern shown in Figure 11.14.

for each selected record the QuantityOrdered is multiplied by the ProductPrice and then added to the running total stored in Sum

$$InvoiceTotal = Sum([QuantityOrdered] * [ProductPrice])$$

after all selected records have been processed, the value of Sum is stored in InvoiceTotal

Using Built-In Functions

Before building a custom function, the twins would like to add an invoice total to the Invoice form. This operation requires modifying the OrderDetails subform using the built-in Sum function. Like all functions, the Sum function stores the result of its execution in the function name (Sum in this case).

The arguments provided to the Sum function outline what values are to be summed. Arguments must be fields in the form's data source or calculations based on those fields. Arguments cannot reference other calculated controls like ItemTotal, so the item total calculation (QuantityOrdered*ProductPrice) is used as the Sum argument. When Sum function is completed, its value is displayed in the form's ItemTotal text box.

Using the Sum function to summarize OrderDetails subform data:

1. With **ac11KoryoKicks.mdb** open, complete the following

2. Open the **InvoiceOrderDetail** form in Design View

tip: *Maximizing the form may make the following tasks easier*

3. Set the form to display a footer
   a. Right-click on the Form Footer divider bar and select **Properties**
   b. Set the footer's Height property to **.25**
   c. Set the footer's Visible property to **Yes**

4. Set the form's properties
   a. Select **Form** from the drop-down list in the Properties dialog box
   b. In the Default View property, select **Continuous Forms**
   c. Close the Properties dialog box

5. Add a Text Box control with its associated Label control to the Form Footer

6. Resize and position the text box and label as shown in Figure 11.15

7. Double-click on the new Label to access its Properties pages and set the Caption property to **Invoice Total**

8. Click on the new Text Box to open its Properties pages and select the **All** tab
   a. Set the Control Source property to
      =Sum([QuantityOrdered]*[ProductPrice])
   b. Set the Format property to **Currency**
   c. Set the Decimal Places property to **2**

ACCESS

FIGURE 11.15

The revised
InvoiceOrderDetail
subform

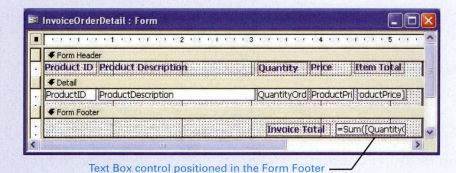

Text Box control positioned in the Form Footer ─────

9. Close the Properties dialog box and the OrderDetails subform saving your changes

10. Open the Invoice form in Form View and move through the customers observing the Invoice Total amount

tip: *The Invoice Total for CstmrID **22** Order **44** should be $184.46. For customers with more line items than will display in the space provided, you will need to scroll through the line items*

11. Close the Invoice form

The invoice total controls were added to the Footer section of the subform because they should display only once after the detail data, while the data in the Detail section displays once for each line of data. The properties of the form and the footer had to be changed so that the footer would display when the form was in Form View. The DefaultView of the main form controls whether or not footers display in it and all of its subforms. The Continuous Forms setting displays footers, while the Datasheet setting does not.

Creating a Custom Function

Each function starts with a Function statement and terminates with an End Function statement. The VBA statements needed to complete the function's task are placed inside these bookends. The last statement in a function is typically used to assign the return value to the function name. Once a custom function procedure has been coded, it is executed in the same fashion as a built-in function.

help yourself *Use the Type a Question combo box in the Microsoft Visual Basic window to improve your understanding of Function procedures by typing **VBA functions**. Review the contents of* Visual Basic for Applications Functions *to see a list of built-in functions and* Writing a Function Procedure *to learn more about writing a custom function. Close the Help window when you are finished*

Opening a New Standard Module

Functions can be either public (available everywhere) or private (belonging to a particular form or report module). While the function names follow the general naming rules already discussed for procedures and variables, more care is typically needed to select appropriate function names. Remember that functions are often used in expressions and so need to be short but descriptive. Additionally, most functions are public in scope and must be unique across all modules.

Missy and Micah would like to develop a function that will display the due date of each invoice on the Invoice form. Although it is being developed for the Invoice form, the DueDate function will need to be used from multiple forms and so will be placed in a Standard module making it public.

task reference Creating a Standard Module

- In the Database Window, click the **Modules** object
- Click **New** on the Database Window toolbar

Creating a new Standard module:

1. With **ac11KoryoKicks.mdb** open, complete the following
2. Click the **Modules** object in the Database Window
3. Click **New**

Multiple functions and procedures can be added to a Standard module. Typically, related functions and procedures are placed in the same module. Like modules that are associated with a particular form or report, Standard modules begin with the General Declarations section. The Option Compare Database statement is automatically added by Access to specify that normal alphabetical order using the language settings specified on your computer will be used. No other General Declarations statements are needed for the DueDate function to work properly.

Building the DueDate Custom Function

The DueDate function will determine when a particular invoice is due based on its OrderDate. Two values will be passed to the DueDate function: the order date and the number of days until the due date. The DueDate function will add the specified number of days to the order date and return it as DueDate.

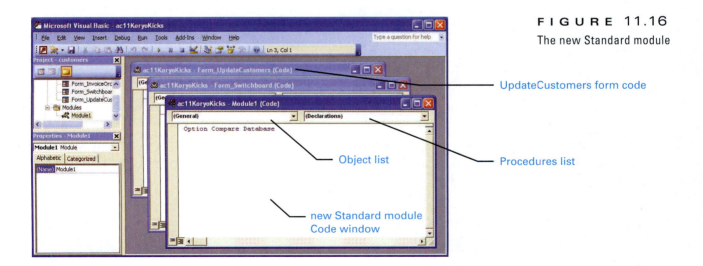

FIGURE 11.16
The new Standard module

UpdateCustomers form code

Object list

Procedures list

new Standard module
Code window

ACCESS

FIGURE 11.17

The DueDate Function
declaration statement

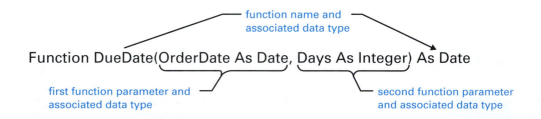

Function DueDate(OrderDate As Date, Days As Integer) As Date

Recall that function names are actually variables that will store the value being returned by the function. Each function name is therefore associated with a data type that determines what it can store and how it can be processed. Because the DueDate function accepts two arguments (values), two additional variables called *parameters* are specified in the Function declaration statement. Each parameter is also declared with a data type. Review Figure 11.17 to understand the Function declaration statement for DueDate.

The DateAdd built-in function will be used within the custom DueDate function to add specific time periods to a known date. The benefit of using this built-in function is that it keeps track of all the calendar variables such as leap years and century changes. The interval added to the date can be specified in several ways including months (m), weeks (ww), week days (w), calendar days (d), and hours (h).

The basic format of the DateAdd function is DateAdd(interval, quantity, date), where interval specifies the unit being added, quantity specifies the number of units, and date is the beginning date. For example, *DateAdd("d", 60, OrderDate)* would add 60 days to the value of OrderDate. Negative quantities will subtract intervals from the date.

---

task reference **Testing Procedures in the Immediate Window**

- In the Visual Basic code window, click **View** and then **Immediate Window**

- Type a question mark (**?**), the procedure name, and any required arguments in parentheses

- Press **Enter** to execute the procedure and display the results

---

Coding and testing the DueDate function:

1. Verify that the Standard code module created in the previous steps is open

2. Add the code shown in Figure 11.18

3. Test the function by clicking the **Immediate Window** option of the **View** menu

4. To execute DueDate with the arguments 12/28/2003 (OrderDate) and 45 (Days) type **?DueDate(#12/28/2003#,45)** in the Immediate window and press **Enter**

tip: *OrderDate was declared with a Date data type, so its arguments must be enclosed in pound signs(#). If the correct results are not produced, revise the code using Figure 11.18*

5. Test other OrderDate and Days arguments and verify the result on a calendar

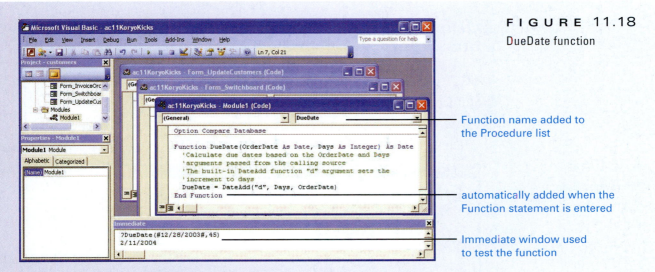

FIGURE 11.18

DueDate function

Function name added to the Procedure list

automatically added when the Function statement is entered

Immediate window used to test the function

6. Click the **Save** button on the Standard toolbar and name the module **KoryoKicksProcedures**

7. Close the Visual Basic Editor window

tip: *KoryoKicksProcedures should now display as in the Modules list of the Database Window*

This custom function consists of a single assignment statement that stores the results of an expression (on the right-hand side of the equals sign) in the name of the function, DueDate. The completed function can be used almost anywhere in Microsoft Access that accepts an expression. For example, code in another procedure or function module could use the DueDate function.

You have probably noticed that the Visual Basic Editor provides tips as you are typing code statements. When the editor recognizes the statement being entered, the arguments needed to complete it or a list of valid values are provided. These tips significantly improve the likelihood that your code is syntactically correct. Additionally, each time that you move to a new line in the editor, the completed line of code is tested for syntax errors. Syntax errors generate a dialog box describing the error, and the erroneous code is displayed in red. Syntax errors must be corrected before testing for logic errors.

The DueDate function was tested for logic errors using the Immediate window to execute it with a variety of argument values. When invalid values result, there is an error in the logic of the procedure that must be repaired to produce valid results. It is critical to test each procedure thoroughly to ensure valid results are produced through its use.

Using the DueDate Custom Function

Since the DueDate function was stored in a Standard module, it is available throughout Access like any built-in function. To demonstrate this concept, the function will be used on an existing KoryoKicks form and to create a printed invoice report.

Updating the Invoice Form

Now that the DueDate custom function is complete, it can be used to add the due date for each order to the Invoice form. This operation requires modifying the Orders subform using the custom function. This use of DueDate will parallel the use of the built-in Sum function earlier in this session.

Using the DueDate function to display the order due date on the Orders subform:

1. With **ac11KoryoKicks.mdb** open, complete the following

2. Open the **InvoiceOrderSubform** form in Design View

3. Add a Text Box control with its associated Label control below the existing Detail section controls, increasing the height of the form if needed

FIGURE 11.19

The revised Orders subform

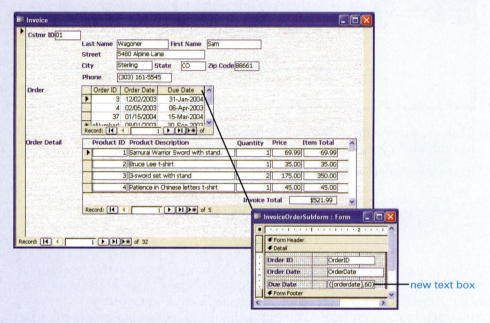

new text box

4. Click on the new text box to open its Properties pages and select the **All** tab

   a. Set the Control Source property to =**DueDate([OrderDate],60)**

   tip: *DueDate is the custom function created in a previous set of steps. OrderDate is the Name of the text box on the Orders subform containing the current record's order date, and 60 is the number of days to be added to the order date*

   b. Set the Format property to **dd-mmm-yyyy** (to match Order Date)

   c. Set the Text Align property of the Format tab to **Right**

5. Click the new label and set the Caption property to **Due Date**

6. Change to Form View and adjust the column widths

7. Close the Properties dialog box and the subform saving your changes

8. Open the **Invoice** form in Form View and move through the customers observing the Due Date value

9. Switch to Design View and widen the Orders subform to display all of the Due Date control

10. Return to Form View and scroll through records

    tip: *The Due Date for CstmrID 028 OrderID 19 should be 01-Jan-2004*

11. Close the Invoice form

Controls that reference data on a subform can be added to the main form, but are most easily added to the subform, in this case the Orders subform. In a text box, an assignment statement is used to call the DueDate function. Function calls must always include arguments for the parameters defined in the function declaration statement, in this case OrderDate and Days. The arguments are passed to the DueDate function, processed, and then a DueDate is returned to be displayed in the text box.

Creating the Invoice Report

Although you have been working on the Invoice form for several chapters, a report version that can be mailed to customers has not been developed. The twins would like the printed report to mimic the Invoice form, but contain the KoryoKicks logo, show all the order details, and issue a page break between each order. You will complete the report that the twins have started.

Using the DueDate function to display the order due date on the Invoice report:

1. With **ac11KoryoKicks.mdb** open, complete the following

2. Click on the **Reports** object in the Database Window, select **Invoice**, and click the Design View button

3. Explore the existing report components

4. Add a Text Box control with its associated Label control to the right of existing OrderID Header section controls

5. Select the new label and use cut and paste to place it into the Customer_CstmrID Header

   a. Move the label to the right of Order Date
   b. Double-click on the label to open its Properties pages
   c. Set the Caption property to **Due Date**
   d. Set the Text Align property on the Format tab to **Right**

6. Resize and position the text box and label as shown in Figure 11.20

FIGURE 11.20

The revised Invoice report

new Label control

new Text Box control

7. Click on the new text box to open its Properties pages and select the **All** tab

   a. Set the Control Source property to **=DueDate([OrderDate],60)**

   tip: *DueDate is the custom function created in a previous set of steps. OrderDate is the text box on the form containing the current record's order date, and 60 is the number of days to be added to the order date*

   b. Set the Format property to **dd-mmm-yyyy** (to match Order Date)

   c. Set the Text Align property to **Right**

8. Close the Properties dialog box

9. Use the Format Painter to copy the OrderDate text box's properties to the new text box

10. Open the Invoice report in Print Preview View

11. Return to Design View

The Invoice report will be completed using a subreport control. A *subreport control* is used to imbed a table, query, form, or report inside an existing report. There are two benefits of the subreport control. First, existing forms and reports can be reused, saving time and simplifying maintenance. Second, the subreport can be used to add additional header and footer sections within the body of a report.

A subreport can be added to any section of a report but, like any other control, the section selected determines how the subreport behaves. When you want subreport data to appear only once for the report, put it in either the Report Header or Footer section. When the subreport data are to appear once for each record, the data should be placed in the Detail section.

The KoryoKicks Invoice report will use the Invoice form's OrderDetail subform/subreport to simplify its creation. Since this subform/subreport already contains the controls needed to display the items ordered, the item total, and the invoice total, those features do not need to be rebuilt. Because the data in the subreport are to appear once for each record, the data will be placed in the Detail section of the Invoice report.

task reference   Adding a Subreport Control to an Existing Report

- Open the exiting report in Design View

- Click the **Control Wizards** button in the toolbox, if Control Wizards are not already active

- Determine the appropriate section for the subreport control

- Click the **Subform/Subreport** control in the toolbox

- Click in the desired report section

- Follow the SubReport Wizard to select content for the subreport control

- Use Print Preview to evaluate your updates

- Move and resize the control as needed

Creating a subreport control on the Invoice report:

1. Verify that the Invoice report is open in Design View from the previous steps

2. If Control Wizards are not turned on, click the **Control Wizards** button in the toolbox

3. In the toolbox, click the **Subform/Subreport** control

4. Click in the Detail section below the OrderID text box

tip: *The SubReport Wizard will initiate*

5. In the SubReport Wizard
   a. Click **Use an Existing report or form**, then select the **InvoiceOrderDetail** Subform from the list, and click the **Next** button
   b. Click **Next** to accept the default link method

tip: *The link method is a SQL statement that defines how the subreport is linked to the main report*

   c. Click **Finish** to accept the default subreport name

6. Enlarge the subreport area to display all of its controls and insert a PageBreak control below it (just above the Page Footer section)

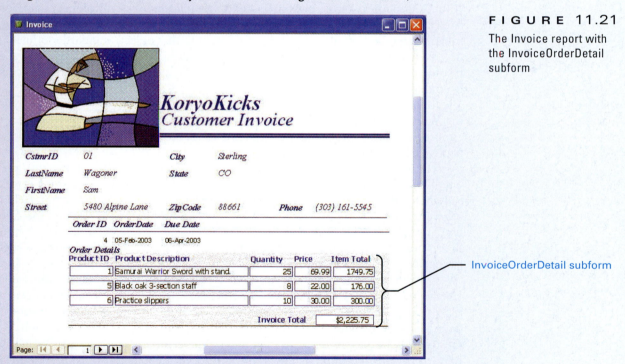

FIGURE 11.21
The Invoice report with the InvoiceOrderDetail subform

InvoiceOrderDetail subform

7. Edit the OrderDetails Subform label to read **Order Details**

8. Change to Print Preview View to evaluate your changes

9. Make any necessary updates in Design View

10. Close the report, saving your changes

When printed, this invoice report should place each customer order on a separate page, displaying customer data only when the data change. By reusing the OrderDetail subform in the Invoice report, development was significantly simplified. Additionally, changes made to the OrderDetail subform will be reflected in both the Invoice form and report based on that subform, reducing overall maintenance.

SESSION 11.2

making *the grade*

1. How do you determine what module will hold a new VBA procedure?

2. What is the purpose of concatenation?

3. What differences exist between the structure of an Event procedure and that of a Function procedure?

4. How do you know what arguments to pass a function?

SESSION 11.3 SUMMARY

Microsoft Visual Basic for Applications (VBA) provides the ability to create fast, customized, user-friendly features for any Access database. The VBA code statements necessary to complete a task are stored in a procedure. Procedures can respond to events (Event procedures), return a value (Function procedures), or stand alone. Groups of related procedures are stored in Code modules. Each Access report and form has an associated module to contain procedures relevant to that object. Standard modules are a new database object used to hold Public procedures. Public procedures are available throughout Access, while those placed in a form or report module can only be accessed from that object.

Most forms and reports already contain VBA code that was generated by your menu or Wizard selections. This code can be modified, or new procedures can be added as needed to customize the user environment. VBA code statements follow a strict syntax using keywords, arguments, and punctuation.

The Visual Basic Editor provides a Code window where VBA statements are entered. The VBA Editor checks syntax as code statements are entered, issuing errors on statements that it cannot understand. Such errors are called syntax errors. Help and other programs are a good source of VBA syntax examples. In the VBA Editor, color is used to identify various components of each statement. Green text indicates a comment that is not processed during program execution. Blue text identifies keywords such as String, If, Function, and End. Red text identifies syntax errors.

Once the syntax of new code has passed the VBA Editor, it is time to check for logic errors. Logic errors occur when VBA statements are used inappropriately. For example, if the wrong argument is passed to a function or a function is applied in the wrong situation. Logic errors are uncovered by running the code and observing the result. When the result is not accurate, there must be a logic error in the code. The Visual Basic Editor provides the Immediate window and other debugging tools to help uncover logic errors.

Visit www.mhhe.com/i-series/ to explore related topics.

MICROSOFT OFFICE SPECIALIST OBJECTIVES SUMMARY

- No specific MOS objectives were addressed in this chapter

making the grade *answers*

SESSION 11.1

1. A Sub procedure is a programmatic structure beginning with Sub and ending with End Sub that contains all of the VBA statements needed to accomplish a particular task. An Event procedure is a special type of Sub procedure that is triggered by an event such as a button click.

2. Select the Event procedure that will trigger the VBA code in response to the desired event. For example, select the Click event of a command button to enter code that will run when the button is clicked. Some objects like a form have multiple events that are triggered by a single user action (**Open** $\Rightarrow$ **Load** $\Rightarrow$ **Resize** $\Rightarrow$ **Activate** $\Rightarrow$ **Current**). In such cases, selecting the best event requires research into the features that each option provides.

3. If YearsOfService <= 5 Then Message = "5 Vacation Days"

   Else

   Message = "10 Vacation Days"

   End If

4. Click the Procedure View button in the bottom left-hand corner of the Code window.

SESSION 11.2

1. New VBA procedures can be placed in an existing form/report module or in a Standard module. Procedures, such as Event procedures, that are tied to a particular form or report should be placed in the module for that form or report. Such procedures have a Private scope. Procedures that are accessed from multiple forms or reports should be placed in a Standard module. These procedures have a Public scope.

2. Concatenation is used to combine various string values into a single value by joining them end-to-end. The methodology allows variables and values from other sources to be added to a static portion of a string. For example, a SQL Where clause can be built to incorporate values displayed on a form.

3. An Event procedure begins with a Sub statement and terminates with an End Sub statement. The name of the procedure is a combination of the object and event, cmdOpen_Click(), for example. Function procedures begin with the Function statement and terminate with the End Function statement. The developer chooses the name of a function, but it must be unique. Additionally, a function returns a value in the function name, so the function name has a data type. The last statement of a function generally assigns the return value to the function name.

4. As you type a function in the VBA Code window, the arguments needed for that function are provided in a pop-up. When Access functions in other areas, use Help to determine the correct arguments.

task reference *summary*

Task	Page #	Preferred Method
Viewing an object's event properties	AC 11.4	• In Design View, right-click on the object • Select **Properties** from the pop-up menu • Click the **Event** tab and explore the available event properties
Saving an Access database as an MDE file	AC 11.16	• Close all open copies of the database • Create a backup copy of the database using Windows Explorer • On the Tools menu, point to **Database Utilities**, and then click **Make MDE File** • In the Database To Save As MDE dialog box, select the drive, folder, and filename of the Access database to be converted • Click **Make MDE** • In the Save MDE As dialog box, specify the drive, folder, and filename of the MDE file

ACCESS

task reference *summary*

Task	Page #	Preferred Method
Creating a Standard module	AC 11.23	• In the Database Window, click the **Modules** object • Click **New** on the Database Window toolbar
Testing procedures in the Immediate window	AC 11.24	• In the Visual Basic code window, click **View** and then **Immediate Window** • Type a question mark (**?**), the procedure name, and any required arguments in parentheses • Press **Enter** to execute the procedure and display the results
Adding a subreport control to an existing report	AC 11.28	• Open the exiting report in Design View • Click the **Control Wizards** button in the toolbox, if Control Wizards are not already active • Determine the appropriate section for the subreport control • Click the **Subform/Subreport** control in the toolbox • Click in the desired report section • Follow the Subreport Wizard to select content for the subreport control • Use Print Preview to evaluate your updates • Move and resize the control as needed

TRUE/FALSE

1. VBA comment lines are executed to produce program output.

2. The result obtained by executing a function is stored in the function name.

3. After a custom function has been coded, it is executed using the function name with any necessary arguments in parentheses.

4. A subreport control is used to add an existing table, query, form, or report to the report being designed.

5. The Form Load event is the only event that occurs when a form is opened.

6. *Private Sub Form_Load()* is a variable assignment statement.

FILL-IN

1. _____ the code modules of an Access database converts the VBA statements to machine code.

2. VBA code is entered in the _____ of the Visual Basic Editor.

3. VBA procedures that are related are stored in a(n) _____.

4. The process of attaching string values end-to-end is called _____.

5. A(n) _____ is an action that can be completed by an object.

6. A variable or procedure declared with a scope of _____ is available to all procedures in all modules.

7. A(n) _____ statement is used to store a value in a variable.

MULTIPLE CHOICE

1. The _____ VBA statement is used to control processing based on the result of a condition check.
   a. Assignment
   b. If
   c. Condition
   d. all of the above

2. If a procedure is being called from an assignment statement and returns a value, it must be a _____ procedure.
   a. Function
   b. Declaration
   c. Private
   d. all of the above

3. Which of the following lines of code would store a concatenated value in the variable txtThankYou?
   a. txtThankYou = "Thank you for your business " & txtFirstName
   b. txtThankYou = "Thank you for your business"
   c. "Thank you for your business " & txtFirstName = txtThankYou
   d. none of the above

4. A procedure that will be available only to the current form should be declared with _____ scope.
   a. Local
   b. Public
   c. Private
   d. Global

5. A variable's data type determines _____.
   a. valid values for storage
   b. the size of the storage area in RAM
   c. whether the stored value can be used in mathematical calculations
   d. all of the above

REVIEW QUESTIONS

Each of the following topics should be addressed in one to three paragraphs.

1. Discuss why the last statement of a function is typically an assignment statement.

2. Describe the use of the General Declarations section of a Code module.

3. Explain how to create the string "Welcome to SkillsTracking. The current date and time is: " with a display of the current system date and time.

4. How would you add your name to a list of names stored in the string variable strNameList? Each name on the list appears on a new line.

5. What is the focus?

CREATE THE QUESTION

For each of the following answers, create the question.

ANSWER	QUESTION
1. It returns a value	_____
2. FunctionName(argument1, argument2, . . .)	_____
3. Clicking, double-clicking, and dragging	_____
4. Click in a code statement and press F1	_____
5. Standard module	_____
6. Dim strDemo as String	_____
7. Place a single quote (') before the line of code	_____

FACT OR FICTION

For each of the following, determine whether the statement is fact, fiction, or both and present your arguments for that conclusion.

1. The If statement is used to execute some code statements and not others based on the evaluation of a condition.

2. The Visual Basic Editor's Code window always displays all of the procedures for the current module.

3. When storing a value in a string variable, double quotes ("") must be placed around text such as "F".

4. Sub procedures can be used in assignment statements.

5. Each procedure must have a unique name within the active database.

6. The Function name in a Function declaration statement is assigned a data type.

7. In the VBA Code window, blue text identifies Visual Basic keywords.

1. Building Visual Basic Procedures for Gibbs Foods—Part I

Gibbs Foods is an international distributor of specialty foods. Visual Basic code is needed to enhance existing database functionality.

1. Open **ac11GibbsFoods.mdb**

2. Open the Products table in Datasheet View and review Units In Stock, Units On Order, and Reorder Level. When the sum of Units In Stock and Units On Order is below the Reorder Level, it is time to order more product. Close the table

3. Open the **ProductReorders** query in Datasheet View and review the records retrieved. Switch to Design View and review the last field (scroll right) used to retrieve rows that need to be reordered. Notice that this calculated value does not display. Close the query

4. Open the **SuppliersReorders** report in Report view. The ProductReorders query is the data source for this report. Close the report

5. To improve the functionality of the SuppliersReorders report, the optimal number of units to order needs to be calculated using a custom function

   a. Switch to Design View and minimize the window to free space to work in the Code window

   b. In the Database Window, click **Module** and then **New** to create a new Standard module

   c. Create the function OrderQty by typing the following code

   Function OrderQty(Class As Integer, ReorderQty As Integer) As Integer

   If Class = 1 Or Class = 2 Then

   $OrderQty = 5 + ReorderQty * 1$

   ElseIf Class = 3 Or Class = 4 Then

   $OrderQty = 5 + ReorderQty * 1.5$

   Else

   $OrderQty = 5 + ReorderQty * 2$

   End If

   End Function

   d. Use the Immediate window to perform two separate tests of the function with **?OrderQty(2,20)** and **?OrderQty(4,20)** (The results should be 25 and 35, respectively)

   e. Close the Visual Basic Editor

6. Open the **SuppliersReorders** report in Design View

   a. Add a Text Box control to the Detail section of the form

   b. Cut the label portion of the control and paste it in the Suppliers.SupplierID Header section between the double lines to the right of Reorder Level

   c. Position the text box below the label in the Detail section

   d. Set the properties of the label so that the caption reads **Order Qty** and the formatting is the same as the other labels

   e. Set the Control Source property of the text box to **=OrderQty([CategoryID], [ReorderLevel])**

   f. Switch to Print Preview View and evaluate the result of using the custom OrderQty function

7. Close the report, saving your changes

F I G U R E 11.22

The new SuppliersReorders report

second page · values calculated with the new OrderQty function

2. VBA Automation for the Recycling Database

The Recycling.mdb database is used to track the recycling habits of selected recyclers in order to track patterns and understand recycling behavior. The ultimate goal is to better understand consumers so that services can be matched to consumer behavior. You will be adding automation features to simplify movement between objects in the database.

1. Start Access and open **ac11Recycling.mdb**

2. Review the contents of the Customer and RecyclingPickup tables. The RecyclingPickup table contains one record for each recycling pickup and is linked to the Customer table using CstmrID

3. Open the Customer form in Design View

   a. Create a message to display when the form first displays on the user's screen. Open the Form Properties and click on the On Load event

      i. Use the Build (…) button to open the Code Builder

      ii. Add the code needed to use a MsgBox to display the message **Recycling is not a production database. It should be used for statistical analysis only.**

   b. Widen the form to make space for command buttons

   c. Verify that the Control Wizards are active and then place a new command button to the right of the Phone field. This button will print the contents of the current form

      i. In the Command Button Wizard, select **Form Operations**, **Print Current Form**, and then click **Next**

      ii. Display the Printer icon

      iii. Name the button **cmdPrint** and click **Finish**

      iv. Open the Properties of cmdPrint and review the code added to the On Click event procedure created by your Wizard selections

   d. Add a second command button to the right of the First Pickup field and cancel the Command Button Wizard

   e. This new command button needs to be coded to open the RecyclingPickup form displaying pickups for the customer displayed in the Customer form

      i. Open the Properties pages for the new command button

      ii. Name the button **cmdRecyclingPickup**

      iii. Set the button Caption to **Pickups**

      iv. Open the On Click Event Code Window

      v. Add the code shown in Figure 11.23

4. Test the new features and make any needed repairs

5. If your work is complete, exit Access; otherwise, continue to the next assignment

F I G U R E 11.23

Customer form and cmdRecyclingPickup_Click() Event procedure

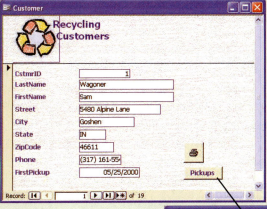

challenge!

1. Building Visual Basic Procedures for Gibbs Foods—Part II

The Visual Basic procedures for Gibbs Foods were started in the Practice project with the creation of the OrderQty function. Additional Visual Basic procedures are needed to complete database development.

1. Open your copy of **ac11GibbsFoods.mdb**. If you did not complete the Practice assignment for this chapter, complete it now

2. Add a new Visual Basic function to the existing Standard module. Name the function **DeliveryEstimate**, and make it a Date data type with no arguments (The parentheses in the Function declaration statement are empty when no values are being passed)

   a. Use the Dim statement to dimension the variable TodaysDate and use the built-in Now() function to store the current date there

   b. Use the built-in DateAdd function to add 10 week days to TodaysDate and store it in DeliveryEstimate

   c. Test the function in the Immediate window with **?DeliveryEstimate** and verify the result with a calendar

3. Add a text box to the SuppliersReorders report using Figure 11.24 as a guide

   a. Make the label read **Estimated Delivery**

   b. Make the Control Source of the text box use the custom function DeliveryEstimate to display the anticipated delivery date for the order

   c. Format the text box to display the date in **Short Date** format

   d. Evaluate the results

4. Open the **ProductReorders** form

   a. Use the Properties dialog box to change the Height property of the Footer section to **.25**

   b. Add a text box to the Footer section

   c. Make the label read **Orders placed today should be received by**

   d. Use the custom DeliveryEstimate function to assign the value to the text box

   e. Format the text box to display a short date

   f. Add a text box to Detail section of the form to the right of the existing controls

   g. Cut the label and place it in the Form Header to the right of existing controls

   h. Set the label's Caption to Order Qty

   i. Use the custom OrderQty function created in the Practice project to assign a value to the new text box

5. Code the Form Load procedure for the ProductOrders form that displays a message indicating that you have updated the user interface and use the Tools menu to set it as the startup form

6. Create a .mde file

FIGURE 11.24

DeliveryEstimate added to the SuppliersReorders report

Estimated Delivery Date assigned with a custom function

2. Automating the PuppyParadise User Interface

PuppyParadise is a distributor of pet supplies. The PuppyParadise database is a mature database with a number of tables, queries, forms, and reports. An Invoice form and report were recently added to the database and need to be finalized using a custom function.

1. Start Access and open **ac11PuppyParadise.mdb**

2. Review the existing tables, queries, forms, and reports

3. Create a new Standard module

   a. Create a **CalcDueDate** function procedure in the new Standard module

   b. The function should accept one argument, the order date

   c. Use the DateAdd built-in function to add 90 days to the order date

4. Open the Orders subform of the Invoice form in Design View

   a. Add a Text Box control to the Form Footer

   b. Label the control **Total**

   c. Use a built-in function to calculate the invoice total

   d. Set the format to **Currency**

   e. Change to Datasheet View and verify the calculation

5. Open the Orders subform of the Invoice form in Design View

   a. Add a Text Box control to the right of the Order Date control

   b. Label the text box **Due Date**

   c. Use the CalcDueDate custom function

   d. Set the display format to **dd-mmm-yyy**

   e. Adjust the width of the subform to allow full display of all data

6. Open the Invoice form in Datasheet View and move through the records verifying the Due Date calculation

7. Open the Invoice report in Design View

   a. Add a Text Box control to the right of the Order Date

   b. Label the new text box **Due Date**

   c. Set the Control Source property of the new control to use the CalcDueDate function to add 90 days to the Order Date

   d. Set the form of the control to **dd-mmm-yyy**

   e. Verify the results in Print Preview View

8. If your work is complete, exit Access; otherwise, continue to the next assignment

FIGURE 11.25

PuppyParadise Invoice form and report

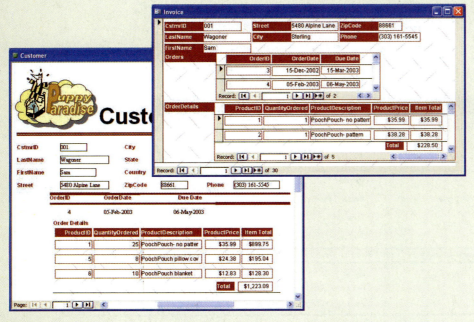

e-business

WebToys Visual Basic Procedures

WebToys is an Internet portal providing shopping bots that search Internet toy sales storefronts for products specified by the visitor. The current Web site does not store any customer data. You have been asked to create a form that will gather customer data so that orders can be placed through WebToys rather than through the individual retailer sites.

1. Open **ac11WebToys.mdb**

2. Open the **CustomerData** form in Form View and review the controls

3. Switch to Design View

    a. Check the Name properties of the two text boxes

    b. If the Toolbox Control Wizard is on, click it off

    c. Add a Command Button control to the bottom right-hand corner of the form. Set its Name to **cmdValidate** and Caption to **Validate**

    d. Create the On Click event procedure for cmdValidate (see Figure 11.26). The procedure should verify that txtLastName and txtFirstName text boxes on the form contain data since they will be required fields in the final form. Before a text box can be validated, it must have the focus. The .SetFocus method is used to give an object the focus. The .Text

property of each text box is tested for a "" (no data) value because it stores data entered by the user. If no data exist in the control, its background is turned yellow and a message box with an error message is displayed. The variable strErrorFlag is used to keep the procedure from issuing multiple errors. strErrorFlag is set to "N" at the beginning of the procedure and "Y" when the first error is encountered

    e. Test the procedure with a blank form, data entered in txtLastName only, data entered in txtFirstName only, and data entered in both fields

4. Add a third Text Box control to the CustomerData form below the First Name

    a. Make the label read **Street Address** and set the Name property of the text box to **txtStreetAddress**

    b. Add the code to the cmdValidate_Click procedure to ensure that data are entered in txtStreetAddress. Be sure to issue an appropriate error message and turn the background yellow when there is an error

    c. Test the procedure with all combinations of data/no data values

FIGURE 11.26

cmdValidate_Click procedure

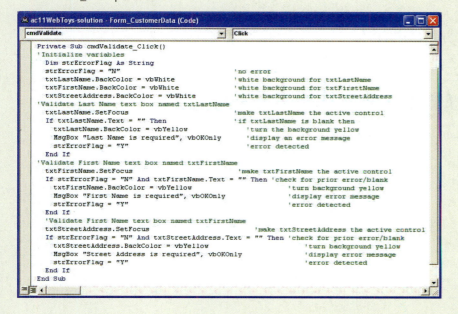

```
ac11WebToys-solution - Form_CustomerData (Code)

cmdValidate                                    Click

    Private Sub cmdValidate_Click()
    'Initialize variables
    Dim strErrorFlag As String
    strErrorFlag = "N"                          'no error
    txtLastName.BackColor = vbWhite             'white background for txtLastName
    txtFirstName.BackColor = vbWhite            'white background for txtFirsttName
    txtStreetAddress.BackColor = vbWhite        'white background for txtStreetAddress
    'Validate Last Name text box named txtLastName
    txtLastName.SetFocus                        'make txtLastName the active control
    If txtLastName.Text = "" Then               'if txtLastName is blank then
        txtLastName.BackColor = vbYellow        'turn the background yellow
        MsgBox "Last Name is required", vbOKOnly 'display an error message
        strErrorFlag = "Y"                      'error detected
    End If
    'Validate First Name text box named txtFirstName
    txtFirstName.SetFocus                       'make txtFirstName the active control
    If strErrorFlag = "N" And txtFirstName.Text = "" Then 'check for prior error/blank
        txtFirstName.BackColor = vbYellow       'turn background yellow
        MsgBox "First Name is required", vbOKOnly 'display error message
        strErrorFlag = "Y"                      'error detected
    End If
    'Validate First Name text box named txtFirstName
    txtStreetAddress.SetFocus                   'make txtStreetAddress the active control
    If strErrorFlag = "N" And txtStreetAddress.Text = "" Then 'check for prior error/blank
        txtStreetAddress.BackColor = vbYellow   'turn background yellow
        MsgBox "Street Address is required", vbOKOnly 'display error message
        strErrorFlag = "Y"                      'error detected
    End If
    End Sub
```

2. Automating the Golden Cream Bakery Graphical User Interface

Golden Cream is a bakery specializing in restaurant desserts. Orders are accepted from an Internet Web site. For processing, the data are loaded into a Microsoft Access database. Although this database is working well, it needs automation to improve functionality.

1. Open **ac11GoldenCream.mdb**. Peruse the current tables and queries.

Review the existing forms and reports

2. Create a new Standard module named **PubCalcs**

   a. Create a **CalcDueDate** function procedure in PubCalcs

   b. The function should accept one argument, the order date

   c. Use the DateAdd built-in function to add 90 days to the order date

3. Open the Order subform of the CustomerOrder form in Design View

   a. Add a Text Box control below the Order Date control

   b. Label the text box **Due Date**

   c. Use the CalcDueDate custom function

FIGURE 11.27
Golden Cream Invoice form and report]

d. Set the display format to **dd-mmm-yyy**

e. Adjust the width of the subform to allow full display of all data

4. Open the Sales subform of the CustomerOrder form in Design View

   a. Add a Text Box control to the right of Unit Price. Adjust the new label and text box to match Figure 11.27

   b. Add the calculation = [**Unit Price**] * **Qty** as the Control Source and label the control **Total**

   c. Set the Form Footer height to .25 and add a Text Box control. Use a built-in function to calculate the invoice total

   d. Set the format of both calculated controls to **Currency**

   e. Change to Datasheet View and verify the calculation

5. Open the Invoice form in Datasheet View and move through the records verifying the Due Date calculation

6. Open the CustomerInvoice report in Design View

   a. Add a Text Box control to the right of the Order Date

   b. Label the new text box **Due Date**

   c. Set the Control Source property of the new control to use the CalcDueDate function to display the due date calculated from the Order Date

   d. Set the form of the control to **dd-mmm-yyy**

   e. Calculate the Item Total and Invoice Total and have them display **Currency** format

   f. Verify the results in Print Preview View

7. Close the database and exit Access if your work is complete

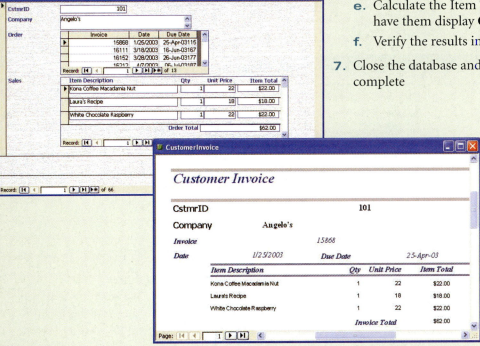

1. Book Club Visual Basic Procedures

Book Club is an organization of avid readers who share books. The books table of the BookClub database lists the current inventory. A new BookRequest table has been created to allow members to request specific books. You have been asked to customize database features with Visual Basic.

1. Use Web search tools to locate and document at least 10 books in several different categories (Novel, Suspense, Romance, Technology, Women, Fiction, Self-help, etc.)

2. Open **ac11BookClub.mdb**

3. Open the **BookRequest** form in Design View
    a. Click off Toolbox Control Wizards if they are on
    b. Add a Command Button control to the bottom right of the form (If the Command Button Wizard initiates, cancel it)
    c. Set the command button properties so that the text **Help** displays in the button and it is named **cmdHelp**
    d. Use the On Click Event from the Properties dialog box to open a Visual Basic Code window and use the DoCmd statement to open the BookRequestHelp form
    e. Test the procedure by clicking the command button in Form View

4. Open the **Books** form in Design View
    a. Add a Command Button control to the bottom right of the form (If the Command Button Wizard initiates, cancel it)
    b. Set the properties to name the button **cmdHelp** and have it display the word **Help**
    c. Write the procedure to cause the Help button to open the BooksHelp form

5. Open the **Switchboard form** in Design View and activate the Form properties dialog box
    a. Open the **Form Load** Event procedure
    b. Create code to determine the time of day and greet users with **Good Morning! before noon, Good Afternoon! between noon and six p.m., and Good Evening! between six p.m. and midnight**
    c. Display a message box with the greeting and a message to contact you with concerns about interface modifications

6. Open the **Switchboard form** in Form View and use it to test both Help buttons. Add the data from your research using the BookRequest form

7. Create a .mde file

FIGURE 11.28

Help forms and opening dialog box

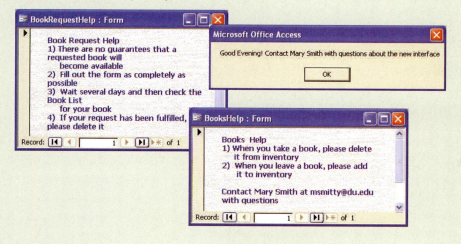

around the world

1. Professional Tennis Earnings

Professional tennis players' earnings are tracked to evaluate their success and value as endorsers of products. As earnings increase, so does public visibility and marketing value. Although professional players are from various countries, earnings are tracked in U.S. dollars.

1. Open **ac11Tennis.mdb**

2. Open the **PlayersIncome** form in Datasheet View and review the data

3. Switch to Design View

   a. Add a Text Box control below the existing controls. Make the label display **Market Appeal** and name the text box **txtAppeal**

   b. Close, saving your changes

4. Open a new Standard module

   a. Create a function named Appeal that accepts Income as a String argument (all Text Box controls display String data) and returns a string value

   b. The function should convert Income from String to Currency and then evaluate Income to assign the market appeal value. Appeal values are low (<150000), moderate (150000–350000), and high (>350000). Review Figure 11.29

5. Open the **PlayersIncome** form in Design View and activate the Properties dialog box for the txtAppeal text box. The value for this control is determined using the Appeal function created in the previous steps with the value held in txtWinnings as the argument. Set the Control Source property to =**Appeal([txtWinnings])**

6. Switch to Datasheet View, verify the results of the Appeal function, and close the form

7. Open the **PlayersIncome** report in Design View

   a. Add a Text Box control to the Detail section of the report to the right of existing controls

   b. Cut the label, place it in the Header section above the text box, and cause it to display **Market Appeal**

   c. Align the text box and use the Appeal function created earlier to display the market appeal value (The control holding the income value is named Winnings)

   d. Switch to Print Preview View, verify the results, and close

8. Open the **PlayersIncome** form in Design View

   a. Click off Toolbox Control Wizards if they are on

   b. Add a Command Button control to the bottom right of the form (If the Command Button Wizard initiates, cancel it)

   c. Set the command button properties so that the text **Help** displays in the button and it is named **cmdHelp**

   d. Use the On Click Event from the Properties dialog box to open a Visual Basic Code window and use the DoCmd statement to open the PlayersIncomeHelp form

   e. Test the procedure by clicking the command button in Form View

FIGURE 11.29

Appeal function code and result

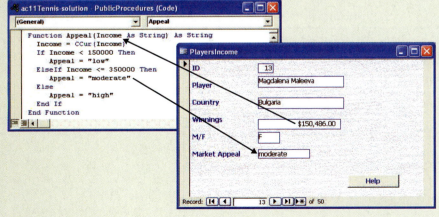

running project: TnT web design

TnT Visual Basic Procedures

The graphical user interface for the TnT database needs some finishing touches that require the use of Visual Basic. Use your copy of the database to complete this exercise.

1. Open your copy of **AC10TnT.mdb** (after completing Chapter 10), remembering to hold down the Shift key
2. Delete your copy of tblEmployees and use the Get External Data option of the File menu to import a revised copy from the ac11TnT.mdb database for this chapter. Delete the Employees form and retrieve the updated version
3. Close and use Windows to rename your copy of ac10TnT.mdb to **ac11TnT.mdb**
4. Open your copy of **ac11TnT.mdb**
5. Open **tblEmployees**, review the hire dates, and then close the table
6. Create a new Standard module
   a. Create a Function named Vacation that returns an Integer and accepts DateHired as an argument
   b. Use the DateDiff built-in function to calculate the number of years between the hire date and today
   c. If the number of years between hire date and today is less than or equal to one, Vacation equals zero. If the number of years is greater than one and less than or equal to five, Vacation equals five. Otherwise Vacation is equal to ten
   d. Open the Immediate window and test the function by typing ?**Vacation(#4/25/95#)** and pressing **Enter**
   e. Save and close
7. Open the **Employees** form in Design View
   a. Add a Text Box control to the form below Phone
      i. Set the properties of the label so that it displays **Hire Date**
      ii. Set the Control Source property of the text box to display **DateHired** using the drop-down list
      iii. Set the Name property to **txtDateHired**
   b. Add a second Text Box control to the form below Job Class
      i. Set the properties of the label so that it displays **Vacation Days**
      ii. Set the Control Source property to **=Vacation([txtDateHired])**
   c. Switch to Form View, verify the result, and save your changes
8. Open the **EmployeesByJobClass** report in Design View and add two Text Box controls with properties set to display DateHired and Vacation (Place the controls in the Detail section of the form and then cut and paste the labels to the Header section)

F I G U R E   11.30

Vacation function and the revised Employees form

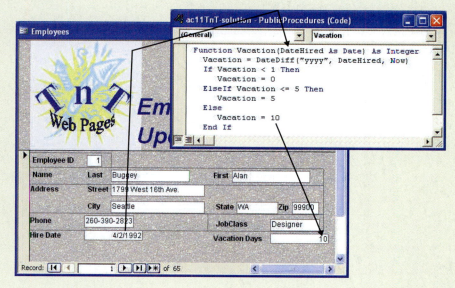

1. VBA Automation for Presbyterian Hospital

Open your copy of the database named **ac10 PresbyterianHospital.mdb** containing the updates from Chapter 10's Level Four project. This database is used to track various hospital operations. Review each existing database object and design processes automation using VBA. Submit your database and documentation of the new features added.

VBA automation should include

- Issuing a message when the database opens
- Use of a Command Button to print form content
- Use of a Command Button to open related data in another form
- A Custom Function used by at least two database objects

2. VBA Automation for your Multitable Database

Locate any multitable database with a switchboard that you have worked with during the course of this class. The database should include at least two queries and at least two reports. Take a look at your current database objects and determine processes that could be automated using VBA. Submit your database and documentation of the new features added.

VBA automation should include

- Issuing a message when the database opens
- Use of a Command Button to print form content
- Use of a Command Button to open related data in another form
- A Custom Function used by at least two database objects

Advanced Forms and Data Sharing

did you know?

the *shortest known war was between Britain and Zanzibar in 1896 and lasted only 38 minutes.*

Leonardo da Vinci *was the first to record that the number of rings in the cross section of a tree trunk revealed its age and that the width between the rings indicated the annual moisture.*

a giraffe *can clean its ears with its tongue.*

Venus *spins from east-to-west while the other planets in our solar system spin from west-to-east.*

there *is no synonym for the word* thesaurus.

the *actual name of the # symbol is octothorpe (not pound or number sign).*

to *find out the longest word found in abridged dictionaries that can be typed using only the fingers of the right hand, visit www.mhhe.com/i-series.*

Chapter Objectives

- **Save PivotTable and PivotChart Views to Data Access Pages— MOS AC03S-4-2**

- **Add Web browser control to Access forms**

- **Import XML documents into Access**

- **Export Access data to XML documents**

- **Understand the upsizing options provided by Microsoft SQL Server technology**

KoryoKicks: Building Tabbed Forms and Using XML

KoryoKicks has come a long way from offering a few self-defense classes to augment Missy and Micah's college income. As in most growing organizations, the needs for and uses of data have dramatically changed due to expansion and changes in the business environment. The organization now consists of over 20 full-time employees scattered throughout the United States.

Databases are now used to track customers, employees, orders, payments, shipments, inventory, and expenses. While each of these applications functions to support a specific business area, it is time to consolidate, organize, and redesign user interfaces to be more effective. Even when the original database design is sound and all of the database objects are functioning appropriately, revisions to the user interface can improve employee performance and satisfaction.

One way to enhance a functioning user interface is the use of Tabbed forms. Tabbed forms allow multiple forms to be combined on a single interface. The content of the forms can be linked so

F I G U R E 12.1

Tabbed pages for the most commonly used forms

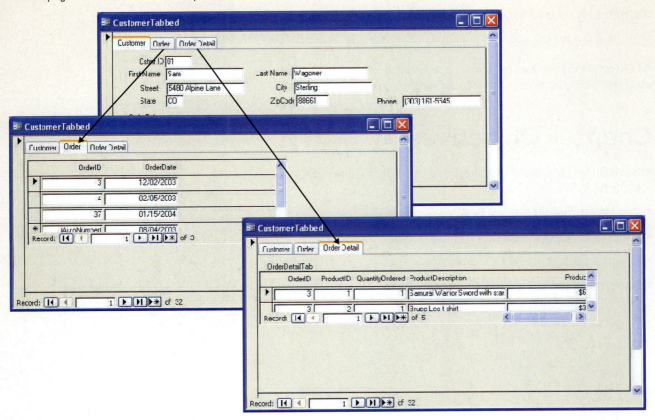

that selections on one form are reflected in the data displayed on another form. The most commonly used forms at KoryoKicks are based on the Customer, Orders, and OrderDetails tables. With the current design, each table can be opened independently or through a main form/subform interface. While the main form/subform interface contains all the necessary components, they are crowded and visually confusing. Redesigning this form to use linked tabbed pages will make the form easier and faster to use.

KoryoKicks, like most growing businesses, has an ever-changing need to reorganize and evaluate data in order to support decision making. PivotTables and PivotCharts are ideal for reorganizing and charting data to help decision makers see patterns. Both are features supported by Access tables, queries, and forms, and both can be placed on Data Access Pages to provide Web-based interaction with live data.

The twins are also interested in improving customer service by allowing Web-based ordering and payment processing. They believe that these services can be purchased from existing Web services retailers, but understand that a way of sharing data among the organizations and applications is needed. Extensible Markup Language (XML) is the platform most recommended for sharing data, so an XML transfer of KoryoKicks data needs to be completed and evaluated. Finally, KoryoKicks is outgrowing the capabilities of Microsoft Access and methods of upsizing using Microsoft SQL Server 2000 must be planned.

SESSION 12.1 EMPLOYING ADVANCED FORM FEATURES

Forms provide the backbone for user interaction with the data contained in any Access database. Making smarter and easier forms is a key component of improving user satisfaction and database performance.

Creating Multipage Forms

One way to make forms easier to use is to provide multiple pages of related data from the same form. With proper organization, multipage or *tabbed forms* make most information and data maintenance fields available from one form.

Now that KoryoKicks users understand how they access and use their data, Missy and Micah are ready to reorganize the interface to match that usage. The most fundamental change is to make the Invoices form easier to use and understand by placing the subforms on separate pages of the Customer form. This will provide the same functionality as the current form without the cluttered look. Additionally, the new form will use the standard Windows colors because the colors on the existing form become harsh on the eyes over time.

AC 12.3

ACCESS

Defining the Queries for Complex Forms

Although some of the existing KoryoKicks queries and forms could be used to make the new tabbed Customers form, they were created for other purposes and would not result in the most efficient form. When reorganizing the user interface, it is advisable to revisit database design and rebuild existing queries to perform exactly the operations needed in the new interface. Streamlining the queries will improve performance.

The new Customers form will contain data from each of the KoryoKicks tables: Customer, Order, OrderDetail, and Product. The Customer data will appear on the main form, the first subform will allow the user to select an order, and the details of that order will be on the second subform. Since all the data from the Customer and Order tables will be used and no calculations are involved, there is no need to create a query to support their use in the new Invoice form.

The details of the order on the second subform require a combination of data from the OrderDetail (ProductID and QuantityOrdered) and Product (ProductDescription and ProductPrice) tables. The total price for each line item is obtained by multiplying QuantityOrdered by ProductPrice. To provide the most efficient processing, a query will be created to select the fields from both tables and calculate the line totals.

Creating the InvoiceLineItems query:

1. Open the **ac12KoryoKicks.mdb** database

   tip: *You will need to hold the **Shift** key while the database loads to activate the development environment*

2. Select the **Queries** object from the Database Window

3. Double-click **Create query by using wizard**

4. In the Simple Query Wizard
   a. Select the **OrderDetail** table and move all of the fields to the Selected Fields list
   b. Select the Product table and move **ProductDescription** and **ProductPrice** to the Selected Fields list
   c. Click **Next** twice (until you can name the query)
   d. Name the query **InvoiceLineItems**
   e. Click **Finish**

5. Verify the query results and then change to Design View

6. In the Field Row of the first blank column, add a calculated field by typing **Item Total:QuantityOrdered*ProductPrice**

7. Switch to Datasheet View to verify the calculation

8. Close the window, saving your changes

Developing a query to select and calculate only the data that are necessary for the form results in more efficient form processing. It is also easier to verify the calculation before it becomes part of the report.

Building the Default Form

Although any form can be built from scratch in Form Design View, it is usually faster to develop most form functionality using Wizards and then customize to obtain the

FIGURE 12.2
InvoiceLineItems query

OrderID	ProductID	QuantityOrdered	ProductDescription	ProductPrice
3	1	1	Samurai Warrior Sword with stand.	$69.99
4	1	25	Samurai Warrior Sword with stand.	$69.99
5	1	1	Samurai Warrior Sword with stand.	$69.99
6	1	50	Samurai Warrior Sword with stand.	$69.99
7	1	10	Samurai Warrior Sword with stand.	$69.99
10	1	1	Samurai Warrior Sword with stand.	$69.99
13	1	1	Samurai Warrior Sword with stand.	$69.99
14	1	25	Samurai Warrior Sword with stand.	$69.99
15	1	100	Samurai Warrior Sword with stand.	$69.99
16	1	45	Samurai Warrior Sword with stand.	$69.99
17	1	50	Samurai Warrior Sword with stand.	$69.99
19	1	1	Samurai Warrior Sword with stand.	$69.99
20	1	1	Samurai Warrior Sword with stand.	$69.99
21	1	22	Samurai Warrior Sword with stand.	$69.99

Record: 1 of 184

desired result. Before adding tabbed pages to the UpdateCustomers form, a new form using subforms will be built from the Wizard.

Building the basic CustomerTabbed form with subforms:

1. Verify that the **ac12KoryoKicks.mdb** database is open, with no active database objects
2. Select the **Forms** object from the Database Window
3. Double-click **Create form by using Wizard**
4. Select the **Customer** table and move all of its fields to the Selected Fields list
5. Select the **Order** table and move all unduplicated fields to the Selected Fields list
6. Select the **InvoiceLineItems** query, move all of its fields except OrderID to the Selected Fields list, and click **Next**
7. Verify that the by Customer view and Form with subforms are both selected and then click **Next**
8. Select **Tabular** as the layout for *each* subform (click Tabular in each option button group) and click **Next**
9. Select **Standard** as the Style and click **Next**
10. Set the form name to **CustomerTabbed**, set the first subform's name to **OrdersTab**, and the second subform's name to **OrderDetailsTab**
11. Click **Finish** and compare your result to Figure 12.3
12. Change to Form Design View

The best strategy when using a Wizard to create forms for customization is to place all controls that will contain data on the form. This approach ensures that the correct field names are bound to each control and that the proper relationships are maintained between data from different tables.

FIGURE 12.3

CustomerTabbed form before modifications

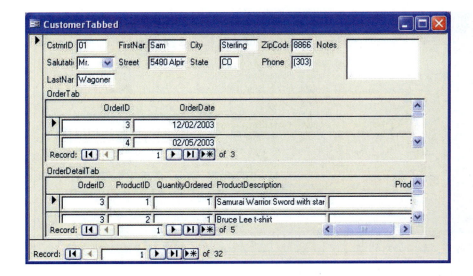

At this point, a new version of the KoryoKicks Invoice form has been created using the standard Windows color scheme. Now that the basic controls are on the form, modifications can be applied. The default controls need to be resized, reorganized, and re-captioned to better present the data.

Reorganizing the main form of the CustomerTabbed form:

1. Verify that the **ac12KoryoKicks.mdb** database is open, with the CustomerTabbed form in Design View

2. Make the form **6** inches wide using the ruler

tip: *It may be easier to complete these steps with the form maximized*

3. Move the two subforms down to provide workspace to manipulate the Customer controls

4. Add spaces between the words in labels

5. Adjust size of the labels and add needed spaces (Last Name, First Name) on the main form so that all characters can be read

tip: *Move the controls to allow space for this operation*

6. Roughly double the size of the Last Name text box and then make First Name, Street, City, and Phone text boxes the same size

tip: *Select all of the text boxes and then use the Size option of the Format toolbar to facilitate this operation*

7. Arrange the controls as shown in Figure 12.4

8. Change to Form View and verify that all data and labels display correctly

9. Make any necessary adjustments and save

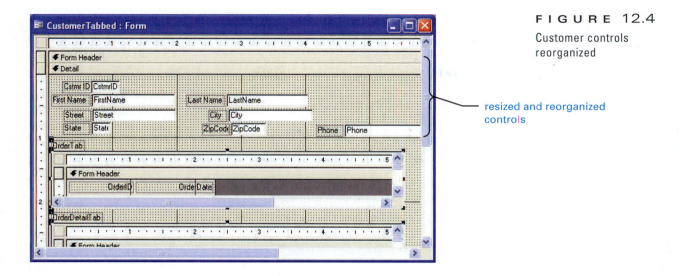

FIGURE 12.4
Customer controls
reorganized

resized and reorganized
controls

When customizing forms, it is generally best to work from top to bottom and left to right. The form width was determined by properly sizing the controls and then arranging them in the order that they are used. The form size is then adjusted to comfortably contain the controls. To facilitate opening multiple forms, it is best not to build full-screen forms. Unless all forms in an application are to be a standard size, it is best to size the form to fit its content.

Adding Tabbed Pages to a Form

Several of the controls available from the Form toolbox are designed to contain other controls. In fact, a form is a control that can contain other controls. Subforms and Tab controls are also built to hold other controls. Such controls are called *containers*. Controls contained by other controls must be either drawn directly on that container or pasted (using Microsoft Windows cut/copy and paste operations) directly on that container. For example, a text box must be drawn or pasted onto a specific page of the Tab control to be accessible from that tab in Form View.

Adding tabbed pages to the Customer form:

1. Verify that the **ac12KoryoKicks.mdb** database is open, with the CustomerTabbed form in Design View

2. Select all the controls on the main form (excluding the subforms) that were organized in the previous steps and use the **Cut** button to place them on the Clipboard

3. Click the Tab Control from the toolbox and draw it to fill an area 6 inches wide and 3.5 inches tall using the ruler. Place the Tab Control flush against the left form margin

4. Click the first tab and use the **Paste** button to place the controls on the first page of the tabbed form

5. Double-click on the tab to open the Properties pages and set the Caption property to **Customer**

6. Select the OrderTab subform and **Cut** it from the main form

7. Click the second tab, set its Caption property to **Order**, and then **Paste** the Order Tab subform

8. Select the OrderDetail subform and **Cut** it from the main form

9. Right-click on the Order tab and select **Insert Page** from the pop-up menu

10. Click on the new page, set its Caption property to **Order Detail**, and then **Paste** the OrderDetails subform from the Windows Clipboard

11. Drag the Footer divider until the Detail section of the form is even with the bottom of the tabbed pages

12. Change to Form View, test the tabs, and return to Design View

F I G U R E   12.5

Tabbed pages added to the CustomerTabbed form

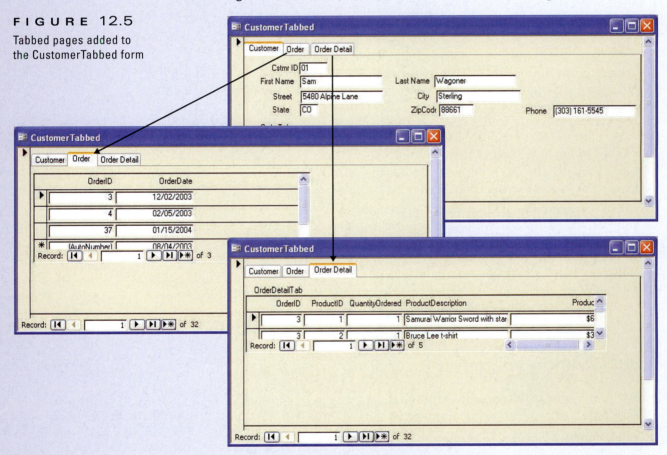

To create tabbed pages for the CustomerTabbed form, the Tab control was added to the form and then existing controls were pasted to its pages. The Customer, Order, and Order Detail tabbed pages are properly linked because the Wizard built the links between the main form and subforms used to construct them. These links were maintained by pasting the main form controls as a unit and then pasting each subform.

The Customer tab is well organized and properly displays all its data, but the Order and Order Detail tabs need to be restructured. Moving fields and sizing them to suit the data creates a more user-friendly environment by providing visual clues for valid data entry.

For the Order tab, the subform needs to be resized and the controls adjusted to suit their data. A new text box and associated label will be added to display each order's due date, which is calculated from the OrderDate value.

Restructuring the Order tabbed page:

1. Verify that the **ac12KoryoKicks.mdb** database is open, with the CustomerTabbed form in Design View

2. Click the **Order** tab

3. Select and delete the label containing the text Order Tab

4. Switch between Form View and Design View as needed to complete the following steps
    a. Select the subform and resize it to fill the tabbed page
    b. Widen the subform to fill the subform area
    c. Narrow the OrderID label and text box to better suit the size of the data
    d. Narrow the OrderDate label and text box to better fit the data

5. Add new label and text box controls to the right of the current OrderDate controls

tip: *Add a text box to the Detail section and then use Cut and Paste to move the label to the Form Header section*

    a. Make the Caption of the label **Due Date** and set the Text Align property to **Right**
    b. Set the Control Source property of the text box to **=DueDate([OrderDate],60)**
    c. Set the Format property of the text box to **dd-mmm-yyyy** to match the Order Date format
    d. Resize and align the controls to match Order Date

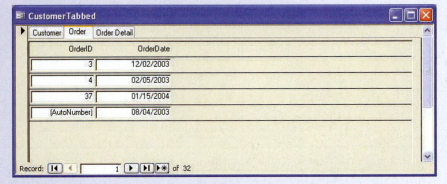

FIGURE 12.6

Restructured Order tab

6. Click the Order subform selector box (the square between the rulers) to open the Properties dialog box. Set the Scroll Bars property to **Neither** and Navigation Buttons to **No**

tip: *These settings remove the scroll bars and navigation buttons from the subform, result-ing in a simpler display. If there are more orders than can be displayed in the space, the scroll bar will display*

7. Change to Form View and test the tabs by selecting a customer and then clicking the Order tab to see their orders

8. Save

The Order tab now displays its data in a much less cluttered and confusing format. The due date was calculated using the custom DueDate function created in Chapter 11.

The function requires two arguments, a beginning date (OrderDate) and the number of days to add to that date (60), to determine the due date.

Restructuring the Order Detail tabbed page:

1. Verify that the **ac12KoryoKicks.mdb** database is open, with the CustomerTabbed form in Design View

2. Click the **Order Detail** tab

3. Select and delete the label containing the text Order Detail Tab

4. Switch between Form View and Design View as needed to complete the following steps

   a. Select the subform and resize it to fill the tabbed page
   b. Widen the subform to fill the subform area
   c. Hold down the **Ctrl** key and press **Enter** between words in the labels to make two-line headings. Increase the height of the Form Header if needed
   d. Narrow the OrderID, ProductID, QuantityOrdered, ProductPrice, and ItemTotal labels and text boxes to better suit the size of the data
   e. Lengthen the label and text box for Product Description so that complete descriptions display
   f. Arrange the fields as shown in Figure 12.7

FIGURE 12.7

Restructured OrderDetails tab

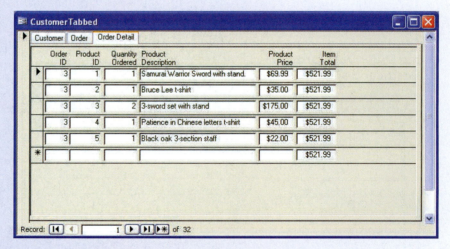

5. Set the Height property of the Form Footer to **.25**

6. Add a new Text Box control to the OrderDetail subform footer. Line the text box up with ItemTotal

   a. Make the Caption of the label **Order Total** and set the Text Align property to **Right**
   b. Set the Control Source property of the text box to **=Sum([QuantityOrdered]*[ProductPrice])**
   c. Set the Format property of the text box to **Currency**

7. Click the subform's selector (the box between the rulers). Set the Scroll Bars property to **Neither** and Navigation Buttons to **No**

8. Change to Form View and test the tabs by selecting a customer from the Customer tab, selecting an order from the Order tab, and then reviewing the Order Detail associated with that order

9. Close, saving your changes

Using tabbed pages, KoryoKicks employees are now able to access any data related to a customer from a single form. This simplified interface will improve customer service by allowing faster access to all customer data. It will also speed data entry and maintenance, since all customer and order data can be accessed on the same easy-to-navigate form.

Tabbed pages can be added to any form to contain data from different sources, or simply to organize large records into manageable subgroups. For example, the data from an organization's Employee table could be split into personal and employment pages. Similarly, a dialog box could be created to be used as a switchboard with a page for each database object (tables, queries, forms, reports, and so on).

Understanding PivotTable and PivotChart Views

It is often difficult to understand trends and analyze patterns in the large volumes of data typically stored in a database. To facilitate the analytical process, PivotTable and PivotChart views were added to Microsoft Access 2002. If you are familiar with Microsoft Excel, you have probably been exposed to the use of pivot tables and pivot charts to summarize list data. Pivot tables create output similar to a Crosstab Query by summarizing data on multiple fields. Such summaries provide analytical views of the data that can be used to support the management decision process.

Defining a PivotTable View

Any table, query, or form can be used as the foundation for interactive analysis using either PivotTable or PivotChart View. Pivot data can be summarized using standard functions such as Count, Sum, Average, Max, or Min. Data displayed on a pivot table or chart can be filtered to summarize only records that meet a specified criterion. When a new PivotTable or PivotChart View is opened, an empty diagram displays with a list of fields in the data source. The data source fields are dragged and dropped to areas on the diagram to create the pivot chart.

The twins would like to be able to interactively analyze KoryoKicks sales. The InvoiceJoinWithCalc query is ideal for this application because it combines key fields from each KoryoKicks table and includes the calculation to total each invoice detail line. The twins would like to start by viewing total sales organized by state and date.

Creating a PivotTable View based on the InvoiceJoinWithCalc query:

1. Verify that the **ac12KoryoKicks.mdb** database is open with all objects closed

2. Click the Queries object and double-click **InvoiceJoinWithCalc** to view its output in Datasheet View

3. Drop-down the View list by clicking the down arrow to the right of the Design View button and click **PivotTable View**

4. Explore the Pivot Table Field List noting the available fields and clicking the plus (+) signs to view the subfields available for OrderDate by Month

5. Drag **ProductDescription** from the field list and drop it in the **Drop Row Fields Here** area of the diagram

tip: *If you drop a field in the wrong area, simply drag it to the correct area. If you drag the wrong field, drop it outside the diagram*

ACCESS

FIGURE 12.8

Empty pivot table diagram

empty pivot
table diagram

fields that can be used
to create the pivot table

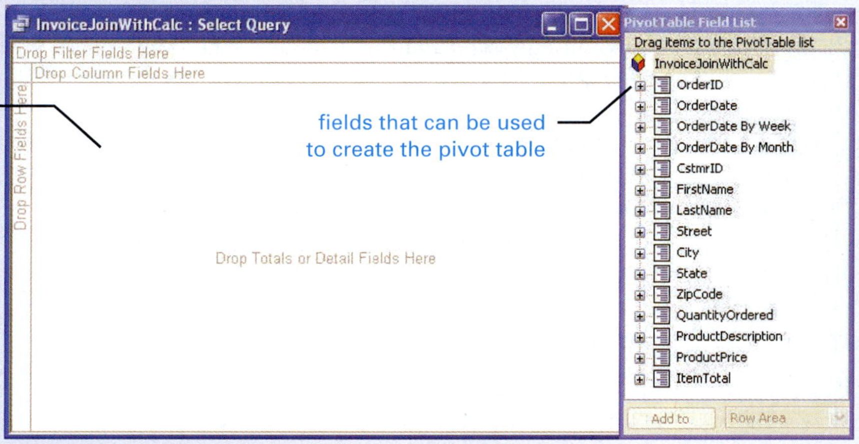

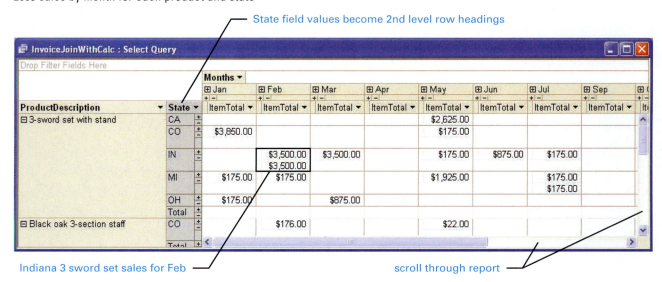

6. Drag **State** from the field list and drop it to the right of
   ProductDescription in the **Drop Row Fields Here** area of the diagram

7. Drag **Months** from the OrderDate by Month group to **Drop Column
   Fields Here**

8. Drag **ItemTotal** to **Drop Totals or Detail Fields Here**

9. Click the **State** button and use the Formatting (PivotTable/PivotChart)
   toolbar to change the font, font color, and fill color to settings of your
   choice

10. Save

Notice that fields that have already been placed on the pivot table diagram are
bolded in the field list. Notice also that there are several *fieldsets* or versions of the
OrderDate field and that each version supports different subfields. It is important to select the fieldset with the subfields that are effective for your needs.

Text and values in the pivot table can be formatted using the Formatting
(PivotTable/PivotChart) toolbar. Toolbar adjustments include font, font size and font

FIGURE 12.9

2003 sales by month for each product and state

State field values become 2nd level row headings

Indiana 3 sword set sales for Feb

scroll through report

color, fill color, bold, underline, italic, and alignment. In addition, the Properties dialog box can be used to change number, time and date formats, captions, and other report features.

Saving a PivotTable View does not impact what is displayed on the Datasheet View of a table, query, or form but, the next time the PivotChart View is opened, the saved table will display. Once a chart has been developed, it can be used to evaluate data by manipulating row and column values or adding filters. The Show/Hide Details buttons display as plus (+) and minus (−) signs on each field and are used to control the level of detail displayed for the field.

Each field button also includes a drop-down arrow that can be used to filter (select) specific values to display for that field. For example, in the InvoiceJoinWithCalc PivotTable View, the State button can be used to select specific states, the Years button can be used to select dates, and the ProductDescription button can be used to select products.

Using Field buttons to select InvoiceJoinWithCalc data:

1. Verify that the **ac12KoryoKicks.mdb** database is open, with the InvoiceJoinWithCalc query open in PivotTable View

2. Drop down the State button list and uncheck **CA**, **CO**, and **OH** and then click **OK**

3. Drop down the Months button list and uncheck **Qtr3** and **Qtr4** and then click **OK**

4. Drop down the ProductDescription button and uncheck everything but 3-sword set with stand and Samurai Warrior Sword with stand

tip: *You can also uncheck the All option and then check the desired options*

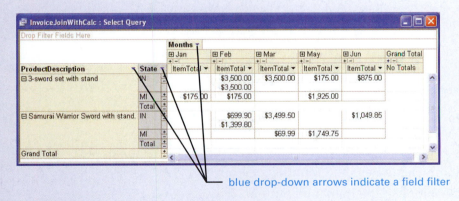

blue drop-down arrows indicate a field filter

F I G U R E 12.10

Pivot table with Field button filters

5. Click **OK**

6. Remove the Field button filters by dropping down each button list, checking **All**, and then clicking **OK**

tip: *There should be no blue drop-down arrows when this step is complete*

7. Drag **LastName** from the field list and drop it in the **Drop Filter Fields Here** area of the diagram

tip: *Filter fields select data before they are summarized using the other Pivot Table fields*

FIGURE 12.11

Gray, Guo, Hill, and Wagoner business

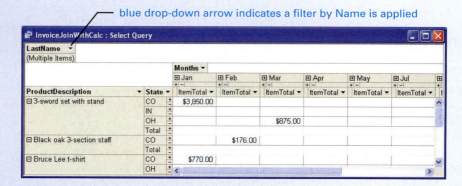

blue drop-down arrow indicates a filter by Name is applied

8. Assume that **Gray, Guo, Hill**, and **Wagoner** have formed a partnership, and you would like to see how much business you can expect from that partnership. Use the **LastName** button to select only these customers

9. Remove the **LastName** filter

10. Save

Dragging and dropping field buttons onto the pivot table diagram controls the detail values that display in each cell of the table. The drop-down filter feature of buttons already in the grid can be used to select only records meeting criteria based on displayed fields. Additional fields can be dropped in the Drop Filter Fields Here area and then used to select data. Filters are cumulative, so it is important to remove existing filter(s) before applying new ones.

Summarizing PivotTable Data

Finding trends in lists of detail data is difficult. Managers often use summary values to represent data without viewing each detail row. Once the organization of the data has been set up by dragging and dropping fields to the pivot table design, summarization methods such as Sum, Count, or Average can be selected.

Summarizing InvoiceJoinWithCalc PivotTable View:

1. Verify that the **ac12KoryoKicks.mdb** database is open, with the InvoiceJoinWithCalc query open in PivotTable View

2. Drag Product Description off the chart and drop it. Move **State** to Drop Column Fields Here and **Months** to Drop Row Fields Here

3. Click on one of the **ItemTotal** buttons

4. Drop down the AutoCalc Σ▾ button on the PivotTable toolbar and select **Sum**

5. Drop down the AutoCalc Σ▾ button and select **Min**

6. Drop down the AutoCalc Σ▾ button and select **Max**

7. Click the plus sign (+) to the left of each month and the Grand Total in the pivot table design (see Figures 12.12 and 12.13)

tip: *Screen Tips display Show/Hide Details when the cursor pauses over these buttons*

8. Save

Show/Hide Details buttons

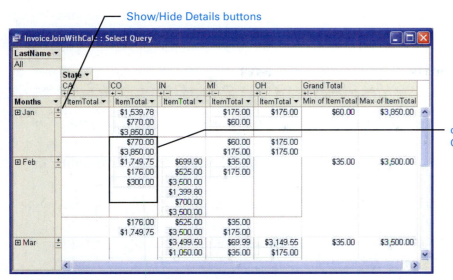

detail records for CO and Feb

FIGURE 12.12

Summary pivot table without month details displayed

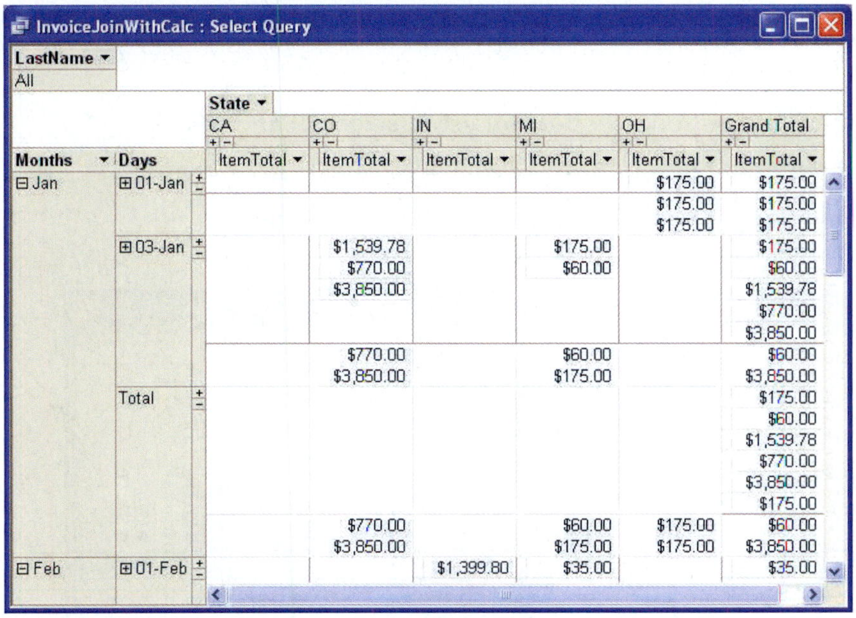

FIGURE 12.13

Summary pivot table with month details displayed

As you experienced in the steps, multiple summary functions can be simultaneously applied to pivot table data. Notice that each summary function is added as a subfield of both the Total and Grand Total fieldsets. The button for each added summary can be dragged to reorganize fields in the table. Dropping a summary button outside the table will delete the summary from the view, but not from the PivotTable field list. Only one PivotTable View can be stored for a database object.

Creating a PivotChart View

PivotChart View is used to create a graphic representation of table, query, or form data. When PivotChart View is first opened, an empty design displays with the Chart field list, unless the PivotTable View has already been used to summarize data. Changes made in PivotChart View impact PivotTable View and vice versa.

Fieldsets or fields can be dragged from the Chart field list and dropped on the pivot chart design to create various graphic representations of selected data. In pivot chart design, *categories* are used to summarize the data and appear on the x (horizontal) axis of most charts, while *data fields* contain the numeric data to be plotted, and a *data series* is used to determine data field values for each category. Each data series is plotted in a different color and represented on the legend.

Using InvoiceJoinWithCalc PivotChart View:

1. Verify that the **ac12KoryoKicks.mdb** database is open, with the InvoiceJoinWithCalc query open

2. Change to PivotChart View and drag existing field buttons off the edge of the design

3. If the Chart field list is not visible, activate it using the Field List button on the Pivot Chart toolbar

4. Drag **Months** item from OrderDate by Month to the Drop Category Fields Here design area

5. Drop **ProductDescription** to the left of Months (OrderDate by Month)

6. Drag **Item Total** to the Drop Data Fields Here area

7. Drop **State** in the Drop Series Fields Here area

8. Use the State button's drop-down list to select **IN** and **OH**

9. Use the Month button's drop-down list to select **Qtr1** only

10. Click the **Show Legend** 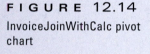 button on the Formatting (PivotTable/PivotChart) toolbar

FIGURE 12.14

InvoiceJoinWithCalc pivot chart

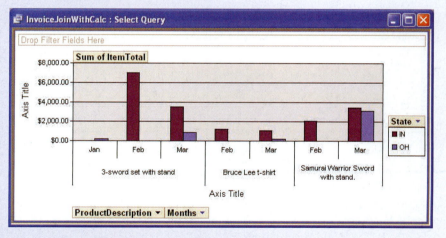

11. Click the **By Row/By Column** button, evaluate the result, and then click it again to return to the original chart

12. Save

The InvoiceJoinWithCalc pivot chart uses multiple categories to organize the data. The fields that are closest to the data (ProductDescription) are referred to as *inner fields*, while the other fields (Years) are called *outer fields*. An alternative to having two categories is to plot the outer field values in separate charts using multiple plot options.

Creating multiple pivot charts:

1. Verify that the **ac12KoryoKicks.mdb** database is open, with the InvoiceJoinWithCalc query open in PivotChart View

2. Click the **Multiple Plots** button on the Formatting (PivotTable/PivotChart) toolbar

   tip: *The Drop MultiChart Fields Here drop area should be added to the design*

3. Drag **ProductDescription** from the category field drop area to the Drop MultiChart Fields Here area

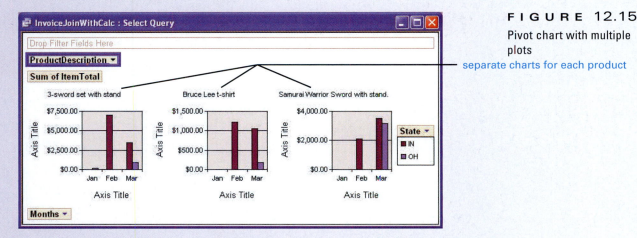

FIGURE 12.15

Pivot chart with multiple plots

separate charts for each product

4. Notice that each chart has a unique scale for the y (vertical) axis

5. Click the **Multiple Plots Unified Scale** button and notice that all charts now use the same scale

6. Click the **Multiple Plots Unified Scale** button a second time and notice that charts use a different scale again

7. Click the **AutoFilter** button to remove all applied filters

8. Click the **AutoFilter** button again to reapply all filters

9. Save

The basic layout of a pivot chart is created by dragging and dropping fields into the appropriate drop areas. Each drop area can hold multiple fields. Adjustments to the layout are accomplished by dragging fields to new drop areas. Fields are removed from the layout by dragging them off the chart area.

Filters should be removed before adjusting pivot chart layout because filter settings are not changed by moving or removing a field. When a data series or category field is removed and then later added back, the original filter values are retained.

Formatting PivotChart View

If you have used Microsoft Graph or Microsoft Office Chart, the formatting features of Access's PivotChart View will be familiar. Formatting options include the ability to select from a variety of chart and subchart types, change data series colors, and customize text formatting. New chart elements such as explanatory text, trend lines, and error bars can be added as needed.

Formatting pivot charts:

1. Verify that the **ac12KoryoKicks.mdb** database is open, with the InvoiceJoinWithCalc query open in PivotChart View. Refer to Figure 12.16 as you complete these steps

2. Move ProductDescription back to the categories drop area in front of Months

3. Click the **Multiple Plots** ⊞ button to remove the Drop MultiChart Fields Here drop area

4. Right-click on the vertical Axis Title text and select **Properties**

   a. Click the **Format** tab

   b. Set the Caption property to **Invoice Value**

   c. Select a blue font color from the Font Color drop-down list

   d. Select another font and point size

5. With the Properties dialog box still open, click the horizontal Axis Title text

   a. On the Format tab, set the Caption property to **Products by Month**

   b. Set the other properties to match the previous step

6. Select the **General** tab and click **Chart Workspace** in the drop-down list

   a. On the **Border/Fill** tab, select the lightest gray, **Gainsboro**, for the Fill color

tip: *Pause the cursor over an object to see its name*

   b. Click the **Type** tab and review the available chart/subchart types. Select **Smooth Line** as the chart type with markers displayed at each data point as the subtype

7. On the **General** tab, select **IN** from the drop-down list

   a. Click the **Add Trendline** button

   b. On the **Line Marker** tab, select **Sea Green** as the Line Color and **Star** as the Marker Shape

8. On the **General** tab, select **OH** from the drop-down list

   a. Click the **Add Trendline** button

   b. On the **Line Marker** tab, select **Royal Blue** as the Line Color and **Triangle** as the Marker Shape

9. On the **General** tab, select **OH Trendline 1**

   a. On the **Line Marker** tab, choose **Royal Blue** as the Line Color

   b. Set Weight to **Thick**

10. On the **General** tab, select **IN Trendline 1**

    a. On the **Line Marker** tab, choose **Sea Green** as the Line Color

    b. Set Weight to **Thick**

11. Close the Properties dialog box

12. Save

FIGURE 12.16
Formatted pivot chart

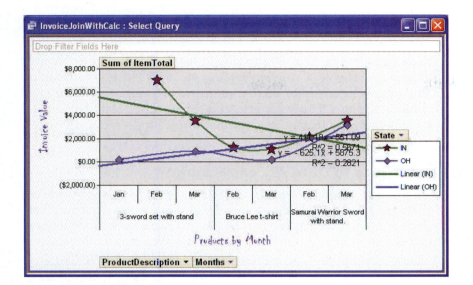

help yourself *Use the Type a Question combo box in the Microsoft Visual Basic window to improve your understanding of PivotTables and PivotCharts by typing* **pivottable**. *Review the contents of* About designing a PivotTable or PivotChart view *and* About formatting a PivotTable or PivotChart view. *Close the Help window when you are finished*

The steps demonstrated a few of the available formatting options such as the chart type, trend lines, text formats, and line colors. A complete exploration of the chart properties dialog box would reveal many formatting options that were not applied. Dramatic effects can be achieved by rotating 3D charts to change the view angle and using pictures or gradients to fill plotted columns. Conditional formatting based on data values can also be applied to emphasize problems or trends. With practice, PivotChart View provides the tools to create dramatic visual representations of data for analysis and presentation.

making the grade

1. What are the benefits of tabbed forms?

2. Explain how to customize the color and contents of a label.

3. What database objects support PivotTable and PivotChart Views?

4. Explain the mechanics of creating a PivotTable or PivotChart View.

SESSION 12.2 USING EXTENDED WEB FEATURES

PivotTables and PivotCharts can be saved on Data Access Pages so that they can be placed on an intranet or on the Web. The most common Web data-sharing format is Extensible Markup Language (XML). Access can both import and export this format. Full use of these features requires the use of Microsoft Internet Explorer 5.01 with Service Pack 2 or later.

Placing PivotTables and PivotCharts On Data Access Pages

Data Access Pages (see Chapter 8) are built using Dynamic HTML to provide live-interactive access to Access objects from an intranet or the Internet. The resulting Dynamic HTML documents are stored on a server where they can be viewed using a Web browser. Internet Explorer 5.01 or above is required to create a Data Access Page. Older versions of Internet Explorer and other manufacturers' browsers can view pages, but may not provide full interactivity.

Saving PivotCharts to Data Access Pages

Data Access Pages consist of an exported HTML page and a new database object that links the HTML file to a database object. Because the connection to a database object (table, query, form, or report) is maintained, Data Access Pages can be used to view, edit, update, delete, filter, group, and sort live data using a Web browser. Data Access Pages can also contain components from spreadsheets, PivotTables, or PivotCharts.

Existing PivotChart Views can be saved as interactive Data Access Pages using the Save As option of the File menu. When Data Access Pages are placed on an intranet or Internet server, a Web browser such as Internet Explorer can be used to manipulate chart elements based on live data stored in the Access database. Most of the capabilities of PivotChart View, such as dragging and dropping fields and using field button drop-down lists to filter chart data, are maintained.

---

task *reference*　　Saving PivotTable or PivotChart
View to a Data Access Page

- Create the PivotTable or PivotChart View

- On the File menu, click **Save As**

- Type a filename, select **Data Access Page** from the As drop-down list, and then click **OK**

- Navigate to the desired folder

- Click **OK**

- Review the page in the Access Browser Window that opens automatically

---

Converting a PivotChart to a Web page:

1. Verify that the **ac12KoryoKicks.mdb** database is open, with the InvoiceJoinWithCalc query open in PivotChart View

2. Click **File** and then **Save As**

3. Type **InvoiceJoinWithCalcPivotChart** in the Save As text box

4. Choose **Data Access Page** from the As drop-down list and click **OK**

5. Navigate to the drive and folder for your files and click **OK**

6. Wait for the page to open in the Access Web Browser window
   a. Maximize the browser window
   b. Drop down the Months button, select **Qtr2** only, and click **OK**
   c. Experiment with other live changes to the chart, such as filtering, moving fields, or adding new fields

tip: *Right-click on the chart to open the Chart Field List*

7. Close the browser window

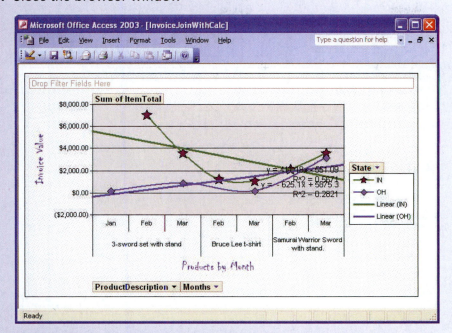

FIGURE 12.17
PivotChart viewed from a Data Access Page

tip: *If the browser window is maximized, the X in the blue Title bar will close Access, the one below it will close the browser window. Double-clicking the name of a Data Access Page in the Pages object of the Database Window will reopen the browser window*

Most options available in PivotChart View can be accessed from a chart saved as a Data Access Page. Users can adjust filters and drop zone fields with immediate results. While the Data Access Page chart will reflect any changes made to the underlying data, it cannot be used to update the PivotChart View stored with the query.

Saving PivotTables to Data Access Pages

Like PivotChart Views, PivotTable Views can be saved as interactive Data Access Pages using the Save As option of the File menu. Such pages can be viewed and altered using an Access Web Browser Window or using a Web browser.

Converting a PivotTable to a Web page:

1. Verify that the **ac12KoryoKicks.mdb** database is open, with the InvoiceJoinWithCalc query open in PivotChart View

2. Change to PivotTable View

3. Click **File** and then **Save As**

4. Type **InvoiceJoinWithCalcPivotTable** in the Save As text box

5. Choose **Data Access Page** from the As drop-down list and click **OK**

6. Navigate to the drive and folder for your files and click **OK**

7. Wait for the page to open in the Access Web Browser Window

    a. Maximize the Access Web Browser Window

    b. Drop down the Months button, select **Qtr1**, and click **OK**

    c. Experiment with other live changes to the PivotTable, such as filtering, moving fields, or adding new fields

FIGURE 12.18

PivotTable viewed from a Data Access Page

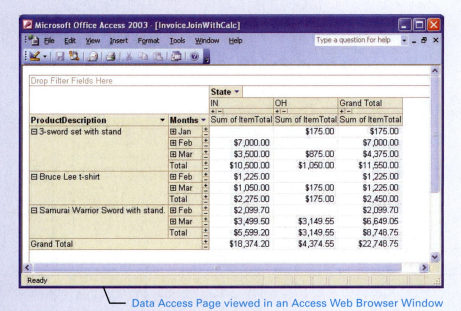

Data Access Page viewed in an Access Web Browser Window

tip: *Right-click on the chart to open the PivotTable field list*

8. Close all open objects

tip: *The X in the blue Title bar will close Access, the one below it will close the browser window*

Although the page saved in the steps resides on a local disk, it would behave the same way when opened from an intranet or the Internet. Geographically distributed users can thereby benefit from the analytical powers of PivotCharts and PivotTables without directly using Access or maintaining a local copy of the database.

Using Design View to Create PivotTables and Charts on Data Access Pages

The Design View of a Data Access Page provides the most complete control over the layout and content of the page. The toolbar provides tools to add an Office PivotTable control or an Office Chart control to other content organized on the page. Missy and Micah would like the ability to create a PivotTable and see its graphical representation on the same page. Design View is the only way to create such a page.

Building a PivotTable on a Data Access Page:

1. Verify that the **ac12KoryoKicks.mdb** database is open, with no open objects

2. Click the **Pages** object in the Database Window

3. Double-click on **Create data access page in Design view**

4. Title the page **Sales Analysis**

5. Expand the design grid to **6** inches wide (large squares) by **5** inches tall

tip: *Use the View button to display the grid, if needed*

6. Click the **Office PivotTable** tool in the toolbox and drag it to be **6** inches wide by **3** inches tall

7. In the PivotTable Field List, open the **Queries** folder and then open the **InvoiceJoinWithCalc** list

   a. Drop **ProductDescription** in the Drop Row Fields Here drop zone

   b. Drop **State** in Drop Column Fields Here drop zone

   c. Drop **ItemTotal** in the Drop Totals or Detail Fields Here drop zone

8. Use the field button filters to display only CO and IN state values

9. Use the field button filters to display only 3-sword set with stand and Samurai Warrior Sword with stand

10. Select an ItemTotal field button, click the AutoCalc button on the PivotTable controls' toolbar, and select **Sum**

11. Use the minus (−) sign next to each product to display only the sum

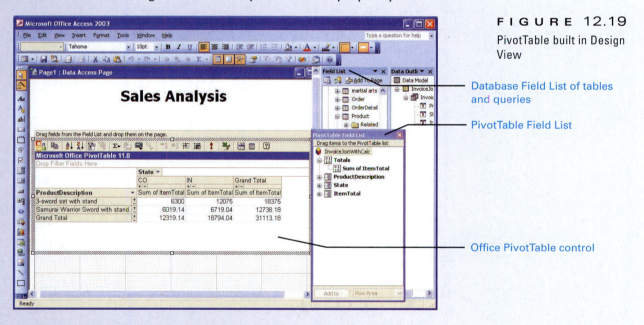

FIGURE 12.19
PivotTable built in Design View

Database Field List of tables and queries

PivotTable Field List

Office PivotTable control

12. Save the page as **SalesAnalysis**

Like the PivotTable saved to a Data Access Page from the PivotTable View of an object, this PivotTable is fully interactive. It was not necessary to add data to the table before building the chart, but data make it easier to see that the chart is performing properly.

Adding a linked Office Chart to a Data Access Page:

1. Verify that the **ac12KoryoKicks.mdb** database is open, with the SalesAnalysis Data Access Page in Design View

2. Click the **Office Chart** tool in the toolbox and drag to fill the remaining design grid area as shown in Figure 12.20

FIGURE 12.20

PivotTable with linked Office Chart

CA added to PivotTable and Chart

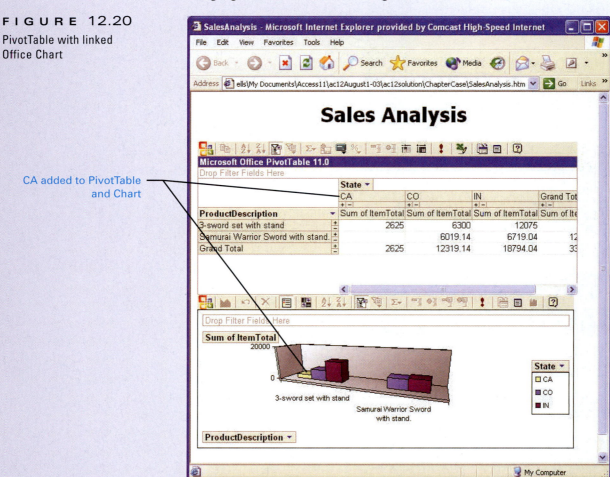

3. If the Office Chart control is not already selected, click to select it and then click it again to display the Commands and Options dialog box
   a. Click **Data from the following web page**
   b. Verify that PivotTable: PivotTable0 is selected
   c. On the **Type** tab, experiment with chart types and then select **3D Column Clustered**
   d. Click the **Show/Hide Legend** button on the Office Chart control's toolbar
   e. Explore the Chart Type and other buttons on the Office Chart control's toolbar
   f. Return the chart to its pre-exploration state (see Figure 12.20)

4. Save

5. Open Internet Explorer (IE) by selecting the **Web Page Preview** view from the View button drop-down list

6. In the PivotTable, change the State filter to include **CA** and observe the result on both the PivotTable and Chart

7. In the Office Chart, remove CA from the State filter and observe the result on both the Chart and PivotTable

8. Pause over each toolbar button available for the PivotTable and Office Chart objects to see ToolTips

9. Click the **ProductDescription** field button and sort it in reverse alphabetical order

10. Close the IE Window

11. Close the SalesAnalysis Data Access Page

The PivotTable and Office Chart created in the steps are linked so that each reflects updates made to the other. The fields available to these controls were determined by what was placed in the PivotTable template during design. Placing more fields in the template allows the user a broader range of selections.

The data source of the Office Chart was defined to be the PivotTable, but other Commands and Options settings would allow it to be linked to any valid data source. If you leave the Commands and Options dialog box open, the tabs and options presented will be valid for the selected object. Many options can be adjusted while viewing the page in a browser, but the data source and chart type must be updated from page Design View.

The twins are happy with the Web page developed. They believe it will allow employees operating from the various company sites, or even on the road, to select and evaluate KoryoKicks sales to help complete their jobs.

Adding a Web Browser Control to Form Pages

The Form Design toolbar contains the controls most commonly used to create Access forms. These include the text box, label, command button, combo box, and rectangle controls, which are referred to as built-in or intrinsic controls. The controls were designed for use within the Office environment.

ActiveX controls are controls that have been developed for use by a variety of applications and across platforms. These controls are similar in behavior to intrinsic controls, but they provide more reliable Web performance and are not directly available from the toolbox. ActiveX controls are available from a wide variety of sources including Microsoft.

A number of ActiveX controls are installed with Microsoft Office. Two popular ActiveX controls are the Calendar control, which can be used to add various types of calendar functions to a form, and the Microsoft Web Browser control, which will display Web pages from a form. The available ActiveX controls are listed by clicking the More Tools button on the Form Design toolbar. Once a control is selected from the list, it can be drawn on the form.

KoryoKicks employees have continual access to the network and the Internet. To complete the redesign of the Customers form, the twins would like a Web tab added that will allow users to browse without leaving the KoryoKicks interface.

task reference   Adding a Web Browser
                                          Control to a Form

- Open the form in Design View
- Click the **More Controls** button on the toolbox
- Select **Microsoft Web Browser** from the list
- Click the form to add the control
- Move and resize the control as necessary
- Create a procedure that will control the browser window display

Adding a Microsoft Web Browser control to the CustomerTabbed form:

1. Verify that the **ac12KoryoKicks.mdb** database is open, with no open objects

2. Select the **Forms** object and open **CustomerTabbed** in Design View

3. Right-click on an existing tab and choose **Insert Page** from the pop-up menu

4. Place a Text Box control near the top of the new page

5. Double-click the new page tab to open the Properties dialog box and set its Caption property to **Web Browser**

6. Click the label portion of the Text Box control and use the Properties dialog box to set its Caption property to **Web Address**

7. Click the text box and set its Name property to **txtWebAddress**

8. Click the **More Controls** 🔳 button in the toolbox, select **Microsoft Web Browser** from the list, and click the form

   tip: *Be sure to review the other available ActiveX controls*

9. Use the Properties dialog box to name the Web Browser control **WebBrowser**

10. Close the Properties dialog box

11. Resize and position the controls as shown in Figure 12.21

12. Switch to Form View to evaluate your results

13. Save

Now that the needed controls are on the form, they must be linked using Visual Basic code. When the user types a new local (usually the C: drive), intranet, or Internet file address in the Web Address text box, the file specified should display in the Web Browser control. To accomplish this, code will be added to the text box's On Exit event.

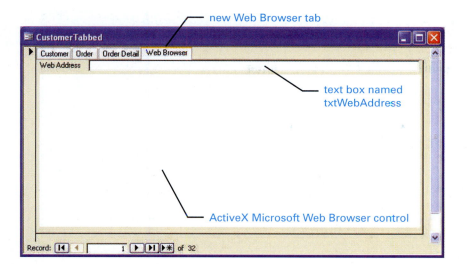

FIGURE 12.21
Microsoft Web control

Coding a Microsoft Web Browser control on the CustomerTabbed form:

1. Verify that the **ac12KoryoKicks.mdb** database is open, with the CustomerTabbed form open in Design View

2. Right-click on the Text Box control and select **Properties**

3. Click **On Exit** in the **Event** tab

   a. Click the Build (ellipsis) button to the right of On Exit and choose **Code Builder**

   b. Type **WebBrowser.Navigate txtWebAddress** in the *Private Sub txtWebAddress_Exit(Cancel As Integer)* procedure

   c. Close the Microsoft Visual Basic window

   d. Close the Properties dialog box

4. Switch to Form View

5. Click the **Web Browser** tab, type www.microsoft.com in the text box, and press **Enter**

   tip: *An active Internet connection is necessary to retrieve Web pages. If the page cannot be displayed in the browser window, either the address entered is invalid, the controls are not properly configured (revisit the steps), or there is not an active Internet connection (test with a local file on your A: or C: drive)*

6. Type another valid Web address, for example, your school's Web site

7. Save and close the CustomerTabbed form

The txtWebAddress_Exit procedure contains one line of Visual Basic code that will execute each time the txtWebAddress control is exited. A control can be exited by pressing Enter, tabbing to a new control, or clicking in another control. The line of code instructs the Web Browser control to navigate to the address stored in the txtWebAddress control. Navigate is a method of the Web Browser control.

F I G U R E 12.22

Microsoft Web page
displayed in the
CustomerTabbed form

type a valid Web address and press
Enter or move to another control

Introducing Extensible Markup Language (XML)

Although networks have made the process of sending and receiving data very efficient, the inability to properly process data of different formats is pervasive. Data cannot be used unless the format is understood by the local software. The World Wide Web has made data sharing more complex by expanding the audience needing to share data resources.

As you browse and use Web documents, any number of behind-the-scenes activities are required to retrieve, format, and process your requests. Many of these activities involve sharing data with multiple organizations or gathering data from multiple organizations. Web business partnerships abound where one company warehouses and ships the product while another processes credit cards and still another provides customer service. In such partnerships, each organization must receive data in a format that will interact with its normal business systems. Looking up a product requires submitting a query (probably in SQL) to the vendor's database, retrieving the results, transporting them to your computer, and displaying them in an understandable format. Web portals search multiple sources, retrieve data stored in different formats, and present them on a single Web page. Such data interactions are at the heart of Web-based research and e-commerce.

About XML

Extensible Markup Language (XML) was developed to address the growing need to share files from any data source and has become the standard for transporting data on the Web. The first XML standard definition was published in 1998 by the World Wide Web Consortium (W3C). Current standards can be viewed from the W3C Web page located at www.w3.org.

HTML is used to describe the visual components of Web pages, while XML is used to port (move) data gathered from the user to a server and send queried data back to the requesting machine. If you submit a Web form, its contents are most likely communicated to the server using XML. Similarly, if you request specific information like a category of books, XML is normally used to transport the data retrieved by the query so that they can be displayed in a Web page for your evaluation. Microsoft Access is able to both import and export data using XML formats.

XML is a language designed to describe both the data structures (such as the fields of an Access table) and the data values stored in those structures. XML uses a data interchange format that separates the data from the data presentation so that the data can be interpreted by diverse software applications into presentations consistent with their programming. XML files are fully self-describing and platform-independent. Similar to HTML, XML tags and their attributes are used to delimit data components. Unlike

HTML, however, XML tags are not predefined and so are fully open to interpretation by the application receiving it. XML tags are also case sensitive.

An XML document typically begins with a declaration statement identifying it as an XML document and specifying the version. For example, *<?xml version="1.0">* identifies an XML version 1 document. There must be a unique root element, or a pair of tags that enclose the entire document. The <DATAROOT></DATAROOT> tags are often used for this purpose. All other tags must be paired ensuring that for each start tag there is a corresponding end tag.

Exporting to XML

The mechanics of exporting an Access database object in an XML file format are simple, but understanding the impacts of the options selected is more involved. In Access, you can choose to export only the data, only the structure (schema), or both. Additionally, a style sheet can be exported to describe the display of the data.

Missy and Micah are considering the use of Web-based forms and order processing. They have evaluated several options for processing Internet orders and believe that outsourcing will be the most cost effective. Since order and payment data will need to be shared across organizations, XML is the logical format. The twins have asked you to evaluate Access's XML capabilities. A three-item Products table named ProductsXML has been created to simplify the evaluation process.

task reference — Exporting a Table, Query, Form, or Report as an XML File

- In the Database Window, click the name of the object to be exported
- Click **File** and then **Export** on the menu
- In the Save as type drop-down box, **click XML Documents (*.xml)**
- Select the drive and folder for the XML document
- Enter the filename in the File name box
- Click **Export**
- Check the appropriate options in the Export XML dialog box
  - Click **Data** (XML) to export the object's data to an XML document
  - Click **Schema** of the data to export the object's structure to an XML file
  - Click **Presentation** of your data (XSL) to export a file describing data formatting
- Click **OK**

Exporting ProductsXML as an XML file:

1. Verify that the **ac12KoryoKicks.mdb** database is open, with no open objects
2. Select the **Tables** object and double-click **ProductXML**
3. Review the table's fields and their contents so you will be able to assess the XML file created

4. Click the **File** menu and then click **Export**

5. In the Save as type box, click **XML (*.xml)**

6. Select the drive and folder for the resulting XML file

7. Click **Export All**

tip: *If the item being exported is not open, the button will read Export rather than Export All*

8. Verify that **Data (XML)** and **Schema of the data** are checked and then click **OK**

9. Minimize Access, navigate to the ProductsXML.xml file, and double-click to open it

tip: *There should be two files created by this process: ProductsXML.xml and ProductsXML.xsd (the schema file). ProductsXML.xml may open in either your default Web browser or editor*

10. Explore the code to determine how it represents the data

11. Close the window displaying the code

12. Close ProductXML

F I G U R E 12.23

ProductsXML.xml open in Microsoft Internet Explorer

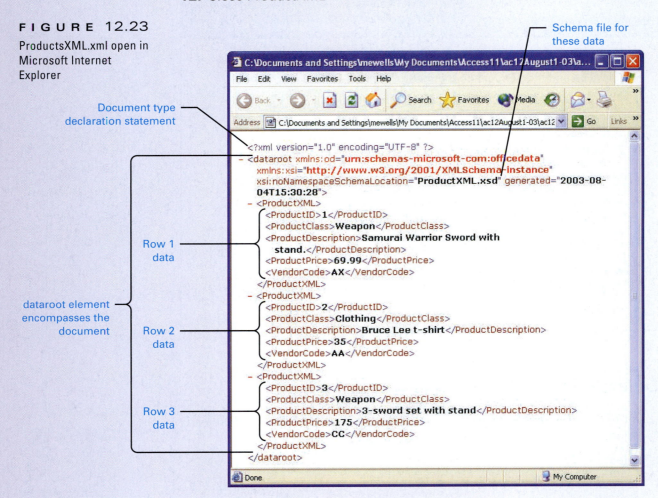

Schema file for these data

Document type declaration statement

dataroot element encompasses the document

Row 1 data

Row 2 data

Row 3 data

The XML file created by the export process uses the <dataroot> </dataroot> tags to enclose the document. The <ProductsXML> and </ProductsXML> tags enclose each row of data. The value stored in each field is indicated by start and end tags using the field name from the Access table design. Each XML tag is case sensitive and tag sets must be properly nested within each other. Exporting the schema information as well as the data allows other applications to determine the structure of the data and evaluate how that structure might be impacted by the receiving application. Advanced options are available from the Export XML dialog box to customize export settings in order to better match those needed by a receiving application.

help yourself *Use the Type a Question combo box in the Microsoft Visual Basic window to improve your understanding of XML by typing* **xml**. *Review the contents of* About XML and data access. *Close the Help window when you are finished*

When an XML file is imported by another application, the field names exported from Access may not apply to the import database structure. For example, the ProductDescription values exported from Access could be imported to a database field called MerchandiseDescription.

Importing from XML

Database functionality is dependent on rapidly gathering accurate data. Often these data have been organized, stored, and used in a variety of software applications making data consolidation difficult. Using XML files, it is easier and more accurate to transform data from dissimilar external sources into a format usable by Access. XML allows Access to share data with virtually a limitless number of applications and formats, regardless of how similar or dissimilar they are to Access.

External data can be imported to a new Access table using the XML tags to determine the table and field names. In Access 2003, both data and schemas (table design specifications) can be imported, so a table resulting from an XML import will have property settings such as Data Type or Field Size assigned based on its schema.

Micah has been keeping track of employees' salaries, hire dates, and birthdays in his personal digital assistant (PDA). He would like to import these data to create an Access table. This could be accomplished by exporting to an Excel or comma-delimited text file, but an XML file should provide more reliable results. Micah has exported from the proprietary PDA file format to an XML file format. The XML file needs to be imported into Access and the results assessed.

---

task reference   Importing an XML File
                                              as an Access Table

- Click **File**, point to **Get External Data**, and click **Import**

- Change the Files of type value to **XML Documents (*.xml;*.xsd)**

- Navigate to the folder containing the XML file

- Select the XML file and then click the **Import** button

- On the Import XML dialog box, click the **Options** button, and set the import options

- Click **OK**

- Click **OK** to close the finished importing document dialog box

---

Importing data from an XML file:

1. Verify that the **ac12KoryoKicks.mdb** database is open, with no open objects

2. Use Windows Explorer to navigate to the files for this chapter. Double-click **ac12Employee.xml** to open it in the browser. Review the XML code and then close the browser

3. In Access, click **File**, point to **Get External Data**, and click **Import**

4. Change the Files of type value to **XML Documents (*.xml;*.xsd)**

5. Navigate to the files for this chapter, select **ac12Employee.xml**, and click **Import**

6. Click the **Options** button, verify that both the structure and data will be imported, and click **OK**

7. Click **OK** to close the finished importing document dialog box

8. Open the Employee Data table in Datasheet View and review the records

9. Switch to Design View and notice that all fields have the same Field Size and Data Type

10. Close the Datasheet View

FIGURE 12.24

ac12Employee.xml imported as an Access table

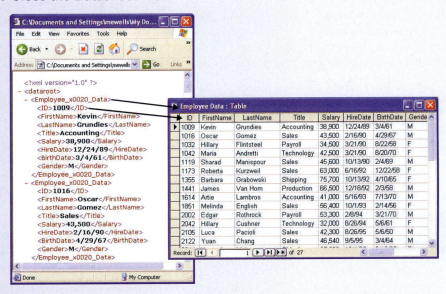

Although the XML import demonstrated in this chapter created a new table, the import process can be used to append records to an existing table. Any record that cannot be imported is placed in an ImportErrors table to preserve the data. Errors can be ignored or manually added to the table.

Understanding Access Projects and SQL Server Technology

Over time successful Access database applications support a growing number of users and are adapted to fit changing business needs. As systems evolve, they can exceed the capabilities of the original Access development environment. Access applications can be *upsized* in a variety of ways using Microsoft SQL Server technology.

Scaling an Access application is very similar to using the Database Splitter Wizard to create a front end/back end application where data are stored centrally, but each user can customize their interface. With SQL Server technology, the application to centrally store data is called the *server* while the user interface installed on multiple computers is called the *client*. In this case, the client application consists of the code-based objects (forms, reports, Web pages, along with the names and locations of other objects) of the application while the SQL server database contains all data-based (tables and stored procedures) objects.

The native database engine used by Access is *Microsoft Jet*. The Jet database is designed to provide database services to a small number of simultaneous users with a relatively simple development environment. Although the Jet can support front end/back end (client/server) applications, it is not the best tool for that job. By contrast, *Microsoft SQL Server 2000* is a full-service database engine designed to support client/server applications involving large networks and thousands of users.

Microsoft SQL Server 2000 Desktop Engine provides much of the functionality of Microsoft SQL Server 2000 in a format optimized for desktop computing. Like the default Jet engine, databases have a size limit of 2 gigabytes and only five simultaneous queries (threads) can operate at a time. Unlike the Jet, excess threads are spooled and addressed later by the processor. Additionally, the Desktop engine provides more efficient processing and better security in a multiuser environment. Applications developed in or converted to Microsoft SQL Server 2000 Desktop Engine reside in an environment developed for client/server computing and are 100 percent compatible with Microsoft SQL Server 2000 (the full-scale database). Access applications that use data resources stored in any SQL Server database are called *Access projects*.

To the user, working with an Access project is very similar to working with an Access database. Datasheets are used to display table and query data; the process of creating new forms, reports, pages, and macros is almost indistinguishable from native Access. Common Wizards such as the Form Wizard, Report Wizard, and Page Wizard function similarly from an Access project. Developing tables and queries is, however, noticeably different. While the Database Designer, Table Designer, Query Designer, Query Builder, and SQL Text Editor are similar to Access, all will require a small learning curve to become fully comfortable and productive.

Microsoft SQL Server 2000 Desktop ships with Office System but is not part of the standard installation. Before an Access database can be converted to SQL Server or a new SQL Server application can be developed, the Desktop software must be installed using the Office System installation disk.

making the grade

SESSION 12.2

1. Why would you place a pivot table or pivot chart on a Data Access Page?

2. How is XML beneficial?

3. What is an ActiveX control?

4. What is upsizing and why is it important?

SESSION 12.3 SUMMARY

The topics of this chapter centered on improving the user interface and accessibility of data stored in Access. More efficient interfaces improve user satisfaction and increase productivity. One way to achieve this is to provide a single entry location for the most commonly performed tasks using a tabbed form. Tabbed forms can be organized by function or object with the goal of putting everything the user needs one click (at most) away. A Web Browser control is an ActiveX control that can be added to any form to provide browser capabilities.

Access 2003 tables, queries, and forms support PivotTable and PivotChart Views. These views allow live data to be manipulated to uncover trends and improve forecasting. PivotTables display numbers organized into a table defined by dragging and dropping fields onto a design layout. Once placed, fields can be summarized and filtered to provide the level of detail needed to support the decision-making process. Only one view can be stored per object.

PivotTable and PivotChart Views can be saved to Data Access Pages using the Save As option of the File menu. Like their Access-native counterparts, these pages provide full access to live data using a Web browser from an intranet or the Internet. Pivot tables and pivot charts can be built from scratch on a Data Access Page in Design View using the Office PivotTable control and the Office PivotChart control. Building in Design View allows the pivot table and pivot chart to be linked so that they both reflect the same data.

Extensible Markup Language (XML) is a case-sensitive tag-based language similar to HTML. XML is designed to document data so that data can be ported across hardware and software platforms efficiently and without data loss. Microsoft Access is able to both import and export XML files to facilitate data sharing.

Microsoft Access is also designed to be fully compatible with Microsoft SQL Server 2000 Desktop Engine and Microsoft SQL Server 2000 (the full edition) to provide growth, networking, and distribution options when Access is no longer sufficient. Any Access application that uses SQL Server features is referred to as an Access project. Visit www.mhhe.com/i-series/ to explore related topics.

MICROSOFT OFFICE SPECIALIST OBJECTIVES SUMMARY

- Using PivotChart View—MOS AC03S-4-2

making the grade *answers*

SESSION 12.1

1. Tabbed forms allow vast quantities of data to be organized for easy access. The data can be from a single data source, or multiple tables. Tabbed forms are more attractive and easier to navigate than forms with subforms.

2. Use the Properties dialog box to update any property of a control. To open the Properties dialog box, click the label, right-click, and then select Properties from the pop-up menu. The Fore Color property controls the text color and the Caption property controls what displays. Both of these properties can be found on either the All or Format tab of the Property Sheet.

3. Table, query, and form objects support PivotTable and PivotChart Views.

4. When a PivotTable and PivotChart View is opened for the first time, a blank design grid and field list are displayed. The user drags fields from the field list to the target areas on the design to create the view. If a field is dropped in the wrong area, it can be moved by dragging. To remove a field from the view, drag it off the edge of the design. The Field buttons on the design can be used to filter data to present only records that meet a specified criteria.

SESSION 12.2

1. Data Access Pages use DHTML to create dynamic Web pages capable of interacting with live data. Pivot tables and pivot charts placed on a Data Access Page reflect the current status of data and allow the user to manipulate live data from an intranet or the Internet.

2. Extensible Markup Language (XML) is used to port data and its structure across hardware and software platforms allowing data sharing by dissimilar systems.

3. An ActiveX control is not natively listed on the Form Design View toolbox, but is accessed using the More Controls button. These controls have been designed to provide improved performance across platforms and are a good choice for forms that will display on the Web.

4. Upsizing is a term used to describe moving an application from one platform to another to accommodate growth. For example, Microsoft Access is fully compatible with Microsoft SQL Server Desktop and the complete version of Microsoft SQL Server. This compatibility provides options for growth without re-creating the application.

task reference *summary*

Task	Page #	Preferred Method
Saving PivotTable or PivotChart View to a Data Access Page	AC 12.20	• Create the PivotTable or PivotChart View • On the File menu, click **Save As** • Type a filename, select **Data Access Page** from the As drop-down list, and then click **OK** • Navigate to the desired folder • Click **OK** • Review the page in the Access Browser Window that opens automatically
Adding a Web Browser control to a form	AC 12.26	• Open the form in Design View • Click the **More Controls** [icon] button on the toolbox • Select **Microsoft Web Browser** from the list • Click the form to add the control • Move and resize the control as necessary • Create a procedure that will control the browser window display

task reference *summary*

Task	Page #	Preferred Method

Exporting a table, query, form, or report as an XML file	AC 12.29	• In the Database Window, click the name of the object to be exported
		• Click **File** and then **Export** on the menu
		• In the Save as type drop-down box, click **XML Documents (*.xml)**
		• Select the drive and folder for the XML document
		• Enter the filename in the File name box
		• Click **Export**
		• Check the appropriate options in the Export XML dialog box
		  • Click **Data** (XML) to export the object's data to an XML document
		  • Click **Schema** of the data to export the object's structure to an XML file
		  • Click **Presentation** of your data (XSL) to export a file describing data formatting
		• Click **OK**

Importing an XML file as an Access table	AC 12.31	• Click **File**, point to **Get External Data**, and click **Import** • Change the Files of type value to **XML Documents (*.xml;*.xsd)** • Navigate to the folder containing the XML file • Select the XML file and then click the **Import** button • On the Import XML dialog box, click the **Options** button, and set the import options • Click **OK** • Click **OK** to close the finished importing document dialog box

TRUE/FALSE

1. ActiveX controls provide more reliable Web performance.

2. Forms with multiple pages are called multipart forms.

3. A control such as a Form, Subform, or Tab control is a container for other controls.

4. Microsoft Access can both import and export XML data.

5. A PivotTable or PivotChart saved to a Data Access Page is fully interactive and based on live database data.

6. Microsoft Access databases are most commonly upsized to Oracle databases when they outgrow Access's capacity and functionality.

FILL-IN

1. The _____ control adds multiple pages to a form.

2. _____ on an object to open its shortcut menu.

3. A _____ in the field list allows a variable like date to be grouped.

4. The _____ button is used to summarize PivotTable data.

5. _____ is used to port data between dissimilar hardware and software platforms.

6. A _____ is used to display Web pages on a Microsoft Access form.

7. In an XML export the _____ exports the structure of the data being described.

MULTIPLE CHOICE

1. An Extensible Markup Language (XML) document is made up of case-sensitive paired _____.
   a. assignments
   b. PDAs
   c. tags
   d. all of the above

2. The native database engine used by Microsoft Access is _____.
   a. Microsoft Jet
   b. Microsoft SQL Server
   c. Microsoft project
   d. all of the above

3. A fieldset _____.
   a. is used in a PivotTable
   b. contains multiple values
   c. provides alternate ways to group data
   d. all of the above

4. Tabbed pages of a form _____.
   a. use the Tab control
   b. are not linked
   c. are private
   d. none of the above

5. When redesigning an interface, it is best to _____.
   a. use existing queries and forms
   b. build new queries and forms
   c. use VBA
   d. none of the above

review of concepts

REVIEW QUESTIONS

Each of the following topics should be addressed in one to three paragraphs.

1. In the chapter, why was the Wizard used to create a form with subforms that was then converted to a tabbed form?

2. Why do most forms created with a Wizard need to be customized?

3. Explain the impact of saving a PivotTable View on other views of a query.

4. How are filters removed from a PivotTable or PivotChart?

5. Discuss the options available for upsizing an Access database.

CREATE THE QUESTION

For each of the following answers, create the question.

ANSWER	QUESTION
1. Right-click the tab and choose Insert Page	_____
2. Draw or paste the controls directly on the page	_____
3. =functionname(argument1 argument2, . . .)	_____
4. Used to summarize data and normally displays on the X-axis of a PivotChart	_____
5. Click Save As from the File menu and choose Data Access Page in the As drop-down list	_____
6. Microsoft SQL Server 2000 Desktop Engine	_____
7. Draw or paste the control directly on the Tab control page	_____

FACT OR FICTION

For each of the following determine whether the statement is fact, fiction, or both and present your arguments for that conclusion.

1. It is OK to use existing queries when redesigning an interface.

2. The Caption property of a label always holds the text displayed by the label.

3. A PivotTable View can be filtered by any field included in the design.

4. Clicking a plus sign (+) in a PivotTable shows more detail.

5. Each data value is plotted in a different color on a PivotChart.

6. A PivotChart stored as a Data Access Page can be formatted without impacting database data or views.

7. Extensible Markup Language uses predefined tags that are not case sensitive.

practice

1. Altamonte High School Booster Club Donation Tracking—Part I

Creating PivotTable and PivotChart Views: Altamonte High School Booster Club is an organization of students, teachers, parents, and community members who sponsor high school activities through the donations of their members and fund-raising. The Boosters are using an Access database to track donations.

1. Start Access and open **ac12AltamonteBoosters.mdb**

2. Open each table and review the data. Click the Relationships button and review table relationships

3. Build a Select Query named **DonationsByClass** that retrieves **DonationClass** and **Name** from the Boosters table and **DonationDate** and **DonationAmount** from the Donations table. Run the query to verify the results

4. Change to PivotChart View

   a. Drag **Years** from the DonationDate by Month fieldset to the Drop Category Fields Here area

   b. Drag **DonationAmount** to Drop Data Fields Here

   c. Drag **DonationClass** to the Drop Category Fields Here area and drop it to the right of Years

   d. Use the DonationClass drop-down button to select only classes **3** and **4**

   e. Click on the Chart and then click the Chart Type button. Select the **3D Column**

   f. Save

5. Switch to PivotTable View

   a. Notice that the selections made in the PivotChart View are reflected in the PivotTable View

   b. Use the plus sign (+) to display the details for Category 3 in both years

   c. Click the **DonationAmount** button and then click the **AutoCalc** drop-down list and click **Average** (The Average displays below the total for each Donation Class and is added to the field list)

6. Switch to PivotChart View

   a. Drag the Years button from the Category area and discard it

   b. Change the chart type to line and select the 3D Line subtype

   c. Save and switch to PivotTable View to see the impact

7. Save the PivotTable View as a Data Access Page named **DonationsByClassPivotTable**. Close the preview window without making any changes

8. Save the PivotChart View as a Data Access Page named **DonationsByClassPivotChart**. Close the preview window without making any changes

9. Save the Donations table in an XML format named **Donations.xml**. Export both the data and the structure. Review the results in your browser by double-clicking the filename from Windows Explorer

F I G U R E 12.25

DonationsByClass PivotTable and PivotChart

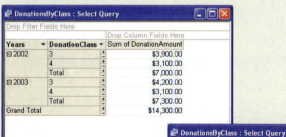

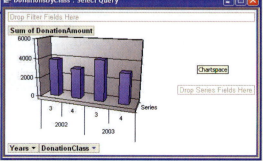

2. MicroWarehouse: PivotTable/Chart Data Access Pages

MicroWarehouse is a retail supplier of computing products. Sales are completed from a Web storefront and a number of brick-and-mortar sites throughout the United States. Their Microsoft Access database tracks products, orders, customers, and suppliers.

1. Start Access and open **ac12MicroWarehouse.mdb**

2. Review the contents of the existing database objects

3. Build a Select Query named **SalesByManufacturer** that retrieves

   a. **PartNumber**, and **QtyOrdered** from the OrderLine table

   b. **OrderDate** from the Order table

   c. **Manufacturer** and **Price** from the Product table. Create a calculated field **Total: QtyOrdered*Price**

4. Review the query results from Datasheet View and then switch to PivotChart View

   a. Drag **OrderDate** to the Drop Category Fields Here area

   b. Drag **QtyOrdered** to the Drop Data Fields Here area

   c. Drag **Manufacturer** to the Drop Category Fields Here area below OrderDate

   d. Use the Manufacturer drop-down button to select **American Power Conversion**, **Adobe Systems**, and **Macromedia**

   e. Click on the chart and then click the Chart Type button. Select the **Clustered Bar**

   f. Save

   g. Save the PivotChart View as a Data Access Page named **ManufacturerPivotChart**. Close the preview window without making any changes

5. Switch to PivotTable View

   a. Change the summary function of Total to **Average**

   b. Display all of the details using the plus signs (+)

   c. Save the PivotTable View as a Data Access Page named **ManufacturerPivotTable**

6. Minimize Access and open ManufacturerPivotChart in Internet Explorer. Experiment with formatting and other updates. Return the chart to its original state

7. Open ManufacturerPivotChart in Internet Explorer. Format the chart by changing the bar colors. Close IE

8. If your work is complete, exit Access; otherwise, continue to the next assignment

FIGURE 12.26

PivotTable/Chart Data Access Pages

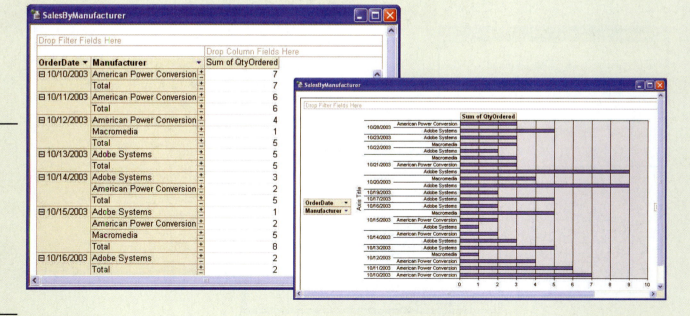

1. Altamonte High School Booster Club Donation Tracking—Part II

Updating the user interface:

1. Start Access and open your copy of **ac12AltamonteBoosters.mdb** (If you did not complete the Practice assignment, you will need to do so now)

2. Use the Form Wizard to create a main form/sub-form for Boosters and their donations

   a. The main form should display all of the Boosters table fields

   b. The subform should display all of the Donations table fields

   c. Set the data to be viewed **by Boosters**

   d. Use **Tabular** layout for the subform

   e. Use the **Blueprint** style

   f. Name the form **BoostersDonations** and the subform **DonationsSubform**

   g. Customize the main form and subform so that all of the labels display and the field sizes are appropriate

3. Place a Tab Control on the form large enough to hold the Booster data. Set the Back Style property to **Transparent**

4. Place the Booster data on the first tabbed page and label the tab **Booster**

5. Place the Donations data on the second tab and label it **Donations**

6. Set the Scroll Bars property of the subform (click on the scroll bar in Design View) to **Vertical Only**

7. Use the form to add another donation for Matthew Hoff for the current date and **$700**. Change his DonationClass to **6**

8. Add a third page to the Tab control labeled **Browse**

9. Place a Text Box control and Web Browser control on the third page. Set the properties of the label to display Address. Set the Name property of the text box to **txtAddress** and the Name property of the browser to **WebBrowser**. Write the procedure that causes WebBrowser to display what is typed in txtAddress

10. Test the browser control with a live Internet connection, and then close the form saving your changes

11. Open the Donations table and note the current number of records

12. Import the data in the **NewDonations.xml** file into the Donations table. Use the Options button of the Import XML dialog box to select **Append Data to Existing Table(s)**

13. Open the Donations table and review the imported records. Review any errors placed in the ImportErrors table

F I G U R E 12.27

BoostersDonations tabbed form

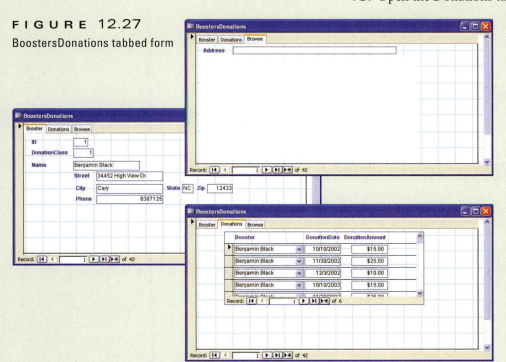

2. Completing the PuppyParadise User Interface

PuppyParadise is a distributor of pet supplies. The PuppyParadise database is a mature database with a number of tables, queries, forms, and reports. A tabbed form, XML export, and Web access need to be finalized to complete the user interface.

1. Start Access and open **ac12PuppyParadise.mdb**

2. Create a query named **InvoiceLineItems** that retrieves all fields from the OrderDetails table, **ProductDescription** and **ProductPrice** from the Products table. Include a calculation for Item Total

3. Build a form named **CustomerTabbed** with tabular subforms that displays all customer data in the main form, OrderId and OrderDate from Orders, and data from the InvoiceLineItems query in subforms

4. Add tabbed pages to CustomerTabbed and organize the Customer, Order, and Line Items tabs using Figure 12.28

5. Export the Customer table data as an XML file named **ac12Customer.xml**. Do not export the schema

6. Create a PivotTable from the InvoiceJoinWithCalc query

   a. Place **State** in the Drop Column Fields Here area

   b. Place **ProductDescription** in the Drop Column Fields Here area

   c. Place **OrderDate** by Month in the Drop Row Fields Here area

   d. Place QuantityOrdered in the Drop Data Fields Here area

   e. Select data from CA, CO, and OH

   f. Save the PivotTable as a Data Access Page named **InvoiceJoinWithCalcPivotTable**

7. Change to PivotChart View

   a. Reorganize the chart until OrderDate by Month is the category field, Sum of Item Total is the data field, and State is the series field

   b. Show the legend

   c. Customize the color of the bars

8. Use Internet Explorer to verify the functionality of your Data Access Pages

9. If your work is complete, exit Access; otherwise, continue to the next assignment

F I G U R E 12.28

PuppyParadise CustomerTabbed form

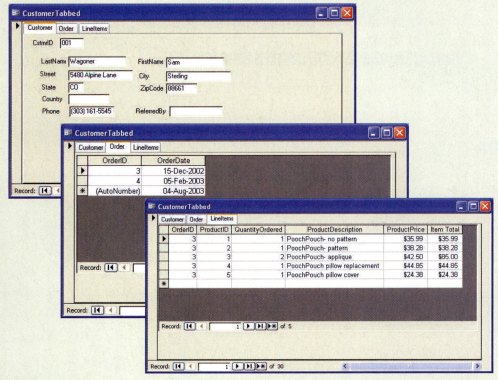

1. Curbside Recycling

Curbside Recycling is enhancing its Web presence to include pivot tables, pivot charts, and data sharing. You will be enhancing its database in preparation for posting forms and reports on the Web.

1. Open the **ac12CurbsideRecycling.mdb** database

2. Open the **CustomerRecords** table and review the records

3. Import the XML file **ac12CustomerRecordsImport.xml** appending it to the CustomerRecords table

4. Verify that the records were added to the **CustomerRecords** table and then export the full table and schema in XML format named **UpdatedCustomerRecords.xml**

5. Use the Form Wizard to create a form with all the fields from the Customer table and all fields of the CustomerRecords table except CstmrID. Display the data by customer using subforms; select Tabular as the subform layout and Sumi Painting as the style. Name the form **Customers** and accept the default subform name

   a. Place a Tab control on the form large enough to hold the Manufacturers data. Set the Back Style property to **Transparent**

   b. Place the Customer data on the first tabbed page and label the tab **Customer**

   c. Place the CustomerRecords data on the second tab and set the tab label to **Records**

   d. Adjust the controls as needed to properly display all data

   e. Add a third page to the Tab control labeled **Browse**

   f. Place a Text Box control and Web Browser control on the third page. Set the properties of the label to display **Address**. Set the Name property of the text box to **txtAddress** and the Name property of the browser to **WebBrowser**. Write the procedure that causes WebBrowser to display what is typed in txtAddress

   g. Test the browser control with a live Internet connection, and then close the form saving your changes

6. Use the Query Wizard to create a query named **CustomerData** that retrieves all fields from Customer and CustomerRecords except CustID

7. You have been asked to compare the effectiveness of employee 218 with that of employee 382. Open the PivotChart View of the **CustomerData** query

   a. Arrange Years and EmployeeID so that the names appear on the X-axis (Categories) and both WeightPaper and WeightOther are charted

   b. Activate the legend

   c. Can you draw any conclusions from the chart?

   d. Save the view

   e. Create a Data Access Page named **CustomerData.htm** from the view

FIGURE 12.29

Customer tabbed form

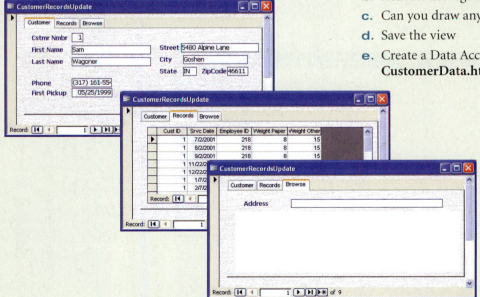

2. Finalizing the Golden Cream Bakery Graphical User Interface

Golden Cream is a bakery specializing in restaurant desserts. Orders are accepted from an Internet Web site. The GoldenCream database is a mature database with a number of tables, queries, forms, and reports. A tabbed form, XML export, and Web access need to be finalized to complete the user interface.

1. Open **ac12GoldenCream.mdb**. Peruse the current tables and queries

2. Create a query named **InvoiceLines** that retrieves all nonduplicate fields from the Order and Sales tables. Include a calculation for Item Total

3. Build a form named **InvoiceTabbed** with tabular subforms that displays all customer data in the main form and data from the InvoiceLine query in subforms

4. Add tabbed pages to CustomerTabbed and organize the Customer and Invoice tabs as shown in Figure 12.30. Close form when done

5. Export the Customer table data as an XML file named **ac12GoldenCream.xml**. Do not export the schema

6. Create a PivotTable from the InvoiceLines query

   a. Place **ItemDescription** in the Drop Row Fields Here area

   b. Place **Months** from the Date by Month fieldset in the Drop Row Fields Here area

   c. Place Item Totals in the Drop Totals or Detail Fields Here area

   d. Select only Item Descriptions with Chocolate in them

   e. Save the PivotTable as a Data Access Page named **InvoiceLinesTable**

7. Change to PivotChart View

   a. Reorganize the chart until an ItemDescription is the category field, Sum of Item Total is the data field, and Quarters is the series field

   b. Show the legend

   c. Customize the color of the bars

   d. Save the PivotChart as a Data Access Page named **InvoiceLinesChart**

8. Use Internet Explorer to verify the functionality of your Data Access Pages

9. Close the database and exit Access if your work is complete

FIGURE 12.30

Golden Cream tabbed form

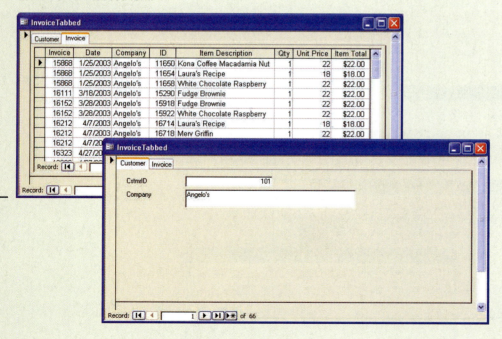

1. EduWare Software

EduWare Software is a local mall store selling educational software. You are improving their existing Access database.

1. Use a search engine to locate at least 10 math, English, and science educational software titles and prices

2. Open the **ac12EduWare.mdb** database and review the contents of each table

3. Create a query that retrieves Manufacturers.Name, Titles.Name, Titles.Category, Titles.Quantity, and Titles.Price. Name the query **ManufacturersTitles**

4. You have been asked to evaluate the impact of dropping one of the manufacturers. The first step is to compare the products provided by each manufacturer. Open the PivotChart View of the **ManufacturersTitles**

   a. Arrange Manufacturers.Name and Quantity so that the names appear on the X-axis and the quantity is charted (data field)

   b. Add Category as a series field

   c. Activate the legend

   d. Can you draw any conclusions from the chart?

FIGURE 12.31

MfgTitles tabbed form

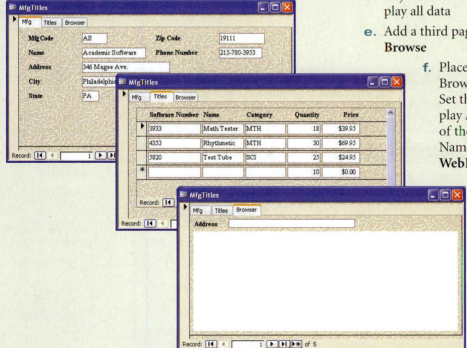

e. Save the view

f. Create a Data Access Page named **ManufacturersTitles.htm** from the view

5. Add your records to the Titles table. Evenly divide them between Academic Software (AS) and Edusoft (EI)

6. Revisit the PivotChart. Does the new data impact your evaluation?

7. Save the Titles table in an XML format named **Titles.xml**. Export both the data and the structure. Review the results in your browser

8. Use the Form Wizard to create a form with all of the fields from the Manufacturers table and all fields of the Titles table except MfgCode. Display the data by manufacturer using subforms, select Tabular as the subform layout and Ricepaper as the style. Name the form **MfgTitles** and use the default subform name

   a. Place a Tab control on the form large enough to hold the Manufacturers data. Set the Back Style property to **Transparent**

   b. Place the Manufacturers data on the first tabbed page and label the tab **Mfg**

   c. Place the Titles data on the second tab and set the tab label to **Titles**

   d. Adjust the controls as needed to properly display all data

   e. Add a third page to the Tab control labeled **Browse**

   f. Place a Text Box control and Web Browser control on the third page. Set the properties of the label to display Address. Set the Name property of the text box to **txtAddress** and the Name property of the browser to **WebBrowser**. Write the procedure that causes WebBrowser to display what is typed in txtAddress

   g. Test the browser control with a live Internet connection, and then close the form saving your changes

around the world

1. TechRocks Seminars

TechRocks Seminars provides onsite technical training to large businesses around the world.

1. Open the **ac12Seminars.mdb**

2. Create a query named **EnrollmentQuery** that displays a Count of LastName Group by SeminarID

3. Create a query named **SeminarsQuery**

   a. Retrieve Seminar ID, Description, Cost, and Trainer ID from the Seminars table

   b. Retrieve Count of LastName from the EnrollmentQuery. Rename the field Enrollment by placing **Enrollment:** before CountOfLastName

   c. Create a calculated field in the first empty column by placing **Extended Cost: [Cost]*[Enrollment]** in the Field row

   d. Change to Datasheet View to see the query result

4. Open the PivotChart View of SeminarsQuery

   a. Make the category fields SeminarID and Description

   b. Chart ExtendedCost

   c. Check the PivotTable View and then save both views in separate Data Access Pages named **SeminarsPivotChart** and **SeminarsPivotTable**

   d. Which seminar is currently making the most money?

5. Use the Form Wizard to create a form named **SeminarData** with all fields from all three tables except Seminars.Trainer Id and Enrollment.Seminar ID

   a. View the data by Facilitators and use subforms

   b. Make both subforms tabular

   c. Use the SandStone style

6. Customize the SeminarData form

   a. Place a Tab control on the form and set the Back Property to **Transparent**

   b. Caption the first tab Facilitators and place the data from the Facilitator table there

   c. Caption the second tab Seminars and place the Seminars subform there. Set the Scroll Bars property of the subform to **Neither**

   d. Create a third tab named Enrollment and place the Enrollment subform there. Set the Scroll Bars property of the subform to **Neither**

   e. Adjust the size of the fields and subforms to suit the data. Use Figure 12.32 as a guide

   f. Add a fourth page with a Text Box control and a Web Browser control. Set the properties and code the procedure that will allow pages to display

7. Save the SeminarQuery in an XML format named **ac12SeminarData.xml**. Export both the data and the structure. Review the results in your browser

F I G U R E 12.32
SeminarData tabbed form

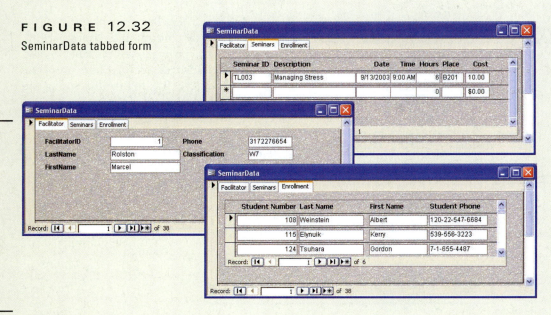

running project: TnT web design

Tabbed Forms and Pivot Charts for TnT

As TnT grows, so does the complexity of its database. Tori and Tonya now have over 65 employees and several hundred customers. Employees and projects are spread across the United States, so it is becoming critical to have simple Web-based data entry and reporting.

1. Create a backup of your AC11TnT.mdb file named **ac12TnT.mdb** using Windows Explorer

2. Start Access and open your copy of the **ac12TnT.mdb** database. Remember to hold down the **Shift** key to bypass startup processing

3. Delete the CustomersAndSites and tblCustomerSites subform forms

4. Use the Form Wizard to create a form named **CustomerSiteData** with all fields from tblCustomers and tblCustomerSites except tblCustomerSites.CustID and tblCustomerSites.Employee. Add Employee LastName, FirstName, and Phone from tblEmployees

    a. Use subforms and display the data by tblCustomers

    b. Select **Tabular** as the subform layout

    c. Select **Sumi Painting** as the style

FIGURE 12.33

CustomerSiteData tabbed form

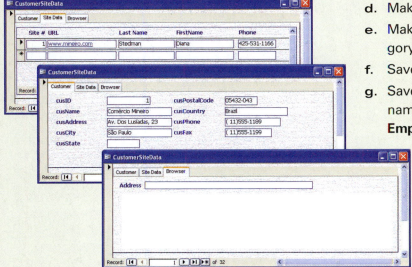

    d. Add a Tab control to the form and set the Back Style property to **Transparent**

    e. Place the customer fields on the first page of the form and label it **Customer**

    f. Place the subform on the second page labeled **Site Data**

    g. Adjust the caption text and form and field sizes to suit the data. Use Figure 12.33 as a guide

    h. Add a third page with a Text Box control and a Web Browser control. Set the properties and code the procedure that will allow an address to be entered in the text box and the browser control to display the page

5. Create a query in Design View named **EmployeeSiteCount** to count the number of sites built by each employee

    a. Retrieve tblEmployees.EmployeeID, tblEmployees.LastName, tblEmployees.FirstName, and tblCustomerSites.URL. Use the Totals button to Group by the first three fields and count the last

    b. Change the URL field heading to **Sites Built:URL** to modify the heading

    c. Test the query and then switch to PivotChart View

    d. Make Sites Built the data field

    e. Make LastName and FirstName the category fields

    f. Save the view

    g. Save a Data Access Page from the view named **EmployeeSiteCountPivotChart.htm**

1. Tabbed Forms and XML for Presbyterian Hospital

Open your copy of the database named **ac12 PresbyterianHospital.mdb**. This database is used to track various hospital operations. Export the employee table as an XML file named **ac12PresEmployee.xml**. Review existing database objects and design a tabbed form to improve the user interface. Submit your database and documentation of the new features added. The tabbed form should include

- A page to update Units
- A page to update Employees
- A page to update Employee Remediation
- The Employee and Employee Remediation pages should be linked to display information for the same employee

2. Tabbed Forms and XML for Your Multitable Database

Locate any multitable database with multiple forms that you have worked with during the course of this class. The database should include at least three forms. Export the most important table as an XML file named **ac12MultiTable.xml**. Review existing database objects and design a tabbed form to improve the user interface. Submit your database and documentation of the new features added.
The tabbed form should include

- A minimum of three pages
- A page with a functioning Web browser
- Linked data on different tabbed pages

reference 1

Access *File Finder*

Location in Chapter	Data File to Use
CHAPTER 1	
Session 1.1	
Opening the Customer database	ac01Customers.mdb
Session 1.2	
Opening the Customer table	ac01Customers.mdb
Hands-on Projects	
Practice Exercise 1	ac01CurbsideRecycling.mdb
Practice Exercise 2	ac01LalierConstruction.mdb
E-Business Exercise 2	ac01DelroyTravel
Around the World Exercise 1	ac01AGC.mdb
Running Project	ac01TnT.mdb
CHAPTER 2	
Session 2.1	
Reorganizing datasheet columns	ac02Customers.mdb
Session 2.2	
Building the Orders table	ac02KoryoKicks.mdb
Populating the Order table	ac02KoryoKicks2.mdb
Hands-on Projects	
Challenge Exercise 2	ac02NewVideoReleases.mdb
E-Business Exercise 2	ac02Calendar.mdb
Running Project	ac01TnT.mdb copied and renamed to AC02<yourname>TnT.mdb
CHAPTER 3	
Session 3.1	
Filtering the Customer table	ac03KoryoKicks.mdb
Session 3.2	
Selecting Software table records	ac03KoryoKicks.mdb
Adding a Graphic to InventoryValueByClass	ac03KoryoKicksLogo.gif

REFERENCE

Location in Chapter	Data File to Use
Hands-on Projects	
Practice Exercise 1	ac03CurbsideRecycling.mdb ac03Curbside.tif
Practice Exercise 2	ac03BestBakery.mdb ac03Food.jpg
Challenge Exercise 1	ac01LittleWhiteSchoolHouse.mdb or ac03Lwsh.mdb ac03Lwsh.tif
Challenge Exercise 2	ac03Software.mdb ac03Software.gif
E-Business Exercise 1	ac03Cars.mdb ac03ClassicCars.tif
E-Business Exercise 2	ac03GovernorsUniversity.mdb ac03Study.gif
On the Web Exercise 1	ac03IRI.mdb ac03IRI.tif
Around the World Exercise 1	ac03Populations.mdb ac03Globe.gif
Running Project	ac03TnT.mdb ac03TnT.tif
CHAPTER 4	
Session 4.1	
Selecting Customer table records with Between	ac04KoryoKicks.mdb
Session 4.2	
Adding a Memo field to the Customer table	ac04KoryoKicks.mdb
Hands-on Projects	
Practice Exercise 1	ac04Merrill.mdb
Practice Exercise 2	ac04Recruiting.mdb
Challenge Exercise 1	ac04CurbsideRecycling.mdb
Challenge Exercise 2	ac04Lacrosse.mdb
E-Business Exercise 1	ac04SportsPix.mdb
E-Business Exercise 2	ac04USDA.mdb
On the Web Exercise 1	ac04IRI.mdb
Around the World Exercise 1	ac04Populations.mdb
Running Project	ac04TnT.mdb Ac04TnT.tif

Location in Chapter	Data File to Use
CHAPTER 5	
Session 5.1	
Creating the Customer form in Design View	ac05KoryoKicks.mdb
Adding content to the Form Header	ac05KoryoKicks.gif
Session 5.2	
Customizing the Customer AutoReport	ac05KoryoKicks.mdb
Adding the Report Header to the Customer report	ac05KoryoKicks.gif
Hands-on Projects	
Practice Exercise 1	ac05Cyberia.mdb ac05Cyberia.tif
Practice Exercise 2	ac05GradeBook.mdb ac05GradeBookLogo.gif
Challenge Exercise 1	ac05CyberiaChallenge.mdb ac05Cyberia.tif
Challenge Exercise 2	ac05GradeBookChallenge.mdb ac05GradeBookLogo.gif
E-Business Exercise 1	ac05SportsPix.mdb ac05SportsPix.tif
E-Business Exercise 2	ac05NMOEnergy.mdb ac05NMOLogo.gif ac05DiamondBullett.emf
On the Web Exercise 1	ac05TerraPatrimonium.mdb ac05TerraPatrimonium.tif
Around the World Exercise 1	ac05Seminars.mdb ac05TechRocks.tif
Running Project	ac05TnT.mdb ac05TnT.tif
CHAPTER 6	
Session 6.1	
Viewing KoryoKicks relationships	ac06KoryoKicks.mdb
Session 6.2	
Creating a multitable query, InvoiceJoin	ac06KoryoKicks.mdb
Creating a logo and title for the InvoiceJoinWithCalc report	ac06KoryoKicksLogo.gif

REFERENCE

Location in Chapter	Data File to Use
Hands-on Projects	
Practice Exercise 1	ac06AltamonteBoosters.mdb
Practice Exercise 2	ac06NMOEnergy.mdb
Challenge Exercise 1	ac06AltamonteBoosters.mdb
Challenge Exercise 2	ac06NMOEnergy.mdb
E-Business Exercise 1	ac06CurbsideRecycling.mdb
E-Business Exercise 2	ac06CommunityHospital.mdb ac06Nurse.gif
On the Web Exercise 1	ac06Software.mdb
Around the World Exercise 1	ac06Seminars.mdb
Running Project	ac06TnT.mdb
CHAPTER 7	
Session 7.1	
Customizing the Customer table input masks	ac07KoryoKicks.mdb
Session 7.2	
Splitting the KoryoKicks database	ac07KoryoKicks.mdb
Hands-on Projects	
Practice Exercise 1	ac07AltamonteBoosters.mdb
Practice Exercise 2	ac07BBsShoes.mdb
Challenge Exercise 1	ac07AltamonteBoosters.mdb
Challenge Exercise 2	ac07HealthCare2Go.mdb
E-Business Exercise 1	ac07CurbsideRecycling.mdb
E-Business Exercise 2	ac07SportBabies.mdb
On the Web Exercise 1	ac07Software.mdb
Around the World Exercise 1	ac07SSeminars.mdb
Running Project	ac07TnT.mdb
CHAPTER 8	
Session 8.1	
Creating a report with a chart	ac08KoryoKicks.mdb
Linking a Word document to the OrdersByStateChart report	ac08OrdersAnalysis.doc
Importing ac08NewCustomerContacts.mdb	ac08NewCustomerContacts.mdb
Importing ac08Importers.xls	ac08Importers.xls

Location in Chapter	Data File to Use
Session 8.2	
Exporting Importers.html	ac08KoryoKicks.mdb
Adding an Image to ImportersDataAccess.htm	ac08Warrior.gif
Importing WebImporters.htm as an Access table	ac08WebImporters.htm
Entering and repairing a hyperlink in WebImporters	ac08KoryoKicksHome.htm
Hands-on Projects	
Practice Exercise 1	ac08AltamonteBoosters.mdb
Practice Exercise 2	ac08ScaleModels.mdb
Challenge Exercise 1	ac08AltamonteBoosters.mdb ac08AltamonteSummary.doc
Challenge Exercise 2	ac08ScaleModels.mdb ac08ScaleModel.gif
E-Business Exercise 1	ac08CurbsideRecycling.mdb ac08Competition.xls
E-Business Exercise 2	ac08xXtreMeSportz.mdb ac08xXtreMeSportzLinks.xls ac08xXtreMeSportz.gif
On the Web Exercise 1	ac08Software.mdb ac08SoftwareTitles.xls
Around the World Exercise 1	ac08Seminars.mdb ac08Seminars.gif
Running Project	ac08TnT.mdb
CHAPTER 9	
Session 9.1	
Using the Crosstab Query Wizard	ac09KoryoKicks.mdb
Session 9.2	
Locating duplicate records in the Customer table	ac09KoryoKicks.mdb
Hands-on Projects	
Practice Exercise 1	ac09LWSH.mdb
Practice Exercise 2	ac09xXtreMeSponsors.mdb
Challenge Exercise 1	ac09SuccessTraining.mdb
Challenge Exercise 2	ac09xXtreMeSponsors.mdb
E-Business Exercise 1	ac09LumberOnline.mdb
E-Business Exercise 2	ac09xXtreMeSponsors.mdb
On the Web Exercise 1	ac09InternetCafe.mdb

REFERENCE

Location in Chapter	Data File to Use
Around the World Exercise 1	ac09WorldPopulation.mdb
Running Project	ac09TnT.mdb
Analysis	ac09CommunityHospital.mdb
CHAPTER 10	
Session 10.1	
Creating a macro to run and print the CustomerOrdersJoin query	ac10KoryoKicks.mdb
Session 10.2	
Beginning the KoryoKicks switchboard	ac10KoryoKicks.mdb
Beautifying the KoryoKicks switchboard	ac10KoryoKicksLogo.mdb
Hands-on Projects	
Practice Exercise 1	
Practice Exercise 2	ac10xXtreMeSportz.gif
Challenge Exercise 1	ac10RoseUniversity.mdb ac10RoseGraphic.wmf
Challenge Exercise 2	ac10TechRocks.mdb ac10TechRocks.tif
E-Business Exercise 1	ac10LumberOnline.mdb ac10OnlineLumber.wmf
E-Business Exercise 2	ac10Cheesecake.mdb ac10Cheesecake.gif
On the Web Exercise 1	ac10InternetCafe.mdb ac10InternetCafe.wmf
Around the World Exercise 1	ac10WorldPopulations.mdb ac10WorldPopulations.wmf
Running Project	ac10TnT.mdb ac10TnT.tif
Analysis	ac10PresbyterianHospital.mdb
CHAPTER 11	
Session 11.1	
Viewing UpdateCustomers event properties	ac11KoryoKicks.mdb
Session 11.2	
Creating the cmdOpenInvoice_Click event	ac11KoryoKicks.mdb

Location in Chapter	Data File to Use
Hands-on Projects	
Practice Exercise 1	ac11GibbsFood.mdb
Practice Exercise 2	ac11Recycling.mdb
Challenge Exercise 1	ac11GibbsFood.mdb
Challenge Exercise 2	ac11PuppyParadise.mdb
E-Business Exercise 1	ac11WebToys.mdb
E-Business Exercise 2	ac11GoldenCream.mdb
On the Web Exercise 1	ac11BookClub.mdb
Around the World Exercise 1	ac11Tennis.mdb
Running Project	
Analysis	
CHAPTER 12	
Session 12.1	
Creating the InvoiceLineItems query	ac12KoryoKicks.mdb
Session 12.2	
Converting a PivotChart to a Web page	ac12KoryoKicks.mdb
Importing data from an XML file	ac12Employee.xml
Hands-on Projects	
Practice Exercise 1	ac12AltamonteBoosters.mdb
Practice Exercise 2	ac12MicroWarehouse.mdb
Challenge Exercise 1	ac12AltamonteBoosters.mdb NewDonations.mdb
Challenge Exercise 2	ac12PuppyParadise.mdb ac12Customer.xml
E-Business Exercise 1	ac12CurbsideRecycling.mdb ac12CustomerRecordsImport.xml
E-Business Exercise 2	ac12GoldenCream.mdb
On the Web Exercise 1	ac12EduWare.mdb
Around the World Exercise 1	ac12Seminars.mdb
Running Project	
Analysis	Ac12PresbyterianHospital.mdb

REFERENCE

reference 2

Access Microsoft Office Specialist Certification Guide

Microsoft Office Specialist Objective	Task	Session Location	End-of-Chapter Location
CHAPTER 1	**Understanding Relational Databases**		
AC03S-1-1	Starting Access and opening a blank database	1.1	AC 1.35
AC03S-1-2	Using the Create Table Wizard	1.2	AC 1.35
AC03S-1-7	Querying the Customer table	1.2	AC 1.35
AC03S-1-7	Sorting the query results	1.2	AC 1.35
AC03S-1-8	Using AutoForm	1.2	AC 1.35
AC03S-2-2	Opening the Customer table	1.2	AC 1.35
AC03S-4-3	Printing the Customer table's design	1.2	AC 1.35
AC03S-4-3	Printing Forms with data	1.2	AC 1.35
CHAPTER 2	**Maintaining Your Database**		
AC03S-2-1	Finding and replacing values in the Customer table	2.1	AC 2.36
AC03S-2-1	Using wildcards to find Customer table data	2.1	AC 2.36
AC03S-2-1	Adding New Records to the Customer table	2.1	AC 2.36
AC03S-2-1	Deleting a record from the Customer table	2.1	AC 2.36
AC03S-2-1	Using the Office Clipboard with the Customer table	2.1	AC 2.36
AC03S-2-1	Populating the Order table	2.2	AC 2.36
AC03S-3-4	Sorting the Customer table	2.1	AC 2.36
AC03S-3-4	Hiding and unhiding columns of the Customer table	2.1	AC 2.36
AC03S-3-4	Freezing and unfreezing columns of the Customer table	2.1	AC 2.36
AC03S-3-5	Reorganizing datasheet columns	2.1	AC 2.36

REF 2.1

REFERENCE

Microsoft Office Specialist Objective	Task	Session Location	End-of-Chapter Location
AC03S-3-5	Sorting the Customer table	2.1	AC 2.36
CHAPTER 3	**Introducing Queries, Filters, Forms and Reports**		
AC03S-1-7	Creating a Customer table query	3.1	AC 3.38
AC03S-1-7	Formatting the Customer table query	3.1	AC 3.38
AC03S-1-7	Sorting the Customer table query	3.1	AC 3.38
AC03S-1-7	Selecting Software table records	3.2	AC 3.38
AC03S-1-7	Creating an expression field with the Expression Builder	3.2	AC 3.38
AC03S-1-7	Summarizing grouped data	3.2	AC 3.38
AC03S-1-8	Using the Form Wizard	3.2	AC 3.38
AC03S-1-9	Changing the AutoFormat of the InventoryValue form	3.2	AC 3.38
AC03S-1-10	Using the Report Wizard	3.2	AC 3.38
AC03S-1-10	Changing the AutoFormat of the InventoryValueByClass report	3.2	AC 3.38
AC03S-1-10	Changing the labels of the InventoryValueByClass report	3.2	AC 3.38
AC03S-1-10	Making mailing labels for software venders	3.2	AC 3.38
AC03S-1-10	Adding a graphic to InventoryValueByClass	3.2	AC 3.38
AC03S-3-1	Creating an expression field with the Expression Builder	3.2	AC 3.38
AC03S-3-1	Creating an expression by typing	3.2	AC 3.38
AC03S-3-1	Summarizing selected data with aggregate functions	3.2	AC 3.38
AC03S-3-1	Summarizing grouped data	3.2	AC 3.38
AC03S-3-2	Changing the AutoFormat of the InventoryValue form	3.2	AC 3.38
AC03S-3-6	Filtering the Customer table	3.1	AC 3.38
AC03S-3-6	Excluding records from the Customer table	3.1	AC 3.38
AC03S-3-6	Filtering the Customer table with Filter by Form	3.1	AC 3.38
AC03S-3-6	Filtering the Customer table with an Or condition	3.1	AC 3.38

Microsoft Office Specialist Objective	Task	Session Location	End-of-Chapter Location
AC03S-3-6	Filtering the Customer table with Filter For	3.1	AC 3.38
AC03S-3-6	Filtering the Customer table with Advanced Filter/Sort	3.1	AC 3.38
CHAPTER 4	**Compound Queries and Database Utilities**		
AC03S-1-3	Setting a lookup field for vendors in the Product table	4.2	AC 4.33
AC03S-1-3	Adding a Memo field to the Customer table	4.2	AC 4.33
AC03S-1-4	Deleting a field from the Customer table	4.2	AC 4.33
AC03S-1-4	Moving a field in the Customer table	4.2	AC 4.33
AC03S-1-4	Changing field properties in the Product table	4.2	AC 4.33
AC03S-1-4	Setting an input mask for the OrderData field	4.2	AC 4.33
AC03S-1-7	Selecting Customer table records with Between	4.1	AC 4.33
AC03S-1-7	Selecting Customer table records with In	4.1	AC 4.33
AC03S-1-7	Selecting Customer table records with Like	4.1	AC 4.33
AC03S-1-7	Selecting Customer table records with compound criteria	4.1	AC 4.33
AC03S-1-7	Selecting Customer table records with Not	4.1	AC 4.33
AC03S-1-7	Joining the Order and Customer tables in a query	4.1	AC 4.33
AC03S-1-7	Create a Cartesian product	4.1	AC 4.33
AC03S-1-7	Repairing a Cartesian product	4.1	AC 4.33
AC03S-1-7	Analyzing sales with a Crosstab Query	4.1	AC 4.33
AC03S-4-5	Using Access to backup KoryoKicks	4.2	AC 4.33
AC03S-4-6	Compacting and repairing the KoryoKicks database	4.2	AC 4.33
AC03S-4-6	Compacting and repairing the unopened KoryoKicks database	4.2	AC 4.33
AC03S-4-6	Setting the Automatic Compact and Repair option for KoryoKicks	4.2	AC 4.33

REFERENCE

Microsoft Office Specialist Objective	Task	Session Location	End-of-Chapter Location
CHAPTER 5	**Customizing Forms and Reports**		
AC03S-1-9	Changing form properties	5.1	AC 5.42
AC03S-1-9	Repositioning Customer form controls	5.1	AC 5.42
AC03S-1-11	Customizing the Customer AutoReport	5.2	AC 5.42
AC03S-1-11	Building the Customer report in Design View	5.2	AC 5.42
AC03S-1-11	Editing label captions	5.2	AC 5.42
AC03S-1-11	Aligning Customer report controls	5.2	AC 5.42
AC03S-1-11	Adding the Customer report date and time	5.2	AC 5.42
AC03S-3-2	Creating the Customer form in Design View	5.1	AC 5.42
AC03S-3-2	Changing labels	5.1	AC 5.42
AC03S-3-2	Changing text boxes	5.1	AC 5.42
AC03S-3-2	Adding Form Header/Footer	5.1	AC 5.42
AC03S-3-2	Adding content to the Form Header	5.1	AC 5.42
AC03S-3-3	Adding page numbers to the Customer report	5.2	AC 5.42
AC03S-3-3	Adding the Report Header to the Customer report	5.2	AC 5.42
AC03S-3-3	Adding separators to the Customer report	5.2	AC 5.42
AC03S-3-3	Adding a report total (Count) to the Customer report	5.2	AC 5.42
AC03S-3-3	Adding Sorting and Grouping to the Customer report	5.2	AC 5.42
AC03S-3-3	Adding State Header and Footer content	5.2	AC 5.42
AC03S-3-3	Hiding duplicate State values	5.2	AC 5.42
AC03S-3-5	Finding form records	5.1	AC 5.42
AC03S-3-5	Filtering form records	5.1	AC 5.42
AC03S-4-2	Querying an Open Form	5.1	AC 5.42
AC03S-4-2	Customizing the Customer AutoReport	5.2	AC 5.42
AC03S-4-2	Building the Customer report in Design View	5.2	AC 5.42

Microsoft Office Specialist Objective	Task	Session Location	End-of-Chapter Location
AC03S-4-2	Previewing and printing reports	5.2	AC 5.42
CHAPTER 6	**Defining Table Relationships**		
AC03S-1-5	Viewing KoryoKicks relationships	6.1	AC 6.39
AC03S-1-5	Viewing KoryoKicks relationship properties	6.1	AC 6.39
AC03S-1-5	Building a one-to-one relationship	6.1	AC 6.39
AC03S-1-5	Deleting a table and its associated relationships	6.1	AC 6.39
AC03S-1-5	Building a one-to-many relationship	6.1	AC 6.39
AC03S-1-6	Viewing KoryoKicks relationship properties	6.1	AC 6.39
AC03S-4-1	Viewing KoryoKicks object dependencies	6.2	AC 6.39
CHAPTER 7	**Maintaining Databases**		
AC03S-1-4	Customizing the Customer table input masks	7.1	AC 7.35
AC03S-1-4	Customizing the Order.OrderDate field format	7.1	AC 7.35
AC03S-1-4	Adding default values to the KoryoKicks database	7.1	AC 7.35
AC03S-1-4	Requiring fields in the KoryoKicks database	7.1	AC 7.35
AC03S-1-4	Adding field validation to the KoryoKicks database	7.1	AC 7.35
CHAPTER 8	**Integrating with Other Applications**		
AC03S-1-12	Using the Page Wizard to create ImportersDataAccess.htm	8.2	AC 8.46
AC03S-1-12	Adding scrolling text to ImportersDataAccess.htm	8.2	AC 8.46
AC03S-1-12	Adding an Image to ImportersDataAccess.htm	8.2	AC 8.46
AC03S-1-12	Applying a Theme to ImportersDataAccess.htm	8.2	AC 8.46
AC03S-2-3	Linking a Word document to the OrdersByStateChart report	8.1	AC 8.46
AC03S-2-3	Embedding a Word document in the OrdersByStateChart report	8.1	AC 8.46

REFERENCE

Microsoft Office Specialist Objective	Task	Session Location	End-of-Chapter Location
AC03S-2-3	Importing ac08NewCustomerContacts.mdb	8.1	AC 8.46
AC03S-2-3	Linking ac08NewCustomerContacts.mdb	8.1	AC 8.46
AC03S-2-3	Importing ac08Importers.xls	8.1	AC 8.46
AC03S-2-3	Importing WebImporters.htm as an Access table	8.2	AC 8.46
AC03S-2-3	Confirming the import	8.2	AC 8.46
AC03S-4-4	Exporting ProductByStateCrosstab.rtf	8.1	AC 8.46
AC03S-4-4	Exporting OrderData.xls	8.1	AC 8.46
AC03S-4-4	Exporting Importers.html	8.2	AC 8.46
CHAPTER 9:	**Using Queries to Analyze and Maintain Data**		
AC03S-1-7	Creating and modifying Crosstab, Unmatched, and Duplicate queries	9.1	AC 9.36
AC03S-1-7	Using the Crosstab Query Wizard	9.1	AC 9.36
AC03S-1-7	Creating a Crosstab Query in Design View	9.1	AC 9.36
AC03S-1-7	Restricting crosstab column headings	9.1	AC 9.36
AC03S-1-7	Locating duplicate records in the Customer table	9.2	AC 9.36
AC03S-1-7	Locating customers without orders	9.2	AC 9.36
CHAPTER 10:	**Automating Database Tasks**		
No MOS Objectives			
CHAPTER 11:	**Using Visual Basic for Applications**		
No MOS Objectives			
CHAPTER 12:	**Advance Forms and Data Sharing**		
AC03S-4-2	Using Datasheet, PivotChart, Web page, and Layout views	12.1	AC 12.34
AC03S-4-2	Using InvoiceJoinWithCalc PivotChart View	12.1	AC 12.34
AC03S-4-2	Creating multiple pivot charts	12.1	AC 12.34
AC03S-4-2	Formatting pivot charts	12.1	AC 12.34
AC03S-4-2	Converting a PivotChart to a Web page	12.2	AC 12.34
AC03S-4-2	Converting a PivotTable to a Web page	12.2	AC 12.34

reference 3

Task	Page #	Preferred Method
Opening an Access object	AC 1.19	• Click the type of object that you would like to open in the Database Window's Objects bar • Select the object that you would like to open • Click the **Open** button
Activating Access Wizards	AC 1.24	• Click the object (Queries, Forms, Reports) whose Wizard you would like to access in the Database Window's Objects bar • Click **New** in the Database Window's toolbar • The available Wizards will be listed • Select the Wizard and respond to its questions
Getting help	AC 1.32	• Click in the Type a Question drop-down text box in the Access menu • Type in keywords relevant to your topic. Full sentences are not necessary and do not improve the performance of the search • Press **Enter** • Select from the topics provided or adjust the keywords and search again
Finding specific data values	AC 2.6	• Click in the column that you would like to search • Click the **Find** button • Enter the Find What criteria using the data value that you would like to find. Remember that a question mark (?) can be used as a wildcard for one character and an asterisk (*) is a wildcard for multiple characters • Click the **Find Next** button. If multiple rows match the Find What criteria, you may need to repeat this step until the row you are searching for is found
Office Clipboard: collect items to paste	AC 2.14	• Display the Office Clipboard by selecting **Office Clipboard** from the **Edit** menu • Select the item to be copied • Click the **Copy** or **Cut** button in the Standard toolbar • Continue placing items on the Clipboard (up to 24) until you have collected everything that you need

Office Clipboard: paste collected items	AC 2.14	• Display the Office Clipboard if it is not already present. If the Office Clipboard option of the Edit menu is not available, you are in an application or view that does not support the Office Clipboard
		• Click or select the area where you want to place items
		• Do one of the following:
		  • Select the **Paste All** button to paste the entire contents of the Office Clipboard
		    or
		  • Select a Clipboard item and choose **Paste** from its drop-down menu

Office Clipboard: remove items	AC 2.14	When the Clipboard is open • To clear one item, click the arrow next to the item you want to delete and then click **Delete** • To clear all Clipboard contents, click the **Clear All** button • Placing more than 24 items on the Clipboard will replace existing items beginning with the oldest item

Task	Page #	Preferred Method
Hiding datasheet columns	AC 2.16	• Open a table, query, or form in Datasheet View • Click the field selector of the column to be hidden • Click **Hide Columns** on the **Format** menu
To unhide a column	AC 2.16	• On the **Format** menu, click **Unhide Columns** • Select the names of the columns that you want to show from the Unhide Columns dialog box
Freezing and unfreezing datasheet columns	AC 2.17	• Open a table, query, or form in Datasheet View • Select the column(s) that you want to freeze or unfreeze • To freeze column(s), select **Freeze Columns** on the **Format** menu • To unfreeze column(s) select **Unfreeze All Columns** on the **Format** menu
Defining a Table field	AC 2.26	• Click **Tables** in the Options bar • Click the **Design View** button on the toolbar • Enter a field name • Select a data type • Define other field attributes as needed
Filter By Selection	AC 3.4	• Open the table in Datasheet View • Select the field and character(s) of the search criteria (see Figure 3.2) • Click the **Filter By Selection** ⚡ toolbar button to return values matching the selection or • Right-click and choose **Filter Excluding Selection** to filter the selection out of the data • Evaluate the results of the filter • Click **Remove Filter** ▽ on the Access toolbar
Filter By Form	AC 3.6	• Open a table in Datasheet View • Click the **Filter By Form** 🔳 toolbar button • Build the filter criteria by selecting from the drop-down list for a field or typing your own value • Click the **Filter** ▽ toolbar button • Review the filtered data to be sure they are what you expected • Work with the filtered data • Click **Remove Filter** ▽ on the Access toolbar when you are done
Filter For Input	AC 3.8	• Open a table in Datasheet View • Right-click the field to be filtered • Type the filter criteria in the Filter For text box using wildcards, operators, and values • Press **Enter** to activate the filter • Review the filtered data to be sure they are what you expected • Work with the filtered data • Click **Remove Filter** ▽ on the Access toolbar when you are done
Advanced Filter/Sort	AC 3.9	• Open a table in Datasheet View • On the **Records** menu, point to **Filter**, and then click **Advanced Filter/Sort** • Add criteria fields to the design grid • Enter the filter and sort criteria • Click the **Apply Filter** ▽ button on the toolbar • Review the filtered data to be sure they are what you expected • Work with the filtered data • Click **Remove Filter** ▽ on the Access toolbar when you are done
Saving a filter as a query	AC 3.10	• Display the filter in either the Filter By Form window or the Advanced Filter/Sort window (recall that any filter can be displayed in these windows regardless of how it was created) • Click the **Save As Query** 💾 button on the toolbar

Task	Page #	Preferred Method
		• Type a name for the query and click **OK** • The new query will appear with the other query objects in the Database Window
Create a Select Query	AC 3.12	• Select the **Queries** object from the Database Window • Verify that **Create query in Design View** is selected • Click **New** on the toolbar • Select the **Design View** 🖉 ▾ button from the New Query dialog box and click **OK** • Double-click the name of each table that contains relevant data from the Show Table dialog box • Double-click each table field that is to be contained in the query result to place it in the Field row of the design grid. The order of the columns is the order of the output • Enter sort criteria in the Sort row of the design grid • Enter selections in the Criteria row of the design grid • Click the **Datasheet View** 🔲 ▾ button on the toolbar to see the query results • Click the **Design View** 🖉 ▾ button on the toolbar to update the query criteria • Click the **Save** 🔚 button to save the query criteria
Create an expression using Expression Builder	AC 3.20	• Click in the Field row of the QBE grid column that will display the calculation • Click the **Build** 🔨 button in the query design toolbar • Select expression elements and operators to create the desired calculation • Click **OK** to place the calculation in the QBE grid
Modify the format of a form	AC 3.27	• Open the form in Design View • Click the **AutoFormat** 🖥 button in the Form Design toolbar • Select from the same formats that were available in the Wizard
Modify the format of a report	AC 3.30	• Open the report in Design View • Click the **AutoFormat** 🖥 button in the Report Design toolbar • Select from the same formats that were available in the Wizard
Add a graphic to a report or form	AC 3.35	• Open the report or form in Design View • Select the section that is to display the graphic • Select **Picture** from the Insert menu • Navigate to the folder containing the image and change the file type selector to the image file type • Select the file and click **OK** • Move and size the image as needed
Creating a Crosstab Query	AC 4.13	• Click the **Queries** object in the Database Window, select **Create query by using wizard**, and then click **New** • Select **Crosstab Query Wizard** from the New Query dialog box and then click **OK** • Follow the Wizard's instructions to choose the data source, row heading, column heading, and aggregate functions for the query • Name the query and then view the results
Creating a Lookup field	AC 4.14	• Verify the relationship between the table that will have the Lookup field and the table where the field is being looked up. The most likely relationship is one-to-many, where the child (many sides of the relationship) table will look up the key value of the parent table (one side of the relationship) • Open the child table and change the data type to **Lookup Wizard** • Follow the Lookup Wizard instructions

REFERENCE

Task	Page #	Preferred Method
Creating an input mask	AC 4.21	• Open a table in Design View • Select the field for which you want to define an input mask • From the General tab select the **Input Mask** property and either • Click the **Build** button and follow the Input Mask Wizard instructions (Text and Date fields only) or • Type the input mask definition (Numeric and Currency masks must be entered manually)
Compact and repair the open database	AC 4.25	• On the **Tools** menu, point to **Database Utilities**, and then click **Compact and Repair Database**
Compact and repair an unopened database	AC 4.26	• Access must be running with no open database • On the **Tools** menu, point to **Database Utilities**, and then click **Compact and Repair Database** • In the **Database to Compact From** dialog box, specify the Access file you want to compact, and then click **Compact** • In the **Compact Database Into** dialog box, specify a name, drive, and folder for the compacted Access file • **Click** Save
Setting Automatic Compact and Repair	AC 4.27	• Open the Access database that you want to compact automatically • On the **Tools** menu, click **Options** • Click the **General** tab • Select the **Compact on Close** check box
Setting Detect and Repair for Microsoft Office	AC 4.28	• On the **Help** menu, click **Detect and Repair** • To restore the program shortcuts to the Windows **Start** menu, make sure the **Restore my shortcuts while repairing** check box is selected • Click **Start**
Database backup with Access	AC 4.30	• Open the database to be backed up. All database objects should be closed • From the **File** menu select **Back Up Database** • In the Save Backup As dialog box, indicate the drive, folder, and filename for the backup • Click **Save**
Open a new form in Design View	AC 5.6	• In the Database Window of an open database, click the **Forms** object • Click the **New** button on the Database Window toolbar • In the New Form dialog box, click **Design View** • Select the table or query that will be the record source for the form and click **OK**
Select and move form controls	AC 5.9	• Select the control to be operated on by clicking it. The Shift key can be used to select multiple controls • Drag the control(s) to the new location. Use the large move handle to independently move components of a bound control
Set control properties	AC 5.11	• Right-click the control to open the pop-up menu • Select **Properties** from the pop-up menu • Select the appropriate Properties tab (usually Format) • Navigate to the property and change its setting
Show Form Headers and Footers	AC 5.15	• Open a form in Design View • Select **Form Header/Footer** from the **View** menu
Add Toolbox controls to a design	AC 5.16	• Open a form or report in Design View • If necessary, activate the toolbox using the **Toolbox** button on the Form Design toolbar

Task	Page #	Preferred Method
		• Verify that the Toolbox **Control Wizards** button is depressed (a blue outline will show around it) • Click the Toolbox control that is to be added to the form • Click in the Form section that will contain the control • Set the control's properties using the Properties pages activated with the Properties button
Query an open form with a saved filter	AC 5.21	• Open a form in Form View • Click the **Filter By Form** button • Click the **Load From Query** button • Select the query to be applied and click **OK** • Click the **Apply Filter** button
Create a report in Design View	AC 5.27	• In the Database Window click the **Reports** object and click the **New** button • Click **Design View** as the way to develop the report, select the record source from the drop-down list, and click **OK**
Add page numbers to a report in Design View	AC 5.32	• Display the report in Design View • Choose **Page Numbers** from the **Insert** menu • Select the formatting, position, and alignment options that you want and click **OK**
Control Sorting and Grouping in a report	AC 5.37	• Display the report in Design View • Click the **Sorting and Grouping** button on the toolbar • Use the Field/Expression drop-down list box to select each field that you want to use to sort or group data. Each selected Field/Expression will be on a different line of the grid • Select the Sort order for each Field/Expression listed. The order of multiple fields determines their priority in the sort • Select the grouping option(s) for each field • Close the Sorting and Grouping dialog box • Add the necessary controls and content to any Group Headers and Footers created
View table relationships	AC 6.4	• Click the **Relationships** button on the Database toolbar • If relationships exist, they will be displayed. If there are no current relationships, you can add tables and build relationships between them
View relationship properties	AC 6.6	• Click the **Relationships** button on the Database toolbar • If relationships exist, they will be displayed. If there are no current relationships, you can add tables and build relationships between them • Double-click the relationship line that you would like to view • The Edit Relationships dialog box displays the properties of that relationship
Create a relationship	AC 6.8	• Click the **Relationships** button on the Database toolbar • If relationships exist, they will be displayed • Click the **Show Table** button on the toolbar • Select the table that you want to relate and click the **Add** button. Repeat this process for each table to be related • When you have added all of the necessary tables, click **Close** • Click the primary table field of the relationship and drag to the secondary field to initiate the relationship • Select the Referential Integrity options in the Edit Relationships dialog box • Click **OK** to close the Edit Relationships dialog box • Repeat this process for any other relationships to be built • Close the Relationships window

REFERENCE

Task	Page #	Preferred Method
Index a table field	AC 6.13	• Open the table in **Design View** • Select the field to be indexed from the Field Name column • Set the Indexed field property to **Yes (Duplicates OK)** or **Yes (No Duplicates)** • Close the table design and save the changes
Delete an index	AC 6.14	• Open the table in **Design View** • Select the field whose index is to be removed from the Field Name column • Set the Indexed field property to **No** (this does not impact the field or its data) • Close the table design and save the changes
View the indexes of a table	AC 6.14	• Open the table in **Design View** • Click the **Indexes** 📝 button of the toolbar • Click an index to review its properties
Viewing object dependencies	AC 6.37	• Open the task pane and use the drop-down arrow to select **Object Dependencies** • In the dependency pane • Review the list of objects that use the selected object • To view the list of objects that are being used by the selected object, click **Objects that I depend on** at the top of the pane • To view dependency information for an object listed in the pane, simply click on the expand icon (+) next to it
Controlling blank data values	AC 7.11	• Open the table in Design View • Click the field whose blank values you would like to control • Set Required to **Yes** to disallow blank values (Allow Zero Length should be set to No)
Defining field validation rules	AC 7.14	• Open the table in Design View • Click the field that will be monitored by the validation rule • Select the **Validation Rule** property for that field • Type the validation expression or use the Expression Builder by clicking the ellipsis to the right of the Validation Rule text box • Click the Validation Text property box for the same field and enter the text that is to display when the validation rule is broken • Save the table update • If the validation rule has been set for a field that already contains data, Access will ask if you want to apply the new rule to existing data • If there are no existing data in the field, there will be no prompt
Splitting a database	AC 7.16	• Back up the database • On the Tools menu, point to **Database Utilities**, and then click **Database Splitter** • Follow the Database Splitter Wizard instructions
Optimizing database objects	AC 7.18	• Open the database to be optimized • Click the **Tools** menu, then **Analyze**, and then **Performance** • Select the tab for the database object (table, query, report, form, etc.) that you would like to analyze • Click the check box of each object to be evaluated or click Select All to select all objects in the list • Select objects from other tabs if desired • Click **OK** • Review and apply results as needed

Task	Page #	Preferred Method
Replicating a database	AC 7.20	• Open the database to be replicated • Remove any password protection and ensure that the database is not open by any other users • On the **Tools** menu, point to **Replication**, and then click **Create Replica** • Click **Yes** when prompted with: The database must be closed before you can create a replica • Answer **Yes** when prompted with: Converting a database into a Design Master results in changes . . . • In the Location of New Replica dialog box • Navigate to the location for the replica • Set the **Priority** • Check the **Prevent deletes** check box to prevent record deletions in the replica • In the Save as type box, select the replica visibility • Click **OK**
Synchronizing replicated databases	AC 7.23	• Open the replica to be synchronized • On the **Tools** menu, point to **Replication**, and then click **Synchronize Now** • Select the other replica set member to be synchronized from the Directly with Replica drop-down list box • Click **OK** • Respond **Yes** when prompted to close the database for synchronization • Respond **OK** when notified that the process has been completed
Hiding a database	AC 7.26	• Open Windows Explorer • Navigate to the file to be hidden • Right-click on the file to be hidden • Click the **Properties** option • Click the **Hidden** attribute • Click **OK**
Encoding a database	AC 7.28	• Open Access with no open database • Open the **Tools** menu, pause over **Security**, and click **Encode/Decode Database . . .** • Enter a folder and a name for the database to be encoded and click **OK** • Enter a folder and name for the encoded database and click **Save**
Password protecting a database	AC 7.29	• Open Access with no open database • Click the **Open** button on the Database toolbar • Navigate to the folder and select the file to be password protected • Click the Open button's list arrow and select **Open Exclusive** • Open the **Tools** menu, pause over **Security**, and then click **Set Database Password** • Type the password in the Password text box, repeat the same password in the Verify text box, and then press **Enter**
Setting user-level security	AC 7.32	• Open the Access database to be secured • On the **Tools** menu, pause over **Security** and then click **User-Level Security Wizard** • Follow the Wizard instructions
Create a Microsoft Graph	AC 8.4	• Click the **Reports** object in the Database Window • Click **New** to activate the New Report dialog box • Select **Chart Wizard**, use the drop-down list to select the query or table containing the data to be charted, and then click **OK** to initiate the Chart Wizard • Follow the instructions to select the field(s) with the data to be charted, select the chart type, specify the layout, and add a chart title

Task	Page #	Preferred Method

Importing with an unbound object frame on a form or report	AC 8.11	• Open the Design View of the form or report to contain the imported object
		• Click the **Unbound Object Frame** tool in the toolbox
		• Click and drag the area on the form or report that will contain the object
		• In the Microsoft Access dialog box
		  • Click **Create From File**
		  • Browse to the file for import
		  • Click the Link check box to create a linked object or leave it unclicked to create an embedded object
		  • Click **OK**

Import or link to another Access database	AC 8.16	• Open the Access database that is to contain the imported data
		• Open the **File** menu, point to **Get External Data**, and then do one of the following:
		  • Click **Import** to create Access tables from the external data
		  • Click **Link Tables** to create links to tables that remain in the source location
		• In the Import or Link dialog box
		  • Use the Files of Type drop-down list to select **Microsoft Office Access (*.mdb, *.mda, *.mde)** as the type of file to be linked or imported
		  • Use the Look in box to select the drive, folder, and filename of the file to be imported or linked
		  • Select the import tables and click **Import**

Import or link to an Excel spreadsheet	AC 8.18	• Open the Access database that is to contain the imported data
		• Open the **File** menu, point to **Get External Data**, and then click **Import**
		  • Click **Import** to create Access tables from the external data
		  • Click **Link Tables** to create links to tables that remain in the source location
		• In the Import or Link dialog box
		  • Use the Files of Type drop-down list to select **Microsoft Excel (*.xls)** as the type of file to be linked or imported
		  • Use the Look in box to select the drive, folder, and filename of the file to be imported or linked
		  • Follow the Import Spreadsheet Wizard instructions

Export an Access object to Microsoft Word	AC 8.22	• Open the Access database with the object to be exported
		• Select the object to be exported in the Database Window (it is best to preview the object before exporting)
		• Open the **Tools** menu, point to **Office Links**, and then either
		  • Select **Merge It with Microsoft Word** to use an Access table or query as the data source for a Word merge document
		  or
		  • Select **Publish It with Microsoft Word** to create an .rtf file in the default database folder (usually C:\ My Documents or the folder containing the database) with the same name as the exported object

Export an Access object to an Excel spreadsheet	AC 8.23	• Open the Access database that contains the data to be exported • Select the object to be exported in the Database Window (it is best to preview the object before exporting) • Open the **Tools** menu, point to **Office Links**, and then click **Analyze It with Microsoft Excel**

Export an Access object to a static HTML page	AC 8.26	• Open the Access database that contains the data to be exported
		• Select the object to be exported in the Database Window (it is best to preview the object before exporting)
		• Open the **File** menu and click **Export**
		• In the Export To dialog box
		  • Use the Save In box to select the drive and folder for the Web page
		  • Set the Save As Type to **HTML Documents (*.html; *.htm)**

Task	Page #	Preferred Method
		• In the File Name box, enter the name for the Web page (it is best not to use spaces in these names) • **Save Formatted** should be clicked to retain the formatting applied to the datasheet in Access and activate the next two options • Check **AutoStart** to display the page in your default browser • In the HTML Output Options dialog box • Apply an HTML template to standardize formatting (Optional) • Click **OK**
Use Internet Explorer to view a static HTML page	AC 8.28	• Open Access • From the **View** menu, pause over **Toolbars** and then click **Web** • On the Web toolbar, drop down the **Go** list and select **Open Hyperlink** • Click the **Browse** button in the Open Internet Address dialog box • Use the Browse dialog box to navigate to the file to be viewed • Select the file and click **Open** • Click **OK**
Use the Page Wizard to create a Data Access Page	AC 8.30	• Open the database containing the data for the Data Access Page • Click the **Pages** object in the Database Window • Double-click **Create data access page by using wizard** • Follow the Wizard instructions
Repair broken Data Access Page links	AC 8.38	• Open the Data Access Page with a broken database link in Design View • Click **Update Link** in the informational dialog box • Navigate to the network folder containing the Data Access Page • Select the page and click **OK** • Click **OK** in the dialog box explaining that the connection needs to be repaired • On the right-hand side of the Data Access Page Design View, click the **Page connection properties** option in the Field List Window • On the Connection tab, click the ellipsis (…) and update the database name • Click **Open** • Click the **Test Connection** button • When the test works, click **OK** • Click **OK** again to end the update
Importing an HTML document as an Access table	AC 8.39	• Open the database to hold the imported table • Verify that the layout of the data to be imported is either a list or a table • On the **File** menu, point to **Get External Data**, and then click **Import** • Select the HTML file for import and click **Import** (be sure to set the Files of Type to HTML documents) • Complete the Wizard dialog boxes
Construct a Web page or file hyperlink	AC 8.43	• Open the form, report, or Data Access Page in Design View • Click the Insert Hyperlink 🔗 button in the toolbox and drag the display area on the form, report, or Data Access Page • In the Insert Hyperlink dialog box • Select the type of object to **Link to** (Existing File or Web Page, Object in This Database, Create New Page, or E-Mail Address) • Enter the **Text to display** for the hyperlink (if this is blank, the URL will display) • Enter the **Screen Tip text** (if this is blank, the URL displays when the user pauses the cursor over the link) • In the Address box, type or browse to the path of a file or a URL • Click **OK**
Create a Crosstab Query in Design View	AC 9.5	• Create a Select Query to retrieve the rows and columns to be cross-tabulated • Open the Select Query in Design View and use the **Query Type** 🔲 ▾ button on the toolbar to select **Crosstab**

Task	Page #	Preferred Method
		• Set the Crosstab property of the field to appear across the query answer set to **Column Heading** and the Total property of this field to **Group by** • Set the Crosstab property of the field to appear down the left-hand side of the query answer set to **Row Heading** and the Total property of this field to **Group by** • Set the Crosstab property of the field to be cross-tabulated to **Value** and select an appropriate aggregate function for the Total property • Move to Datasheet View to verify the query answer set
Create a parameter query	AC 9.8	• Create and test a Select Query with static criteria to retrieve the desired rows and columns • Open the Select Query in Design View and type prompt(s) contained in square brackets in the Criteria row of field(s) that will prompt the user for data retrieval criteria • Run the query to test the prompts and parameters
Create an Append Query	AC 9.13	• Create and test a Select Query with the data to be appended to another table • In Query Design View, click the **Query Type** button and select **Append** • In the Append dialog box • Enter the name of the table where records are to be appended • Select the database location • Click **OK** • Use the **View** button to preview the records that will be appended • Use the **Run** button to execute the query responding **Yes** to the prompt indicating the number of rows that will be updated
Create an Update Query	AC 9.15	• Back up the data to be updated to protect against update errors • Create and test a Select Query with criteria to retrieve the desired data • Verify the Select Query • Use the **Query Type** button to change the query to an Update Query • Place the update expression in the Update To row of the Query Design grid • Run the query responding **Yes** to the update prompt notifying you of the number of records to be updated • Verify the update
Create a Delete Query	AC 9.18	• Create and test a Select Query to retrieve the data to be deleted • In Query Design View, click the **Query Type** button and select **Delete Query** • Use the **View** button to preview the records that will be deleted • Use the **Run** button to execute the query responding **Yes** to the prompt indicating the number of rows that will be deleted
Create a Make-Table Query	AC 9.20	• Create and test a Select Query to retrieve the data to be moved • In Query Design View, click the **Query Type** button and select **Make-Table Query** • Use the **View** button to preview the records that will be copied to a new table • Use the **Run** button to execute the query responding **Yes** to the prompt indicating the number of rows that will be deleted
Create a Find Duplicates Query	AC 9.22	• Select the **Queries** object in the Database Window • Click the **New** button in the Database Window • Select **Find Duplicates Query Wizard** and click **OK** • Follow the instructions provided by the Find Duplicates Query Wizard
Create an Unmatched Query	AC 9.23	• Select the **Queries** object in the Database Window • Click the **New** button in the Database Window • Select **Find Duplicates Query Wizard** and click **OK** • Follow the instructions provided by the Find Unmatched Query Wizard

Task	Page #	Preferred Method
Create a Top Values Query	AC 9.24	• Create a Select, Make-Table, or Append **Query** that returns all records meeting the desired criteria • In Query Design View, enter the number of percent of records to be selected in the Top Values text box on the Query Design toolbar • Run the query
Create a Self-Join Query	AC 9.25	• Select the **Queries** object and double-click **Create query in Design view** • Add two copies of the self-join table to the design grid and close the Show Table dialog box • Define the relationship between the two copies of the self-join table by clicking and dragging from the one side of the relationship to the many side of the relationship • Right-click on the relationship line and set the join properties • Select the query fields, define the selection criteria, and run the query
Create an Aggregate Query	AC 9.28	• Select the **Queries** object and double-click **Create query in Design view** • Add the needed table(s) to the design grid and close the Show Table dialog box • Add the fields to the design grid (only fields that will be used to aggregate or select should be added) • Click the **Totals** Σ button on the Query Design toolbar • Set the Total row option for each field in the grid
Create a query using SQL	AC 9.29	• Select the **Queries** object and double-click **Create query in Design view** • Without adding fields to the design grid, close the Show Table dialog box • Click the **SQL View** button on the Query Design toolbar (you may need to drop down the View list for this selection to be visible) • Enter SQL statements and run the query
Create a macro	AC 10.4	• In the Database Window, click **Macros** • Click the **New** button on the Database Window toolbar • Add an action to the macro using the drop-down list in the Action column of the Macro design grid • Use the lower part of the design grid to set the arguments for the action • Add additional actions and set their arguments as needed • Close, save, and name the macro
Adding conditional operations to a macro	AC 10.6	• In the Database Window, click **Macros** • Click the **New** button to open a new macro or select the macro and click **Design** to open an existing macro • Add the actions and arguments to be performed in the macro • Click the **Conditions** button on the Macro toolbar • Enter a condition in the Condition column of the Action row to be conditionally executed • Close, save, and name the macro
Creating a macro group	AC 10.9	• In the Database Window, click **Macros** • Click the **New** button on the Database Window toolbar • If the Names column is not visible in the Macro design grid, click the **Macro Names** button on the Macro Design toolbar • Type the name for the first macro and then enter the conditions, actions, and action arguments for that macro • On the line under the last action of the first macro, enter the second macro name, and then enter the conditions, actions, and action arguments associated with this macro • Continue adding macro names, conditions, actions, and action arguments to complete all of the macros in the group • Close, and name the macro group

Task	Page #	Preferred Method
Displaying Macro Name and Condition columns by default	AC 10.11	• On the Tools menu, click **Options** • Select the **View** tab • In the Show in Macro Design section of the View tab, check the **Names column** and/or the **Conditions column** check boxes
Executing a macro	AC 10.11	Do one of the following • From the Macro Window, click the **Run** ![icon] button on the Macro Design toolbar to run a stand-alone macro or the first macro in a macro group • From the Database Window, select the **Macros** object and then double-click macro name to run a stand-alone macro or the first macro in a macro group • On the **Tools** menu, point to **Macro**, click **Run Macro**, and then select the macro from the Macro Name list to run any individual macro
Single stepping a macro	AC 10.12	• Open the macro to be diagnosed in Design View • Click the **Single Step** ![icon] button on the Macro Design toolbar • Click the **Run** ![icon] button on the toolbar • Click **Step** to carry out an action and evaluate its result • Click **Halt** to stop the macro and close the Macro Single Step dialog box
Setting the On Click event procedure	AC 10.14	• With a form or report open in Design View, right-click on the object that will respond to a click and select **Properties** • Click the **Event** tab • Click in the text box to the right of the On Click event property • Either select a macro name from the drop-down list or use the Build (…) button to create an expression or event procedure
Creating a switchboard	AC 10.17	• Open the database to contain the switchboard • On the Tools menu, point to **Database Utilities**, and then click **Switchboard Manager** • Respond **Yes** if prompted to create a new switchboard • The default Switchboard page named Main Switchboard is created • Click **Edit** to add items to the switchboard. This will open the Edit Switchboard dialog box • Click **New** on the Edit Switchboard page dialog box to add a new item to Main Switchboard. This will open the Edit Switchboard Item dialog box • Enter the text to display on the switchboard • Select the command to execute when this item is activated from the drop-down Command list • Select any arguments needed for the command • Click **OK** • Repeat the previous step to add additional items to the switchboard. When all items have been added, click **Close** • **Close** the Switchboard Manager
Defining shortcut keys in a switchboard	AC 10.21	• On the Tools menu, point to **Database Utilities**, and then click **Switchboard Manager** • Select the switchboard page and click **Edit** • Select the item and click **Edit** • Insert an **&** (ampersand) before the shortcut character in the Text field • Click **OK** on the Edit Switchboard Item dialog box • **Close** the Edit Switchboard Page dialog box • **Close** the Switchboard Manager
Reordering switchboard items	AC 10.22	• On the Tools menu, point to **Database Utilities**, and then click **Switchboard Manager** • Select the switchboard page and click **Edit** • Select the item to be moved or deleted • Use the appropriate (Move Up, Move Down, or Delete) button to modify the item

Task	Page #	Preferred Method
		• Click **Close** to close the Switchboard Item dialog box • Click **Close** to close the Switchboard Manager dialog box
Setting startup options	AC 10.29	• On the Tools menu, click **Startup** • Select the options or enter the desired settings
Bypassing startup options	AC 10.31	• Open Access with no active database • Click the **Open** button • Navigate to the file and click to select it • Hold the **Shift** key while clicking the **Open** button • Release the Shift key when the database load process has completed • Explore the development interface
Viewing an object's event properties	AC 11.4	• In Design View, right-click on the object • Select **Properties** from the pop-up menu • Click the **Event** tab and explore the available event properties
Saving an Access database as an MDE file	AC 11.16	• Close all open copies of the database • Create a backup copy of the database using Windows Explorer • On the Tools menu, point to **Database Utilities**, and then click **Make MDE File** • In the Database To Save As MDE dialog box, select the drive, folder, and filename of the Access database to be converted • Click **Make MDE** • In the Save MDE As dialog box, specify the drive, folder, and filename of the MDE file
Creating a Standard module	AC 11.23	• In the Database Window, click the **Modules** object • Click **New** on the Database Window toolbar
Testing procedures in the Immediate window	AC 11.24	• In the Visual Basic code window, click **View** and then **Immediate Window** • Type a question mark (**?**), the procedure name, and any required arguments in parentheses • Press **Enter** to execute the procedure and display the results
Adding a subreport control to an existing report	AC 11.28	• Open the existing report in Design View • Click the **Control Wizards** button in the toolbox, if Control Wizards are not already active • Determine the appropriate section for the subreport control • Click the **Subform/Subreport** control in the toolbox • Click in the desired report section • Follow the Subreport Wizard to select content for the subreport control • Use Print Preview to evaluate your updates • Move and resize the control as needed
Saving PivotTable or PivotChart View to a Data Access Page	AC 12.20	• Create the PivotTable or PivotChart View • On the File menu, click **Save As** • Type a filename, select **Data Access Page** from the As drop-down list, and then click **OK** • Navigate to the desired folder • Click **OK** • Review the page in the Access Browser Window that opens automatically
Adding a Web Browser control to a form	AC 12.26	• Open the form in Design View • Click the **More Controls** button on the toolbox • Select **Microsoft Web Browser** from the list • Click the form to add the control • Move and resize the control as necessary • Create a procedure that will control the browser window display

REFERENCE

Task	Page #	Preferred Method

Exporting a table, query, form, or report as an XML file	AC 12.29	• In the Database Window, click the name of the object to be exported
		• Click **File** and then **Export** on the menu
		• In the Save as type drop-down box, click **XML Documents (*.xml)**
		• Select the drive and folder for the XML document
		• Enter the filename in the File name box
		• Click **Export**
		• Check the appropriate options in the Export XML dialog box
		  • Click **Data** (XML) to export the object's data to an XML document
		  • Click **Schema** of the data to export the object's structure to an XML file
		  • Click **Presentation** of your data (XSL) to export a file describing data formatting
		  • Click **OK**

Importing an XML file as an Access table	AC 12.31	• Click **File**, point to **Get External Data**, and click **Import** • Change the Files of type value to **XML Documents (*.xml;*.xsd)** • Navigate to the folder containing the XML file • Select the XML file and then click the **Import** button • On the Import XML dialog box, click the **Options** button, and set the import options • Click **OK** • Click **OK** to close the finished importing document dialog box

glossary

Absolute address: An address to a Web page, local file, or other object that contains values for every address component. Moving files will cause an absolute address to be invalid.

Access project: A Microsoft Access database that uses resources of a Microsoft SQL Server database.

Access Window: The main window of the Microsoft Access user interface. Other windows display inside it.

Action: The building block of a macro consisting of a self-contained instruction. Actions are combined to automate tasks.

Action arguments: Properties of a macro Action that define how the action is to be accomplished.

Action queries: Queries that update the data in a database in some fashion. For example, to delete a group of records that meet a criterion, to update a group of records, to add records to an existing table, or to add records to a new table.

Active Server Page: A Web page designed to display up-to-date read-only data. The data are selected by the server and displayed in a table format. Opening or refreshing an ASP file from a Web browser causes the page to be dynamically created from current values and sent to the browser.

ActiveX: A class of controls that are built to be used across platforms and so are suitable for forms used on the Web.

Advanced Filter/Sort: The most comprehensive filtering method that presents a grid of the table being filtered and allows you to enter record selection criteria.

Aggregate function: Access predefined calculations used to summarize groups of data (e.g., Sum and Avg).

Alternate keys: A table field that could have been assigned as the primary key but was not.

And: The logical operator that combines two conditions that must both be true to retrieve a record.

Append Query: A query that will select records from one table and append them to another.

Argument: The value used to replace a parameter when a function or procedures executes.

Assignment statement: A Visual Basic code statement that stores a value in a variable or constant.

AutoExec: The name of a macro that will automatically run when the database is opened.

Back-end: The centralized data storage of a split database.

Between: The relational operator used to select records whose values fall between the stated upper and lower bounds. For example, Between 14 and 18.

Bound controls: Any control on a form or report that displays data from a record source.

Calculated field: A field of a query that contains an expression.

Call: The method used to run or execute one procedure from another procedure.

Candidate key: Each table field that could be defined as the primary.

Caption: The table field property that determines what displays as the label for the field in Datasheet and other views.

Cascade Delete Related Records: Referential integrity setting that causes the related records to be deleted when a primary record is deleted.

Cascade Update Related Fields: Referential integrity setting that causes an update in the primary table to also be applied to the related table.

Category: Groupings of data used to summarize data when charting. The category is usually displayed on the x-axis.

Chart: A graphical representation of numeric data. For example, a pie chart.

Chart types: Microsoft Graph setting that determines the type of chart (for example, pie, line, column, and bar).

Chart Wizard: An Access Wizard that walks you through the process of creating a chart based on table data.

Client: The end-user interface that can be installed on multiple computers with access to the centrally stored server database in a SQL Server database environment.

Client/server databases: DBMSs that are designed to support multiple users in a networked environment.

Code window: The window of the Visual Basic Editor used to enter and debug Visual Basic statements.

Coding: The process of adding statements to a procedure.

Compact on Close: The database option that causes a database to automatically compact each time it is closed.

Compacting: The process of removing excess space from a database.

Compiling: The process of converting a programming language to the computer's language of zeroes and ones.

Composite key: The result of multiple attributes being combined for the primary key.

Concatenation: The process of combining multiple string values using the ampersand (&) operator.

Condition: The method of entering selection criteria using operators such as >, <, >=, <=, and <>.

Conflict Viewer: Access tool used to resolve synchronization conflicts in replication sets.

Container: An Access control that can contain (hold) other controls, such as a Tab control, which holds controls for a form page.

Control Wizards: Wizards set from the form or report design toolbox that walk the user through the process of setting up complex controls.

Count: Function that counts the number of non-blank entries in a text or numeric field. =Count(fieldname)

Crosstab Queries: Queries that are used to analyze data by grouping data and calculating values for each group.

Crosstab Query: A query format that allows data to be tabulated by two variables: a row header and a column header.

Data access language (DAL): RDBMS language for rapidly retrieving and organizing stored data. SQL is the standard.

Data Access Pages: Web pages that allow a Web browser to be used to view and update table data via a live connection to the data in your database.

Data definition language (DDL): The language provided by RDBMS for structuring the data tables and their relationships.

Data fields: Provide the values to plot in a PivotChart. Data field values are typically plotted on the Y-axis.

Data integrity: A term used to describe the reliability of data.

Data redundancy: Storing the same data such as a customer's last name multiple times. Redundant data increase the likelihood that data will not be updated properly in all locations and so reduce data integrity.

Data series: Determine the data field value for each category and series. On a line chart each series is a different line. On a bar chart, each series is a different color.

Data type: The table field property that determines what type of data it can store and how much storage space it will require.

Data validation rules: Rules that verify data entered are within appropriate bounds. For example, Gender should contain only M for male or F for female.

Data value: The intersection of a table row and column containing data pertaining to one attribute of one entity.

Database: A file that organizes Access objects (tables, queries, forms, reports, and so on) that are related to each other.

Database management system (DBMS): The software used to store data, maintain those data, and provide easy access to stored data.

Database Window: The window displaying an open Access database.

Datasheet View: The default grid layout used to display Access table data.

Declaration statement: A Visual Basic code statement that creates a named storage location (variable or constant) whose value can change during processing.

Default Value: The table field property that determines the value that will automatically be loaded for the field in a new record. The user can overtype the default value.

Delete Query: A query used to select and delete multiple records based on the specified criteria.

Design grid: The form used to specify fields and criteria in a query.

Design Master: The original database of a replica set that keeps track of all replicas.

Design View: The view of an object that is used to change the structure of the object.

Detect and Repair: A facility to detect and repair problems with Office software.

Direct synchronization: The synchronization method used when the replica set shares a network and can directly connect to each other.

Domain: All valid entries for one table attribute (column).

Embedded: A distinct copy of an object placed in a destination document that retains a link to the program that developed it, called the source program. Double-clicking an embedded object will open the source program in edit mode.

Encryption: A method of coding a file so that it is indecipherable without the conversion algorithm.

Entity: A person, place, object, idea, or event about which data are being collected.

Event: An action, such as clicking a button, that triggers a stored procedure.

Event procedure: A set of stored instructions outlining programmatic steps to be completed in response to an event.

Event property: The properties of an object that can be set to control how it responds to an event.

Event-driven: Programming languages, such as Visual Basic, that are used to code event procedures.

Exclusive: A type of database access that locks out all other users. Use the Open button drop-down list to access this mode.

Executable statement: A Visual Basic code statement that performs an action.

Explicit permissions: Those permissions granted directly to a user account.

Expression Builder: A tool for building expressions by selecting fields from tables, operators, and other calculation components.

Extensible Markup Language (XML): Language developed to address the growing need to share files from any data source. It is the standard for transporting data on the Web.

Extranet: A combination of Internet and intranet technologies capable of securing and sharing data and information both locally and via the World Wide Web.

Field: A table column representing a unique property of an entity such as LastName, BirthDate, or Quantity; it can also be referred to as an attribute.

Field list: The listing of fields for a table used to select fields to be included in a query.

Field name: The attribute of a table field that identifies it and is used to refer to it in queries, forms, reports, and modules.

Field selector: The button containing the field name that can be used to select an entire column of a datasheet.

Fieldset: Subgroupings of field data that can be used to create PivotTable or PivotChart Views. For example, quarterly and monthly are subgroups of a date field.

Field size: The table field property that determines the maximum value that the field can store, how much space is required to store it, and how fast it can be processed.

Filter by Form: A method of filtering or selecting records using an empty version of the current datasheet where you can type match values.

Filter by Selection: The simplest type of filter, which selects records that match the datasheet value you have selected.

Filter Excluding Selection: A method of selecting records that do not meet the stated criteria.

Filter for Input: A filter initiated from the pop-up menu that provides a text box for entering record selection criteria.

Find Duplicates query: A query used to find duplicate values in a field or fields so that their validity can be evaluated.

Focus: The active control or object in a Window is said to have the focus.

Foreign key: The value used to match the attributes from one table to those in another table.

Form: A user-friendly way to view and update data on a computer screen.

Form View: The view used to manipulate data in a form.

Form Wizard: An Access Wizard that walks you through the process of building a form by selecting fields from multiple tables and queries.

Format: The field property of a table definition that controls how data display to the user after they have been entered.

Format Painter: A tool available on the Standard toolbar that will pick up formatting applied to text and allow you to paint it onto other text.

Freezing columns: Keeping the leftmost columns of a datasheet on the screen when scrolling through columns to the right. The leftmost columns would scroll off of the screen if they were not frozen.

From: SQL keyword used to specify the tables containing the fields of a query.

Front-end: In a split database, this is the part that is customized for each user.

Function procedure: Visual Basic code statements that accept data and return a value.

Global chart: A type of chart that is based on all of the available data. Totals or averages from the data are usually charted.

Graphical user interface: A user interface composed of windows, menu bars, pull-down menus, dialog boxes, and icons.

Group by: Query grid option used to set a field or fields that will be used to calculate subtotals. SQL keyword used to specify field(s) used to group data for aggregate operations.

Groups bar: A bar in the Access Database window to allow users to group database objects for easier manipulation.

GUI: See Graphical user interface.

History table: A table used to store inactive records from a production table.

Hot key: See shortcut key.

HTML: See Hypertext Markup Language.

Hyperlink: A link between two objects that allows the user to navigate from object to object. Text hyperlinks are usually underlined and a different color. When the cursor is over a hyperlink, it changes to a pointing hand.

Hypertext Markup Language: A tag-based language used to create and link Web pages for delivery on a local computer, the Internet, an intranet, or an extranet.

Implicit permissions: Those permissions inherited from the group to which the user belongs.

In: The relational operator used to select records whose values match those listed. For example, In ("CO", "IN", "CA").

Index: Used to speed data access and sorting by allowing direct access to a specific value. Works like the index of a book.

Indexed: The field property of a table definition that determines whether or not this field indexes the table.

Inner field: The category closest to the data when multiple categories are used to create a PivotChart View.

Inner join: A type of table relationship that creates rows in the query answerset when the related fields have matching values.

Input masks: A property used to create "field template" that uses literal display characters to control how data is entered in a field.

Internet: A worldwide network of computers used to distribute and share data and information.

Internet Service Provider: An organization that provides e-mail and Internet service to another entity via a connection through one of their servers.

Intranets: A local network used to share data and information using Web pages and other Internet technologies.

Joining: The process of using a foreign key from one table to link to the data in another table.

Label: A control used to display descriptive text that cannot be updated by a user on a form or report.

Left outer join: A type of table relationship that creates rows in the query answerset for all of the records in the first (left) table and adds the data from the second table when the related fields have matching values.

Like: The relational operator used to select records using wild cards (*, ?, #).

Linked: A picture of an object displays in the destination document but there is only one copy of the object, which can be maintained only from the source program.

Logic error: Errors in a procedure caused by misplacing, misusing, or misapplying program statements. For example, using the correct keyword with an inappropriate argument.

Lookup field: A tool to ease data entry by listing valid values from a related table. Lookup fields are created using a Wizard in table Design View.

Macro: An action or series of actions used to automate repetitive database tasks.

Macro group: Related macros stored under the same name.

Macros: Used to automate repetitive database tasks using a series of actions; a self-contained instruction or command.

Main form: The outer form in a main form/subform pair. The main form typically displays data from the primary table and a subform displays related records.

Make-Table Query: A query that will select records from a table or tables and create a new table for them.

Many-to-many: A table relationship that exists when one row in the first table matches with multiple rows in the second table and one row in the second table matches with multiple rows in the first table. Many-to-many relationships can't be directly modeled in relational databases, but are broken into multiple one-to-many relationships (abbreviated M:N or ∞:∞).

Max: Function that returns the maximum number from the entries in a date or numeric field. =Max(fieldname)

MDE file: An Access file type that compiles all of the VBA modules and compacts the database resulting in the smallest and fastest access to data. Caution: MDE files do not allow forms, reports, queries, or VBA code to be edited.

Method: An action that operates on objects or controls.

Microsoft Graph: The application that is used by the Chart Wizard to create a chart.

Microsoft Jet: The database engine designed to support 5 simultaneous threads (queries) and used to power Microsoft Access.

Microsoft SQL Server 2000: A full-service database engine designed to support thousands of networked users.

Microsoft SQL Server 2000 Desktop Engine: A PC version of Microsoft SQL Server 2000 similar in size to the Jet engine, but with superior spooling, processing speed, and security.

Microsoft Visual Basic: A high-level version of the Basic programming language developed by Microsoft for building Windows applications.

Microsoft Visual Basic for Applications (VBA): The programming language based on Microsoft Visual Basic that is provided with Microsoft Office products such as Access.

Min: Function that returns the minimum number from the entries in a date or numeric field. =Min(fieldname)

Module: A collection of Visual Basic statements and procedures that are organized and stored together to be accessed as a unit.

EOB 1.3

MsgBox: A small dialog box containing a message. The message can be a simple warning or allow the user to choose a course of action.

Not: The logical operator that negates the condition that it precedes.

Now: Function that returns the current date and time. =Now()

Null: A field is said to be null or contain null values when nothing has been entered. This is used to differentiate between spaces and nothing entered in a field.

Nz: Null zero function used to convert null values to zero so they are included in aggregate calculations.

Object: Virtually anything—traditional data, a moving image, people talking, a photograph, narrative, text, music, or any combination.

Object bar: A bar displaying icons in the Access Database Window for each of the objects that can be created for a database.

Object linking and embedding: The Microsoft technology that allows objects to be placed in other objects. Such objects are either linked to the source object or embedded with no link to the source.

Object-oriented: Programming languages, such as Visual Basic, that create and manipulate objects. Tables, queries, command buttons, and text boxes are examples of objects that can be manipulated in code.

OLE: See Object linking and embedding

One-to-many: The table relationship that exists when one row of the first table matches to multiple rows in the second table (abbreviated 1:M or 1:∞).

One-to-one: The table relationship that exists when one row of the first table matches to one and only one row of the second table and both tables have the same primary key (abbreviated 1:1).

Optimizing: A series of performance-enhancing operations that will result in a more efficient database.

Or: The logical operator that combines two conditions when either one or both of the conditions can be true to retrieve a record.

Outer field: The category furthest from the data when multiple categories are used to create a PivotChart View.

Owner: The user who created a database object is the owner of that object and has all security rights to that object.

Parameters: Variables declared in a Function declaration statement to hold arguments passed to that function. For example, the function declaration *DateAdd(interval,quantity,date)* has three parameters: interval, quantity, and date.

Parameter queries: A query that will prompt the user for criteria when run. Parameters are specified in the Query Design grid using square brackets.

Parameter query: A query that prompts the user for criteria that will be used in selecting data from the database.

Password: A password is used to allow only authorized users to access a database.

Permissions: Permissions establish the level of access a user has to a specific object. The level of permission determines whether the user can see, update, print, modify, and perform other operations on an object.

Personal databases: Systems like Microsoft Access that work best in single-user environments.

Primary key: A table field or fields that uniquely and minimally identify an entity.

Primary sort: The first field that is used to order rows of data.

Primary table: The table on the one side of a one-to-many relationship.

Private: A Visual Basic keyword used to indicate the scope of a sub procedure or variable. Private sub procedures are available only within the current module.

Private Sub: A series of Visual Basic statements that accomplish a specific task needed by the current object.

Procedure: A series of program language statements that accomplish a specific task, such as resetting an object's properties.

Public: A Visual Basic keyword used to indicate the scope of a Sub procedure or variable. Public Sub procedures accessed from other objects and other code modules.

Public Sub: A series of Visual Basic statements that accomplish a specific task and is available to be called from multiple objects.

Query: Questions that are posed to a relational database using *Structured Query Language (SQL)*.

Read-Only: A type of database access that will not allow updates to the database. Use the Open button drop-down list to access this mode.

Record: One row in a relation (table) representing the unique data for one *entity* (person, place, object, idea, or event); it also can be referred to as a tuple.

Record Navigation toolbar: A toolbar on a Data Access page that will allow you to save edits, delete records, move through the records, and other maintenance tasks.

Record selector: The buttons to the left of records in Datasheet View used to select a row.

Record-bound chart: A type of chart that reflects the data of the current record and changes when another record is active.

Related table: The table on the many side of a one-to-many relationship.

Relational database: A collection of data relations defined using related tables.

Relational database management systems (RDBMS): A type of DBMS that stores data in interrelated tables. Tables are related by sharing a common field.

Relational operator: The operators (>, < >=, <=, <>) used to set conditions in queries.

Relationships window: The window used to set or edit table relationships. Accessed using the Relationships button on the toolbar.

Relative address: An address to a Web page, local file, or other object that does not contain all of the address components. The missing components are assigned the values of the current object.

Repair: The process of fixing errors in the structure of database objects.

Replica: A copy of a database that must be synchronized with the Design Master to maintain accuracy among all of the replicas.

Replica set: The Design Master and all of its replicas.

Report: RDBMS object used to format data for printing.

Required: The table field property that determines whether or not the user must enter a value in this field.

Right outer join: A type of table relationship that creates rows in the query answerset for all of the rows in the second (right) table and adds the data from the first (left) table when the related fields have matching values.

Scope: Defines the visibility of a procedure, constant, variable, or other programmatic structures. Typical scopes are Public and Private.

Secondary sort: The second field that is used to order rows of data.

Select: SQL keyword used to specify fields to be returned by the query.

Select Queries: The most common type of query used to retrieve (select) data from one or more tables.

Server: The central storage location for data in a SQL Server database environment.

Shared: A type of database access that allows multiple users to be logged on to the same database simultaneously. The default open mode.

Shortcut key: Underlined letters in the user interface that can be used in combination with the Alt key to select options. For example, Alt+F will open the File menu in a standard Windows application.

Single stepping: A tool used to debug macros by stepping through each macro action and displaying its result.

Snapshot table: A copy of a table as of a specific period in time.

Sort Ascending: Toolbar button used to cause an ascending sort based on the selected column(s).

Sort Descending: Toolbar button used to cause a descending sort based on the selected column(s).

Static HTML: Web pages used to publish a snapshot of the data, which have to be updated manually.

Standard module: The database object created from the Modules option in the Database Window and used to hold public procedures (Sub) and functions.

Startup options: The options that control how a database opens such as what form opens.

Statement: One instruction (usually one line) in a procedure.

Structured Query Language (SQL): The language used to pose questions or queries to a relational database; SQL has been standardized by the American National Standards Institute (ANSI).

Sub: A Visual Basic keyword used to indicate the beginning of a sub procedure.

Sub procedure: A series of Visual Basic code statements that perform operations necessary to complete a task.

Subdatasheet: A small datasheet that presents over the main datasheet to display related data. Activated by clicking the plus (+) sign on the main datasheet.

Subform: The inner form in a main form/subform pair. The main form typically displays data from the primary table and the subform displays related records.

Subreport control: A control available from the report toolbox that is used to nest a form, report, table, or query inside another report.

Sum: Function that returns the sum of the entries in a date or numeric field. =Sum(fieldname)

Switchboard: A special form used to create a graphical user interface for a database.

Switchboard Manager: The Access interface used to build and edit switchboards.

Synchronization: The process of retrieving updates from replicas and applying them to the members of the replica set so that they all reflect the same data, queries, forms, and reports.

Syntax: The grammatical rules used when coding.

Syntax error: Errors in a procedure caused by violating the rules of the language. For example, misplacing a comma or using an invalid keyword.

Tabbed form: A form that contains multiple pages accessed by clicking a tab.

Table: Rows and columns used to store data in a relational database management system.

Top Values property: A property that can be set for a query to cause it to return a specified number of values.

Uniform Resource Locator: The address that identifies an object on a computer. An Internet address consists of the protocol, server address, path, and filename.

Unmatched Query Wizard: A Wizard that creates a query used to find records that do not have matching values in another table.

Update Query: A query that will select records based on criteria and then apply a change to them to update value(s) in the selected records.

Upsize: One of a group of terms used to describe moving a database application to another platform, such as moving a Microsoft Access application to Microsoft SQL Server.

URL: See Uniform Resource Locator.

User interface: The visual display and methods of interacting with a software application.

User-level security: Complex security such as that found on larger computers. Users belong to user groups that carry permissions for levels of access to each database object.

Validation: The table field property that contains the rule or rules that govern what data are acceptable for that field of a table.

Variable: A named storage location in RAM used by program statements during processing to save values.

Visual Basic Editor: The program used to create and maintain Visual Basic code.

Web browser: The software that allows you to view Internet documents. For example, Microsoft Internet Explorer.

Web servers: Computers that store documents for Internet distribution.

Where: SQL keyword used to specify the conditions for retrieving records in a query.

Wizards: Provide the user with step-by-step instructions on common tasks such as creating simple queries, forms, and reports.

World Wide Web: A network of linked documents made available through the Internet.

WWW: See World Wide Web.

Zero-length strings: Entered as " ", this indicates that the field is not supposed to contain data.

Zoom box: An enlarged area for entering long expressions activated by pressing Ctrl+F2.

index